BEYOND BULLETS

The Suppression of Dissent
in the United States

BEYOND BULLETS

The Suppression of Dissent
in the United States

Jules Boykoff

Beyond Bullets: The Suppression of Dissent in the United States
by Jules Boykoff

ISBN 978-1-904859-59-8
Library of Congress Number: 2006933529

Cover Design: Jon Resh
Layout: C. Weigl

AK Press
674-A 23rd Street
Oakland, CA 94612
www.akpress.org
akpress@akpress.org
510.208.1700

AK Press U.K.
PO Box 12766
Edinburgh EH8 9YE
www.akuk.com
ak@akedin.demon.co.uk
0131.555.5165

Printed in Canada on 100% recycled, acid-free paper by union labor.

TABLE OF CONTENTS

Acknowledgments

I have many, many people to thank for their support, assistance, and love during the writing of this book. A great deal of this work passed through the "Mom Filter." Big thanks to my mom, Sue Schoenbeck, and my mom-in-law, Meg Eberle Ainsworth, for their thoughtful reading of this project.

I would like to thank Robin Hahnel for putting me in contact with the collective members at AK Press. It's a real honor for me to publish this book with AK Press, a publishing house I have long admired for its political integrity, egalitarian organizational structure, and incorrigible vitality. This book benefited massively from the careful attention of Charles Weigl of AK Press. To say Charles is a thoughtful, judicious, sagacious editor is to egregiously understate his thoughtfulness, judiciousness, and sagacity. He has the skills, savvy, and principle that would make Alexander "Straight Thinking" Berkman proud. It has been a complete and total pleasure to work with him; I couldn't have asked for a more competent, kind editor.

Big thanks go to Sara Lozito for in-the-clutch research assistance. Thanks also to the Thombo Clipping Service and to Ben Holtzman from Routledge. Previous versions of work from this book first appeared or are forthcoming in *Antipode, New Political Science, Social Movement Studies, Encyclopedia of Activism and Social Justice, XCP: Cross Cultural Poetics, Common Dreams*, and *The Suppression of Dissent: How the State and Mass Media Squelch USAmerican Social Movements* (Routledge). I thank the editors of these publications for supporting this work.

Numerous friends, comrades, and colleagues have made their imprint on my thinking, and have helped me get this research out into the world in various ways. Thank you Stephen "Kelly" Ainsworth (1946–2002), Bill LeoGrande, Joe Soss, Peter Kuznick, Robin Hahnel, Kristen Sheeran, Father Paul Surlis, Sahar Shafqat, Celia Rabinowitz, Daniel Ellsberg, Mike Schmidt, Ryan Scott King, Carolyn Forché, Harry Mattison, Andrea Murray, Pam Hickman, Sandi Nunn, Jeff Betts, David Buuck, Rod Smith, David Barsamian, Tom Orange, Susana Gardner, Eric Schlosser, Charlie Benjamin, Bob McChesney, James K. Rowe, Dave Pauli, and Susan Schubothe. Special thanks to my colleagues at Pacific University who generously offered constructive criticism and encouragement: Bob Van Dyk, Jeff Seward, Pam Kofstad, John Hayes, Larry Lipin, Chris Wilkes, and Cheleen Mahar.

My family has always been super-supportive of me and my work. Deep thanks go to Thomas Boykoff, Sue Schoenbeck, Dick Hose, Molly Boykoff, Max Boykoff, Neal Sand, Meg Eberle Ainsworth, Al and Marge Schoenbeck, Marge and John Pratt, Rob Huddleston, Monica Boykoff, Chuckie and Harry Johnson, Steve and Beryl Sand, Emily Boykoff, Joan Baron Boykoff, and Reuben Baron.

For inspiration, I thank Quinton Huddleston, Indigo Huddleston, Elijah Boykoff, Calvin Boykoff, Dominic Betts, and Stella Gardner.

Finally, I simply would not have been able to write this book without the intellectual and emotional support of Kaia Sand. Kaia assisted with every stage of this project, treating the work (and me!) with patience, smart criticism, and good cheer. I'm deeply grateful for Kaia's indomitable intellect and zestful way. This book is dedicated to her.

1
The State, Mass Media, and Dissent

On 24 May 1990, as Earth First! members Judi Bari and Daryl Cherney drove Bari's Subaru station wagon through downtown Oakland, a pipe bomb exploded beneath the driver's seat, injuring both environmental activists. Bari, who was driving, had her spine dislocated and her pelvis shattered, while Cherney, who was riding in the front passenger seat, received lacerations on his face and injuries to his eye. As emergency paramedics and fire personnel worked to assist Bari and Cherney, members of the Federal Bureau of Investigation's (FBI) domestic terrorism squad swooped in and, in concert with the local police, took control of the investigation. As members of Earth First!, a radical environmental organization, Bari and Cherney were placed under immediate scrutiny and suspicion. The police quickly obtained a search warrant against the activists, asserting in an affidavit that they were "members of a violent terrorist group involved in the manufacture and placing of explosive devices." Upon release from the hospital the day of the bombing, Cherney was taken into custody and charged with possession and transportation of explosives. The next day, Bari was arrested in her hospital bed where she lay flitting in and out of consciousness. The mass media picked up the story, transmitting the police's assertion that the bomb belonged to Bari and Cherney and that it detonated inadvertently.[1] Two months later, lacking any credible evidence, these charges were dropped. The FBI assured the victims it would pursue the case, but no arrests have been made. Six years later, after a vertiginous whirl of civil litigation, Bari learned that before the bombing, she and Cherney were being investigated by the FBI as suspected terrorists.[2]

But the FBI's interest in Earth First!—and environmentalists more generally—didn't begin with Judi Bari and Daryl Cherney. In 1970, the Bureau sent agents to surveil Earth Day rallies in more than forty U.S. cities. A decade later, in 1980, it opened a file on Earth First!, soon after the group was established.[3] In 1989, the FBI arrested Earth First! founder Dave Foreman as the culmination of a two and a half year investigation that cost more than $2 million and involved between fifty and a hundred Bureau agents.[4] The arrest was facilitated by extensive surveillance: over sixty phone taps were put on people who were in communication with Foreman. One of those people was Judi Bari. The Bureau also coordinated the infiltration of an agent provocateur, Michael Fain. Once, while being taped, Fain inadvertently, though clearly, explained the Bureau's goals to other FBI agents in his company: "This [Foreman] isn't really the guy we need to pop, I mean in terms of an actual perpetrator. This is the guy we need to pop to send a message. And that's all we're really doing."[5] By the early-1990s, considering his own safety, Dave Foreman stopped engaging in environmental "monkeywrenching" to express his political beliefs.[6] This deprived the environmental movement of one of its most prominent, charismatic leaders.

How do we make sense of this concerted effort of the U.S. government to squelch the actions of a dissident group? Is the suppression of Earth First! similar to what other dissidents have experienced in other times and places? Or is history too singular to try to pinpoint common forms of suppression that thread through the years?

In *Beyond Bullets: The Suppression of Dissent in the United States*, I argue that the state takes recurring actions, sometimes in concert with the mass media, in order to suppress dissent. Through an exploration of the relationship between dissidents, the state, and the mass media, I identify and categorize the ways in which the state and mass media have done this. By sifting through a wide range of contentious political activity and distilling the swirl of state, mass media, and dissident interaction into discrete categories, we can better understand the hidden interstices of U.S. history where suppression regularly resides. I try to shine a light on the underbelly of U.S. history, revealing patterns of containment that recur across space and time, making sense of the dynamic interactions between activists and the state both historically and contemporarily.

Dissident citizenship—replete with creativity, consciousness, and courage—is a crucial cog in the complex machine of democracy. As a force that challenges privilege and repudiates the thinning of political discourse, social critics serve the important democratic function of seeking out forms of authority and domination, and vigorously questioning their legitimacy. Therefore, understanding the role of the dissident citizen is critical to understanding democracy as it is practiced in the United States.

In *Beyond Bullets*, I identify and classify the actions the state and mass media take to stunt opposition and thus damage democracy. I spotlight the modes of suppression that feed into the process of dissident demobilization: when people cease from making contentious political claims. In fact, these modes of suppression are the pavement on the road to social movement demobilization. Chapters 2 through 13 explore each mode of suppression, using dissident histories to show how these modes play out in the real world. Along the way, I bring into focus the dialectic of restriction and resistance as I explore a number of activists and social movements engaged in a variety of struggles—from the anarchists of the early-twentieth century to the Communists of the 1950s to the Black Panther Party in the 1960s and 1970s to today's global justice movement.

Beyond Bullets addresses the following questions: How has the state taken action to squelch the practice of dissent in the United States? How has the state interacted with the mass media to achieve this goal? How do these state actions get individuals and groups to stop participating in social movements or opt to never join them in the first place?

Repression and Suppression

In this chapter, I'll lay some groundwork for thinking about the suppression of dissent in the United States. First, I will explain what I mean by the terms repression and suppression. Then, I'll explore the idea of dissident citizenship and how dissent and criminality have often been falsely equated in the United States. Finally, I'll outline what role the media play in this process, introducing concepts like media "framing" and journalistic norms like personalization, dramatization, and indexing along the way.

Clearly, repression affects the ability of dissident citizens and groups to engage in collective action. Nevertheless, political repression rarely gets defined in studies of dissidence. Frequently, the term "repression" is used to denote state-sponsored violence—or what David Snyder calls "governmental coercion"—carried out against people who contest existing power arrangements, and the term is often used in the context of research on revolutions and democratization.[7] Within these definitions, the direct violence component is prominent, and indeed central. But by focusing on the direct use of force, either through assassination, murder, torture, or beating, these definitions fail to consider subtler means of short-circuiting radical activity.

In *Beyond Bullets*, I differentiate between repression and suppression. Repression is violent, while suppression, a broader term, also encompasses other, more subtle modes of silencing opposition. I prefer to use "suppression" where others might use "repression." "Suppression" is less drastic or dramatic and lets us see beyond more spectacular instances of governmental coercion. The term suppression is especially appropriate for a study that focuses on the United States, where direct violence isn't used nearly as frequently as subtler forms of social control. So, "suppression" is a broad term that encompasses both repression—or, what I call "direct violence"—as well as subtler modes of silencing or preventing dissent. I use the term "repression" synonymously with "direct violence."

While authoritarian regimes tend to implement more direct violence against dissidents, liberal-democratic regimes, like the United States, tend to rely more on quieter methods.[8] In democratic societies, the state can't engage in open coercion too often without losing legitimacy. Thus, the state must come up with subtler ways to maintain social control. I agree with Mayer Zald's definition of social control as "the process by which individuals, groups, and organizations attempt to make performance, the behavior and operations of other groups, organizations, and individuals, conform to standards of behavior or normative preferences."[9] This is a negotiated process and not a wholly imposed one, although the negotiation between dissidents and the state occurs on uneven socio-political terrain. Because the subtler modes of suppression are more difficult to observe, and therefore harder to measure, many social movement researchers have sidestepped the issue entirely. Granted, there are many reasons why it's harder to gather this sort of data. First of all, activists often internalize the effects of suppression. Many won't discuss their demobilization because they feel ashamed they're no longer active or that the social movement they were part of failed to reach its goals. At the same time, state agents (e.g. from the FBI) may be unwilling to share information about their role in the process because it might incriminate them or their colleagues. Regardless of these hurdles, this book's central concern is the subtle, difficult-to-detect modes of suppression that don't necessarily include the bullet and the baton.

Robert Justin Goldstein describes suppression as "government action which grossly discriminates against persons or organizations viewed as presenting a fundamental challenge to existing power relationships or key governmental policies, because of their perceived political beliefs."[10] Building from this definition but altering it slightly, I define suppression as *a process through which the preconditions for dissident action, mobilization, and collective organization are inhibited by either raising their costs or minimizing their benefits.* This definition differs from Goldstein's in two important ways. It doesn't limit suppression to "government action" since there are often mediating forces and factors (such as self-censorship and mass-media practices) that play a large a role in silencing activists and social critics. Also, as Jennifer Earl points out, "private actors—particularly private organizations—have an immense capacity to repress movements."[11] While I agree with her that counter-demonstrators and groups like the KKK as well as private corporations move to squelch dissent, in this book I focus on the state and mass-media—a rich and variegated topic in itself—although occasionally I make reference to suppression carried out by private individuals or groups: what I call "outsourced suppression."[12] Secondly, the "gross discrimination" aspect of Goldstein's definition implies that suppression only affects the government's selected targets. However, I argue that suppression also affects the general public and other potential social movement allies. Finally, my definition specifies more clearly what suppression entails. As Charles Tilly notes, "repression is any action by another group which raises the contender's cost of collective action." This can be done in two ways: by focusing on "the target group's mobilization or directly on its collective action/activities," which means that a social movement's actions as well as its actors can be coerced and channeled into inaction.[13] However, it's also important to keep in mind that there are subtler forms of suppression (such as derogatory mass-media portrayals of activists) that do not so much raise the costs as minimize the benefits of mobilization. The definition I employ in this study lets us identify and examine the subtle nuances and mediating factors that often play important roles in suppression.[14]

So, if suppression is a process through which the preconditions for dissident action, mobilization, and collective organization are inhibited by either raising their costs or minimizing their benefits, what do I mean by "the preconditions of collective action"? The preconditions of collective action are factors that organizationally, operationally, strategically, or tactically make dissent more possible. More precisely, they involve the ability to:

1) Maintain solidarity (i.e. sustain the morale and commitment of current recruits)
2) Attract new recruits
3) Create, nurture, and support leaders / leadership[15]
4) Generate media coverage (preferably favorable)
5) Mobilize support from potentially sympathetic "bystander publics"
6) Carve out the tactical freedom to pursue social-change goals (rather than put resources toward defensive maintenance needs)[16]

When the modes of suppression that we'll be looking at come into play, either alone or in combination, dissident social movements are less able to meet these six preconditions. In fact, such suppressive tactics affect many of the preconditions for collective action at once, thus highlighting the interrelatedness of these state and mass-media actions. Conversely, each precondition may be inhibited by many of the forms of suppression, which highlights the complexity of suppression. As we'll see in the following chapters, the modes of suppression make these preconditions less likely, negate them, or prevent them from being achieved, thereby impinging upon the practice of dissent.

Suppression Under the Scholarly Microscope

Despite the importance of state suppression in the emergence, growth, and longevity of social movements, scholars have not explored the topic as much as one might think. Social-movement scholars Doug McAdam, Sidney Tarrow, and Charles Tilly view suppression and the threat of suppression as an "underemphasized corollary" of the study of mobilization and activism. They suggest that the lack of academic attention to subtler forms of coercion might have something to do with the particular historical moment in which the field of social movement studies emerged. "Its genesis in the relatively open politics of the American 'sixties,'" they write, produced "more emphasis on opportunities than on threats, more confidence in the expansion of organizational resources than on the organizational deficits that many challengers suffer." They go on to note that social-movement scholars have "focused inordinately on the *origins* of contention rather than on its later phases" such as movement maintenance and decline.[17] While most studies on dissident citizens and social movements explore the emergence, growth, and effectiveness of social movements, they virtually ignore the *failure* of movements to emerge, grow, become influential, maintain solidarity, meet their collective goals, and the factors—both internal and external—that play into this failure. In other words, scholars of social movements and activists involved in such movements haven't fully or systematically considered the suppression of dissent or the demobilization of social movements. As Kim Voss puts it, "Failure is an unpopular subject among social movement scholars. Like death and taxes at social gatherings, it is a topic that many of us avoid. In contrast, the birth of insurgency is eagerly debated. As a result, our theories of movement emergence are much more sophisticated and convincing than our models of movement development and decline."[18] On the activist front, contemplating the bleak reality of state suppression can sometimes be viewed as a paranoia-inducing, solidarity-puncturing endeavor.

This book will try to ameliorate this theoretical gap by offering a straightforward theory on the state and mass media's role in the suppression of dissent. At the same time, I hope to document the grim history of suppression in a way activists find useful. I believe that a deeper awareness of what the state and mass media have done in the past can help activists and social movement participants trace a path toward a more just future. Knowing the forms of state and mass media suppression in advance allow progressives to sidestep such debilitating actions and therefore become more effective activists.

The existing research that does take up the topic of dissent suppression has significant shortcomings. First of all, a predominant swathe of previous research focuses on the policing of protests and demonstrations at the expense of other, less obvious modes of suppression.[19] This makes sense, since researchers can often access documents—such as police records—that detail openly observable protests that happen in public spaces. Yet, radicals do much more than attend protests and there are many more modes of social control than policing. Research that only considers protest policing obscures the wide range of alternative oppositional tactics and the variety of subtler ways the state attempts to quash them.[20] While such research is compelling, its focus is unnecessarily narrow: it fails to explore the quiet, difficult-to-observe interstices of history where suppression is often located.

Studies that move beyond protest policing and attempt to categorize coercive tactics also have notable limitations. Marwan Khawaja has remarked that few of them "provide clear criteria for conceptually distinguishing among the many manifested forms of repression."[21] In fact, aside from two recent works,[22] one must go all the way back to 1979 and Gary Marx's seminal "External Efforts to Damage or Facilitate Social Movements: Some Patterns, Explanations, Outcomes, and Complications" to find a study that tries to comprehensively categorize external strategies against social movements.[23] In this work, Marx addresses other researchers' biased focus on factors *internal* to social movement organizations, such as sectarian squabbling, rather than *external* factors like the role of the government functionaries. Almost two decades later, Deborah Balser voiced the same critique.[24]

Other studies zero-in on specific movements and dissident groups during short time periods. In *Beyond Bullets*, I look at a variety of social movements over a wide range of times and places. For instance, Michael Carley explores the "successful state repression" of the American Indian Movement (AIM), while David Cunningham looks at the FBI's treatment of the New Left and the Ku Klux Klan.[25] Both researchers focus on the role that the FBI played against the groups they studied, while I look at how additional agents—such as police forces and the National Guard—fit into the picture. Moreover, Cunningham looks at how the FBI increased the *costs* of social-movement participation, whereas I also consider how the state *minimizes the benefits*.[26] Both Carley and Cunningham explore short time periods: Carley considers the 1970s, while Cunningham looks at the period between 1961 and 1971. This book, on the other hand, investigates an array of cases ranging from the early-twentieth century to the early-twenty-first century.[27]

Neither Carley nor Cunningham make much mention of the role of the mass media, whereas this book highlights the ways the media help hobble dissident citizens and social movements. In fact, these authors are not alone in downplaying the role that media play in the suppression of dissent. Few studies include mass media outlets, let alone explore in detailed descriptive terms the role they sometimes perform.[28] While the state is a crucial component in the process, so are the mass media, especially since most people learn what they know about social movements through mass-media sources. As we will see in Chapters 10 through 13, the mass media can depict social movements in negative, degrading ways. Their transmission of the state's unfavorable portrayals of dissidents, has important effects not only on social movement participants, but also on potential recruits and supporters.

Over the past thirty years, a number of studies have traced the effect of suppression on dissident activity in an effort "to discover the 'true' relationship between repression and dissent."[29] These studies range in topic from the conditions affecting the use of political repression to the timing of suppression as well as its scope and intensity.[30] They range in geographical location, from Germany and Northern Ireland to Argentina, Iran, and Belarus.[31] Charles Brockett notes a well-known paradox that state violence "smothers popular mobilization under some circumstances, but at other times similar (or even greater) levels of violence will provoke mass collective action rather than pacify the target population."[32] In fact, the range of empirically supported relationships between suppression and dissent is striking: there is little agreement. Some claim that suppression decreases mobilization, while others say it increases it. Some say mobilization decreases suppression, while others argue the opposite. *Beyond Bullets*, however, shifts focus away from the *effects* of suppression, and instead considers its *forms* and how the state responds to dissent. I don't try to come to any universal conclusion that would apply to both democratic and authoritarian states. Rather, I focus on suppression in the United States. While previous social movement scholars have provided an array of coherent, historically specific descriptions of how particular individuals and social movements were denigrated and derailed, I step back and consider the bigger picture, offering an explanation of dissident suppression in twentieth and twenty-first century USAmerica.

What Is Dissident Citizenship?

The suppression of dissent is usually couched in the syntax of exceptional circumstances and justified in a rhetoric of peril. Dangerous situations, the forces of order tell us, require drastic measures. The state and mass media often invoke the language of crisis as they shrink social space for dissidents and their ideas and actions. Crisis language and exceptionality work powerfully together to tacitly, and sometimes explicitly, warn activists that they should not continue to engage in oppositional behavior. In such a milieu, dissenters collectively become a negative symbol representing a complex web of forces and figures that are perceived as a devious, dangerous, dishonest threat to the social order. Certainly many dissidents *are* a threat to the social order.

In fact, being such a threat is their unambiguous intention, since the social order is unjust, exploitative, and ethically lopsided. Yet these activists do not aim to be flattened into symbols of derision designed by the state and news media for public consumption. This erroneous symbolism whereby the state and mass media portray dissidents as treacherous and unprincipled can be a powerful cultural concoction with devastating effects.

In the perpetual societal trade-off between freedom and security, there is frequently a noticeable shift in emphasis toward the latter when dissident citizens challenge the status quo. Exceptionality functions in an important way on both the international and domestic levels. The state, in concert with the mass media, delimits what are considered "appropriate" words and deeds during "exceptional" moments when state action is ostensibly needed to in-stall order. In moments of alleged "crisis," the existing government's desire to maintain order and defend the rule of law usually gains greater currency,[33] or, as Giorgio Agamben puts it: "the state of exception requires that there be increasingly numerous sections of residents deprived of political rights."[34] According to Ricardo Blaug, in times of crisis, "people tend to pathologize those who hold views different from their own."[35] Activists come to learn this quickly during "exceptional" moments when the suppression of dissent is proceeding in full force and they find that oppositional political practice is discouraged, if not by the police baton, then by more subtle means.

On the political terrain of crisis, radicals are often depicted negatively by the state and mass media as offering nothing but criticisms and objections, which downplays their regenerative qualities rooted in creativity, conscien-tiousness, and courage. Dissenting citizens not only speak to perceived dan-gers and problems in society, but also to the opportunities and possibilities of vigorous political life. They challenge the axiomatic, taken-for-granted "realities" of the prevailing social order. They question the silences, omis-sions, and limitations of society as we know it. In historical hindsight, dis-sident citizens are often held up as national heroes. Certainly this is the case in the United States, from Sam Adams and his revolutionary comrades to Harriet Tubman and the slavery abolitionists, from César Chávez to Martin Luther King, Jr. It is difficult to deny the importance of these people in U.S. history; they are held up as model USAmericans precisely because their dis-sident philosophies strongly challenged the prevailing social norms of the time and because of their persistent commitment in the face of risk, fear, and sometimes even danger.

But what, more precisely, is dissent and what is dissident citizenship? Dissent came into English in the late sixteenth century as both a general term meaning disagreement in outlook or sentiment and as a specific term meaning difference of opinion in regard to religious doctrine or worship.

With both meanings, it signified the opposite of consent or assent. It is by definition conflictual and presents significant challenges to the social order. Yet for dissident citizens, conflict is not an end: it is a means of public education and possibly even the creation of newfound consensus.

In its most general sense, dissent indicates the rejection of commonly held views or disagreement with majority opinions (e.g. the dissenting opinion of a judge). However, dissent goes beyond disagreement. It's much more active than that. Dissident citizens don't just disagree with predominant political ideas; they take action to change things. Dissent is the collective mechanism for activating social change.

This involves both a dedication to autonomous thinking and a willingness to act on behalf of nonconformist principles and ideals. Dissident citizens disregard the resilient, pervasive social pressures to conform not only their thinking, but also their behavior. They actively push to meet the goals and aims of causes bigger than themselves. They disagree with and actively oppose dominant doctrines and attempt to widen the path of freedom and improve the vibrancy of civil society. In short, they widen social dialogue.

Erik Doxtader defines dissent as "a moment of conflict in which taken-for-granted rules, topics, and norms of public deliberation are contested, opposed or transgressed."[36] Dissenting citizens break many of the rules of deliberative democracy and discourse. McAdam, Tarrow, and Tilly distinguish two types of oppositional politics: "contained contention," in which all contenders are previously recognized actors who make political claims in conventional ways and "transgressive contention," in which some contenders are new political actors on the scene who engage in innovative, sometimes unorthodox political action that is either unprecedented or prohibited.[37]

Clearly, the people we're talking about fall into this latter category. They move beyond the normal activity of deliberative citizens who actively participate in the contained politics of institutionalized, representative democracy. They see the deliberative role, regardless of how critical it may be, as merely a starting point, and they expand the official definition of "politics" itself to include things like direct action and self-organization outside the electoral and legislative realm. They act vigorously against "received wisdom," hegemonic ideas, and unjust institutions.

Rather than relying on voting, petitioning, and letter writing, dissident citizens create a variety of unconventional public spaces and events—such as protest marches, picket lines, worker strikes, consumer boycotts, and street theater—on the margins and in the fractures of the polity. Dissident citizens can come from anywhere on the political spectrum, but they share a propensity to engage in alternative forms of political engagement that are radically democratic, innovative, and oppositional.

Dissent and the Public Sphere

Dissident citizens don't move beyond the deliberative, sanctioned public sphere just for the heck of it. They understand that the seemingly benign call for cool-headed deliberation can actually be a sly way to dictate the terms of discourse, thereby dismissing and subordinating social criticism. Feminist activists and scholars, among others, have questioned oversimplified portrayals of the public sphere. Nancy Fraser critiques the deliberative realm of conventional politics, established actors, and traditional rules—emphasizing its "*bourgeois, masculinist*" nature.[38] She says the idea of the public sphere, supported by people like Jurgen Habermas and others, is actually an exclusionary device that marginalizes significant groups of people, including women, "the plebeian classes," and other groups.[39] Fraser argues that orderly deliberation, a crucial element in the idea of the public sphere, "can serve as a mask for domination," particularly when a dissident group's rhetoric can be construed as opposing deliberative democracy. Deliberative processes in public spheres will tend to operate to the advantage of dominant groups and to the disadvantage of subordinates," writes Fraser.[40] In societies where vast inequality exists, it can be very difficult to carve out safe spaces where such power relations don't hold sway. Therefore, the public sphere is founded upon a central contradiction: the political procedures and practices that are supposed to enhance the freedom, liberty, and autonomy of all citizens are the same ones that exclude many individuals and groups, as well as their ideas, interests, and grievances. This chasm between democratic principle and on-the-ground democratic practice leads dissident citizens to forge alternative modes of participation. Rather than relenting to false consensus, Fraser notes that members of historically subordinated groups—like women, racial minorities, gays and lesbians, and workers—form alternative spaces of dissent, or what she calls "subaltern counterpublics."[41] The dissent practiced in such spaces checks the exclusionary nature of consensus-building procedures that are central to deliberative democracy in the public sphere.

Jane Mansbridge seconds Fraser's safe space-creating function of subaltern counterpublics, and highlights the crucial role these safe spaces play in democratic society. Were it not for these subaltern counterpublics, many dissident citizens would be unable to process, adapt, and reformulate their ideas, strategies, and tactics. These zones of opposition provide safe arenas from which alternative ideas and principles can be catapulted into the mainline public sphere, thereby widening democracy.[42] As such, these subaltern counterpublics are crucial spaces for the practice of dissent.

Yet many of these subaltern counterpublics are not simply working outside the pathways of institutional power in order to muster the confidence to ask for a seat at the state-sanctioned table. Nor do many of them have the desire to make the table bigger. Rather, many of the dissidents featured in *Beyond Bullets* want to throw out the table altogether because they believe true democracy is impossible if the existing institutions aren't destroyed and replaced by new social relations. Many members of these progressive, oppositional groups believe that nothing truly transformative ever makes it to the institutional table if it's not backed up by massive activity thrumming in the streets and thronging in workplaces. Many dissidents would say that real change, especially anything that threatens the power or wealth of the dominant classes, never originates within the institutions of our "democratic society." As long as there are rulers and ruled, owners and owned, any meaningful social change will be forced from below. In fact, they argue, often convincingly, that formal politics within the institutional pathways of power is the problem; unequal dealings with the government only pave the path of co-optation and domestication, of legislated appeasement that takes the wind out of the sails of social movements and replaces their ideals with a pale, government-sanctioned facsimile.

In *Beyond Bullets*, dissident citizens and groups are defined by the following three criteria: (1) They publicly challenge prevailing structures of power and / or the underlying logic of public policy, (2) they engage in some extra-institutional, oppositional tactics, though they may be flexible actors who operate both inside and outside the institutional pathways of political power, and (3) on at least some issues, they have marginal stances that are not consistently entering the dominant political discourse.[43]

When faced with dissent, the state has four options: (1) suppression; (2) appeasement; (3) co-optation; and (4) disregard. These are not mutually exclusive categories. For instance, in its dealings with the environmental movement, the state can work with name-brand environmental groups like the Sierra Club and the Environmental Defense Fund, sometimes appeasing them with what they want and sometimes only offering part of what they want in return for a seat at the proverbial table. At the same time, the state can be suppressing more direct-action-oriented environmentalists from groups like Earth First! and the Earth Liberation Front.

The state's efforts to suppress dissent, to discourage organized resistance and prevent it from widening, are a common reaction. According to Christian Davenport the state's tendency to resort to suppression when challenged by a domestic threat is one of the "few relationships in the social sciences that [has] stood the test of time." He notes that this finding "has been supported with political-historical as well as statistical evidence concerning most countries in the world over varied time periods from the late eighteenth century to the present."[44] Frances Fox Piven and Richard Cloward adamantly assert that the state suppresses dissent not only to preserve political and social stability, but also to maintain the stability of capitalism itself, a point that should not be left out of the explanatory mix.[45]

The Criminalization of Dissent

According to constitutional scholars David Cole and James Dempsey, "Political freedom is a society's safety valve, allowing the passionately critical a nonviolent way to express their dissatisfaction with the status quo. Dissent is the mechanism for initiating social change. Shutting off this safety valve only encourages those who have no desire to see the process of peaceful change work."[46] This book illuminates the complex set of state and mass-media actions that, when combined, place serious limits on political freedom, and therefore restrict the peaceful—and sometimes not-so-peaceful—quest for social justice. As I explore the relations between dissidents, the state, and the mass media, I underscore the tendency to falsely equate crime and radical dissent.

While Cole and Dempsey are correct that dissent can be "society's safety valve," many of the revolutionary dissidents in this book would reply that advocating "the process of peaceful change" is itself a surreptitious form of social control rooted in political freedoms that are in large part illusory. For such revolutionaries, questions of violence and non-violence are beside the point in a world where the state and powerful corporations confect a political and economic system that is saturated with violence, discrimination, and injustice. In the face of such a system, these people often deliberately express their dissent through illegal acts. Such acts are the radical core of civil disobedience. Under this long-established logic, to *not* engage in illegal activity is to afford the state a veneer of legitimacy despite its silence in the face of inherently violent poverty and inequality. This important critique aside, many activists have rooted their opposition in the protections afforded by the U.S. legal system.

While the U.S. Constitution affirms the freedom of speech, assembly, and the petitioning of grievances, in reality the state has regularly trampled these rights when it comes to dissenters. This has especially been the case during times of war. In these moments, which include declared wars and metaphorical wars such as the "War on Terrorism," dissent is cast by the state as disloyalty, and in some cases disloyalty that crosses the line into illegality. As historian Geoffrey R. Stone notes, "the United States has a long and unfortunate history of overreacting to the perceived dangers of wartime… Time and time again, Americans have suppressed dissent, imprisoned and deported dissenters, and then—later—regretted their actions."[47] The First Amendment (freedom of speech, assembly, and the right to petition grievances), the Fourth Amendment (protection against unreasonable searches and seizures) and the due process guarantee of the Fifth Amendment would all seem to be legal weapons of defense for activists during these fear-laden, intensity-drenched historical moments; however, these are usually the constitutional rights that dissidents have been forced to forfeit.

The judicial branch of government has not always protected these cherished constitutional rights when power relations are being contested. In fact, U.S. political culture—shades of which are reflected in the courts—has exhibited significant levels of intolerance for political minorities. Political scientist James Gibson, in his study of civil liberties during the post-World War II Red Scare, notes that, "Although intolerance may not be pervasive in everyday politics, when a crisis emerges, the political culture helps structure the response."[48] In moments of crisis the state may engage in "legal repression," whereby government officials must balance the need to exert social control in the short term and the need for long-term legitimacy based on respect for due process and the rule of law.[49] In many cases, emphasis is placed on the former, while constitutional rights get temporarily brushed aside or conveniently reinterpreted to suit the political moment. This was especially the case during the early-twentieth century, when the U.S. Supreme Court upheld convictions for giving speeches against the draft and against war. For example, in *Schenck v. United States* (1919), the Court upheld the conviction of Charles Schenck for printing a pamphlet that argued the draft was unconstitutional, morally dubious, and carried out for the benefit of the rich.[50] In this case Justice Oliver Wendell Holmes offered the "clear and present danger" test for determining when speech could be legally limited by the government.[51] Holmes wrote that if one's speech were significantly and imminently dangerous, then it could be deemed illegal. Neither a speaker's intent nor the value or veracity of his or her words were as important as whether the expression created a clear and present danger of serious harm.

Despite the promising ring of such a standard, these criteria were then used to uphold Schenck's conviction. The Court ruled his efforts to undermine the draft had the "natural and probable tendency" to deflate men's compliance to conscription, although the Court neither offered nor required any evidence of such an effect. As Justice Holmes wrote for the unanimous majority upholding the conviction, "The question in every case is whether the words used are used in such circumstances and are of such a nature as to create a clear and present danger that they will bring about the substantive evils Congress has a right to prevent." He added, "It is a question of proximity and degree. When a nation is at war many things that might be said in time of peace are such a hindrance to its effort that their utterance will not be endured so long as men fight and no Court could regard them as protected by any constitutional right."[52] In other words, according to Robert K. Murray, the Supreme Court "could not refrain from holding that ideological nonconformity, even though no criminal act was involved, constituted in itself a clear and present danger."[53] In this way, dissident efforts to discourage military enlistment were reframed by the Court as conspiracy to obstruct recruitment, thus transmogrifying speech acts into criminal behavior.

This logic also reigned in the 1950s, as McCarthyism unfolded. Laws like the Internal Security Act of 1950, which made it illegal to try to establish a "totalitarian dictatorship" in the United States and which required Communist organizations to register with the U.S. Attorney General, provided significant tests for the First Amendment. According to Robert Justin Goldstein: "The Internal Security Act was clearly one of the most massive onslaughts against freedom of speech and association ever launched in American history."[54] Large majorities in both chambers of Congress condoned this "massive onslaught" on the Bill of Rights, passing the Act over President Truman's veto. It was not until the McCarthy Era had passed that these laws began to be vigorously challenged—and ultimately overturned—in the courts.

In the last four decades, the U.S. Supreme Court has more adamantly protected the First Amendment's assurance of free speech and association. For example, in the case of *Brandenburg v. Ohio* (1969), the Supreme Court ruled that it was legal for people to make statements advocating the use of force or other illegal behavior unless those statements are "directed to inciting or producing imminent lawless action and is likely to incite or produce such action."[55] This case, which concerned the free speech of a member of the Ku Klux Klan, threw out the "clear and present danger" criteria—or at least expanded the criteria to require actual clear dangers that were both serious and imminent—thereby broadening the scope of the First Amendment. Therefore, the Court asserted that speech which *advocated* crime was protected by the Constitution. Later, the Supreme Court ruled that speech that creates a climate of violence is also constitutionally protected.[56] In effect, imminent incitement became the criteria by which dissidents could be prosecuted. The Court has also protected the right to political association, asserting in 1972 that First Amendment rights could not be denied on the basis of "guilt by association alone, without [establishing] that an individual's association poses the threat feared by the Government."[57] Rather, the government was given the burden of establishing a knowing affiliation with a group or organization pursuing illegal aims. The government must also demonstrate a specific intent to further those unlawful goals. Essentially, it was legal for activists to associate with individuals or groups engaged in illegal endeavors, but it was *not* legal to explicitly attempt to advance or expand these endeavors. However, as we will see, guilt by association has been resolutely resuscitated by the Bush administration in the wake of the terrorist attacks of 11 September 2001.

All together, these rulings serve, in theory, to constrain the ability of the government to legally suppress its political foes. However, even with the Supreme Court's propensity to protect First Amendment rights, the courts have, according to Cole and Dempsey, "erected procedural barriers that make it difficult for the victims of political spying to obtain judicial relief."[58] For instance, in the 1972 case *Laird v. Tatum*, the Supreme Court declared that Vietnam War protesters could not legally contest the far-reaching governmental surveillance programs that were monitoring their organizing efforts. This ruling was based on the "standing doctrine," which means that police or FBI surveillance can only be legally challenged in the courts if the dissident groups can demonstrate that the surveillance is not only intrusive, but also injurious.[59] Even if such legal challenges emerge, the glacier-like cycle of governmental suppression, dissenter objection, and judicial vindication can take years and can simultaneously drain dissident resources. In general, the Supreme Court has been disinclined to place limits on FBI investigations and surveillance. This is especially the case in times of war when, as Howard Zinn notes, the courts have exhibited "historic subservience" to state authority.[60] This will be explored in much greater detail in Chapter 5 during the discussion of surveillance as a form of state suppression.

The Fourth Amendment and its guarantees against unreasonable searches and seizures would also, at first glance, appear to afford legal protection for dissident citizens. But, much like the historical interpretation of the First Amendment, the Fourth Amendment, in practice, has not been as useful for the defense of dissent as one might expect. While the courts have consistently asserted that, in criminal cases against dissident citizens, physical searches and wiretaps can only be conducted when a judge has issued an order based on probable cause that a crime is in process or about to be carried out, and that the search will unearth evidence of this crime, search warrants are almost never denied. For example, between 1987 and 1997, law enforcement officials made 8597 requests for wiretaps and only three were refused by judges at the federal, state, or local levels. This translates to a denial rate of 0.03%.[61] When a foreign dissident group is involved, the courts have offered even thinner protection. As transnational dissident activity surges with the rise of economic and cultural globalization, this is becoming increasingly relevant.[62] Also, the U.S. Supreme Court has ruled that information gathered by FBI informants, infiltrators, and undercover agents is not protected under the Fourth Amendment. According to Cole and Dempsey:

Under the "invited informer" principle, the Court has reasoned that a person or political organization has no legitimate expectation of privacy in information voluntarily shared with a third party in the mistaken belief that the information will not be turned over to the government. Thus, an informant can record his own phone conversations with activists who have invited him into their group or "wear a wire" to record conversations at meetings for the government, without any court order or probable cause showing.[63]

The lack of legal restraint on the infiltrator and informer has deep historical roots, as will be discussed in Chapter 6, which focuses on infiltration, badjacketing, and the use of agent provocateurs as methods of state suppression.

Finally, dissident citizens might expect, at the very least, that they will enjoy the right to due process under the Fifth Amendment. Again, though, dissidents can sometimes find themselves wallowing in a yawning chasm between the written laws that are designed to constrain government conduct and the real-world application of such laws. This is especially the case in recent times with the "War on Terror." While the Fifth Amendment assures that in criminal proceedings the government cannot use secret information that is not available to the defendant and his/her lawyer, recently, in terrorism-related deportation hearings and criminal proceedings, secret evidence has been deemed admissible.[64] In October, 2001, Attorney General John Ashcroft signed a directive entitled "National Security: Prevention of Acts of Violence and Terrorism," which, under the aegis of fighting terrorism, permits the Department of Justice to handpick specific prisoners for "special administrative measures." These measures include complete isolation and the total denial of communication and contact with the outside world. The new regulations also allow intelligence agencies to command the Bureau of Prisons to detain an inmate incommunicado for up to one year, with additional one-year periods of detention being considered. And when prisoners are allowed to correspond with their lawyers, they find themselves under closer scrutiny, as previously private attorney-client interactions may now be monitored, as delimited by the USA PATRIOT Act.[65] Renewed battles over these facets of the Fifth Amendment continue to be waged in the courts. Due process matters will be considered in more detail in Chapters 8 and 9 during the discussion of two modes of suppression: (1) harassment arrests, and (2) extraordinary laws and rules. I will offer a critical assessment of the USA PATRIOT Act in Chapter 14.

The First, Fourth, and Fifth Amendments to the Constitution are often retracted, if temporarily, in the name of national security. Supporters of this logic reason that in moments of national crisis, unity should be the tune of the day, and those who refuse to sing along—dissident citizens and others—are dangerous denizens who are jeopardizing national security. Suppressing the actions of these people is thus seen as more acceptable by the general public. State suppression is rationalized rhetorically in ways that emphasize exceptional, perilous circumstances.

Virtually every time in U.S. history when the civil liberties of dissident citizens were curtailed, the declared rationale was to protect "national security." Nevertheless, "national security" is a notoriously slippery term, often invoked by state functionaries to explain away the violation of civil liberties. Historian Melvyn Leffler defines national security policy as "the decisions and actions deemed imperative to protect domestic core values from external threats." But this definition is vague and unhelpful analytically.[66] What are "domestic core values"? "External threats"? Actions "deemed imperative"? By whom? As Murray Edelman puts it:

> The very term "national interest" encourages people to redefine their concrete interests to make them consonant with the interests that are already strong in domestic political interplay. "National interest" is a totally ambiguous term in the sense that it can mean whatever an individual or group chooses to read into it, even though the various meanings are often different and often conflicting. Its very semantic hollowness makes it all the more potent symbolically, however. Once an official governmental agency defines a policy as in the national interest it is endowed with compelling emotional effect flowing from....various social psychological processes....This effect is especially potent if the government defines the national interest by publicized action as well as by its words. This general interest is perceived as transcending the concrete interests of specific groups and so draws support even from some people who are hurt by it. Its lack of semantic precision enables it to condense for each person a set of empirically unobservable but emotionally compelling beliefs and meanings consonant with their perception of the national interest.[67]

This malleability of meaning is a crucial element to the suppression of domestic dissent. It's worth noting, though, that the Supreme Court has not always exhibited "historic subservience" when it comes to the issue of national security and the freedom of speech. For example, in the 1971 case of Daniel Ellsberg and the Pentagon Papers he helped bring to public attention, the Supreme Court allowed the *New York Times* to publish what the Nixon administration claimed was sensitive information. Ellsberg and his co-defendant Anthony Russo were charged with, among other things, conspiracy to defraud the government from withholding classified information from the public, embezzlement of the Papers, and giving national-defense-related documents to people not permitted to obtain them.[68] The final charge was made under the Espionage Act of 1917, a wartime law that was only in effect because President Harry Truman had declared a state of emergency in 1950 over the Korean War, and this declaration had never been revoked.[69] In the end, the Court ruled that the Pentagon Papers did not threaten vital national security, and this set an important precedent for the relationship between the press and government over such issues.[70]

All the News That's Fit to Suppress:
The Role of the Mass Media

"Information," said Thomas Jefferson, "is the currency of democracy." In the modern era, the mass media are a crucial linchpin in the dissemination of information. Therefore it is important to ask—in the context of the state's suppression of dissent—how are dissidents portrayed in the mass media? Additionally, how do members of various social movements (leaders, follow-ers, anti-leaders, supporters, fellow travelers) perceive media coverage of their groups' efforts, and how does mass-media coverage affect the subsequent strategies and tactics they adopt? To fully comprehend how opposition is demobilized in the United States, it is important to consider the relations the mass media have with both the state and dissident citizens.

It is especially important to examine how the U.S. "prestige media" de-pict dissent, given the distribution and influence of these national news out-lets. Throughout *Beyond Bullets* I use terms like "prestige press" and "prestige media." The former means the most influential newspapers in the United States: the *New York Times*, the *Washington Post*, the *Los Angeles Times*, *Boston Globe*, *USA Today*, and the *Wall Street Journal*. The "prestige media," a larger umbrella term, also include the major television networks: ABC, CBS, CNN, Fox, and NBC.

The mass media have played an important historical role in suppressing dissent in the United States. They tend to look more favorably on people who operate within the system and to disparage those whose oppositional activi-ties move beyond sanctioned forms of action. While activists are sometimes able to frame issues and grievances in a manner satisfactory to them, they are more often frustrated by what they deem inadequate—and sometimes even derisive—mass-media coverage. Coverage frequently fails to focus on the issues and ideas of dissident citizens and social movements and actually depicts the participants negatively, thereby undermining their efforts.

Mass-media coverage—or a lack thereof—influences the nature, form, and development of social movements, as well as the ability of these movements to reach their goals.[71] Understanding the role of the mass media is crucial to comprehending how social movements coalesce, build, and maintain themselves, as well as how they decide to frame their dissident messages.[72] Despite the substantial resources that social movements expend to obtain media attention and to sculpt this attention into positive coverage, social-movement scholars Dominique Wisler and Marco Giugni assert that, for the most part, the effects mass media have on the practice of dissent have been "largely overlooked" in theories and research on social movements.[73]

The interplay between social movements and the mass media creates a situation in which activists feel pressed to amp up or escalate their tactics. Escalation is both a reaction to the ability of social-movement opponents to adapt to previous tactics as well as the result of the mass media's unquenchable penchant for novelty. Dissident challengers, who are almost by definition at a disadvantage in terms of social status and resources, often try to make up for these limitations by engaging in exceptional, creative actions that are designed to gain mass-media attention. Contained, sanctioned actions are not likely to garner mass-media attention, but disruptive, novel events improve the chances of mass-media interest. This relationship with the media creates a dialectic of escalation whereby activists feel perpetually compelled to foment protest activities that are novel and attention-grabbing enough to be newsworthy. Yet, this creates a dilemma in that such actions can be easily dismissible as gimmicky, violent, or weird. Also, such actions can distract target audiences or trivialize the short- and long-term goals of social movements. Initiating effective dissident actions that are not eminently rejectable by both the media and the general public can be a fine line to walk. Even if social movements garner mainstream press, they nevertheless have to ceaselessly adapt, since what is considered exceptional, and therefore newsworthy, keeps changing. This all leads to carrying out "pseudo-events" characterized by inflated rhetoric and militancy beyond the group's capabilities, which sets the table for mass-media deprecation. Such media deprecation will be fully explored in Chapter 12.

At the same time, sociologists John D. McCarthy and Clark McPhail assert that, since the late-1960s, there has been a gradual but persistent "institutionalization of protest" whereby protest has "become a normal part of the political process, its messages seen as a legitimate supplement to voting, petitioning, and lobbying efforts to influence government policy and practice." Simultaneously, "the recurring behavioral repertoires of both protesters and police, and their interactions with one another, have become institutionalized and therefore routinized, predictable, and, perhaps as a result, of diminishing impact."[74] This "diminishing impact" occurs in part because the state has enjoyed an increase in its ability to control the timing, locale, and mode of dissident action, even as the right to protest has been legally fortified in the United States. But, importantly, this "diminishing impact" is also due to the way protest activity is framed by the mass media.[75] The routinization of protest affects how much attention social movements get from the media. What was formerly riveting and fresh can quickly become prosaic and ever-so-yesterday.

When trying to explain deficient media coverage, activists and scholars often correctly insist we consider who owns the media. Media scholar, critic, and activist Robert McChesney explores historical trends in ownership and media composition, as well as the structure of the mass media, in an attempt to understand constraints on the collection, processing, and dissemination of information.[76] Asserting the existence of a "corporate media cartel," McChesney argues that "the striking structural features of the U.S. media system in the 1990s are concentration and conglomeration."[77] This rampant concentration of media power, which has spilled over into the twenty-first century, has a deleterious effect on democracy and dissident citizenship in the United States, he asserts, as it steers the public down the rutty road of mass depoliticization. In other words, what is good for the media firms on Wall Street is not always good for the general public. McChesney characterizes the structure of the corporate media system as a locale where "the wealthy and powerful few make the most important decisions with virtually no informed public participation."[78]

In late capitalism, with mass-media conglomeration the order of the day, journalists must also acknowledge, if subconsciously, formidable economic constraints. Efficiency and profit increasingly shape the news business, and this compulsion has led many mass-media outlets to slash their investigative journalism budgets.[79] Mass-media concentration has important implications in terms of news content. For example, a study that looked at mass-media coverage of the 1996 Telecommunications Act found "systematic evidence that the financial interests of media owners influence not only newspaper editorials but straight news reporting as well."[80] Activists who are able to garner media attention may do so more because of the logic of the capitalist market and the economic interests of news organizations than because of the inherent value of their ideas. Capitalist media firms privilege drama and newness since they help sell their products, so if radicals carry out innovative, dramatic events they may well rouse journalists to cover them.

Mass-media concentration affects newsmaking in less direct ways, too. With an ever-shrinking number of media firms controlling the news terrain, mass-media workers have fewer options for employment. This creates a subtle form of discipline, as it swerves workers, whether consciously or subconsciously, away from controversial stories and perspectives that rock the boat and toward safer stories that don't offend their manager, supervisor, or media owner. Incorrigible boat-rockers, if reprimanded for writing stories that don't fit the corporate line or support corporate interests, may have a harder time finding work. Informal blacklists are easier to maintain the fewer "competitors" there are in the field.

Some social commentators characterize the mass media as a metaphorical marketplace of ideas that rests upon two real-world markets: the political and the economic.[81] While some argue that the marketplace allows journalists to achieve excellence, media scholar Robert Entman asserts that "the competition prevents journalists from supplying the kind of news that would allow the average American to practice sophisticated citizenship."[82] Edward Herman and Noam Chomsky's institutional analysis of the mass media employs a "propaganda model" that takes the critique of the marketplace of ideas a step further:

> the mass media serve as a system for communicating messages and symbols to the general populace. It is their function to amuse, entertain, and inform, and to inculcate individuals with the values, beliefs, and codes of behavior that will integrate them into the institutional structures of the larger society. In a world of concentrated wealth and major conflicts of class interest, to fulfill this role requires systematic propaganda.[83]

Their "propaganda model" zeros in on wealth and power inequality and demonstrates how this affects mass-media interests and news selection. They show how the prestige media primarily function as a transmitter of state propaganda; the very structure of the mass media in the United States prevents it—for the most part—from disputing the version of events emanating from governmental and other politically important sources.[84] Todd Gitlin, professor of journalism and sociology at Columbia University, contends that, despite being embedded in a hegemonic corporate structure, mass-media journalists actually have more leeway and autonomy than many media critics give them credit for.[85] Nevertheless, individual journalists must work within the constraining ideological matrix that thrives inside the corporate media culture. In this environment, fundamental questions about the way society is organized are discouraged. That is not to say, of course, that specific claims that state officials make through the mass media are never disputed. The mass media can be an arena of sharp-edged contention, especially when significant sectors of the political and/or economic elite challenge each other in the public sphere over policy decisions.[86] However, this disagreement usually takes the form of deliberative democracy—or "contained politics"—rather than dissident citizenship and "transgressive politics."

Patrick O'Heffernan has proposed an alternative model to explain the relationship between the state and the mass media: the mutual exploitation model. By this he means that now—with the rise of the global media industry and the worldwide U.S. foreign policy and diplomatic community—the relationship between government and media is sometimes competitive and sometimes cooperative, but that this relationship is only incidental to each group's self-interest. He describes the government and media as "two very desegregated, aggressive ecosystems constantly bargaining over a series of 'wants' while they manipulate both the structure and output of the other for their own advantage. Sometimes the result is mutually beneficial and sometimes it is not."[87] While it is important to consider these bigger-picture models for understanding the role of media in society, one can also gain insights by looking at the on-the-ground, in-the-newsroom micro-operations mass-media workers abide by and are constrained by.

Framing Dissent: The Machinations of Deprecation

Working journalists face a barrage of professional and logistical pressures. They all must deal with organizational dictates, both temporal and spatial. Ever-shrinking page space and airtime affect journalistic decision-making, while deadlines and space considerations constrain journalists,[88] as do editorial preferences,[89] and pressure from publishers.[90] Imminent deadlines may lead to one-source stories,[91] and the single source is likely to be an authoritative official with ties to the state.[92] Story placement—whether an article appears on the front page or is buried deep in the newspaper—affects how social movement actions and statements are interpreted by the general public. Also, headline selection and photograph placement—which are often editorial decisions—can significantly influence how the news consumer construes social-movement-related events and situations.[93]

The mass media present social movements and their actions through a process of framing, in which easily identifiable lenses refract the news and shape public opinion.[94] A frame is "an interpretive schemata that simplifies and condenses the 'world out there' by selectively punctuating and encoding objects, situations, events, experiences, and sequences of actions within one's present or past environment."[95] Newspaper articles or television news stories use certain frames to organize the presentation of opinions and facts. A news story covering an anti-war protest could adopt a frame that portrays the dissidents as committed humanitarians who hold grounded, well-thought-out positions based on compassion and kindness and who take democracy seriously. Alternatively, the news story could represent these same activists as uninformed rabble-rousers with a penchant for cheap thrills, negative attitudes, and facial jewelry.

Frames present structured cross-sections of perpetually-evolving public affairs. According to Robert Entman, framing "involves selection and salience. To frame is to select some aspects of a perceived reality and make them more salient in a communicating text, in such a way as to promote a particular problem definition, causal interpretation, moral evaluation, and/or treatment recommendation for the item described."[96] Therefore, by framing socio-political issues and controversies in specific ways, news organizations present—if tacitly—the foundational causes and potential consequences of a social problem or issue, as well as possible remedies.

Frames not only overlap and reinforce each other, but also frequently compete. For instance, mass-media coverage of social movements that features a frame emphasizing violence clashes with—or at least challenges—injustice frames that the group may be trying to highlight. On one level, coverage of dissidence can be seen as a framing contest whereby different social actors and groups present their frames in an effort to gain social currency, the contested topography of public discourse. However, at the end of the day, the mass media collectively serve as the arbiter of these framing contests by implementing and synthesizing their own frames. Framing, as Entman notes, "plays a major role in the exertion of political power, and the frame in the news text is really the imprint of power—it registers the identity of actors or interests that competed to dominate the text."[97] By focusing more on the events organized by social movements and the characteristics of participants and less on the social issues that galvanized the contention and the context that informs it, the mass media depict protest activity (and dissidence more broadly) in ways that can undercut the agendas of these movements.

Dissidents are often depicted as violent, disruptive, or downright strange. But why is this the case? Clearly, language practices affect the way that activists are rendered in the press and on television. The word choice and phrasing of viewpoints put forth in the mass media can influence the opinions and behavior of news consumers.[98] The subtle connotations of word choice and phraseology tap into wellsprings of history that are drenched in emotional valence, and are therefore powerful forces of perception.[99] As we will see, use of certain phrases and specific imagery tends to strip dissidents of credibility and to make them appear irresponsible, fringe-like, and sometimes even violent. This translates to both themes of deviance and ludicrousness, and these deprecatory themes affect the ability of dissident citizens and social movements to meet their objectives.

The mass-media's negative depiction of social movements is not so much a conspiracy born in a cigar-smoke-filled, secret room, as it is a collection of ever-unfolding tactical responses of journalists to the real world, as guided by professional norms, rules, and values. Mass-media accounts that make members of dissident social movements look like wide-eyed idealists, wild-eyed fringe characters, or red-eyed peaceniks who are out of touch with mainstream views do not necessarily indicate an overt ideological bias on the part of individual journalists, editors, and publishers. Generally speaking, individual journalists do not deliberately attempt to frame dissidents and their activities in derogatory light, disseminating misinformation in conscious, calculated collusion with the values and interests of their employers. Rather, such deprecatory framing can be linked to mass-media workers' faithful adherence to the journalistic norms and values that undergird U.S. news production.

Since deprecatory coverage of dissidence emerges from the interaction between social movements and the norms, values, and biases that inform the decisions of the modern mass-media workers,[100] consideration of these factors affords great leverage in understanding mass-media output regarding social movements. Indeed, these norms, values, and biases—which may coexist and reinforce each other—play into the dialectic of escalation social movements invariably face and are crucial in the framing battle that social movements must engage in.

Contemporary journalism favors stories that flare with novelty and drama.[101] As Stocking and Leonard put it: "It ain't news unless it's new," and this leads to an "issue-of-the-month syndrome" that submerges chronic social problems in favor of concentrated crises.[102] Because journalists perceive a need for a "news peg" upon which they can hang their stories, dramatic situations and accounts are deemed suitable while others are not. The preference for novelty and drama leads to both the trivialization of news content as well as the disregarding of news that lacks a strong whiff of freshness or drama.

Personalization—or, the downplaying of structural factors in favor of ostensible personal agency—is another norm that guides news production. The tribulations, misfortunes, and victories of individuals are valued, while political and economic structures earn little consideration. Relatedly, the fragmentation norm isolates news stories from their origins and contexts, which makes it difficult to see the wider view. Finally, the authority-order norm is the tendency for reporters to rely in moments of crisis on authority figures as sources who can promise that order will soon be restored.[103]

These informational biases and how they translate into mass-media coverage (or a lack of coverage) of dissidents are also related to the important concept of "indexing," which media scholar W. Lance Bennett defines as "the journalistic practice of opening or closing the news gates to citizen activists (and, more generally, a broader range of views) depending on levels of conflict or political difference among public officials and established interests with the capacity to influence decisions about the issue in question."[104] In other words, mainstream mass-media journalists, editors, and publishers are inclined to "index" the range of perspectives and positions both in hard news and in editorials so as to be in alignment with the range of perspectives being bandied about in governmental debate on any given topic. When conflict between governmental and corporate decision makers occurs, more dissident (or "non-official") viewpoints are allowed to enter the discussion. As a general rule, these dissident voices are only included in news stories and editorials when these voices express viewpoints and opinions that have already emerged in governmental or corporate (i.e. "official" or elite) circles. Voices that fall outside the range of "acceptable" ideas are occasionally permitted space on the mass-media terrain, but often their price of admission is subjection to ridicule, condemnation, and old-fashioned public scolding. "Indexing" is important for the practice of dissent since it directly relates to a number of preconditions of collective action, such as the mobilization of support from potentially sympathetic "bystander publics" as well as the precondition of pursuing social-change goals (rather than putting resources toward defensive social-movement maintenance). The concept of indexing has been tested in a number of real-world cases and has proven to be a useful way of explaining mass-media coverage.[105]

Many of these mass-media norms are interrelated, and, in some instances, a challenge to disentangle. Nevertheless, these norms and values, when put into practice, coalesce into biased coverage. However, when I use the term "bias" I am not referring to ideological bias. The ideological bias of the U.S. mass media—whether it is conservative or liberal—has been widely discussed elsewhere.[106] When I employ the term "bias" I am referring to informational biases—or predilections—that hinge on the journalistic norms of novelty, dramatization, personalization, fragmentation, and deference to authority figures.[107] These informational biases lead to episodic framing of news, rather than thematic framing of news, which in turn leads to shallower—and in some instances, misinformed—understandings of political and social issues.[108]

In order to garner mass-media attention, social movements must engage in the dialectic of escalation, organizing novel, more dramatic events. In other words, as Smith, et al point out, "social movements often seek *thematic* media attention to some broad social concern by generating an *episode* or event that may be newsworthy in itself."[109] However, the downside for social movements is that such episodic newsworthiness is often framed as violent or bizarre. Social movements therefore are forced to sacrifice deeper, thematic coverage on the altar of episodic mass-media attention. By obscuring a richer, wider understanding of social problems that pays heed to political complexity—social problems that dissident social movements are often trying to bring under public scrutiny—the combination of these informational biases lead to negativity and cynicism, and this often discourages social-movement participation in democratic life. This in itself serves to undermine participation in social movements, but, as we shall see, these informational biases also contribute to the suppression of these dissident citizens and social movements once they have been integrated into journalistic accounts.

In short, understanding the organizational structure and professional norms of the mass media in the U.S. helps us better understand how and why some news ultimately makes it onto the page or screen and some does not. Portrayals of certain groups or individuals as deviant are derived from the micro-processes of newsmaking, processes that involve mass-media workers acting under a pressure-pressing assortment of constraints. These constraints often translate into mass-media output that suppresses dissent by stripping activists of credibility through unflattering, hyperbolic, inaccurate, or simplistic portrayals.

Modes of Suppression: A Brief Introduction

Social-movement theorist Jack Goldstone has made the plea for students of dissent to widen the standard notion of repression—state agents violently clashing with protesters in the open—in order to incorporate the state's extensive repertoire of sanctions, including non-violent ones, that it carries out against its dissident citizens.[110] This is precisely what *Beyond Bullets* sets out to do.

In the following chapters, I focus on left-of-center dissident citizens and social movements that have experienced state and mass media suppression, since the state has historically focused its suppressive energy on such groups.[111] In each chapter I isolate a single form of state suppression and demonstrate how it has played out in specific historical moments. I reconstruct these case studies using FBI internal memos, mass-media accounts, social movement archives, police records, government documents, and secondary sources.

After combing twentieth and twenty-first century U.S. history, I have developed a comprehensive list of the ways in which dissent is suppressed by the state and the mass media. In the short run these modes of suppression slow down—or in some cases paralyze—the practice of dissent. In the long run they demobilize dissent by discouraging *future* action. Some of these state and media methods of suppression, in fact, are designed more to affect future actions than to have immediate dissent-stunting effects. Sometimes

these actions are directed toward particular individuals, while other times
they are aimed at groups of people. What follows is a list of the modes of
suppression that will be explored through detailed case studies in the following chapters:

1) Direct Violence
2) Public Prosecutions and Hearings
3) Employment Deprivation
4) Surveillance and Break-ins (including "black bag jobs")[112]
5) Infiltration, Badjacketing, and Agent Provocateurs
6) Black Propaganda[113]
7) Harassment and Harassment Arrests
8) Extraordinary Rules and Laws
9) Mass Media Manipulation
10) Bi-level Demonization
11) Mass Media Deprecation
12) Mass Media Underestimation, False Balance, and Disregard

While the first eight modes zero in on the actions of the state, the final
four modes focus on how the structures, norms, and values of the modern
mass-media system dovetail with the state's suppressive objectives. These suppressive tactics almost always work in various combinations and sequences;
only very rarely does a mode operate unconnected from others.

Some readers may have reached this point of the book saddled with
a sense of bafflement as they ask themselves, "Our government uses violence against its own dissidents?" and "The U.S. government goes *beyond*
using bullets against dissenters? I didn't even know they used bullets in the
first place!" In a country like the United States, where historical amnesia is
systematically encouraged, such questions and comments may not be uncommon. Yet this ideologically prevalent notion is more myth than reality.
Before we explore how the state moves *beyond* bullets, which is the central
purpose of this book, it is important to consider how, despite the fact that the
United States is putatively a liberal democracy, its state apparatus has indeed
resorted to violence in order to quell dissent. This callous reality is acutely
evident in the death of Black Panther Party leader Fred Hampton, which is
explored in the next chapter.

2
Direct Violence

In the U.S., dissent is often repressed with direct violence. From nineteenth-century attacks on anarchists to early-twentieth-century confrontations with members of the Industrial Workers of the World (IWW) to beatings of protesters at the 1968 Democratic Party's National Convention to strikes on the MOVE organization in Philadelphia in the 1970s and 1980s to police violence directed at protesters of the World Trade Organization (WTO) in Seattle in 1999, dissident citizens in the United States have experienced direct repression in the form of beatings, bombings, shootings, and other forms of violence. The state often carries out this violence directly via the military, police, FBI, or National Guard. This chapter explores two such cases of state violence: (1) the fatal National Guard shootings at Kent State in May 1970, and (2) the murder of Black Panther Party members Fred Hampton and Mark Clark in December 1969.

Kent State University:
Not Your Standard-Issue "Demonstrating School"

Kent State University is a public school in Kent, Ohio. At the time, it had approximately 20,000 enrolled students, four-fifths of whom had also attended high school in Ohio. Although Kent State wasn't known as "a demonstrating school,"[1] and the non-student population in the area was "conservative, even right-wing,"[2] there was significant dissident organizing on campus in the years prior to the infamous National Guard attack on 4 May 1970. In 1968, members of Students for a Democratic Society (SDS) and the Black United Students (BUS) orchestrated a five-hour sit-in against campus recruiters from the Oakland, California police department.[3] Student council vice president Bob Pickett, an African-American from New Jersey, claimed, "The city of Oakland's Police Department has perpetrated a system of racism upon the black people of Oakland and they have made repeated attempts to kill Black Panther Chairman Huey P. Newton."[4] In this case, campus administration was open to the students' demands. After the 250 black protesters involved were granted amnesty by university officials, Kent State launched an Institute of African-American Affairs and agreed to consider adding more courses oriented toward black studies. In the spring of 1969, SDS made four specific demands to the Kent State administration: elimination of the ROTC program, expulsion of the Liquid Crystals Institute (a Defense Department-funded research center), removal of a state crime laboratory located on campus, and the abolition of Kent State's degree program in law enforcement. These demands sparked a violent interchange between protesters and student counter-protesters backed by university police. Several protesters were charged with assault and battery. Subsequently, the Kent State administration revoked SDS's charter, banning the group from campus.[5]

Meanwhile, student activism, and a broader anti-Vietnam War movement, was on the rise. Nationally, SDS membership increased from approximately 10,000 in October 1965 to more than 80,000 in November 1968. Attendance at anti-war protests was also increasing. While 40,000 took part in the Washington, DC protest in November 1965, 300,000 attended subsequent demonstrations in San Francisco and New York in April 1967, and approximately 500,000 people were present at the November 1969 rallies in San Francisco and Washington, DC. While there were about 400 protests nationwide in 1966–67, there were 3,400 during the 1967–68 academic year, and 9,408 in 1968–69.[6] As the number of protests increased and the protests became larger, the more radical edges of the movement(s) sharpened. More aggressive tactics emerged and violence eventually increased. Sit-ins became a common tactic to either slow down university processes seen as illegitimate, harmful, or otherwise deceitful, or to block these processes entirely. This tactic was used with various degrees of success to challenge the recruiting efforts of the FBI, CIA, police, and U.S. military. Sometimes activists varied their tactics by attacking the buildings that housed recruiting efforts or research that aided the war.

The level of protest activity and the intensity of violence increased greatly with and after the events at Kent State. Though not seen as "a demonstrating school," a campus-wide poll in 1968 found that only 22 percent of all students supported the Vietnam War.[7] Active resistance really heated up on 30 April 1970, when President Richard Nixon announced the U.S invasion of Cambodia as a "protective response" to the supposed existence of a National Liberation Front of Vietnam (NLF) headquarters there.[8] Many students saw this as a sharp reversal of his previous policy of withdrawal from Vietnam. Within the hour, protests popped up on a number of college campuses across the nation. That night, Kent State students went into downtown Kent and spray-painted anti-war slogans like "Get Out of Cambodia!" and "Power to the People" on the walls of a number of businesses.[9]

The next day, on the Kent State campus, student activists carried out a symbolically powerful protest in which a copy of the U.S. Constitution was buried near the Victory Bell, a former Erie & Lackawanna railroad bell that students rung after Kent State football victories. One student explained, "If a nation can launch a war on Cambodia without declaring it, the Constitution as we know it is really dead."[10] Approximately 500 students attended the non-violent burial ceremony, which was organized by a group of history graduate students called WHORE (World Historians Opposed to Racism and Exploitation). The energy and excitement continued into that night, when students threw bottles at passing police cars and ignited a bonfire in the street. Kent Mayor LeRoy Satrom declared a state of emergency and County police used tear gas to disperse the students. Fifteen students were arrested, mostly for disorderly conduct.[11] These activities triggered an escalating spiral of dissent.

Around this time, students at Yale University called for a national student strike. Dissident students at Brandeis University organized a National Strike Information Center.[12] Students from over sixty campuses went on strike in the days that followed.[13] Spontaneous strikes on college campuses were decisive. Perhaps the biggest was at Princeton, where approximately 2,500 students and faculty (out of about 6,000) voted to strike.[14]

Back at Kent State, on 2 May, Mayor Satrom formalized the state of emergency, forbidding the sale of beer, liquor, and firearms. Gas could only be purchased if pumped directly into the tank of an automobile. He also obtained the support of seventy-five additional deputies from the Portage County Sheriff and established a dusk-to-dawn curfew (from 8 p.m. to 6 a.m.), which, later that afternoon, he modified to a 1 a.m.-to-dawn clampdown.[15]

That evening, the ROTC building on the Kent State campus was set on fire by individuals who were part of a swarm of about 1,000 students roaming campus and chanting slogans against the war. When members of the fire department arrived students promptly slashed their hoses. Mindful of their own safety, fire department personnel retreated without extinguishing the fire. Around this time, Mayor Satrom called both the Highway Patrol and the Assistant Adjutant General Sylvester Del Corso of the Ohio National Guard, requesting their assistance. John McElroy of the governor's office assured Mayor Satrom that National Guard troops would be available if needed.[16] Portage County law enforcement appeared on campus shortly thereafter, decked out in full riot gear and toting shotguns, carbines, and handguns. One deputy told a reporter, "If anybody gets near that fire truck, I have orders to put a little round hole in him."[17] The National Guard used tear gas liberally to quell the uprising, but windy weather made this largely unsuccessful. According to one account, "Del Corso ordered his junior officers to form the troops into a skirmish line. Bayonets were fixed. The troops broke into platoon-sized units and, rifles ready, advanced on the students, who broke into smaller groups."[18] In the ensuing chaos, National Guardsmen attacked Kent State students with bayonets. A number of students were injured including a twenty-one year old senior who, after being chased by two Guardsmen, received an eight-inch bayonet wound on his right cheek and a deep stab wound in the leg.[19] However, due to their late arrival, the Guard failed to apprehend whoever had torched the ROTC building, which burned to the ground at a cost of $86,000. In this context, "Student resentment against the Guard continued to grow."[20]

At a 10 a.m. news conference the next day, 3 May, the governor of Ohio, James A. Rhodes, proclaimed that the violence on the Kent State campus was "probably the most vicious form of campus-oriented violence yet perpetrated by dissident groups and their allies in the state of Ohio" and assured the people of Ohio that "we are going to employ every force of law that we have under our authority."[21] Rhodes's toughly worded law-and-order speech, during which he emphatically thumped his fist on the table as he spoke, was probably influenced by the fact that it was election time in Ohio. Rhodes was enmeshed in a tight battle for the Republican senatorial nomination with Robert Taft, Jr. With the primary election a mere two days away, and knowing he was trailing Taft in the polls, Rhodes likely saw this as an opportunity to appear strong.[22]

Regardless of whether Rhodes's table thumping stemmed from political calculation or genuine anger, his unforgiving, law-and-order approach to the situation set the tone for what followed. Rhodes offered this assessment of the dissident students on the Kent State campus:

> These people just move from one campus to another and terrorize the community. They are worse than the brown shirt and the communist element and also the nightriders and the vigilantes. They're the worst type of people that we harbor in America. Now I want to say this, they are not going to take over a campus. [The campus] is no sanctuary for these people to burn buildings down of private citizens and of businesses, in the community, then run into a sanctuary. It is over with in the state of Ohio.[23]

This tone emanated from the top of the U.S. government. On 1 May, as President Nixon walked out of a briefing at the Pentagon, he slowed down to express his estimation of college-age dissidents to a group of supporters and reporters: "You know, you see these bums, you know, blowin' up the campuses. Listen, the boys that are on the college campuses today are the luckiest people in the world, going to the greatest universities, and here they are, burnin' up the books, I mean, stormin' about this issue, I mean, you name it—get rid of the war, there'll be another one."[24]

Governor Rhodes moved beyond criticizing college students to promising a response to their dissent: "We are going to eradicate the problem. We are not going to treat the symptoms." Rhodes was followed by General Del Corso, who asserted that "We have sufficient force in the area, [and] we will apply whatever degree of force is necessary to provide protection for the lives of our citizens and his property." Later in the press conference, Del Corso, with haunting prescience, added, "As the Ohio law says, any use of force that's necessary even to the point of shooting. We don't want to get into that but the law says that we can if necessary."[25]

The afternoon was relatively calm on campus. Protester Allison Krause, a freshman, even slotted a lilac into the barrel of one National Guardsman's M-1 rifle. When one of his superiors saw the flower and ordered the guardsman to remove it, Krause said "Flowers are better than bullets." These words were later etched into her gravestone.[26] Later, at around 8 p.m. that night, students held a rally on the campus Commons. This eventually led to a sit-in at the intersection of Lincoln and Main Streets where students used a bullhorn to make a number of demands including the abolition of the school's ROTC program, the removal of the National Guard from campus, and the termination of the town curfew. Students insisted on speaking directly to Mayor Satrom and the Kent State University President Robert I. White. Around 11 p.m., students were told that neither Satrom nor White would agree to speak with them. The National Guard read the students the Riot Act and changed the curfew from 1 a.m. to 11 p.m. Students threw rocks. The Guard launched tear-gas and drew its bayonets. In the ensuing melee, a female student was stabbed as she attempted to crawl into a window. Using gun barrels as lilac vases hadn't lessened tensions and resentments. More than fifty people were arrested, bringing the grand total to more than one hundred.[27] This violence, however, pales in the context of the next day's gruesome events.

The next morning, on 4 May, as relations on campus became even more tense, students organized a noon rally on the campus Commons. Just before it began, a Kent State patrolman, backed by three National Guardsmen, announced through a bullhorn that the pending gathering would be illegal and that students should disperse. This announcement was met with jeers, lewd gestures, and some stones. The National Guard replied by lofting teargas canisters into the area where the students were assembled, but a 14 mph wind prevented the gas from inhibiting the students' efforts.[28] Students even threw the canisters back at the National Guardsmen. Brigadier General Robert H. Canterbury ordered the troops to drive away the students. According to one account, when a student spokesperson approached Canterbury asking him to not march into the students, General Canterbury replied "These students are going to have to find out what law and order is all about."[29] Canterbury's troops formed a skirmish line and marched forward. The students retreated and split into two main groups, which eventually settled on either side of the Guard, hemming them in.[30] Just before 12:20 p.m. ten guardsmen knelt and assumed the firing position, aiming their rifles at some of the more raucous protesters. This increased tensions momentarily, but eventually General Canterbury gave the order to cease this bellicose stance and to retreat. Then, at 12:24 p.m., in mid-retreat, twenty-eight members of the National Guard wheeled around and opened fire for *Thirteen Seconds*, strafing approximately 200 unarmed students with sixty-one bullets.[31] The attack left four dead and nine wounded. The four students killed were Allison Krause, Jeffrey Miller, Sandra Scheuer, and William Schroeder. Many of the wounded, and even one of the dead, William Schroeder, were bystanders, not demonstrators. Schroeder was actually a member of the ROTC.[32] Sandra Scheuer was walking to her one o'clock class.[33] Of the four students who were killed, the nearest to the National Guardsmen was almost "a football field away."[34] All thirteen victims were students at Kent State. Two were shot in the front, seven in the side, and four in the back.[35] Joseph Lewis, who was wounded that day, remarked, "I first noticed bits of dirt flying up in front of me it was then that I realized the bullets were real and I was simultaneously shot. I was shocked that the guns were loaded first of all and could not believe that they shot me."[36] By 5 p.m. that evening the campus was virtually deserted. Hanging from the window of a building on campus was a makeshift sign made of bedsheets that, in large red letters, simply read "Why?"[37]

This paroxysm of violent repression, while temporarily silencing the assembled dissenters on the Kent State campus, galvanized massive student resistance to the war and to the direct violence that was being used to repress this resistance. According to historian Kirkpatrick Sale, in the four days that followed that repression at Kent State (5 May through 8 May):

> there were major campus disruptions at the rate of more than a hundred a day, students at a total of at least 350 institutions went out on strike and 536 schools were shut down completely for some period of time, 51 of them for the entire year. More than half of the colleges and universities in the country (1350) were ultimately touched by protest demonstrations, involving nearly 60 percent of the student population—some 4,350,000 people—in every kind of institution and in every state of the Union. Violent demonstrations occurred on at least 73 campuses (that was only 4 percent of all institutions but included roughly a third of the country's largest and most prestigious schools), and at 26 schools the

demonstrations were serious, prolonged, and marked by brutal clashes between students and police, with tear gas, broken windows, fires, clubbings, injuries and multiple arrests; altogether, more than 1800 people were arrested between May 1 and May 15.[38]

Additionally, the Weather Underground bombed National Guard headquarters in response to the naked act of violent aggression at Kent State.[39]

Kent State wasn't the only college campus to experience violent repression during this time. Following Nixon's 30 April pronouncement on Cambodia, the National Guard shot one protesting student from a distance of 200 feet at Ohio State University.[40] At the University of Buffalo, police shot and wounded a dozen students. Ten students were stabbed with bayonets at the University of New Mexico.[41] Ten days after Kent State, during protests at Jackson State University, an all-black school in Jackson, Mississippi, state police killed two female students and wounded fourteen by strafing the ground level of their dormitory with bullets. As critical historians like Kirkpatrick Sale and Fred Halstead have pointed out, the Jackson State killings attracted neither the same amount of press coverage as Kent State (the *New York Times* only gave the Jackson State killings a one-column headline and six inches of print, while Kent State had received a four-column headline and fifty-one inches of print), nor the level of student protest in direct response to the incident (only fifty-three campuses protested and most of these were all-black colleges).[42] Prior to Kent State, in 1968, police opened fire on students who were protesting segregation on the University of South Carolina, Orangeburg campus—three students were killed and forty were wounded. The "Orangeburg Massacre" resulted in acquittals in federal court for nine state police officers, and the only person convicted in the melee was Cleveland L. Sellers Jr., a protester convicted of rioting charges and sent to prison.[43]

At Kent State, no National Guardsmen were ever indicted for the fatal, thirteen-second fusillade, even though an FBI report concluded "We have reason to believe that the claim made by the National Guard that their lives were endangered by the students was fabricated subsequent to the event."[44] U.S. Attorney General John Mitchell refused to start an investigation or to assemble a grand jury.[45] In fact, in the immediate aftermath of the killings, White House Press Secretary Ron Ziegler implied that the deaths were really the fault of the protesters, commenting that the incident "should remind us that when dissent turns to violence it invites tragedy."[46] Indeed, twenty-five students and faculty—who became known as the "Kent 25"—were brought up on charges by a Portage County grand jury.[47] This juridical maneuvering reflected the fact that many people in Kent, and in the nation at large, wished *more* students had been killed. For example, a local hotel clerk said, "You can't really help but kind of think they've been asking for it and finally got it."[48] Another local woman said, "I'm sorry they didn't kill more [students]. They were warned and they knew what was happening and they should've moved out."[49] In a national *Newsweek* poll, 58 percent of the respondents blamed the students for what happened at Kent State and only 11 percent blamed the National Guard.[50] These attitudes dovetail with the mass-media portrayal of these dissidents.[51] The families of the students who were killed did, after years of litigation, receive $675,000 in compensation from the state of Ohio. The state also issued an official apology. This was in 1979.[52]

Fred Hampton and the Black Panther Party: "We Want Freedom"

Richard Hofstadter asserted that, in the United States, "we have a remarkable lack of memory where violence is concerned and have left most of our excesses a part of our buried history."[53] A harrowing, illuminating example of the state's use of direct violence and how it can become "buried history" is the assassination of Black Panther Party leader Fred Hampton. Exploring Hampton's murder also highlights how numerous modes of suppression can combine to form a vicious concoction of suppression.

The Black Panther Party for Self-Defense was founded in October 1966 by Huey P. Newton and Bobby Seale, two black students at Merritt College in Oakland, California. Explaining the selection of the panther as a symbol, Seale said, "It's not in the panther's nature to attack anyone first, but when he is attacked and backed into a corner, he will respond viciously and wipe out the aggressor."[54] The Black Panthers committed themselves to feeding, clothing, and providing medical services to members of their communities by building networks of cooperation and mutual aid. They made a concerted effort to engage in praxis, reflectively moving back and forth between theory and practice. The BPP's newspaper, *The Black Panther*, explained how the Breakfast for Children Program successfully blended the abstract and the concrete: "theory's cool, but theory without practice ain't shit. You got to have them both of them—the two go together. We have a theory about feeding kids free. What'd we do? We put it into practice. That's how people learn."[55] This free food program began in April 1969. According to Ron Satchel, a participant in the program,

> We served an average of one hundred and fifty children per day. Then
> we served breakfast to about one hundred seventy-five children at St.
> Dominic's Church near the Cabrini Green homes. A hundred children

were served at a church near the Henry Horner homes. Another hundred at the Baptist church on Jackson Boulevard near Western, and another ninety at a restaurant called the Soul Cafeteria. At the peak, we had somewhere between eight to ten different sites where we served children before they went to school. We felt that nutrition would help them learn.[56]

With this program and the BPP's other activities, the Panthers forged deep inroads in the African-American community.

The Black Panther Party built from the previous work of the Community Alert Patrol (CAP), which emerged in the wake of the 1965 uprising in Watts. In an effort to shield blacks from police harassment and excessive force, CAP members served as observers who went to the scene of police arrests or other actions; CAP squads also informed blacks of their legal rights. The Panthers took this watchdog role a dramatic step further by creating armed patrols designed to curtail police brutality toward blacks. This was legal, though many law enforcement officials found it to be incendiary. Robert Allen notes that since they were aware of the extra state scrutiny they were sure to garner, "the Panthers scrupulously avoided violating the law." Not only did the Panthers bring arms to the scenes of alleged crimes, but they also "habitually carried with them law books from which they could quote the appropriate section of the legal code being violated by the police."[57] Explaining the logic behind this approach, and the Black Panther Party's political philosophy more broadly, Bobby Seale commented:

> We tried to establish an organization that would articulate the basic desires and needs of the people and in turn try to organize black people into having some kind of power position so they can deal with the power structure. The party realizes that the white power structure's real power is its military force; is its police force. And we can see our black communities are being occupied by policemen just like a foreign country might be occupied by foreign troops. Our politics comes from our hungry stomachs and our crushed heads and the vicious service revolver at a cop's side which is used to tear our flesh, and from the knowledge that black people are drafted to fight in wars, killing other colored people who've never done a damn thing to us. So how do we face these cops in the black community? We have to face them exactly how they come down on us. They come down with guns and force. We must organize ourselves and put a shotgun in every black man's home. Our political stand is that politics is war without bloodshed, and war is politics with bloodshed.[58]

This worldview vibrates throughout the Panthers' ten-point "Party Platform and Program," released in October 1966. This wide-ranging document starts off with the line "We want freedom" and sets numerous concrete goals to improve the daily lives of blacks in the United States and globally. More than forty years later, African Americans are still pursuing many of these aims, such as full employment, better housing, improved education, and the elimination of police brutality against blacks.[59]

According to historian and activist Manning Marable, "By the late-1960s, the Black Panthers had become the most influential revolutionary nationalist organization in the U.S."[60] The Black Panther Party's success, as well as its emphasis on revolutionary politics and armed self-defense, quickly drew the attention of the U.S. government and its intelligence networks. In an effort to roll back the Panthers' progress and influence, the U.S. government turned to the FBI, and more specifically to its "Counter Intelligence Program," or what is known as COINTELPRO. The Church Committee wrote that COINTELPRO, "was designed to 'disrupt' and 'neutralize' individuals deemed to be threats to domestic security."[61] These covert programs were aimed at five main targets: (1) the Communist Party (1956–71); (2) the Socialist Workers Party (1961–69); (3) White Hate Groups (1964–71); (4) "Black Nationalist—Hate Groups" (1967–71), and; (5) the New Left (1968–71).[62] As such, COINTELPRO has a specific, historical meaning. Nevertheless, Ward Churchill and Jim Vander Wall correctly note that "in popular usage [COINTELPRO] came to signify the whole context of clandestine political repression activities, several of them—such as unwarranted electronic surveillance—related to but never formally part of COINTELPRO at all."[63]

COINTELPRO lasted from 1956 to 1971. It ended, at least nominally, only after the intrepid efforts of a dissident group. On 8 March 1971, the Citizens Commission to Investigate the FBI burgled an FBI office in Media, Pennsylvania and made off with thousands of pages of information from classified files. When the *Washington Post* printed a summary of these documents the next week, people first became aware of the FBI's vast network of counter-intelligence efforts. Attorney General John Mitchell pleaded with the press to not publish information from the documents, claiming that such information "could endanger the lives or cause other serious harm to persons engaged in investigative activities on behalf of the United States" and "could endanger the United States and give aid to foreign governments whose interests might be inimical to those of the United States." The group also delivered documents to Senator George McGovern, a Democrat from South Dakota, and Parren J. Mitchell, a Democrat from Maryland. Both members of Congress promptly returned the documents to the Bureau and chastised those who carried out the daring theft. McGovern, who had been a critic of J. Edgar Hoover, said stealing the documents constituted illegal acts that "only serve to undermine reasonable and constructive efforts" to scrutinize the FBI's policies.[64] Unfazed, the Citizens Commission to Investigate the FBI vowed to contact previously undercover agents and urge them to cease their efforts to suppress dissent. It said it would also inform the affected dissidents of their FBI records and then publicly reveal the names of infiltrators and informants. In the group's letter to FBI informants, it wrote, "We regret that this action was necessary, but these are troubled times, and the struggle for freedom and justice in this society can never succeed if people continue to betray their brothers and sisters."[65] The members of Citizens Commission to Investigate the FBI were never apprehended.

According to Ward Churchill and Jim Vander Wall, the FBI has been implicated in the assassination of select political figures, "either for 'exemplary' reasons or after other attempts at destroying their effectiveness had failed."[66] An example of such state-sanctioned vigilantism occurred in Chicago in the pre-dawn hours of 4 December 1969, when the Chicago Police raided a Black Panther Party flat at 2337 West Monroe Street and killed Panther leaders Fred Hampton and Mark Clark. Hampton was the twenty-one-year-old Chairman of the Black Panther Party of Illinois, while Clark, age twenty-two, was a Panther official from Peoria, Illinois.

Hampton was a special target of the FBI, as he was a charismatic and effective leader who was able to build alliances with such disparate groups as Students for a Democratic Society and the Blackstone Rangers, one of Chicago's biggest gangs. Nikhil Pal Singh considers Hampton "one of the Party's most innovative organizers" due to his ability to establish an unprecedented "rainbow coalition" comprised of "the Blackstone Rangers, the Young Patriots, and the Young Lords, the city's largest Black, White, and Puerto Rican youth gangs."[67] Noam Chomsky dubbed Hampton "one of the most promising leaders of the Black Panther Party."[68] Akua Njeri (formerly Deborah Johnson), who was pregnant with Hampton's child and with him in bed when the police raided, said about Hampton: "You knew this man really believed in what he was doing. He wasn't in it for any power or fame or glory trip. This man was going to live and fight and die for the people. And you just knew that."[69] BPP lawyer Charles Garry said Hampton "was a brilliant, aggressive, down-to-earth young man with tremendous understanding combined with great affability."[70] Fellow Panther David Hilliard described Hampton as "a powerful spokesman and a strong leader effortlessly combining love, determination, and anger."[71]

Hampton graduated high school in Maywood, Illinois with academic honors. From there, he became youth director for the Maywood branch of the NAACP, where he was admired for building a vibrant chapter. Eventually he moved to Chicago and became involved with the Black Panthers.[72] By the end of 1967, the FBI had opened a file on him, which would grow to more than 4,000 pages by the time of his death. That same year, he was convicted on charges of stealing $71 worth of ice cream and was given a two- to five-year prison sentence. However, after securing an appeal bond, he was released early from Menard Prison, despite the protestations of an Illinois official who testified Hampton was "a professed revolutionary."[73] Upon release, he turned his full attention to local organizing and eventually rose to assume the chairmanship of the Illinois BPP. As Chairman of the Illinois chapter, Hampton was a rising star, both on the local level and in the Panther's national organizational structure. Working with the Black Panther Party, Hampton had set up a number of successful community programs to help residents meet their medical, health, and education needs. In the years before the violent police raid on 4 December 1969, Hampton was deeply involved in a number of the BPP's community programs including the free Breakfast for Children Program, the campaign to shift to a community policing model, the establishment of free health clinics for blacks, and the formation of black-liberation schools that instilled pride in young blacks and offered radical, alternative history lessons. These activities, and an outspoken approach that sometimes drew from Maoist principles, earned him a slot on the FBI's Rabble Rouser Index, a list of dissidents formulated in August 1967 to facilitate the apprehension of so-called "racial agitators and individuals who have demonstrated a potential for fomenting racial discord." In November 1967, these already vague standards were widened to include any dissidents who had a "propensity for fomenting" that endangered "internal security." The FBI defined a "rabble rouser" as "a person who tries to arouse people to violent action by appealing to their emotions, prejudices, et cetera; a demagogue."[74]

On 4 December 1969 at 4:45 a.m., police officers from the Special Prosecutions Unit (SPU) of the Cook County Illinois State's Attorney's Office raided the flat where Hampton was sleeping. The SPU was an elite group created to deal with gang activity. It also worked closely with the regular police Gang Intelligence Unit (GIU) and the Chicago Police Department's Anti-Subversive Unit of the Intelligence Division (a.k.a. the "Red Squad"). The SPU, which was formed in February 1969, operated directly out of the State's Attorney's Office.[75] It was known to focus its attention on the Black Panther Party in Chicago during the late-1960s.[76]

The raid on the Panther flat was part of the FBI's COINTELPRO against "black nationalist—hate groups."[77] In fact, almost 80 percent of the FBI's admitted COINTELPRO operations against groups or individuals it considered to be "Black nationalists" were carried out against the BPP (233 of 295 actions).[78] That night, police bashed down the front door of the flat and, armed with twenty-seven firearms ranging from .38 caliber revolvers to a sawed-off 12-gauge shotgun and a .45 caliber submachine gun, proceeded to spray more than ninety bullets around the apartment, wounding four and killing Mark Clark instantly with a pointblank shotgun blast to the chest.[79] The only shot that the Panthers fired occurred when Clark's shotgun discharged as he fell dead to the ground. Police fired a shot that hit Hampton in the left shoulder as he slept in his bed, seriously wounding him.

Deborah Johnson, Hampton's eight and one-half month pregnant fiancée, who was in the bed with Hampton, described the scene:

> All this time, the bed was vibrating. Bullets were going into the mattress. I looked up at the doorway, and I could see sparks of light, because it was dark back in that area. I thought I was dead then and I was just seeing this as a spirit or something. I didn't feel any pain. I wasn't shot, but I just knew, with all this going on, it was all over. Then Louis Truelock [another Panther on the scene] yelled out: Stop shooting! Stop shooting! We have a pregnant sister in here." At some point they stopped shooting. Fred didn't move anymore. That was it, the one time he raised his head and laid it back down, like a slow-motion movie.[80]

Forty-two of the approximately ninety shots were aimed at the head of Hampton's bed. Such a convergence of bullets occurred because the Chicago police were working off a blueprint of the flat that had been supplied to them through the FBI by William O'Neal, a Bureau informant who had worked his way up through the Black Panther Party ranks, all the while reporting to Special Agent (SA) Roy Mitchell, a member of the FBI's "Racial Matters Squad" in the Chicago Field Office.[81] According to an FBI memorandum, prior to the police raid on 4 December, the informant supplied

> a detailed inventory of the weapons and also a detailed floor plan of the apartment....In addition, the identities of BPP members utilizing the apartment at the above address were furnished. This information was not available from any other source and subsequently proved to be of tremendous value in that it subsequently saved injury and possible death to police officers participating in the raid...on the morning of 12/4/69. The raid was based on the information furnished by the informant.[82]

After Hampton was wounded, a second group of policemen smashed its way through the back door. Two policemen, Edward Carmody and another unidentified officer, entered Hampton's bedroom and, according to eyewitnesses, identified Fred Hampton. One of them asked "Is he dead?... Bring him out." The other officer replied, "He's barely alive; he'll make it." Then witnesses heard two shots. "He's good and dead now," said a voice presumed to be Carmody's.[83] The two shots that killed Hampton were fired pointblank into his head, both of them "entering on the right side at approximately the same angle from above and slightly to the rear of the subject."[84] In other words, Fred Hampton was shot in the head from above and behind as he slumped harmless and immobile. He was then dragged by his wrist to the doorway of the bedroom where he was left, face down, to die.

Then the two sub-groups from the SPU returned their attention to the other eight people in the apartment (though one of them, Clark, was already dead). One member of the SPU, Joseph Gorman, sprayed submachine gun fire at them, inflicting wounds on Ron "Doc" Satchel (hit four times), Verlina Brewer (hit twice), and Blair Anderson (hit twice).[85] Satchel, Brewer, and Anderson were all taking cover on the floor. Eventually the gunfire stopped and the SPU collected its victims, beating them and taunting them along the way.

Satchel, who was the Minister of Health for the Illinois Panthers, later described what happened:

> After the shooting stopped, they came in with their flashlights. I saw two people in the doorway with guns pointed at me. I remember hearing a voice say, "If Panthers kill police, police will kill Panthers." They told me to turn the light on. I said I was hit and hurting and couldn't get up. They said, "If you don't get up, we're going to kill you." I tried to make my way around the foot of the bed, using the wall to support myself, and limped to the doorway. They started calling me, "Nigger!" "Black bastard!" "Motherfucker!" I hopped once or twice more toward the back of the house—then I was kicked in the rear. I fell flat on the floor in the dining room area, on my chest and stomach....I was told to put both of my hands behind my neck, and handcuffs were placed on my wrists, real tight. I was in a very awkward position. My stomach was in pain. I had pain in my leg. Raising my arms over my neck caused more intense pain. The cuffs cut off circulation in my arms....I seemed to be passing out. I thought I was going to die....I was kicked on one of my feet and told, "Get up nigger." I tried. But I was dizzy and blacking out periodically. The same voice said, "Get up or I'll kick your ass." I don't know how I managed to get up—maybe it was a rush of adrenalin—but I did. I had to walk to the front door and down the stairs and all the way to the paddy wagon. It was freezing cold. I was in excruciating pain, and I kept passing out. I didn't get a wheelchair till I

got to Cook County Hospital. There the policemen photographed me
and took my fingerprints. They handcuffed my leg to one of the poles
of my hospital bed, and they supplied a twenty-four-hour guard. That's
the way it was for fourteen days.[86]

The seven Panthers who were still alive—Blair Anderson, Harold Bell,
Verlina Brewer, Brenda Harris, Deborah Johnson, Ronald Satchel and Louis
Truelock—were pulled out into the street during the dead of winter and
were arrested, and eventually indicted, on charges of attempted murder,
"armed violence," illegal possession of firearms, and an assortment of other
felonies.[87]

On the morning after the raid, Cook County's State's Attorney Edward
V. Hanrahan—after a thirty-minute, secret meeting with FBI officials—
held a press conference with the entire SPU that had carried out the raid.
During the press conference he maintained that the raiding policemen were
acting in self-defense, and that the Panthers had opened fire on them as
they attempted to serve a warrant. Sergeant Daniel Groth of the Chicago
Police Department, an organizer of the raid, said that he and his men had
"defended themselves" against the "extremely vicious" Black Panthers. In the
immediate aftermath of the raid, this police-friendly account was transmitted at face value throughout the mass media, especially by the Chicago newspapers and television stations, who even staged a police-dictated reenactment
that "demonstrated conclusively" that the SPU had acted valiantly and in
self-defense.[88] The *Chicago Tribune* turned to Sergeant Groth who said the
Panthers "staged a wild gun battle" when the police tried to present their
search warrant.[89] Groth's fantasy fusillade was also cited in a front-page story
in the *New York Times*, where he claimed he opened the apartment door to
find a woman lying on a bed who opened fire on them with a shotgun. He
added, "There must have been six or seven of them firing."[90] The police also
maintained that they had probable cause to carry out the attack because an
informant had provided information that the Panthers' flat was home to an
illegal arms cache.[91] The *Chicago Tribune* gave front-page consideration to
this theme the morning after the attack as it ran a photograph of a collection
of weaponry sporting the caption "Part of a weapons cache seized after a
raid on west side apartment used as secret headquarters of the Black Panther
Party."[92]

Less than a week after the raid, some critical and questioning voices
emerged, however. Many of these also denounced the Panthers, even as they
punched holes in the police account of events. For example, Mike Royko,
writing as a columnist for the *Chicago Daily News*, asserted that the Panthers
were "racists" who "hoard guns and preach violence."[93] Voices critical of the

official storyline appeared in part because the flat was left open for the public for two weeks after the attack; thousands filed through the apartment, and "simply viewing the bullet-torn walls of the apartment" was a "deeply disturbing experience" for these post-raid observers who witnessed "a heavy concentration of machinegun and shotgun fire at one living room wall and in two bedrooms."[94] A wide range of people, both black and white took the somber tour. The *New York Times* described the scene like this: "There are youths, workmen in paint-stained clothes, middle-aged women in flowered hats, neatly dressed office workers, elderly people and postal workers in gray uniforms. Many give a clenched fist salute as they leave."[95] Five African-American members of Congress also walked through the flat. One of them, Representative Charles C. Diggs, a Michigan Democrat, commented, "There are certain obvious conclusions to a layman. All the projectiles were coming from one direction—going in." The other Congress members—all Democrats—were Louis Stokes (Ohio), Adam Clayton Powell (New York), John Conyers Jr. (Michigan), and William Clay (Missouri). These Congressmen vowed in the *New York Times* to open their own investigation into the violent raid.[96] Such media coverage led State's Attorney Hanrahan to assert "there has been an orgy of sensationalism in the press and on TV that has severely damaged law enforcement and the administration of justice."[97]

Closer inspection of the flat revealed that the Chicago Police's version of events had serious deficiencies. For instance, dark spots on the flat's doors that the SPU alleged were "photographic evidence" of bullets fired by the Panthers were found merely to be nail heads.[98] Even the overtly biased Grand Jury that was called to investigate the raid to judge whether the rights of the Black Panthers had been violated pointed to "the irreconcilable disparity between the detailed accounts given by the officers and the physical facts and evidence."[99] The Grand Jury even went so far as to say: "The great variance between the physical evidence and the testimony of the officers raises the question as to whether the officers are falsifying their accounts."[100] Furthermore, the Grand Jury found that the Chicago Police Crime Laboratory, which carried out its own investigation of the raid, "indicated a serious lack of professionalism and objectivity" as it was responsible for "a totally inadequate search and for a grossly insufficient analysis" of the premises.[101] Nevertheless, even though it was willing to make these damning assertions, the Grand Jury concluded:

> While there is a serious lack of corroboration of the officers' accounts, no one has appeared before the Grand Jury with a specific allegation of wrongdoing by them. Unquestionably, the raid was not professionally planned or properly executed and the result of the raid was two deaths,

four injuries and seven improper criminal charges. The grave issues of professional law enforcement raised by these facts are discussed elsewhere. The question here is whether the facts establish probable cause to believe that the officers involved intentionally committed acts which deprived the occupants of federally protected rights, contrary to law. The Grand Jury is unable to reach that conclusion. The physical evidence and the discrepancies in the officers' accounts are insufficient to establish probably [sic] cause to charge the officers with a willful violation of the occupants' civil rights.[102]

So, stunningly, though perhaps not surprisingly, members of the SPU who conducted the raid and leaders from the Chicago Police Department who helped plan it were let off the criminal hook.

One glaring omission from the Grand Jury investigation was the thoroughgoing involvement of the FBI. This occurred because of the FBI's obfuscation and outright lying, and because of illegal collusion with officials from the Department of Justice.[103] For example, on 11 February 1970, Special Agent (SA) Marlin Johnson testified before the Grand Jury that FBI involvement in the "Hampton-Clark affair" was minimal at most. While in front of the Grand Jury, SA Johnson opted not to mention FBI informant O'Neal's infiltration of the Party or the fact that he provided a floor plan to the SPU.[104] Meanwhile, SA Roy Mitchell was penning a confidential memo to FBI Headquarters requesting that its star BPP infiltrator and agent provocateur, William O'Neal, be allowed to stay on the payroll at $575 per month.[105] In fact, O'Neal received a $300 bonus from the FBI for what they saw as his "uniquely valuable services" in preparation for the pre-dawn raid.[106]

The FBI document requesting this bonus, and a host of other documentation that linked the Bureau to the raid, was suppressed without much difficulty. This was largely because the Grand Jury's prosecutor was Jerris Leonard, a Nixon administration Department of Justice employee who had worked for years to eradicate the Black Panther Party. Realizing that a murder trial for any of the seven surviving Panthers could lead to the unsealing of these secret files and the unearthing of the FBI's involvement in the raid, Leonard, in consultation with Attorney General John Mitchell, cut a deal: The federal grand jury wouldn't hand out indictments against any of the participants in the raid, so long as Hanrahan promised to drop the state indictments on attempted murder charges of the Panthers.[107] So, on 5 May 1970, one day after the National Guard attacks that left four protesters dead at Kent State University, the Illinois State's Attorney, already informed of the Grand Jury's planned report and the brokered deal, asserted that his review of the evidence brought him to the conclusion that "all the indictments of the survivors should be dismissed in the interest of justice."[108] Accordingly, ten days later, the Grand Jury issued its report devoid of indictments against the SPU.

The Multiplier Effect:
Forms of Suppression in Combination

Clearly, in the case of the political murders of Fred Hampton and Mark Clark, the direct violence mode of suppression dovetails with other modes, including: (1) infiltration, badjacketing, and the use of agent provocateurs (2) black propaganda, and (3) mass media deprecation. These suppressive tactics, in combination, had massively deleterious effects on the Black Panther Party.

When William O'Neal met SA Mitchell in late-1968, O'Neal had already accumulated two criminal charges: interstate car theft and impersonation of a federal officer (FBI, actually). In exchange for paying O'Neal's $300 cash bond on the impersonation charge, dropping both charges, and providing a monthly stipend, O'Neal agreed to infiltrate the BPP in Chicago. Frank Donner estimates that O'Neal made approximately $30,000 between 1969 and 1972, not including car maintenance and bonding fees, which the FBI also paid for.[109] SA Mitchell, who had just signed on to the Chicago Panther COINTELPRO Unit, and who was working under the auspices of SA Robert Piper, asserted that by February 1969 O'Neal was the "number three man" in the Chicago branch of the BPP.[110] O'Neal quickly gained the confidence of Panther leader Bobby Rush (Chicago's Minister of Defense) as well as of Hampton, whose security guard he ultimately became. He was swiftly promoted to "Captain of Security," and, along the way, so as to maintain credibility, he was arrested frequently on a number of charges, from attempting to illegally purchase firearms to drug possession to "openly threatening the life of a woman."[111]

O'Neal also played the role of agent provocateur, as he adopted a consistently militant stance in relations with external groups like the Blackstone Rangers as well as in BPP internal matters. In April 1969, O'Neal personally initiated the first violent collision between the BPP and the Blackstone Rangers, while he also advocated the use of nerve gas and electrocution to take care of BPP informants. He even went so far as to design and build an "electric chair" that could be used to torture infiltrators. This ferocious proposal was rejected out of hand by the BPP leadership, as was his suggestion that the Chicago BPP should obtain an airplane in order to bomb city hall. He once bullwhipped a Panther who he alleged was an informant and he enticed other BPP members to engage in crimes like burglary under the ostensible rubric of "fundraising." O'Neal also supplied the Panthers with high-tech explosive devices and weapons training, while the FBI footed the bill. He proposed schemes like blowing up an armory and robbing a McDonald's restaurant. He conspicuously contributed to the BPP's outwardly militaristic stance, habitually donning a .45 automatic in a shoulder holster, while keeping two 12-gauge shotguns and an M-1 carbine on hand. "Always go armed" became his motto.[112]

O'Neal was at least partially successful in creating an atmosphere of distrust, suspicion, and violence within the Chicago chapter of the BPP. According to Ron "Doc" Satchel, O'Neal brought drugs onto Panther premises, even though most Panthers opposed drug use.[113] In fact, Satchel remarked, "I never used drugs. But I got introduced to drugs from an FBI informant, William O'Neal, inside the party. The first time I smoked marijuana, I got it from him."[114] Commenting on O'Neal's penchant for breeding suspicion, Satchel recalls:

> I didn't like the methods he used to screen out "police provocateurs," so-called agents. Those people were no agents. He would accuse them of being informants, and he wanted to question them and beat them. I couldn't agree with that. And I got real quiet and withdrawn for a while. Other people objected, too, but they were afraid to say anything because they would be accused of being agents themselves. There was a big mistrust among the members.[115]

This is the textbook definition of badjacketing, or snitchjacketing, which Churchill and Vander Wall define as "the practice of creating suspicion—through spreading rumors, manufacture of evidence, etc.—that bona fide organizational members, usually in key positions, are FBI/police informers, guilty of such offenses as skimming organizational funds and the like."[116] The purpose of "badjacketing"—which will be discussed in much greater detail later in the book—is to foment distrust and to isolate targeted social-movement participants.

Informant O'Neal was a crucial player in what many, including black alderman A.A. (Sammy) Rayner, were calling an assassination.[117] In mid-November 1969, a few weeks prior to the raid that left Hampton and Clark dead, O'Neal met SA Mitchell at the Golden Torch Restaurant in downtown Chicago. It was there that he offered a detailed floor plan of the flat on Monroe Street, including such details as the placement of furniture and, most importantly, the precise spot where Fred Hampton slept.[118] The information O'Neal furnished was passed along to the Chicago police who used it to plan for the deadly raid of 4 December.[119] M. Wesley Swearingen, a former FBI agent, independently corroborates the FBI's involvement in the Hampton / Clark assassination and O'Neal's role as an informant (though he does not refer to O'Neal by name).[120]

As if providing the FBI with floor plans of the apartment were not enough, O'Neal almost assuredly drugged Hampton with seconal (a barbiturate) by surreptitiously mixing it into his Kool-Aid; O'Neal made dinner that night at the flat, which included the Kool-Aid.[121] Indeed, a vial for barbiturates was recovered by police after the raid.[122] Also, during Hampton's autopsy, a toxicological study of his blood found "high levels" of seconal in his system, approximately "the level of 4.5 milligrams percent."[123] These reported drug levels contradict sources close to Hampton who said he never used drugs. Strangely, that night Hampton dozed off in mid-sentence as he spoke to his mother on the telephone. BPP member Louis Truelock's subsequent efforts to wake him up in the immediate moments after the raid commenced were unsuccessful, despite the fact that Hampton was usually a light sleeper.[124]

In the aftermath of the fatal raid, O'Neal actually went out to Hampton's mother's house, ostensibly to console her, but also, seemingly, to start circulating a rumor that one of the other Panthers in the flat during the raid was a police informant.[125] His cover didn't last forever, though, and his role as informant surfaced in 1973 during the prosecution of an unrelated case.[126] In the end, O'Neal died a violent death. According to Churchill and Vander Wall, "William O'Neal apparently committed suicide in late February 1990 via the messy expedient of running down an embankment onto Chicago's Stevenson Expressway and being hit by an oncoming taxi."[127]

Black Propaganda:
"There's supposed to be a hit out for you."

The FBI's treatment of Hampton prior to the December 1969 raid constitutes a quintessential example of another mode of suppression: "black propaganda." Black propaganda is schism creation through the manufacturing of false documents purporting to come from the target organization. The FBI fabricated a number of letters to and from Jeff Fort, the leader of the Blackstone Rangers, to foment discord, and even violence, between the BPP and the Blackstone Rangers.

In late-1968 and early-1969, the FBI attempted to rupture a developing alliance in Chicago between the Black Panther Party and the Blackstone Rangers, a youth gang that the Church Committee described as "a heavily armed, violence-prone organization."[128] BPP leader Fred Hampton had been trying to unite the Panthers and the Rangers so as to strengthen efforts toward shared social-justice goals. According to Kenneth O'Reilly, "The Panthers hoped to politicize the Rangers, to turn the black youths who flocked to the city's gangs away from street crime and toward constructive community action."[129] Negotiations over a potential merger snagged over whether the Panthers would join the Rangers, as Ranger leader Jeff Fort wanted, or whether the Rangers would join the Panthers, which is what BPP leadership was pushing for.

The FBI, concerned about the potential power of such a coalition, suggested sending an anonymous, forged letter to Fort, telling him that BPP leaders were badmouthing him over his "lack of commitment to black people more generally." According to the FBI, this letter was designed to encourage "his refusal to accept any BPP overtures to the Rangers and additionally might result in Fort having active steps taken to exact some form of retribution toward the leadership of the BPP."[130] In other words, the FBI not only hoped to prevent the Rangers and the Panthers from joining forces, but it also aimed to incite violence between the two groups.[131] J. Edgar Hoover authorized the mailing of the following anonymous letter, which was sent to Jeff Fort:

> Brother Jeff:
> I've spent some time with some Panther friends on the west side lately and I know what's been going on. The brothers that run the Panthers blame you for blocking their thing and there's supposed to be a hit out for you. I'm not a Panther, or a Ranger, just black. From what I see, these Panthers are out for themselves, not black people. I think you ought to know what they're up to, I know what I'd do if I was you. You might hear from me again.
> (sgd.) A black brother you don't know[132]

The FBI itself explained in an internal memo that the objective of the letter—and more specifically the phrase "there's supposed to be a hit out for you"—was to "intensify the degree of animosity between the two groups and occasion Fort to take retaliatory action which could disrupt the BPP or lead to reprisals against its leadership." In the winter of 1970, in front of a federal grand jury, SAC Marlin Johnson exhibited Orwellian flair when he maintained that the word "hit" didn't mean a murder contract. Rather, he insisted that it meant "something non-violent in nature."[133]

Clearly the FBI was trying to incite inter-group violence, as its internal memos reveal. The FBI opted not to send a similar letter to the Black Panthers. It felt it likely wouldn't be "productive" since "the BPP at present is not believed as violence prone as the Rangers to whom violent type activity—shooting and the like—is second nature."[134] In reality, however, the Bureau did send anonymous letters to Panther leadership with the aim of creating dissent between the BPP and the Blackstone Rangers. For example, the following unsigned letter was mailed to Fred Hampton. "Brother Hampton: Just a word of warning. A Stone friend tells me [name deleted] wants the panthers and is looking for somebody to get you out of the way. Brother Jeff is supposed to be interested. I'm just a black man looking for blacks working together, not more of this gang banging." Clearly this letter was meant to forge deep distrust between Hampton and Ranger leader Jeff Fort. These letters were followed by "a series of violent clashes."[135] It's impossible to tell how much of the subsequent animosity and violence between the Panthers and the Rangers—who never did join forces—was the result of this forged correspondence, but undoubtedly these letters didn't help improve relations.[136]

Media Coverage of the Black Panthers

By the early-1970s the Party was in suppression-induced shambles. Many of its leaders were in jail; others had been killed, either by the state—like Hampton—or by rival groups. According to Charles Jones, the BPP's "national influence began to subside after 1971" though "the organizational life span of the BPP lasted until 1982."[137] The killing of Fred Hampton and Mark Clark was an important piece of this sharp slide into disarray. In fact, according to Michael Staub,[138] the assassination of Hampton and Clark constituted a pivotal moment that catalyzed a "moral panic" that took the form of a "full-scale rhetorical campaign *against* the Panthers" carried out by the mainstream media. It this way, mass media deprecation intersects with direct violence in a significant way. Mainstream mass-media coverage of the Black Panthers facilitated the Black Panther Party's internal fracturing and social isolation.

According to Staub, in the aftermath of the fatal pre-dawn raid on 4 December 1969 in Chicago:

> the Panthers were…turned into folk devils. From this point on, media representations amplified and distorted the Panthers' dealings far more than they had before. But while most scholarship on the moral panic scenario has assumed that folk devils are caricatured and demonized in a fairly straightforward, uniform fashion, an examination of the media coverage of the Panthers reveals a discordant jumble of representations, a set of metaphoric images and associations that were both vigorously fearmongering *and* sniggeringly derisive.[139]

While *Harper's* magazine drew the comparison between Bobby Seale and Adolf Hitler ("Both are anti-rational. Hitler's injunction to 'think with your blood' is echoed by Bobby's appeal to the impulses of the Black Soul"),[140] others, like Tom Wolfe, extended the attack beyond members of the BPP to people who merely supported the stance of the Panthers. In "Radical Chic: That Party at Lenny's," an article that appeared in the *New York* magazine, Wolfe wrote about a party at Leonard Bernstein's apartment that doubled as a fundraiser for the defense of twenty-one Black Panthers who were on trial in New York for planning to kill New York City police officers and bomb department stores. In covering this cross-class event, Wolfe put forth a merciless mixture of condemnation and ridicule, as he focused on Bernstein's flamboyant style, the wealth of the guests, and the Jewishness of the partygoers. This acerbic portrayal followed similarly skeptical coverage of this event that appeared in the prior months in the *New York Times*.[141]

In her study of the national press's treatment of the Black Panther Party, Jane Rhodes also found that the media undermined the Panthers. She asserts that the media by and large depicted the Panthers as "wrongheaded, antisocial, and a national threat" and that the national press failed to provide the historical context that gave rise to the Panthers. Rather, "The ideologies about race and social protest disseminated by the national press were quite explicit; black power advocates were a problem population to be addressed by law enforcement practices of containment."[142] A 1967 editorial by the *New York Times* titled "The Spirit of Lawlessness" epitomizes this. The editorial starts with examples of the Panthers flouting traditional approaches to redressing one's grievances before launching a paternalistic, pedantic tirade about the sanctity of law. The *Times* concluded that "the Black Panthers and the 'black power' zealots" who defied the law constituted "forces of anarchy" that deserved no compromise. If J. Edgar Hoover were to have read this, he couldn't have considered it anything other than a gleaming green light from the country's most influential newspaper.[143]

As mentioned previously, local media outlets in Chicago offered coverage of the siege on the Panther flat that favored the views of law enforcement and marginalized voices in support of the BPP. In a comparative analysis of a mainstream newspaper, the *Chicago Tribune*, and a newspaper from the black press, the *Chicago Defender*, Todd Fraley and Elli Lester-Roushanzamir conclude that the *Tribune's* coverage helped create an anti-Panther moral panic whereas the *Defender* situated the killing of Hampton and Clark within the larger context of racism and the potential for abuse of power by local officials. According to the authors, the *Chicago Tribune* consistently put forth coverage in which "the Panthers became equated with the disintegration of society and the police became the friend of the people and the saviors of traditional values."[144] The *Chicago Defender* stressed the human rights of the Panthers and the idea that they deserved equal protection under the law. While the *Tribune* marginalized Panther voices, recorded the comments local officials at face value, painted the Panthers as deviant, and treated Hampton as an object rather than a human, the *Defender* included the BPP's goals and demands, critically examined the statements of local officials, pushed for deeper investigation of the raid, and framed Hampton as a person with numerous positive qualities. Such findings point to the importance of subaltern counterpublics: safe spaces where dissent can be cultivated and proliferated.[145] The role of the mass media in the suppression of dissent will be explored in much greater detail later.

Fred Hampton was a magical orator with the struggle for justice bubbling in his blood. He once asked, "Why don't you live for the people? Why don't you struggle for the people? Why don't you die for the people?"[146] Hampton died for the people, and at much too young an age. Others struggled on, however, to preserve his legacy. The brutality of the fatal attack galvanized members of Weatherman/SDS to go underground as the Weather Underground. As David Gilbert put it, "It was the murder of Fred Hampton more than any other factor that compelled us to feel [that] we had to take up armed struggle."[147] The Hampton and Clark families pressed onward through the legal system. In 1982, the families were rewarded for their persistence and awarded a settlement of $1.85 million in a civil suit. Their attorney, Flint Taylor, described the settlement as "an admission of the conspiracy that existed between the F.B.I. and Hanrahan's men to murder Fred Hampton." Part of the awarded money ($36,000) went to William O'Neal for testifying as a witness. Hampton's family used the money to set up the Fred Hampton Scholarship Fund for young African-Americans who wish to study law.[148]

3
Public Prosecutions and Hearings

Political radicals have long been confronted with legalized suppression in the form of public prosecutions or hearings. As part of the "Red Scare" of 1919–1920, militant anarchists Nicola Sacco and Bartolomeo Vanzetti were charged with first-degree murder and robbery in Massachusetts. Prior to the charges, neither had a criminal record, yet both were active labor organizers and anti-war activists, which drew the attention of the authorities. After working their way through a highly prejudicial, indisputably corrupt legal labyrinth, the state executed Sacco and Vanzetti by electric chair in 1927. Fifty years later, Massachusetts Governor Michael Dukakis asserted in a public statement that the defendants' experiences in the criminal justice system were "permeated by prejudice against foreigners and hostility toward unorthodox political views." Dukakis also remarked, "the trial and execution of Sacco and Vanzetti should serve to remind all civilized people of the constant need to guard against our susceptibility to prejudice, our intolerance of unorthodox ideas and our failure to defend the rights of persons who are looked upon as strangers in our midst."[1] Such "hostility toward unorthodox political views" has become a distinctive feature of U.S. political culture, and it has led to the legal persecution of numerous dissidents. Many political dissidents have found themselves testifying at hostile hearings and defending themselves in court, including Angela Davis, Geronimo Pratt, Russell Means, the Chicago Eight, Thomas McGrath, and numerous protesters in the Civil Rights and Vietnam anti-war movements.

Public prosecutions of and hearings on dissidents—especially events that are mass-media publicized—suppress dissent on two levels: (1) dissidents are often put in jail or so traumatized as to drop their political stances or temporarily put them on hold, and (2) current supporters and potential supporters are discouraged from putting forth dissident views. When dissidents are publicly questioned—and sometimes punished—by the state, their reputations can be tarnished, if not destroyed, in the public sphere, thereby lessening the inclination to join these individuals' groups, to support these groups, or even to make an effort to figure out exactly what these groups are saying.[2] Public trials can also lead to hefty legal fees, vanishing wages, and other monetary losses that put a dent in activist organizing.[3]

According to Carey McWilliams, members of Congress applied intense coercive pressure on witnesses—especially "unfriendly" witnesses—who appeared in front of the House Committee on Un-American Activities (HUAC), and this pressure doubled as "a form of carefully rehearsed psychological warfare against the American people."[4] The Hollywood Ten, who went on trial in 1949, are a quintessential example of the public prosecutions and hearings mode of suppression, but in order to understand what happened in this highly controversial, closely followed court case, one must first get a handle on how these ten Hollywood workers ended up on trial in the first place.

HUAC was created in 1938 as a temporary, special investigating committee under the chairmanship of Texas Democrat Martin Dies, an inveterate red-baiter and a longtime proponent of deportation for foreign political radicals. Dies often alleged that the federal government's bureaucracy was brimming with "hundreds of left-wingers and radicals who do not believe in our system of private enterprise."[5] In 1945, the Committee shed its temporary status and became a permanent standing committee, the only investigative committee in the House with subpoena powers. Under the 79th Congress's Public Law 601, the Committee had the authority to investigate: "(1) the extent, character, and objectives of un-American propaganda activities in the United States, (2) the diffusion within the United States of subversive and un-American propaganda that is instigated from foreign countries or of domestic origin and attacks the principle of the form of government as guaranteed by our Constitution, and (3) all other questions in relation thereto that would aid Congress in any remedial legislation."

With the political embers from World War II still glowing, the House Un-American Activities Committee turned its attention to domestic dissidents of the red-hued variety. The Hollywood Ten emerged in October 1947 when HUAC began formal hearings on the alleged Communist infiltration of the film industry. From the moment the hearings began in the Caucus Room of the Old House Office Building on 20 October until the moment they ended at 3 p.m. on 30 October, witnesses—both "friendly" and "unfriendly"—were brought in front of the committee in order to find out whether they were Communists, Communist sympathizers, or willing participants who would "name names" of suspected Communists. HUAC Chairman J. Parnell Thomas exhibited a hyper-focus on Communism, even though in 1947 less than one percent of the Hollywood workforce—fewer than 300 out of 30,000—was either a past or present Communist. As the Cold War became hotter and hotter, Hollywood progressives found themselves with less and less political support for their dissident ideas. Not even Franklin Roosevelt was safe from vicious criticism. In May 1947, the Committee alleged that Roosevelt had urged the creation of "flagrant Communist propaganda films." It also leveled the allegation that Roosevelt's National Labor Relations Board (NLRB) had "infiltrated" Communists into the motion picture industry.[6]

In May 1947, HUAC—which by this point "thirsted for liberal-radical blood" according to Larry Ceplair and Steven Englund—traveled to Los Angeles to hold closed hearings at the Biltmore Hotel with fourteen "friendly" witnesses such as Sam Wood, Lela Rogers, and Adolphe Menjou, who rattled off the names of real, suspected, and imagined Communists.[7] Wood was the first president of the Motion Picture Alliance for the Preservation of American Ideals (MPAPAI). As Fariello points out, "The MPAPAI openly invited HUAC to investigate Hollywood and supplied the committee with an extensive list of Reds and fellow travelers."[8] Known as a militantly anti-Communist reactionary, Wood was subpoenaed again in September 1947. Rogers was the mother of actress Ginger Rogers. Chairman Thomas later referred to the elder Rogers as a "friendly" witness. He considered her part of a group of "volunteers of information" whose "Americanism is not questioned."[9] She alleged that her daughter, Ginger Rogers, had been asked to speak the communistic line "Share and share alike—that's democracy" in "Tender Comrade," a film written by Dalton Trumbo. She pegged both Trumbo and playwright Clifford Odets as Communists, the latter because she had read in a newspaper column that he was, and she had never encountered a denial from him.[10] Menjou, like Wood, was known for his reactionary beliefs. He was an officeholder in the MPAPAI. Testifying before HUAC in May 1947, Menjou said, "Hollywood is one of main centers of Communist activity in America."[11] In response to a question from committee member Richard Nixon, a Republican from California, Menjou frothed, "I am firmly convinced of the evils of Stalinism or Marxism. It is so evil and such a menace to the American people that I think it should be watched and watched and watched."[12] This is exactly what many members of the Committee wanted to hear.

These witnesses—almost all of them associated with the Motion Picture Alliance—were so loquacious that Thomas ended up extending his stay so as to hear all the witnesses at length. With the ammunition afforded by these friendly, finger-pointing witnesses, the Thomas Committee came to the conclusion that Hollywood was producing "some of the most flagrant Communist propaganda films" in circulation.[13] Therefore, Thomas and the rest of the Committee proceeded to go after the Hollywood producers, hoping to swing them onto HUAC's side, since these producers could fire studio employees, and could therefore wield the hiring-and-firing stick as a form of economic restriction and disciplinary control.

Many of the film producers went along reluctantly, as they didn't want to relinquish control of their filmmaking. According to Ceplair and Englund: "Only when the Committee convinced the producers that their profits and control were imperiled by seeming solidarity with the 'unfriendly' witnesses would studio management abandon [their support for left-wing screen artists] for one of grudging compliance with HUAC." Jack Warner was the first to fracture the producer solidarity when in April 1947 he advocated "An All Out Fight On Commies." Warner "behaved before the Committee like a cornered villain from one of his studio's gangster movies, blurting out the names of every left-winger or liberal he could think of (all of whom he labeled 'Communist')."[14] Once the film producers capitulated into full cooperation with HUAC, a subpoena was suddenly transmogrified from an invitation for ideological and constitutional battle with Committee members into an invitation to one's own film-industry funeral. The possibility of being blacklisted upped the stakes in an already high-stakes affair.

In these May 1947 investigation proceedings in Los Angeles, members of the House Un-American Activities Committee exerted calculated, ideological discipline. Chairman Thomas applauded people like Lela Rogers as "friendly witnesses cooperating with the Committee" while witnesses deemed uncooperative, like the musical composer Hanns Eisler, earned the Committee's scorn and derision. Eisler also earned a return trip to the Committee in September 1947 where he was dubbed "the Karl Marx of Communism in the musical field" by Robert E. Stripling, a HUAC staff member.[15] In September, Eisler, who had fled Hitler's Germany in 1933, was grilled mercilessly by Stripling, earning special attention because he had "made application" to the German Communist Party two decades prior. Even though Eisler claimed to have "neglected the whole affair" and not participated in Party meetings, he earned no compassion from the Committee.[16] For his troubles, the Committee leveled perjury charges at him, called him "the murderous little Moscow agent," and requested that the Immigration authorities deport him.[17] After a compulsory hearing, the immigration authorities obliged, issuing Eisler a deportation warrant in February 1948. He and his wife, Louisa, left for Czechoslovakia the next month after signing a declaration vowing never to return to the United States.[18] All this happened despite the efforts of prominent USAmericans like Eleanor Roosevelt and the *New Republic*'s Malcolm Cowley, who publicly lobbied the State Department on Eisler's behalf. The futile efforts of such influential people sent a strong message to the general population: HUAC was a powerful body that was difficult to challenge. Also, Eisler's "voluntary" deportation was the potential fate of dissidents who had come to the United States from abroad, and this didn't go unnoticed at the time. The Eisler family's experiences offered lessons that affected other foreign-national dissidents, like the German poet and playwright Bertolt Brecht, whose time before the Committee was still to come.

HUAC's spring hearings were an effort to gather injurious grist that could later be used in an all-out frontal attack on Hollywood leftists. HUAC needed more specific information about Communism in Hollywood, beyond the unsubstantiated blatherings of the Motion Picture Alliance. The hearings were also designed to test the Hollywood film industry's mettle. How much resistance would Hollywood put up? Who could be relied upon to display paroxysms of patriotism and to attack their fellow workers? Throughout 1947, Chairman Thomas continued to rev up anti-communist sentiments as he declared, through the largely compliant mass media, that the Committee's central objective was to "expose activities by un-American individuals and organizations which, while sometimes being legal, are nonetheless inimical to our American concepts and our American future." In a radio address, Thomas further explained that the Committee's objective "is based upon the conviction that the American public will not tolerate efforts to subvert or destroy the American system of government, once such efforts have been pointed out."[19]

Meanwhile, Eric Johnston, a HUAC-compliant film producer, proposed a three-point plan to his fellow producers who were most assuredly due to stumble into HUAC's crosshairs at some future moment. His plan suggested that the producers: (1) publicly demand that HUAC's future investigative hearings be open; (2) hire Truman's former Secretary of State James Byrnes to be their public representative; and (3) not employ "proven Communists" in positions that dealt with film content. Producers, in general, were willing to go along with the first two tenets of the plan, but they found the third unpalatable. Producers didn't want their hiring and firing processes dictated by others, let alone the government.[20] However, as the pressure-cooker of HUACian humiliation began to crank, more and more producers were willing to acquiesce to the third tenet of Johnston's plan.

On 21 September 1947, forty-three Hollywood workers from the film industry received subpoenas to appear before HUAC in October.[21] The Committee expected about nineteen of these to be "unfriendly," and of these nineteen, many were either current or former members of the Communist Party. The nineteen were a collection of screenwriters (Alvah Bessie, Lester Cole, Richard Collins, Gordon Kahn, Howard Koch, Ring Lardner Jr., John Howard Lawson, Albert Maltz, Samuel Ortiz, Waldo Salt, and Dalton Trumbo); writer-directors (Herbert Biberman and Robert Rossen); directors (Edward Dmytryk, Lewis Milestone, and Irving Pichel); a playwright (Bertolt Brecht); a writer-producer (Adrian Scott); and an actor (Larry

Parks). Of these nineteen, eight didn't end up appearing before HUAC in 1947, and of these eight, three (Collins, Parks, and Rossen) later emerged as "friendly" witnesses.[22]

Aside from the fact that all nineteen were men, they all resided in Hollywood and had been actively involved at some point in their careers in pro-Soviet pursuits. Ten were Jewish, sixteen had at some point been writers, and a large majority of them were members of the Communist Party of the United States (CPUSA).[23] In an interview years after the Hollywood Ten trial, Ring Lardner Jr. said that the nineteen also

> agreed that we should challenge the committee's rights, that Congress had no right to investigate the screen because it was protected by extension of the freedom of the press clause in the First Amendment. If they had no right to legislate in that area, then they had no right to investigate it, or the political beliefs of individuals, for that matter.[24]

Finally, many of the nineteen shared political and professional experiences with the "friendly" witnesses who were to testify devastatingly against them. Ceplair and Englund also note that the nineteen might really be considered eighteen since Bertolt Brecht "wanted to be left free to work out a position that would not risk the loss of his recently issued exit visa—to Switzerland— as soon as the hearings had ended. He feared that close associations with the Americans would be used as an excuse to delay his departure. The other eighteen understood."[25]

In contrast to the "unfriendly" witnesses who were often cut off by the Committee questioner, and generally treated brusquely, the "friendly" witnesses were often allowed to speak at length. While Chairman Thomas pounded his gavel like an angry carpenter when "unfriendly" witnesses failed to answer the Committee's queries in a straightforward, direct manner, "friendly" witnesses were able to expand on their ideas at length. Walt Disney, Jack Warner, Ayn Rand, Adolphe Menjou, and Robert Taylor were all given ample opportunity to discuss the perils of Communism. Another "friendly" witness, future-president of the United States and then-president of the Screen Actors Guild, Ronald Reagan, was able to portray himself as the victim of Communist conniving, as he firmly stated his hatred for Communists. He said, "I detest their philosophy, but I detest more than that their tactics, which are those of the fifth column, and are dishonest."[26] Nevertheless, Reagan suggested that democracy need not be subverted in order to stop Communism in Hollywood. He remarked, "at the same time I never as a citizen want to see our country become urged, by either fear or resentment of this group, that we ever compromise with any of our democratic principles through that fear or resentment. I still think that democracy can do it."[27] Yet, according to Fariello, "As the head of the Screen Actors Guild, Reagan regularly informed on his members to the FBI."[28] Athan Theoharis corroborates this assertion, writing, "FBI officials in fact knew that Reagan could provide the desired information and would be cooperative. Recruited as a confidential informant for the FBI in 1943, Reagan had regularly briefed his FBI contact about the political activities of his Hollywood associates."[29] Many years later, in 1979, Reagan gave a backhand defense of Joseph McCarthy's actions, claiming "The senator used a shotgun when a rifle was needed, injuring the innocent along with the guilty. Nevertheless, his broadsides should not be used today to infer that all who opposed Communist subversion were hysterical zealots." In 1983, Reagan's Attorney General Edwin Meese toasted McCarthy as "a truly great senator" before clinking glasses with Ronald and Nancy Reagan.[30]

In 1947, "friendly" witnesses like Reagan provided the Committee with plenty of condemnatory grist, which came in handy the following week when the "unfriendly" witnesses were called to the stand. Prior to their appearance in front of HUAC for the second week of investigation, the subpoenaed nineteen assembled quietly to discuss legal strategy, in light of the accusations that had been hurled around the committee room the previous week. In general, they had three strategic objectives: "1) opposing HUAC, while 2) not discrediting themselves in studio executives' eyes with 'indecorous' outbursts of intransigence, and 3) providing the constitutional basis for a favorable Supreme Court opinion."[31] Regarding this third objective, rather than pleading the Fifth Amendment, as some of their attorneys had recommended, the men, as a group, decided to hinge their defense on the First Amendment. They feared that use of the Fifth Amendment would imply guilt and thereby not engender public support whereas a defense hinged on the much more widely accepted First Amendment—freedom of speech—would allow them to find resonance with a wider audience. But aside from the fact that the nineteen wanted to appear credible before the invisible jury of public opinion, they also wanted to develop a case that the Supreme Court would be more likely to consider. At that point in time, the Supreme Court had yet to rule on the use of the First Amendment by witnesses testifying in front of Congress. Therefore, the nineteen had a better chance in their anticipated court case—once it wended its way through the lower courts—of earning consideration from the highest court in the land. The dissident witnesses also agreed that each of them would lead off his testimony with a personal statement, and then, during questioning, they vowed to evade queries about their group affiliations, whether they were with political, religious, or union organizations.

So when asked the now-famous question "Are you now or have you ever been a member of the Communist Party?" members of the Hollywood Ten responded neither with silence nor with a straight answer, but rather by questioning the questioner. One by one—though each in his own way—they asserted that the Committee didn't have the right to even pose such a query. Some commentators, like Victor Navasky, argue retrospectively that this strategy was less effective by virtue of the fact that the Ten didn't consistently stress that they felt the Committee had no right to ask the Are-you-now-or-have-you-ever-been question, but rather they answered the question each in his own way. Therefore, instead of sounding like conscientious civil libertarians testing the boundaries of the First Amendment, they often ended up sounding more like aggressive and obstinate (if creative and dramatic) witnesses who were pushing the limits of the First Amendment.[32]

The first of the "unfriendly" witnesses, John Howard Lawson, came out of the gates on 27 October with verbal guns firing. While HUAC never divulged its process for determining the order of the "unfriendly" witnesses, some have conjectured that the order was decided according to the amount of ostensibly incriminating evidence the committee investigators had previously collected on each of the nineteen. Anticipating hostility, Lawson requested to read his statement immediately upon being sworn in, an indulgence that had been afforded to many of the "friendly" witnesses without any resistance from Committee members. But before allowing Lawson to read his statement aloud, Chairman Thomas demanded to pre-screen the statement. Displeased with Lawson's prepared remarks, he refused him the right to read it out loud, thereby preempting one of the central strategies of the nineteen witnesses.

In his statement, Lawson wrote, "Rational people don't argue with dirt." Later he questioned the "evidence" being brought against him, asserting that it derived from "a parade of stool-pigeons, neurotics, publicity-seeking clowns, Gestapo agents, paid informers, and a few ignorant and frightened Hollywood artists." He even singled out Chairman Thomas as "a petty politician, serving more powerful forces" that "are trying to introduce fascism in this country."[33] Unable to read this, Lawson tried his best to disseminate these views, even when they didn't match up perfectly with the question he was asked. When asked about membership in certain groups, like the Screen Writers Guild, Lawson argued, "the raising of any question here in regards to membership, political beliefs, or affiliation" was "absolutely beyond the powers of this Committee." Nevertheless, he continued to respond to the questions, saying that the answers were actually "a matter of public record." Throughout the testimony, the Committee Chairman gaveled Lawson into silence, and at one point put forth a not-so-thinly veiled threat:

Mr. Lawson, you will have to stop or you will leave the witness stand. And you will leave the witness stand because you are in contempt. That is why you will leave the witness stand. And if you are just trying to force me to put you in contempt, you won't have to try much harder. You know what has happened to a lot of people that have been in contempt of this Committee this year, don't you?[34]

Lawson responded with feistiness, proceeding even as Chairman Thomas banged his gavel and appealed for order: "I am glad you have made it perfectly clear that you are going to threaten and intimidate the witnesses, Mr. Chairman. I am an American and I am not at all easy to intimidate, and don't think I am." Not long after accusing the Committee of "using the old technique, which was used in Hitler Germany in order to create a scare" Lawson was ordered off the stand. Officers removed him as he continued to try to speak. Lawson's final recorded words were "I have written Americanism for many years, and I shall continue to fight for the Bill of Rights, which you are trying to destroy." Lawson's extrication from the stand was greeted by a boisterous mélange of applause and boos from the assembled spectators.[35] As Lawson was carted away, HUAC investigator Louis J. Russell stepped up to the stand and, reading from a prepared text, alleged thirty-five of Lawson's "Communist affiliations."[36]

A number of potential supporters in bystander publics abhorred the witnesses' aggressiveness, which sometimes took the form of barely bridled yelling and angst-ridden pleas in response to intimidation and rough treatment from Committee members. By cagily scheduling one of the most contentious and undeniably Communist witnesses first, Thomas managed to facilitate the alienation of a number of liberals from the nineteen's cause. In the short-term, Lawson's sharp-edged testimony put off apparent supporters like Eric Johnston, whose acquiescent statement in front of HUAC later that afternoon sent shock waves through the ranks of the nineteen Hollywood workers and their supporters. Johnston assured the Committee that film producers would do anything they needed to do in order to keep subversive ideas, themes, and motifs from finding their way to the screen. "I have never objected to your investigating Hollywood," he said. "I told you we welcomed it, and we sincerely do."[37] His words wedged doubt into the minds of the nineteen. This statement was strikingly different than the tough stance he had taken previously in defense of the nineteen, such as when he asserted, "As long as I live I will never be a party to anything as un-American as a blacklist, and any statement purporting to quote me as agreeing to a blacklist is a libel upon me as a good American....We're not going to go totalitarian to please this committee."[38] Clearly times had changed. The witnesses couldn't help but wonder if the producers would in fact abandon them in this crucial moment.

Hostile exchanges—similar to the Lawson testimony and punctuated by forced removal from the Committee hearing room—continued throughout that week, though some of the witnesses were more measured and subdued. In the end, of the "unfriendly" nineteen, only eleven witnesses were called to testify. Ten of them took the position that the Committee had no right to question them in such a manner and on such matters. The eleventh witness, Bertolt Brecht, agreed with the Ten in principle, but after his comically evasive and contradictory testimony, he decided to leave the United States for East Germany. Hence, the name for the group—the Hollywood Ten—emerged.

While Brecht may have agreed with the Ten in principle, he categorically denied, while on the stand, that he was a Communist. After seeing how the previous ten "unfriendly" witnesses answered the are-you-or-have-you-ever-been question, Brecht opted to soften up the Committee by saying that "I am a guest in this country and do not want to enter into any legal arguments, so I will answer your question fully as well I can. I was not a member, or am not a member, of any Communist Party."[39] From there, Brecht worked the Committee into a dizzying swirl of literary interpretation and faulty memory, justifying his reading of Marx by arguing that "as a playwright who wrote historical plays, I, of course, had to study Marx's ideas about history. I do not think intelligent plays today can be written without such study."[40] Brecht's verbal oscillations were at times comical:

> **Mr. Stripling:** Mr. Brecht, since you have been in the United States, have you attended any Communist Party meetings?
> **Mr. Brecht:** No, I don't think so.
> **Mr. Stripling:** You don't think so?
> **Mr. Brecht:** No.
> **The Chairman [Thomas]:** Well, aren't you certain?
> **Mr. Brecht:** No—I am certain, yes.
> **The Chairman** You are certain you have never been to Communist Party meetings?
> **Mr. Brecht:** Yes, I think so. I am here six years—I am here those—I do not think so. I do not think that I attended political meetings.
> **The Chairman** No, never mind the political meetings, but have you attended any Communist meetings in the United States?
> **Mr. Brecht:** I do not think so, no.

The Chairman You are certain?

Mr. Brecht: I think I am certain.

The Chairman: You think you are certain?

Mr. Brecht: Yes, I have not attended such meetings, in my opinion.[41]

Brecht's savvy manipulations, combined with his droll selective memory, seemed to have an effect on Committee members. As Chairman Thomas concluded Brecht's testimony he thanked him, adding that he was "a good example" to the other witnesses.[42]

After Lawson, the other witnesses who took the stand before the final witness, Brecht, were Dalton Trumbo, Albert Maltz, Alvah Bessie, Samuel Ornitz, Herbert Biberman, Edward Dmytryk, Adrian Scott, Ring Lardner, Jr., and Lester Cole. As Ceplair and Englund note, generally speaking, their testimonies "alternated between statements of constitutional principle and the rights of American citizens on one hand, and criticism of HUAC's 'fascistic' intentions on the other."[43] Some memorable moments include Lardner's response to the question of whether he was a Communist that "I could answer that, but if I did I'd hate myself in the morning" and Ornitz's pensive remark that "I say you do raise a serious question for me when you ask me to act in concert with you to override the Constitution."[44] Following each witness's uniquely worded refusal to answer the are-you-or-have-you-ever-been question, HUAC Investigator Russell was paraded out to offer specific, damaging information about the witness in question, from Edward Dmytryk's "Communist Party book No. 84961 for the year 1944" to Adrian Scott's Communist Political Association identification cards.[45] Even though this information was a calculated concoction of hearsay, circumstantial evidence, and outright fabrication, it was allowed to stand.[46] After Russell made his incriminating statements, Chairman Thomas would declare the witness should be cited for contempt.

The hearings ceased on 30 October, although a satisfying explanation for the abatement was not, and never has been, offered. Adjourning the hearings that Thursday, Chairman Thomas stated:

> While we still have heard 39 witnesses, there are many more to be heard. The Chair stated earlier in the hearing he would present the records of 79 prominent people associated with the motion-picture industry who were members of the Communist Party or who had records of Communist affiliations. We have had before us 11 of these individuals. There are 68 to go...I want to emphasize that the committee is not adjourning sine die, but will resume hearings as soon as possible.[47]

Such proclamations notwithstanding, the hearings did not resume. Perhaps such capriciousness from HUAC should be expected, since over time the Committee was consistently inconsistent.

On 24 November 1947, U.S. Congress voted to cite the Hollywood Ten for contempt of Congress. In the days leading up to the issuance of contempt citations, members of Congress took the opportunity to viciously attack individuals from the Hollywood Ten. For example, John McDowell, a Republican from Pennsylvania, pilloried Albert Maltz, saying, "This man was the most arrogant, the most contemptible, the most bitter of all these people who do not believe in their own country. Here is a typical Communist intellectual, burning with a bitter hatred of the country he was born in, its Government, its officials, and its people."[48]

Meanwhile, fifty leading film executives met secretly for two days in the Waldorf-Astoria Hotel in New York City, deciding in the end to fire the members of the Hollywood Ten, because, they argued, the Ten's "actions have been a disservice to their employers and have impaired their usefulness to the industry."[49] In this way, the blacklist began. A number of informal, unofficial blacklists were enforced at the time, but the blacklist that came closest to "official" was "Red Channels." This list, which was released on 22 June 1950, a mere three days before the Korean War and a few days before the sentencing of eight of the Hollywood Ten, included 151 allegedly subversive directors, writers, and performers, including Leonard Bernstein, Lena Horne, Langston Hughes, Arthur Miller, Dorothy Parker, Pete Seeger, Gale Sondergaard (who was married to Herbert Biberman of the Hollywood Ten), and Orson Welles.[50]

Numerous liberals failed to support the Hollywood Ten, instead offering critiques of how the group could have better performed in front of the Committee.[51] Ceplair and Englund sum up this logic when they write about Hollywood liberals who "provided everyone with what appeared to be the best face-saving device: the separation of people and principle. In effect, the liberal formula ran along this line: 'we support the right of people to freedom of expression, but we do not stand behind the Ten who are denied that right.' As transposed into the managerial key, the tune ran: 'we are opposed to a blacklist, but we are not going to hire Communists.'"[52] Thus the Hollywood producers summarily sacrificed the Ten on the altar of future economic profit. But, at the same time, they also decided to launch a significant counter-attack that might dissuade HUAC from further damaging the reputation of these firms and their films. These producers believed at the time that by forming a limited blacklist they might be able to make this their final fight against HUAC. Little did they know that this was really their first battle in a war that would stretch deep into the next decade.

On 3 December 1947, the producers issued their "Waldorf Statement," which made plain their plan to ostracize the Ten because their actions supposedly stained the film industry's reputation. Members of the Association of Motion Picture Producers vowed to "discharge or suspend without compensation those in our employ and we will not re-employ any of the ten until such time as he is acquitted or has purged himself of contempt and declares under oath that he is not a Communist."[53] Thus, the "Waldorf Statement" signaled the firing of the Hollywood Ten and vowed not to "knowingly employ a Communist or a member of any party or group which advocated the overthrow of the Government of the United States by force or by illegal or unconstitutional methods."[54] The abandonment of the Hollywood Ten was complete.

Shortly thereafter, on 5 December, the Hollywood Ten were indicted for contempt of Congress by a federal grand jury at the request of Attorney General Tom Clark. Eight of the Ten were accused of refusing to answer questions about membership in the Communist Party and the Screen Writers Guild, while the other two were only charged with refusing to answer the question about the Communist Party.[55] Individuals from the Hollywood Ten toured the United States in an effort to drum up support for their cause. Initially, big stars like Frank Sinatra, Gene Kelly, Lucille Ball, Lauren Bacall, Judy Garland, Burt Lancaster, and Humphrey Bogart supported them. Calling themselves the Committee for the First Amendment, this ad hoc group of liberals and moderates took out ads, underwrote nationwide broadcasts, and traveled to Washington, DC to question the way HUAC was attacking Hollywood artists. This group was not so much acting in support of the Ten as it was in defiance of HUAC. But once the producers slotted the blacklist into place, the Hollywood Ten adopted an aggressive approach in the committee hearings, and their real Communist connections were established, this liberal and moderate support for the Ten quickly dwindled.[56] Not even the guilds came to the Ten's defense, and therefore, by the end of the year, they were, as artists, personae non gratae in the industry and their careers were imperiled.[57] Soon after their grand-jury indictment, the Ten's request for a collective trial was rejected by a federal district court. This meant each person would have to face trial individually, thereby increasing the group's expenses many times over.

Lawson appeared in court first, followed by Trumbo. A federal judge found Lawson guilty of contempt of Congress on 19 April 1949, a mere week after his trial commenced. Trumbo was similarly convicted on 5 May. After these convictions, the government's prosecution and the defense teams of the other eight agreed that, rather than continuing to try each member of the Ten individually in the lower courts, the remaining eight would avoid what promised to be a lengthy appeal process by accepting the likely verdict in advance.

Then, on 13 June 1949, Bennett C. Clark, the Chief Justice of the Circuit Court of Appeals, ruled in *Lawson v. United States* and *Trumbo v. United States* that "the House Committee on Un-American Activities, or a properly appointed subcommittee thereof, has the *power* to inquire whether a witness subpoenaed by it is or is not a member of the Communist Party or a believer in communism."[58] The Ten were not deeply discouraged, though, since they anticipated a favorable First Amendment interpretation from the Supreme Court, given that it had among its ranks liberal, Roosevelt-appointed justices like Hugo Black, William O. Douglas, Robert Jackson, Frank Murphy, Wiley Rutledge, and Harlan F. Stone. However, to the shock of the Ten and their supporters, Justices Murphy and Rutledge unexpectedly died on 19 July 1949 and 10 September 1949 respectively. They were replaced by the staunchly anti-Communist Attorney General Tom Clark and the liberal-turned-conservative Sherman Minton, and soon thereafter, in April 1950, the Supreme Court refused to hear the Lawson and Trumbo cases, with only Black and Douglas dissenting. Lawson and Trumbo were both handed one-year sentences, which they began serving in June 1950. In an odd twist of events, Lester Cole and Ring Lardner Jr. were assigned to the federal prison in Danbury, Connecticut where their paths crossed once again with former HUAC Chairman J. Parnell Thomas, who was convicted in 1948 of defrauding the government by bolstering his office's payroll.[59]

In addition to their prison sentences, Lawson and Trumbo were also handed monetary fines. Everyone from the Hollywood Ten received a one-year sentence except Herbert Biberman and Edward Dmytryk, who only received six-month terms. This may have been due to the distraction of the Korean War, which began between the sentencing of Dalton and Trumbo and the rest of the Ten. In their sentencing proceedings, many of the defendants made impassioned statements that addressed matters of civil liberties. For instance, Lester Cole harkened to a previous Supreme Court ruling that stated: "If there is a fixed star in our constitutional constellation, it is that no official, high or petty, shall prescribe what shall be orthodox in politics, religion, nationalism, or in matters of opinion, or force citizens to confess by word or act their faith therein." Responding to these words from the Court, Cole said:

> I am guided by that star today, as I was when I appeared before the
> Committee on Un-American Activities two and a half years ago. For
> I believe it is in the light of that fundamental concept that there can
> exist the freedom of thought and conscience necessary to guide our na-

tion to the path of democracy and the world to the road of peace and fraternity.[60]

Cole's eloquence sailed off into the ether. Meanwhile, HUAC's investigations of Hollywood were de-prioritized as the Hollywood Ten's case wove its way through the juridical pylons. However, once the Supreme Court refused to review the case, HUAC re-fixed its attention on Hollywood in 1951 with Chairman John S. Wood, a Georgia Democrat, calling Larry Parks as its first witness of the new phase. Parks ended up being HUAC's first full-blown informant from Hollywood.[61] "Thereafter," as Victor Navasky has pointed out, "the informer came into his own, and the blacklist became institutionalized. No Hollywood Communist or ex- who had ever been accused, or called to testify, or refused to sign a studio statement would get work in the business—at least under his own name—unless he went through the ritual of naming names."[62] This shift in witness attitude was part of a larger process that set the stage for McCarthyism.

Although the fate of the Hollywood Ten seemed severe at the time, it was only a preview of the devastating, reactionary hurricane that was to rip through Hollywood in the near future. Between 1948 and 1950, when the Ten were embroiled in litigation, seven of the Ten were still able to sell their writing and screenplays, albeit anonymously.[63] The ability of the Ten to continue working under different names should not be overstated, however. According to Bernard Dick, "Whatever art the Ten were still capable of producing was hindered, curtailed, and in some instances, terminated in 1947 by a committee's attempt to investigate an area over which it had no jurisdiction."[64] As Ring Lardner said in an interview years later, "We were able to get some kind of work for greatly reduced fees."[65] But even these diminished employment opportunities would evaporate with the rise of Republican Senator Joseph McCarthy and his vituperative, aggressive, spittle-sputtering attacks on those he deemed political subversives. The congressional assaults on these alleged subversives in Hollywood and elsewhere—which were made in collaboration with the nation's political and social elites—multiplied in the wake of the Hollywood Ten's jailing. This sent reverberations throughout U.S. civil society, chilling the practice of dissent.

The fact that these suppressive reverberations permeated the general population is important. As Carey McWilliams noted in regards to the Hollywood Ten:

> It can be a short step from "informing" the public to intimidating the public. And this, in effect, is precisely what happened to the Hollywood Ten. The House Committee on Un-American Activities, in the guise of

"informing" the public and Congress on Communistic infiltration in the motion picture industry, proceeded to interdict a vast range of social, economic, and political ideas and to proscribe those identified, in any manner, with any of these ideas. The action had a clear tendency to dissuade other people from listening to an exposition of these ideas or from reading about them or from being associated with those interested in them.[66]

Under such conditions of state intimidation, Hollywood leftists found it extremely difficult to—in terms of the preconditions of collective action mentioned in Chapter 1—maintain solidarity, attract new recruits, and mobilize support from potentially sympathetic "bystander publics." All this precluded them from being able to carve out the tactical freedom to pursue social-change goals through their films. Rather, they were forced to put their resources toward defending themselves. Once the public was intimidated, the suppression-induced silence spread surreptitiously across space, filling the arenas where dissent might have flourished. Such a dynamic has applied to numerous dissident groups and individuals throughout U.S. history.

Blacklisted and incarcerated, the Hollywood Ten suffered the consequences of both public prosecution and employment deprivation. By depriving dissidents of employment, the blacklists also encouraged self-censorship. McWilliams asserts that in the case of the Hollywood Ten,

> writers were discharged from their positions and blacklisted in the motion picture industry as a result of direct pressure applied by a congressional committee. If the committee had subpoenaed ten editorial writers from ten newspapers, all identified with a similar point of view, and had then told their employees to fire them, it could not have been any clearer that the intention was censorial. This, indeed, is how censorship is accomplished under the guise of protecting "the freedom of the screen." No laws are necessary; all that is needed is a little pressure, strategically applied.[67]

Indeed, censorship was implemented, if silently, as the Hollywood Ten were placed in the public spotlight. Hollywood films were certainly affected. One study found that in 1947, 28 percent of all films produced had a "serious social bent." By 1953, however, after the implementation of the blacklist, a mere 9 percent of films featured such concerns.[68] Additionally, many film producers heeded HUAC member Richard Nixon's suggestion to make more films that portrayed communism in a negative light. Films like "I Married A Communist" were produced despite the fact that there was very little public demand for anti-Communist films.[69]

It was this sort of professional pressure that led one of the Ten—Edward Dmytryk—to recant his radical affiliations entirely when he was brought back in front of HUAC on 25 April 1951. In his testimony, he answered all the questions that were asked of him, along the way naming twenty-six other subversives.[70] Later, in an interview, Dmytryk showed no remorse: "I don't feel sorry for the blacklisted ones," he said. "I knew why I was blacklisted. I knew how to get off the blacklist, and I eventually did."[71] He rationalized naming names by arguing that he was a director while all the rest were writers. While the rest could sell scripts under different names, he couldn't anonymously direct a film or do it under a fake name.

Another important mode of suppression that comes into play in the case of HUAC and the Hollywood Ten is mass media manipulation. According to HUAC scholar Robert Carr, members of the Committee and its staff established tight bonds with specific newspapers and journalists. The Committee and the press regularly shared "confidential information" and the Committee often planted "anonymous or unofficial statements."[72] The Hollywood Ten story conformed to a number of mass-media informational biases—such as dramatization and personalization—which may account for why the story received such heavy—and slanted—coverage. But Carr also asserts that the relationship moves beyond this: "The intimacy which has existed between the committee and certain newspapers has at times been disquieting. With few exceptions, the newspapers enjoying these close contacts have been reactionary journals, and the record makes it clear that they have aided and abetted the committee in some of its most sensational and flamboyant undertakings."[73]

Donner is more polemical in his assessment, charging a segment of the press with having been "a conscious collaborator and tool of the Committee in the exposure process."[74] Nevertheless, this collaboration shouldn't be overstated. In fact, many newspapers, including the *New York Times* and the *Washington Post*, published editorials that attacked the way HUAC was handling the Hollywood hearings.[75]

Other modes of suppression, such as bi-level demonization and mass media deprecation were also in play. Members of the Hollywood Ten, or Communists more generally, were called, among other things, "a direct branch of the Comintern," (by Adolphe Menjou) and "very un-American" (by Gary Cooper).[76] The Hollywood Ten and other people brought in front of HUAC in the late-1940s and early-1950s were scrutinized as potential Russian agents and spies and linked to the depredations—both real and imagined—of the Communists in the Soviet Union. These complex, mass media-related suppressive modes will be explored in much greater detail later in the book.

4

Employment Deprivation

Sometimes the silencing of dissent cuts straight to a person's livelihood. The next mode of suppression involves the deliberate threat of being deprived of one's job or the actual loss of employment because of one's political beliefs. While the dissident citizen's political views and principles are the central reason for dismissal, employers often conceal this motive, conjuring socially acceptable excuses for public consumption. For individual activists, being deprived of employment has both immediate and long-term impacts, especially if a "blacklist" is disseminated to other prospective employers.

Modern-day employment deprivation aimed at political dissidents is rooted in the loyalty programs—replete with loyalty oaths—that began on 22 March 1947 with President Harry S. Truman's Executive Order No. 9835. Political scientist Robert Justin Goldstein marks this moment as "the real beginning of what has been called 'McCarthyism'" since "it was this program, more than any other single action, which set the tone and paved the way for the anti-communist hysteria which gripped the country from 1947 onwards."[1] Echoing this sentiment, Ellen Schrecker asserts, "No other event, no political trial or congressional hearing, was to shape the internal Cold War as decisively as the Truman administration's loyalty-security program."[2] The Truman administration believed that the Soviets were using the Communist Party in the United States to subvert USAmerican democracy and values through espionage and deceit. To undermine these efforts, all prospective and current federal government employees would have to submit to loyalty tests.[3] These loyalty oaths took at least two forms: (1) the affirmative oath, such as a pledge to uphold the Constitution and perform the necessary duties of the job, and (2) the negative oath, or what Goldstein described as the "compulsory disavowal of political beliefs and affiliations which do not involve actual violations of laws meeting clear and present danger standards."[4]

While never explicitly defining disloyalty, Executive Order No. 9835 indicated that it meant membership in or association with groups or organizations that were designated by the U.S. Attorney General as "Totalitarian, fascist, communist, or subversive, or as having adopted a policy of advocating or approving the commission of acts of force or violence to deny others their rights under the Constitution of the United States, or as seeking to alter the form of government of the United States by unconstitutional means." This was one of six types of activity that implicated a federal employee as disloyal. The other five activities were: (1) sabotage, espionage, and related activities; (2) treason or sedition; (3) advocacy of illegal overthrow of the government; (4) intentional and unauthorized disclosure of confidential information; and (5) serving a foreign government in preference to the interests of the United States. The latter five types of activity were already illegal.[5]

Numerous progressive social commentators at the time were skeptical of the merits of such a loyalty program. Carey McWilliams noted, "Not since the time of the Alien and Sedition Acts has the federal government been so intensely and morbidly preoccupied with the loyalty of the American people."[6] The Truman administration ignored vehement, principled critiques like McWilliams's and plunged forward with its loyalty preoccupation.

President Truman's executive order poured the legal foundation for the FBI's enhanced scrutiny of "subversive" groups, ostensibly in order to improve its ability to root out disloyal federal employees. While the loyalty oaths were often meant to be a mere affirmation of loyalty to the United States, in effect, they wedged open the door to the intensified investigation and surveillance of groups deemed dissident, or "subversive." Also, a loyalty program at the federal level invited similar programs at the state level. State government employees, labor union leaders, and lawyers trying to meet state bar standards were forced to take loyalty oaths that forswore association with the Communist Party or communism more generally. By 1952, Utah was the only state that had not passed anti-subversion laws. Thirty-two states had special loyalty oaths on the books for teachers, eleven states denied the right of communists to hold meetings in school buildings, and twenty-eight states passed statutes that prevented "subversives" from gaining public employment. Municipalities passed similar laws. Often the loyalty oaths were not confined to workers with security-sensitive posts, but extended to all government jobs including trash collector, janitor, and secretary. On 18 July 1950, the city of Birmingham, Alabama went as far as to make it illegal for members of the Communist Party to be inside the city limits.[7]

At the federal level, the U.S. Attorney General amassed a list of 275 "subversive" organizations, sucking more than 20 million people into the investigative vortex created by Truman's Executive Order. Nevertheless, not a single case of espionage was unearthed, although more than 490 people were dismissed from their government jobs on loyalty grounds.[8] Many of these investigations occurred during the first few years of the program. By 1953, 13.5 million people—one of every five in the workforce—were subject to loyalty-security requirements. Of the 4,756,705 people examined for government employment, the FBI made 26,000 field investigations, most of which involved alleged associations with organizations on the Attorney General's list of "subversive" groups.[9] While few were dismissed from their jobs, this form of political suppression reverberated throughout the working ranks. According to Mildred Grossman, a New York public school teacher who was questioned menacingly by the FBI about her loyalty, the anti-communist and loyalty oaths "aroused a great deal of fear. People were afraid to touch anything that was controversial. Anything. They just kept quiet. And teachers skirted issues in the classroom. There were teachers who felt this was pressure they couldn't take, and they just resigned. And some people became informers."[10] Under intense pressure from the Bureau, numerous employees opted to name names—sometimes doling out inaccurate lists of ostensible dissidents—in order to get the authorities off their backs.

In the White House, it wasn't only Truman who was concerned about loyalty. In 1953, President Dwight D. Eisenhower issued Executive Order 10450, which maintained almost all the essential features of Truman's federal employee loyalty/security program. It also extended certain aspects, allowing the FBI to conduct a "full field investigation" on any individuals or groups who were a potential security risk. President Truman didn't want the Bureau to hold this power exclusively, despite FBI Director Hoover's clamoring for such authority. According to presidential aide George M. Elsey, Truman was afraid that the FBI might become a "Gestapo." Apparently Eisenhower did not share such concerns.[11]

The executive orders from Truman and Eisenhower had a far-reaching effect on dissident activity. Truman's first order led to a sharp decline in Communist Party membership. Yet, despite the fact that membership in the Communist Party was likely less than 100,000, it was strong in the trade unions and, more generally, on the heels of the Great Depression, a greater swathe of the general population held a healthy skepticism of capitalism. In light of the strong communist presence in trade unions, historian Howard Zinn regards the loyalty programs of Truman and Eisenhower as part of a calculated plan "to weaken and isolate the left," which was gaining broader societal support at the time.[12]

In the process of ascertaining loyalty, anonymous testimony was admissible, thereby preventing the accused from facing his or her accuser. In the end, official charges issued against potentially disloyal employees in front of loyalty boards included the allegations that "Communist literature was observed in the book shelves and Communist art was seen on the walls of your residence" and "You have during most of your life been under the influence of your father, who...was an active member of the Communist Party." Questions asked during the loyalty hearings, ostensibly to determine loyalty to the United States, included: "What do you think of the third party formed by Henry Wallace?"; "Have you ever had Negroes in your home?"; "There is suspicion in the record that you are in sympathy with the underprivileged. Is this true?"; and "Do you read Howard Fast? Tom Paine? Upton Sinclair?"[13] While these questions are taken out of their context, they nevertheless indicate the wide-ranging queries that were deemed acceptable in order to root out disloyalty.

It wasn't until the mid-1960s that the U.S. Supreme Court began to question loyalty oaths on First Amendment grounds. In 1964, it invalidated a loyalty oath for the first time based on its vagueness and overreach. In 1966, the Court struck down a loyalty oath on grounds it didn't require the person in question to ascribe to the unlawful objectives of the group, and, in 1967, the Supreme Court came to the conclusion that a loyalty oath for New York teachers, which had been upheld fifteen years earlier, was unconstitutional due to its imprecision and ambiguousness.[14] Despite these rulings, a number of anti-Communist state laws based on notions of loyalty remained buried in the books.[15] As Alexander Cockburn has pointed out, "Emergency laws lie around for decades like rattlesnakes in summer grass."[16] As we shall see later in the book, these rattlesnakes emerged decades later baring their venomous fangs, resulting in long-lasting litigation and sometimes prolonged prison sentences for numerous dissident citizens.

Rabid anti-communism led to a number of firings based on ideology. Many successful careers were snuffed while their flames still burned strong. John Carter Vincent, who served the U.S. government as the American Counselor of the Chinese Embassy in Chungking from 1941 to 1943 and then as the Director of the Office of Far Eastern Affairs, came under attack in 1947 for "losing China" to the Communists (and this was a full two years before the final fall of Chiang Kai-Shek and the Nationalists to Mao and the Communists). Vincent's loyalty was further questioned in February 1950 when Senator Joe McCarthy proffered to the Senate a list of alleged communists in the State Department. In terms of importance, Vincent found himself placed in the number two slot, which, in part led to him being accused in 1951 of having been "under Communist discipline" while working in Chungking. This web of charges was spun by Louis Budenz, a former editor of the *Daily Worker* who had subsequently swung sharply to the right. Budenz had been a member of the Communist Party in the United States for ten years. During that time, he served as managing editor of the major party organ. After quitting the Communist Party and becoming a Catholic, he taught economics, first at Notre Dame, and then at Fordham University.

Although Budenz made damaging claims against Vincent, he didn't provide evidence to support such allegations. Despite a dearth of hard evidence, Budenz served as a prolific witness for the state. He claimed to have testified before the FBI for more than 3000 hours between 1946 and 1949. Never during this extensive debriefing did he ever mention Vincent's name. Even when testifying in front of Millard Tydings's Senate Foreign Relations Subcommittee, he said he was unsure whether Vincent had communist ties or not. Only later did he tell the Senate Internal Security Subcommittee (SISS) that he was sure Vincent was a member of the Communist Party, and he stated vaguely that he knew this "from official reports I have received."[17] After Budenz's damaging accusations, Vincent worked his way through the labyrinth of loyalty review boards, and was even cleared by the State Department's.own Loyalty and Security Board. Nevertheless, in December 1952, the President's Loyalty Review Board ruled in a three-to-two vote that it had "reasonable doubt as to Vincent's loyalty to the U.S." Vincent was immediately suspended from his position as Minister to Morocco. Shortly thereafter, Vincent was informed that he could either select retirement or he would be fired.[18] Between being suspended and being offered the choice of retirement or dismissal, Vincent's case was sent to an ad hoc committee run by Judge Leonard Hand who ruled that Vincent should be kept. However, when John Foster Dulles became Secretary of State, he attacked Vincent's loyalty and essentially fired him.[19]

The Case of Frank Wilkinson

In a way, John Carter Vincent had it easy: at least he was presented with the option of choosing retirement. Others did not enjoy such alternatives. Frank Wilkinson was a member of the Los Angeles Housing Authority who for years fought for integrated, affordable, public housing. From 1942 through 1952 while working on housing projects, he took a number of loyalty oaths, vowing that he was not a communist. During an August 1952 eminent do-main hearing regarding the Chavez Ravine area in Los Angeles, Wilkinson, who was representing the Los Angeles Housing Authority as an expert wit-ness, was asked what organizations, political or otherwise, he had belonged to since 1929. Since, as he put it, he was "feeling sick and tired of trying to prove I'm loyal," he refused to answer the question. His testimony was then struck from the record and his status as expert witness was annulled.[20] The L.A. City Council requested that the House Un-American Activities Committee investigate the Housing Authority. Wilkinson was subpoenaed by the California State Senate's version of HUAC, and, when he refused to answer questions about his political beliefs and affiliations, Wilkinson was promptly fired by the Housing Authority.[21]

Wilkinson's wife, Jean, who also was subpoenaed to testify in California and who also refused to answer questions, was summarily fired from her position as a public school teacher.[22] She was blacklisted until 1965, when she was finally able to secure a job in the Berkeley area.[23] In order to squeeze out a living, Frank Wilkinson was forced to take on janitorial work in a department store at one dollar an hour, and he was only hired on the condition that he would not tell anyone where he worked.[24]

The FBI began tracking Wilkinson's actions in 1942 when—after being named the manager of the first integrated housing project in Watts—he was dubbed a national security risk. Over the next thirty-eight years, the FBI built a 32,000-page file on Wilkinson at the expense of more than seventeen million dollars, despite the fact that none of the information the Bureau gathered on him uncovered any criminal activity. When he later worked with the Southern Christian Leadership Conference and the Southern Conference Educational Fund, the FBI placed him under twenty-four-hour surveillance.[25]

Wilkinson was later brought in front of a special convening of the House Committee on Un-American Activities in Atlanta where he refused to offer any information but his name, "as a matter of conscience and responsibility."[26] Wilkinson was cited for contempt of Congress, and was ultimately sentenced to a year in prison.[27] The ACLU used Wilkinson's case as a way to challenge HUAC's investigative powers, successfully bringing the case all the way to the U.S. Supreme Court. Yet, in a bitterly divided decision, the Court ruled 5 to 4 in favor of HUAC, upholding its right to investigate dissidents thought to be communists.[28] Writing in dissent, Justice Hugo Black asserted, "There are not many people in our society who will have the courage to speak out against such a formidable opponent...If the present trend continues, this already small number will necessarily dwindle as their ranks are thinned by jails."[29]

After losing this Supreme Court split-decision, Wilkinson was one such dissident who was sent to jail. While behind bars, he was kept under continued, intense surveillance.[30] "Everything we did was attacked," he said. "I just got a stack of documents with every letter that was written to me or that I wrote while I was in prison. The FBI copied everything."[31] Also, the Wilkinsons' home was bombed, Frank's office was bombed, and their children, ages nine and seven, were refused entrance to YMCA camp. Only after the Wilkinsons promised not to visit their kids at camp were the children allowed to attend.[32] People who fought for the clemency of Wilkinson and Carl Braden—a journalist-turned-civil-rights-worker who was also handed a one-year sentence for refusing to answer HUAC's questions—were also surveilled.[33] Wilkinson obtained documents through the Freedom of Information Act that indicate the FBI was aware of an assassination attempt that was scheduled to take place, and, rather than trying to prevent it from happening, instead opted to "stake out the residence to witness the assassina-tion." When the assassination did not occur, a memo written the next day to Bureau Headquarters said, "No attempt was made on the life of Wilkinson last night, we'll watch for further developments."[34]

The experiences of the Wilkinson family were not unique. According to the Church Committee's Final Report, "The Bureau often tried to get targets fired, [and] with some success." The FBI went to great lengths to be-smirch the reputations of dissidents, especially during the COINTELPRO era. The Bureau periodically wrote letters to employers to tell them about the political activities of dissidents, in hopes of getting them fired.[35] The FBI also sent letters to credit bureaus and potential social-movement donors relating information about political dissidents in order to make them less appealing to creditors and possible supporters.[36] Revelations made by the Church Committee in the mid-1970s led to some reforms in the way the Bureau carried out its work. Only a few years later, President Reagan pro-ceeded to water down these reforms, establishing a tradition of civil-liber-ties encroachment that the administrations of George H.W. Bush and Bill Clinton continued. This process went into fast-forward on 30 May 2002 when Attorney General John Ashcroft eliminated post-Church-Committee-imposed limits on the discretion of individual FBI agents, thereby widening the possibility for unsupervised surveillance, intelligence collection, and file opening. Ashcroft removed rules that prevented FBI agents from—in the "preliminary inquiry" stage of an investigation—interviewing a potential suspect's employer and/or co-workers.[37] These relaxed rules pave the way for increased use of employment deprivation as a form of dissent suppression.

Trying to Re-educate the "Red-ucators": The Case of Thomas McGrath

The Bureau has historically taken special interest in the actions of teach-ers, since, on one hand, they are in the unique position to "plant the seeds of communism…in the minds of unsuspecting youth," as one internal FBI document put it, and, on the other hand, they have the ability to give "added prestige" to political causes.[38] The realm of higher education is one place where, despite notions of academic freedom, dissident views have been at-tacked and jobs have been lost.[39] From the beginning, professors deemed progressive—or, what Griffin Fariello calls "Red-ucators"—were at the center of the loyalty inquisition, and since then, they have remained un-der varying degrees of pressure to conform in order to avoid losing their jobs.[40] In 1953, organizations like the Association of American Universities (AAU) were issuing unambiguous statements like: "Present membership in the Communist Party…extinguishes the right to a university position" and "free enterprise is as essential to intellectual as to economic progress."[41] There are numerous examples of teachers and professors who lost their jobs either because of their political affiliations or because of the subject matter they taught or the way they taught it.[42]

Thomas McGrath was a poet and political organizer from the Midwest who, from a young age, was concerned with patterns of authority and domination. And as a member of both workers' struggles and the progressive professoriat, McGrath wasn't afraid of challenging the legitimacy of these patterns. Growing up on his father's farm in North Dakota in the 1920s, he came into contact with a variety of radical political organizers, from the Industrial Workers of the World (his father was a member of the IWW, or the Wobblies), to anarcho-syndicalists to communists and socialists, who were all welcomed at the farm by his father.[43] McGrath soon developed, as he put it, "a Marxist view of things" and before long he became a member of the Communist Party, "a card-carrying and dues-paying type."[44] Literary critic Terrence Des Pres described McGrath's political approach as "an insurrectionary stance that in its Marxist emphasis might have been international but which, nourished by the grainland countryside west of Fargo, is decidedly homegrown."[45] Never a fan of "benevolent gradualism," and always outspoken about the injustice of "the general distribution of goods in this world," McGrath naturally entered the crosshairs of the powerful, and, more specifically the crosshairs of HUAC.[46]

After returning from Europe where he dropped out of the Rhodes Scholar program at Oxford, McGrath worked various jobs in Los Angeles, eventually settling into a teaching position at Los Angeles State College. According to McGrath, while working as a college professor of English, "I still went out and distributed leaflets in the railroad yards, and all that kind of stuff which I had done before."[47] Such behavior—in addition to his open, unabashed affiliation with radical political groups and his politically laced poetry—attracted the attention of the House Un-American Activities Committee, which called him to testify in the April 1953 hearings it held on "Communist activities in the motion picture and educational field in Los Angeles." While in front of the Committee, McGrath said:

> When I was notified to appear here, my first instinct was simply to refuse to answer committee questions out of personal principle and on the grounds of the rights of man and let it go at that. On further consideration, however, I have come to feel that such a stand would be mere self-indulgence and that it would weaken the fight which other witnesses have made to protect the rights guaranteed under our Constitution.

Therefore I further refuse to answer the committee on the grounds of the fourth amendment. I regard this committee as usurpers of illegal powers and my enforced appearance here as in the nature of unreasonable search and seizure.

I further refuse on the grounds of the first amendment, which in guaranteeing free speech also guarantees my right to be silent. Although the first amendment expressly forbids any abridgement of this and other freedoms, the committee is illegally engaged in the establishment of a religion of fear. I cannot cooperate with it in this unconstitutional activity. Lastly, it is my duty to refuse to answer this committee, claiming my rights under the fifth amendment as a whole and in all its parts, and understanding that the fifth amendment was inserted in the Constitution to bulwark the first amendment against the activities of committees such as this one, that no one may be forced to bear witness against himself.[48]

McGrath's stand, rooted in Constitutional freedoms, may have earned him the respect of his students, to whom he said he felt a great responsibility, but it didn't leave a positive impression on the president of Los Angeles State College who swiftly fired McGrath, fearful of the political and economic damage that a faculty member acting as an uncooperative witness might have on the school's reputation.[49] Despite student protests demanding McGrath's reinstatement, he was placed on a blacklist, which made it virtually impossible for him to secure another academic post. McGrath's firing is emblematic of a deeper trend in the intersection of Hollywood, education, and HUAC. One study found that during a two-year period of hearings, of the sixty-four "unfriendly" witnesses who testified in front of HUAC, fifty lost their jobs.[50]

After losing his position at Los Angeles State College, McGrath tried to obtain another teaching position, and by concealing crucial facts about his background, he was, in fact, able to secure another job. However, a subsequent letter of recommendation that arrived late revealed McGrath's controversial past, and the offer for the position was quickly rescinded.[51] McGrath was forced to eke out a living performing a variety of jobs. In a letter dated late-1956, McGrath wrote, "Since the Committee got my teaching job I've been working at several things, mostly very tiring and dull—and also bad paying. A very hard period."[52] Although McGrath was a trained machinist, he was unable to get work because machinist employers in Los Angeles were associated with the defense industry, and, in light of his radical past, there was no way he could earn security clearance. McGrath ended up plying his trade as a writer, living "on the fringes of the Hollywood blacklist," anonymously penning movie scripts for pay.[53] In a 1961 letter, written after he left Los Angeles for New York, McGrath described his situation:

> It's been a hard year. I've been working a lot in documentary and other kinds of film, trying to make enough to buy myself a little time for my own stuff. And so far I've lost three jobs this year as a result of committees, blacklists etc. The first two were in colleges and either of them would have been permanent. I like teaching and the security would have allowed me to write. The latest one was doing documentary work for NBC. The pay is very good and I had a dream of doing about three months work a year and having the rest of the time myself. The dream lasted just long enough for them to check their files (I never imagined I'd be there since I've never worked for the likes of NBC) and I suppose it's a duplicate of the FBI file since it's run by retired FBI types. So the dream ended pretty abruptly.[54]

Such a stressful, unstable existence not only took a toll on the blacklisted individual, but on his or her family as well. Representative of what many blacklisted academics were experiencing at the time, McGrath wrote: "I would say that the episode *destroyed* a life....I would say that it was largely responsible for destroying a marriage and a family because of lack of money to live on, lack of security, the resultant anxieties."[55] For many, the marital, professional, societal, and financial insecurities coalesced into a nerve-wracking life shaded by paranoia and ill-will. It wasn't until the 1960s that McGrath was able to secure a teaching position, when he took a job at North Dakota State University.[56]

Surveilling the Ivory Tower

The difficulty that McGrath experienced when searching out employment as a blacklisted academic was not uncommon.[57] Neither was the FBI's suppression of university professors, and the Bureau's pressure wasn't limited to the humanities. Prominent leftist scholar-activist Michael Parenti asserts that despite the public conception that the ivory tower is a safe space for independent thought, "academia is not a universe of free discourse and exchange of ideas." He said, "you're expected to be monastic if you're in academia, to show forbearance, restraint, objectivity." Getting involved in activism means "crossing a line" that will raise administrative eyebrows and often costs academics their jobs.[58] Social scientist David Price corroborates Parenti's contentions in *Threatening Anthropology: McCarthyism and the FBI's Investigation of Anthropologists*. In this book, Price engages in deep archival research that demonstrates how the FBI tracked and intimidated numerous activist anthropologists in the 1940s and 1950s in order to curb their radicalism. Price also details how the Bureau was able to convince these anthropologists' colleagues to spy on their politically active brethren on behalf of the state.[59]

Anthropologists were not the only group of academics facing extensive Bureau scrutiny. In *Stalking the Sociological Imagination*, Mike Forrest Keen explores how the FBI took an intense interest in sociology professors, even ones who were by no means purveyors of radical politics. Through the Freedom of Information Act, Keen secured more than 2,700 pages of FBI documents on only fourteen renowned sociologists. These sociologists were Jane Addams, Herbert Blumer, Ernest Burgess, Erving Goffman, George Lundberg, Helen and Robert Lynd, C. Wright Mills, William Ogburn, Talcott Parsons, Pitirim Sorokin, Samuel Stouffer, Thorstein Veblen, and Florian Znaniecki.[60] Clearly, even the elite professoriat was not exempt from persecution. A full decade after McGrath's blacklisting, Staughton Lynd, a distinguished history professor at Yale University with a panoply of accolades to his credit, was terminated at the behest of the Yale trustees after he accompanied Tom Hayden of the SDS and communist Herbert Aptheker to Vietnam in 1966 in clear violation of State Department regulations. The FBI played a role in Lynd's dismissal, and there is evidence that the Bureau trailed him to Illinois where it prevented him from getting hired at a number of universities. After being rejected in Illinois, Lynd had to leave academia.[61]

Unlike these sociologists, anthropologists, and Thomas McGrath, many professors continued to be deprived of employment beyond the 1960s. Another prominent example is the case of Angela Davis, a professor of philosophy at University of California at Los Angeles (UCLA), who was fired for her radical political activity. Davis was an active member of the Che-Lumumba Club, a leftist political group affiliated with the Communist Party, and she was also working with the Black Panther Party. In 1969, when this came to the attention of the Governor of California—Ronald Reagan—and the California Board of Regents, a secret hearing was called to ascertain whether or not Davis was, in fact, a Communist.[62] At Governor Reagan's request, the chancellor at UCLA asked Davis if she was a Communist, since if she were, an obscure regulation from 1949 outlawing the hiring of Communists that remained in the Board of Regents' Handbook—one of Cockburn's emergency-law rattlesnakes lurking in the grass—provided the legal justification for her firing. Rather than invoking the Fifth Amendment, as many expected she would, Davis answered, as she later put it, "with an unequivocal affirmation of my membership in the Communist Party. I strongly protested the posing of the question in the first place, but made it clear to them that I was prepared to fight openly, as a communist."[63]

While the philosophy department wholly supported Davis, as did the Chancellor of UCLA and a majority of the students, the Board feared that Davis, as a member of the Communist Party, would, whether she tried to or not, indoctrinate UCLA students. Also, her public affirmation that she was a member of the Communist Party earned her Governor Reagan's unwavering contempt. Reagan, who in the midst of the controversy unequivocally stated that "Membership in the Communist Party is a bar to working at the University of California," made every effort to have her fired.[64] In the end, despite the recommendations of the UCLA administrative and academic committees involved in the process, the Board of Regents fired Davis for her political beliefs, stating that her speeches were "so extreme…and so obviously false" that she was unsuitable to teach in the California system.[65] Davis took her case to the courts and won a favorable decision that the government could not fire an employee solely based on her political beliefs. The State Supreme Court passed down a ruling in support of Davis's right to teach at UCLA, and then the U.S. Supreme Court refused to hear the case, therefore allowing the state court's decision to stand.[66]

Then, on 19 June 1970, the Board of Regents voted not to renew Davis's contract, which constituted a de facto firing. This decision was based on her involvement with the Soledad Brothers Defense Committee and other radical causes (the Soledad Brothers were George Jackson, Fleeta Drumgo, and John Cluchette, three black prisoners who were charged with the death of a prison guard at Soledad Prison in California).[67] As another battle for Davis's job heated up, state officials intensified their efforts to denigrate Davis. In the following exchange on the evening news in August 1970, Governor Reagan demonstrated his relentless opposition to Davis and her political stance:

> **Reporter:** Governor Reagan would you consider Angela Davis dangerous?
>
> **Reagan:** Yes, she is a Communist.
>
> **Reporter:** Tell me Governor, how did the police department determine the guns used in the Marin County Massacre were all registered to Angela Davis?
>
> **Reagan:** Simple, she was a Communist.
>
> **Reporter:** Governor, it had been rumored that one of the weapons used was in fact a weapon recovered in an earlier raid that was never returned to Angela Davis. Is this true?
>
> **Reagan:** Is Angela Davis a Communist?
>
> **Reporter:** Thanks Governor. Back to you, Tom [the host].

Davis had become embroiled in another controversy involving Jonathan Jackson, brother of George Jackson, the most prominent member of the Soledad Brothers.[68] This incident will be explored below in the discussion of harassment and harassment arrests.

Michael Parenti is another example of an academic who was forced out of his job. Parenti, who taught at the University of Vermont in the early-1970s, did not have his contract renewed by the school's Board of Trustees, despite the fact he was immensely popular with students and widely respected by his colleagues. The *New York Times* reported that his dismissal "set off a campus uproar."[69] In fact, once word spread that the Board might terminate his contract, he was supported by his students as well as by his colleagues in the political science department. Even the school's president, provost, faculty senate, and council of deans came out in support of keeping Parenti at the university, but the Board of Trustees overruled them all, claiming his dissent against the Vietnam War amounted to "unprofessional conduct."[70] According to Will Miller, a colleague of Parenti and member of the Philosophy Department, the Board concocted the professional-conduct requirement "after the fact to justify their decision." Miller described Parenti's dismissal as a "political firing" that was "an extraordinary overturning of the usual procedures for academic reappointment."[71] It also caused a campus-wide imbroglio that lasted throughout the 1971–1972 academic year. Nevertheless, the Board of Trustees' decision stood, rooted in its contention that Parenti's conviction for fighting with police during riots at the University of Illinois after the Kent State shootings, and before he joined the faculty in Vermont, was a mark against the university. Thus, they claimed the need to dismiss him in order "to protect the image of the university."[72] Reflecting on his termination, Parenti drew the distinction between his radical views and his boots-to-the-pavement activism, asserting it's hard enough to survive as an academic with radical views, but to get involved organizing students often meant putting one's job at risk. Parenti's own activism drastically affected his employability. After his experiences at the University of Vermont, he had brief stints at a few institutions, but, as he put it, "I never got another regular academic appointment again." He sent in job applications to more than 110 schools, but the job offers never rolled in, despite the fact that his publishing and teaching record was often stronger than anyone in the departments where he was applying.[73]

Other examples of the use of employment deprivation to suppress dissent in higher education include Morris Starsky (Arizona State University), Peter Bohmer (San Diego State University), and Bruce Franklin (Stanford University).[74] More recently, Sami Al-Arian, a tenured professor of computer science at the University of South Florida (USF), was fired based on his political commentary after the terrorist attacks of 11 September 2001. His case will be considered in more detail in Chapter 14.

While dissident teachers are frequently suppressed through the firing and hiring process, there are subtler means that can also be used to channel behavior and suppress dissent. One of these involves denying funding to dissident academics. As a way to quiet them and to deter other academics from assuming such dissident stances, funding sources—such as foundation grants—can suddenly dry up. In July 2003, Kathleen Sullivan, Dean of Stanford Law School, explained this process clearly and succinctly: "The government uses research funding as a carrot to induce people to refrain from speech they would otherwise engage in. If it were a command, it would be unconstitutional."[75] Historically, radical writers and teachers were refused literary grants, scientists had their funding canceled in the middle of the funding cycle, and the social sciences experienced similar constrictions in money flow.[76] Their behavior channeled, some political scientists, as Ira Katznelson points out, cultivated their relations with the state, "including its emergent national security apparatus, building on the personal and institutional relationships forged between social scientists and the government during World War II."[77] On the one hand, as R.C. Lewontin notes, "The state has deeply penetrated higher education as a means for the production of a large managerial and technical cadre without which a successful economy is not possible."[78] On the other hand, the FBI and CIA have funded various projects at many colleges and universities around the United States, which creates a pecuniary incentive for behavior in academia—in terms of both the research questions asked (and not asked) and the methodological approaches assumed (and not assumed)—that coheres with the values of these organizations.[79]

Clearly, other forms of suppression intersect with employment deprivation. As the case of Frank Wilkinson demonstrates, surveillance may lead up to or coincide with a dissident citizen losing his job. Similarly, harassment and harassment arrests often serve as the initial pavement on the road to eventually losing one's job. This will be explored in more detail later, when we revisit the case of Angela Davis. Also, the use of false mail, as with the derogatory letter that was sent out to create a schism between Morris Starsky and his colleagues, will also be examined later, when we discuss black propaganda. Finally, as we have already seen, employment deprivation intersects in a very direct way with public prosecutions and hearings, as it did in the case of Thomas McGrath.

5
Surveillance and Break-ins

Surveillance is a facet of all social relationships. Surveillance scholar David Lyon defines surveillance as "a shorthand term to cover the many, and expanding, range of contexts within which personal data is collected by employment, commercial and administrative agencies, as well as in policing and security."[1] Surveillance is also intricately linked with social control, as Lyon indicates when he writes, it "is any collection and processing of personal data, whether identifiable or not, for purposes of influencing or managing those whose data have been garnered."[2] In the context of dissident citizenship, surveillance is the ongoing observation of and collection of information about a person or group suspected of being involved in radical political activity. In the United States, the surveillance of dissident citizens is carried out by the domestic political surveillance apparatus, which has historically consisted of three interrelated networks: local police, the FBI, and military intelligence. Of these, the FBI and the police—often operating in tandem— are the most important, especially today. Surveillance of dissident citizens is one of the most common forms of state suppression. In part, this is because it can generate intense, reverberative effects at a relatively small cost. Many dissidents who have posed significant challenges to the status quo have been placed under state surveillance.

Surveillance may be carried out in ostentatious fashion in order to let dissidents know they are being monitored. Brian Glick calls this "conspicuous surveillance," and argues that the objective is "not to collect information (which is done surreptitiously), but to harass and intimidate," thereby "scaring off potential activists and driving away those who [have] already become involved."[3] A common mode of ostentatious surveillance includes FBI or police interviews of dissidents. During these interviews, investigators can, either furtively or unequivocally, let dissidents know that their actions have been or are being tracked by state authorities. In a document titled "New Left Notes—Philadelphia," filed on 16 September 1970, an FBI agent described the merits of carrying out intensive interviews with dissidents and their "hangers-on." The agent declared that the investigative interviews not only "enhance the paranoia endemic in these circles" but also "further serve to get the point across there is an FBI agent behind every mailbox."[4] This document only became public because, on 8 March 1971, the Citizens' Commission to Investigate the FBI burgled an FBI office in Media, Pennsylvania and made off with thousands of pages from classified files. When the *Washington Post* printed a summary of these documents the next week, people first became aware of the FBI's dense network of covert counter-intelligence efforts, or COINTELPRO.[5]

Intelligence gathering is another important aspect of surveillance. This intelligence can later be used to harass, intimidate, prosecute, and rally institutional support against dissident citizens. Indeed, it may be the most common activity of "control agents," as well as a prerequisite to other forms of suppression.[6] More often than not, state "control agents" transmogrify intelligence gained through surveillance into ideological grist that state agents use selectively to reinforce or reinstitute the political status quo.[7]

The state gathers political intelligence on activists through many forms of surveillance: wiretapping, mail opening, file storage, and electronic surveillance.[8] Also, there are "black bag jobs," which the Church Committee defined as "warrantless surreptitious entries for purposes other than microphone installation, e.g., physical search and photographing or seizing documents."[9] Thus, surreptitious entries, or break-ins, constitute the wider category, and "black bag job" is a more specific term. As we've already seen, surveillance can be—and often has been—facilitated by informants who infiltrate the social movement under observation. Most surveillance is shrouded in secrecy, and cloaked in deception. Nevertheless, even if it is exposed, it can implant second-guessing within a surveilled individual's skull, a social movement's collective relations, or both.

The state has used surveillance to track the activities of a number of dissident groups, from the Black Panther Party to Students for a Democratic Society to the Socialist Workers Party to modern-day protesters of corporate-driven globalization. In a memorandum to the Church Committee in October 1975, the FBI itself estimated—using incomplete records, as there was no central index for such files—that between 1960 and 1975, "509 surreptitious microphone installations took place against 420 separate 'targets of counterintelligence, internal security, and intelligence collection investigations.'" Yet, according to the Church Committee, "It is impossible to determine from the FBI estimates exactly how many of these installations involved a surreptitious entry because other techniques were also utilized, such as installing a microphone prior to the occupancy of the target or encapsulating it in an article which was sent into the premises." The FBI also estimated that it carried out 491 surreptitious entries to embed electronic surveillance devices against 396 targets of criminal investigations between 1960 and 1975.[10]

The FBI and Martin Luther King, Jr.

Perhaps the quintessential "target of counterintelligence" was Martin Luther King, Jr. His intense surveillance was carried out by the FBI, in concert with local police forces, when King emerged as an important leader in the Civil Rights movement. It occurred in three sequential phases.

Phase 1: Forging Communist Connections

According to King scholar David J. Garrow, "No other black leader came in for the intensive and hostile attention that Dr. King was subjected to in the mid-1960s."[11] Additionally, the Church Committee's Final Report maintains that "From December 1963 until his death in 1968, Martin Luther King, Jr. was the target of an intensive campaign by the Federal Bureau of Investigation to 'neutralize' him as an effective civil rights leader."[12]

Actually, the Senate report is wrong to date the beginning of the FBI's interest in King as December 1963. In fact, the FBI had been tracking King and his associates long before the tumultuous sixties. In September 1957, J.G. Kelly, a member of the FBI, clipped and mailed a newspaper article about King's Southern Christian Leadership Conference (SCLC) to the FBI's field office in Atlanta. Kelly found the SCLC's stated position against segregation as well as its two-pronged public promise to combat racial injustice and fight for voting rights for blacks to be worthy of FBI attention. Without offering specific proof, Kelly asserted that the SCLC was "a likely target for communist infiltration," and therefore "in view of the stated purpose of the organization you should remain alert for public source information concerning it in connection with the racial situation."[13] FBI Director J. Edgar Hoover was responsive to such suggestions; he had already, in March 1956, sent a collection of reports to the White House alleging Communist influence within another group fighting for rights for blacks, the National Association for the Advancement of Colored People (NAACP).[14] He responded to Kelly's submission by sending out a memo on 20 September 1957 that, echoing Kelly's words, told agents not to conduct an investigation, but to "remain alert for public source information" on King and the SCLC "in connection with the racial situation."[15]

This memo, albeit speculative, opened the door for surveillance, and, in October 1962, Hoover called for a COMINFIL investigation of the SCLC, with a focus on its leader. COMINFIL was the FBI code name for Communist Infiltration investigations. The COMINFIL program was initiated in the 1950s to probe and track the activities of a number of groups and individuals whose work spanned the labor, social-justice, and racial-equality movements. This COMINFIL was ordered despite the fact that the Atlanta

Field Office reported that its sources "had no information regarding any Communist Infiltration of the SCLC."[16] The Bureau had only tenuous, circumstantial evidence: King had been approached by black Communist Party member Benjamin Davis, after King presented a guest sermon at a church in Harlem in 1958; King associated with the Progressive Party when he was an undergraduate at Morehouse College in Atlanta in 1948; he had also publicly thanked the Socialist Workers Party for its backing in the Montgomery bus boycott, had voiced appreciation to Davis for donating blood after King was stabbed in 1958 while participating in a book signing, and had written an article for the *Nation* magazine that supported speeding up integration.[17] The lack of an established Communist link aside, the inertial process of intense surveillance was set into motion.

A major part of the rationale for King's surveillance that Hoover offered to high-level officials like Attorney General Robert F. Kennedy was King's connection with Stanley Levison and Jack O'Dell, two men who had previous ties—some real and some imagined—with the Communist Party. Levison had broken with the Communist Party by fall 1955 and he had no active ties with the Party in 1956 when he began working with King. O'Dell, who had been hired by Levison to work in the SCLC's New York office, never denied that he had worked with the Communist Party. He had been a member and party organizer from the late-1940s through the mid-1950s.[18]

In March 1962, with Robert Kennedy's authorization, FBI agents placed a wiretap on the telephone in Levison's New York office, where they also broke in to install an electronic bug.[19] The FBI sent summaries of subsequent phone calls between Levison and King to Vice President Lyndon B. Johnson, Attorney General Kennedy, and President John F. Kennedy's aide Kenneth O'Donnell.[20] Although the alleged Communist ties the FBI used to justify its surveillance of Levison and (eventually) King were never substantiated, except through FBI agent and CP infiltrator Jack Childs, the suspicions alone allowed for continued surveillance.[21] Indeed, by squawking about King's supposed communist connections—which was largely a pretext for state suppression—the surveillance was actually ramped up. Hoover and the FBI fashioned a pattern whereby once they used surveillance to establish ties—however tenuous—between King and Communism, they were able to continue to justify to the Attorney General—whether it was Kennedy, Nicholas Katzenbach, or Ramsey Clark—the need for continued or even heightened surveillance. Essentially, they devised a circle of self-reinforcing justification that, in the 1960s, played well not only in the highest echelons of political power, but also with the general population.

King responded to allegations of Communist infiltration by saying that there were "about as many Communists in this freedom struggle as there are

Eskimos in Florida."[22] Years later, the Church Committee corroborated this assessment, saying of King's relationship with Levison and O'Dell that "we are unable to conclude whether either of these two Advisers was connected with the Communist Party when the 'case' was opened in 1962, or at any time thereafter. We have seen no evidence establishing that either of those Advisers attempted to exploit the Civil Rights movement to carry out the plans of the Communist Party." The report went on to declare, "the FBI has stated that at no time did it have any evidence that Dr. King himself was a Communist or connected with the Communist Party."[23] Nevertheless, the government exerted great pressure on King and the SCLC to disassociate from anyone with a red-hued past. At the behest of Attorney General Kennedy, who feared that King's associations with Communists might jeopardize the civil rights legislation that was being proposed by the Kennedy administration, John Seigenthaler, Kennedy's administrative assistant, warned King that he was consorting with alleged Communists.[24] Assistant Attorney General Burke Marshall pressured reluctant White House Civil Rights Adviser Harris Wofford to do the same. King, who knew Wofford quite well, said that he trusted Levison more than the FBI, especially since the Bureau was unwilling to ante up its supposedly damning information on Levison. Finally, on 17 June 1963, pressure on King reached the highest level when President John F. Kennedy took King on a stroll through the Rose Garden, telling him that in order to salvage the civil rights legislation being proposed, he needed to ditch Levison and O'Dell. "They're Communists. You've got to get rid of them," he reportedly said. The President also noted, "there was an attempt (by the FBI) to smear the movement on the basis of Communist influence" and warned King, saying, "I assume you know you're under very close surveillance." King stood up for Levison, demanding that Kennedy provide proof.[25] King later joked with Andrew Young about the incident. According to Young, "Martin came back saying that the President was afraid to talk in his own office, and he said—and he was kinda laughing about it—he said, 'I guess Hoover must be buggin' him, too.'"[26]

Jokes aside, due to this intense pressure, King opted to end regular, direct contact with his much-valued consultant, Levison, instead communicating with him through a third party, Clarence B. Jones. However, as Frank Donner points out, "the secrecy and caution bred by repression in turn became proof of subversion" and so, even after King severed his direct ties to Levison and publicly disassociated himself from O'Dell, surveillance continued.[27]

Part of the reason for increased surveillance was the intense personal disdain that J. Edgar Hoover had for King, and for blacks more generally. Hoover referred to King as "no good," among other things, and, on 11 May

1962, an internal FBI memo stated that King "should be placed in Section A of the Reserve Index and tabbed communist."[28] According to FBI regulations, during a "national emergency," people who were placed in Section A of the Reserve Index would be rounded up because they "are in a position to influence others against the national interest or are likely to furnish material financial aid to subversive elements due to their subversive associations and ideology."[29] This would give the FBI the legal pretext to detain King in the case of a "national emergency."[30]

In November 1962, King fanned the flames of ire between himself and Hoover when, in response to a report by Howard Zinn and the Southern Regional Council about the police and FBI's unfair treatment of protesters in Albany, Georgia, King said the Bureau and local police forces combined efforts to enforce segregation.[31] This critique followed previous unfavorable assessments of the FBI. For example, in February 1961 King wrote an article for the *Nation* that alluded to racial discrimination in the federal law enforcement agencies. King's November remarks, which were reported in newspapers across the United States, ignited a firestorm at the Bureau. During an interview the next day, Hoover told a gaggle of reporters that "In view of King's attitude and his continued criticism of the FBI...I consider King to be the most notorious liar in the country." Hoover also said that King was "one of the lowest characters in the country" and that he was "controlled" by the Communists who were advising him.[32] Hoover expanded his verbal assault in a subsequent speech at the Chicago Loyola medical school where, in reference to King and the SCLC, he attacked "pressure groups that would crush the rights of others under heel," and whose members "think with their emotions, seldom with reason." His attack built to a crescendo, as he said that these dissident groups "have no compunction in carping, lying and exaggerating with the fiercest of passion, spearheaded at times by Communists and moral degenerates."[33] William Sullivan, who was one of Hoover's top-level associates at the FBI, and who played a major role in the surveillance and harassment of King, explained to the Church Committee in November 1975 the belief system from which Hoover's hatred for King arose: "I think behind it all was the racial bias, the dislike of Negroes, the dislike of the civil rights movement....I do not think he could rise above that."[34]

Phase 2: Discrediting King's Character

In 1963 and 1964, the combination of this racism-fueled animosity and the desire to stop King—an increasingly effective civil rights leader with an ever-widening critique—led to two important shifts in the surveillance of Martin Luther King, Jr.: (1) surveillance increased markedly, and (2) its purpose changed from focusing on ostensible connections between King and Communists to a preoccupation with King *as a person*.[35] The FBI's bigger goal remained the same: to undermine the Civil Rights movement and maintain the socio-political status quo. Yet the path to achieving this goal shifted from a focus on communism—or, radical activism more generally—to a focus on King as an individual. In 1963–64, the Bureau began to actively pursue King's "neutralization," reflecting the will to besmirch his reputation by bringing his private affairs before the public eye.

After King's "I Have A Dream" speech in Washington in the summer of 1963, a speech the FBI deemed "demagogic," the Bureau, in an internal memo penned by William Sullivan, came to the conclusion that "King stands head and shoulders over all other Negro leaders put together when it comes to influencing the great masses of Negroes. We must mark him now, if we have not done so before, as the most dangerous Negro in this Nation from the standpoint of communism, the Negro and national security."[36]

In October 1963, the FBI received the go-ahead from Attorney General Robert Kennedy to place wiretaps on King's home as well as on his SCLC office lines in Atlanta and New York. Attorney General Kennedy had previously, in July 1963, rejected an FBI request to place a wiretap on King's home and office.[37] He allegedly changed his mind for political reasons. Edwin O. Guthman, Press Chief for the Justice Department during Kennedy's tenure as Attorney General, testified to the Church Committee that Kennedy eventually approved the wiretap on King because "he felt that if he did not do it, Mr. Hoover would move to impede or block the passage of the Civil Rights Bill."[38] Kennedy was also miffed by King's unwillingness to cut off ties with Levison.[39] The wiretaps were installed shortly thereafter. The FBI used them to track communication involving the SCLC's Atlanta offices from 24 October 1963 to 21 June 1966, and King's home from 8 November 1963 to 30 April 1965, when the King family moved.[40]

Also, Hoover and the FBI liberally interpreted Kennedy's authorization so that it also applied to King's hotel rooms. Indeed, at that time, FBI guidelines didn't necessitate obtaining the Attorney General's permission in order to install microphones in King's hotel rooms.[41] Shortly after *Time* magazine named King its "Man of the Year" for 1963, the FBI planted bugs in the Willard Hotel in Washington, DC, where he was staying. The "Man of the Year" honor was only one of many King received around this time. He was awarded a number of honorary degrees by universities and colleges. He was also invited to speak at a ceremony in Germany that honored President Kennedy after his assassination. He also met with Pope Paul VI in Rome and, in October 1964, was named as the Nobel Peace Prize winner, an award he would receive that December. These awards only deepened

Hoover's fury toward King and hardened his resolve to bring him down. In fact, the Bureau attempted to prevent King from receiving such honorary degrees, from earning an audience with the Pope, from gaining the support of church groups, and even from having a "welcome home" party after he received the Nobel Prize.[42] The planted bugs at the Willard Hotel were the first time the FBI used such methods to surveil King.[43] The FBI had fairly specific hopes for what that bug would turn up, and their hopes would not go unfulfilled.

While Kennedy may have been concerned about King's associations with Communists, the FBI had other reasons for the heightened surveillance. According to internal memos, they wanted to paint King as "a fraud, demagogue, and scoundrel" in order to "take him off his pedestal and to reduce him completely in influence."[44] FBI Director Hoover had even more direct aims: "to neutralize or completely discredit the effectiveness of Martin Luther King Jr., as a Negro leader."[45] To reach this goal, the FBI set out— through stepped-up surveillance—to collect information about Dr. King's personal life. The Bureau focused on his extra-marital relationships with women and his drinking. Internally, the FBI was quite explicit about why it was surveilling King; in the words of William Sullivan, the Bureau did this so that "we may consider using this information at an opportune time in a counterintelligence move to discredit." He also declared that "We will at the proper time when it can be done without embarrassment to the Bureau, expose King as an immoral opportunist who is not a sincere person but is exploiting the racial situation for personal gain." Sullivan vowed to, as soon as possible, "expose King for the clerical fraud and Marxist he is."[46]

It didn't take long for the FBI to generate material to use toward these goals. Bugs installed at the Willard Hotel in Washington, DC on 5 January 1964 captured nineteen reels of tape, and these reels included exactly the kind of information the Bureau had anticipated: drinking and extra-marital sex. According to Sullivan, when a "highlight" reel was spliced together and presented to Director Hoover, he exclaimed, "This will destroy the burrhead." Hoover, who deemed Dr. King "a 'tom cat' with obsessive degenerate sexual urges," pressed forward with electronic surveillance of King in hopes of turning up even more discrediting information from his hotel stays.[47] Over the course of 1964–1965 the FBI placed at least fifteen microphones in King's hotel rooms in various cities spanning the United States.[48]

With information gathered from the Willard Hotel and other hotels in which King stayed in the early months of 1964, the FBI cobbled together an eight-page "Top Secret" report that it distributed to key individuals—including Attorney General Kennedy—in order to inject doubts into their minds about King's moral character.[49] This report was periodically updated and disseminated to members of Congress, UN Representatives Adlai Stevenson and Ralph Bunche, prominent church leaders, and other influential figures who considered forming alliances with King.[50] "Highlights" from the hotel surveillance audiotapes—replete with episodes of drinking and carousing with assorted women—were also compiled into a single tape, which was sent to King at the SCLC Atlanta office in November 1964, approximately a month before he was due to receive the Nobel Peace Prize (to be precise, this was thirty-four days before he was to receive the prize, hence the number mentioned in the letter). A note to King accompanied the tape. It read, in part:

KING,

In view of your low grade...I will not dignify your name with either a Mr. or a Reverend or a Dr. And, your last name calls to mind only the type of King such as King Henry the VIII....King, look into your heart. You know you are a complete fraud and a great liability to all us Negroes. White people in this country have enough frauds of their own but I am sure they don't have one at this time that is anywhere near your equal. You are no clergyman and you know it. I repeat you are a colossal fraud and an evil, vicious one at that. You could not believe in God....Clearly you don't believe in any personal moral principles.

King, like all frauds your end is approaching. You could have been our greatest leader. You, even at any early age have turned out to be not a leader but a dissolute, abnormal moral imbecile. We will now have to depend on older leaders like Wilkins a man of character and thank God we have others like him.[51] But you are done. Your "honorary" degrees, your Nobel Prize (what a grim farce) and other awards, will not save you. King, I repeat you are done.

No person can overcome facts, not even a fraud like yourself....I repeat—no person can argue successfully against facts. You are finished....And some of them pretend to be ministers of the Gospel. Satan could not do more. What incredible evilness....King you are done.

The American public, the church organizations that have been helping—Protestant, Catholic and Jews will know you for what you are—an evil, abnormal beast. So will others who have backed you. You are done.

King, there is only one thing left for you to do. You know what it is. You have just 34 days in which to do this (this number has been selected for a specific reason, it has definite practical significance). You are done. There is but one way out for you. You better take it before your filthy, abnormal fraudulent self is bared to the nation.[52]

The "grim farce" may have actually been that the FBI thought it could get King to commit suicide after receiving such a letter, if that was indeed what the Bureau was attempting to achieve. At the very least, though, the Bureau hoped to create a rift between Dr. King and his wife, Coretta Scott King. In fact, it was Coretta Scott King who first came across the tape and threatening letter when on 5 January she was cataloguing tapes of her husband's public speeches that were received at the SCLC office. Upon discovering that this tape wasn't the usual public appearance, and then finding the accompanying letter, she called her husband immediately. King listened to the tape three times, and then called a meeting of his most respected advisors—Ralph Abernathy, Bernard Lee, Joseph Lowery, and Andrew Young— and they listened to the tape together. King realized that the hotel rooms had been bugged and that he should expect such treatment in the future. He and his advisers also came to the conclusion that this surveillance was the work of the FBI. Clearly rattled by the episode, and feeling like a moral failure, King said, "They are out to break me."[53]

President Johnson's Attorney General, Nicholas Katzenbach, readily grabbed the baton of surveillance authorization from his predecessor, Robert Kennedy. While, in March 1965, Katzenbach insisted that the Bureau resubmit all its wiretaps for reauthorization, he proceeded to approve the wiretap on the Atlanta SCLC office.[54] He changed procedures slightly by making Attorney General approval a requirement for both wiretaps and the implantation of bugs; prior to this procedural modification, the FBI had been able to freely bug places via surreptitious entry (and this, at the same time, allowed them to sidestep getting Attorney General approval for wiretaps). Elsur bugs are more intrusive and more thorough in their capability to capture information.[55] Nevertheless, although he tightened formal procedures regarding black bag jobs and the installation of electronic surveillance, Katzenbach approved Elsurs of King's hotel rooms in July 1965.[56] Even when President Johnson released a directive that limited wiretaps to national security matters (as certified by the Attorney General), the level of King's surveillance didn't abate, in large part because of Katzenbach's compliant attitude toward Hoover's requests. This only changed in 1966 when Senator Edward V. Long of Missouri instigated an investigation of the use of electronic surveillance by federal police and law enforcement agencies. Concerned that the FBI's complex network of surveillance activity against one of the most revered USAmericans might be exposed to the public, Hoover opted to cease electronic surveillance of King. In the final two years of his life, King didn't experience microphone surveillance.[57] This tightening of standards also had something to do with the new Attorney General Ramsey Clark, who curtailed the placement of wiretaps on the SCLC office in Atlanta.[58] Accordingly, the

FBI's investigation of King and the SCLC "was strikingly quiet from the summer of 1966 through February 1967."[59] Nevertheless, this phase in the surveillance of Martin Luther King, Jr. and the SCLC allowed the FBI to identify potential pressure points within the Civil Rights movement.

Phase 3: Predicting Civil Rights Movement Activities

In light of these procedural changes for intelligence activities, and the over-all decrease in surveillance, a notable shift occurred in terms of the reasons for the surveillance of Martin Luther King, Jr. According to Garrow, in the fall of 1965, the objective of surveillance shifted from a desire to discredit King to "a desire to know ahead of time what events would be occurring in the civil rights movement."[60] In other words, this phase of surveillance was designed to gain political intelligence.

The new approach was facilitated by the infiltration of an informant. The FBI had at least one informant working inside the SCLC. Because of the onerous transcribing and paperwork that a wiretap or Elsur generates, the Bureau had been looking for an infiltrator/informant since at least the middle of 1963.[61] By the fall of 1965, the Bureau had its man: James A. Harrison, a young accountant in the SCLC who agreed to double as an FBI informant. Codenamed "AT 13878-S," Harrison worked closely with Atlanta Agent Alan G. Sentinella; they met weekly, with Harrison providing particulars on King's itinerary and travel plans.[62] They also communicated by telephone. Harrison also recounted for the FBI specific conversations between King and his top aides, proffered lists of cities and rural areas where King aimed to recruit supporters, and accompanied King and a number of other SCLC workers to Memphis during the final weeks of King's life. Harrison produced substantial information on the SCLC's internal affairs to the FBI. For his efforts, the Bureau paid Harrison a larger salary than the one King and the SCLC paid him.[63]

This shift in surveillance strategy also coincided with King's radical turn, when he deeply and publicly questioned U.S. militarism and imperialistic tendencies. Along the way, he began to interrogate capitalism as the system that gave rise to such trends by objectifying human beings. Therefore, Garrow writes, "In the last twelve months of his life King represented a far greater political threat to the reigning American government than he ever had before. An intensified interest in his political activities was perfectly in keeping with that development."[64]

King's cross-examination of capitalism and its intersection with militarism was articulated forcefully on 4 April 1967 in the anti-Vietnam War speech he delivered at Riverside Church in New York, where he said that the

U.S. was "the greatest purveyor of violence in the world today." Mainstream media coverage of this speech was scathing. *Newsweek* called his speech "an extravagantly vituperative attack on his government" that "carelessly mixes political and economic arguments," engages in "specious arithmetic," and conflates moral and political values. The magazine concluded, "He can only serve his people poorly in any case, by essaying the smoothest mimicry of their roughest extremists."[65] The *Washington Post* attacked King for offering irresponsible analysis based on "sheer inventions and unsupported fantasy." The *Post* concluded, "Many who have listened to him with respect will never again accord him the same confidence. He has diminished his usefulness to his cause, to his country, and to his people."[66] *Life* magazine went further, asserting in an editorial titled "Dr. King's Disservice to His Cause" that King "goes beyond his personal right to dissent when he connects progress in civil rights here with a proposal that amounts to abject surrender in Vietnam" and that therefore he "comes close to betraying the cause for which he has worked so long." *Life*'s editorial condemned the speech as "demagogic slander that sounded like a script for Radio Hanoi."[67]

The FBI responded aggressively to King's speech and his mounting anti-imperialist critique of the military-industrial complex by initiating a COINTELPRO against the SCLC under the "Black Nationalist—Hate Group" rubric. The stated purpose of the FBI's Black Nationalist—Hate Group COINTELPRO was to "expose, disrupt, misdirect, discredit, or otherwise neutralize the activities of black-nationalist, hate-type organizations and groupings, their leadership, spokesmen, membership and supporters to counter their propensity for violence and civil disorder." King was listed specifically as a "primary target" of the COINTELPRO. All FBI Field Offices received official directives that delineated the following "long-range goals":

> 1. Prevent the coalition of militant black nationalist groups....An effective coalition of black nationalist groups might be...the beginning of a true black revolution.
> 2. Prevent the rise of a "messiah" who could unify and electrify the militant black nationalist movement. Malcolm X might have been such a "messiah;" he is the martyr of the movement today. Martin Luther King, Stokely Carmichael, and Elijah Muhammad all aspire to this position. Elijah Muhammad is less of a threat because of his age. King could be a real contender for this position should he abandon his supposed "obedience" to "white, liberal doctrines" (nonviolence) and embrace black nationalism....
> 4. Prevent militant black nationalist groups from gaining respectability, by discrediting them...[68]

This COINTELPRO was in effect through King's assassination on 4 April 1968 in Memphis, Tennessee. While the FBI intensely tracked King until his death, it actually continued to besmirch his name even after he was assassinated on 4 April 1968. For example, the Church Committee found that, in March 1969, the FBI tried to prevent Congress from passing a law declaring King's birthday a national holiday. The Bureau's Crime Records Division recommended that key members of Congress be briefed by FBI agents about why "King was a scoundrel." Then in April 1969, a memorandum from the Atlanta office to Hoover recommended "to entertain counter-intelligence action against Coretta Scott King and/or the continuous projection of the public image of Martin Luther King."[69] Hoover replied to Atlanta that "the Bureau does not desire counterintelligence action against Coretta Scott King of the nature you suggest at this time."[70]

In the end, Garrow asserts: "Neither the 1975–1976 Church Committee investigation, nor the House Assassinations Committee probe two and one-half years later…provided a complete and accurate public explanation of the Bureau's conduct in the King and SCLC security investigations."[71] William Pepper, in *An Act of State: The Execution of Martin Luther King*, takes this critical assessment a step further. He has assembled convincing evidence that the FBI and the U.S. Army were surveilling King right up until his death, and that, in fact, this surveillance may have been an important piece in the assassination puzzle.[72] While it was years after King's assassination that Pepper meticulously tracked the intersection between the work of federal law agencies and the efforts of Martin Luther King, Jr., the first public disclosure that King had been wiretapped came a mere two months after his death.[73] This was done for political reasons: to taint the reputation of presidential candidate Robert F. Kennedy, since it had been the Attorney General who approved surveillance of King and the SCLC. However, when Kennedy himself was assassinated in June 1968, the story died with him.

Surveillance and Break-ins, Then and Now: Extensions and Reverberations

Warrantless surreptitious entries constituted an important aspect of the surveillance of Martin Luther King, Jr. These break-ins have at least three purposes, none of which are mutually exclusive: (1) causing fear and/or paranoia; (2) implanting electronic surveillance; and (3) gathering information via theft (or in FBI parlance "black bag jobs"—a method William Sullivan heralded in a 1966 internal FBI memo as an excellent way to root out "materials held highly secret by subversive groups and organizations which consisted of membership lists and mailing lists of these organizations").[74] In January

1976, the FBI reported to the Church Committee that it had carried out, at minimum, 239 surreptitious entries against at least fifteen unidentified domestic organizations from 1942 until 1968.[75] These are only the warrantless surreptitious entries that the FBI has publicly acknowledged carrying out itself. This number does not include outsourced black bag jobs or break-ins left to local police forces. In fact, the FBI admitted that agents were "unable to retrieve an accurate accounting" of the exact number of warrantless entries because there is no central index for such files. The 239 they admitted to were derived from the memories of FBI agents based at headquarters as well as from extant FBI files.[76] These break-ins were approved in writing by FBI Director Hoover or Associate Director Clyde Tolson, and a "'Do Not File' procedure was utilized, under which most records of surreptitious entries were destroyed soon after an entry was accomplished"[77]

In 1966, J. Edgar Hoover officially abolished black bag jobs, though in practice surreptitious entries continued, if at a reduced rate. The fact that they continued despite the official ban is evident from the aforementioned statistics. The FBI admitted to carrying out those 239 surreptitious entries "from 1942 until *1968*."[78] Also, break-ins for the purpose of microphone installation were not prohibited by Hoover's directive—and the ban didn't apply to foreign surveillance targets. In 1970, presidential assistant Tom Charles Huston tried to revive the practice of black bag jobs against "urgent and high priority internal security targets"—while at the same time acknowledging their illegality—but Hoover opposed this effort.[79] Despite the attempts of the Church Committee to place restrictions on the surveillance activities of the FBI, the Bureau was hardly de-toothed. In fact, in 1981 President Ronald Reagan issued Executive Order 12333, which allowed the FBI to again more freely engage in wiretaps and black-bag-job type break-ins.[80]

Recent legislation—such as the 1996 Anti-Terrorism and Effective Death Penalty Act and the USA PATRIOT Act of 2001—makes it markedly easier for the FBI to carry out surveillance on potential dissidents. The PATRIOT Act will be discussed in greater detail in Chapter 14. In a sense, the watchword "Communism" has been replaced by "terrorism," and, because it weakens the probable cause requirements for surveillance, this legislation has afforded the FBI renewed and expanded space to carry out widespread surveillance for allegedly anti-terrorism, national-security purposes.

Clearly, the surveillance of Martin Luther King, Jr. and the SCLC affected morale and altered tactics within the Civil Rights movement. According to his colleagues and friends, King would often make jokes about how the FBI was surveilling him, saying that any offhanded remark might be captured, chronicled, and commemorated by one of the FBI's concealed microphones.[81] Because "they were bugging just about every place we went," recounted Andrew Young, "we had a running joke of who all was a member of the 'FBI Golden Record Club'....When somebody said something a little fresh or flip, Martin would say, 'Ol' Hoover's gonna have you in the Golden Record Club if you're not careful.'"[82] Jack O'Dell later recalled,

> Surveillance by the FBI and for the FBI and the whole range of dirty tricks were constantly part of our problem. I mean, I can remember in Albany when we used to hold meetings at Dr. William Anderson's house. Dr. King had to get out of that house to talk about what we were going to do. He operated on the assumption that the place was bugged and the phones were tapped and the house was under surveillance and that any information they got would be used against us. We were always operating in a treacherous environment.[83]

By early January 1965, when King sat with his closest advisors and listened to the FBI's tape of him carousing with women, he was "worried about spies and microphones to the point of whispering."[84]

But a lowered voice was only a part of King's surveillance-induced problem. "Inevitably, surveillance and even the fear of surveillance on the part of those not actually monitored," asserts Donner, "produce a pervasive self-censorship."[85] Harry Wachtel, one of King's lawyers and confidantes, told the Church Committee how the political intelligence gathered through surveillance impinged on the group's ability to plan effectively:

> It affected the strategies and tactics because the people you were having strategies and tactics about were privy to what you were about. They knew your doubts....Decision-making...had to be limited very strongly by the fact that information which was expressed by telephone, or which could even possibly be picked up by bugging, would be in the hands of the President.[86]

Surveillance also led to the attrition of key social-movement figures. As O'Dell put it, "If Martin was speaking somewhere, I'd stay clear because I'd figure they were surveilling it." It was because of intense surveillance that O'Dell knew he had to resign from the SCLC, because his former ties to the Communist Party were leading to intense pressure on King.[87]

Finally, as Gary Marx has pointed out, "Knowing that agents are gathering information on it may make the social movement less open and democratic, require that limited resources be devoted to security, and may deter participation."[88] As open and democratic as the Civil Rights movement was, relatively speaking, the fact that it was so heavily surveilled most assuredly affected the overall flexibility of its organizational apparatus. The Church Committee concluded that the FBI's surveillance and smear campaigns made an "unquestionable" impact on the movement. Surveillance and the spreading of rumors also, according to Church Committee findings, "had a profound impact on the SCLC's ability to raise funds."[89]

The fervor with which federal and local law enforcement groups tried to curtail the dissident activities of Martin Luther King, Jr. can be seen by the number of suppressive tactics they used. First of all, the FBI conducted a number of activities designed to harass King and his associates, thereby demobilizing the Civil Rights movement. Working in conjunction with the Internal Revenue Service, they carefully scrutinized King's and the SCLC's tax returns for the most minor infraction. Having the SCLC's tax returns in hand also meant that the FBI also had access to their donor list. When the FBI's meticulous audit failed to turn up any irregularities, the Bureau suggested in an internal memo that it obtain SCLC stationery and write a letter to donors informing them that the group was being audited. The goal here was to "cause considerable concern and eliminate future contributions."[90]

Also, as we have seen, the Bureau's surveillance dovetailed with another method of suppression: the infiltration of an informant. In Chapter 2, we saw how this worked with William O'Neal's infiltration of the Chicago branch of the Black Panther Party, and how this eventually led to Fred Hampton's assassination. As noted, the FBI also had at least one informant working inside the SCLC.

Attempts at bi-level demonization—forging a connection between King and Communism—have already been noted. Importantly, the Bureau also manipulated the media—another common tactic—farming out the alleged King-Communism connection to sympathetic journalists. The FBI's media campaign took two major forms: (1) the placement of derogatory stories about targeted groups or individuals, and (2) the leaking of information intended to discredit dissidents and social movements.[91] Combining the two forms, the FBI "consciously cultivated the news media" through the strategic release of leaks. According to Theoharis, "Cognizant of the potential vulnerability of these leaks, FBI officials identified 'friendly' media sources who would both keep this relationship confidential and support the Bureau's interests."[92] A false story the FBI distributed in October 1962, which said that the "acting executive director" of the SCLC was "a concealed member of the national committee of the Communist Party," appeared in a number of papers, including the *Augusta Chronicle, Birmingham News, St. Louis Globe Democrat, New Orleans Times-Picayune,* and *Long Island Star Journal.* Interestingly, all these newspapers ascribed their condemnatory information to "a highly authoritative source."[93] The Bureau also tried to plant derogatory stories about King in the most influential of U.S. publications; for instance, Cartha "Deke" DeLoach and the Crime Records Division attempted to get *Newsweek*'s Washington Bureau Chief Benjamin Bradlee to run damning information on King that had been accumulated through electronic surveillance. Bradlee refused to oblige. FBI officials proceeded to try to peddle photographs of King leaving a hotel with a woman, transcripts of unflattering King commentary, and actual recordings of King and his associates to a number of prominent publications, including the *New York Times*, the *Los Angeles Times*, and the *Atlanta Constitution*.[94]

Technology has advanced significantly since King's day. And, as it has, so has the possibility of ever more surreptitious forms of surveillance. Long ago Herbert Marcuse wrote, "Technology serves to institute new, more effective, more pleasant forms of social control and social cohesion."[95] With the Internet and ever-advancing tracking technologies, this assertion has never been more true.[96] As Gary Marx pointed out, "Computers qualitatively alter the nature of surveillance—routinizing, broadening, and deepening it."[97] Data warehouses allow for the storage of information that may seem innocuous today but that may be incriminating tomorrow.[98] Marcuse astutely points us toward an important dialectic for dissidents to consider: the relational nature of technology-facilitated opportunity and suppression. The combination of high technology and recent legislation like the USA PATRIOT Act is likely to extend surveillance as a staple method of suppression for years to come. This suppression becomes all the more complicated to address in an era in which, as David Lyon notes, "Surveillance always carries with it some plausible justification that makes most of us content to comply."[99] Such is the surveillance-drenched context dissident citizens face as they express their ardent desires for social change.

6

Infiltration, "Badjacketing," and Agent Provocateurs

Another of the state's methods for suppressing dissent involves the infiltration of informants who engage in intelligence gathering, create internal dissension, and/or incite illegal activities. The use of informants is quite common. In fact, according to the Church Committee, "the paid and directed intelligence informant is the most extensively used technique in FBI domestic intelligence investigations" of dissident groups and individuals. More specifically, a 1976 Government Accounting Office study titled "Domestic Intelligence Operations of the FBI" found that eighty-five percent of domestic intelligence investigations involved informants, while only five percent involved electronic surveillance.[1] Historically, the U.S. Army has also infiltrated and surveilled domestic political groups, although it has not received the same public attention as the FBI.[2] The IRS also has a sophisticated informant system.[3] As of 30 June 1975, the FBI had more than 1,500 informants engaging in domestic intelligence gathering on dissident citizens, and these informants were bound by few standards in terms of the scope of their activities. In fact, at the time, the domestic political intelligence program's budget was more than twice that of the organized crime informant program budget.[4] In a conservative estimate, Donner reports that between 1940 and April 1978 the FBI hired approximately 37,000 informants, more than 29,000 of them working under the rubric of "security" and almost 8,000 working under the category of "racial and extremist."[5]

Donner lists four main types of intelligence informants: (1) the "planted infiltrator" who has not previously been associated with the group; (2) the already embedded member of the group who, for whatever reason, decides to start offering information to the state; (3) the courtroom witness; and (4) the irregularly reporting, ad-hoc informant who is more likely to participate in debriefing sessions where dissidents are identified in photographs after a march or similar action.[6] The discussion of informants in this section does not consider one-time volunteers of information—tipsters—though they are quite common. Rather, I focus on paid informants from categories (1) and (2), many of whom are not completely willing volunteers. These informants can also be divided by occupation—whether they are civilians or state agents from the police or FBI—and by motive—whether they become informants for ideological reasons, because of police pressure, to make material gains, to satisfy personal ends, or some combination thereof.[7] Regardless of when or why one becomes an informant, in order to be an effective, fully infiltrated agent, one must become a trusted member of the group or organization. Abstracting outward to the bigger picture, Marx asserts that the "latent reason" to have infiltrated agents "may be to harass, control and combat those who, while not technically violating any laws, hold political views and have life-styles that are at odds with the dominant society."[8] This most assuredly applies to the FBI's treatment of numerous dissident citizens and social movements from the twentieth and twenty-first centuries.

From the perspective of the law enforcement agency interested in hiring an informant to infiltrate targeted organizations, there are a number of potential problems and pitfalls to consider. First, many recruits come from criminal backgrounds. The case of William O'Neal—who had a prison sentence waived in exchange for becoming an informant in the Black Panther Party—isn't uncommon. However, these recruits may have deep-seated distaste for law enforcement agencies based on previous personal experience, and may therefore be unreliable. Also, because they are often not constrained by precise guidelines for action, they may veer toward illegal activities, especially since they know they will likely receive immunity from the state in exchange for their informant work. According to Gary Marx, "The price of gaining cooperation of informers may be to ignore their rule breaking in other settings....Undercover situations lend themselves well to exploitation by informers for their own criminal ends, apart from their role as agents of law enforcement."[9] There is also the possibility that informants will develop bonds with the people who they're gathering political intelligence on, and might therefore misreport or not provide the state with the information it desires, or, in the extreme case, become a "double agent" who also spies on the state on behalf of the social movement under surveillance.[10] Finally, if informants feel pressure to produce information for the agent with whom they're working, they may fabricate information if unable to come across it otherwise, especially if their paycheck is contingent on producing relevant information. Also, in the case of the agent provocateur, report-worthy information may be generated through violence or the encouragement of violence. For these reasons, one federal agent complained: "Trying to control informers is an ulcer factory."[11]

Infiltrators who serve as informants have been used to hamper the political activities of a variety of social movements, from situations we have already explored—like William O'Neal's infiltration of the BPP and James Harrison's informant work within the SCLC—to Mary Jo Cook's infiltration of Vietnam Veterans Against the War (VVAW) and the infiltration of the Women's Liberation Movement.[12] Another specific example is Douglass Durham's penetration of the American Indian Movement (AIM), which clearly demonstrates how this tactic can diminish social movement activity.

The American Indian Movement and "Red Power"

AIM emerged from a "dynamic of historical antagonism" between the United States government and Native American peoples.[13] U.S.-Indian relations consist of a violent history of deceit and duplicity with few intervals of conciliation and appeasement. Nebraska federal judge Warren Urbom has referred to these relations as an "ugly history" that "white Americans may wretch at the recollection of."[14] It is from this "ugly history" of persecution that a more militant and activist mode of resistance emerged among Native Americans in the mid-1960s. Compared to previous tribal administration, AIM addressed the long-term social problems that Indians faced with "a new vigor, a more militant rhetoric, and a more active and urban style derived largely from the protest movements of the 1960s."[15] Comparable to the rise of Stokely Carmichael and H. Rap Brown's notions of Black Power, people like Clyde Warrior, a Cherokee, organized Indians under the slogan of "Red Power."[16] Mirroring strategies put forth by groups like the BPP, proponents of "Red Power" did not rule out violence as a strategy. Within this charged milieu, two Chippewa activists, Dennis Banks and George Mitchell, founded AIM in Minneapolis in 1968.[17] AIM deliberately modeled itself on the Black Panther Party's community self-defense approach launched by Huey P. Newton and Bobby Seale in Oakland two years earlier, and AIM chapters quickly emerged in other U.S. cities where there were pockets of active Native American resistance, like Cleveland and Denver.[18]

Despite attracting media attention through creative protests, AIM leaders experienced perpetual disappointment as numerous promises that the federal government made during demonstrations were quickly reneged upon once the protests concluded.[19] AIM officials felt they had to up the ante, so they organized "The Trail of Broken Treaties." "The Trail" was a massive action that, beginning in California, snaked across the country before settling at the Bureau of Indian Affairs (BIA) building in Washington, DC. The timing of the event—just prior to the presidential election of 1972—attracted Indians from around the country, as well as mass-media and FBI attention. Although it wasn't pre-planned, once the caravans converged on Washington, DC, a group of delegates sat down with BIA officials and began negotiations on a set of twenty demands, which were hammered out en route in Minnesota.[20] Meanwhile, Indians waiting for the results of the negotiations were hassled by BIA security guards, but, rather than submitting to the

guards' demands to vacate the premises, they overwhelmed security personnel with force and occupied the BIA federal building. This led to a standoff,
which lasted from 3 November to 9 November when negotiators struck a
deal whereby the occupiers would leave in exchange for $66,000 in travel
money, a promise that criminal charges wouldn't follow, and the BIA's assurance that it would respond to AIM's twenty demands within sixty days.[21]

As AIM members evacuated the building, a number of them pilfered
boxes of BIA records. Hank Adams, a Trail of Broken Treaties delegate,
agreed to remain in DC until the documents were returned to BIA headquarters, but, in the process of giving back the stolen documents, Adams was
arrested by the FBI. Les Whitten, who was helping Adams transport the documents, was also arrested. Whitten was renegade columnist Jack Anderson's
assistant, and Anderson's investigative journalism had long been a thorn in
the U.S government's side. According to Native American historian Vine
Deloria, Jr., Adams and Whitten "were kept most of the day while the F.B.I.
changed the affidavits that were used to justify their arrest—it seemed that
the F.B.I. had planned on arresting Jack Anderson, not Les Whitten, and had
sworn statements to support their arrest warrants stating that Jack Anderson
was to pick up the papers and use them for his own purposes."[22]

In the end, a federal grand jury shelved charges due to entrapment orchestrated by FBI infiltrator John G. Arellano. Apparently, Arellano was only
one of many FBI agents who had infiltrated AIM and participated in the BIA
building takeover.[23] FBI internal memos obtained through the Freedom of
Information Act reveal a plan whereby "local police put [AIM] leaders under
close scrutiny, and arrest them on every possible charge until they could no
longer make bail." Meanwhile, according to Churchill and Vander Wall,
the FBI was assembling "detailed profiles of AIM members and leaders as
part of an 'Extremist Matters' investigation."[24] The infiltration of Arellano
and others, as well as the ramped up surveillance and tracking of individual
members of AIM, were only the beginnings of what became a full-fledged
effort to squelch the dissent of AIM members. American Indians have been,
according to Ward Churchill, "demonstrably one of the most victimized
groups in the history of humanity," so perhaps we should not be surprised
that they received so much FBI attention when they vigorously challenged
the status quo.[25] If Arellano was the FBI's amateurish rehearsal of infiltration, then Douglass Durham was its award-winning performance.

Escalation: Douglass Durham in Action

Douglass Durham wasn't an Indian, though he claimed to be one-quarter
Chippewa from the Lac Court O'Reilles Indian Reservation in Hayward,

Wisconsin.[26] When later asked about his heritage by Senator James Eastland's Subcommittee on Internal Security, he said he was "Scottish-Irish, English and German," not Native American.[27] Before becoming a paid infiltrator for the FBI, Durham was a police officer in Des Moines, Iowa for three years.[28] The FBI enlisted Durham's services in 1973, assigning him to infiltrate AIM, gain the trust of AIM members, and try to move up the hierarchy of power within the organization as quickly as possible. Durham later testified that he officially worked for the FBI from March 1973 through March 1975, and that he was paid "on an escalating scale" over that period of time. In the end, he said he earned approximately $20,000. He first made contact with AIM in the spring of 1973, during the seventy-one day siege at Wounded Knee on the Pine Ridge Reservation, where he operated undercover, ostensibly as a photographer for the magazine *Pax Today*. Durham turned over photographs he snapped at Wounded Knee, as well as a detailed report, to the FBI.[29]

After becoming acquainted with many AIM members during the Wounded Knee standoff, Durham joined AIM's Des Moines chapter. He quickly gained the trust and friendship of AIM's Midwest Regional Coordinator, Ron Petite, and began to move into positions of power within the AIM command structure. Because of Petite's confidence, Durham quickly entered the inner circle of Dennis Banks, a nationally renowned and tactically creative AIM leader. Durham became AIM's National Security Director, which meant that, among other things, he served as Banks's personal bodyguard and pilot. Importantly, Durham was also named to a security post in the Wounded Knee Legal Defense/Offense Committee (WKLDOC—pronounced "Wickle-dock").[30] Such positions of power entailed access to high-level planning sessions, both for future AIM actions in general and more specifically for legal defense strategies. In fact, aside from Banks and Means, their attorneys, and other legal workers, Durham was the only person with "access to the defense strategy room." Moreover, "he controlled security clearance for both the attorneys and the defense volunteers."[31] He himself bragged, "I exercised so much control that you couldn't see Dennis or Russell without going through me, you couldn't contact any other chapter without going through me, and if you wanted money you had to see me."[32] Since AIM leaders as well as rank-and-file members were perpetually engaged in legal squabbles—per the FBI's explicit blueprint of harassment—these were important gatherings in terms of the future of the organization, and Durham was privy to all the strategies and tactics discussed.

Durham's insider knowledge proved immensely valuable to the FBI during the Wounded Knee Trials, which began in January 1974. Although seven AIM leaders had been indicted on conspiracy charges, high-profile figures Dennis Banks and Russell Means were isolated from the others and put on trial first.[33] This trial—a skirmish between AIM and the Nixon administration that was covered heavily by the mass media—featured famous lawyers like William Kunstler and Mark Lane representing the defendants, and celebrities like Harry Belafonte, Dick Gregory, and Marlon Brando standing up publicly in their defense.[34] All the while, Durham was listening in on important defense strategy meetings. Although he claimed that he was counseled by the FBI to not hand over his insider knowledge on Wounded Knee defense plans, scholars like Churchill and Vander Wall have asserted that "intelligence information gleaned by Durham *was* used to improperly influence the course of the judicial proceedings."[35] For example, he proffered a report to his contacts at the FBI alerting them to the fact that Banks had met privately with trial judge Fred Nichol and Nichol's wife at their home after a pretrial hearing in October 1973. This information led the U.S. Attorney's Office in Sioux Falls to file "a very strongly worded motion of prejudice" against Nichol, requesting that he voluntarily disqualify himself from the rest of the trial.[36]

Not only did Judge Nichol adamantly refuse to recuse himself, but he also became visibly annoyed at what appeared to be a concerted effort to intimidate him. His annoyance was only exacerbated by what he perceived as the FBI's lack of integrity and openness. For instance, when defense attorney Kunstler requested a petition signed by the residents of Wounded Knee that demanded the government "cease and desist from firing upon our guest members of the American Indian Movement," the FBI provided him with a falsified petition, as it was ostensibly unable to locate the original. Nichol was "greatly disturbed" by this suspicious mishandling, and proceeded to lash out against the Bureau: "I used to think that the FBI was one of the greatest bureaus that ever came down the pike." Now, however, he said that the FBI had "deteriorated and I don't care how many FBI agents are here in court listening to me."[37] This evidentiary legerdemain led to a request from the defense to view all the relevant FBI files. The Bureau complied, turning over 5,239 volumes worth. In all, there were 315,981 documents—or "serials."[38] Nevertheless, according to Churchill and Vander Wall, the FBI and the prosecution team had "deliberately suppressed at least 131 pieces of exculpatory evidence which might have served to exonerate the defendants."[39] In response to the unearthing of evidence tampering, state prosecutor R.D. Hurd and FBI Agent Philip Enlow visited Nichol and pledged that the petition issue had been a mere aberration. "In no way has the FBI attempted to hide or conceal anything in connection with [Nichol's] court orders or evidence the defense has a right to have," Enlow assured the media afterwards. "There was a misunderstanding in the handling of the case, and as soon as we found the error, it was corrected and the court was so notified."[40]

However, this wasn't the only "error" or subtle prevarication executed by the prosecutor in concert with the FBI.

In early April 1974, when defense lawyers requested full disclosure of any information about potential FBI infiltration of the defense team, state prosecutor R.D. Hurd put forward a sworn affidavit to Judge Nichol asserting that a thorough inspection of FBI documents turned up no evidence of infiltration. Durham's name was included on a potential informant list that WKLDOC turned in to the government, but Hurd assured the defense that FBI records "contained no material which could arguably be considered as evidence of the invasion of the defense legal camp."[41]

Yet Durham had been meeting "regularly" with his FBI contacts, Ray Williams and Robert Taubert, throughout the trial.[42] Johanna Brand asserts that FBI Agent Joseph Trimbach said Durham had met with his FBI contacts "nearly fifty times."[43] SAC Raymond Williams, one of Durham's contacts, corroborated this under oath.[44] Hurd's claim was also contradicted by Durham himself. Testifying in front of the Eastman Subcommittee, he said that he "advised the FBI that I had been asked to accompany Banks to the trial, and they said they wanted to hold a very thorough briefing for me prior to the beginning of that trial."[45] Also, Hurd admitted on record that in fact he was aware of FBI informants who were close to one of the defendants.[46]

Durham, when later trying to cover his tracks, said, "If Dennis [Banks] and I were sitting in a room and an attorney would walk in and start talking, I couldn't jump up and say, 'I can't be here. The FBI won't allow it.'"[47] So, Durham remained infiltrated in the legal defense committee. In fact, during the trial, Durham's FBI salary actually *increased* from $900 to $1,100 per month, further proof that he was providing the FBI with insider information.[48] He later admitted that he had a special, secret telephone number to call the FBI during the trial, and that he communicated regularly with a three-person FBI team headed by Special Agent Williams.[49] Despite the FBI's denials, Kenneth Tilsen, another member of the WKLDOC, said, "There was no person other than defense counsel and the defendants themselves who knew more about the total plans, concerns, and stratagems of the defense than Douglass Durham."[50] In sum, the Bureau and the U.S. Attorney's office—using Durham as a key infiltrator and informant—joined forces to subvert due process for Dennis Banks and Russell Means. However, their efforts did not succeed, at least not in the short term. Disgusted with FBI malfeasance, Judge Nichol dismissed the defendants' charges in September 1974, saying he was "very angry" about the way the trial had transpired and "ashamed" of the way the government had handled the case.[51] Judge Nichol said, "It's hard for me to believe that the FBI, which I have admired for so long, has stooped so low."[52]

Nichol's dismissal preceded the revelation that Durham was in fact an FBI informant. On 7 March 1975, while working their way through a set of papers released by a U.S. Attorney in a Wounded Knee-related case in Arizona, WKLDOC lawyers came across an informant report that was signed by Durham. When confronted with the document, Durham admitted he was an FBI infiltrator and informant.[53] In an interview with the *New York Times*, Durham said he was "relieved" to have been revealed as an informant, and that he had come to respect AIM leaders like Dennis Banks. He also said AIM was a "legal, social organization that wasn't doing anything wrong."[54] On 12 March 1975, AIM organized a press conference in Chicago where Durham admitted publicly he was an FBI informant and that he felt bad about it since he saw AIM as "an organization attempting to effect social change in America."[55] Durham then held his own press conferences in Minneapolis and Chicago, explaining in detail his covert, FBI-funded trajectory.[56]

Durham later appeared before the Eastman Subcommittee on Internal Security, where he fully discarded his sympathy for AIM, portraying it as heavily influenced by Communists and "a violent group" that was "dedicated to the overthrow of our Government."[57] The transcript from his testimony was consequently published in a report called *Revolutionary Activities Within the United States: The American Indian Movement*, which was "widely distributed" and "quickly accepted as a primary source of background information for reportage and scholarship on AIM."[58] Durham also emerged as "the most popular speaker on the John Birch [Society] circuit," where he made a number of outrageous, anti-AIM claims. For instance, he said AIM had "established training camps around the country in which political indoctrination, marksmanship, and guerrilla warfare are taught" in order to disrupt the Bicentennial celebration that was planned for 1976. He also said AIM intended to carry out "indiscriminate killings of whites."[59] He regularly told conservative, John Birch Society audiences that AIM was "a threat to freedom" due to the fact that its members were "Communist controlled."[60]

"Badjacketing," or "Snitchjacketing"

Sometimes individuals who infiltrate dissident social movements engage in badjacketing, or snitchjacketing: intentionally generating the suspicion that legitimate, committed members are actually FBI or police informants. They often target social-movement leaders or members in important positions, and sometimes resort to fabricating evidence. In a spurious psychological turn, infiltrators paint legitimate group members as corrupt, deceitful, and untrustworthy, when, in fact, the opposite is the case. The Church Committee came to the conclusion that "The 'snitch jacket' is a particularly nasty technique even when used in peaceful groups. It gains an added dimension of danger when it is used—as indeed, it was—in groups known to have murdered informers."[61] To be sure, a number of alleged informants—including badjacketed individuals—have experienced violence as a result of being perceived as a snitch, but, more commonly, targeted individuals are excluded from the movement, banished from participation. In addition to violence and ostracism, Brian Glick notes that badjacketing "generates confusion, fuels distrust and paranoia, diverts time and energy from a group's political work, turns co-workers against one another."[62]

Badjacketing was a common "neutralization" technique under COINTELPRO.[63] It was an explicit tenet in a twelve-point plan outlined in an internal, COINTELPRO—New Left document that was part of the "Counterintelligence Program, Internal Security, Disruption of the New Left." In this document, as a "suggestion for counterintelligence action" that could "be utilized by all offices," the FBI advocated "The creating of impressions that certain New Left leaders are informants for the Bureau or other law enforcement agencies."[64] FBI-supported badjacketing extended well beyond the New Left, however.

Informants have snitchjacketed countless dissidents over the years, including thirty-year veteran and Communist Party leader, William Albertson. Albertson, who had been a committed Communist since he was a young man, was, after being falsely fingered as an informant, kicked out of the Party in 1964, despite the fact that he was completely innocent of such charges. In fact, the Bureau falsified an informant's report, making it look as if it had been written by Albertson, even imitating his handwriting. An FBI informant then planted this report in a car Albertson had been riding in to make it seem like he had accidentally left it behind. Albertson offered to take a lie-detector test to prove his innocence, but Communist Party officials were convinced by the strikingly similar handwriting and refused his fervent appeals.[65]

The FBI also made an effort to badjacket SDS founder Tom Hayden. In an internal memo dated 10 May 1968, the FBI's Newark office identified Hayden as one of a number of "key leaders" who should "become the object of a counterintelligence plot to identify them as government informants." The plan was to "Accuse them of selling out to 'imperialistic monopoly capitalism.'" In regards to Hayden, the Newark office opined: "It might be possible to attach the stigma of informant or Government 'fink' to HAYDEN because of the apparent unlimited finances at his disposal, enabling him to take numerous trips in and out of the U.S., without any job or other means of financial support. Also, the ease with which he travels to communist countries, his reception there, the privileges afforded him, and his eventual return with no actual remonstrations by this Government." The FBI planned on using timely news releases and "cooperative news media" to propagate doubt about Hayden's money sources and his integrity more generally.[66] The FBI used similar tactics in an attempt to pigeonhole SNCC leader Stokely Carmichael as a stool pigeon by having an informant plant false correspondence ostensibly written by him to federal law enforcement agents.[67]

Badjacketing was also used to fracture and factionalize the American Indian Movement. Not surprisingly, Douglass Durham engaged in the practice. Two specific examples demonstrate his efforts. The first involved John "Two Birds" Arbuckle, a Native American who had founded an AIM chapter in Lincoln, Nebraska. The badjacketing of Arbuckle began after the events at Wounded Knee, when AIM was holding its national convention in Oklahoma from 25 July through 5 August 1973. According to Richard B. Williams, another member of the Lincoln chapter of AIM, once the group arrived for the convention,

> just about the first thing that happened was that a bunch of heavy se-
> curity guys came around and just interrogated the hell out of John. It
> seems that some of the national leadership had been put on notice that
> he was working for the police and they wanted to deal with that....Well
> John was pretty cool about it, he dealt with the questions and every-
> thing, but it was really humiliating, you could tell...and from that mo-
> ment on, there was a lot of mistrust and bad feeling between Lincoln
> AIM and some of the national leadership circles. They were never really
> able to rely on us...and we never really forgave *them* for the accusations
> that were made.[68]

It didn't take long for some members of AIM to figure out who was be-
hind the "whispering campaign." Aaron Two Elk, an AIM member from Des Moines, fingered Durham as the rumor instigator, asserting, "Right off, [Durham] started telling Ron Petite that John Arbuckle...was a pig...an undercover cop. Now, a couple of us knew Arbuckle, and had our doubts about this...but, still, the story got around pretty fast, and I guess a lot of people believed it."[69] These rumors affected Arbuckle's credibility, and he never emerged as a national leader, despite the fact that he was highly respected on the local level.

Badjacket-induced paranoia led to actual violence inside of AIM.
Durham also spread rumors about Carter Camp, who had sided with Arbuckle at the national convention. Such support for an alleged informant

made Camp suspect, too. Clyde Bellecourt believed Camp "was being paid off" as an informant. When Bellecourt made his theory public, Camp shot him pointblank in the stomach.[70] Reflecting on that episode, Aaron Two Elk said that when Durham "bad-rapped people, other people listened" due to his connections with leaders on the national level. "I'm not saying that Durham was responsible all by himself for what happened between Carter and Clyde, but he sure helped things along. And, after that, the unity of the Movement really began to come apart."[71]

Another of Durham's badjacketed victims was committed AIM member Anna Mae Aquash. Aquash was a young Native American woman from Nova Scotia, Canada. According to Peter Matthiessen, she was "an intelligent, energetic person" who was dedicated to making Indian cultural history more widely available and willing to take part in direct actions—such as the Trail of Broken Treaties and the events at Wounded Knee—in order to bring attention to the plight of Indians in North America.[72] Rex Weyler viewed her as "a symbol for Indian people throughout North America as a dedicated freedom fighter."[73] Perceptive as she was, Aquash was one of the first AIM members to conclude that Durham was an informant for the state.[74] Yet, despite her impressive credentials, rumors began to circulate that Aquash herself was an FBI informant. Many involved in the struggle felt that and the incipient uncertainties about Aquash originated with Douglass Durham, who according to Matthiessen, "tried to discredit anyone he did not control."[75]

As these rumors proliferated, the AIM leadership felt it was necessary to confront Aquash, and this task fell to Leonard Peltier, one of AIM's security heads. Peltier described the interaction this way:

> I run into Anna Mae on the Trail of Broken Treaties, but we never talked hardly; we never really got to know each other really until we were part of the support group for Russ and Dennis at [their trial in] St. Paul. She was involved in a lot of stuff, and she could have done a *lot* of damage if she was an informer. Anyway, I trusted her. So we just went over and sat in a car and bullshitted a little while, and that was all there was to it.[76]

Peltier walked away from their conversation feeling confident that Aquash wasn't an informant, and he passed this sentiment along to the national leadership. Aquash did not leave the car with the same equanimity. She felt betrayed by AIM's lack of trust in her, despite all she had risked for the organization. She even considered returning to Nova Scotia and suspending her work with AIM, thereby depriving the group of one of its most active, courageous, and dedicated members.[77] Soon after Peltier confronted Aquash, it became public knowledge that Durham was an FBI agent. This haunted AIM leaders, especially Dennis Banks who had trusted Durham for so long. According to Russell Means, "Banks was so paranoid after Douglass Durham that he thought *everyone* was an informer, even Anna Mae."[78] Such is the power of the badjacket.

The revelation that Durham was an FBI agent did not end Aquash's badjacketing. John Stewart, another FBI informant who had infiltrated AIM, continued to besmirch Aquash's name. The FBI maintained an intense interest in Aquash, harassing her at every opportunity. By 1975, she feared for her life; she told her sister that the FBI was out to get her.[79] Her refusal to cooperate with the FBI—who thought she was a witness to the killing of two agents—only deepened her predicament. On 24 February 1976, a rancher found a partly decomposed body in a riverbed on the Pine Ridge Indian Reservation. The BIA and FBI whisked the body away for examination, and shortly thereafter a BIA pathologist asserted that the woman had died from exposure. Unable to identify the woman, they severed her hands and sent them off to be examined. Meanwhile, the body was buried in an unmarked, "Jane Doe" grave. Tests on the hands revealed that the body was that of Anna Mae Aquash. Subsequently, her family demanded a second autopsy, and after the body was exhumed and inspected, a bullet was found in her skull. Apparently Aquash had been murdered, execution-style with a .32 caliber handgun. The BIA doctor who performed the original autopsy remarked, "A little bullet isn't hard to overlook."[80]

The "optimal result" of a badjacket, from the point of view of the police or the FBI, is when a snitchjacketed individual actually *does* become an informant when the individual realizes that he or she isn't appreciated by the group anyway. This is rather rare, though, and more commonly, badjacketed activists stop participating in the social movement, resigning themselves to inaction; in FBI parlance, they are "neutralized."

Agent Provocateurs

A final dimension of this mode of suppression is the work of agent provocateurs, "undercover agents who urge others to violent activity, train others in violent methods, and consciously provoke violence."[81] These informants move beyond the information-gathering function and instead deliberately attempt to swerve the plans and actions of the social movement in a violent direction. According to Gary Marx, the agent provocateur may also "set up a situation in which the group *appears* to have taken or to be about to take illegal actions," and "this may be done to gain evidence for use in a trial, to encourage paranoia and internal dissension, and/or to damage the public image of a group."[82] Churchill and Vander Wall add that agent provocateurs infiltrate targeted organizations "expressly for the purpose of fomenting or engaging in illegal activities which could then be attributed to key organizational members and/or the organization as a whole. Agents provocateurs were also routinely assigned to disrupt the internal functioning of targeted groups and to assist in the spread of disinformation."[83] Essentially, once the agent provocateur suggests violence, he or she must engage in violence, too, since to do otherwise would be to risk credibility with the group and therefore risk one's usefulness as an informant. The fact that agent provocateurs know they may be immune from prosecution allows them to act more freely, and violently.[84] Also, the fact that an agent provocateur might lose his or her job as an informant if they don't inspire illegal activities, leads to a tendency to escalate violence. As Marx points out, agent provocateurs "may encourage internal divisiveness and lines of action that are self-defeating or not in the best interests of the organization."[85]

Many social movements and political groups have been infiltrated by agent provocateurs. We have already seen how informant William O'Neal did his part to amplify the violent image of the Black Panthers. Another example of violent provocation, also during the Vietnam era, involved Horace L. Parker, who infiltrated SDS and the Weathermen at the University of Washington. Parker moved in with some members of the Weathermen in a Seattle duplex.[86] He even "supplied campus radicals with drugs, weapons, and materials used for preparing Molotov cocktails."[87] Under cross-examination during the "Tacoma Conspiracy Trial" in 1970, Parker said that he was willing to "do anything necessary" in order to protect his identity as an FBI operative, including the use of "acid, grass, speed and mescaline."[88] He also provided two cases of paint—paid for by the FBI—used to vandalize the federal courthouse in Seattle in early-1970, an act that directly led to federal charges (conspiracy to damage federal property) being brought against otherwise peaceful demonstrators. Parker also stoked tensions by participating in attacks that the Weathermen carried out against ROTC buildings on the University of Washington campus.[89]

Not surprisingly, Douglass Durham also served the FBI as an agent provocateur. From the beginning, Durham demonstrated "a propensity for visible displays of armed resistance."[90] On one hand this overt willingness to engage in violence earned him credibility within the organization as someone who was willing to put himself on the line for AIM and its causes. On the other hand, for the outside world, it played into the stereotype that Native Americans were violent and dangerous, which, in turn, allowed the state to more freely suppress their dissent.

Durham later testified that in the early-1970s there was "considerable concern regarding potential violent activities emanating from the Des Moines, Iowa, chapter" of AIM.[91] Indeed there was, and in large part that was because of the agent-provocateur work of Durham himself. According to Matthiessen, "While subverting the AIM national office, Durham had also remained active in Iowa; by encouraging rash, inflammatory acts, he had all but destroyed Iowa AIM."[92] Churchill and Vander Wall concur, noting that when Durham was in St. Paul at the trial of Dennis Banks and Russell Means, he was "openly and persistently advocating 'guerrilla warfare' despite the efforts of numerous AIM members to dissuade him."[93] Furthermore, Durham was fashioning and disseminating a violent image for AIM by writing and releasing to the public a number of unauthorized memoranda suggesting the possibility of AIM instigating a campaign of "systematic violence."[94]

Aaron Two Elk, who Durham tersely described in front of the Eastman Subcommittee as "the resident militant," claimed it was Durham, in fact, who advocated an extreme militancy.[95] Durham was "always right out front, urging everybody to get it on," he said. "His thing was that if you didn't have continuous confrontations going on, you weren't really serious, that if we weren't engaged in confrontations, we couldn't generate any sort of progress for Indian people." In fact, according to Two Elk, Durham went over the head of AIM's Midwest coordinator, Ron Petite, and sent out a memo commanding all people in AIM to "carry arms at all times."[96] This is the quintessential characterization of the agent provocateur.

Durham's maneuverings did not stop there. He began to alter major AIM policies, guiding them in a violent direction he could control. For example, in a confidential, internal AIM document from the fall of 1973 called "Operation Goals of National AIM," Durham proposed establishing an "AIM Center," which would "act as image, vanguard, political force, planner and policy formulator for the movement."[97] Durham was to be at the hub of the Center, in that he was to assume operational authority over an important part of the plan, called "Railroad Operations." This section of the document called for the creation of a "railroad system" designed to allow "Indian warriors to freely move in the execution of their appointed tasks." Durham was in charge of some crucial tasks in this underground operation. According to the document, which Durham dutifully passed on to the FBI, he would "validate identities and personnel" and "know at all time where personnel are located."[98] As Churchill and Vander Wall wryly note, "no COINTELPRO theorist could have envisioned a neater scenario than one in which an infiltrator was placed in a position to order a targeted organization's membership to engage in clandestine activities, *all* of which were to be reported—directly and immediately—to the infiltrator."[99]

Finally, Durham plotted at least two kidnappings designed to attract mass attention. One involved kidnapping Robert D. Day, the Governor of Iowa, and the other concerned an AIM nemesis, South Dakota's Deputy Attorney General, William Janklow. In both cases, AIM leadership put a quick stop to such audacious ideas that were sure to make AIM and its demands all the more dismissible, stigmatizable, and, indeed, demonizable.[100]

The Effects and Reverberations of Infiltration

Infiltration took a heavy toll on Native American social-movement organizing. Although COINTELPRO was officially disbanded in April 1971, the infiltration work done by Douglass Durham demonstrates that the program's spirit continued. Agent provocateurs like Durham surreptitiously managed to encourage both internal and external conflict, as they embedded themselves in the inner workings of the group. Internal FBI memoranda explicitly reveal the Bureau's general plan to demobilize AIM.

> The key to the successful investigation of AIM is substantial, live, quality informant coverage of its leaders and activities. In the past, this technique proved to be highly effective. [Redacted section here]. As a result of certain disclosures regarding informants, AIM leaders have dispersed, have become extremely security conscious and literally suspect everyone. This paranoia works both for and against the movement and recent events support this observation.[101]

According to Matthiessen, this assessment is correct: "After two years of disruption and harassment by Durham and other informers," he writes, "AIM was fragmented by fear of infiltration; as a national organization, it was virtually defunct."[102] Sayer agrees, adding: "By 1975, AIM had become increasingly wary of its own membership, and open debate over future plans and recruitment of new members had all but ceased."[103] The closing down of debate, in turn, leaves social movements open to charges that they are anti-democratic and run by a handful of power-hungry leaders. Ironically, once debate is crippled, and a small circle of powerful leaders emerges, groups are even more vulnerable to the work of agent provocateurs, if the agent is able to infiltrate this power circle, as Durham did. Agent provocateurs, as we have seen, can move social-movement policies and actions in a violent direction that, in turn, conveniently provides the state with the propagandistic grist required to demonize the group through the media and to use the legal system to repress the group. In this way, the FBI made full use of Durham, utilizing his statements as evidence that AIM was "violence-prone."[104] The

extreme policies advocated by the agent provocateur, in turn, allowed bystander publics to simply dismiss AIM members "as renegades, urban hoodlums, criminals, youthful adventurers, and the like."[105] The state's concerted
suppression of Native American radical dissent certainly achieved its goals.
Sayer asserts that "by the end of 1975 the Indian movement had lost its momentum. Although local work continued, AIM had ceased to be a force as a
national organization."[106]

Clearly, these tactics intersect with a number of other modes of suppression that, in combination, hobble social movements. Surveillance, mail
opening, and wiretapping often pave the way for the infiltration of informants and agent provocateurs, because such practices offer glimpses of a
social movement's weak spots and indications of small cracks in relations
that might possibly be wedged wider by an agent provocateur. State agents
are always on the lookout for weak links who can be pressured and exploited. As with surveillance, the idea is not only to induce paranoia, but also
to fracture solidarity and induce deep internal suspicion. The case of AIM
demonstrates that informants and agent provocateurs also facilitated harassment and harassment arrests. The fabrication of evidence was also common.
Cornell describes how such tactics affected the preconditions for collective
action: "Harassment and infiltration exacerbated factional divisions within
some groups and fostered crippling internal suspicions. Court cases tied
up resources." According to one AIM leader Cornell interviewed in 1978,
"We've been so busy in court fighting these indictments we've had neither
the time nor the money to do much of anything."[107] Certainly the expansive and expensive trials diverted the precious resources of time, money, and
energy toward defensive purposes, resources that could have been used in a
more positive way.

Durham's testimony in front of the Eastman Subcommittee also
played into bi-level demonization in the mass media, linking AIM explicitly to Communists.[108] Durham alleged that AIM actions were funded by
the Communist Party of Canada and that AIM leaders considered having
Dennis Banks seek refuge in Cuba where he could establish contact with
Fidel Castro, and perhaps even the Algerian radical Ahmed Ben Bella.[109] By
saying that AIM received funding from England, France, Germany, Ireland,
Canada, and South America, Durham made AIM appear to be a mere tool
of leftist power centers in foreign lands. Durham's allegations regarding the
violent plans of AIM also justified the direct violence being used against it.
In light of AIM's ostensibly hyper-militant stance, the state violence perpetrated against it appeared to be justified and condonable by bystanders who
had no way of knowing any better.[110]

The Church Committee concluded that these suppressive tactics also affected people's employment possibilities: "The use of informants in the investigation of groups and individuals involved in political activity may chill the exercise of First Amendment rights. For example, citizens…may fear an informant's report will prevent their gaining a job requiring security clearance, even though in fact they supported no unlawful activity."[111]

Finally, as we will see momentarily, the role of the agent provocateur can be closely related to the use of black propaganda. While badjacketing leads to internal rifts *within social-movement groups*, black propaganda engenders rifts *between* them.

7

"Black Propaganda" and the Creation of Schism

Black propaganda involves the use of fabricated documents assiduously designed to forge schisms or prevent solidarity between social movement organizations.[1] These false documents purportedly originate with one organization—the target of state suppression—and are sent to other organizations that are current or potential allies. In fact, these extant or prospective allies may *also* be targets of state suppression. By design, these controversial, offensive, and sometimes vicious documents are meant to foment dissension between the groups. These publications and missives engender confusion about and animosity toward the targeted social movement organization, as they "misrepresent their positions, goals or objectives in such a way as to publicly discredit them."[2] So, while infiltration, badjacketing, and agent provocateurs often lead to dissension and violence *among* group members, black propaganda provokes conflict *between* dissident social movement organizations. These organizations' social-change efforts, goals, and actions are sidetracked as they are forced to divert resources to defensive maintenance activities. Also, violence may result, which can lead to dwindling bystander support, shrinking possibilities for new-member recruiting, and plummeting morale among current supporters. In these ways, this mode of suppression can lead to social movement breakdown as it mires organizations on the bitter shoals of inter-group strife.

As with the cultivation of informants within social movements, the creation of schisms between social movements was explicitly included in the FBI's twelve-point plan to demobilize the New Left. In the aforementioned internal COINTELPRO—New Left document, the author, a special agent in the Albany office, noted "a definitive hostility among SDS and other New Left groups toward the Socialist Workers Party (SWP), the Young Socialist Alliance (YSA), and the Progressive Labor Party (PLP)." He recommended that "*this hostility should be exploited wherever possible*" by the FBI.[3] This internal memo also espouses "the use of cartoons" and the proliferation of "misinformation." These same tactics were also applied to the Bureau's COINTELPRO for "Black Nationalist—Hate Groups."

When the "Black Nationalist—Hate Group" target list was assembled in August 1967, the Black Panther Party wasn't on it. However, in September

1968, J. Edgar Hoover added the BPP to the list of groups to be "neutralized," contending that it was:

> the greatest threat to the internal security of the country. Schooled in the Marxist-Leninist ideology and the teaching of Chinese Communist leader Mao Tse-tung, its members have perpetrated numerous assaults on police officers and have engaged in violent confrontations with police throughout the country. Leaders and representatives of the Black Panther Party travel extensively all over the United States preaching their gospel of hate and violence not only to ghetto residents, but to students in colleges, universities and high schools as well.[4]

In the end, the Panthers came to dominate the FBI's attention under this COINTELPRO. As previously mentioned, nearly four of every five COINTELPRO operations against groups or individuals the FBI considered to be "Black nationalists" were aimed at the Black Panther Party.[5] While this COINTELPRO was ostensibly designed to prevent and decrease violence, aspects of the Bureau's overall strategies actually fostered and even fomented violence. Black propaganda was an important dimension of this process.

Historically, the state has used a number of methods to generate tensions, aggravate fractures, and imbue group relations with an artificial, contentious sense of dire urgency. For example, the FBI often engaged in the anonymous mailing of Bureau-authored articles and letters.[6] Fearful of the power that a Panther-SDS alliance might wield, the FBI penned a number of hostile letters supposedly from concerned members of one of the two groups. In one such letter, the FBI—posing as an SDS member—attacked a BPP leader from New Jersey, and the Panthers more generally:

> To Former Comrade [name]
> As one of "those little bourgeois, snooty nose"—"little schoolboys"—"little sissies" Dave Hilliard spoke of in the "*Guardian*" of 8/16/69, I would like to say that you and the rest of your black racists can go to hell. I stood shoulder to shoulder with Carl Nichols last year in Military Park in Newark and got my a-- whipped by a Newark pig all for the cause of wineheads like you and the rest of the black pussycats that call themselves Panthers....
>
> Who the hell set you and the Panthers up as the vanguard of the revolutionary and disciplinary group. You can tell all those wineheads you associate with that you'll kick no one's "a--," because you'd have to take a three year course in spelling to know what an a-- is and three more years to be taught where it's located....

Brains will win over brawn. The way the Panthers have retaliated against the US is another indication. The score: US-6: Panthers-0.

Why, I read an article in the Panther paper where a California Panther sat in his car and watched his friend get shot by Karenga's group and what did he do? He run back and write a full page story about how tough the Panthers are and what they're going to do. Ha Ha—B—S—.

Goodbye [name] baby—and watch out. Karenga's coming.

"Right On" as they say.[7]

"US" stands for United Slaves. The group's acronym also denoted its conflict-based approach—US as opposed to "THEM."[8] This organization pushed a black cultural nationalist approach that was strongly influenced by United Slaves leader Maulana Karenga. Karenga, who was born as Ronald Everett in 1941, articulated the theoretical underpinnings of black cultural nationalism, which propelled United Slaves into the center of the Black Power movement of the 1960s and 1970s.[9] The animosities that the FBI stoked between US and the BPP are discussed in much greater detail below. By taunting the Panthers for their inability to retaliate against US, this letter demonstrates how the Bureau was angling in on—and indeed exacerbating—these animosities from a number of different directions, taking the opportunity to fan the flames of US-BPP dissension in any way it could. Such mail was clearly designed to create ill will between SDS and the Panthers, in hopes that these groups would not coordinate their social-change energies.

In another letter penned to the editor of a *Black Power* magazine, ostensibly from "Soul Brother Jake," the presumably African-American author racializes relations with SDS, with a spate of red-baiting thrown in for good measure:

Editor:

What's this bull---- SDS outfit? I'll tell you what they has finally showed there true color. White. They are just like the commies and all the other white radical groups that suck up to the blacks and use us. We voted at our meeting in Oakland for community controls over the pigs but SDS says no. Well we can do with out them mothers. We can do it by ourselfs.

OFF THE PIGS – POWER TO THE PEOPLE

Soul Brother Jake.[10]

Specific details from meetings—which were sometimes gleaned from electronic surveillance or through informants—offset what were often paltry attempts to catch the colloquial flavor of the group from which the letter ostensibly emanated.

A third example of a fabricated, inflammatory letter-writing campaign to prevent an alliance between SDS and the Panthers involves a 1970 note purportedly composed by a disgruntled Panther who interrogates the integrity of SDS and, along the way, incites class tensions:

> Dear Brothers and Sisters,
>
> Since when do us Blacks have to swallow the dictates of the honky SDS? Doing this only hinders the Party progress in gaining Black control over Black people. We've been ------ over by the white fascist pigs and the Man's control over our destiny. We're sick and tired of being severely brutalized, denied our rights and treated like animals by the white pigs. We say to hell with the SDS and its honky intellectual approaches which only perpetuate control of Black people by the honkies....
>
> The damn SDS is a paper organization with a severe case of diarrhea of the mouth which has done nothing but feed us lip service. Those few idiots calling themselves weathermen run around like kids on Halloween... they call themselves revolutionaries but take a look at who they are. Most of them come from well heeled families even by honky standards. They think they're helping us Blacks but their futile, misguided and above all white efforts only muddy the revolutionary waters.
>
> A time has come for an absolute break with any non-Black group and especially those ------ SDS and a return to our pursuit of a pure black revolution by Blacks for Blacks.
>
> Power!
>
> Off the Pigs!!!![11]

This letter was sent to BPP leaders as well as a number of organizers in the New Left. On occasion, though not in these three cases, the state forges social-movement stationery or produces replica business cards so as to enhance the credibility of its forgeries. In one instance in which the Bureau used "facsimiles of BPP letterhead," letters were sent to BPP Solidarity Committees throughout Europe ostensibly from David Hilliard, an ally of Panther leader Huey Newton. In part, the letter read, "The Supreme Servant of the People, Huey P. Newton, with concurrence of the Central Committee of the Black Panther Party, has ordered the expulsion of the entire Intercommunal Section of the Party at Algiers. You are advised that Eldridge Leroy Cleaver is a murderer and a punk without genitals."[12] Such inflammatory rhetoric exacerbated the piano-wire tensions between the Newton and Cleaver factions of the BPP.

The Bureau also forged social-movement schisms by creating front organizations, or "notional," fictitious organizations. The Church Committee categorized these "notionals" into three types: (1) organizations whose members were all FBI informants; (2) organizations with a mix of informants and unsuspecting social-movement participants; and (3) completely fictitious organizations with no members. These "notionals" were simply pseudonyms used for bogus mailings.[13] Many were Bureau-inspired underground newspapers that disseminated misinformation and derogatory information that created tension among and between social movement organizations. The *Armageddon News* at Indiana University was made up of FBI agents based in Indianapolis. It attacked radical activist organizations as devious manipulators who wanted "to seize the university and to strike at the heart of the democratic system." Hoping to undermine support for such groups, the FBI front organization suggested, alternatively, that, "This is a situation we can and should deal with at the polls."[14] Besides facilitating factionalism, these newspapers also competed for scarce funding, while alienating potential supporters or recruits by portraying dissidents as "a disruptive minority." Similar newspapers using parallel tactics with comparable effects emerged at the University of Texas–Austin, with *Longhorn Tale*, and at American University in Washington, DC, where the *Rational Observer* was published.[15] According to Linfield, "In addition to creating bogus 'underground' papers, the FBI established three phony news services, the Pacific International News Service in San Francisco, the Midwest News in Chicago, and the New York Press Service on the east Coast." These news services offered to cover demonstrations and marches, sending their photographers and writers.[16]

Other prominent examples of black propaganda include the FBI-induced rift between Tom Hayden of SDS and Black Nationalist poet and playwright Leroi Jones;[17] the NY Black Muslim FBI informants who forged a schism between the followers of Malcolm X and the SWP;[18] the rift created between the SWP and the YSA;[19] the Bureau-instigated split between the YSA and the Revolutionary Youth Movement (RYM—a splinter from SDS);[20] and the Bureau's concertedly stoked violence between the BPP and the Blackstone Rangers.[21]

Culture Clash:
The Black Panthers and the United Slaves Organization

A prime instance of the state's attempt to foment violence between the Black Panthers and a rival group, in order to either prevent the formation of an alliance or to fracture an extant or budding partnership, is the concerted wedge that the southern California FBI constructed in order to set the Panthers and the United Slaves Organization (US) against each other. The Bureau produced imaginative black propaganda in an effort to facilitate this rift.

US was a west-coast-based black nationalist group led by Maulana Karenga that emerged after the Watts insurrection of 1965. US countered the revolutionary political nationalism of the BPP with its own brand of cultural nationalism. US believed a cultural revolution was necessary before political revolution could occur. According to Karenga, "To go back to tradition is the first step forward," and so US adopted an Africa-centric stance that manifested itself in group members' dress, artistic production, language, and social relations.[22] According to Van Deburg, members of US—who called themselves "advocates"—were highly disciplined and intensely committed to the idea that "black culture *was* Black Power," and Karenga forcefully asserted the idea that, "black liberation was impossible, by definition unthinkable, without breaking the white culture's domination of black minds."[23] To facilitate this breaking away from the dominant values of white society, the creation of new black cultural forms was crucial. *Kawaida*, the ideological backbone for cultural and social change, permeated the practice of US and many of its allies.[24] Before signing on as an advocate, one had to take a seven-week course in the US doctrines and practices. Upon completing the class, the advocate pledged allegiance to US by taking an oath called the *Kaipo* whereby one promised to remain committed to Karenga as the Master Teacher and to the principles of US more generally.[25]

Amiri Baraka—who before his cultural black nationalist turn was known as Leroi Jones—followed Karenga's doctrine for eight years. He described Karenga as "quick-witted, sharp-tongued, with a kind of amusing irony to his putdowns of white people, America, black people, or whatever."[26] Being an artist, Baraka was drawn to the centrality of cultural work in Karenga's program, as well as the group's "tight organization and military-like rank and discipline," which made the cadre seem "much more 'together' than most of the other militants."[27] Baraka notes that Karenga's social theory was "eclectic" in that it borrowed widely, from Elijah Muhammad to Frantz Fanon to Julius Nyere to Marcus Garvey. Karenga distilled ideas from these diverse sources into the three C's: Color (race), Culture, and Consciousness—and in order to be considered legitimate, any black nationalist, cultural, or arts movement had to have all three C's.[28] Karenga's theoretical eclecticism aside, soon after meeting him, Baraka adopted his doctrine and promoted it widely.[29] Karenga's tough, charismatic disposition and original, culture-based approach had a lot to do with Baraka's—and many other advocates'—attraction to the group. US created an array of new holidays, including *Kwanzaa*, a seven-day celebration rooted in traditional African harvests, that is celebrated today by a wide range of African Americans.[30]

Karenga insisted that US didn't believe in the notion of class struggle. He once asserted, "The international issue is racism, not economics. White people are racists not just capitalists. Race rules out economics and even if it doesn't wipe it out completely it minimizes it. Therefore we conceive of the problem today not as a class struggle but a global struggle against racism."[31] Such analysis alienated possible supporters of a socialist or Marxist bent.[32] This outlook—and US's Afro-centrism and emphasis on artistic production—led to allegations from the Panthers and others that US was a collection of bourgeois black nationalists, or what Earl Anthony called "pork chop niggers" and "those niggers with the bongos in their ears."[33] Amiri Baraka scathingly put it this way, years after he left US:

> The idea that we somehow had to go back to pre-capitalist Africa and extract some "unchanging" black values from historical feudalist Africa and impose them on a 20th-century black proletariat in the most advanced industrial country in the world was simple idealism and subjectivism. Cultural nationalism uses an ahistorical, unchanging never-never-land Africa to root its hypotheses. The doctrine itself is like a bible of petty bourgeois glosses on reality and artification of certain aspects of history to make a recipe for "blackness" that again gives this petty bourgeoisie the hole card on manners to lord it over the black masses, only this time "revolutionary" manners.[34]

Other critics disdained what they saw as a cult of personality orbiting around Karenga. This "Maulana Complex," as Baraka dubbed it, invited the condemnation that US was a "reactionary" group with an approach that "might possibly lead to a kind of black fascism."[35] Others noted disapprovingly that, Karenga's ideological approach was borderline evangelical.[36] Many decried the male chauvinism that permeated US relations.[37]

More directly related to the eventual schism that the FBI exacerbated between US and the Black Panthers were barbs exchanged by the two groups in the late-1960s as they attempted to position themselves as the premier black revolutionary social-change group, often by attacking, oversimplifying, or misrepresenting the other group's approach. In an interview that was published as a pamphlet by *The Movement*, Huey Newton directly assailed the US ideology:

> Cultural nationalism, or pork chop nationalism, as I sometimes call it, is basically a problem of having the wrong political perspective. It seems to be a reaction instead of responding to political oppression. The cultural nationalists are concerned with returning to the old African cul-

ture and thereby regaining their identity and freedom. In other words, they feel that the African culture will automatically bring political freedom. Many times cultural nationalists fall into line as reactionary nationalists.[38]

Karenga himself entered the rhetorical ring to spar with the Panthers, calling them "a front group" for white radicals. Karenga often referred derisively to the BPP as part of "the left," which came across as borderline red-baiting.[39]

The Panthers' disapproval of US support for "Black Capitalism" also served as a fundamental ideological difference between the two groups since, according to Newton, "to be a revolutionary nationalist you would by necessity have to be a socialist."[40] The fact that, in the wake of the assassination of Martin Luther King, Jr., Karenga met with Governor Ronald Reagan in order to try to prevent rioting didn't gain any favor with the Black Panthers either, even though Karenga later said meeting Reagan at the governor's request was "the wrong move."[41] When Karenga suggested that the notoriously racist LAPD help with security at the Black Congress in LA in the late-1960s, the Panthers were fervently opposed. In response to this proposal Panther leader David Hilliard wrote in his autobiography, "We can't support stuff where you got police who oppress and kill Panthers standing around and talking about being *security*!....You know, we say a pig is a pig!"[42]

Belligerent public comments and printed essays by cultural nationalists didn't help ease tensions. For example, Baraka, then a proponent of Karenga's brand of cultural nationalism, wrote in an essay titled "Nationalism Vs PimpArt" that

> Frankly the Panthers, no matter the great amounts of sincere but purposefully misled brothers, getting shot up because some nigger was emotionally committed to white people, are extreme examples of PimpArt gone mad. It is a spooky world when the Negro Ensemble Theater and The Black Panther Party (post Huey) can both suddenly exist as large manipulative symbols of white power and white ideology.[43]

Such provocations didn't go unnoticed. By the fall of 1968, L.A. Black Panther Alprentice "Bunchy" Carter observed, "There's real bad blood between the Panthers and US."[44] This tension also arose, in part, because of attempts by the BPP to establish a deeper presence in Los Angeles, where US was strongest and in San Diego, where Karenga also had great influence.[45]

The FBI, aware of the tension between the two groups, seized its opportunity by promptly authoring black propaganda designed to exacerbate these feelings of mistrust and ill will. A memo from FBI Headquarters to the

Baltimore Field Office observed that the rivalry between US and the BPP was "taking on the aura of gang warfare with attendant threats of murder and reprisals." The message went on to suggest that the Bureau take an active role in encouraging the rivalry. Hoover wrote: "In order to fully capitalize upon BPP and US differences as well as to exploit all avenues of creating further dissension in the ranks of the BPP, recipient offices are instructed to submit imaginative and hard-hitting counterintelligence measures aimed at crippling the BPP."[46] Beginning in December 1968, each FBI office was to send a letter to Headquarters outlining such "imaginative" ideas and detailing "accomplishments obtained during the previous two-week period."[47]

The Shootout at UCLA

The US and BPP's pressure-cooker relationship led to the violent murder of two Black Panther Party members—Alprentice "Bunchy" Carter and John Huggins—on 17 January 1969 in Campbell Hall on the campus of UCLA. Disagreement between the two groups had erupted over how the university's Black Student Union would select a director for the newly created Black Studies Program. US and BPP members who were enrolled in the school's "High Potential Program"—a special project created for talented students of color who had struggled academically in past educational endeavors—fervently diverged on who should take the helm at this new and important post.[48] Both victims who died in the attack were participants in the High Potential Program.[49] Huggins was the chair of the criteria committee to select the new director.[50] Five men associated with US—Larry Watani-Stiner, George Ali-Stiner, Donald Hawkins-Stodi, Claude Hubert-Gaidi, and Harold Jones-Tawala—were charged with the killings. Brothers Larry Watani-Stiner and George Ali-Stiner surrendered themselves to the police along with Donald Hawkins-Stodi. Neither Claude Hubert-Gaidi nor Harold Jones-Tawala were ever apprehended. Watani-Stiner, Ali-Stiner, and Hawkins-Stodi were convicted on two counts of second-degree murder as well as conspiracy to murder. The Stiner Brothers were given life sentences while Hawkins-Stodi went into youth detention since he was only twenty.[51]

Churchill and Vander Wall assert that the Stiner brothers and Claude Hubert-Gaidi were very likely "police infiltrators of US, injected as an expedient to raise the level of tension between US and the BPP." In other words, they were agent provocateurs. The fact that the Stiner brothers escaped from San Quentin in 1974—an "unprecedented feat" at the time—lends some credence to this contention.[52] This has also been corroborated by Darthard Perry, an FBI informant who infiltrated the BPP. He said in a sworn affidavit for a BPP lawsuit against the U.S. Government that he knew the murderers were employed by the FBI and that, in fact, the Bureau had a hand in their escape.[53] Former FBI Agent M. Wesley Swearingen supports this account.[54] Others, including Scot Brown, author of *Fighting for US: Maulana Karenga, the US Organization, and Black Cultural Nationalism*, are skeptical that the killing of Carter and Huggins was a planned assassination. They view the killings as more spontaneous than orchestrated.[55] Regardless of whether or not a conspiracy generated the murders, the inter-group tensions, which were deliberately exacerbated by the FBI, played a significant role in the killings.

According to Baraka, after Carter and Huggins were killed, the intensity of the situation increased. "From that point on," he wrote, "the FBI escalated their 'intervention' into the conflict. They'd shoot at one organization, knowing that the other would get blamed, and that the organization shot at would retaliate in kind. That is just what happened."[56] Indeed, in the wake of the murders, the FBI moved quickly to thicken the bad blood. The Bureau's San Diego office came up with the idea of drawing cartoons that would generate anger—and perhaps even violent retaliation—from both groups. The FBI was explicit about its goal: "The purpose of the caricatures is to indicate to the BPP that the US organization feels that they are ineffectual, inadequate, and riddled with graft and corruption," said one memo.[57] The idea was quickly approved and put into action. In early March, the Bureau's first cartoon was mailed to five Panthers as well as to two underground newspapers. Internal FBI communication indicates that the Panthers did indeed blame the US for the cartoon, considering it an attack.[58]

The black propaganda seemed to be achieving the Bureau's goals, as well. In mid-March, members of US critically wounded a Panther at a rally in Los Angeles. The BPP retaliated by shooting at the home of a US member. A hundred miles south in San Diego, however, temperatures seemed to be cooling as members from both groups were willing to try to hammer out their differences at the negotiating table. Such cool-headed civility galvanized the Bureau to pencil more inflammatory cartoons. After receiving approval from Headquarters, the San Diego branch drew up three more cartoons that ridiculed the BPP and strategically mailed them to specific Panthers.[59] FBI agents and informants also posted copies of these black propaganda cartoons on lampposts, telephone poles, and bulletin boards throughout black neighborhoods.[60] The delicate harmony in San Diego promptly came to an end. Per the FBI plan, a number of scuffles and skirmishes between US and the BPP followed, and the San Diego branch of the Bureau was quick to posit a causal relationship in its internal communications:

> The BPP members...strongly objected [to] being made fun of by cartoons being distributed by the US organization (FBI cartoons in

actuality)....[Informant-name deleted] has advised us on several occasions that the cartoons are "really shaking up the BPP." They have made the BPP feel that US is getting ready to move and this was the cause of the confrontation at Southcrest Park [in San Diego] on 4/4/69.[61]

As spring became summer, the inter-group violence skyrocketed. In late May, Black Panther John Savage was killed by US member Jerry Horne (a.k.a. Tambuzi). In keeping with its bi-weekly reports of "accomplishments obtained," the San Diego Field Office reported to Headquarters with satisfaction—albeit in a major understatement—that altercations between the two groups had escalated from "mere harassment up to and including beating of various individuals"[62]

Despite the fact that FBI surveillance indicated that US was fortifying its armament stocks and engaging in ramped up firearms training exercises, Bureau Headquarters approved sending a forged, incendiary letter to the Oakland BPP office that was ostensibly penned by a disgruntled San Diego Panther. The letter intimated that a San Diego Panther leader had a white girlfriend and that the US was freely inflicting violence on members of the San Diego BPP without an appropriately forceful response from the Panthers. The bogus letter challenged the Panthers to take a more aggressive approach with the rival United Slaves. In the wake of this letter, a spate of violence ensued. On 14 August 1969, US gunmen wounded two Panthers, and the next day killed BPP member Sylvester Bell. The Panthers replied by bombing US offices.[63] The San Diego Field Office responded to the murder in an internal memo: "In view of the recent killing of Sylvester Bell, a new cartoon is being considered in hopes that it will assist in the continuance of the rift between the BPP and US." It also said: "Efforts being made to determine how this situation can be capitalized upon for the benefit of the Counterintelligence Program."[64] The Church Committee reported in 1976 that the FBI's San Diego office—which was working under a system that included cash incentives based on how agents achieved "accomplishments"—"pointed with pride to the continued violence between black groups."[65] In a memorandum from San Diego to FBI Headquarters in September 1969, under the heading TANGIBLE RESULTS, a Bureau official reported: "Shootings, beatings, and a high degree of unrest continues to prevail in the ghetto area of southeast San Diego. Although no specific counterintelligence action can be credited with contributing to this overall situation, *it is felt that a substantial amount of the unrest is directly attributable to this program.*"[66]

Bureau intelligence indicated that Maulana Karenga was intensely concerned about his personal safety, fearing assassination by the Panthers. According to Scot Brown, "The taxing combination of the threat of retaliation from the Black Panther Party alongside police and FBI surveillance, disruption, and attacks had a transformative impact on the organization's structure and internal operations." Brown points to a "rapid militarization" in which "every facet of US…had to shift its main activities to ones relating to protecting the organization's leader from the immediate threat of an attack from the Black Panther Party or the police."[67] Witnesses like Amiri Baraka have related that "Karenga had a machine gun sitting in his living room facing the front door, on a tripod" in case of a Black Panther attack.[68]

The FBI's San Diego Field Office received permission from Headquarters to attempt to exacerbate Karenga's stress by mailing him a letter, ostensibly from a San Diego US member, which referred to an article from a BPP newspaper that verbally attacked Karenga. The FBI explanation attached to the proposal reasoned that, "The article, which is an attack on Ron Karenga of the US organization, is self-explanatory. It is felt that if the following letter be sent to Karenga, pointing out that the contents of the article are objectionable to members of the US organization in San Diego, the possibility exists that some sort of retaliatory action will be taken against the BPP."[69] The deliberate fueling of paranoia was clearly meant to demobilize the US leadership. Undoubtedly it moved US away from its socio-cultural agenda and towards the basic goal of self-preservation.

In January 1970, FBI Headquarters—buoyed by its successes of the past—approved the distribution of a new batch of cartoons to be sent to Black Panthers in San Diego, Los Angeles, and San Francisco. These drawings portrayed Karenga as a dominating figure "who has the BPP completely at his mercy." According to a memo sent from the San Diego Field Office to FBI Headquarters, the explicit "purpose of the caricatures" was "to indicate to the BPP that the US Organization considers them to be ineffectual, inadequate, and [considers itself] vitally superior to the BPP."[70] More specifically, one cartoon portrayed the BPP as abusive toward black women and children, while another blamed the BPP for an LAPD raid on US headquarters.[71]

A few months later, when special agents from the Bureau came across an aggressive article in the Panther newspaper titled "Karenga King of the Bloodsuckers," the FBI again pushed itself to come up with ways to exploit this seething hostility. It not only considered penning additional threatening attacks to send to US from the BPP, but also sending communication to the Panthers since, as they saw it, the article was an "admission by [the] BPP that it has done nothing to retaliate against US for [the] killing of Panther members attributed to US and Karenga, an admission that the BPP has been beaten at its own game of violence." The Los Angeles Field Office reacted to this suggestion from Headquarters by saying that in fact the killings *had* resulted in retributive violence, but further violence was hindered by Panther temerity in the face of intimidating US force. Nevertheless, the FBI in Los Angeles was hopeful that further violence might be sparked. More specifically, Los Angeles wrote back to Headquarters:

> The Los Angeles Division is aware of the mutually hostile feelings harbored between the organizations and the first opportunity to capitalize on the situation will be maximized. It is intended that the US Inc. will be appropriately and discretely advised of the time and location of BPP activities *in order that the two organizations might be brought together and thus grant nature the opportunity to take her due course.*[72]

Aside from the essentialist view that it was part of these groups' very "nature" to engage in violence, the wording of the memorandum—"will be appropriately and discretely advised of the time and location of BPP activities"—implies that informants were embedded in US who the Bureau could rely on to facilitate the groups being "brought together" at the desired moment. In any case, as Donner has observed: "The Bureau, it is clear, was criminally complicit in the violence that enveloped the two groups."[73]

All these FBI activities—and the violence they generated—led to intense feelings of distrust and paranoia, or what Baraka called "a foxhole mentality," whereby formerly active members of social movements holed up for safety purposes instead of hitting the pavement and organizing.[74] Instead of attracting recruits, sustaining the morale of current members, or pressing for social change, these groups instead felt compelled to go on the defensive or to disengage from their socio-political agendas. The violence-drenched images of the groups undermined their efforts to gain wide-reaching, consistent community support.[75] In terms of the Black Panther presence in southern California after the US / BPP violent schism, the L.A. district attorney's office offered the following assessment: "The Panthers in Southern California are now a pretty small group of leftovers."[76] Meanwhile, according to Brown, "US had become increasingly isolated and vilified." In June 1971, Karenga was sent to prison on assault and false imprisonment charges, stemming from the brutal treatment he and two others inflicted on Gail Idili-Davis and Brenda Jones, two US members. While Karenga languished in prison, US membership shrank markedly, and by 1974 "its ranks had dwindled to only a handful of committed members."[77]

Intersections with Other Modes of Suppression

In practice, schism-creation between groups through the use of inflammatory black propaganda ties in with a number of other modes of suppression.

As the Church Committee demonstrated, it frequently intersects with mass media manipulation. As the FBI-induced schisms took form, the Bureau often leaked information—and sometimes even pre-written stories—to sympathetic members of the news media.[78] This practice—which has been dubbed "gray propaganda"—aims to discredit the dissident social movements in question and to tacitly rationalize any forceful suppression of these groups that may occur.[79] Such calculating use of the press was an explicit tenet in the FBI's COINTELPROs of the 1960s and early-1970s, and the Bureau even had a literal "list of 'friendly' news media sources" that could be relied upon to write disparaging stories about the Black Panthers and US Organization.[80] Donner has noted that "'Cooperative news media' were supplied with a steady stream of discrediting stories and, more ambitiously, plans were made to use 'established and reliable sources in the television and/ or radio field' to prepare programs discrediting the BPP."[81] In the context of the exacerbation of tensions between the BPP and US, Van Deburg has gone as far as to say that "The press and the electronic media were manipulated shamelessly."[82] For example, FBI Headquarters asked all of its field offices to disseminate copies of a scathing column penned by labor columnist Victor Riesel that advocated a nationwide boycott against *The Black Panther* newspaper.[83]

Surveillance is also closely related to black propaganda. Reliable surveillance—either through wiretaps, bugs, or informants—allows for more believable letters, cartoons, and communiqués from rival organizations. Correspondence bolstered with surveillance-captured information seemed more credible, and, in some occasions, more threatening. In the case of the rift between US and the BPP, surveillance afforded the Bureau the knowledge that US was stockpiling weapons, which galvanized it to further inflammatory propaganda.[84] As we have seen, agent provocateurs also played a role in all this.[85] Additionally, harassment arrests led to suspicions that rival groups were supplying information to the police.[86] Taken further, this noxious combination of suppressive tactics massively hindered the social-change endeavors of both the Black Panther Party and United Slaves Organization.

Harassment and Harassment Arrests

Another mode of suppression that diminishes dissident activity is the state's execution of harassment and harassment arrests. Dissidents are arrested for minor charges that are often false, and that are sometimes based on obscure statutes that have remained on the books, buried and dormant but nevertheless vessels for legal persecution. Harassment arrests can have a devastating effect. Such charges, even if false, thrust dissidents into legal labyrinths that consume social-movement resources, divert activists from their social-change goals, undermine morale of social-movement participants, and discourage support from potential recruits or bystander publics, as these groups often tense up at the possibility of consorting with alleged criminals. As Churchill and Vander Wall note, harassment arrests also "increase paranoia, tie up activists in a series of pre-arraignment incarcerations and preliminary courtroom procedures, and deplete their resources through the posting of numerous bail bonds (as well as the retention of attorneys)."[1] Social-movement leaders—who are often the target of harassment arrests—are, at the least, temporarily paralyzed as they spend time planning their defense. If convicted, they are shelved away in prison, sometimes for years, where it's more difficult to effect change. Importantly, harassment arrests shift focus away from the ideas, institutions, and individuals that the activists are critiquing and onto the dissidents themselves. These arrests also tend to generate negative media coverage, which usually overshadows any acquittals or dropped charges that may follow.

Sociologist Jennifer Earl makes two often overlooked observations about harassment arrests: (1) despite being considered relatively "softer" than direct violence, harassment arrests can be painful, physically challenging experiences, and (2) "the costs imposed on defendants through their sheer entanglement with the criminal justice system are imposed on the innocent and guilty alike."[2] Forest activist Kim Marks asserts we need to be aware of the dialectical relationship between state agents and dissidents. Arrests can result from overzealous cops and agents, but, as activists, "if you don't know what your exit strategy is, there often can be more accidental arrests."[3]

Yet state harassment need not result in arrest to be an effective tactic. Countless activists have been harassed by the police and FBI, whether in the form of being followed, "greeted" ostentatiously outside their residences, pulled over while driving or biking, brusquely reminded of upcoming grand jury appearances, or given extra inspections at the airport. Environmental activists are no strangers to state harassment. Craig Rosebraugh, a spokesperson for the radical environmental organization the Earth Liberation Front (ELF), an underground group that engages in direct-action economic sabotage in order to discourage environmental destruction, wasn't actually arrested, but repeatedly harassed by federal agents and brought in front of a grand jury on numerous occasions. Grand juries can in themselves be a method of suppression. A witness can plead the Fifth Amendment so as not to give self-incriminating testimony, but a judge can force testimony. Failure to cooperate in a grand jury can mean jail time for contempt of court and can also lead to criminal charges. On top of that, grand juries meet for eighteen months at a time and this can be renewed in perpetuity. Also, the state's prosecuting attorney can, and sometimes does, prep grand jury members to be hostile before the activist even steps in the room to testify. Lawyers are not allowed to accompany their clients into the grand jury room, and lawyers and activists are not allowed to watch other witnesses' testimony. Information not admissible in a regular court, such as hearsay, is often allowable in a grand jury.[4] All together, this amounts to "the conversion of the grand jury system into a major instrument for harassing and intimidating political radicals."[5] This experience contributed to Craig Rosebraugh's decision to quit his position as ELF spokesperson.[6] Harassment can also take the form of military conscription and reclassification, as was the case in the 1960s with Muhammad Ali as well as SNCC leaders John Lewis and Bob Moses.[7] In this chapter, however, I will focus on harassment that eventuates in arrest.

Harassment arrests compose part of what Isaac Balbus has called "legal repression," which he describes as the crushing of dissent by the "formal rationality" of a legal apparatus. This legalized squelching "tends to depoliticize the consciousness of the participants, delegitimate their claims and grievances, and militate against alliances between participants and other nonelites or elite moderates." This minimizes the possibility of social change and maximizes the ostensible legitimacy of the state apparatus. Balbus continues: "Long-run legitimacy and the need to maintain an ongoing repressive mechanism are hopelessly at odds with one another. The response on the part of court authorities to this contradiction has been to maintain verbal and symbolic adherence to formal rationality yet at the same time to develop a covert sanctioning system which departs at every important stage from its dictates."[8] By maintaining an outward commitment to criminal justice and law enforcement, the state can bolster its legitimacy with the general public, even as it uses the criminal justice system as a tool to suppress dissent in both the short and long term.

Harassment Arrests: The Dominant Features

Balbus's conception of "legal repression" manifests in many forms, and one of them—on the front end of the criminal justice path—is harassment arrests, which often share a number of features. Frequently, dissidents are selectively arrested for minor crimes that, when committed by the general population, go unpunished. They are often given inflated bails to post, and, if convicted, exorbitant jail sentences. Also, harassment arrests often have a pre-emptive dimension: their aim is to prevent future political dissidence. Finally, the violation of due process procedures is common, as is the fabrication of evidence in order to frame dissidents for crimes they did not commit. Many of these core features occur in concert.

The tradition of harassment arrests based on dubious charges extends far back into U.S. history. The Palmer Raids, which will be discussed in more detail later in the book, led to numerous arrests of political radicals under dodgy circumstances. Later, in the early-1960s, the state used harassment arrests to smother the Southern Civil Rights movement. According to scholar Steven Barkan, in Albany, Georgia alone, "Most of the more than 1,200 arrests that took place through the summer of 1962 were without legal merit."[9] The tactic was codified as an explicit part of the FBI's plan under COINTELPRO. The Church Committee found that the FBI—together with local law enforcement and regulatory agencies—engaged in "selective law enforcement" of the actions of COINTELPRO targets whereby "state and local agencies were frequently informed of alleged statutory violations which would come within their jurisdiction" even though "this was not always normal Bureau procedure." Also, these agencies were not only provided information about alleged violations, but they were encouraged by the FBI "to find evidence of violations—*any* violations—[in order] to 'get' a target." According to FBI agent George Moore, "Ordinarily, we would not be interested in health violations because it is not my jurisdiction....But under this program, we would tell our informants perhaps to be alert to any health violations or other licensing requirements or things of that nature, whether there were violations and we would see that they were reported."[10] An internal FBI memo from 1968 lavished praise on the Philadelphia Field Office for its success in having local dissidents "arrested on every possible charge until they could no longer make bail" and therefore "spent most of the summer in jail." In another internal memo, FBI agents were counseled that because the purpose of such harassment charges "is to disrupt" that "it is immaterial whether facts exist to substantiate the charge."[11]

FBI cooperation with local police departments was common in attempting to disrupt—or "neutralize"—the Black Panther Party. For example, according to the Church Committee's Final Report, in San Diego the Bureau worked closely with the San Diego Police Department (SDPD), "supplying it with informant reports to encourage raids on the homes of BPP members, often with little or no apparent evidence of violations of State or Federal law." The Bureau also encouraged the SDPD to crack down on the Panthers for traffic violations. Internal FBI memos show that after the San Diego Field Office obtained information that Panthers staying at the BPP Headquarters were "having sex orgies on almost a nightly basis," the Bureau pressured the SDPD to come up with a legal justification for conducting a raid. The SDPD came through with the requisite rationale—outstanding traffic warrants—and proceeded to carry out a raid of the Headquarters, which failed to uncover a sex orgy, but nevertheless resulted in the arrest of six people. According to an FBI memo from the San Diego Field Office, the raid led to the seizure of a rifle, three shotguns (one of which was stolen), one canister of tear gas, and four gas masks. The Bureau also noted, "as a result of this raid, the six remaining members of the BPP in San Diego were summoned to Los Angeles on 11/28/69....Upon their arrival, they were informed that due to numerous problems with the BPP in San Diego, including the recent raid on the BPP Headquarters, the BPP Branch in San Diego was being dissolved."[12] The author of the memorandum also remarked that, "as a direct result of the raid [informants] have reported that [name deleted] has been severely beaten up by other members of the BPP due to the fact that she allowed the officers to enter BPP Headquarters the night of the raid." A separate memo indicates that, during the raid, confidential BPP files were "obtained" as well.[13] As this case demonstrates, harassment arrests can create destructive spirals that tornado through the ranks of a social movement organization.

Another common aspect of harassment arrests is the imposition of inflated or exorbitant bails and jail sentences. During the protests that coincided with the Republican Party's national convention in Philadelphia in 2000, John Sellers, Director of the Ruckus Society, an organization based in Berkeley, California that offers training in non-violent resistance and civil disobedience tactics, was arrested as he walked down the street chatting on his cell phone after a small, peaceful protest. Although he was only charged with misdemeanors, his bail was set at $1 million, much more than most bails for felony charges.[14] Sellers was charged with conspiracy, possession of an instrument of crime, reckless endangerment, and obstruction of justice. Sellers's attorney, Larry Krasner, called the bail "intergalactic" and remarked, "It's a ridiculous, punitive, unconscionable pre-emption of his going to the rest of the Republican Convention and the upcoming Democratic convention."[15] Bail for three other protesters who the Philadelphia police labeled "ringleaders" was set at $400,000 to $500,000, although only one of them was charged with a felony, throwing a bicycle at Philadelphia Police Chief

John Timoney.[16] Later, a judge lowered Sellers' exorbitant bail to $100,000, but not before Sellers and his lawyers were forced to expend significant time and resources that could have been directed toward political dissent.[17] During those same protests in Philadelphia, police also raided a warehouse where protesters were making art. The art was confiscated, seventy protesters were arrested on misdemeanor charges such as refusing to identify oneself, and bails were set in many cases at $50,000, uncharacteristically high for such petty charges.[18]

In terms of inflated jail sentences, one need not look farther than the jailing of Fred Hampton in Maywood, Illinois for the alleged theft of $71 worth of ice cream bars. For this minor crime, Hampton was sentenced to two to five years. The mayor of Maywood testified at Hampton's trial that the police's key witness who pointed out Hampton in a line-up had a "vendetta" against the young Panther leader. The mayor's testimony wasn't heeded, however, and Hampton was sent away to Menard Prison.[19] Similarly when George Jackson—one of the three Soledad Brothers—was eighteen years old he was handed an indeterminate sentence in prison—one year to life—for his role as driver when an acquaintance stole $70 from a gas station.[20]

Dissidents are also sometimes held in jail for long periods after being detained with no charges being brought against them, or with charges changed as time goes by. Jailed protesters at the "Battle of Seattle" protests against the World Trade Organization in 1999, for instance, were forced to sit on public buses for hours with their hands bound and no public restrooms available.[21] Another example is the "Los Angeles 8," a group of Palestinians and one Kenyan who were arrested by the INS and FBI in January and February 1987 for their affiliation with the Popular Front for the Liberation of Palestine (PFLP). While the six who were resident aliens were charged by the INS with technical visa violations, the other two, who were permanent residents, were charged under the 1952 McCarran-Walter Act for advocating the "doctrines of world communism." When Congress repealed this Act in 1990, the charges conveniently shifted to association with a group that advocates the destruction of property, and then later to affiliation with a group that advocates attacks on government officials. Finally, the U.S. government settled on the charge of providing material support to a foreign terrorist organization (FTO). According to Cole and Dempsey, "As the case progressed, it became clear that the INS was seeking to deport the LA 8 precisely because the FBI disapproved of their political activities." The deportation proceedings dragged on through 1999, when the U.S. Supreme Court handed down a decision that argued the LA 8 did not have a right to object to their possible deportation based on the First Amendment, even though, had they been U.S. citizens, they would have enjoyed this protection.[22]

As already mentioned—and as evident in the arrest of the Ruckus Society's John Sellers—harassment arrests often have a pre-emptive hue. To state the obvious, if dissidents can be kept in jail—even if only temporarily—they can't participate as activists. This logic was also prevalent during the urban rebellions in Los Angeles, Detroit, and Chicago in 1965 through 1968, when "in each city bail was set so as to ensure that those arrested would be 'kept off the streets' at least for the duration of the revolt." In all three cities, "both judges and prosecutors publicly articulated this policy of preventive detention."[23] Similarly, in late September 2002, during the IMF and World Bank protests in Washington, DC, nearly 650 protesters were preemptively scooped up and arrested for failing to obey a police order while participating in a rally in Pershing Park and Freedom Plaza. However, according to eyewitnesses, no police order to disperse was ever communicated, and, in fact, people who attempted to vacate the area were physically stopped by the police and re-corralled into the mass of people. One protester—who wasn't resisting arrest—had his ribs broken when police knocked him down. The Friday afternoon demonstration was attended by many who planned to spend the entire weekend protesting. Instead, many of them sat in jail. The cordoning-off and execution of strategic arrests at a peaceful rally also set the tone for the weekend: if one were a protester, one knew in the back of one's mind that one could, at any moment, be encircled by police and arrested, if not physically injured.[24] Two of the groups involved have filed suit for what they see as unconstitutional arrests. The DC City Council's Judiciary Committee also voted to begin an investigation of alleged police misconduct for wrongfully arresting protesters and for using excessive force.[25] In January 2005, DC government was forced to pay out $425,000 to seven of the protesters who were wrongfully caught up in this mass arrest. A number of other lawsuits are still pending, including a class-action suit filed on behalf of all the protesters who were arrested that day.[26]

Harassment arrests also sometimes entail violations of due process procedures, as well as the fabrication of evidence to provide the state with grounds to arrest, and sometimes even to convict. In early May 1971, when dissidents blocked traffic at intersections and on bridges in Washington, DC in order to protest the Vietnam War, the police responded by arresting 7,000 people. "In effect," remarked Fred Halstead, "the cops used preventive detention, suspending their normal procedures and making no pretense of concern for civil liberties." In order to deal with the approximately 12,000 protesters, the state amassed 5,000 police officers, 2,000 members of the National Guard, and 8,000 soldiers and Marines. On 3 May, these forces were assembled to meet a protest march at the edge of the Fourteenth Street Bridge. One witness described the convening of war protesters and state forces this way:

"A cop hit someone in the front line over the head with a club. The tear gas started going off all around us. There was a Black kid shouting that the cops had broken his arm. There was no way to hold the march together."[27] Amid the pandemonium, law enforcement forces arrested people in broad sweeps; as a result, a number of innocent bystanders were inadvertently arrested, including a couple on their way to their wedding ceremony, an off-duty police officer, a U.S. Army lieutenant, medics who were giving aid to the injured, and a reporter from the *Washington Star*. Because the DC-area jails were jam-packed, those detained were funneled into the local stadium and coliseum where they were left without food or bathrooms for many hours. Some detainees had it much worse. According to one witness-participant, Jot Kendall,

> They packed seventeen of us in one small holding-cell for forty-eight hours. It was dirty, no water in the toilet. We had to organize rotation to lie down. It was so tight one person at all times had to stand on the toilet, or sit on it if they could bear it. The Red Cross sent us sandwiches the first day, but the jailers didn't give them to us until the next day and they were loaded with mayonnaise. A lot of us got very sick from it. I still think the cops did that deliberately.[28]

While the sweeping arrests and "preventive detention" cleared the streets of many protesters, they did not result in many arrests that could hold up in court. In the end, there were less than one hundred convictions. The American Civil Liberties Union (ACLU), representing a group of the falsely arrested, later won a $12 million judgment.[29]

Churchill and Vander Wall view evidence fabrication as a "widely used FBI tactic" that allows for the detention, arrest, or prosecution of "key individuals," as well as "the withholding of exculpatory evidence which might serve to block the conviction of these individuals." Under this rubric, they also include witness intimidation and the exploitation of physical, emotional, and mental coercion to acquire damaging, albeit false, testimony.[30] Of course, the fabrication of evidence has a long history in the U.S. One case from the early-twentieth century, involves Marcus Garvey, the founder of the Universal Negro Improvement Association (UNIA), the most extensive black nationalist movement in the history of the United States.[31] After arriving in the United States from Jamaica in March 1916, Garvey quickly built up a mass following, relying largely on the support of the black poor. It did not take long for Garvey to attract the interest of alienated blacks who felt disillusioned by the de facto disenfranchisement they experienced, as well as by the many unfulfilled promises of white USAmerica. It also did not take him long to get the attention of the FBI, which viewed him as a serious threat. In fact, Churchill and Vander Wall note, "the decision to bring about his elimination had been made at the highest level of the Bureau long before any hint of criminal conduct could be attached to him."[32] In a letter written in 1919 from future FBI Director J. Edgar Hoover to the U.S. Attorney General, Hoover was clearly fishing for a pretext to have Garvey deported:

> Unfortunately, however, he has not as yet violated any federal law whereby he could be proceeded against on the grounds of being an undesirable alien, from the point of view of deportation. It occurs to me, however, from the attached clipping that there might be some proceeding against him for fraud in connection with his Black Star Line propaganda and for this reason I am transmitting the communication to you for your appropriate attention.[33]

Black Star Line was a shipping line established under the umbrella of the UNIA in 1919. It was used to carry people, mail, and freight, and was an important logistical component of Garvey's "back to Africa" repatriation project.[34]

The Bureau didn't simply search for damning information from the outside: infiltrators were also inserted into the UNIA in an effort to dredge enough evidence to begin deportation proceedings. This indirectly led to a number of charges being brought against Garvey, from conspiracy to tax evasion to the charge that ultimately led to the single—but necessary, from the state's perspective—conviction: using the mail to defraud. With questionable evidence injected into the court proceedings, Garvey was convicted of mail fraud and sentenced to five years in jail. After two years in an Atlanta federal prison, President Calvin Coolidge commuted his sentence and Garvey was deported as "an undesirable alien."[35] In the end, the U.S. government was able to suppress the dissidence of someone who, in Hoover's estimation, was "one of the most prominent Negro agitators" and "an exceptionally fine orator" skilled at "creating much excitement" among black people, excitement that could coalesce into concerted efforts toward racial and social justice.[36]

Suppressing the Press

Looking at media coverage of the Vietnam War, conventional wisdom supports the oppositional media thesis, which asserts that as the war proceeded—and especially after the Tet Offensive of 1968—an increasingly oppositional news media emerged to challenge governmental authority.[37] A corollary to this thesis is that the press was free from governmental interference and that this freedom extended to the underground press as well. This is, according to Michael Linfield, a myth:

> The underground papers during the Vietnam War faced the same type of governmental repression as did the opposition press during the Alien and Sedition Acts 160 years earlier—editors were jailed, presses were bombed, reporters were harassed, news vendors were arrested, newsrooms were infiltrated by government spies, businesses were intimidated from advertising in the papers and numerous publications were forced to close due to government harassment.[38]

By 1969, there were at least five hundred underground papers in the United States.[39] The more these publications printed investigative accounts of governmental malfeasance, the more governmental attention they received. Newspaper editors and writers were arrested on minor charges not directly related to their political statements, but related to the acts these statements inspired. According to underground media scholar Geoffrey Rips, these arrests constituted "a deliberate attempt to silence an adversary voice." Faced with the prospect of trials on minor charges, unable to meet high court costs, and besmirched by public allegations of illegal activity, many underground papers were driven out of business, and therefore fully suppressed. Many of these charges stemmed from the alleged use of illicit drugs, and raids of underground paper headquarters were also justified on such grounds. Even when drugs were not found during a raid, equipment was often damaged by raiding state agents. The state also leveled obscenity charges in order to crush the dissident underground press.[40]

Another way the state squelched the dissident press—and dissident social movements generally—was through fine-toothed Internal Revenue Service audits of their finances. The CIA had a particularly close relationship with the IRS, and frequently had it investigate the Agency's political foes. When *Ramparts* was about to break a story about the CIA's covert funding of the National Student Association, the Agency tried to invent a legal rationale that would enable the courts to prevent publication. When these efforts failed, the CIA pressured the IRS to audit *Ramparts'* corporate tax returns, as well as the personal tax returns of Edward Keating, its publisher.[41] When such harassment failed to turn up any wrongdoing, the CIA pressed forward, initiating a propaganda campaign against *Ramparts* through "friendly" mass-media sources like nationally syndicated columnist Carl Rowan.[42] The IRS also worked closely with the FBI to audit "key activists" as part of COINTELPRO.[43] After investigating the IRS/FBI relationship, the Church

Committee concluded that "the FBI has had free access to tax information for improper purposes," and that the FBI used legally acquired tax information supplied by citizens to the government "as a weapon against the tax-payer."[44] A wide range of dissidents were harassed through the IRS, including New Left activists as well as Martin Luther King Jr. and the SCLC. When the IRS was unable to unearth any illegal activity on the part of King and the SCLC, Director Hoover reportedly scribbled, "what a farce" across the memo that conveyed this information.[45] The IRS's extra-meticulous audits of the tax returns of individual dissidents and social movement organizations provided the requisite material for both the harassment arrests of individuals as well as the revocation of non-profit status for activist organizations.

Taking Aim at AIM Again (and Again)

The American Indian Movement was also the victim of harassment arrests. In 1981, the Subcommittee on Civil and Constitutional Rights in the House of Representatives found that the Battle of Wounded Knee in 1973 resulted in 562 arrests. Federal grand juries indicted 185 people, and out of these there were only fifteen convictions, which the Subcommittee viewed as "a very low conviction rate considering the usual rate of conviction in Federal Courts and a great input of resources in these cases."[46] Indeed, this was "a very low conviction rate." Fifteen convictions out of 562 arrests translated to a less than 3% arrest-to-conviction rate, and many of the arrests that did not result in convictions may be considered harassment arrests, in the sense that, even when convictions were not obtained, the arrests reverberated throughout the Indian community. According to one of AIM's attorneys in the Wounded Knee trials, Ken Tilsen, these arrests were carried out "to neutralize an organization whose politics the FBI objects to by tying up the organization in an unending series of trials and pretrial incarcerations, and in bankrupting the organization by forcing it to meet massive amounts of bail."[47] As Churchill and Vander Wall describe the case of AIM leader Russell Means:

> Means was charged with a total of thirty-seven felonies and three mis-demeanors between 1973 and 1976. Of these he was exonerated thirty-nine times. The fortieth charge, which resulted in a conviction costing him a year in the South Dakota State Penitentiary, wasn't filed as a result of *any* of the "criminal activities" the Bureau attributed to him. Rather it was levied as a result of his frustrated and allegedly illegal behavior in court, near the end of the seemingly interminable Bureau-fostered trials which had drained his time, energy and other resources for more than two years.[48]

This case may well constitute the quintessential—or at least most egregious—example of harassment arrests as a suppressive tactic.

Angela Davis:
"The country's number one terrorist fugitive."

Another egregious instance involves Angela Davis. Davis, as a member of the Communist Party, an associate of the Black Panther Party, and a professor of philosophy at UCLA had earned the attention—indeed the wrath—of powerful state and national politicians like Ronald Reagan and Richard Nixon, as well as commanding federal investigative organizations like the FBI. Davis's dismissal from her teaching post at UCLA was not the end of her experiences with suppression. As previously mentioned, Davis was heavily involved with the Soledad Brothers Defense Committee. The Soledad Brothers were three African American men—John Cluchette, Fleeta Drumgo, and George Jackson—who were accused of murdering a prison guard at Soledad Prison in California.

On 7 August 1970, Jonathan Jackson, who had been working side-by-side with Davis to prevent the "legal lynching" of his brother, George, entered the Marin County Courthouse heavily armed. After sitting in the court's spectator section for a short while, Jackson leaped up—carbine in hand—and said, "All right gentlemen. This is it. I'm taking over now."[49] He proceeded to arm three of the prisoners and take the judge, an assistant district attorney, and three jurors hostage. Jackson and his cohorts demanded the release of the Soledad Brothers. When the group went outside and hopped into a rented van, they were met with a shower of bullets that killed four—Jackson, two prisoners, and the judge—and paralyzed the assistant district attorney for life.[50]

The story was actually much more complicated. The FBI—in concert with a number of California law enforcement agencies—had concocted the plan for Jackson using an infiltrator/agent provocateur, Melvin "Cotton" Smith who provided weaponry and logistical support. A number of Black Panthers were supposed to be involved in the action, but at the last minute, they backed out. However, no one informed Jackson of this, and he decided to proceed on his own. As planned by the Bureau, sharpshooters waited for the hostages and hostage-takers to leave the building. While they may have been surprised at the small number of people involved in the operation, this did not prevent them from firing upon the group.[51]

Soon it came to light that four of the guns that Jackson brought into the courtroom had been had been purchased by Angela Davis.[52] California law at the time dictated that anyone who abetted a murderer before the act of murder was also guilty of the crime, and so a warrant was issued for her arrest.[53] The law, Section 31 of the California Penal Code, read: "All persons concerned in the commission of a crime, whether it be a felony or misde-meanor, and whether they directly commit the act constituting the offense, or aid and abet in its commission, or, not being present, have advised and encouraged its commission...are principles in any crime so committed." Section 31 was passed into law in 1872 and had rarely been used. Its use in this instance therefore constituted selective enforcement, and many questioned its constitutionality.[54]

Within hours of the incident, Davis went underground, setting off a massive search. President Nixon called her "the country's number one terrorist fugitive."[55] FBI Director Hoover placed her on his list of "Ten Most Wanted" criminals in the United States, which thereby made Davis, according to her chief counsel, Howard Moore Jr., "a shooting target for any law enforcement officer, stomp-down racist or nut, had she shown her face. Any of them could have shot her down without so much as asking the time of day on the pretext they were slaying an escaping felon to prevent a failure of justice."[56] Many observers suspected she would resurface in Algiers, where Black Panther Eldridge Cleaver was seeking sanctuary, but in October the FBI found and arrested her in New York City. President Nixon congratulated the FBI on national television. In an editorial, the *New York Times* also back-slapped the FBI for its "brilliant investigative effort" as it condemned Davis supporters for wanting "to politicize her case, and to deflect attention from the specifics of the charges against her." The *Times* closed its editorial with a passage that glistened with paternalism: "Whatever the eventual outcome, the tragedy is that one who might have made a significant contribution to the nation's *normal* political debate and to its needed processes of peaceful change became so alienated that she finally went over to revolutionary words and perhaps even worse."[57] This editorial demonstrates in crystalline fashion how power defines what is "normal" and what is not.

After two months of legal battles over her extradition, Davis was ferried to California. In June 1971, she was denied bail entirely, despite the recommendation of the Marin County Chief Probation Officer. The judge himself said she was a solid candidate for release, but that his hands were tied because of his reading of an obscure section of the penal code for capital cases. The section in question was Section 1270, which said that all people charged with crimes were entitled to bail except in capital cases when the presumption of guilt was strong or when there was overwhelming evidence to convict.[58] On 18 February 1972, the California Supreme Court abolished the death penalty, deeming it cruel and unusual punishment, and thereby eliminating the category of capital offense.[59] After a massive outpouring of "Free Angela" energy from both international and domestic sources, the judge soon set bail for Davis at $100,000, noting the enormity and intensity of public demand.[60] On 4 June 1972, in what historian Bettina Aptheker viewed as "a trial reeking with chauvinist demagoguery, male supremacist stereotypes and anti-communism melodrama," the jury found Davis not guilty on all charges.[61] One of Davis's lawyers, Leo Branton, Jr., said in the aftermath of the acquittal, "If Angela Davis were not Angela Davis, she would never have been prosecuted."[62]

Hounding the Panther:
The Harassment of Elmer "Geronimo" Pratt

A final example of harassment arrests is the case of Elmer "Geronimo" Pratt. After graduating from high school in Morgan City, Louisiana, Pratt opted to join the Army. He did this in order to gain the skills necessary to become part of "a new generation of black warriors," who could protect his people from the Ku Klux Klan, which had a strong presence where Pratt grew up.[63] Pratt was shipped to Vietnam where he served two tours (a year and a half in total), earning almost twenty combat decorations including the Silver Star, the Bronze Star, and the Purple Heart.[64] In Vietnam, he began thinking critically about the war, and U.S. society more generally: "After a while I began to see the war as another kind of racism. In boot camp and advanced infantry training all we ever heard was 'gooks,' 'Buddha-heads,' 'slopes,' same way our daddies heard 'Krauts' and 'Japs.' You got to make people subhuman before you kill 'em. I saw things I don't want to remember. I *did* things I don't want to remember." Pratt decided he had enough, and the Army granted him an honorable discharge.[65]

Upon returning to Morgan City, a town elder suggested he contact Alprentice "Bunchy" Carter, who was also from Louisiana, but was now living in Los Angeles where he had founded a branch of the Black Panther Party. Pratt acted on this advice and drove to Los Angeles where he met Carter. The two took to each other immediately, and soon Carter gave Pratt a new name: Geronimo ji Jaga, or "Geronimo of the Jaga," a respected group of African warriors. Many people continue to refer to Pratt by this name.[66]

Pratt became Carter's bodyguard and, following Carter's lead, he enrolled in UCLA's High Potential Program. When not in class, Pratt immersed himself in Panther organizational work and trained his fellow Panthers in infantry and munitions.[67] Pratt was considered such an effective organizer and motivator that he was seen by BPP higher-ups as a future Panther leader. In fact, when Carter and John Huggins were gunned down by the United Slaves organization in January 1969, the LA-BPP found an audiocassette tape that Carter had left in case he was killed. On this tape, Carter named Pratt as his successor as top man in the LA-BPP as well as the chapter representative on the Party's national Central Committee.[68]

Around this time, Pratt was also attracting the attention of the FBI and the LAPD's Urban Counterinsurgency Task Force, a group also known as "the Panther Unit." At the FBI's Los Angeles Field Office he was added to the "Key Black Extremist" list and placed on the National Security Index.[69] Once designated a "Key Black Extremist" by the FBI, Pratt found himself the victim of a series of harassment arrests.

This sort of thing wasn't devised especially for Pratt, however. It was already an established practice in the state's dealings with the Panthers. Between May 1967 and December 1969 members of the BPP were slapped with 768 arrests, and $4,890,580 had to be diverted from other Panther projects in order to post bail. Obviously, this was a tremendous drain on the BPP's resources.[70] Also, according to Panther lawyer Charles R. Garry, of this almost $5 million in bail money, more than $200,000 of it was non-refundable bail-bond premiums.[71] This was all occurring in a time when the BPP was growing, and these resources surely would have furthered that growth.

While President Nixon was pushing his "law and order" message and Assistant Attorney General Jerris Leonard was making public comments like "The Black Panthers are nothing but hoodlums and we've got to get them," FBI Field Offices across the country were given the green light to concoct creative ways to have Panthers arrested. The San Diego Field Office, for example, in an attempt to shut down the BPP's newspaper, *The Black Panther*, suggested three specific statutes that might be used against them: a state tax law regarding printing equipment, a "rarely used transportation tax law," and a zoning law concerning businesses in residential areas.[72] In Los Angeles, the LAPD's Urban Counterinsurgency Task Force turned up the throttle on its harassment of the Panthers. According to Jack Olsen, this Task Force,

> stepped up its program of stopping Panther cars and rousting the occupants. Party documents were thrown into gutters. Bundles of the newspaper the *Black Panther* disappeared in sewers. Police would order a driver to the curb, break his taillight, then stop him a few blocks away for defective lights. Panthers were arrested on suspicion of crimes ranging from reckless driving to murder and held in the labyrinthine 77th Division station, the oldest in the city, where they were interviewed, photographed and had their names added to intelligence files as high-risk offenders. At night officers shuttled detainees from precinct to precinct so they couldn't be bailed out. Sometimes the arresting officers

drew their guns, ordered their victims to their knees and fired random shots into the ground or over their heads.[73]

An official statement by the ACLU in December 1969 came to the conclusion that "the style of law enforcement applied to the Black Panthers has amounted to provocative and even punitive harassment, defying the constitutional rights of Panthers to make political speeches or distribute political literature." The statement also pointed out that, despite the wide array of charges leveled at individual Panthers, "Seldom have these charges held up in court [and] often they have been dropped by the prosecutor prior to trial."[74]

Geronimo Pratt's treatment at the hands of the Los Angeles police and the FBI mirror this general pattern. An internal FBI document dated 26 June 1970 refers to the fact that "constant consideration is given to the possibility of the utilization of counterintelligence measures with efforts to being directed toward neutralizing PRATT as an effective BPP functionary." The teletype concluded by saying that the Bureau "Will continue to follow and report activities of ELMER PRATT in view of his being the BPP Minister of Defense." This document also acknowledged the existence of a "Black Nationalist Photo Album" that the FBI maintained, and it noted that Pratt's picture was included in it.[75]

This close attention from the Bureau makes sense, given the treatment Pratt was receiving on the streets even before the memo was written. In early April 1969, he was arrested by the LAPD along with another BPP leader, Roger "Blue" Lewis, on a supposed tip for the possession of an explosive device. The case did not go to trial until 1972. Later that month he was arrested again, this time for the kidnapping of BPP member Ollie Taylor. He was acquitted of these charges in April 1971. In mid-June 1969, Pratt was brought in for questioning regarding the murder of BPP member Frank Diggs. All charges against Pratt in this case were soon dropped.[76] It appears that the FBI had even bigger plans for Pratt; internal Bureau memos indicate that the FBI was making a concerted effort to implicate Pratt in a bank robbery. The document reads: "A bank robbery conspiracy case is being opened in the Los Angeles Office on ELMER PRATT…appropriate investigation *to attempt to develop a conspiracy case* will be considered."[77] This plan was later dropped, as there was no evidence of BPP involvement in the bank robbery.

An arrest warrant was later written for Pratt, accusing him of aiming a machinegun at a passing police car. Evidence was never brought to bear on this charge, but it was part of the justification for the LAPD's raid of the LA-BPP's Headquarters four days after the Chicago police had killed Fred Hampton and Mark Clark. As a result of this raid-turned-shootout, "a grab bag of seventy-two counts" was brought against Pratt.[78] In the end, nine Panthers, including Pratt, were convicted of conspiring to possess illegal weapons. As for the rest of the charges, Pratt was found not guilty. Johnnie Cochran, his lawyer at the time, later remarked: "I had never heard so many 'not guiltys' in my life."[79]

While awaiting trial after the shootout, Pratt was forced to remain in jail for two months until he could raise the $125,000 bail.[80] While in jail, more charges mounted. At one point, he was charged with felony assault when prison deputies claimed that he tried to attack them with a pencil. He was acquitted of this charge.[81] Later, when Pratt failed to show up for a court date because he was in Texas, a federal warrant was issued charging him with interstate flight to avoid prosecution. He was tracked down and brought back to California where he was put in jail without bond.[82]

Meanwhile, Panther politics raged. A rift that developed between Eldridge Cleaver and Huey Newton led to Newton purging Cleaver supporters like Pratt, Pratt's wife Sandra, and many others from the Party. Then, on 11 November 1970, Pratt was told that his wife—who was eight months pregnant at the time—had been murdered and left along a freeway in Los Angeles. He was not allowed to attend the funeral.[83]

While in jail, Pratt learned that he was also being charged with the murder of Caroline Olsen, which had occurred on 18 December 1968. This case—nicknamed "the Tennis Court Murder"—was the only one in which major charges against Pratt would not end in acquittal. Although, as the murder was being committed in Santa Monica, Pratt was at a BPP meeting in Oakland, 400 miles away, charges were brought against him. There were massive holes in the prosecution's case, some of which were filled by completely fabricated evidence. When the FBI was asked for its surveillance records of the BPP meeting Pratt had attended at the same time as the murder, these records had mysteriously disappeared.[84] Also, the eyewitness to the crime—the victim's husband, Kenneth Olsen—identified Pratt as the killer, but only after he had already positively identified another man in a police line-up. Both Olsen and another eyewitness who fingered Pratt were coached by the LAPD, although neither this fact nor the fact that Olsen had first identified another man as the murderer of his wife were admitted in court.[85] Third, the murderer was clean-shaven, but Pratt had facial hair his entire adult life.[86] Nevertheless, Pratt was convicted of first-degree murder in July 1972 and sent to San Quentin Prison. His harassment arrests culminated in a frame-up job that landed him in prison for twenty-seven years.

After being denied parole sixteen times, Pratt was finally released from prison in 1997 when California Superior Court Judge Everett Dickey ruled that Pratt's murder trial was severely tainted because the prosecution relied on perjured evidence from infiltrator/agent-provocateur Julius "Julio" Butler, a key witness in Pratt's trial who had testified under oath that Pratt had bragged to him about the murder. The judge said that, if the defense had known that Butler was actually a paid informant for the FBI and LAPD, that information "could have put the whole case in a different light."[87] In 1999, a state appeals court refused to reinstate Pratt's murder conviction, ruling that it was "unable to profess confidence in a guilty verdict based solely on evidence unconnected to Butler."[88] Numerous supporters, including celebrities like Marlon Brando and Sean Penn, were able to finally rejoice in Pratt's freedom.[89] In April 2000, there was more reason to celebrate, as Pratt won approximately $4.5 million in a false imprisonment and civil rights lawsuit against the federal government and the City of Los Angeles.[90]

Pratt's case not only illuminates many common facets of harassment arrests—selective enforcement, exorbitant jail sentences, fabrication of evidence—but it also sheds light on many of the previously discussed modes of suppression, including surveillance, infiltration, badjacketing, and the use of agent provocateurs (both Melvin "Cotton" Smith and Julius "Julio" Butler played crucial roles in Pratt's arrests and convictions), as well as division-creating black propaganda, since Pratt was featured in a number of inflammatory cartoons penned by the FBI.[91]

Harassment arrests tend to combine with other suppressive tactics in common patterns. Clearly, surveillance allows the state an opportunity to gather information it can use to make harassment arrests, as it did with the surveillance of Maxwell Sanford's Revolutionary Action Movement in Philadelphia and protesters at the Republican National Convention in the same city more than three decades later.[92] Extraordinary rules and laws also intersect with harassment arrests. When the Soledad Brothers were on trial in 1970, there was tremendous public pressure on Judge Gordon Campbell. Protesters organized rallies outside the courthouse, and sometimes things even got rowdy inside the courtroom. This energy once led Judge Campbell to admonish members of the mostly black courtroom audience to "conduct themselves properly and not sit as if they were in a pool hall or at a barbecue table." He also pressured a state senator to introduce legislation that would make it illegal to picket outside the courthouse where he worked. Such pressure led to the passage of a law in September 1970 that read: "Any person who pickets or parades near a building which houses a court of this state with the intent to interfere with, obstruct, or impede the administration of justice, or with the intent to influence any judge, juror, witness or officer of the court in the discharge of his duty shall be guilty of a misdemeanor." This law enabled police to carry out even more harassment arrests.[93] The effect of such laws on the practice of dissent will be explored in the next chapter.

9
Extraordinary Rules and Laws

Extraordinary rules and laws are another form of "legal repression." During "exceptional" moments when the state is seriously challenged by dissident groups or individuals, it often responds in a way that allows it to both reassert order and maintain legitimacy. It sometimes does this by promulgating and executing laws and rules that are then used to suppress the challenge and stifle dissent.

According to Michael Hardt and Antonio Negri, in these crisis situations the state has two crucial advantages:

> (1) the capacity to define, every time in an exceptional way, the demands of intervention; and (2) the capacity to set in motion the forces and instruments that in various ways can be applied to the diversity and the plurality of the arrangements in crisis. Here, therefore, is born, in the name of the exceptionality of the intervention, a form of right that is really *a right of the police.* The formation of a new right is inscribed in the deployment of prevention, repression, and the rhetorical force aimed at the reconstruction of social equilibrium.

They further argue that the "juridical power to rule over the exception and the capacity to deploy police force are thus two initial coordinates" that characterize "the imperial model of authority."[1] In his essay, "In This Exile (Italian Diary, 1992–94)" social theorist Giorgio Agamben suggests that we are currently "living in the state of exception that has now become the rule."[2] This has serious implications for dissident citizens. Political scientist James L. Gibson designates this method of suppressing dissent as "repressive public policy." By this, he means "a statutory restriction on *oppositionalist political activity*" that affects "some, but not all, competitors for political power."[3]

U.S. history provides a plethora of examples of extraordinary rules and laws that, once enacted, have facilitated the state's three-pronged pursuit of maintaining order, sustaining legitimacy, and squelching dissent. As Howard Zinn has noted:

> It is ironic, but a historic truth, repeated again and again, that exactly at those moments when citizens need the greatest freedom to speak their

minds, exactly when life and death issues are involved, that is, when the
question is war or peace, it is then that our liberties are taken away. The
juggernaut of war crushes democracy, just when the nation claims it is
fighting for democracy.[4]

In this chapter, I explore three eras when laws and rules emerged as "the
juggernaut of war" rolled forward: (1) the Palmer Raids and the ensuing deportations during the World War I era; (2) the Japanese internment camps
during World War II; and (3) the post-9/11 roundup of potential dissidents
and the establishment of military tribunals as part of the so-called "War on
Terrorism." In a sense, the third case is a combination of the first two, in that
it is a mixture of summary deportation and open-ended detention.

U.S. history is full of instances when the U.S. government—tromping
the topography of "crisis"—wrote laws and acted on rules or executive orders that suppressed dissent, freezing activists in their tracks either temporarily or permanently. In fact, the historical roots of this sort of suppression
reach at least as far back as the crime of seditious libel—or statements that
impugn the authority of government. For a long time, sedition was pros-
ecutable regardless of whether what one said was true or not. The Sedition
Act of 1798—which codified seditious libel as "any false, scandalous and
malicious" writings, utterances, or publications against the government,
Congress, or the president, with intent to defame them, bring them into
contempt or disrepute, or excite against them the hatred of the people"—was
rescinded under the rule of President Thomas Jefferson. Even though the law
had been overturned, Leonard Levy, writing in 1960, asserted that, "seditious libel was—and still is—the principal basis of muzzling political dissent."[5] Seditious libel, whether explicitly delineated as such or not, wormed
its way into a number of pieces of legislation—even after Jefferson rescinded
the Act. In 1964, the U.S. Supreme Court ruled in *New York Times Co.
v. Sullivan* that seditious libel prosecutions violated the First Amendment.[6]
Thus Levy's characterization of seditious libel as "the principal basis of muzzling political dissent" needs to be updated and imbued with some nuance,
because, despite such court rulings, the spirit of seditious libel's criminality
lives on.

Many extraordinary laws and rules, it should be noted, were later repealed, rescinded, or otherwise abandoned once the crisis passed. Indeed
many are now looked back upon with historical disfavor. The Espionage Act
of 1917, passed in the throes of World War I, is one example. This Act made
it illegal to "willfully utter, print, write or publish any disloyal, profane, scur-
rilous, or abusive language" about the United States, or to "cause or attempt

to cause, or incite or attempt to incite, insubordination, disloyalty, mutiny, or refusal of duty, in the military or naval forces of the United States."[7] When this wasn't seen as strong enough, the law was amended in 1918 and became known as the Sedition Act. Violation of either Act could lead to a twenty-year prison sentence and/or a fine of $10,000.[8]

The Smith Act (a.k.a. the Alien Registration Act) of 1940—the first national sedition law during peace-time since the Alien and Sedition Acts of 1798—prohibited "the advocacy of insubordination, disloyalty, mutiny or refusal of duty in the military" as well as "the advocacy of the overthrow or destruction of any government in the United States by force or violence."[9] The McCarran Act, or the Subversive Activities Control Act of 1950, made it a crime for any group deemed a Communist-front organization to mail anything that was to be read by two people or more, unless the envelope in which it was sent was clearly marked with the warning label: "Disseminated by _____, a Communist organization." Also, Section 6 of the Act prohibited the granting of passports to "subversives." This was specifically meant for members of the Communist Party or any "Communist-front organization" who, if they applied for a passport, could receive a five-year prison sentence and a $10,000 fine.[10] As U.S. Secretary of State Dean Acheson explained in 1952, it was his legal obligation to refuse or withhold a passport to anyone he had "reason to believe" was a communist or whose "conduct abroad is likely to be contrary to the best interest of the United States."[11] Among the many dissidents who were denied passports were W.E.B. DuBois, Arthur Miller, Paul Robeson, Howard Fast, Paul Baran, Owen Lattimore, Ring Lardner Jr., and Supreme Court Justice William O. Douglas.[12] Countless others never even bothered to apply for passports, knowing they would be denied.[13]

Similarly, many foreign artists, scholars, and intellectuals were banned from entering the United States. According to informed estimates, by 1955, at least one hundred, and quite probably several hundred, foreign scientists had been denied visas.[14] From the 1940s through the 1970s, other "subversives" who were denied visas and therefore prevented from entering the U.S. included Pablo Picasso, Czeslaw Milosz, Graham Greene, Pablo Neruda, Dario Fo, Gabriel García Márquez, Hortensia Allende (widow of Salvador Allende), Julio Cortazar, Simone de Beauvoir, and anarchist historian George Woodcock.[15] In 1985, Farley Mowat, author of the teen literary classic *Never Cry Wolf*, was denied entrance by the Reagan administration for a book tour he had planned in the United States. Mowat, a Canadian, was turned away by the INS based on provisions in the 1952 McCarran Act.[16]

Once inside the U.S., visa revocation was also a possibility. Colombian journalist Patricia Lara had her visa revoked in 1986 when the State Department deemed her a threat who might engage in "subversive activities." She was expelled because, according to the Reagan administration, she had previously been a member of a group that was now considered to be a terrorist organization. Proof of her membership was never offered.[17]

In the wake of the attacks of 11 September 2001, the state has revived restrictions on travel. As part of the Aviation and Transportation Security Act of 2001, Congress mandated a federal "No Fly" list that, in theory, was meant to detect potential terrorists before they boarded airplanes. In practice, many dissident citizens have been stopped and questioned because their names were on the terrorist list. Twenty anti-war activists from a group called Peace Action Wisconsin were detained, forcing them to miss their flight, even though they had done nothing illegal, and even though only one of the twenty had a name that resembled a name on the no-fly list. Many months after the incident, the activists from Wisconsin still had not learned from the government why they were stopped.[18]

In 2003 Aquil Abdullah, member of the United States national rowing team, was stopped at Newark International Airport because his name appeared on the no-fly list. According to Andrew Kurpat, a police officer with the Port Authority in Newark, "What this means is that anyone with a common Muslim name has to be checked out, to see if it's an alias, to see if he's on a terrorist list."[19] Wade Henderson, a civil rights activist, responded to Abdullah's detention by writing, "Profiling is deeply ingrained in the culture of law enforcement. Not simply a matter of bad apples or a few rogue cops, profiling is systemic and demands reform at the highest levels of policy-making."[20] Profiling based on race, ethnicity, and religion sits at the heart of numerous post-9/11 anti-terrorism policies put forth by the Bush administration.

One reason the Transportation Security Administration (TSA) has experienced difficulty executing the no-fly list is its computer software, which relies on a 120-year-old indexing system used by many airlines' reservations systems. This airlines-reservation software mixes up the similar spelling or sounds of guiltless passengers' names with the names of supposed terrorists on the list, therefore creating "false positives." For example, due to assonance and syllabic similarity, the software cannot tell the difference between the names of terrorist leader Osama bin Laden and punk-rock star Johnny Rotten Lydon.[21] Also, people who find their names on the no-fly list, even though they are not terrorists, continue to be stopped, searched, and scrutinized, even after they had cleared their names and demonstrated their innocence. For example, everyone with the name "David Nelson" can expect to be "pulled from ticket lines, quizzed about their identities, asked to unpack their bags and told to slowly pull each ID and credit card from their wallets" regardless of whether they have gone through the entire routine before.[22] In short, the harassment of leftists plus computer glitches equals complications for dissident citizens attempting to fly.

Not only have extraordinary federal laws and regulations affected the practice of dissent, but so have state and local laws and rules. For instance, with anti-communism building to a crescendo after the Russian Revolution and the post-WWI strike wave in the U.S., thirty-three states passed "red-flag" state sedition or syndicalism laws during 1919–1920 alone. With the exception of four states, these laws were still in place at the onset of World War II.[23] Some state laws also banned certain dissidents from publicly speaking in certain places. For instance, in 1947, the Illinois legislature passed a law that forbade Communists to speak on University of Illinois system campuses.[24] The state of Texas went even further in the 1950s. Although the Governor of Texas was advocating the death penalty for communists, he settled for the Communist Control Act of 1951, which required communists who were visiting the state for more than five days to register themselves with the Department of Public Safety. Registration included fingerprinting and the answering of any questions the Department of Public Safety viewed as relevant. Violation of the law was a felony with a ten-year maximum prison sentence and a $10,000 maximum fine. Perhaps tired of the paperwork associated with this law, the Texas legislature decided to ban the Communist Party altogether in 1954. The sentences and fines also doubled those of the 1951 Act, vaulting to a twenty-year prison term and a $20,000 fine.[25]

More recently, localities have promulgated laws that mandate waiting periods for obtaining protest permits. In Dearborn, Michigan, for example, one must wait thirty days or risk a 90-day jail term and a $500 fine.[26] Also, recently, many protesters have been confined to "designated protest zones," usually located far away from the people whom the protesters are trying to influence. People who refuse to limit their protest activities to these designated areas or who try to leave the zones to protest elsewhere have been arrested. These rules were exercised in Philadelphia and Los Angeles in 2000 at the Republican and Democratic National Conventions as well as more recently at the Democratic and Republican parties' 2004 national conventions. "Designated protest zones," which are ironically also called "free speech zones," have become commonplace on the outskirts of President George W. Bush's public appearances. At a Labor Day rally in Pittsburgh in 2002, people carrying pro-Bush signs were allowed to line the streets wherever they liked, while people with signs that were critical of the president were relegated to a protest zone that was a third of a mile away from the route. Those who refused to move—such as 65-year-old steelworker William Neel, who donned a sign reading "The Bushes must love the poor; they've created so many of us"—were arrested, though the charges were later dropped.[27]

The Palmer Raids

When the United States declared war on Germany in April 1917, radical dissident groups were wielding substantial influence in electoral politics, union policy, and other day-to-day organizational activity. These groups made major inroads with previously inactive citizens, especially throughout the rest of 1917. Not surprisingly, given the threat they posed, these groups became the concern of state officials who wanted to maintain the status quo, if not tighten their grip on power. Therefore, according to Goldstein, "Organizations which identified themselves as against the war, or which were identified as such in the public mind" experienced "a vicious campaign of repression against them on the part of the federal, state and local governments."[28] This suppression, which was tremendously effective in silencing or otherwise minimizing the success of the anti-war movement, continued into 1919. When there was a subsequent resurgence of radical activity, it was met with what became known as the Red Scare of 1919. According to Goldstein, this Red Scare "was a very rational response on the part of government and business elites who accurately perceived that extremely serious threats to the status quo were developing."[29] This "rational response" culminated in the Palmer Raids of 1919–1920.

A. Mitchell Palmer was the Attorney General under President Woodrow Wilson. Known as an ardent foe of radical politics, Palmer was a major proponent of the Espionage and Sedition Acts of 1917 and 1918. He also attempted to persuade J. Edgar Hoover—a twenty-something lawyer who was head of the Justice Department's Alien Radical Division at the time—that a peacetime sedition law was necessary in order to thoroughly thwart the publication and distribution of any and all radical texts.[30] As Palmer once phrased it, "There could be no nice distinction drawn between the theoretical ideas of the radicals and their actual violations of any national laws." Palmer felt the U.S. simply needed to get rid of these "criminal aliens" whom he considered "alien filth."[31]

According to historian Robert K. Murray, "The word 'radical' in 1919 automatically carried with it the implication of dynamite," and in June of that year, as part of a string of violent political actions, Attorney General Palmer's house was bombed by anarchists. Palmer saw the bombings as an outward manifestation of a Bolshevik master plot to overthrow the U.S. government and to institute communism.[32] Palmer's allegations not only represented an attempt to demonize dissidents, but also demonstrated his ignorance of the differences between anarchists and Bolsheviks. Murray B. Levin explains that in this time frame—the late-1910s and early-1920s—all labor actions, including strikes, were incorrectly seen as proof of Bolshevik influence. The press framed events so as to encourage such a viewpoint.[33] With such monomaniacal simplemindedness as a backdrop, the bombing of the Attorney General's house galvanized the "Red Raids"—what became known as the Palmer Raids—which have been characterized by Michael Linfield as "one of the most massive campaigns of civil liberties violations against non-Third World minorities in U.S. history."[34]

By July 1919, immigration officials had received orders from their upper ranks to concentrate on "alien radicalism." Later that summer, the Commissioner General of Immigration, Anthony Caminetti, interpreted these new orders quite plainly for the House Appropriations Committee: "A dragnet inquiry would be made and search instituted for suspected anarchists and radicals of all kinds."[35] The dragnet was put into action on 7 November when Palmer, working in concert with the FBI, executed a nationwide raid against the Union of Russian Workers in which approximately 250 union leaders and members were apprehended. This was followed by a bigger raid the following night, when, in New York City alone, seventy-three centers of dissident activity were raided, resulting in the arrest of more than 500 people. In the end, 246 of those detained were deemed deportable.[36] Then, on 21 December, 249 "Reds" were loaded aboard the *Buford* and shipped to Soviet Russia. Among the deportees were the well-known anarchists Emma Goldman and Alexander Berkman.[37] Before she left, the *New York Times* reported Goldman said, "Incidentally, I am coming back. I am not going to stop my work as long as life remains."[38] Upon their departure, William J Flynn, the Director of the FBI, said the deportees represented "the brains of the ultra-radical movement," a phrase that was plastered throughout the mass media. The 249 were sent off so hastily that a number of them were not even allowed to secure warm clothes for what promised to be a frigid voyage.[39]

Then, on 30 December 1919, in preparation for the largest of the Palmer Raids, the Department of Labor re-instituted a vague but revealing rule that stipulated foreigners would only be able to obtain legal counsel *after* the interests of the U.S. government had first been safeguarded.[40] Or, as Caminetti spun it for the House Appropriations Committee, an "alien" would be able to testify by "telling the truth in most instances as he saw it, *without being hampered by the advice of counsel.*"[41] Three days later, on 2 January 1920, the FBI turned its attention to communists, simultaneously raiding the meeting halls, headquarters, and newspaper editorial offices of the Communist Party and the Communist Labor Party in thirty-three cities.[42] Almost every single local and national leader from these two parties was arrested. In the end, at least 4,000 non-citizens were apprehended, and many—approximately 1000 of them—were summarily deported. Other estimates of those detained during the raids range upwards of 10,000.[43] In this synchronized swirl of activity, formalities like arrest warrants were often abandoned. Once in detention, many prisoners were kept incommunicado and prevented from seeking legal counsel. Prison conditions were horrific.[44] One detainee, Mrs. Vasilierwska, was held for six hours daily in a filthy bathroom, before she was taken to Deer Island Prison where conditions were intensely cold and the weather severe. In Detroit, more than 100 detainees were held in a police pen a mere twenty-four by thirty feet. Also, 800 people were kept for up to six days at a time in a dark, windowless hallway where they shared a single toilet and were occasionally denied food.[45]

While January 1920 was the height of the Great Red Scare, the Palmer Raids continued through May 1920, snatching up dissidents based on their political beliefs. These raids had a devastating effect on the Communist parties in the United States, driving them underground. As evidence of its outward demise, dues-paying members in the Communist Party declined from more than 27,000 in October 1919, the month before the initial raids, to about 1,700 in January 1920.[46] Attorney General Palmer offered an explanation for the raids in a subsequent article for *Forum* magazine. He said it was necessary "to tear out the radical seeds that have entangled American ideas in their poisonous theories" because "Like a prairie-fire, the blaze of revolution was sweeping over every American institution of law and order" and was "eating its way into the homes of the American workman, its sharp tongues of revolutionary heat were licking the altars of the churches, leaping into the belfry of the school bell, crawling into the sacred corners of American homes, seeking to replace marriage vows with libertine laws, burning up the foundations of society." Palmer wrote that he felt compelled to act, since information at the Department of Justice "showed that communism in this country was an organization of thousands of aliens, who were direct allies of Trotsky. Aliens of the same misshapen caste of mind and indecencies of character, and it showed that they were making the same glittering promises of lawlessness, of criminal autocracy to Americans, that they had made to the Russian peasants."[47]

Palmer's hyperbolic prose aside, with the "Red Raids" the U.S. government stood on shaky legal ground. According to historian Howard Zinn, "The Constitution gave no right to Congress to deport aliens, but the Supreme Court had said, back in 1892, in affirming the right of Congress to exclude Chinese, that as a matter of self-preservation, this was a natural right of the government."[48] Schmidt concurs, writing, "the Justice Department and the Bureau were acting without any legitimate legal basis whatsoever."[49] J. Edgar Hoover was aware of, though not impeded by, this fact. In an internal memorandum he admitted there was "no authority under the law permitting this Department to take any action in deportation proceedings relative to radical activities."[50] Palmer, too, acknowledged this dearth of legal standing, albeit in characteristically flashy fashion, saying, "we have been compelled to clean up this country almost unaided by any virile legislation."[51] The deportations after the raids were not subject to the ruling of a judge or jury since they were not criminal proceedings per se. They were conducted by immigration officials who could change the ground rules at a moment's notice—and did. Nevertheless, regardless of the paucity of legal justification, the Palmer Raids, as carried out on the back of extraordinary rules, decimated dissident groups, undoing years of social-movement activity.[52]

Japanese Internment Camps

During the lead-up to the United States' entrance into World War II, and throughout the war itself, expressing dissenting views made one vulnerable to being labeled a "subversive." Goldstein goes as far as to write, "by virtually any measure, World War II was pretty much a disaster for civil liberties." He found the "ratio of repression to dissent" extremely high, in that "there was probably more repression during World War II in *relation* to the amount of dissent voiced, than in any period in American history, with the possible exception of the 1950–54 period."[53] Even people who were not expressing dissent found themselves yanked into the vortex of state suppression. The most egregious example of this is the internment of Japanaese and Japanese-Americans in the early-1940s. This tragic example of overzealous state control is an instructive precursor to the "preventative detention" that the U.S. government carried out after the terrorist attacks of 11 September 2001.

Analysts in the early-1940s tended to offer positive assessments of the Roosevelt administration's respect for civil liberties during the war. For instance, the ACLU wrote in June 1944 that under Roosevelt's watch there had been an "extraordinary and unexpected record of the first two years [of the war] in freedom of debate and dissent on all public issues and in the comparatively slight resort to war-time measures of control or repression of opinion." The ACLU went on to note the striking contrast between the state of civil liberty in the first eighteen months of World War II and the massive clampdown on dissent during World War I, remarking that the "country in World War II is almost wholly free of those pressures which in the first World War resulted in mob violence against dissenters, hundreds of prosecutions for utterances...in savage sentences for private expressions of criticism; and in suppression of public debate of the issues of the war and of the peace."[54] These alternative assessments aside, one situation that almost all commentators tend to agree was an unnecessary wartime precaution—at least in retrospect—is the preventive detention of the Japanese and Japanese-Americans in internment camps, a euphemism for concentration camps.[55] Milton S. Eisenhower—who was charged with the responsibility of running the camps—preferred to use the terms "relocation camps" and "evacuation centers."[56] Nevertheless, President Roosevelt himself unintentionally referred to the evacuation centers as "concentration camps."[57]

On 19 February 1942, shortly after the bombing of Pearl Harbor, Franklin Delano Roosevelt's Executive Order 9066 authorized the evacuation, relocation, and detention of 110,000 people of Japanese ancestry who were living on the West Coast.[58] Under the order, all people of Japanese ancestry were moved from the western areas of Oregon and Washington, the southern part of Arizona, and all of California. Some of this occurred voluntarily, but much of it was imposed by the U.S. Army.[59] Almost two-thirds of those detained were born in the United States, and Roosevelt offered no evidence that those detained were working to support the Japanese war effort or fomenting sustained dissident opposition to the war.[60]

This is the same Roosevelt who called the Japanese perpetrators of the attack on Pearl Harbor "barbarous," "uncivilized," "inhuman," and depraved."[61] The president and others were malicious toward people of Japanese descent, whether they were Issei (Japanese immigrants), Nisei (people born in the United States with Japanese immigrant parents), or Sansei (U.S.-born grandchildren of Japanese immigrants). According to Richard Drinnon, Roosevelt "viewed the Japanese and their descendents as innately bad, wherever they were, and as such fit for the great roundup."[62] In fact, according to Greg Robinson, "Several years before World War II started, Roosevelt became personally engaged in efforts to monitor Japanese Americans and to prepare plans for dealing with them as part of preparations for war with Japan, and he approved surveillance and tolerated racial discrimination in defense industries on the assumption that Nisei could not be trusted."[63] So, on Roosevelt's command, tens of thousands of U.S. citizens, who were not charged with any crime, were penned into enclosures with barbed-wire perimeters. Drinnon sets the number interned at precisely 119,803.[64] He described the encampments this way:

> In each camp were about a square mile of flimsy barracks, usually tar-papered, mess halls, schools, hospitals, stores, police stations and administration buildings. Military police patrolled the perimeters, served as sentries at the gates, and manned the guard towers, but were under orders to move into the centers only upon formal request from the WRA [War Relocation Authority].[65]

These camps also entailed forced labor, physical abuse, coercive draft-ing of young men for U.S. military service, and "the basic denial of com-mon decency." If the detainees attempted to escape these enclosures they could expect to be shot.[66] The U.S. government and Army also censored reading materials and seized Japanese phonograph records belonging to the detainees.[67] In terms of personal property, official internment policy only al-lowed relocated Japanese to bring what they could carry, forcing many to sell whatever they could before they left, or to simply abandon—and in many cases lose—their property.[68] In fact, the U.S. Federal Reserve calculated that Japanese-Americans lost approximately $400 million in property.[69] Robert J. Maeda, who as a child was sent to a concentration camp in Poston, Arizona, described his overall experience at camp as "a disruption of childhood, a fraying of those family intimacies that so often make childhood memories pleasurable."[70] In other words, being herded into these camps had the ef-fect of violently stretching, and sometimes even ripping, the social fabric of Japanese and Japanese-Americans living in the United States.

In sum, President Roosevelt willingly sent the Nisei to concentration camps, which clearly violated the constitutional rights usually granted to people born in the U.S.—rights like due process, habeas corpus, and equal protection under the law. In 1944, he was supported in doing this by the U.S. Supreme Court, which in *Korematsu v. the United States* upheld the constitutionality of Japanese internment, arguing that Roosevelt's Executive Order did not violate the Constitution's equal protection clause.[71] This dras-tic, wide-reaching policy was undertaken to preempt the possibility that any-one of Japanese ancestry would adopt a dissident stance in support of the Japanese during World War II.

It wasn't until the spring of 1943 that the WRA began to offer "leave clearance" to certain Japanese, letting them depart the camps and begin the resettlement process. Loyalty examinations were requisite to being granted such clearance.[72] The exclusion orders were not officially rescinded until 2 January 1945, when resettlement kicked into high gear.[73] Decades later, a "Redress Movement" successfully lobbied for a congressional inquiry into the matter of internment, and in 1980, Congress responded by creating the Commission on Wartime Relocation and Internment of Civilians (CWRIC), which in 1983 issued a report called "Personal Justice Denied." In this report the Commission asserted: "Executive Order 9066 was not justified by mili-tary necessity, and the decisions that followed from it—exclusion, detention, the ending of detention and the ending of exclusion—were not founded upon military considerations. The broad historical causes that shaped these decisions were race prejudice, war hysteria, and a failure of political leader-ship." Five years later, in 1988, President Reagan signed Congress's redress bill, which allotted $20,000 (tax-free) to each individual who had been sent to a concentration camp.[74] Reparation payments to the 60,000 survivors began in July 1990, a full forty-five years after World War II.[75]

The internment of Japanese and Japanese-Americans is striking in its intensity and scope. What many historians of the era gloss over is the concerted, courageous dissent that emerged from the Nisei and Issei who were rounded up and constricted in camps. In fact, there was organized resistance in internment camps across the country. Preemptive suppression generated a new dissent in response to that suppression. People of Japanese descent challenged internment in the courts, as with the *Korematsu* case. Some intentionally violated curfew laws and ignored evacuation orders, asserting such measure violated their Fifth Amendment rights. Still others deliberately plowed under their crops in order to undermine the war effort.[76] Cultural resistance within the camps also flourished, with Japanese language schools and ethnic places of worship well-attended. Unions also organized and even struck occasionally. After barbed wire fences and watchtowers were constructed at the Heart Mountain detention center in Wyoming, more than half the adults in the camp signed a petition in protest.[77] After a Kitchen Workers Union member was beaten by government authorities at the Manzanar relocation center in California, 3,000 to 4,000 detainees organized a march to protest. Eventually, the military police were called in to quell the dissent, spraying tear gas into the crowd and firing directly at the protesters, killing one and wounding more than ten others.[78]

This was not the only death from the barrel of a military police gun. On 11 April 1943, military police fired on James Hatsuaki Wakasa, a 63-year-old who was shot in the chest near the perimeter fence that surrounded the Topaz Relocation Center in Utah.[79] A year later, a sentry keeping watch fatally shot Soichi James Okamoto at the Tule Lake Camp in Northern California. The gunman was fined $1 for "the unauthorized use of government property" and then acquitted. Cultural resistance bubbled to the surface after Okamoto's cold-blooded killing, with numerous internees writing haiku in response:

> Dandelion has bloomed
> a moment of bitterness—
> of what consequence?

> Death of brethren
> mourning intensely
> rain falling drearily

Sending off comrade's hearse
last day of May
rain falling[80]

As these poems demonstrate, the psychological and corporeal violence of internment sliced powerfully into the traditions of natural and seasonal imagery common to haiku as a poetic form.

The Tule Lake Internment Camp became "the focal point of resistance" when it emerged as the place to segregate incorrigible, activist evacuees.[81] In early-1943, the WRA distributed a notorious loyalty questionnaire with two key questions. Question #27 read, "Are you willing to serve in the armed forces of the United States on combat duty, wherever ordered?" and Question #28 asked, "Will you swear unqualified allegiance to the United States and faithfully defend them from any or all attack by foreign or domestic forces, and forswear any form of allegiance or obedience to the Japanese emperor, or any other foreign government, power, or organization?" People who answered "yes" to both questions were dubbed "loyal" by the U.S. government and therefore made eligible for resettlement in another part of the U.S. or for service in the U.S. military. Those who answered "no" to one or both questions—or who refused to answer the questions entirely—were labeled "disloyal" and sent to Tule Lake.[82] This is how the Tule Lake camp became a segregation center that was, according to internment historian Barbara Takei, "a community filled with the most articulate dissident leaders and organizers from the other WRA camps."[83] Those who responded "no" to both questions eventually became known as "No-No's" or "No-No Boys," and they often found themselves under the piercing attention of the WRA's Internal Security police.[84] The WRA inserted infiltrators into the dissident ranks and used stockades to punish activist leaders. Thus, "the stockade became the omnipresent reminder of the keepers' arbitrary use of power at Tule Lake."[85] These drastic measures demonstrate the great lengths to which authorities were willing to go to produce docile bodies within the internment camps.

Preventive Detention and Military Tribunals after 9/11

Although there is wide support for the notion of civil liberties in the United States, Gibson has noted, "U.S. political culture has long distinguished between 'true Americans' and others and has always been willing to deny civil liberties to those who are 'un-American'….Thus citizens learn that civil liberties are indeed important to protect, but only for those who have a 'legitimate' right to liberty."[86] The preventive detention—or, internment—of the Japanese during World War II is a poignant example of this observation.[87] In moments of alleged national crisis, extraordinary rules and laws are fashioned and allowed to stand, even though they wouldn't earn serious consideration under "normal" conditions and have massive repercussions for the practice of dissent. Both the Palmer Raids and the Japanese internment are examples of the U.S. government's willingness to cast a wide net in the name of national security. This theme—civil liberties for some and not for others, usually foreigners—continues to rear its head, most recently with the detention of Arab and Muslim men in the wake of the terrorist attacks on 11 September 2001. Indeed, many aspects of the U.S. government's response to the events of September 11 borrow from extraordinary laws and rules from the past, including deportation, preventive detention, and an overall devaluing of the legal rights of foreign nationals.

After 9/11, the U.S. government—with Attorney General John Ashcroft leading the charge—moved quickly to detain foreign nationals who were allegedly connected to "terrorism" in any way. In the weeks after the attacks of September 11, more than 1,200 foreign nationals residing in the U.S. were arrested and detained indefinitely without any criminal charges being brought against them. The detentions were part of what the Justice Department was dubbing the largest criminal investigation in U.S. history. "It's an extraordinary number of people [to detain]," commented Beth Wilkinson, a former U.S. attorney who prosecuted the Oklahoma City bombing case, "but this is an extraordinary crime and investigation."[88] Of the 1,200 detainees, 718 were arrested for alleged immigration violations, while the rest, it may be presumed, were arrested either for criminal violations, as material witnesses, or on "unspecified suspicions." Approximately 40 percent of those detained were of Pakistani origin, while most of the rest were either Arab, Muslim, or both. Almost none of the detainees have been identified publicly by the U.S. government—aside from the 93 who were charged with criminal violations—owing largely to the highly secretive aura that has shrouded the detentions from the beginning.[89]

Stephen J. Schulhofer, a professor at New York University Law School, notes that these detentions may be unconstitutional, for three reasons: "the strict conditions of *secrecy* that surround the program, the *length* of the detentions, and the absence of any *judicial review* at key stages."[90] Over time, Ashcroft and the Justice Department have offered four rationales for such intense secrecy: (1) for the detainees' own protection, since "for us to either advertise the fact of their detention or to provide the suggestion that they are terrorists…would be prejudicial to their not only privacy interest but personal interest." It could even lead to violence being perpetrated against them, even if they were, in the end, not terrorists; (2) revealing the names of the detainees "may deter them from cooperating"; (3) releasing their names "would reveal the direction and progress of the investigation"; (4) abandoning such secrecy "could allow terrorist organizations and others to interfere with the pending proceedings by creating false or misleading evidence."[91]

Criticism like Schulhofer's even emerged from within the Justice Department itself. In a report issued in early-June 2003, the Justice Department Inspector General Glenn A. Fine reported that federal authorities detained many foreign nationals for excessive periods of time. Fine also concluded that there were "significant problems in the way the Sept. 11 detainees were treated," which included "a pattern of physical and verbal abuse by some correctional officers" where detainees were being jailed. For many detainees, conditions of confinement were, in sum, "unduly harsh."[92] The horrifying revelations that emerged from the Abu Ghraib prison scandal in the Spring of 2004 did nothing to improve the world's confidence in the way the U.S. government was treating its detainees.

The creation and use of military tribunals constitute another example of the principle that non-citizens are not necessarily entitled to the same constitutional rights as citizens when the government claims the country is in the midst of a "crisis." On 13 November 2001, President Bush signed a Military Order authorizing the establishment of military tribunals—or what some prefer to call "military commissions"—to try foreign nationals for terrorism-related charges. Military tribunals are essentially military courts with officers serving as judges. They operate separately from U.S. civil and criminal courts, and are designed to try non-U.S. citizens. According to Section 4 of Bush's order, "Any individual subject to this order shall, when tried, be tried by military commission for any and all offenses triable by military commission that such individual is alleged to have committed, and may be punished in accordance with the penalties provided under applicable law, including life imprisonment or death." Under the rules governing Bush's military tribunals, both conviction and sentencing only requires "the concurrence of two-thirds of the members of the commission present at the time of the vote, a majority being present."[93] Therefore, someone could be sentenced to death without a unanimous decision.

Barbara Olshansky and the Center for Constitutional Rights point out that this "unprecedented order" applies to more than 20 million non-citizens residing in the United States, most of whom are legal residents.[94] Defending the creation of the tribunals, Bush said he needed the unusual measure, "should we ever bring one of these Al Qaeda members in alive." He remarked in November 2001 that "The option to use a military tribunal in the time of war makes a lot of sense," especially in light of the notion that the nation was battling "against the most evil kinds of people, and [so] I need to have that extraordinary option at my fingertips."[95] A couple weeks later, in a different venue, he said, "The enemy has declared war on us. And we must not let foreign enemies use the forums of liberty to destroy liberty itself."[96]

The Military Order applies to non-U.S. citizens, which means legal permanent residents of this country as well as any other status for foreign nationals including people entitled to citizen status who have not officially been accorded that status. These non-citizens may be tried in front of a military tribunal if the president claims he has "reason to believe" that they are members of al-Qaeda, are involved in international terrorism, or have "knowingly harbored" people who meet those criteria. The Military Order never explicitly defines "international terrorism," however. According to Olshansky, it also "appears to extend the jurisdiction of the military commissions beyond trials concerning 'violations of the laws of war,' to those concerning violations of all 'other applicable laws.' This broad phrase could be easily invoked by the executive branch to use military commissions to try people accused of committing state and federal crimes that have no relationship whatsoever to any terrorist activity."[97] The military order affords the president remarkable discretion in terms of identifying who will be brought in front of the tribunals, creating the rules that will guide the operation of the tribunals, appointing the judges, prosecutors, and defense lawyers who will be involved, and delineating the sentence upon conviction as well as any appeals process that might take place.[98] Also, evidence typically not allowed in the civilian court system—such as hearsay—is admissible in the tribunals. Defendants can be tried and convicted with evidence neither they nor their lawyers were permitted to view. While evidence obtained through torture is inadmissible, any testimony coerced through methods a sliver shy of torture is acceptable.[99] In general, such procedures favor the prosecution and codify subservience to the executive branch.

Dick Cheney, summing up the rationale for military tribunals, asserted in November 2001: "The mass murder of Americans by terrorists, or the planning thereof, is not just another item on the criminal docket. This is a war against terrorism. Where military justice is called for, military justice will be dispensed."[100] Others have justified the tribunals by pointing to U.S. history. They note that the Supreme Court has traditionally supported presidential initiative in setting up military tribunals. In 1942, an eighteen-day, behind-closed-doors, military tribunal took place, resulting in the conviction—and subsequent execution—of eight German saboteurs dispatched by the Nazis to enter Florida and Long Island to wreak violence on U.S. war industries. The U.S. Supreme Court consented to these convictions in *Ex parte Quirin* in 1942. Also, in 1946, the Court condoned the conviction of a Japanese military commander operating in the Philippines. This case also resulted in a state execution.[101]

Moreover, during World War II, the Governor of Hawaii declared martial law and, as part of the Hawaii Organic Act, military tribunals replaced civilian courts.[102] In the 1946 case, *Duncan v. Kahanamoku*, the Supreme Court placed restrictions on these military courts, however, ruling that civilians could not be tried in them.[103] Nevertheless, Goldstein notes that when martial law was in place, the suppression of dissent "was so severe that martial law could not even be discussed in the mass media. During over twenty-two thousand military trials conducted in 1942, about 99 percent of defendants were found guilty; in some cases they were forced to give blood or purchase war bonds in addition to suffering jail sentences and fines."[104] Martial law was rescinded in Hawaii in 1944.

Military courts were previously instituted by President Lincoln during the civil war, resulting in the trials of up to 30,000 civilians. Habeas corpus was abandoned with abandon. Only at the end of the Civil War did the Supreme Court begin to curb Lincoln's wartime emergency powers. In 1866, the Court ruled in *Ex parte Milligan* that a civilian—Lambden P. Milligan—should have been tried in a civilian court rather than in front of a military tribunal since a civilian court was available and operating.[105]

Regardless of whether one believes tribunals are justifiable, they may well affect the practice of dissent. Their conceptual vagueness and elimination of a number of checks and balances may lead to the prosecution of dissidents who were not delineated under the original scope of the Military Order. This could have a serious chilling effect on potential activism. As the Pentagon continues to refine and adapt the rules under which the tribunals will operate, dissidents may well slip into the scope of tribunal justice, and this may be facilitated by terminology like "domestic terrorist."

On 3 July 2003, President Bush declared six unnamed "enemy combatants" eligible to be tried in front of a military tribunal. The Bush administration had adamantly refused to call detainees "prisoners of war" since that would mean treating them in accordance with the Geneva Conventions. The term "enemy combatants" gives the U.S. government legal reason to detain these individuals indefinitely. It appears the Bush administration wants to keep the option of using military tribunals when it can't obtain a conviction in the criminal courts.[106]

The Bush administration claims it can detain U.S. citizens as "enemy combatants," and it has the support of influential establishment organizations like the Council on Foreign Relations. William Haynes, in an article written for the Council's website, asserts that "The President has unquestioned authority to detain enemy combatants, including those who are U.S. citizens, during wartime." Reflecting the right-of-center position, Haynes defines an "enemy combatant" as "an individual who, under the laws and customs of war, may be detained for the duration of an armed conflict. In the current conflict with al Qaida and the Taliban, the term includes a member, agent, or associate of al Qaida or the Taliban. In applying this definition, the United States government has acted consistently with the observation of the Supreme Court of the United States in *Ex parte Quirin*." "Enemy combatants" come in two varieties: lawful and unlawful. According to Haynes, "Lawful combatants receive prisoner of war (POW) status and the protections of the Third Geneva Convention. Unlawful combatants do not receive POW status and do not receive the full protections of the Third Geneva Convention."[107] As David Cole has noted, "It is generally the case that in times of fear, people place security above all, and they are quite willing to cede to the government extraordinary authority. We love security more than we love liberty."[108] Such "extraordinary authority," when combined with the pliant nature of military tribunals' operating procedures, invites state manipulation and misuse.

Early court rulings supported the Bush administration in its executive power grab. In January 2003, a federal appeals court in Virginia decided that the president had the legal authority to designate U.S. citizens as "enemy combatants," and that the Bush administration could hold them in military custody as long as they are deemed a threat to national security.[109] But just when everything seemed to be going Bush's way, the Supreme Court ruled in June 2006, in *Hamdan v. Rumsfeld* that military tribunals were neither sanctioned by federal law, nor militarily necessary, and were in violation of Common Article 3 of the Geneva Conventions.[110] Law scholar David Cole noted that this ruling had "sweeping implications for many aspects of the Bush doctrine, including military tribunals." In the wake of the Supreme Court decision, he wrote, "At bottom, the *Hamdan* case stands for the proposition that the rule of law—including international law—is not subservient to the will of the executive, even during wartime."[111]

According to the *Washington Post*, the *Hamdan* ruling forced the Bush administration to select one of two relatively unpalatable choices: "operate the commissions by the rules of regular military courts-martial, or ask Congress for specific permission to proceed differently."[112] In other words, the president had to either afford the foreign "enemy combatants" the same rights as U.S. military personnel who were court-martialed or had to get Congress to pass a law making the tribunals legal. President Bush vigorously followed the second track, with administration appointees speaking in front of various congressional committees in an attempt to sway Congress toward its positions. Attorney General Alberto Gonzales told the Senate Armed Services Committee that "In the midst of the current conflict, we must not share with captured terrorists the highly sensitive intelligence that may be relevant to military commission proceedings."[113] All this lobbying paid off when in September 2006 Congress passed the Military Commissions Act, which gave the president the ability to press forward with his military tribunals.[114] The law—which also took away the federal courts' jurisdiction to hear petitions for writs of habeas corpus from non-citizens, thereby essentially preventing detainees from challenging their detention in court—will be discussed in more detail in Chapter 14.

Mixing and Melding the Modes of Suppression

Several modes of suppression intersect with extraordinary rules and laws. Employment deprivation, for instance, has dovetailed with this method of suppression: In fact, the loyalty security program—as well as other related laws from the Truman-McCarthy era—may well be considered extraordinary laws and rules in themselves. Also, as we have seen, public prosecutions and hearings are often justified by extraordinary laws and rules. These laws and rules form the legal grid that allow the public prosecutions and hearings to function, lubricating the gears of such prosecutions and hearings once they are set in motion. This mode of suppression also clearly and frequently relates to harassment arrests. Extraordinary rules and laws may be applied selectively to targeted dissidents. Also, exorbitant jail sentences, fines, and bails—a feature of harassment arrests—often follow the implementation of extraordinary rules and laws, as evidenced by the state laws in Texas regarding communism discussed above. Finally, in the United States today, the Justice Department seems willing to combine extraordinary rules and laws with harassment arrests if this combination yields the desired end result. One unidentified official from the Justice Department, when reminiscing on the arrest of Al Capone on tax violations, said this tactic might serve as a model for dealing with those dubbed "terrorists." "If we are dealing with people who are potentially linked to terrorists," the official said, "we will prosecute them to the fullest extent of the law. We don't care if it's chump change."[115] The bottom line is that when there are wars—whether they are declared by Congress or metaphorical wars against abstract concepts—extraordinary rules and laws are soon to follow. These laws often target activism, thereby squelching dissent.

10
Mass Media Manipulation

The Relationship Between the
Mainstream Mass Media and Dissent

The mass media form a crucial site for the construction of "reality," an ever-unfolding discursive locale that deeply influences public opinion on social issues and significantly affects the assumptions that bracket how we talk about politics. In the contemporary era, the mass media play an important role carving the course of history. Historian Rodger Streitmatter has observed, "As the news media report and comment on the events of the day, they wield enormous *influence* on those events." He continues, "news media have shaped American history. Absolutely. Boldly. Proudly. Fervently. Profoundly."[1] Reinforcing a central point, Murray Edelman adds, "The concepts and categorizations that language constructs are therefore not instruments of expression but *potent creators of what we accept as reality*."[2] With this in mind, mass-media coverage or a lack thereof most assuredly influences the nature, form, and development of social movements, as well as the ability of these movements to reach their goals.[3]

Generating favorable media coverage is one of the critical preconditions for collective action. Therefore, understanding the role of the mass media is crucial to comprehending how social movements coalesce, build, and maintain themselves, as well as how they decide to frame their dissident messages. "Because the mass media play such a central role in modern societies," writes social-movement scholar Bert Klandermans, "social movements are increasingly involved in a symbolic struggle over meaning and interpretations."[4] Therefore, media discourse is not only vital in terms of framing social issues and problems for the general public, but it's also a place where activists and state actors can struggle over ideology and ideas. In the big picture, the relationship between any dissident citizen or social movement and the mass media has at least two dimensions: a structural dimension (the battle over access) and a cultural dimension (the battle over meaning).[5]

The mass media have played an important historical role in suppressing dissent in the United States. While dissidents are sometimes able to frame issues and grievances in a manner satisfactory to them, they are more often

frustrated by what they deem inadequate—and sometimes even derisive—
mass-media coverage. Describing this double-bind, Sidney Tarrow adds a
layer of complexity:

> The influence of the media on the perception of movements' actions
> is double-edged. On the one hand, a growing "frame" of the media
> is that public life is corrupt, a point of view that is comfortable for
> readers and viewers because it justifies inaction or demobilization. On
> the other hand, the interest of movement-mounted dramatic activities
> quickly fades for the media unless they change or escalate their routines.
> When protests escalate, the media will continue to offer coverage, but
> are quick to give priority to their violent or bizarre aspects.[6]

The interplay between social movements and the mass media therefore
results in a dialectic of escalation in which dissidents feel pressed to amp up
their tactics. Not only is escalation a reaction to the ability of state agents to
thwart previous tactics, but it's also the result of the mass media's unquenchable penchant for novelty. The dialectic of escalation will be explored in the
following chapter when I analyze mainstream media coverage of the modern-day global justice movement.

As mentioned previously, media scholars John McCarthy and Clark
McPhail argue that, since the late-1960s, mass public protests have been
institutionalized and thus have become "normal" political activity that has,
over time, generated a "diminishing impact."[7] This "diminishing impact"
not only affects the desire of activists to continue to participate in social
movements, but it also affects the attention that social movements garner
from the press. For activists, the routinization of protest activity paves the
way to being disregarded by the mass media. Social movements and dissident citizens must contend with this reality as they move forward with their
strategies and tactics.

Objectivity is another important journalistic guiding principle that affects mass-media coverage of social movements. Media historian Michael
Schudson asserts that objectivity "is not just a claim about what kind of
knowledge is reliable. It is also a moral philosophy, a declaration of what
kind of thinking one should engage in, in making moral decisions."[8] This
moral compass is not only characterized by personal detachment, but also by
the notion that journalists are supposed to be politically neutral writers who
critically examine important social issues and offer impartial coverage.[9]

Even though objectivity became "the emblem of American journalism,"
now it's seen more as the mythical tune journalists whistle around the water
cooler.[10] As Entman notes, "The objectivity creed contains yet simultaneous-

ly camouflages codes and conventions that journalists use in making their news choices."[11] In response to critiques like this, the Society of Professional Journalists removed the term "objectivity" from its ethics code in 1996. In the vacuum left behind, alternative definitions of objectivity abound, leading *Columbia Journalism Review* editor Brent Cunningham to quip, "Ask ten journalists what objectivity means and you'll get ten different answers."[12] Many contemporary journalists avoid the term "objectivity," preferring instead the terms fairness, balance, accuracy, truth, and comprehensiveness.

Even if journalists follow the rules for "objective" reporting, they often present a news frame that does not give the audience an opportunity to make an informed assessment. Entman argues that "because [journalists] lack a common understanding of framing, journalists frequently allow the most skillful media manipulators to impose their dominant frames on the news," as when the media assume government press releases are factual and report their claims as such rather than investigating them.[13] This may be true, but it also affords an opportunity for activists to reframe social debates in ways that help their causes, as when dissidents supply journalists with fact sheets that favor their conclusions. In the end, Miller and Riechert argue, "objectivity obliges reporters to report facts, but it does not assure that they are getting the right facts."[14] Social-movement participants know this from experience.

While the dialectic of escalation, the institutionalization of protest, and putative objectivity can all swerve mass-media coverage of dissent in a denigrating direction, negative coverage also results from the state's direct manipulation of "friendly" media sources. Sometimes the mass-media-related suppression of dissent arises from an accumulation of tactical responses rooted in the everyday norms and practices of journalism, although occasionally it arises from concerted conspiring between media workers and state agents. I am referring to the state's direct interference in mass-media production as "mass media manipulation," which I will examine in this chapter. In Chapters 11 through 13, I will explore subtler mass-media-related methods of suppression.

Mass Media Manipulation

There are two types of mass media manipulation: (1) story implantation, and (2) journalist strong-arming. Story implantation is tantamount to the state writing and leaking denigrating portrayals of activists to media allies. Strong-arming is designed to prevent journalists from publishing unwanted information and to deter the use of undesirable frames in future mass-media accounts. Press censorship—including coerced self-censorship—is an important dimension of the latter.

Sometimes the state makes use of friendly press contacts who publish government-generated articles verbatim, or with minor adjustments. Such articles can be "gray propaganda": when the state deliberately disseminates information that is based on half-truths and subtle prevarications. Ostensibly, this information comes from a neutral source, whereas, in reality, it does not. "Gray propaganda" is based on half-truths whereas "black propaganda," a previously mentioned government tactic, is based on outright lies. Churchill and Vander Wall highlight the interrelation between modes of suppression when they write that with "gray propaganda" the state "systematically released disinformation to the press and electronic media concerning groups and individuals, designed to discredit them and foster tensions. This was also seen as an expedient means of conditioning public sentiment to accept Bureau/police/vigilante 'excesses' aimed at target organizations/individuals, and to facilitate the conviction of those brought to trial, even on conspicuously flimsy evidence."[15]

Often, there is a fine line between "gray propaganda" and government "spin." Calculated misinformation is inherent to "gray propaganda" and is carried out in order to create or sustain a negative public image of a dissident group, thereby undermining one of the preconditions for collective action: the generation of preferably favorable media coverage. This form of suppression also indirectly affects a number of other preconditions for collective action, such as the morale and commitment of adherents, which may suffer from such negative coverage, as well as the support of potentially sympathetic bystander publics, which may be less inclined to collaborate with activists who are saddled with an unfavorable image.

Media scholar Melvin Small has noted that "The media generally do not look favorably upon movements that oppose official policy."[16] Tarrow adds, "the capacity of movement organizations to appropriate the media for their own purposes is limited."[17] However, when the state is coordinating its message with "friendly" media so as to write stories that intentionally portray dissidents in a negative light, appropriation is virtually impossible. While the state worked to harass the underground press into submission in the 1960s and 1970s, it simultaneously supplied information—and sometimes even completely written stories—to the mainstream media in order to disseminate its preferred views, and therefore to succeed in what Herbert Schiller called "the slippery business of mass persuasion."[18] Denigrating propaganda can be a powerful tonic in the public sphere.

Instances of direct state creation and implantation of news are relatively rare, and, when they do occur, journalists, editors, and publishers are often loathe to admit it, as they fear looking like prostrate pawns of the state rather than principled practitioners of fairness, accuracy, and balance.[19] Direct intervention, however, is rare for a reason. Journalistic norms and values usually suffice to produce frames agreeable to the elite power structure, and overt tactics—which undermine the predominant democratic belief system—are therefore usually unnecessary. When mass-media values and norms fail to temper news coverage, elite managers—like editors, publishers, and owners—can always step in to modify coverage. Gitlin asserts this happened in media coverage of Vietnam War protest, when bosses in mass media companies interceded in order to "secure moderating frames." Yet he asserts, "Only episodically, in moments of political crisis and large-scale shifts in the overarching hegemonic ideology," do editors and publishers "intervene directly to re-gear or reinforce the prevailing journalistic routines."[20] Direct intervention by editors and management may be atypical, but it is not singular. Using internal-communications archives for the *New York Times*, political scientist Daniel Chomsky has documented the exertion of such control throughout the twentieth century.[21] If the editorial intrusion of mass-media managers fails, the state may have to intervene directly.

Even though direct mass media manipulation is rare in relative terms, specific examples abound. In part, that is because it was an explicit part of the FBI's COINTELPRO New Left twelve-point plan. According to the Church Committee report:

> Much of the Bureau's propaganda efforts involved giving information to "friendly" media sources who could be relied upon not to reveal the Bureau's interests. The Crime Records Division of the Bureau was responsible for public relations, including all headquarters contacts with the media. In the course of its work (most of which had nothing to do with COINTELPRO), the Division assembled a list of "friendly" news media sources—those who wrote pro-Bureau stories. Field offices also had "confidential sources" (unpaid Bureau informants) in the media, and were able to ensure their cooperation.[22]

When New Left groups engaged in "disruptive activities," the internal FBI document advocated that agents talk with "cooperative press contacts" who "should be encouraged to emphasize" aspects of the protests in tune with the general Bureau sentiments on the matter. Articles could, the Bureau felt, "put an end to lengthy demonstrations and could cause embarrassment" to activists. By reporting on the "depravity of New Left leaders and members," the FBI hoped to marginalize them and to alienate potential bystander-public supporters.[23]

In the COINTEPLRO era, there was no dearth of FBI allies in the media. According to Frank Donner, "In March 1965 FBI offices were requested to compile lists of reliable reporters who could be called on for COINTELPRO work. A memo in response from the Chicago field office listed some twenty-five friendly area sources, including leading newspapers, television, and radio stations; similarly, the New Haven, Connecticut office listed twenty-eight media contacts." Clearly the FBI had compliant cronies in media markets both big and small. Bureau efforts led to a number of explicitly anti-New Left accounts in the press, including a seven-part series in the Jackson, Mississippi *Daily News* where the editor—who the Bureau deemed a "friendly, discreet, reliable...loyal American"—made sure that the series was heavily imbued with Director Hoover's viewpoints and opinions.[24]

But state-driven manipulation of the mass media wasn't limited to the suppression of the New Left. The Church Committee found that the FBI planted derogatory articles about a number of dissident groups operating during the COINTELPRO era, including the Nation of Islam, Poor People's Campaign, the Institute for Policy Studies, the Southern Students Organizing Committee, the National Mobilization Committee and other social movement organizations that the Bureau felt "needed to be seen in their 'true light.'"[25]

A representative FBI memo, sent from headquarters, authorized the Boston Field Office to provide "derogatory information about the Nation of Islam (NOI) to established source [name of mass-media contact deleted]." The memo stated:

> Your suggestions concerning material to furnish [name of mass-media contact] are good. Emphasize to him that the NOI predilection for violence, preaching of race hatred, and hypocrisy, should be exposed. Material furnished [name of mass-media contact] should be either public source or known to enough people as to protect your sources. Insure the Bureau's interest in this matter is completely protected by [name of mass-media contact].[26]

Contrary to the information in this directive, FBI witnesses later testified that the Nation of Islam wasn't actually involved in organizational violence.

Use of this mode of suppression has extended to other targets. In the early-1960s, the Bureau used its friendly contacts in the mass media to work up a case against Fred Black, a Washington, DC lobbyist who was appealing a conviction on income tax evasion, and the Socialist Workers Party. In the early-1970s, the FBI furnished derogatory information to local media sources about the Weathermen.[27]

J. Edgar Hoover's record with friendly media contacts stretched all the way back to the 1930s and his chummy relationship with reporter Rex

Collier, a relationship that "blossomed into a lifelong friendship." Collier worked hard to present the FBI in the best possible light on a consistent basis. Another friend of the FBI working in the media industry, Phillips H. Lord, worked with Hoover to produce a multi-episode radio program called *G-Men* that glorified the Bureau's efforts against criminals and political subversives.[28] Lord actually used the Bureau's manipulation of the scripts as a way to gain credibility. Each show commenced with the following opener in Lord's voice: "This series of the *G-Men* is presented with the consent of the Attorney General of the United States and with the cooperation of J. Edgar Hoover, Director of the Federal Bureau of Investigation. Every fact in tonight's program is taken directly from the files of the Bureau. I went to Washington and was graciously received by Mr. Hoover and all of these scripts were written in the department building. Tonight's program was submitted to Mr. Hoover who personally reviewed the script and made some very valuable suggestions."[29] In addition to these films, a series of books glorifying FBI agents was published by the Whitman Publishing Company, under the "Better Little Book" imprint. For example, in a fictional book titled *G-Man vs. the Fifth Column*, Bureau agents do battle with wicked, bomb-tossing "fifth columnists." The book featured Ted Tabor, a clean-cut FBI agent armed with high technology and a handgun, doing battle with a shadowy band of saboteurs with German accents and names like Otto and Adolph. The theme that "the tentacles of the Fifth Column seemed to reach everywhere" permeated the narrative. Inevitably the G-men emerge victorious.[30]

Back in the real world, the FBI attempted to "help" people outside the United States view dissident social movements in their "true light." FBI personnel working in USAmerican embassies abroad—for example, in Tokyo and London—were instructed to do their best to implant stories in the foreign press that downplayed, if not downgraded, the massive anti-Vietnam War protests of October 1969.[31] The CIA participated in similar story implantation activities, and took their efforts a step further by having agents abroad falsely put themselves forward as journalists. In fact, a House Committee investigating U.S. intelligence agencies learned that, in 1975, the CIA had eleven agents working full-time under the cover of being journalists. The CIA also had many informants working in the foreign press. In Europe, the CIA even operated two of its own news services.[32]

Not surprisingly, the FBI also engaged in mass media manipulation in its efforts to suppress the dissent of Martin Luther King, Jr. as well as the activities of his allies and supporters. On 24 October 1962, the Crime Records Division sent a disparaging story about King's associate Jack O'Dell to at least five newspapers: the *Augusta* (Georgia) *Chronicle*, the *Birmingham*

(Alabama) *News*, the *St. Louis Globe-Democrat*, the *New Orleans Times-Picayune*, and the *Long Island Star Journal*. The stories, which highlighted O'Dell's history with the Communist Party, were almost completely identical, and they all named "a highly authoritative source" as the supplier of information for the story. This story led to the public resignation of O'Dell, as well as a lot of damage-control backpedaling on King's part. Just when King might have felt the Bureau-induced scandal was behind him, the Crime Records Division got back to work and influenced the *Birmingham News* to run a front-page story under the headline, "King's SCLC Pays O'Dell Despite Denial." This mass-media "revelation" forced King to make O'Dell's previously temporary resignation permanent, thereby depriving the SCLC of a young, smart, dedicated employee. The story reappeared for a third time less than a week later, though, when the Bureau's New York office convinced *Atlanta Constitution* writer Bill Shipp to pen a story under the headline "Onetime Communist Organizer Heads Rev. King's Office in N.Y.," an account that one King scholar described as "a virtual reprint of the Bureau's assorted facts on O'Dell."[33] Andrew Young, who worked closely with King, has asserted that these stories "chilled contributions" to the SCLC.[34]

The FBI also contacted state-friendly journalists and editors to write derisive stories about the Black Panther Party.[35] A directive that Bureau headquarters sent to nine field offices in January 1970 described the overall plan:

> To counteract any favorable support in publicity to the Black Panther Party (BPP) recipient offices are requested to submit their observations and recommendations regarding contacts with established and reliable sources in the television and/or radio field who might be interested in drawing up a program for consumption depicting the true facts regarding the BPP....All offices should give this matter their prompt consideration and submit replies by letter.[36]

In response to this directive, the Los Angeles field office took action and fingered two news reporters in the area who seemed like excellent prospects for the "preparation of a program which would present the true facts about the Black Panther Party as part of a counterintelligence effort."[37] As soon as July 1970, an L.A. newscaster sympathetic to the FBI's project produced a series of anti-Panther programs using FBI-supplied materials. A few months later, in October, another FBI-inspired television editorial appeared on the L.A. airwaves.

The following month, the Bureau's San Francisco field office focused its attention on Huey Newton after he reportedly rented "a luxurious lakeshore apartment" in Oakland. The Bureau viewed this piece of information as high in "potential counterintelligence value" since the apartment was opulent in comparison with "the ghetto-like 'pads' and community centers utilized by the Party." The Bureau saved this information, however, for February 1971 when the Newton-Cleaver rift was more fully developed. The information was leaked to a friendly source at the *San Francisco Examiner*, who promptly published a story outlining Huey Newton's extravagance and the irreverent hypocrisy of such high living. Not willing to rely solely on the *Examiner*'s distribution, the Bureau proceeded to anonymously mail copies of the article to numerous branches of the Party. It also sent copies to all field offices where the Panthers were active so that these offices could send the article along to sympathetic newspaper editors.[38] The Bureau's efforts in San Francisco seemed to pay dividends. Shortly after the article was published, the San Francisco field office sent a missive to headquarters with a job-well-done tone:

> BPP Headquarters was besieged with inquiries after the printing of the *San Francisco Examiner* article and the people at headquarters refuse to answer the news media or other callers on this question. This source has further reported that a representative of the Richmond, Virginia BPP contacted headquarters on 2/18/71, stating that they had received a xeroxed copy of…the article and believed it had been forwarded by the pigs but still wanted to know if it was true.[39]

The seeds of internal dissension were sown as the reputation of the BPP was publicly besmirched. Summarizing mass-media coverage of the Panthers, Van Deburg forcefully asserts that "The press and the electronic media were manipulated shamelessly."[40]

The Tragic Case of Jean Seberg

Similar suppressive methods were used to assail Panther sympathizers. One of the most harrowing, and ultimately fatal, examples of this concerns the FBI's implantation of information in the mass media about the USAmerican actress Jean Seberg. Seberg, a white woman living in Paris with her husband Romain Gary, was a supporter of the Black Panthers. FBI monitoring of her bank account indicated she had given more than $10,000 to the BPP.[41]

In light of this financial support, the FBI decided she "should be neutralized," as they put it in one internal memo.[42] The Bureau's concerted attack on this actress highlights one of the FBI's explicit tactics in its effort to suppress the BPP. A memorandum that the Bureau's Los Angeles Field Office sent to headquarters noted with satisfaction that the friendly local television contact who was airing an anti-Black Panther series would focus "especially" on "the area of white liberals contributing to the BPP."[43]

In addition to surveilling her bank account, the FBI was also gathering information about Seberg through wiretaps placed on various Black Panthers in California. Through these wiretaps the Bureau learned in 1970 that Seberg was pregnant. Special Agent Richard Held opined that this piece of information would make for tantalizingly vicious grist in the near future. He suggested that the Bureau plant a story with Hollywood gossip columnists spreading the rumor that Seberg was not pregnant by her husband, but rather by a member of the Black Panther Party. Headquarters responded with tactical patience, saying that the "Bureau feels it would be better to wait approximately two additional months until Seberg's pregnancy would be obvious to everyone."[44] According to former FBI operative M. Wesley Swearingen, Held thought that publicizing Seberg's alleged pregnancy with a Panther "would cheapen her image with the movie-going public and be a source of embarrassment for her," thereby quelling her support—and perhaps the support of others—for the BPP.[45] This analysis resembles that of Held himself, who, in a memo to Hoover, wrote, "It is felt that the possible publication of Seberg's plight could cause her embarrassment and serve to cheapen her image with the general public."[46]

In fact, Seberg was not pregnant by her husband, and they were on the verge of getting a divorce. However, she wasn't pregnant by a Black Panther either. Rather, when shooting the film *Macho Callahan* in Durango, Mexico, Seberg had an affair with Carlos Navarra, and he was the father of the child. Seberg's husband, Romain Gary, agreed, though, to assume the responsibility of fatherhood.[47] It isn't clear whether the FBI picked up on the fact that Navarra was the father. It's also not clear whether Bureau officials would have cared. It was far more useful for the FBI to pin the fatherhood on Panther leader Raymond "Masai" Hewitt, which they proceeded to do.

Held's brainstorm was eventually approved by Director Hoover, and the L.A. field office proceeded to send an anonymous letter to a number of Hollywood movie columnists. The letter read:

> I was just thinking about you and remembered I still owe you a favor. So ‑‑‑‑‑‑‑‑ was in Paris last week and ran into Jean Seberg, who was heavy with baby. I thought she and Romain had gotten together again, but she confided the baby belonged to [name deleted] of the Black Panthers, one [deleted]. The dear girl is getting around!
>
> Anyway, I thought you might get a scoop on the others. Be good and I'll see you soon.[48]

The story was picked up and published—albeit with a pseudonym, "Miss A"—in the 19 May 1970 issue of the *Los Angeles Times* by gossip columnist Joyce Haber, who thought she was getting the information from a trusted member of the *Times'* editorial staff. This story was followed up in June and July by stories in the *Hollywood Reporter* that explicitly named Seberg.[49] It vaulted to the national stage when the 24 August issue of *Newsweek* picked it up, replete with Seberg's name and specific details about the father of the child. Once published in *Newsweek*, the story was picked up by a number of other newspapers and magazines across the country.[50]

The pressure on Seberg threw her into a "feverish and depressed state." She penned a letter to BPP lawyer Charles Garry, breaking off her support for the Panthers: "I do not trust the friends of the Panthers or in fact, the sincerity of very, very few Panthers themselves....My reasons for this conviction are multiple."[51] At one point, she even attempted suicide by taking an overdose of sleeping pills, but doctors saved her life by promptly pumping her stomach.[52] Under intense stress, Seberg gave premature birth via a Caesarean section to a girl on 23 August. The girl, who weighed less than four pounds at birth, died two days later, plunging Seberg into a deep depression tinged with paranoia. She feared that infiltrators were everywhere.[53] Her paranoia was exacerbated after she received documents she had requested from the FBI that revealed its COINTELPRO against her. Each year, close to the anniversary of the death of her child, she attempted suicide. She finally succeeded on 8 September 1979 when she wrapped herself in a blanket and overdosed on barbiturates. Two days after her death, Romain Gary held a press conference where he squarely placed responsibility for both the death of his wife and their daughter on the FBI, and more specifically on the method of suppression they executed. "When an important American magazine published the rumor launched by the FBI," he said, "Jean became like a crazed woman. She never got over the calumny, and that's why she lost her child at birth. She wanted the child to be buried in a glass coffin in order to prove that it was white. From then on, she went from one psychiatric clinic to another, from one suicide attempt to another."[54]

The Strong-arm of the Law

Another aspect of mass media manipulation involves the state strong-arming the mass media. In the extreme, this strong-arming takes the form of outright censorship, which has been most common in wartime. During World War II, for example, the "Office of Censorship" was created under President Franklin Delano Roosevelt. According to the office's "Press Codes," journalists were forbidden from engaging in "criticism of equipment, appearance, physical condition, or morale" of U.S. troops or their allies. In subsequent wars, this was accomplished more subtly through a state-run journalist accreditation process and by carefully delineating lists of topics that couldn't be published without first obtaining military clearance. During the Vietnam War, for example, the Pentagon produced a list of fifteen types of information that could not be reported on without its approval, including casualty numbers and the unannounced movement of soldiers in the field.[55] During the Gulf War in the early-1990s, censorship was achieved through tight, choreographed circumscription of where reporters were allowed to travel and to whom they were allowed to speak.[56]

In addition to these forms of media control, the White House has a long history of a subtler brand of mass-media strong-arming. In 1959, President Eisenhower ordered the FBI to hassle *New York Times* writer E.W. Kenworthy after Kenworthy reported leaks from the State Department regarding future ambassadorial appointments.[57] The FBI didn't always wait for the president's cue, especially when FBI practices were being critiqued in the mass media. In fact, the FBI, and especially its longtime director, J. Edgar Hoover, have never been known for their ability to take criticism constructively. In the early-1940s, for example, when responding to criticism during a radio interview, Hoover said, "Your FBI is respected by the good citizens of America as much as it is feared, hated and vilified by the scum of the underworld, conspiring Communists and goose-stepping bundsmen, their fellow travelers, mouthpieces and stooges."[58] Not surprisingly, then, when members of the press wrote stories criticizing the Bureau, they were treated like the Communists—who were a Hooverian synecdoche for dissident citizens—the FBI was trying to stop. For instance, Hoover, who often tried to intimidate editors and journalists by telling them that their work was "the sort of material I might expect to find on the front page of the *Daily Worker* or *Pravda*," sent agents to the *Chicago Tribune* after it published an article that was critical of the way the FBI dealt with Patty Hearst's disappearance. Also, in 1970, when Jack Nelson wrote an article for the *Los Angeles Times* detailing the Bureau's direct involvement in a deadly KKK firebombing in Mississippi, Hoover went to great lengths to have Nelson fired. He even attempted to spread nasty rumors about Nelson's personal life and moral character in order to persuade the *Times* to dismiss him.[59] In fact, Otis Chandler, the publisher of the *Los Angeles Times* went to Washington where he met with Hoover, who shared with him a number of FBI reports on Nelson's drinking patterns. Other journalists attacked by the FBI after they wrote critical stories or columns about the Bureau include Alan Barth, op-ed writer for the *Washington Post*, Fred Cook of the *Nation*, James Wechsler of the *New York Post*, and Harry Hoffman, editor of the *Charleston Gazette*.[60]

President Eisenhower's intimidation efforts were paltry compared to the laborious lengths to which subsequent presidents went. Lyndon Johnson, for example, would go as far as to call newscasters—like CBS's Dan Rather—in the middle of a newscast to refute, correct, or applaud information that was being presented.[61] He also intimidated journalists by telephoning their bosses when he was unsatisfied with the news frames they adopted. In August 1965, when Morley Safer narrated a documentary on CBS that revealed, in the face of official government denials, that a U.S. Marine had set fire to a peasant's home using a lighter, Johnson phoned the president of CBS, Frank Sutton, and kicked off his conversation with these harsh words: "Frank, are you trying to fuck me? Frank, this is your president and yesterday your boys shat on the American flag." Johnson then demanded that a security check be carried out on Safer, a Canadian. This aggressive strong-arming seemed to take effect with the networks. Later that month, CBS offered a four-part series called "Vietnam Perspective," composed of material that was almost entirely sympathetic to the Johnson administration's position. The other major networks followed suit with similar programming.[62]

Knowing that access to governmental information and presidential pronouncements is important to journalists, Johnson cagily used this political reality to his advantage. For example, in 1967, when Charles Bartlett wrote a scathing piece about Johnson for the Los Angeles Times—explaining the government's "demoralization" in response to the president's "petty vindictiveness, which seeps out of the White House, curls its way through the corridors of the bureaucracy and the salons of Georgetown, and settles upon the city like a dank, uncomfortable chill"—Johnson proceeded to show Bartlett what vindictiveness really was, refusing to share information with the Los Angeles Times for a short while thereafter.[63] Downey and Rasmussen assess the president's overall approach this way: "In essence, Johnson's monitoring of his opponents turned into counterattacks involving both rebuttal and intimidation. His tactics served to muzzle popular and political opposition through obstructionist, self-serving actions."[64]

Such strong-arming and intimidation emerging from the White House were not unique to Lyndon Johnson. President Richard Nixon continued Johnson's rancorous relationship with the press in many ways. When it came to dealing with the media, Nixon "regularly moved beyond threats to actions employing the machinery of the government."[65] In 1972, for example, when faced with the sharp criticism of columnist Jack Anderson, the CIA began—on behalf of the president—"Project Mudhen," an intense, systematic surveillance program designed to track Anderson and his staff. The Nixon administration also took aim at journalists Daniel Schorr and Cassie Mackin, and, in general, the FBI placed wiretaps on a slew of journalists who were deemed unsympathetic. Administration officials explicitly threatened the livelihood of news outlets that challenged the president's policy. In 1972, the White House's director of the Office of Telecommunications Policy, Clay Whitehead, told TV stations that if they continued to produce "biased" stories against the Nixon administration, they might be placing their broadcasting licenses in jeopardy.[66]

In the 1980s, the Ronald Reagan administration used an obscure branch of the State Department—the Office of Public Diplomacy (OPD)—to disseminate "gray propaganda" in hopes of convincing the U.S. public that the administration's Central America policies were apt. Led by Otto Reich, the OPD also suggested that domestic dissident groups, such as the Committee in Solidarity with the People of El Salvador (CISPES) were off-track with their ideas and actions. By staging speaking engagements, radio interviews, and television discussions, and by publishing books, pamphlets, and articles, the OPD spread its pro-Contra, anti-Sandinista views. According to Ross Gelbspan, the OPD "had succeeded in placing a number of op-ed pieces in some of the nation's largest and most influential newspapers, including the *Wall Street Journal*, the *New York Times*, and the *Washington Post*, which were written by authors whose connections to the government operation were never revealed."[67]

More recently, the legacy of mass-media coercion has continued. In the wake of the terrorist attacks on 11 September 2001, Bill Maher, on his television program *Politically Incorrect*, responded to a guest—who had commented that since the terrorists who carried out the attack on 9/11 were willing to die for their cause, they were not cowards—by saying that "We have been the cowards lobbing cruise missiles from 2,000 miles away. That's cowardly." Subsequently, White House Press Secretary Ari Fleischer attacked Maher personally and then issued a more general threat to members of the press and public: "The reminder is to all Americans that they need to watch what they say, and watch what they do, and that this is not the time for remarks like that."[68] This tacit warning to all who might air dissent in the tense moments following the attacks of 11 September had a chilling effect on political discourse. Discursive brackets were set in place that hemmed in what was acceptable to say and report in the mass media and what was not "appropriate." Maher's program was dumped by nineteen ABC affiliates as well as by two major corporate sponsors of the show, Federal Express and Sears. Some of the affiliates returned later, but the corporate sponsors did not.

The Bush administration took a more direct approach to controlling media output when, on 10 October 2001, National Security Adviser Condoleezza Rice persuaded the five major TV news organizations in the U.S.—ABC, CBS, NBC, CNN, and Fox—to agree to abridge future videotaped statements from Osama bin Laden and his al-Qaeda associates, since these statements might contain coded messages for al-Qaeda followers. Andrew Heyward, the president of CBS News, hit the general tenor of the agreement when he said, "This is a new situation, a new war and a new kind of enemy. Given the historic events we're enmeshed in, it's appropriate to explore new ways of fulfilling our responsibilities to the public." The networks also wanted to avoid giving extended airtime to bin Laden. The President of NBC News, Neal Shapiro, said Rice's "biggest point" was that bin Laden "was a charismatic speaker who could arouse anti-American sentiment getting 20 minutes of air time to spew hatred and urge his followers to kill Americans."[69] The next day, Ari Fleischer said he hoped newspapers would also agree to this form of media control. "The request is to report the news to the American people," Fleischer said. "But if you report it in its entirety, that could raise concerns that he's getting his prepackaged, pretaped message out." *New York Times* editor Howell Raines responded to Fleischer's plea by saying "We are always available to listen to any information about security issues."[70]

As usual, this mode of suppression dovetails with other modes. As we have seen, non-compliant journalists were surveilled in some instances. Also, when the state disseminated "gray propaganda" or otherwise damaging information about dissidents to sympathetic members of the press, the goal was often to forge a connection between the dissidents and an enemy of the state (bi-level demonization) or to make the dissidents look ridiculous or out of touch with Middle USAmerica (mass media deprecation). Both of these methods of suppression will be explored below. Finally, it should be mentioned that when "friendly" sources in the mass media are manipulated to create state-friendly news stories, these stories often resemble what journalists and editors would have created anyway due to the values and norms they follow during the production of news. After all, the "gatekeepers" of the mass media veer toward conservative positions, especially during moments of social upheaval and war.[71]

11
Bi-level Demonization

As innovative political scientist Murray Edelman pointed out repeatedly, the presence of external enemies is a significant dimension of person-to-person relations, inter-group dynamics, and geopolitical affairs. Often the state uses the mass media to prime the public to think of certain individuals and groups as enemies and demons and others as friends and allies, and this process greatly affects public opinion. A quieter corollary of the demonization of an external "enemy" can be the debilitating effect this process has on domestic social movements. I place "enemy" in quotation marks since often this demonized individual or group is not, in fact, an enemy of the average U.S. resident, but rather, the antagonist of the U.S. government or corporate capitalism. Bi-level demonization entails the state and mass media linking dissidents to a demonized group or individual from the international arena, even if the activists are not working directly with or supporting the demonized external foe materially or ideologically. As long as the social movement *appears* to be supporting the external demon, even if tacitly, bi-level demonization may kick into motion. Importantly, once a social movement or individual dissident citizen is associated with the external demon, the state's ability to vigorously suppress their dissent without experiencing significant social backlash increases dramatically.

The logic of bi-level demonization proceeds simultaneously on two levels: While an external foe from the international arena is demonized, and therefore depicted as deserving of punishment, a domestic dissident or group is linked to the external demon, and therefore also made vulnerable to state suppression. The linkage to demonized groups or individuals serves to stigmatize domestic dissidents, as the state groups the two together—rightly or wrongly—based on ideology, ethnicity, race, or other social categories. Pertinent to the treatment of domestic social movements, Edelman describes this central dynamic, which operates on both levels of demonization: "Justifications of enmity take the form of constructing a narrative about the past and the future: a story plot that rationalizes draconian measures against supposed enemies on the ground that an evil must be destroyed in order to save the public and the enemies themselves for a better future."[1] The "perceived-friend-of-your-enemy-is-your-enemy" mentality undergirds bi-level demonization, and there are usually debilitating, demoralizing consequences for the domestic social movements and dissident citizens that get pulled into the orbit of this logic.

The term demonization is too often used in a loose, unfocused, extremely ideological way that deprives the term of its useful analytical potential. To counter this, I define the process of external-enemy demonization by four criteria: (1) the state and media focus attention on the inherent nature of the so-called enemy and employ frames that portray this enemy in moral rather than tactical terms; (2) overtly Manichean diction—good versus evil—is used to describe the character of the opponent; (3) the demonological portrayal originates with the state; and (4) no significant, sustained counter-claims emerge from the state to challenge the portrayal.

To be clear, bi-level demonization is an analytical category, a social dynamic that helps us make sense of the state-media-dissident nexus. Bi-level demonization is not necessarily about making truth claims (e.g. there is an actual connection between a domestic dissident and an external demon) or evaluative claims (e.g. the state and media should or should not have done this or that, even though I certainly have my own opinions on these matters). In other words, whether or not there was a real connection between a dissident and an external demon is not the question. Rather, whether the dynamic is at work is the question. With this in mind, when trying to identify bi-level demonization in the real world, I look for state claims regarding connections (real or imagined) between domestic dissidents and the external "enemy." If the state puts forth such connective claims in an effort to discredit the domestic dissidents, and the media pick up on this, then we have bi-level demonization.

With bi-level demonization, the state not only attaches negative emotional valence to the external enemy but also to domestic dissidents. However, for this tactic to work, only the external enemy must meet the four-pronged criteria for demonization. The domestic dissident group or individual need only be associated, not affiliated, with the external demon, regardless of whether they meet all four criteria. Edelman astutely observes:

> Sometimes political enemies hurt their opponents, and often they help them. Because the evocation of a threatening enemy may win political support for its prospective targets, people construct enemies who renew their own commitment and mobilize allies...When an enemy hurts, there is an incentive to end the threat by doing away with him. But the opposite incentive comes into play when the enemy helps marshal support for a regime or cause; in that case those who construct an enemy have every reason to perpetuate and exaggerate the threat he poses.[2]

While bi-level demonization may help "mobilize allies" to crush the external enemy militarily, it also inhibits the preconditions for collective action, suppressing dissent by preventing social movements from carrying out their essential tasks. The charges of maintaining social-movement solidarity and attracting new recruits are complicated tremendously by public association with the demonized external enemy. Specific evidence—whether real, imagined, or fabricated—linking social-movement leaders with the external foe can be equally damaging both to the leadership structure of the social movement and to its ability to gain the ever-crucial support of bystander publics since few people want to ally with, let alone affiliate with an external enemy. Bi-level demonization has the overall effect of putting social movements on the defensive, on the ever-unfolding path of self-explanation, justificatory back-tracking, and damage control. In the social atmosphere that such demonization creates, favorable mass-media coverage is scant. In fact, the mass media proliferate the demonic images. This leaves little time or political space for social movements to pursue their goals, and, even when these goals are pursued, they are more easily dismissed by the state—not to mention potential non-state allies—who view these social movements and their efforts through the countersubversive lens.

Edelman asserts, "The highlighting of foreign enemies to weaken domestic dissent…is a classic political gambit because it is so often an effective one. While this form of displacement is occasionally deliberate, it need not be."[3] In other words, bi-level demonization is not necessarily a conspiracy. Rather, it is an accumulation of tactical reactions on the part of state actors working in concert with journalists.

This "classic political gambit" has emerged in a number of historical situations. Zaller and Chiu note that over a 46-year period (1945–1991), the U.S. press not only bracketed its coverage to only reflect the range of elite opinion emanating from the government, as media scholars suggested it would, but that during "foreign policy crises" it went further, becoming "government's little helper" in that it actually adopted a more hawkish slant than government officials when the external enemy was communist.[4] As they put it, "journalists often simply 'rally round the flag' and whatever policy the government favors."[5] Accordingly, dissident citizens and social movements that challenge the government's policies during foreign policy crises can expect less than favorable coverage.

Bi-level demonization based on leftism scoops much further back into U.S. history than Zaller and Chiu's study, however. In 1877, when a nationwide railway strike was carried out in the midst of a depression—a strike that according to Howard Zinn "shook the nation as no labor conflict in its history had done"—an unnamed official in President Rutherford B.

Hayes's administration called the strike "nothing more nor less than French Communism," thereby equating the strikers with foreign communists.[6] The techniques of bi-level demonization received a massive boost during World War I when the U.S. government endeavored to whip the country into a frenzy of bellicosity.

The Committee on Public Information: Welcome to the Age of PR

When President Woodrow Wilson declared war on Germany in April 1917, popular support was no safe bet, given the prevalence of pacifism and isolationism, as well as the existence of sizable pockets of German-born people and other immigrant communities who came to the U.S. in search of the "land of opportunity" but found instead a landscape of poverty and paucity. In light of this formidable anti-war sentiment and economic-driven disenchantment, Wilson decided to enlist assistance propagandizing the war effort. A major force within this propaganda agenda was the formation of the Committee on Public Information (CPI)—or Creel Committee—on 13 April 1917. According to James Mock and Cedric Larson, authors of *Words that Won the War: The Story of the Committee on Public Information*, the committee eventually became "America's 'propaganda ministry' during the World War, charged with encouraging and then consolidating the revolution of opinion which changed the United States from anti-militaristic democracy to an organized war machine."[7] Noam Chomsky adds that the Creel Committee "succeeded, within six months, in turning a pacifist population into a hysterical, war-mongering population which wanted to destroy everything German, tear the Germans limb from limb, go to war and save the world."[8] Thus the CPI was the chief instigator of bi-level demonization during World War I, and a stunningly effective instigator at that.

One compelling—and perhaps counterintuitive—aspect of the CPI's propaganda program was the alacrity with which many progressives joined the cause. According to historian Stephen Vaughn, "the CPI acted as a veritable magnet, attracting intellectuals, muckrakers, socialists, and other reformers."[9] Even before the United States entered the war, Walter Lippmann, an influential newspaperman of the day, pressured President Wilson to consider how the U.S. government would win over the support of the masses—or engage in the "manufacture of consent"—if it were to enter the war. The day before the CPI was formed, Lippmann suggested that the president create an agency to collect and distribute information on the government's war-related activities, as well as to keep tabs on the foreign media.[10] Other reformers like Arthur Bullard—a muckraker and novelist who wrote the book *Mobilizing*

America—and Charles Edward Russell, a former member of the Socialist Party—joined the cause.[11] As social critic Stuart Ewen notes, the bottom line is that after Wilson declared war on Germany, "an impassioned generation of Progressive publicists fell into line, surrounding the war effort with a veil of much-needed liberal-democratic rhetoric."[12]

President Wilson established the CPI with Executive Order 2564, which stated that the committee should be comprised of the Secretaries of War, State, and Navy and chaired by a civilian. Wilson selected George Creel—a former muckraker who wrote for magazines and newspapers—to chair the committee.[13] He was joined by Secretary of War Newton D. Baker, Secretary of State Robert Lansing, and Secretary of the Navy Josephus Daniels. The CPI was divided into two main components: the Domestic Section, which distributed propaganda on the home front, and the Foreign Section, which monitored the press and citizenry in more than thirty countries. In time, the CPI expanded to more than twenty subdivisions that had offices in the U.S. and numerous other countries.[14] Announcing the formation of the group, the *New York Times* noted bluntly that the CPI would "combine the two functions of censorship and publicity." In a letter penned to President Wilson by Baker, Lansing, and Daniels, the triumvirate directly addressed the need to engage in press censorship. They wrote, "It is our opinion that the two functions—censorship and publicity—can be joined in honesty with profit."[15] Indeed, profit was toward the top of the CPI's agenda. Its first statement discouraged the hoarding of goods, asserting, "We need prosperity in war time even more than when we are at peace." The CPI then made the argument that people shouldn't blame the war for a lagging economy: "The declaration of war can have no real evil effect on business. What bad effects are apparent are purely psychologic and largely of our own foolish making, for our markets are the same in April as they were in March."[16] Bringing together profit, propaganda, and publicity, the CPI, in the words of Creel, "tried to build foundations upon which to erect our house of truth."[17]

One important aspect of this "house of truth," especially in terms of how it fueled bi-level demonization, was the formation of outlets to disseminate the government's propaganda. In May 1917, the CPI began to issue its own daily newspaper, the *Official Bulletin* (later called *Official U.S. Bulletin*), ostensibly because Baker, Daniels, and Lansing were concerned that the newspapers of the day were not printing sufficient amounts of news. A letter from the three that announced the commencement of the CPI contended, "Even though the cooperation of the press has been generous and patriotic, there is a steadily developing need for some authoritative agency to assure the publication of all the vital facts of national defense." The CPI promised to publish official documents from the Wilson administration, as well as "the vast amount of information that it is right and proper for the people to have." The CPI trumpeted a trope that was to be repeated vigorously over the coming years: "America's greatest present needs are confidence, enthusiasm, and service, and these needs will not be met completely unless every citizen is given the feeling of partnership that comes with full, frank statements concerning the conduct of public business."[18] The *Bulletin* was published every day but Sunday, and ranged from eight pages (in May 1917) to thirty-two or more pages (in winter 1919). Daily circulation rates rose from 60,000 in May 1917 to a high of 115,000 in October 1918 before dropping to a low point in March 1919 of 33,000. Mock and Larson judged the *Bulletin* to be "a glorified release sheet," but it was distributed widely, and was doled out for free to newspapers and other agencies that could proliferate the state-concocted information.[19]

In late May 1917, the CPI distributed a "Preliminary Statement to the Press" that laid out the "voluntary" regulations newspapers were supposed to follow. Creel asserted in the statement that it was "dangerous and of service to the enemy to discuss differences of opinion between the allies and difficulties with neutral countries." He also contended, "Speculation about possible peace is another topic which may possess elements of danger, as peace reports may be of enemy origin, put out to weaken the combination against Germany." In the words of Creel and the CPI, the goal was to get the U.S. press to "realize the obligations of patriotism as keenly as those who take the oath of service in the army and navy."[20] Already one could detect the CPI's efforts to portray the Germans as immoral tricksters who weren't above lying their way to victory and the desire to paint those who were not willing to go along with government censorship as unpatriotic. The controversial statement divided news information into three basic types: dangerous, questionable, and routine. Vaughn describes dangerous, not-to-be-reported material as "stories on military or naval operations currently in progress, threats against the life of the President, movement of official missions, and other sensitive matters."[21] According to the CPI's statement, questionable news included, "narrative accounts of naval or military operations, including descriptions of life in training camps" as well as discussions of new military inventions. If journalists were unsure of whether material was "questionable," they were directed to vet the information with the CPI before going to print with it.[22] Later the CPI refined its apparatus of suppression and verification, creating categories like "Passed by the Committee on Public Information," which indicated the information was acceptable to disseminate although not necessarily accurate, and "Authorized by the Committee on Public Information," which designated the material as verified as correct.[23] By this time Creel was already being widely referred to as "the government censor" despite his continuous claims that he was trying to increase rather than decrease the amount of information available to the general public. He wrote in the pages of the *Annals of the American Academy of Political and Social Science*, "We do not touch censorship at any point, because censorship in the United States is a voluntary agreement managed and enforced by the press itself."[24]

At the time, the news media's reaction to this "voluntary agreement" was mixed. Even before the CPI issued its "Preliminary Statement to the Press," numerous newspapers were weighing in on the newly formed committee. Speaking in favor of the CPI, its censorship powers, and censorship legislation Wilson was trying to ram through Congress, the *Nashville Tennessean and American* wrote, "At a time when the safety of the nation, the existence of the nation—aye, the safety and existence of civilization itself—are at stake, the power must be lodged somewhere to lay a hand on the newspaper that would blab the Government's secrets and say it nay." This view was supported by the *Richmond Times-Dispatch*, which editorialized, "Jealously as we guard the right of freedom of speech we must also guard against the menace of unrestrained and even treasonable speech in a time of national peril." Meanwhile, many newspapers came out against the CPI's censorship agenda. The *Oregonian* said it "most forcibly object[s] to a censorship under the control of the very officials who are most exposed to criticism—the heads of the departments which are charged with the conduct of war." The *New York Tribune* railed, "It is not only a wicked thing, but a futile thing, to attempt to silence just criticism and those who honestly seek to destroy evils by exposing them. Tyranny has always founded itself upon the press gag, and the press has always prevailed to the ruin of tyranny."[25]

Given that the CPI was comprised of numerous journalists, it's not surprising that the Division of News—the branch with perhaps the most Orwellian name—was a linchpin in the information dissemination process. In addition to publishing the *Official Bulletin*, the Division put out the *War Digest News*, a collection of pro-U.S. information about the day-to-day happenings of the war. More than 12,000 rural newspapers used the material in their publications. One estimate holds that information from the News Division made its way into at least 20,000 news columns each week.[26]

The CPI's efforts went beyond pressuring journalists and plying newspapers with pro-government cant. Creel and his allies also enlisted artists to the cause. In May 1917, Creel formally requested artists to create pro-war street posters that could be posted far and wide. With the assistance of the Society of Illustrators, he asked every artist in the United States to contribute art to the cause—even if they were not officially members of the Illustrators— keeping "steadily in mind a high ideal of poster art." U.S. artists were asked to emulate skilled European poster artists who "have gone deeply into questions of psychology to find the best ways of reaching that strange region, the public mind."[27] Already we can see the incipient analysis that helped refine propaganda into "public relations." One of the most prominent commercial illustrators of the time—Charles Dana Gibson—rose to Creel's challenge, taking the helm at the CPI's Division of Pictorial Publicity, where he made sure billboards across the U.S. were filled with, in the words of Creel, "posters as beautiful as they are effective."[28]

Gibson's unit worked closely with the Division of Advertising, which President Wilson established on 20 January 1918 in order to "inform public opinion properly and adequately."[29] The Division of Advertising wrote ad copy, penned art designs, and distributed advertisements. William H. Johns, the chairman of the division, and the President of the American Association of Advertising Agencies, described the role of the newly formed group: "In a broad sense, we shall act as an advertising agency. We shall displace no Government advertising departments. We shall simply help those departments, just as the modern advertising agent helps the advertising departments of his clients."[30] Edward Bernays, an Advertising Division enthusiast, described the process more succinctly as "the engineering of consent."[31] The Division of Advertising worked hand in glove with the Division of Pictorial Publicity, mapping designs for the illustrators to hammer out.[32] By the end of the war, Creel estimated the Division of Advertising had scored $2,000,000 in free advertising.[33]

The CPI also launched a national speakers circuit channeled through the Speaking Division. The division tapped the services of a number of prominent reformers of the day, including Ida Tarbell, who represented the Woman's Committee of the Council of National Defense, and Jane Addams, who, even though she was against the war, carried out a lecture tour for the Food Administration. Others who spoke under the CPI banner included Vice President Thomas R. Marshall, Senators Knute Nelson and William S. Kenyon, and a wildly popular French lieutenant named Paul Périgord.[34]

In September 1918, the Speaking Division merged forces with the Four Minute Men, a well-established program that sent speakers to movie theaters to explain the U.S. government line in four minutes or less. The Four Minute Men, comprised of local, voluntary speakers (often businessmen and professionals), grew from 2,500 speakers in July 1917 to 74,500 speakers by the end of 1918. Speakers would stand up at motion-picture theaters across the country and deliver pre-cooked speeches that were passed along to them by the CPI. The Committee sent speakers *Four Minute Men Bulletins* from Washington, with titles like "The Danger to America," "The Danger to Democracy," and "The Meaning of America." The CPI standardized the speeches so the same talk would be dispensed at roughly the same time across the United States. Occasionally, celebrities like former President Theodore Roosevelt and star baseball player Honus Wagner would also do the four-minute drill.[35] The Four Minute Men and their pro-government propaganda were seemingly everywhere. Mock and Larson note, "Wherever an American might be, unless he lived the life of a hermit, it was impossible to escape the ubiquitous Four Minute Men."[36]

The CPI also had a Film Division, which made use of the services of racist filmmaker D.W. Griffith, who had previously released *Birth of a Nation*, as well as other prominent filmmakers of the day such as Cecil De Mille and William Fox. The Division released films like *Pershing's Crusaders*, *America's Answer*, and *Under Four Flags*, and a weekly release called *Official War Review*, all to the tune of a $900,000 profit.[37] Additionally, the Division of Civic and Educational Publications cranked out pamphlets for wide distribution. By June 1917 the Division had begun publishing "war booklets" that were part of a "Red, White, and Blue" series designed "to answer completely and effectively questions concerning our participation in the great war." The Government Printing Office's first print run was sent to newspapers, which were expected to publish them whole cloth. A second batch was circulated to a mass audience across the United States. The booklets were also translated into numerous languages and distributed internationally.[38]

The Committee on Public Information, a well-funded, multi-pronged propaganda organ, set out, as Creel put it, to "fight for the mind of mankind."[39] Creel wrote,

> There was no part of the great war machinery that we did not touch, no medium of appeal that we did not employ. The printed word, the spoken word, the motion picture, the telegraph, the cable, the wireless, the poster, the sign-board—all these were used in our campaign to make our own people and all other peoples understand the causes that compelled America to take arms…What we had to have was no mere surface unity, but a passionate belief in the justice of America's cause that should weld the people of the United States into one white-hot mass instinct with fraternity, devotion, courage, and deathless determination.[40]

To confect this "white-hot mass instinct," well-coordinated, fine-tuned propaganda was imperative. In his book *Propaganda Technique in the World War*, political scientist Harold Lasswell argues that propaganda was necessary to get the general population in line and to snuff out dissent:

> It is no longer possible to fuse the waywardness of individuals in the furnace of the war dance; a new and subtler instrument must weld thou-

sands and even millions of human beings into one amalgamated mass of hate and will and hope. A new flame must burn out the canker of dissent and temper the steel of bellicose enthusiasm. The name of this new hammer and anvil of social solidarity is propaganda.[41]

During this era, the term "propaganda" could carry the derogatory connotations we know today, but it could also serve as a neutral term. Self-proclaimed propagandists—Bernays once called himself a "propagandist for propaganda"—even saw the term through a rose-colored lens, with Creel making the case that they used propaganda "in the true sense of the word, meaning the 'propagation of faith.'"[42]

Value-laden connotations aside, Lasswell enumerated the "major objectives" of propaganda, which included the need "to mobilize hatred against the enemy" and "to demoralize the enemy." Blaming the enemy for the war is a good start, he wrote, "But to make assurance doubly sure, it is safe to fortify the mind of the nation with examples of the insolence and depravity of the enemy" by painting it as "incorrigible, wicked and perverse."[43] The CPI followed this recommendation in textbook fashion.

The first step in bi-level demonization involves establishing the external enemy as a demon. In its literature, the CPI stoked fear by portraying "the brutal, depraved nature of the enemy." A pamphlet called *The Prussian System* made Germans appear to be predatory monsters capable of a wide range of treacherous behavior. The pamphlet concludes that the Prussian system is "monstrous" and "unthinkable" and thus in need of destruction. According to Vaughn, another publication, *German War Practices*, asserted that "terrorism and brutality on the part of the German army was not an aberration but was condoned, even encouraged, by the German high command." Yet another CPI work that zeroed in on ostensible practices of the German army contended that the Germans engaged in "systematic exploitation and wanton destruction," which led to the elderly and the young to die of starvation. German soldiers were portrayed as alcohol-chugging pillagers on bender after destructive bender. Vaughn sums up the publication's central message: "German soldiers were modern Huns." More than 2,225,000 of these pamphlets were circulated in the United States.[44]

A key component to this demonization was the idea that Germans could be infiltrating the patriotic ranks in the United States. Spies, turncoats, and double-agents could be anywhere. Of the 100 million inhabitants of the United States at the time, about 14.5 million were foreign-born, with approximately 8.5 million who considered Germany their country of origin.[45] With foreigners abound, the CPI had no trouble whipping up hyper-vigilance dripping with xenophobia, despite its claims that "the United States has no quarrel with the German people."[46] In a CPI pamphlet titled *The German Whisper*, the Committee wrote that Germany had infiltrated "every community in the United States" where it was spreading its "poisonous" propaganda in order to bring down both the government and mass morale. Similarly, *The Kaiserite in America* claimed German agents were spreading malicious lies about the government and people of the United States. It states:

> You find him in hotel lobbies, smoking compartments, clubs, offices and even in homes. He is a scandal-monger of the most dangerous type. He repeats all the rumors, criticisms and lies he hears about our country's part in the war. He gives you names, places and dates. He is very plausible. But if you pin him down, if you ask him what he really *knows* at first-hand, he becomes vague, non-committal, slippery. He tries to make you think that the Government can fool you, if you are willing to let it—but it can't fool him. No siree! He's too smart. People like that are hurting your country every day. They are playing the Kaiser's game. They are fighting against this country. They are making it harder to win the war. Through their vanity or curiosity or *treason* they are helping German propagandists to sow the seeds of discontent. For every lie that has been traced originated with a German spy. Don't forget that…Get in the fight to stamp out this malicious slander. As you travel about the country or even in your social life at home, run down these lies. Call the bluff of anyone who says he has "inside information." Tell him that it's his patriotic duty to help you find the source of what he's saying. If you find a disloyal person in your search, give his name to the Department of Justice in Washington and tell them where to find him. It is your plain and solemn duty to fight the enemy at home by stamping out these lies.

The CPI printed 437,000 copies of *The German Whisper* and a whopping 5,500,000 copies of *The Kaiserite in America*, making the latter one of the most extensively distributed publications in the history of the Committee.[47]

This demonization was not limited to print publications. The CPI distributed speech preparation materials to the Four Minute Men that delineated the enemy's iniquity and depravity. One "Illustrative Four-Minute Speech"—suggestions for what the Four Minute Men should say in public—read in part:

> Prussian "Schrecklichkeit" (the deliberate policy of terrorism) leads to almost unbelievable besotten brutality. The German soldiers—their letters are reprinted—were often forced against their wills, they them-

selves weeping, to carry our unspeakable orders against defenseless old men, women, and children, so that *"respect"* might grow for German "efficiency." For instance, at Dinant the wives and children of 40 men were forced to witness the execution of their husbands and fathers. Now, then, do you want to take the *slightest* chance of meeting Prussianism here in America?[48]

The Four Minute Men were expected to go out and deliver this gospel according to the CPI.

The CPI undoubtedly exaggerated German atrocities on the battlefield, and it's likely that at least one Committee publication used forged documents.[49] Edward Bernays, who was a ringleader in the CPI's non-stop propaganda circus, admitted that people working with the Committee would, on occasion, get "hysterical." Yet, he noted in their defense, "hysteria was generally prevalent at the time. Reports that the Germans were beasts and Huns were generally accepted. The most fantastic atrocity stories were believed."[50] True, but only with the help of Bernays and his public-relations friends.

Hyperbole-laced psychological warfare on the home front extended to domestic dissident citizens. While the Creel Committee aggressively disseminated pro-USAmerican propaganda, it was also, as Mock and Larson note, "intimately concerned with the negative phases of public opinion management—with suppression of speech or publication inimical to the doctrines for which America believed it was fighting."[51] Such suppression was often carried out through bi-level demonization, linking anyone who disagreed with U.S. foreign policy to German-loving traitors, or "Huns."

A crucial precursor to drumming up bi-level demonization was the establishment of who was a "good citizen." The CPI's literature lauded people who were willing to make personal sacrifices, engage in community service, and exhibit unquestioning obedience to governmental authorities. In a CPI piece titled *The Right Men in the Right Jobs Will Win the War*, the Committee wrote, "The True American wants to work where he will help win the war. *He wants to fit in*."[52] It follows that while the "true American" wanted to conform and support the war effort, the so-called unpatriotic American refused to do so when he or she questioned the rightness of the war. The "good citizen" believed in the ever-malleable idea of "Americanism," which President Wilson defined as "utterly believing in the principles of America and putting them first as above anything that might come into competition with them."[53] With this my-country-right-or-wrong standard firmly in place, there was plenty of room for "patriotic" deviation.

The CPI explicitly depicted the inability or unwillingness to speak English as one such un-American deviation. They printed and circulated a bulletin, the *National School Service*, designed to inculcate the young with a brand of nationalism that emphasized speaking English. Following the slogan "one language and that the best!," teachers were encouraged to train their students to speak and read English, the "clear, clean, beautiful speech."[54]

CPI pamphlets also forged a tight demonological connection between anti-war protesters and German agents. A publication called *The War for Peace* quoted famous lawyer Clarence Darrow hammering away at pacifists: "When I hear a man advising the American people to state the terms of peace, I know he is working for Germany." Darrow's future nemesis, William Jennings Bryan, agreed that dissent must be silenced in wartime. He wrote that open discussion is acceptable before the declaration of war, "but the discussion is closed when Congress acts," at which point "acquiescence on the part of the citizen becomes a duty."[55]

Not everyone was one hundred percent pleased with the efforts of the Committee on Public Information and its chairman George Creel. Yet even quibbles with Creel's comments afforded opportunities to slam domestic dissidents. In April 1918, U.S. Representative Nicholas Longworth of Ohio took to the floor of Congress and skewered Creel for comments he made about the United States' lack of preparedness before the war, describing Creel's remarks as "the most monstrous utterance any American citizen has uttered since we entered this war." He then clicked into bi-level demonization mode, asserting, "The only men who have the right to join this expression of delight at our failure to be at all prepared for this war are the Hindenburgs and Ludendorffs abroad and the I.W.W. and Bolsheviki at home." The *New York Times* reported that Longworth's diatribe "was greeted with prolonged applause" by other members of Congress.[56]

The I.W.W. was regularly attacked in the mainstream press during World War I. An article in the *New York Times* titled "Government May End Outrages by I.W.W.: Action Under Laws Dealing with Treason Expected— Evidence of German Plot" labeled the Wobblies "a menace" whose "leaders are being furnished with German money to carry on a campaign against industry intended to cripple the United States government and its allies." The article went on to claim, "Evidence in possession of the Government indicates that…the leaders of the movement are believed to be Germans or men closely affiliated with German agents. The amount of money that is being spent by the agitators of the organization is so considerable as to excite suspicion on that ground alone."[57] This discursive demonology led to on-the-ground arrests of more than 150 Wobblies, including leaders like William D. "Big Bill" Haywood, in September 1917. Commenting on the arrests, Judge William C. Fitts abandoned even the pretense of neutrality: "The I.W.W. is a degenerate. Its doctrine is treachery built on the teachings of the employment of secret and covert destructive methods intended to wreck the employer, and through destruction of production and transportation disable society and the Government itself, the object at this time being to render the enemy stronger and our dear country weak in the resistance of that strength." The *New York Times* concluded its article by concocting shadowy ties between the arrested Wobblies and Germany. Citing a literal ton of condemnatory data the government had gathered to use against the I.W.W., the *Times* wrote vaguely, "There was evidence that German money was plentifully supplied, as shown in many letters and canceled checks."[58]

While the *New York Times* helped demonize the I.W.W., the U.S. government clamped down on the radical press that questioned the war. In September 1917, U.S. Post Office authorities threatened to shutter the offices of more than a hundred radical publications published by socialists, pacifists, and anarchists because, according to the *Times*, "All of them favor immediate peace with Germany, as a rule on the terms which the Prussian autocracy is said to approve, and all of them are frankly and outspokenly against the Government at Washington." Making use of passive voice, and lumping dissidents into one convenient mass, the *Times* insinuated that the dissident citizens publishing "pro-German and in a great many instances outright treasonable publications," were in direct cahoots with "the Prussian autocracy." The *Times* also took aim at U.S. Senator Robert "Fighting Bob" LaFollette of Wisconsin, whose anti-war remarks were reprinted in the Socialist Party's publication *The American Socialist*.[59] The CPI's Four Minute Men also railed against LaFollette, going so far as trying to drive him out of office. Four Minute Man and former Socialist Charles Edward Russell told the Union League Club in New York City that LaFollette was engaging in treason:

> Disloyal American that disgraces the Congress of the United States, traitor in disguise that has taken the oath of allegiance and goes to the Senate of the United States to do the dirty work of the Kaiser, oh, could I have taken you by the throat, and dragged you to Petrograd to put you up there in the Field of Mars on a Sunday afternoon and let you see the results of your work! For then you would have seen the miserable, fawning, slimy creatures that take the dirty money of Germany, some of them—ashamed I am to tell you of it, some of them with American passports in their pockets. You would have seen them going from crowd to crowd upon that field and repeating your words of treason, quoting you, quoting what you say in the Senate of the United States.[60]

Such vicious ramblings that focus on the moral character of the dissident are the quintessence of bi-level demonization.

In *Mobilizing Civilian America*, Harold Tobin and Percy Bidwell summarize how the state moved beyond bullets to quell domestic dissent:

> The willingness of Americans to bear the war's burdens was strengthened by the work of the Committee on Public Information, which stimulated the people to put forth efforts far in excess of what could have been exacted by legal compulsion...The Committee mobilized all available means of publicity. It bombarded the public unceasingly with enthusiastic reports on the nation's colossal war effort, and with contrasts of our war aims, and those of our Allies, with the war aims of the Central Powers. Dissenting voices were stilled, either by agreement with the press or by the persuasive actions of the Department of Justice. The formidable body of consent resulting from this effort was an effective aid in the mobilization of industry; it buttressed the power of government with the solid support of public opinion.[61]

With mass consent hammered into shape on the anvil of state propaganda, the Wilson administration could proceed full-bore into war.

George Creel was prone to gushing about the CPI's merits, from its "record of stainless patriotism and unspotted Americanism" to its ability to deliver "to every corner of the civilized globe the full message of America's idealism, unselfishness, and indomitable purpose."[62] Creel wasn't the only one who admired the CPI's efforts. So did Adolf Hitler. In *Mein Kampf*, Hitler wrote that from a strategic perspective, U.S. propaganda "was psychologically right" in its portrayal of the German as "a barbarian and a Hun." Hitler wrote effusively about how U.S. spin doctors effectively depicted the "'Hunnish' brutality of the barbaric enemy, without, however, making him think for even a moment that his own weapons could have, perhaps, or even probably, a still more terrible effect."[63]

Immediately after the Armistice, the CPI was disassembled. Yet, as Ewen observes, "the experiences gained in the CPI and its general lessons about the terrain of the public mind would inform the concerns of public relations specialists and affect the contours of American cultural life for decades to come."[64] The sly, strategic strides made in bi-level demonization during World War I would undoubtedly affect future generations of dissidents.

Bi-level Demonization and Communism

For a sizable swathe of twentieth-century U.S. history, domestic dissidents were often linked to the external demon of international communism. During the Great Depression and well into the 1940s, many people in the

United States—particularly young people and intellectuals—were drawn to the ideas behind socialism and communism, since capitalism had failed to offer convincing answers to significant social problems. However, after 1946 when relations between the U.S. and the Soviet Union worsened dramatically and the Cold War sunk its roots, a tremendous ideological force—anticommunism—gained momentum, and this juggernaut didn't spare anyone in the domestic realm who embraced socialism or communism. Such bi-level demonization was an essential ideological building block of Senator Joseph McCarthy's career. As he zealously escalated his crusade against communism, articles on "Reds" dominated the pages of top newspapers like the *New York Times*, earning substantial column inches on a regular basis.

Angela Davis has noted that "The psychological impact of anti-communism on ordinary people in this country runs very deep. There is something about the word 'communism' that, for the unenlightened, evokes not only the enemy, but also something immoral, something dirty."[65] Even Henry Luce, who was far from a radical social critic—he published *Life* and *Time* magazines and his wife was President Eisenhower's ambassador to Italy—commented, while accepting an honorary degree at Temple University in 1953, that "we in America have developed a form of brainwashing under the name of anti-communism."[66]

This fear of socialism, or at least being associated with socialism, reverberated far and wide, even to the outer reaches of the culture industry. For example, in the 1956 Signet paperback edition of *Nineteen Eighty-Four* that was published in the United States, the publisher altered George Orwell's famous phrase that "every line I have written since 1936 has been written, directly or indirectly, against totalitarianism and for democratic socialism as I understand it" by deleting the final eight words. Even claims in support of "democratic socialism" had no space to wriggle in U.S. mainstream political discourse.[67]

When it came to bi-level demonization some central motifs arose: the disloyalty of U.S. communists; their thoroughgoing subservience to Soviet Russia; the U.S. Communist Party's immoral nature and conniving, subterranean activities; the pervasiveness of communism in U.S. culture and in its social institutions; and the Party's desires and plans to overthrow the U.S. government using violence. These motifs soon reverberated in leading newspapers in the United States.

Along with other government officials who perpetually railed against communism, J. Edgar Hoover masterfully tapped many of these powerful motifs throughout his tenure as FBI Director. For instance, in his book on Marxism, *Masters of Deceit: The Story of Communism in America and How to Fight It*, he wrote:

Communism is many things: an economic system, a philosophy, a political creed, a psychological conditioning, an educational indoctrination, a directed way of life. Communists want to control everything: where you live, where you work, what you are paid, what you think, what streetcars you ride (or whether you walk), how your children are educated, what you may not and must read and write. The most minute details, even the time your alarm clocks goes off in then morning or the amount of cream in your coffee, are subjects for state supervision. They want to make a "communist man," a mechanical puppet, whom they can train to do as the Party desires. This is the ultimate, and tragic, aim of communism.[68]

To say Hoover was anti-communist is an extreme understatement. His rabidity on the topic is legendary. Yet the Hooverian brand of anti-communism put forth in *Masters of Deceit* was widespread, and an array of individuals and groups found themselves with an opportunity to exploit this anti-leftist worldview in a variety of political and ideological ways. One of those was bi-level demonization designed to quell radical thought on the domestic front. In *Masters of Deceit*, Hoover makes the link between domestic communists like William Z. Foster—who Hoover quotes directly at times—and international communism:

These statements [above] are confirmed, day after day, by documented reports from areas where communists have already taken over: Hungary, East Germany, Bulgaria, Poland, Roumania [sic], Czechoslovakia, Red China, and other areas. When you read such reports, do not think of them as something happening in a far-off land. Remember, always that "it could happen here" and that there are thousands of people *in this country* now working in secret to make it happen here.[69]

It's not surprising that Hoover and other government officials played the "they're-only-following-orders-from-Moscow" card, given the relationship between the Communist Party and the Soviet regime and in light of the fact that people who disagreed with Stalin's policies were being purged from the Communist Party. How could bi-level demonizers not do this when it was such an easy, obvious, and in large part accurate attack?

Leftist political parties and groups in the United States have a long history of schism.[70] Many people on the left had strong criticisms of the Soviet Union as well as the Communist Party USA, criticisms that, on the surface at least, were quite similar to the state's demonization. For many radicals, the

Soviet Union was indeed a totalitarian state and the Communist Party USA subordinate and far too beholden to it. However, as I stated near the outset of this chapter, my definition of bi-level demonization isn't concerned with whether the state's truth claims and value judgments are legitimate. Certainly, the U.S. government, for the most part, ignored the differences between and ideological variation among dissidents of a reddish hue. Instead, these often quite complex differences were tacitly simplified and quietly compressed into the label "communist," a fact that should make it clear that the purpose of bi-level demonization—the suppression of domestic dissent—has a very tenuous relationship to historical "truth" on any level.

Hoover and other state officials made the connection between domestic communist groups and the demonized Soviet foe, arguing that the tactics of communists in the United States "are part of world-wide communism and are offered as bait to divert and capture our minds."[71] As Senator McCarthy famously put it at the 1952 Republican Party convention,

> I say one Communist in a defense plant is one Communist too many. One Communist on the faculty of one university is one Communist too many. One Communist among American advisors at Yalta was one Communist too many. And even if there were only one Communist in the State Department, that would be one Communist too many.[72]

Such rhetoric paved the way for the suppression of any dissent that could be labeled "communist."

But books and speeches by state officials like Hoover and McCarthy were not the only ways bi-level demonization was propagated in the United States. After all, only so many people could attend these events. These state officials needed the help of the media to proliferate their messages, and, as we'll see in detail, the U.S. press dutifully placed these state leaders in the media spotlight. Indeed, both Hoover and McCarthy were tremendously adept at making use of the mass media, and journalists were attracted to their often outrageous claims. Like the role that the mass media play in contemporary society, the prestige press in the late-1940s and early-1950s constituted a crucial site that connected the words and ideas of elite leaders with the hearts and minds of the general public.[73] In large part the leading newspapers of the day served as a bullhorn for the state that consistently intoned: (1) the demonization of the Soviet Union, and (2) the linkage between domestic radicals and the Soviet Union.

In the following section I draw from *New York Times* articles that appeared in the aftermath of World War II: 1946 through 1955. While this was a heightened period of anti-communism, the trend of demonizing the

Soviet Union—or what President Ronald Reagan famously called the "Evil Empire"—continued through the end of the Cold War. Soon after World War II ended, the Soviet Union became a source of suspicion for some and a wellspring of outright disdain for others. As early as 1946, a number of leaders went on record condemning the Soviet Union as well as communism more generally. For example, Ralph Cooper Hutchinson, the President of Lafayette College in Eastern, Pennsylvania, asserted that despite generous military aid from the United States, the Soviet Union was acting "like a juvenile with a big gun." According to Hutchinson, the Soviets "conquer first, liquidate every Mikhailovitch who in patriotism opposes them. Now they force their teaching. This for them is the beginning of the end."[74] Around this time, the U.S. Chamber of Commerce published and disseminated a booklet called "Communist Infiltration in the United States: Its Nature and How to Combat It."[75] In 1951, a special committee of the American Bar Association—the national body representing the legal profession—made the recommendation to disbar all communist lawyers and sympathizers, justifying this proposed policy by asserting that "communism, like sin, is bad."[76]

Many prominent politicians and sympathetic citizens also appeared in front of congressional committees where they attacked the communist foe in the Soviet Union. Repentant communist Louis F. Budenz, was a veritable one-man demonization crew. He told one congressional committee that the Soviet Union considered the United States its "principle enemy" that needed to be destroyed. "No average American," he claimed, "can appreciate what a concentration camp mentality the Communist Party is."[77] Testifying later in front of HUAC, Budenz asserted that the Soviet Union was involved in "a war of nerves" against the United States, comparing Soviet covert efforts to those of Adolf Hitler, "but with Soviet variations."[78] A few months prior, Budenz had described the Soviet project as "a Hitlerite policy of world domination, to be established step by step through fifth columns."[79] The roots of this equating of communism and fascism reach back to the 1930s, as historian Peter Kuznick notes in his book *Beyond the Laboratory: Scientists as Political Activists in 1930s America*.[80] But equating fascism and communism really hit its stride in the 1940s and 1950s.

President Truman, in his 1949 inaugural address, which was reprinted in the *New York Times*, made a concerted effort to parse out what he saw as the central differences between communism and democracy:

> Communism is based on the belief that man is so weak and inadequate that he is unable to govern himself, and therefore requires the rule of strong masters. Democracy is based on the conviction that man has the moral and intellectual capacity, as well as the inalienable right, to

govern himself with reason and justice. Communism subjects the individual to arrest without lawful cause, punishment without trial, and forced labor as a chattel of the state. It decrees what information he shall receive, what art he shall produce, what leaders he shall follow, and what thoughts he shall think. Democracy maintains that government is established for the benefit of the individual, and is charged with the responsibility of protecting the rights of the individual and his freedom in the exercise of those abilities of his. Communism maintains that social wrongs can be corrected only by violence. Democracy has proved that social justice can be achieved through peaceful change.

He concluded that "the actions resulting from the Communist philosophy are a threat to the efforts of free nations to bring about world recovery and lasting peace."[81] Two years later, in a speech at George Washington University in Washington, DC, Truman, in a less loquacious mood, simply dismissed communism as a "crackpot" notion.[82]

Truman wasn't the only national politician to come out strong against communism. Former Senator John Foster Dulles declared, "The goal of World Communism is world conquest, so that in the end there will be in the world only 'a single state union.' The strategy is one of 'encirclement,' whereby the weaker links are first seized so that the hard core may be slowly strangled."[83] Also, in a 1952 presidential campaign speech General Dwight Eisenhower excoriated the Soviet Union as "the menace of godless communism." "This evil," he said, "denies all dignity to man. It defines him as an organic accident upon the earth's surface, a creature of the same forces that rust iron and ripen corn. It robs him of spiritual meaning or spiritual destiny."[84] All sorts of lesser-known national politicians also chimed in with similar demonizations. For example, Representative James Van Zandt (R–PA) suggested the deportation of all communists to Russia. "Let them demonstrate their sincerity for godless Russia," he commented, "by departing from our shores, and every loyal American will utter a prayer of thanksgiving."[85]

Of course, Senator Joe McCarthy also vigorously condemned communism. Saying that "a rough fight is the only fight Communists can understand," McCarthy chastised his opponents for "hitting [communists] with a perfumed silk handkerchief at the front door while they batter our friends with black knuckles and blackjacks at the back door."[86] HUAC stalwart Martin Dies (D–TX) called communism in any form "a criminal and treasonable conspiracy," while Senator Prescott Bush, a relatively moderate Republican from Connecticut, assured the populace that it wasn't exaggerating the communist threat. "Even a single Communist, if in a sensitive position, can damage our security," he said.[87]

Once it was established that the Soviet Union and its ideology—Stalin's version of communism—was an external demon to be both feared and fought, the next step was to connect domestic dissident groups to this foreign foe. Not surprisingly Louis Budenz, the communist-turned-Fordham-economics-professor, and perpetual state witness for the malevolence of communism, was one of the outspoken USAmericans who made this important connection between external enemies and domestic dissidents. According to a front-page *New York Times* article, Budenz said, in the midst of a three and a half hour testimony, that every single communist in the United States was "a part of a Russian fifth column" propounding "a conspiracy to set up world dictatorship under the control of the dictatorship of the Kremlin." When Budenz became frustrated with himself for not having specific information about "Communist infiltration into the schools, the movies, the radio and the press," Representative John E. Rankin (D–Miss.) assured him that his congressional committee was willing to give Budenz "all the time you want, if it takes from now to Christmas or this time next year."[88]

On another occasion Budenz said, "Never in its entire twenty-five years of existence has the Communist party disagreed one iota with the policies and plans of Soviet Russia." He continued, "Never has it found any flaw, even of the smallest, in the Soviet officials. They are 100 per cent correct always. Everyone else is right or wrong with the Reds, dependent on whether they agree or disagree with the Soviet official statements and actions."[89] He went as far as to say that communists in the U.S. constituted "a direct arm of the Soviet Foreign Department…[that] serves a foreign power and never swerves from such service by a hair's breadth."[90] In a separate spate of testimony, Budenz highlighted the secretive nature of communist planning, asserting that "there is a man who is the agent of the Kremlin who directs all Communist activities in the United States." He added, "this man never shows his face. Communist leaders never see him, but they follow his orders or suggestions implicitly. The average American Communist never heard of him." He concluded, "American Communists are as much a fifth column for Russia as the quislings were for Nazi Germany."[91] Later, in front of the U.S. Senate, the ever-reliable Budenz asserted that communist discipline was so inflexible and unyielding that it "cannot be conveyed to a normal American mind." This damning testimony was featured on the front page of the *New York Times*.[92]

Such portrayals, of course, paved the way for the suppression of domestic communists. Joseph McCarthy colorfully described this suppression, comparing the tracking down of communists to "skunk hunting." "When I was a boy," he told a cheering crowd of 15,000 in Johnstown, Pennsylvania, "we used to hunt skunks that killed our chickens. Some of the boys wouldn't go along because of the odor. We have some nice little boys in the Senate today who won't go out and hunt Communists for the same reason. You can't hunt Communists wearing a top hat and lace handkerchief."[93] Such violent bravado would never have been permitted—let alone applauded—had bi-level demonization not been operating full-throttle, a fact that also smoothed the path for the passage of the Communist Control Act of 1954, which Congress passed on 20 August 1954, with only two votes cast against the bill. Signing the bill into law, President Eisenhower said communism was "a conspiracy dedicated to the violent overthrow of our entire form of Government."[94] It also was related to the FBI's Communist Infiltration investigations—or COMINFIL—which, as we've seen, were carried out against people like Martin Luther King, Jr., even though he wasn't a member of the Communist Party. Also, as Michael Paul Rogin has noted, "Under the COMINFIL program, the Bureau didn't wait to act until it had evidence of Communist activity. Rather, it infiltrated any organization where it suspected it might find Communists."[95] This tendency had dire implications for activists of the time.

Bi-level Demonization Continues

During the Vietnam War, the demonization of the external enemy, the Viet Cong, played into the negative portrayal of dissidents on the home front. As early as 1965, for example, mass-media accounts began to rely more heavily on official statements from government authorities, focusing on the involvement of communists in the anti-war movement and emphasizing both the carrying of Viet Cong flags and the presence of (or potential for) violence in the demonstrations. After the mass media constructed a link between the Viet Cong and anti-war protesters, they framed marches and demonstrations as illegitimate disruptions to the social order rather than thoughtful challenges to reigning bellicosity or as expressions of values fundamental to democracy in the United States. Also, quotation marks were placed around phrases like "peace march" and "silent vigil" in order to cast doubt on the legitimacy of these events, a common device that was used when writing about the more radical protesters, but spared later when describing similar activities of more moderate protester groups that emerged.[96]

The Reagan administration also carried out bi-level demonization. Jeane Kirkpatrick, the U.S. Ambassador to the United Nations and member of the influential National Security Planning Group, made the not-so-subtle suggestion that those who failed to support President Reagan's request for funding for the Contras of Nicaragua were de facto supporters of international communism. In an op-ed she wrote for the *Washington Post*, she asserted,

"There is a plan to create a Communist Central America" that "will have momentous consequences for our security." After detailing close ties between Sandinista leaders and Marxism-Leninism, and asserting that the character of insurgent guerrilla forces in El Salvador were "no more ambiguous than that of Nicaragua's government," she went on to write that congressional Democrats who opposed the Reagan administration's Central America policies were denying the government of El Salvador the help it needed "to stave off a very well armed and advised Marxist insurgency" and preventing the Contras from fighting "a repressive, aggressive Marxist government." She contended that, if Congress were to cease aid for El Salvador and Nicaragua, it would be "the enforcer of the Brezhnev doctrine of irreversible Communist revolution."[97] In response to this final claim, political scientist William LeoGrande notes, "Actually it was Lenin who asserted that Communist revolutions were irreversible. The Brezhnev doctrine, articulated at the time of the Soviet invasion of Czechoslovakia, held that the Warsaw Pact had the right to intervene in any member country's internal affairs if the security of the entire socialist camp was endangered by internal developments. This doctrine of limited sovereignty was not unlike the Roosevelt Corollary to the Monroe Doctrine."[98]

Kirkpatrick's equation of Reagan's congressional adversaries with supporters of Marxism continued after her op-ed was published. She later commented that "some members of Congress would prefer to see a Marxist takeover of the region." A similar mentality could be found in the halls of Congress. Rep. Jerry Solomon (R–NY) interrupted his colleague, Stephen Solarz (D–NY), in mid-sentence to say that he was "not going to stand by while this committee is about to sell the U.S. down the drain by aiding and abetting the spread of communism."[99] After these comments, the U.S Department of State and the Department of Defense issued a background paper on Central America that asserted international opposition to Reagan's Central American policy resulted from communist propaganda operations emanating from the Soviet bloc and Cuba.[100]

Incidentally, bi-level demonization is by no means unique to U.S. political culture. In the wake of 11 September 2001, the Chinese government made a concerted effort to link separatists in Xinjiang province to Osama bin Laden and al-Qaeda. Borrowing from the lexicon of the U.S.-led "War on Terrorism," Chinese officials asserted in a 15-page report that Osama bin Laden and his al-Qaeda network had supplied the Xinjiang separatists with money, weaponry, and training in order to help them "launch a 'holy war' aimed at setting up a theocratic 'Islamic state' in Xinjiang." By linking the ethnic Uighurs—who want to secede from China and start their own country, East Turkistan—to international terrorism, the Chinese government is thereby attempting to justify their ongoing and extremely severe suppression. According to Dilixiadi Rasheed, the spokesperson for the East Turkistan Information Center, this alleged linkage is a complete fabrication: "I can totally deny the assertion by the Chinese government about assistance coming from bin Laden. The reason why they're making it is because they want to crack down on anyone exercising freedom of speech to demand autonomy, by linking them to terrorist crimes."[101] Whether Rasheed's refutation is true or not, he offers a working definition of the dynamic that undergirds bi-level demonization. Other countries, like Indonesia, Russia, India, and the Philippines, have followed a similar pattern, tying domestic dissidents to terrorist organizations while fomenting a spike in suppression.[102]

Even more recently, and back in the United States, protesters have been concertedly, if surreptitiously, linked to terrorism. At the Port of Oakland on 7 April 2003, protesters gathered to show their collective dissent against the War on Iraq. After protesters failed to disperse quickly enough, Oakland Police opened fire, using non-lethal beanbag bullets and wooden dowels, as well as high-tech sting-ball grenades. Oakland Mayor Jerry Brown defended his police force, opting to look on the bright side. He said that at least the police "didn't use pepper spray or batons. They were trying to act in a responsible way, but you can't let people just decide to take over the Port of Oakland and create their own occupation."[103] Police claimed that demonstrators provoked the barrage of bullets by throwing bolts and rocks at the law enforcement officers, but the police department's own videotapes and photographs fail to corroborate this assertion. As Sri Louise, a 35-year-old who was pelted in the jaw by either a rubber bullet or a wooden dowel, put it: "Their evidence is not adding up. All of the violence that day was on the part of the Oakland Police Department."[104] More importantly, it soon became public that the California Anti-Terrorism Information Center (CATIC) had warned the Oakland Police Department almost a week before the protest that violence, illegal activity, and traffic snarls might take place. A spokesperson for CATIC, Hallye Jordan, said that the agency occasionally uses the anti-terrorist warning system for functions other than terrorism alerts.[105] Jordan also assured civil libertarians that CATIC wasn't monitoring the activity of dissident citizens. Her reassuring declarations aside, the *Oakland Tribune* learned that CATIC "routinely has issued warnings to law enforcement about activists and protests since its creation in the wake of the Sept. 11, 2001 terrorist attacks."[106]

Another CATIC spokesperson, Mike Van Winkle, was quite a bit more revealing of the logic swirling through CATIC headquarters. "You can almost argue that a protest against (a war ostensibly against international terrorism) is a terrorist act," he said. "I've heard terrorism described as *anything that is violent or has an economic impact,* and shutting down a port certainly would have some impact. Terrorism isn't just bombs going off and killing people."[107] Since communism has lost its strategic relevance as a useful target for demonization, terrorism has emerged as its ideological replacement. Accordingly, since the Soviet Union's demise in 1991, domestic dissidents are now more likely to be linked to terrorism than communism. Recent legislation such as the USA PATRIOT Act, with its new definition of "domestic terrorism," facilitates this almost seamless justificatory switch.[108]

Bi-level demonization highlights how the state and mass media can work together—whether in conscious collusion or not—to suppress radical thinking and action. At the same time, this mode of suppression forges cohesion among non-dissidents, affording them a pseudo-moral authority that allows them to feel better about themselves as they cast scorn on radical activists. As Edelman notes,

> In constructing such enemies and the narrative plots that define their place in history, people are manifestly defining themselves and their place in history as well; the self-definition lends passion to the whole transaction. To support a war against a foreign aggressor who threatens national sovereignty and moral decencies is to construct oneself as a member of a nation of innocent heroes. To define the people one hurts as evil is to define oneself as virtuous. The narrative establishes the identities of enemy and victim-savior by defining the latter as emerging from an innocent past and as destined to help bring about a brighter future world cleansed of the contamination the enemy embodies.[109]

We have seen this dynamic at work from the days of the Committee on Public Information to the present-day "War on Terrorism."

Bi-level demonization also clears a path for other methods of state and mass-media suppression. Once an individual or group has been demonized through linkage to an external enemy, further suppression can occur with fewer objections from the general population.

12

Mass Media Deprecation

Covering the protests of the World Trade Organization in Seattle in 1999, a front-page article in *USA Today* titled "'This Weird Jamboree': Teamsters and Turtle Protectors on the Same Side" kicked off with the following lead: "President Clinton wants to put a 'human face' on trade, but others want to give it a black eye. A bewildering spectrum of voices has converged on Seattle to disrupt the largest trade meeting ever held in the USA. Their protests and arrests have exposed the huge chasm between those who want to harness globalization and those who intend to stop it." The authors go on to note "the astonishing array of causes, costumes, and voices in the Seattle streets" before quoting Chris Matthews of MSNBC's *Hardball*, who dubbed protesters in Seattle "this weird jamboree of the big-neck boys of labor and the tree huggers."[1]

Such a portrayal depicts protesters as fierce opponents of trade who, when it comes to globalization, simply "intend to stop it." As the black eye metaphor subtly implies, these people might be willing to engage in violence to achieve their ostensible goals. In an attempt to get a handle on the "bewildering spectrum of voices" in Seattle, the author turns to a news celebrity, Chris Matthews, for a quotable moment replete with judgmental name-calling for the dissident demonstrators.

How can we best make sense of this portrayal of dissident citizens in action on the streets of Seattle? Is such a characterization of the anti-corporate globalization movement common? Dissidents have long objected to the coverage they have received in the popular media. Are their concerns about deprecatory media coverage warranted? Michael Hardt and Antonio Negri assert, "there have certainly existed previously numerous mechanisms for shaping public opinion and public perception of society, but contemporary media provide enormously more powerful instruments for this task."[2] Can we pinpoint common framing devices—or "powerful instruments"—that the U.S. mass media use to represent the global justice movement?

I use the terms "anti-corporate globalization movement" and "global justice movement" interchangeably.[3] Also, I concertedly avoid the more common term "anti-globalization movement," since, aside from a slender minority, most of these dissidents are not necessarily opposed to globalization. Rather, they are opposed to the uneven development that corporate-driven economic globalization, based on neoliberal principles, engenders. The global justice movement supports many modes of economic and cultural globalization, not the least of which, as Arundhati Roy points out, is the globalization of dissent.[4] The term "anti-globalization" is not confined to the mass media; academics use the term, too.[5]

This chapter addresses a number of questions. How did major U.S. media outlets portray the anti-corporate globalization movement in two major episodes of boots-to-the-pavement activism: WTO protests in Seattle in 1999 and World Bank / International Monetary Fund (IMF) protests in Washington, DC in 2000? What are the dominant frames the mass media used to depict this social movement? Along the way, I provide a framework for more tractable analysis of media treatment of the global justice movement, a framework that has applicability for this movement working in different locales as well as other contemporary dissident movements.

The concept of framing is crucial to this chapter. Media frames present structured "strips" of everyday affairs, each strip being "an arbitrary slice or cut from the stream of ongoing activity."[6] Thus, simplified snapshots are converted into events, and events are converted into news stories. As I mentioned in Chapter 1, media scholar Robert Entman boils framing down to selection and salience. A frame chooses "some aspects of a perceived reality and make them more salient in a communicating text, in such a way as to promote a particular problem definition, causal interpretation, moral evaluation, and/or treatment recommendation for the item described."[7] Activists and conservatives are perpetually duking it out in verbal framing battles on what Sanford Schram and Joe Soss call "the contested terrain of public discourse."[8] Framing, as Entman notes, "plays a major role in the exertion of political power, and the frame in the news text is really the imprint of power—it registers the identity of actors or interests that competed to dominate the text."[9] When it comes to mass-media coverage of dissident movements, this is not an exaggeration. As Nayda Terkildsen and Frauke Schnell point out, "media frames not only alter issue conceptualizations, but also produce a net shift in citizens' issue support."[10] This support from potentially sympathetic members of society is often important to the success of activists.

The Global Justice Movement

The global justice movement is a diverse collection of groups that focus on a wide range of social issues, from poverty, the environment, sexual politics, and corporate greed to human rights, the AIDS epidemic, labor rights, and the perils of capitalism. A striking range of groups work under the global justice movement umbrella, from non-governmental organizations (NGOs) like Oxfam and Global Exchange to environmental organizations such as Greenpeace and the Blue Water Network, from issue-activists like AIDS Coalition to Unleash Power (ACT UP) to black-bloc anarchists. Additionally, coalitions have emerged to help organize and coordinate protests, such as the Direct Action Network, which was active in Seattle, and the Mobilization for Global Justice, which helped orchestrate protests in Washington, DC.

On the one hand, as Mike Moore, the former Director-General of the World Trade Organization, has written, globalization "has joined imperialism, colonialism, capitalism and communism in becoming an all-purpose tag, which can be wielded like a club in almost any ideological direction."[11] On the other hand, it has come to be seen by its boosters as the neoliberal panacea for poverty and uneven development, the paradigmatic band-aid for a whole host of social maladies. Looking up from below, scholar-activist James Mittelman describes globalization as "a historical transformation: in the economy, of livelihoods and modes of existence; in politics, a loss in the degree of control exercised locally...such that the locus of power gradually shifts in varying proportions above and below the territorial state; and in culture, a devaluation of a collectivity's achievements or perceptions of them."[12] In any case, globalization is the defining economic, cultural, and political phenomenon of the contemporary era, and, as such, it has produced not only ardent supporters, but also a variegated "global backlash."[13]

Recently, many of the larger protests have coalesced around resistance to three major supranational institutions: the WTO, the World Bank, and the International Monetary Fund.[14] These global financial institutions combine to form a synecdoche for a rampant neoliberal capitalism that structurally favors corporate profits over the demands of non-elite citizens. Critics of these institutions assert that they are inherently undemocratic and unjustifiably elitist. Additionally, these institutions often ignore local and national laws, thereby sacrificing the environment, worker rights, and consumer safety on the altar of unbridled trade. Through the trifecta of privatization, deregulation, and trade liberalization, the policies of these institutions promote the free flow of capital and goods (although not workers) and therefore encourage shifting production sites to countries with lower wages and fewer environmental standards. Through their Structural Adjustment Programs, the World Bank and IMF oversee the dismantling of public-sector programs related to education and healthcare.[15] At the same time, the staggering debt accrued by developing countries further affects their ability to serve their populations.[16]

Such criticisms of the WTO, IMF, and World Bank have led scholars and activists in recent years to articulate a wide range of alternatives to neoliberal capitalism. In general terms, Hardt and Negri advocate for a militant "multitude" that "reappropriates space and constitutes itself as an active subject" resisting Empire.[17] Others have delineated more concrete visions of the future. Both collaboratively and individually, Michael Albert and Robin Hahnel have advocated for "participatory economics"—or "parecon"— which promotes economic justice, economic democracy, and social solidarity through self-management, participatory planning, and democratic councils of workers and consumers.[18] Such challenges to globalization from above through alternative globalizations from below also resonate in the work of John McMurtry who promotes "a constitutionally governed, democratically accountable framework" grounded in "life standards" and "life economy principles" such as the repudiation of developing-world debt, the creation of binding environmental standards, and the institution of corporate account- ability.[19] Such complex, intentional alternatives to neoliberal capitalism defy critics who assert that the global justice movement is long on criticism but short on alternatives.[20]

Resistance to corporate-led globalization did not begin with the "Battle of Seattle" in late-1999. In fact, the protests in Seattle emerged out of prior local, regional, national, and transnational mobilizations against the inter- national free-trade regime. Nevertheless, Seattle marked a new era of high- profile protests against these powerful international organizations. Also, this protest, while not the first, cemented the presence of transnational mobilizing structures—coordinating the resistance of citizens and organizations from around the world. Sizable coalitions of labor, environmental, and political organizations worked side by side with consumer groups and extra-move- ment groups like churches, community associations, and friendship net- works. Organizationally, these networks of resistance are relatively non-hier- archical, and they have continued to operate since Seattle, using the Internet as an organizing tool, while attempting to be as unpredictable as possible. During heightened episodes of contention when these networks converge in various cities to protest the WTO, World Bank, and/or the IMF—what ac- tivist Medea Benjamin has called the "unholy trinity"[21]—they have received substantial mass-media coverage.

Such mass-media attention has, in turn, secured the consideration of mass-media scholars. By and large, commentators have found coverage to be insufficient on a number of levels. Looking at newspaper coverage of the WTO protests in Seattle, William S. Solomon found that the media "tended to trivialize and misrepresent the demonstrators' perspectives, thus devalu- ing them and rendering them more compatible with corporate values."[22] Also writing about the Seattle protests, Neil deMause zeroed in on media portrayals of violence, turning coverage on its head by asking why state- sanctioned violence—even with chemical weaponry (pepper spray) banned from international wars—is not critically interrogated as unconstitutional violence.[23] Exploring media coverage of the protests against World Bank and IMF policies in Washington, DC in April 2000, media analyst Rachel Coen took a similar stance as she focused on how the media marginalized protesters through denigration.[24] Considering four protests that occurred after Seattle and Washington, DC, John Giuffo came to the conclusion that "poor coverage of the globalization-related events" is not only problematic due to its "focus on the small percentage of protesters who acted violently," but also because it lacks requisite context. He also asserted that the underlying issues that led to these protests were "often glossed over or misrepresented."[25]

Not everyone agrees with Giuffo. In an article that brings the notion of the Habermasian public sphere into the information age, Kevin Michael DeLuca and Jennifer Peeples use the term "the public screen" to describe the way important public discussions take place on computer and television screens. They argue that the symbolic violence and uncivil disobedience carried out by protesters was actually "a necessary prerequisite" that wedged open media space for "expansive and extensive coverage of the issues surrounding the WTO protests."[26] Andrew Rojecki makes a similar argument in his analysis of the Battle in Seattle, contending that media coverage "followed a trend of evolving understanding of and increased sympathy to movement positions. Initial focus on surface features—costumes and stunts—quickly deepened to the underlying issues they symbolized."[27]

My research in this chapter builds from and questions this work. It both widens the range of mass-media sources and news packets under examination and extends analysis to a second protest a few months later in Washington, DC against the World Bank and IMF. After offering and discussing the five central mass-media frames I discovered in my research, I will discuss a number of the claims found in the work of DeLuca and Peeples as well as Rojecki.

Mass-Media Data Sources

When tens of thousands of demonstrators came together in Seattle in 1999 to protest the policies of the WTO, the media followed. Similarly, when dissidents reassembled in Washington, DC in mid-April 2000 (a.k.a. A16) to protest the World Bank and IMF, the media obliged with substantial coverage. A systematic reading of newspaper articles, op-eds, and television transcripts from major mass-media outlets rendered the empirical data in this study. These articles and reports were collected through the *Lexis-Nexis* advanced search engine and *ABI/Inform* using the search terms "anti-globalization," "protest" and "Seattle" or "Washington, DC." Searches were confined

to ten-day periods that straddled the main events in each episode of contention. For the Seattle protests, the ten-day period ran from 28 November
through 7 December 1999, while for the Washington, DC demonstrations,
the time span extended from 11 April to 20 April 2000. Data sources include six major U.S. newspapers—the *New York Times*, the *Washington Post*,
the *Los Angeles Times*, the *Wall Street Journal*, *USA Today*, and the *Boston
Globe*[28]—and five influential television networks—ABC, CBS, NBC, CNN,
and Fox. Because of geographical circulation, national stature, and influence
on public officials, the general population, and each other, these newspapers
and television entities constitute a powerful and significant segment of the
U.S. mass-media system.

The WTO protests in Seattle garnered significantly more media
coverage than the World Bank / IMF demonstrations in Washington, DC.
Combining newspaper articles and television reports, Seattle coverage totaled 221 news packets (111 newspaper articles and 110 television segments),
while the coverage of DC protests added up to 137 (69 newspaper articles
and 68 television segments). In response to these two prominent episodes
of contention, the eleven news outlets produced 358 news packets in total.[29]
Tables 1 through 4 summarize the data according to episode of contention,
type of media, and source.

**Table 1. Seattle: Newspaper Coverage [28 November through 7
December 1999]**

Source	Articles	Percentage
Boston Globe	9	8.1%
Los Angeles Times	21	18.9%
New York Times	27	24.3%
USA Today	23	20.8%
Wall Street Journal	15	13.5%
Washington Post	16	14.4%
Total	111 articles	100%

**Table 2. Seattle: Television Coverage [28 November through 7
December 1999]**

Source	Reports	Percentage
ABC	26	23.6%
NBC	14	12.7%
CBS	19	17.3%
CNN	42	38.2%
Fox	9	8.2%
Total	110 reports	100%

Table 3. DC: Newspaper Coverage [11 April through 20 April 2000]

Source	Articles	Percentage
Boston Globe	9	13.0%
Los Angeles Times	10	14.5%
New York Times	16	23.2%
USA Today	8	11.6%
Wall Street Journal	8	11.6%
Washington Post	18	26.1%
Total	69 articles	100%

Table 4. DC: Television Coverage [11 April through 20 April 2000]

Source	Reports	Percentage
ABC	10	14.8%
NBC	6	8.8%
CBS	12	17.6%
CNN	34	50.0%
Fox	6	8.8%
Total	68 reports	100%

Framing the Global Justice Movement

For this chapter, I read and coded all 358 of these news packets.[30] This extensive reading of news articles, op-eds, and television transcripts led inductively to the identification of five predominant frames: the violence frame, the disruption frame, the freak frame, the ignorance frame, and the amalgam of grievances frame. These frames often intersect in individual news stories, thereby reinforcing each other. In the analysis that follows, I trace media coverage of both the "Battle of Seattle" and the subsequent A16 protests in Washington, DC, identifying the central frames that were adopted by the media to convert these activist actions into news stories.

Violence Frame

Violent protesters, or the potential for violent protests, was the predominant frame through which news stories on the protests in Seattle and Washington, DC were presented. Even when protesters did not actually perpetrate violence, the frame remained in place as journalists remarked on the lack of destruction, the absence of violence, or the potential for violence based on what transpired in Seattle.[31] As Table 5 demonstrates, almost 63% of news stories covering the WTO protests in Seattle featured the violence frame, with more than half of all newspaper accounts and almost three quarters of every television segment focusing on violent protesters. With the World Bank / IMF protests the following April, the violence frame was less prevalent, although it still factored into more than half of all news segments. Such framing encourages the impression that violence dominates the protest terrain when, in fact, it is the exception rather than the rule.

Table 5. Violence Frame

Seattle	# of articles/reports	% of total articles/reports
Newspaper	57	51.4%
Television	82	74.5%
Total	139	62.9%

DC	# of articles/reports	% of total articles/reports
Newspaper	32	46.4%
Television	41	60.3%
Total	73	53.3%

In the lead-up to the WTO protests in Seattle, the *New York Times* noted, "With so many protesters crowding into Seattle, police officials here say they fear some violence."[32] Similarly, NBC news reported, "police and federal agencies…are giving it the same priority as an Olympics or a papal visit." The report went on to mention that the authorities' preparations for the protest "include more than 400 federal emergency medical and operations personnel stationed in Seattle; 2,000 to 3,000 doses of medicine to handle a potential chemical or biological attack. The authorities say while they're ready for violence, they're not predicting any acts of terrorism."[33] This is a classic example of enthymematic argument or presentation whereby the writer / speaker makes a number of assertions in succession while leaving a gap in the assertions that invites the reader / listener to fill in the missing link.[34] In this case, protesters of the WTO are mentioned in direct proximity to assertions regarding chemical and biological attacks, thereby allowing the reader to make the tacit link that these protesters are capable of committing acts of terrorism involving weapons of mass destruction.

A vocabulary of war was also frequently applied to the protesters. For example, the *Washington Post* opened a front-page story with the lead, "A guerrilla army of anti-trade protesters took control of downtown Seattle to-day, forcing the delay of the opening of a global meeting of the World Trade Organization."[35] A few days later, in another front-page story, the newspaper again keyed on the violence, reporting Seattle Police Chief Norm Stamper's assertion that some of the dissidents were apprehended with "fire-start-ing Molotov cocktails and smoke grenades," and that some demonstrators "pelted officers in some locations with rocks and bottles."[36] The *Washington Post* also reported on page 1 that "A guerrilla army of anti-trade protesters took control of downtown Seattle"[37] while the *New York Times* commented that "The disruptions included a brief bomb scare, the smashing of a window in protests at a McDonald's restaurant and a takeover of a vacant three-story building by a self-described group of anarchists."[38] These anarchists, whom we will return to momentarily, became a magnet for media coverage employing the violence frame. The *Boston Globe* quoted Seattle Police Chief Norm Stamper as saying, "We knew violence would be coming to our city in the form of anarchists; that wasn't a secret."[39] Along the lines of turning to authority figures to restore order, *USA Today* looked to Congressman David Dreier (R–CA), who said he was disgusted with the "mob violence" in the streets that was "being used to stifle debate and dialogue at the World Trade Organization." He asserted that "as Americans, we should be united against violence undermining open debate."[40] *USA Today*'s coverage highlights how media framing is selective. The newspaper could have just as easily framed the protest as an attempt to open the closed-door debates that have contrib-uted to the "violent" immiseration of millions around the globe.

The violence frame also dominated news articles about the A16 pro-tests in Washington, DC. The extensive police preparation was a perpetual theme in pre-protest news articles, which repeatedly noted the similarities or potential similarities with the WTO protests in Seattle. As DC Police Chief Charles Ramsey put it in a widely quoted remark, "They ain't burn-ing our city like they did Seattle. I'm not going to let it happen. I guarantee it."[41] The media anticipated violence, and in some cases expected it. As CBS anchor Russ Mitchell put it on the *Evening News* program, "Police in the nation's capital tonight are already in action for what has the potential to be a busy, violent few days."[42] Similarly, the *New York Times*, in an article titled "Washington Braces to Handle Flood of Globalization Protesters," led off with the details of preparation for the violence of "potential troublemak-ers": "A law enforcement armada from a half-dozen city and federal agen-cies is preparing for mass rallies here this week as organizers try to extend the protest against global economics that plunged Seattle into violent street confrontations in November."[43] Making use of a number of predominant frames, Dan Rather colorfully described police preparations this way on the

CBS *Evening News*: "You might think it was a police convention, but it was just part of the security today aimed at preventing what happened recently in Seattle, Washington, from what's happening this weekend in Washington, DC. It's part of the run-up to the World Bank meeting in the nation's capital and protests bent on disrupting that meeting."[44] As one might expect, comparisons with the violence in Seattle were rampant. More than half of all newspaper accounts (53%) of the A16 protests compared happenings in DC to the violence in Seattle, while more than a third (37%) of television segments did the same.

Once the violence actually began, the violence frame dwarfed all others. The media described "scattered incidents of guerrilla warfare, skirmishes all day between protesters and the police,"[45] and depicted battles that "pitted police, many clad in helmets and weird black gauntlets and shin guards like a baseball catcher's, against some of the more militant protesters, many also wearing black and equipped with goggles and gas masks."[46] Such grim scenes reinforced the framing equation that protests plus police equals violence. When police raided dissident headquarters the day before the major protests were to begin, the potential violence of protesters was also reinforced, as the raid turned up what Gainer described as "instruments of crime": chains, chicken wire and gas masks, and something that Gainer said "looks like a Molotov cocktail." Gainer claimed on the CBS *Evening News* that "I personally saw a Molotov cocktail," but later these allegations were proved to be false.[47] A story on CNN also described the confiscation of "instruments of crime." In this account CNN correspondent Kate Snow explained how police arrested a number of protesters "for possessing so-called 'sleeping dragons,' devices used to lock protesters together." Snow went on to note in a comparative vein that "Those devices were used in Seattle last November when there were protests against the World Trade Organization. Clearly, here in Washington D.C., the concern is that things could get a little bit out of hand, like they did in Seattle. Police here are used to dealing with large crowds, but they don't want things to turn violent."[48] Once again, enthymematic presentation is at work, as the media tacitly encourages the viewer to make the connection between the non-violent tactic of lockboxes to the violent situation in Seattle.

Also focusing on violence, the *Wall Street Journal* described—in graphic detail—the scene in Washington, DC, and then generalized this scene to the entire movement:

> The long-awaited "A16" revolt against the forces of globalization arrived with the three images that are becoming a staple of international economic meetings: protesters, gas masks and pepper spray. Police fired a

few canisters of tear gas at protesters, and squirted pepper spray directly into the eyes of some blocking intersections and access to the World Bank/International Monetary Fund meetings here.[49]

It's remarkable that time and time again the media depicted the protest-ers as engaging in and encouraging "violence," even when, as the previous quote demonstrates, state forces were perpetrating violence at a borderline unbridled clip. A big question looms: why wasn't the violence frame applied with greater frequency to the police? After all, they had the guns, batons, and chemical weapons, and they were the ones inflicting injuries that sent people to the hospital. If one considers relatively minor incidents of property destruction "violence," then most assuredly "violence" occurred. But it seems worth mention that these minor property crimes were committed by a small percentage of protesters. Journalists covering the demonstrations were wad-ing through a sea of people who were accusing the WTO, World Bank, and IMF of extreme structural violence through impoverishment, environmental degradation, the evisceration of cultural practices, and the rampant slashing of social safety nets. Yet, the violence frame was almost never applied to the supranational institutions, despite that being the main message that protest-ers—a majority of players on the scene—were trying to get across. In other words, some graffiti and a few broken windows trumped the dumping of toxic chemicals into rivers, the annihilation of educational programs, and the patenting of indigenous plants. Clearly, the reporters on the scene could have employed different frames that would have sent readers and viewers vastly different messages.

In conformity with the violence frame, black-clad anarchists were never far from the headlines, even when they were inactive or absent. For example, a front-page story in the *Boston Globe* began by dramatizing the presence of anarchists in its lead:

> Thousands of chanting activists, some wearing combat boots and gas masks in preparation for violent clashes with police, mobbed the streets of the nation's capital and tried to disrupt meetings of world finance leaders yesterday, the first such demonstration since the riotous protests against the World Trade Organization in Seattle last fall. Police squirted tear gas at one point, and an isolated group of self-described "anarchists" repeatedly tried to break through police barriers, smashing security car windows and splashing emergency vehicles with red paint.[50]

Similarly, the CBS *Evening News* featured a segment that played up the violence. In dramatic fashion, reporter Lee Cowan described the aggressive behavior of black-clad protesters: "In the shadow of the White House, smoke and scuffles: A week of peaceful protests were peaceful no more. Amidst the 10,000 demonstrators hitting the streets early, an angry few, some in black masks, were looking for trouble, and in a city that was virtually shut down, they found it. Pushing and shoving, they made their way to the headquarters of the IMF and World Bank, where tense fights broke out over issues like globalization and corporate greed."[51] Such coverage was common.

Disruption Frame

The disruption frame, which often dovetailed with the violence frame, appeared regularly in news stories leading up to and during both episodes of contention. In fact, it was the most common frame in coverage of the DC protests. The reported penchant for dissident disruption operated at two levels: (1) the disruption of the scheduled meetings of the WTO, World Bank, and IMF, and (2) the general disruption of the lives of regular, law-abiding (and non-protesting) citizens. The former is reasonable, since disrupting the groups' meetings is often a goal, whereas the latter is less reasonable, since disrupting the lives of the populace is rarely a stated objective. Surely, protesters often voiced the desire to "shut this city down," but the disruption frame was applied unevenly. The media could have blamed the WTO, World Bank, or IMF for having their meetings in the city, thereby being the primary cause of the disruption since the meetings would surely attract significant protest. Alternatively, the media could have recorded the protesters' view that the WTO, World Bank, and IMF were massively disrupting millions of lives through so-called free trade agreements, structural adjustment, and neoliberal policies.

Table 6. Disruption Frame

Seattle	# of articles/reports	% of total articles/reports
Newspaper	40	36%
Television	44	40%
Total	84	38%

DC	# of articles/reports	% of total articles/reports
Newspaper	32	46.4%
Television	51	75.0%
Total	83	60.6%

Even in the lead-up to the WTO protests in Seattle, a front-page *Washington Post* article highlighted disruptive unruliness. When WTO Director-General Mike Moore visited Seattle for a pre-meeting mission, the *Post* reported, "he got a taste of what awaits him" as he "was shouted at, interrupted, contradicted and insulted all day by anti-WTO protesters. The low point came when, during a panel discussion, a heckler compared him to Adolf Hitler."[52] President Bill Clinton also weighed in to denounce these deliberate disrupters: "To those who came here to break windows and hurt small businesses, or stop people from going to meetings or having their say, I condemn them."[53]

Not only were the protests disruptive, but, as Judy Muller of ABC News reported, they were *designed* to disrupt. "They call themselves anarchists," she said. "Dressed in black ski masks, they carried their flag and their mayhem to the streets of Seattle this week, much to the dismay of tens of thousands of peaceful protesters." Later, Muller noted, "'Organized anarchy' might seem like an oxymoron, but no longer. Dozens of young people have been planning for months about ways to incite the crowds at this event."[54] Another theme within this frame was that protesters were not only attempting to disrupt the meetings of these supra-national groups, but they were also disrupting the daily lives of innocent citizens who were just trying to make a living. An editorial in the *Wall Street Journal* remarked that, while "the melee in Seattle was televised around the world," the writer was "especially touched" by the story of "a teary 21-year-old bank teller" who rebuked "vandals who broke the bank's windows in the name of opposition to the World Trade Organization" by shouting "This is my job!…This is how I eat!"[55] In mass-media coverage of Seattle, 17% of all news accounts zeroed in on disruptions to the lives of everyday Seattle residents.

This disruption frame was also common in news stories covering A16 events in Washington, DC. For example, CNN anchor Andria Hall kicked off a story about protests of the IMF and World Bank by noting, "It has been a very busy evening for Washington D.C. Police, and it could get worse this weekend. District officers have arrested hundreds of anti-trade demonstrators who are hoping to disrupt meetings of international-lending organizations."[56] Once it was clear that protesters would not be able to prevent the World Bank and IMF meetings from occurring, even though that was their goal, journalists focused on the disruptions that protesters caused for DC residents and tourists. For instance, in a *Wall Street Journal* article titled "Protesters Can't Stop World Bank Parley, But Do Disrupt Downtown Washington," the authors offer the following lead: "On 'A17,' or day two of their revolt, globalization protesters didn't bother trying to close down World Bank meetings. Instead, they immobilized downtown Washington."

The reporters dubbed the protesters' efforts to disrupt as a "spectacle" that "approached farce."[57] In a front-page story, the *Washington Post* highlighted the disruption to the city, offering an array of specifics:

> It was as if a wildly unpredictable snowstorm were bearing down: A formal dance of 1,000 people has been postponed, a seven-days-a-week beauty salon will not open, a settlement company has spirited financial data to a safe location, a construction company felt it had to shut down a major job site. Although massed demonstrators have yet to try an assault on the World Bank and the International Monetary Fund, their announced intent—and vivid images of Seattle's violence—have disrupted many of the workaday routines of the region, especially downtown Washington.[58]

After both police and protesters claimed success, Fox News reported that, "About the only people who weren't victorious in all this were the thousands and thousands of people who work and live in the Washington, D.C., area who were disturbed by all the chaos, complete disruption in the streets of Washington today."[59] In DC protest coverage, nearly a third (31%) of all coverage offered a disruption frame that made DC residents into victims. On 15 and 17 April, the *Washington Post* even printed "Protest Q and A" guides that offered ideas for how commuters could sidestep the protests but were devoid of any information as to why the protesters were in the streets.[60]

Freak Frame

Another recurrent frame in mass-media accounts of dissidents in Seattle and Washington, DC focuses on the non-mainstream values, beliefs, and opinions of these dissidents, as well as their age and appearance. In her short essay, "Of Magenta Hair, Nose Rings, and Naiveté," Robin Broad describes the overly simplistic and often misleading way in which opponents to current forms of economic globalization are frequently depicted in the mainstream media. She asserts,

> The same images are projected over and over again in the press: rowdy students, black-masked anarchists—desperately in need of a shower— smashing a window or burning a car. Too many journalists write as if this movement were a composite of a caricature: an idealistic privileged student with magenta hair and a nose ring who will one day grow up and understand the way things really are.[61]

With this frame, the more radical elements of the global justice move-ment—in terms of both outward appearance and ideology—are transformed into a symbol for the entire movement. As indicated by Table 7, the freak frame was employed frequently in coverage of the Seattle and DC protests, with 36% percent of all Seattle news packets and 42% of all DC news stories zeroing in on the non-mainstream characteristics of demonstrators. In other words, well more than one in three news stories zeroed in on the non-main-stream aspects of protesters.[62] Once again, the selective nature of framing is glaringly apparent. Somehow, financial ministers and power brokers are con-sidered "normal" and "in touch" with ordinary people—even though they are clearly a nonrepresentative slice of the world population—while those who try to bring to light the depredations and structural violence imple-mented by these so-called world leaders are pegged as fringe characters based on their dress, hair color, or piercings.

Table 7. Freak Frame

Seattle	# of articles/reports	% of total articles/reports
Newspaper	43	38.7%
Television	37	33.6%
Total	80	36.2%

DC	# of articles/reports	% of total articles/reports
Newspaper	35	50.7%
Television	23	33.8%
Total	58	42.3%

For example, a *New York Times* article titled "A Carnival of Derision to Greet the Princes of Global Trade," reported that: "There will be hundreds of protesters in sea-turtle costumes and stilt walkers dressed as monarch but-terflies. Thousands of people will tie up the downtown area during a giant demonstration, and protesters will chain themselves to buildings or scale walls to unfurl banners denouncing the target of their ire: the World Trade Organization."[63] Other news accounts depicted the protesters as young and immature. *USA Today* quoted National Association of Manufacturers presi-dent Jerry Jasinowski as saying, "What's disturbing to me about many of the opponents of expanded trade is their refusal to engage in a mature dia-logue about the benefits and costs of expanding global economic activity."[64] Jasinowski expanded his attack on the "fringe elements" on CNN, asserting how he "was struck by how loopy some of the protesters were. I expected a more serious group that was sort of on message and had some points, but they didn't. They were sort of dancing in the streets, pushing people, acting crazy, breaking windows and throwing things. So, it looked like a group that was out of control."[65]

On Fox News Network *Special Report with Brit Hume*, guest Mara Liasson characterized the protesters as politically marginal: "This is a Pat Buchanan–Ralph Nader moment. This is where the left and the right get together, the far left and the far right. It's where Gary Bauer and Ralph Nader come to agreement." Fellow guest on the show, Fred Barnes, responded by calling the protesters "fringe characters who represent practically no one" while Mort Kondracke, another guest, pondered, "Is Seattle going to be more like Woodstock or more like the '68 Democratic convention? If it's like the '68 Democratic convention, there will be Pat Buchanan in his button-down shirt playing Abbie Hoffman."[66]

The freak frame carried over to coverage of the protests against the World Bank and IMF in Washington, DC, with the CBS *Morning Show* dubbing the protesters "a strange cast"[67] and NBC *Nightly News* reporting that "10,000 angry determined youth laid siege" to downtown DC.[68] Such commentary was bolstered by media accounts that focused on the dress and appearance of protesters. A front-page *Washington Post* story kicked off with the following description:

> In the alley that served as the chow line for the revolution, hundreds of aluminum TV trays were piled with cruelty-free rice, beans, fruit, salad and bread. The same menu fit all, even if the same philosophy and fashion did not. Leather-clad, buzz-cut anarchists squatted and ate with natural-fiber dreadlocked reformers. Clean-cut Ivy League leftists chatted and chewed with skateboard "punx," while gray-haired hippies broke bread with rainbow-haired hippies. They were like members of various religions who called the devil by many different names: free trade, the death penalty, the prison-industrial complex, the Gap, the logging industry, capitalism, the School of the Americas, sanctions against Iraq, the U.S. government, the Burmese government, bioengineering, strip malls, sweatshops, the D.C. financial control board. They could not even agree on a slogan, just a vague, all-encompassing phrase: "global justice."[69]

In a subsequent *Washington Post* story, Police Chief Ramsey was credited with interacting amiably with such "rainbow-haired hippies." According to the account, Ramsey "talked with pink-haired women and shook hands with bandanna-masked men."[70] In *USA Today*, Ramsey paternalistically asserted that protesters were "just kids with a cause."[71]

Columnists and opinion-editorial writers frequently adopted the freak frame. The *Washington Post*'s Jonathan Yardley, in a column titled "They Doth Protest Too Much," asserted that dissidents were engaging in "reductio ad absurdum" since "the demonstrations [were] being staged—and 'staged' is certainly the word for it—by a ragtag band of '60s recidivists and assorted 'activists.'" He went on to say the massive collection of state power was "all deployed to keep a few thousand self-righteous troublemakers from dropping bombs into mailboxes or otherwise exercising their God-given right to make fools of themselves."[72] In an op-ed Michael Kelly called protesters "magenta-haired nose-ringers" on a "great crusade to stop the world's finance ministers from doing lunch."[73] The *Wall Street Journal*'s George Melloan added: "Whoever these groups represent, it is not the world's poor and underprivileged. They are mostly the children (some well along in years) of the vast privileged middle class economic development has created in North America and Europe. Many are rebelling against the 'bourgeois values' of their parents."[74] A *New York Times* op-ed written by David Frum highlighted both the youth of protesters as well as their lack of commitment. On the second day of protests, which was a rainy day, "9,000 of the 10,000 people who had arrived to protest decided to stay in bed. This is the down side of recruiting all those idealistic college students to your cause. They don't go to class when it rains—and class is held in English."[75]

This comment about English is a backhanded swipe at the multi-national, multi-ethnic, multi-lingual flavor of the anti-corporate global justice movement. A more common frame in mass-media accounts of the movement highlights the overwhelming whiteness of the movement. For example, the *New York Times* reported that, "Although one goal of the movement against globalization is to turn the focus away from corporations to the poor nations of the world, there were only a handful of people from what the participants call the global South, or developing nations."[76] This point was hammered home by World Bank Spokesperson Caroline Ansty, who, said on CNN: "I don't believe there are many people on the streets who live on less than $1 a day, which is the number out there in the world, there are 1.3 billion people who live on less than $1 a day and we're here to serve them."[77]

On the domestic front, the day before A16, the *Washington Post* ran a story on the failure of the global justice movement to gain black support in the majority-black Washington, DC: "No matter how hard protesters try, they can't seem to get black District residents involved in their fight against global capitalism. They've tried meetings, and speeches and teach-ins at the Mobilization for Global Justice's huge convergence center at Florida Avenue and 14th Street NW. Time and again, African Americans are largely absent."[78] This whiteness frame, a subset of the freak frame that focuses on outward appearance of dissidents, was less common than I expected, given the amount of self-criticism that the movement levels against itself on the topic. Such criticisms—that the global justice movement is largely white and bourgeois—have continued to this day, from both the media as well as demonstrators who want to make sure they're not replicating the very power relations they're working so hard to transform.

Ignorance Frame

In addition to often being portrayed as out of touch with mainstream USAmerica, protesters are also frequently depicted as ignorant or uninformed. Overall, in mass-media coverage of the episodes of contention in Seattle and Washington, DC, nearly one in five news packets (19%) portrayed activists as ignorant or naïve.

Table 8. Ignorance Frame

Seattle	# of articles/reports	% of total articles/reports
Newspaper	30	27.0%
Television	12	10.9%
Total	42	19.0%

DC	# of articles/reports	% of total articles/reports
Newspaper	21	30.4%
Television	5	7.4%
Total	26	19.0%

In coverage of the WTO protests in Seattle, the *Wall Street Journal* led off a story with the following passage: "One day into the Woodstock of antiglobalization, Debbie Carlson, a bandanna-wearing member of a lesbian-activist group, can't get beyond a few sound bites to explain why she is out in the streets with thousands of other free-trade foes who are opposed to the World Trade Organization."[79] Such deprecatory attacks were routinely woven into mass-media accounts.[80] Journalists writing for *USA Today* introduced readers to Herb Green, "a self-described 'displaced marijuana farmer,' [who] felt strongly enough to leave the mountain home where he lives without electricity." After quoting Green—"The turtles speak to me. I'm a voice for the critters: the four-legged ones and one-legged ones, the trees"—they go on to assert that "it was the naiveté of many demonstrators that irritated some delegates and bystanders." Then they turned to Seattle resident Jack Mackey, who attacked protesters more generally for their ignorance: "I'd like to see half of them spell World Trade Organization," he said.[81] Television news also employed the ignorance frame. ABC News reporter Kevin Reese had the following exchange with a protester on the *World News Now* program:

> **Reese:** "What's the point, man?"
> **Unidentified Man:** "Why? Because it's cool."
> **Reese:** "Do you have any idea what WTO does?"
> **Unidentified Man:** "I don't really give a rat's ass."
> **Reese:** "That's what I thought. Have a nice day."[82]

In A16 coverage, this trend continued. A *New York Times* story described the encounter on the street between a "bearded protester in a Mad Max outfit with chain loops and leather leggings" and Joseph Orlow, who is not described physically, but we are told has "for some time…manned his own quieter protest on 15th Street on behalf of insurance claims by Holocaust victims." Orlow, a member of the Institute for Insurance Ethics, looked at "the ragtag jubilation of the visitors" and said, "I think a lot of these people are not interested in core issues but just want an excuse to demonstrate. I'll bet most of them never heard of HR 3750, a bill that would cut off funding if the I.M.F. doesn't reform."[83] Even potential allies could not resist surmising the alleged ignorance of World Bank and IMF protesters.

Of course, adversaries of the protesters were even more inclined to adopt the ignorance frame. For example, on *The Edge with Paula Zahn*, a show that appears on Fox News, correspondent Brian Wilson discussed his views on the protesters:

> I've been trying to figure out very carefully exactly what it is that they are concerned about. I know that it has to do with the debt of third world nations and the policies of the loaning policies of the IMF and the World Bank. But basically, when you try to start getting to the fine points of this with the protesters, they don't really have all the answers. They don't have all the details. It's just generally that they don't like the policies of the World Bank. That's kind of the way it is. That's their enemy, the World Bank, the IMF. But when you get into the real firm details of what it is specifically that they do that bothers them, they get a little fuzzy on the details[84]

Just as the more outlandish elements of the global justice movement are used as representative symbol for the entire movement, so are individual protesters—replete with their already established ignorance—held up, if tacitly, as typical ambassadors for the movement. For example, a front-page *Washington Post* story introduces the reader to Jeff Slagg, a 21-year-old student from Tennessee who at the time of the interview "was playing a green toy accordion and making up words about peace" and whose "activist lineage" included "his ex-hippie mother and his anti-fascist grandfather." The author of the article, David Montgomery, pointed out that "None of his interests or activities has an overt tie to the World Bank or the IMF" and that Slagg "didn't have a clear set of demands." Slagg is quoted as saying that he was in DC because "whenever you see oppression, you try to find out the root cause, and a lot of times it comes back to these government organizations and international organizations." Such framing makes dissidents appear to be transient protesters-on-demand who are virtually ignorant of the causes they rally against and only able to articulate their ideas in the vaguest of terms. But the author, David Montgomery, did not stop there. He proceeded to extrapolate outwards from Slagg's dearth of clearly delineated demands to the demands of the entire movement: "Whatever the turnout today and tomorrow," wrote Montgomery, "it will be a strange experience for Washington, the capital of protest rallies. Here will be that rarest of creatures—a demonstration without demands."[85]

Not only did straight news portray dissidents as ignorant or uninformed, but so did opinion-editorials, and often in vicious fashion. George Melloan wrote in the *Wall Street Journal* that the protesters "display no understanding of what is visible all around them,"[86] while, in the *Los Angeles Times*, John Micklethwait and Adrian Wooldridge characterized the global justice movement as "a disenfranchised, angry minority with a minimal grasp of economics."[87] In the *New York Times*, Thomas Friedman asked rhetorically, "Is there anything more ridiculous in the news today than the protests against the World Trade Organization in Seattle?" Answering his own question, he wrote, "I doubt it. These anti-W.T.O. protesters—who are a Noah's ark of flat-earth advocates, protectionist trade unions and yuppies looking for their 1960's fix—are protesting against the wrong target with the wrong tools."[88] As a guest on Fox News, David Horowitz also attacked protesters for their ignorant ways. "These are old communist ideas," he said. "I mean, that's really what's going on here and it, you know, goes before Marx even, back to Rousseau. These people do not understand what the market is about, and they have kind of missed the 20th century."[89]

Again, this frame was applied unevenly across the terrain of contention. Journalists could have just as easily interrogated the knowledge of financial

ministers with the same vim they questioned the facts and claims of the protesters. In fact, if reporters were to add the world's power brokers as a target,
we might well see a rise in the frequency of this frame.

Amalgam of Grievances Frame

Often criticized in the mass media for their ignorance, dissidents are also
accused of fighting for too many disparate causes. Such an amalgam of grievances, assert many mass-media accounts, leads to the anti-corporate global
justice movement having no clear message. It should be noted that such
views are not confined to the mass media. Prominent intellectuals on the left,
such as Alex Callinicos, who are sympathetic to the movement's goals, have
offered similar critiques.[90] Yet, most activists and scholars assert that such
decentralization of cause and organizational structure afford a level flexibility that, according to Benjamin Shepard, "allows movement interaction to
remain dynamic rather than dogmatic." Such flexibility also facilitates the
possibility of "engaging, listening, and learning from the multitude of narratives from which different players locate their struggles within the movement."[91] Kate O'Neill asserts that the wide-ranging, inclusive nature of the
transnational global justice movement "builds momentum, attracts participants, and engenders communication across the diversity of groups present,
providing the symbolic glue that holds together similar groups from different
countries."[92] However, this more optimistic viewpoint, which highlights the
ability of protesters to make complex connections between what may on the
surface seem like disparate causes, is rarely aired in mass-media accounts
of global justice movement convergences. In fact, roughly one in four news
stories feature this amalgam of grievances frame, as shown in Table 9.

Table 9. Amalgam of Grievances Frame

Seattle	# of articles/reports	% of total articles/reports
Newspaper	38	34.2%
Television	14	12.7%
Total	52	23.5%

DC	# of articles/reports	% of total articles/reports
Newspaper	24	34.8%
Television	17	25.0%
Total	41	29.9%

The amalgam of grievances frame is an analytical category that can be broken down further in order to interrogate its normative underbelly. In fact, there are three variations on this mass-media frame, whereby such an array of causes and goals are portrayed as: (1) value-neutral, (2) a positive trait, or (3) a negative trait.

Table 10. Amalgam of Grievances Frame

Seattle	# of articles/reports	% of total
Value-Neutral	25 (18 newspaper, 7 tv)	48.1%
Positive	5 (5 newspaper, 0 tv)	9.6%
Negative	22 (15 newspaper, 7 tv)	42.3%
Total	52 (newspaper,tv)	100%
DC	**# of articles/reports**	**% of total**
Value-Neutral	19 (10 newspaper, 9 tv)	46.3%
Positive	1 (1 newspaper, 0 tv)	2.5%
Negative	21 (13 newspaper, 8 tv)	51.2%
Total	41	100%

Combining mainstream-media coverage of both episodes of contention, 47.3% of reports were value-neutral, 6.5% were positive, and 46.2% were negative. All but one of the six positive assessments of movement multiplicity appeared in the op-ed section of the prestige press, whereas the other two categories were prevalent across media and source, across the opinion pages and the hard news. On the whole, these numbers contrast sharply with the general sentiments of the global justice movement.

Negative portrayals of movement diversity were seven times more common than positive representations. For instance, in the article mentioned earlier, *USA Today* reported that "A bewildering spectrum of voices has converged on Seattle" in order to give trade "a black eye." The authors later assert that "Anti-WTO forces are united by a profound mistrust of globalization—and almost nothing else."[93] The *Los Angeles Times* editorialized that protesters were a "bewildering array, ranging from anarchists to environmental activists and labor unionists to rebels without any cause at all. Their message, largely lost in the din of street violence, was muddled, blaming free trade for ills such as poverty, unemployment, child labor and rain forest destruction."[94] Op-ed writers also chimed in. Writing in the *Wall Street Journal*, Francis Fukuyama notes that "The 500-odd organizations on hand

range from staid ones like the Sierra Club and the AFL-CIO to fringe groups
like the Raging Grannies and Dyke Action." Fukuyama further asserted that
"serious people on the left need to repudiate the kooky fellow travelers who
have come to party this week in Seattle. Globalization is too serious a business to be the occasion for a radical nostalgia trip."[95]

This deprecatory nostalgia trope was not uncommon. In deriding the
global justice movement's wide range of issues and goals, commentators
and journalists often compared modern-day dissidents with protesters of
the Vietnam War. In a representative example, Michael Medved, writing
an opinion piece for USA Today, commented that in Seattle there was "utter
confusion about the goals of today's demonstrators. Protesters carried signs
ranging from 'Free Tibet' to 'End the Cuban Blockade' to 'Save the Sea
Turtles.' Anti-Vietnam protests focused on a single goal: End the war and
bring the boys home." Therefore, he concluded that unlike Vietnam War
protesters, "the WTO demonstrators face certain failure."[96] Such criticism
of the global justice movement featured historical blinders, as if the struggle
to end the Vietnam War was not intertwined with civil rights, feminist, and
anti-capitalist struggles.

Coverage of A16 also made use of the amalgam of grievances frame.
On CBS, viewers were told to "Pick a topic, any topic, and chances are,
it's being protested this week in Washington."[97] The Washington Post wrote
that protesters were "representing a grab bag of causes and bearing a raft
of objections to the policies of the target institutions,"[98] while USA Today
was more specific, noting the wide range of causes present in DC: protesters belong to such groups as "the Teamsters, the Green Party, Jamaicans for
Peace and Lesbians for Love. Besides Thursday's AFL-CIO-sponsored rally
on the Capitol steps, the groups are holding everything from salsa dances to
vegetarian potluck dinners, where participants are urged to dress in drag, for
causes ranging from saving the Dupont Circle neighborhood in Washington
from gentrification to Ethiopian famine relief." The article also came to the
conclusion that "Despite whatever views they share, their differences are dramatic and their partnership peculiar."[99] This frame was again echoed in the
editorial sections of major newspapers, such as the Wall Street Journal, where
James Taranto, in an op-ed entitled "Global Village Idiots," said that A16
was not a demonstration, but rather "a massive collection of tiny demonstrations." He went on to write:

> Hammers and sickles haven't been this abundant since the Soviet Union
> fell. Every commie organization imaginable is represented here, from
> the venerable Communist Party USA to the Progressive Labor Party to
> Bolshevik Tendency, publisher of a newsletter called 1917. Single-issue

outfits oppose nuclear power, genetically modified food, the tobacco industry. One group demands "wages for housework for all women from the government." As at any left-wing gathering, there are the obligatory placards and banners in support of Mumia Abu-Jamal, murderer of Philadelphia policeman Daniel Faulkner. Other groups oppose the military government of Burma, America's military presence in Korea, Turkey's treatment of Kurds and the Cameroon-Chad pipeline....It must be frustrating to be a young left-wing demonstrator in 2000, longing for the glory days of the Vietnam era. Back then, protesters had a clear and simple message: End the war. By contrast, nothing of consequence unites today's demonstrators. Do the Mumia Abu-Jamal guys lose sleep over Nicaraguan turtles? Do the hearts of the free-Tibet crowd bleed for the victims of Buddhist persecution in Burma? Has a member of the D.C. Statehood Green Party ever shed a tear for the plight of the Kurds?[100]

In a toned-down version of Taranto's screed, William Safire commented in the *New York Times*: "Under the banner of 'Mobilization for Global Justice,' here come anarchists allied with tree-huggers, prayer vigilantes, foreign-debt cancelers, Luddite globophobes and gutsy human rights activists. They seek to relive the battle of Seattle by disrupting next week's sessions of the I.M.F. and World Bank."

Sometimes the amalgam of grievances frame transmogrified into what might be called an internal dissension frame that highlighted the differences between groups uniting to protest these international organizations. For instance, a *New York Times* article featured the variegation among dissidents: "The protesters now descending on Seattle represent groups pushing environmental, labor and third world development causes, and they do not speak with once voice. Among the divisions is whether the trade group should be abolished or reformed."[101] Another *New York Times* article penned by the same author—a story that focused on the diversity at the Washington, DC protests—also showed a tendency to highlight rifts:

> Some of the main backers worry that the movement's successes to date have been purely tactical—headline-grabbing civil disobedience and a flair for organization. They fear that the coalition could blow apart as quickly as it came together. Already, the strains are showing. Though religious groups are one of the main forces behind debt relief, they have refrained from any direct involvement in the demonstrations this Sunday. Instead, they scheduled their own rally last Sunday. Oxfam and Greenpeace, two of the best-known names in social and environmental activism, have severed formal ties to one of the major coalitions

of protesters, though members of both groups are still participating in the protests. The split came about partly over goals. Oxfam officials, for example, say they have made progress trying to reform the World Bank, and getting governments to agree to debt relief. Global Exchange, in contrast, wants the bank and fund abolished."[102]

Meanwhile, on NBC *Nightly News*, reporter Fred Francis described protesters as the "motley alliance of environmentalist, animal and human rights activists who put 10,000 on the streets yesterday [but] only had a tenth as many today, mainly because they could not agree on a plan. Some wanted more direct action, more confrontation. Others wanted what they did Sunday, non-violence. And many just wanted to go home. And that's what most of them did, though some of those who stayed wanted to fight."[103]

On 29 November 1999 on Fox television, Mara Liasson predicted that "the big story from this meeting is going to be the demonstrators and their message."[104] Liasson was only partly correct. The "big story" was the demonstrators, but only rarely were their ideas—or "their message"—brought to the fore. Additionally, when the protesters' ideas and goals were discussed, these goals were often compressed into either inaccurate or oversimplified news packets or expressed only through vague platitudes. In terms of framing, the amalgam of grievances and internal dissension frames combine to portray protesters as collectively stirring a cauldron of disparate, non-cohesive viewpoints and opinions. The structure of such framing—in combination with other journalistic norms and values—leads mass-media workers down the path of misrepresentation through oversimplification and/or inaccuracy.

Such misrepresentation was common. Media outlets frequently oversimplified protesters' goals and ideas, or reduced them to hollow sound bytes. For example, ABC's *Good Morning America* reported, "The protesters' main message has been that globalization is leaving poor nations behind"[105] while a *USA Today* editorial explained the protesters' message as: "Global institutions are evil. By fostering free trade, they destroy jobs and devastate the environment, all to profit multinational corporations. So, close them down."[106] Sebastian Mallaby opined in the *Washington Post* that "If the demonstrators had their way, there would be no WTO. There would therefore be less trade and hence more poverty,"[107] while the *New York Times* editorialized that protesters were "rallying against what they view as the malign forces of economic globalization." After offering this vague explanation, the *Times* went on to assert: "The dissidents' message is sometimes confused and misplaced, especially in wanting to dismantle essential institutions like the World Bank, the International Monetary Fund and the World Trade Organization" since these goals were "a retreat into nostalgia and economic nationalism."[108]

The mass media were also sometimes inaccurate in their portrayals of dissident citizens. One consistent inaccuracy was the assertion that protest- ers were "anti-trade." In reality, most of the protesters of the WTO, WB, and IMF are no more against trade than protesters of genetically modified organisms (GMOs) are against food. Nevertheless, protesters in Seattle and Washington, DC were consistently characterized as "anti-trade." This label became so firmly affixed that *CBS Morning News* began a story on the DC protests by remarking, "In Washington, this is expected to be a very loud weekend with thousands of people in town to protest against world trade," even though protesters were demonstrating against the World Bank and IMF.[109] Other mass-media accounts went further, first marking protesters as anti-trade, and then dismissing this assigned view as a minority position in the United States. The *Wall Street Journal*, for example, cited a public opinion survey that found only a third of those in the U.S. considered trade harmful, and concluded that "the protesters, rather than serving as a sign of growing social unease, might just as easily represent the fading arguments of a shrinking minority who see harm in the globalization of the economy." To confirm this conclusion, the authors turned to Boston University economics professor Jonathan Eaton who, as they put it, viewed the Seattle protests as "an unusual confluence of extremist views." Eaton remarked, "I certainly don't think this is a movement," since being ostensibly anti-trade "isn't a mainstream position in the United States."[110] Mis-categorizing the global justice movement as anti-trade is not simply an innocuous slip of the pen. Tacitly pointing to the intertwining of deprecatory media frames, DeLuca and Peeples note, "Such media labels are the first step to dismissing the pro- testers as Luddites, Nativists, simpletons, or unruly college kids who are sim- ply against things and do not understand the realities of the world."[111]

Framing Dissent

The five deprecatory frames that emerge from my analysis of news articles and television segments are not mutually exclusive, and they often appear within the same news segment, reverberating and reinforcing each other.

Table 11. Overall Framing Data: Seattle and DC Combined

Violence Frame	# of articles/reports	% of total
Newspaper	89	49.5%
Television	123	69.1%
Total	212	59.2%

Disruption Frame	# of articles/reports	% of total
Newspaper	72	40.0%
Television	95	53.4%
Total	167	46.6%

Freak Frame	# of articles/reports	% of total
Newspaper	78	43.3%
Television	60	33.7%
Total	138	38.5%

Ignorance Frame	# of articles/reports	% of total
Newspaper	51	28.3%
Television	17	9.6%
Total	68	19.0%

A of G Frame	# of articles/reports	% of total
Newspaper	62	34.4%
Television	31	17.4%
Total	93	26.0%

Table 11 combines data from the two protests and summarizes it according to the five analytical frames. In general, the violence frame is the most dominant of the five, as it appears in 59% of all mass-media accounts. In other words, the global justice movement was portrayed as violent in nearly three of every five segments, even though a slender minority of its adherents advocate or engage in violent acts as part of their tactical repertoire. This frame is followed in frequency by the disruption frame, which appeared in 47%—or nearly half—of all mass-media segments during these two episodes of contention. This statistic makes more sense given the fact that shutting down the meetings of the WTO and World Bank/IMF was one of the stated goals of the movement. The high incidence of the disruption frame in relation to the routines and schedules of the general citizenry—more than 22% of all news segments—is more of a surprise, since such disruption is only very rarely a stated goal of the movement. Yet one of every five media accounts detailed how the anti-corporate globalization movement allegedly disrupted the lives of everyday people who were simply trying to make a living. The third most common frame overall was the freak frame, which appeared in 39% of all mainstream media accounts. As mentioned in an earlier footnote, this statistic would have almost assuredly been higher had I not been working almost exclusively with television transcripts, which are, of course, devoid of television's powerful images. The fourth most common frame was the amalgam of grievances frame, which appeared in more than a quarter (26%) of all mass-media accounts. Such a variety of goals and groups was rarely portrayed as a positive characteristic (less than 2% of all accounts); rather, more often such multiplicity was portrayed as a liability (12.0%) or as value-neutral (12%). Finally, nearly one in five (19%) mass-media accounts presented global justice movement participants as ignorant or naïve via the ignorance frame. This is remarkable, given the commitment and dedication exhibited by a large number of individuals and organizations over a sustained period of time.

Combining the data for both protests, however, smoothes over differences between coverage of Seattle and DC, and between newspapers and television news. In fact, there were notable differences in coverage. The disruption frame was used with greater relative frequency in DC, especially the disruptions to DC residents. While both protests led to great use of the violence frame, it was even more common in coverage of Seattle. Not surprisingly, given its visual nature, television news tended to rely on the violence and disruption frames more heavily than the prestige press. While 50% of all newspaper accounts talked about violence, nearly 70% of television segments focused on it. As for the disruption frame, newspapers used the frame 40% of the time while 53% of television segments did. Yet, due to its greater detail and word length, newspapers employed the freak, ignorance, and amalgam of grievances frames with greater frequency than their TV news brethren, 43% to 34%, 28% to 10%, and 34% to 17% respectively.

The media coverage of each protest also followed a different longitudinal pattern. With the WTO protests in Seattle, early coverage tended to rely on the amalgam of grievances and freak frames before moving to the ignorance frame and finally to the violence and disruption frames. In DC, a different pattern materialized: Early coverage started out using the same three initial frames used in Seattle, but also featured the violence frame (based on comparisons with Seattle)—and these frames were quickly supplanted by the disruption frame (first, the disruption of World Bank / IMF meetings, and then the disruption of DC life in general).

This brings us to the question of whether violence, or symbolic violence, led to an increase in substantive coverage of the protesters and their messages, as scholars have previously suggested. As noted earlier, DeLuca and Peeples assert that in Seattle "symbolic violence and uncivil disobedience in concert produced compelling images that functioned as the dramatic leads for substantive discussions of the issues provoking the protests." They go on to write, "Far from discrediting or drowning out the message of the WTO protesters, the symbolic violence generated extensive media coverage and an airing of the issues."[112] Additionally, Rojecki maintains that the media gradually became more engaged with the global justice movement's issues and ideas, eventually eschewing "blanket characterization of movement participants" and instead allowing movement participants to offer their own detailed critiques.[113]

To test whether violence and disruption "drew more attention to the issues"[114] as these scholars suggest, I re-visited each story that featured the violence frame, assigning an additional code: whether such stories contained five or more sentences that explained why the protesters were in the streets. Each sentence that offered a critique of the WTO, World Bank, or IMF, or that explained movement reasoning, goals, or ideas was tallied.[115] Table 12 summarizes the results.

Table 12. Does violence lead to deeper coverage?

Seattle	# of articles/reports with five or more issue-sentences	% of articles/reports with violence frame
Newspaper	8	14.0%
Television	6	7.3%
Total	14	10.1%

DC	# of articles/reports with five or more issue-sentences	% of articles/reports with violence frame
Newspaper	2	6.3%
Television	2	4.9%
Total	4	5.5%

As Table 12 shows, newspaper coverage of the WTO protests in Seattle offered the deepest coverage of protester issues and ideas, although only 14% of all stories that adopted the violence frame also offered five or more sentences explaining why demonstrators had taken to the streets. Only 7.3% of television segments on the WTO protests offered such depth. With the IMF / World Bank protests in DC, the media fared even more poorly, with only 5.5% of the mainstream media digging into protester issues with five sentences or more of depth (6.3% of prestige-press accounts and 4.9% of television segments).[116] Ironically, a number of media accounts featured protesters who were concerned that the vandalism and corporate window-breaking would drown out their message, proceeded to completely ignore that message, offering no explanation of why the protesters were demonstrating.[117] At the end of the day, this study did not come up with convincing empirical evidence to support the claim that violence in the streets—"symbolic violence," or vandalism—was a step on the road to deeper, broader coverage of the issues and ideas that galvanize the global justice movement.[118] I cannot share Rojecki's optimism that the mainstream media "helped articulate a critique that is setting an intellectual foundation for a democratic check on transnational economic institutions. The result is a reenergized pluralism in which the media may play a constructive role in building democratically responsive institutions."[119]

It is possible that I draw less optimistic conclusions because my analysis continues through a second round of protests, whereas Rojecki focuses exclusively on the WTO demonstrations in Seattle. Coverage of the Seattle protests may evince a glimmer of promise, but when one continues media analysis through the DC protests, one can see that in-depth coverage of global justice movement grievances actually trails off. DeLuca and Peeples, whose analysis does extend through the DC protests, if in abbreviated fashion, assert that reduced mass-media coverage of protests in DC and the subsequent WTO meetings in Qatar is proof of the importance of symbolic violence to garnering increased media coverage. Indeed, these protests brought out less "symbolic violence." Yet many other crucial contextual factors were at play in these two cases, from the novelty norm to the fact that Qatar was a borderline totalitarian country where protest—let alone "symbolic violence"—was all but illegal. Part of the discrepancy between my conclusions and those of DeLuca and Peeples stems from the fact that we have different research questions (they are more concerned with the role of images and the "public screen") and therefore different methodologies (they tally up screen minutes on the television or number of front-page stories and visual images in the newspaper, whereas I explore in detail the content of these media accounts).[120] I agree that symbolic violence (which I would prefer to call vandalism or property destruction) can wedge open room for additional media coverage, but the content of coverage needs to be carefully scrutinized in order to decide whether, on balance, it aids the protesters' causes or hinders them. Even if symbolic violence opened up opportunities for dissidents to offer their views, what are the dominant impressions and images a reader or viewer is left with? In a sense, we are all are asking whether symbolic violence is able to undermine the dramatization and fragmentation media biases. Or, alternatively, does it simply trigger the authority-order bias—the media's penchant to turn to authority figures who assure everyone that order will soon be restored?

In sum, while John Kifner of the *New York Times* reported that "Protesters from the Mobilization for Social Justice rejoiced that their once obscure objections to international monetary policy were now on the front pages," this analysis demonstrates that things are more complicated.[121] Nevertheless, the research presented here supports Rojecki's claim that in the op-ed section of the newspaper one finds "anything but a monolithic approach to economic globalization or to its antagonists....Even more remarkable," he notes, "is the combined breadth and depth of the critiques,"[122] While op-eds and editorials sometimes provided a venue for ad hominem attacks and name-calling, as we have seen, they also added space for more comprehensive explanations of protester issues, ideas, and goals. And such in-depth forays were not only encountered on the editorial pages. While conducting this study I came across a number of impressive journalistic efforts that engaged complexity, context, and history with great vim and flair. Jonathan Peterson of the *Los Angeles Times* offered a number of reports from Seattle that clearly and cogently explained why protesters had converged there and Dina Temple-Raston wrote similarly stimulating pieces for *USA Today* during the IMF / World Bank protests in DC.[123]

The Perils of the "Media Spotlight"

The mass media play an important role in the construction of social issues and problems.[124] As Sidney Tarrow points out, "The media are far from neutral in the symbols that they select and transmit." Nor are they neutral in *how* they transmit these symbols. Even if social movements are able to work their way under the "media spotlight," as Wisler and Giugni put it, they may receive mass-media coverage that could do them more harm than good.[125] The news media—through framing practices—set the parameters of acceptable public discourse. Voices that fall outside that range are occasionally permitted space on the mass-mediatized terrain, but their price of admission is often subjection to mass-media deprecation.

Mass-media deprecation may open the door for other forms of dissident suppression. Wisler and Giugni note in their study of protest activity in Europe that, since the police "are in a better position to impose their views on disorders involving countercultural movements" that are portrayed through the freak frame, they "feel more legitimate to exert higher levels of repression. They perceive public tolerance towards countercultural disorders as low, and this translates into the adoption of a tougher line."[126] In this sense they find a connection between direct violence and mass-media deprecation. The media's framing tendencies are not necessarily the result of a conscious conspiracy to demobilize social movements. Rather, less conspicuous and dramatic forces and actions are at work. Journalistic norms and values—such as personalization, dramatization, fragmentation, and the authority-order bias—affect what is deemed news and how that news is framed. Adherence to these norms and values—a sign of journalistic professionalism—often results in deprecatory coverage of participants in the global justice movement.

13
Mass Media Underestimation, False Balance, and Disregard

Aside from these forms of mass-media suppression, activists and social movements may also be denigrated, denounced, or dismissed in the mass media in other subtle ways, including underestimation, false balance, and disregard. This mode of suppression spans the gamut from misrepresentation to little or no representation.

Underestimation

Social movements and the state almost always come up with sharply divergent estimates of crowd sizes for protests, marches, and other forms of activism, with social-movement representatives offering higher numbers and state officials proffering lower ones. Such discrepancies have been consistent throughout the course of the twentieth century. Media historian Melvin Small observed unequivocally that, during the Vietnam War era, "police and government officials underestimated crowd size, movement leaders overestimated," and that this trend continued through the anti-Gulf War demonstrations of January 1991. Small then makes the important point that "Most of the time the media accepted police or government crowd estimates as the 'official' estimates, and usually used those figures in their headlines or first paragraphs."[1] Todd Gitlin supports this assessment. Indeed, he considers "disparagement by numbers (under-counting)" as one of the central framing devices that bolstered deprecatory themes about anti-war protesters.[2]

Since crowd size is an important indicator of mass-media attention, mass media underestimation is no trivial matter from the perspective of social movement participants and potential supporters.[3] From the perspective of the state, crowd-counting is a no-win situation, since the social movement will almost always claim there were more people in attendance than the official count reports. Historically, in the case of Washington, DC, where many large protest events take place, the U.S. Park Police have been charged with the task of estimating crowd size. This has been a consistent source of frustration for them. As one U.S. Park Police officer put it in 1995, "If we say [the crowd] was 250,000, we'll be told it was a half-million. If we say it was a half-million, we'll be told it was a million. Anything short of a million, and you can probably bet we'll take some heat for it."[4] Small notes that disputing the accuracy of crowd enumeration isn't a habit of the left in the United States. Conservatives such as Rush Limbaugh have also disputed crowd estimates for events organized by the right.[5] In terms of Washington, DC protests events, the Park Police have essentially become a perpetual, post-protest punching bag. As a result, the Park Police, having engaged in numerous crowd-counting disputes, became the only law enforcement agency in the country to have its mathematical counting methodology recorded in the Federal Register so as to protect itself from attack.[6]

The already tense relations between U.S. Park Police and protesters were inflamed in 1995 during the Million Man March, which was sponsored by the Nation of Islam and its leader Louis Farrakhan. While the Park Police estimated the crowd was 400,000 people, organizers claimed there were more than a million in attendance, and, when the Park Police refused to revamp its count, Farrakhan threatened to sue the Park Service in order to force it to revise its estimate.[7] Researchers from Boston University fanned the flames of controversy when they came up with an independent crowd estimate of 870,000.[8] Amid a swirl of hostile disagreement and potential litigation, the Park Police eventually relented, amending its calculation. Congress subsequently ordered the Park Police to stay out of further crowd counts on the Mall. This directive was codified in the 1997 appropriations bill for the Department of the Interior, in which Congress barred the National Park Service from carrying out future crowd estimates. The Park Services chief of public affairs seemed almost relieved, saying that the Park Service "is not upset or disappointed" about the legislation since "it has always been a thankless job for the Park Service. Every organization would always cry foul, saying the numbers should be larger."[9] From this moment to the present, if activists wanted their protests and marches counted, they would have to hire an outside agency to do the counting. This has remained the case, though the police sometimes offer informal estimates of crowd size. With the Park Police's official methodology set aside, the possibilities for crowd underestimation have only increased.

Also, as with mass media deprecation, journalistic norms and values often times thwart coverage. With mass media underestimation, the authority-order bias plays an important role. When attempting to ascertain the attendance at a public protest, march, or rally, the mass media look to authority figures, whether it is the Park Police, the Chief of Police, or the president of the United States, to provide official information on crowd size and to tacitly offer reassurance that the temporary disorder caused by the dissident activity is under control or will be under control shortly.[10] During the breakdown of social order that often accompanies social-movement activity, the state is frequently seen by the mass media as an objective source of information and looked to for the restoration of public confidence.

False Balance

Mass media also misrepresent dissent through falsely balancing dissidents with counterdemonstrators. In an exploration of journalistic standards, Ross Gelbspan has noted, "The professional canon of journalistic fairness requires reporters who write about a controversy to present competing points of view."[11] Indeed, since objectivity as a blueprint for journalism writing has become more myth than reality, the notions of balance, fairness, and accuracy have gained greater currency in the news production industry. In fact, balance has become a pillar of "good" journalism.

According to Entman, "Balance aims for neutrality. It requires that reporters present the views of legitimate spokespersons of the conflicting sides in any significant dispute, and provide both sides with roughly equal attention."[12] Similarly, Gans writes: "Political balance is usually achieved by identifying the dominant, most widespread, or most vocal positions, then presenting 'both sides.'"[13] Hallin adds another dimension in his definition of mass-media balance: "News coverage of any political controversy should be impartial, representing without favor the positions of all the contending parties."[14] Despite Hallin's gesture toward nuance and multiplicity, the idea of balance, when translated onto the page or screen, often amounts to a mano-a-mano showdown between two opposing views, rather than the presentation of multiple viewpoints and opinions. This is one factor, among others, that induces oversimplified news in the United States.

When it comes to mass-media coverage of protest activity, balanced coverage often means inaccurate coverage, since the sides being balanced against each other are usually incongruent in terms of size and vociferousness. As Small ponders, "How much space or time should 1000 counterdemonstrators receive compared to 100,000 demonstrators?"[15] This can sometimes be a difficult question, and one that reporters covering major protests events must contend with. The clear answer, however, is not equal coverage for both groups.

In an article in the *Columbia Journalism Review*, Brent Cunningham excavates the term objectivity, asserting that objectivity makes journalists into "passive recipients of news, rather than aggressive analyzers and explainers of it."[16] A similar archaeological effort is needed for the notion of balance since the concept is much more complex than it appears at its surface. Balance is deemed to be fair, but what about the introduction of new and complex ideas into the discourse? These new, complex ideas take more time to explain than old ideas that support the status quo. So in this sense, equal time falls in favor of people proffering easily digestible, not ideologically contrary, viewpoints. In the film *Manufacturing Consent*, Noam Chomsky calls this debilitating phenomenon "the condition of concision." Pierre Bourdieu makes a similar point regarding the unquestioning acceptance of "received ideas" and the difficulties involved in challenging these ossified ideas in the public sphere.[17]

As we have seen, prestige-media coverage of dissident activity exhibits an inclination for personalizing news, and this dovetails in an important way with the journalistic norm of balance. Instead of concentrating on power, context, and process, the prestige press tends to personalize social issues, focusing on the individual claims-makers who are locked in political battle. Bennett goes as far as to call personalization "one of the defining biases of news."[18] With such a bias, the macro is foregone in favor of the micro and institutional analyses are skipped over in favor of personalized stories that stress the trials and tribulations of individuals. As coverage of the global justice movement demonstrates, these personalized stories are seldom linked to deeper social analysis. Personalized news encourages the public to adopt a hyper-individualistic stance toward political and social problems, rather than a collective, community response. The U.S. mainstream media's focus on personalities also encourages passivity and spectatorship. This journalistic norm does not benefit social movements that are attempting to propagate complex ideas that are contrary to the status quo.

With coverage of dissident social movements, the personalization and balance norms combine to create the impression of the dueling protesters. These conflicting protesters, who receive "roughly equal attention," create the appearance of a street debate where roughly equal forces are having at it. This conveniently omits the fact that the forces are unequal, that one side has many more protesters, while the other side may have only a handful of supporters. In turn, this "balance" is a powerful political tool that government officials can use to downgrade dissidents, arguing their numbers are not overwhelming or significant.

This notion of balance as a form of informational bias can be seen in mass-media coverage of protests during the Vietnam War era. In Gitlin's parlance, this framing device was "polarization," or the tendency to underscore counter-demonstrators, neo-Nazi, and ultra-Right groups that were compared with anti-war protesters in an unspoken balance of extremes.[19] This was sometimes achieved by giving roughly equal amounts of column inches to demonstrators and counterdemonstrators.[20] In alignment with Roland Barthes's assertion that "pictures...are more imperative than writing, they impose meaning without analyzing or diluting it," "balance" was also realized through accompanying photographs.[21] For instance, Gitlin described a misleading photograph in the *New York Times* that had the effect of visually equating the anti-war and counterdemonstrators by showing identically sized segments of each group in the frame of the photograph, even though counterdemonstrators were only a small fraction of the size of the anti-war protesters.[22] With a similar effect, newspapers have at other times devoted equal numbers of photographs of protesters and counterdemonstrators, thereby affording the impression of balanced opposition.

State officials have consciously taken advantage of the journalistic tendency to balance dissidents with counterprotesters. During the Nixon presidency, when the Vietnam Veterans Against the War garnered media attention by tossing the medals they had earned in Vietnam onto the Capitol steps, Nixon aide Charles Colson coordinated separate media events comprised of military veterans who supported Nixon's foreign policy. These public-relations media magnets did in fact draw reporters into their orbit and, guided by journalism's balance norm, these pro-Nixon veterans groups received substantial media coverage.[23]

Disregard

Sociologists Pamela Oliver and Gregory Maney divide research on media coverage of protests into two categories: (1) studies that explore the distortion of protest events, and (2) those that examine whether an event will receive coverage at all.[24] Mass media disregard as a suppressive tactic speaks to this latter category.

Many dissident efforts never even make it onto the mass media's agenda, and this is significant, since the processes of agenda setting and priming mass media coverage help shape which controversial political and social issues people think about and how they think about them.[25] Agenda setting is a process whereby social issues and problems that garner prominent attention from the national news media become the social issues and problems that the public sees as most vital. Priming is the way people's standards of evaluation regarding politics change. By focusing on some issues and disregarding others, the national mass media influence the standards people use to assess political leaders, candidates, governments, and public policies. When the mass media disregard social movements, they exert a subtle form of suppression that affects the ability of dissidents to maintain morale, to gain new adherents, or to get taken seriously by potentially sympathetic bystander publics.

Social-movement research has consistently debunked the notion that each protest event has an equal chance of being covered by the mass media. Mainstream media outlets are neither disinterested selectors nor neutral recorders of social events.[26] Nevertheless, the rates of attention and disregard are not necessarily stable across time and place.[27] In general, the mass media have exhibited a "selection bias" in that media agendas and values affect whether protest events are reported, often regardless of the features of the events themselves.[28]

A number of social scientists have looked at media-coverage rates of dissident protest events. For example, McCarthy, McPhail, and Smith found that, in 1982, 13% of all protests in Washington, DC were covered by a major media outlet. In 1991, the coverage rate dropped to 7.1%.[29] In a smaller mass-media market—Madison, Wisconsin—Oliver and Myers discovered that fewer than half of the protests (44%) that took place in this city in 1994 received next-day coverage in the two Madison newspapers.[30] In a separate study of the same city, Oliver and Maney widened their time scope to 1993–1996 and found 46% of message-based protest events received local newspaper coverage. They also note that the content of a protest's message influences its coverage more than its form does.[31]

Oliver and Myers take us toward an understanding of mass media disregard as they point to two factors that most affect whether a protest event will be disregarded or not: (1) the size of protest, and (2) the presence of conflict.[32] Sometimes state officials play a deliberate, calculated role in mass media disregard. President Lyndon Johnson refrained from publicly acknowledging anti-war activity so as to, in Downey and Rasmussen's estimation, "condemn through disconfirmation designed to render the opposition impotent."[33] Johnson also deliberately scheduled events that would be sure to draw media attention away from anti-war efforts. Small argues that, in 1966, he "purposefully stole headlines" from Senate Foreign Relations Committee hearings on the war by convening a conference on the war in Hawaii.[34]

The machinations of ideology may also play a role in mass media disregard of dissident viewpoints and actions. Proponents of the "propaganda framework" of the mass media assert that news outlets often serve the perceived national interests of governments by propagating views rooted in ideological consensus.[35] Accordingly, dissident views in conflict with this zeitgeist of consensus are marginalized and disregarded by the media. Therefore, as Edward Herman argues, when it comes to the U.S. mass-media's treatment of dissident views, "meaningful diversity of opinion may be absent from media coverage of important issues."[36] Building from this foundation, Justin Lewis demonstrates how progressive interpretations of public opinion data are consistently suppressed. Lewis's main point is that the descriptions and interpretations of public opinion data are "of enormous political significance," and that, therefore, such explanations are yet another way that dissident viewpoints and actions are disregarded in the mainstream media.

Lewis writes that the "discursive framework" of "the opinion poll…is often the ideological glue that masks social division and creates the mythical notion of a common set of interests."[37]

When dissidents' views are not completely blocked out of mass-media coverage, they often experience what we might call "relative disregard." As we have seen, the mass media often deny activists an opportunity to offer alternative interpretations of political events while they allow authority figures—often governmental officials—to assume the role of information-provider regarding both domestic and foreign policy. As media critic Daniel Hallin demonstrates, this propensity to confer with state power plays into the marginalization of dissidents in a less intuitive way. While his research finds that "the function of journalism was generally to transmit to the public the government's perspective on the world," he shows that this was done subtly through source selection and stratification of television stories into different types: "dissenters appeared in stories primarily about dissent itself, while official spokespeople appeared in stories which reported the actual news of the war."[38] Thus, the type of story in which dissidents appear also serves to structure thought. This stratification serves as an example of another piece in the mass-mediatized suppression puzzle: Often, if dissident views appear at all, they appear buried in the back pages of the front section, or sometimes even in the Fashion or Style sections of the newspaper, and therefore as not worthy of being a source in "hard news." For example, in covering the protests against the World Bank and IMF in Washington, DC in April, 2000, the *Washington Post* reported that the leaders of the Group of 77 (an organization of developing countries) "said they are the victims of an unfair economic order, and sided squarely with the thousands of protesters."[39] While such international support coming from an organization whose populations comprise more than 80% of the world's people might be seen as important and worthy of serious consideration, the story was buried deep in the front section on page A31. The *Washington Post* often puts stories about protests and marches in the Metro section, since they occurred in the city, even if the protests spoke to national or international issues or if many of the protesters came from outside the city. Thus, story placement allows the views of dissident citizens to be devalued, if they are not ignored completely.[40]

Anti-war Movement: Iraq, 2001–2003

In order to see how these three interrelated actions play out in the real world, the following section focuses on resistance to the George W. Bush administration's drive to a renewed war on Iraq, otherwise known as the Iraq War. In the immediate aftermath of the attacks of 11 September 2001, the Bush cabinet debated the administration's response. From the beginning, Secretary of Defense Donald Rumsfeld wanted to pin the attacks on Saddam Hussein and Iraq. In fact, according to *Time* magazine, he was "so determined to find a rationale for an attack that on 10 separate occasions he asked the CIA to find evidence linking Iraq to the terror attacks." However, to Rumsfeld's chagrin, the CIA "repeatedly came back empty-handed," without the requisite proof.[41] In a post-9/11 cabinet meeting Rumsfeld asked, "Why shouldn't we go against Iraq, not just al Qaeda?" Supposedly, it didn't take long for President Bush's plans to slip into alignment with the Secretary of Defense's skewed vision.[42]

As soon as it became clear that the Bush administration had plans for invading Iraq, protests emerged. Using demonstrations against the Vietnam War as a measuring stick, a number of activists, organizers, and scholars observed that anti-war resistance this time around was unprecedented in that the war had not even officially begun and people were already in the streets. Once protesters put their boots to the pavement, mass media underestimation, false balance, and disregard were immediately observable.

Crowd underestimation occurred in a number of instances and in a few varieties. For example, in October 2002, a number of peace groups organized the largest anti-war protest since the Vietnam War era. While even conservative estimates pegged the crowd at over 100,000 people, *National Public Radio* (NPR) reported on its show *Weekend All Things Considered* that the crowd "was not as large as the organizers of the protest had predicted. They had said there would be 100,000 people here." NPR's Nancy Marshall continued, "I'd say there are fewer than 10,000. However, they did accomplish their goal of actually marching around the White House in one continuous stream of people. It is a little bit thin in some areas, but nonetheless, they have marched around the White House."[43] After a massive outcry from protesters who deemed this an egregious underestimation, NPR released the following post-broadcast apology on 30 October: "On Saturday, October 26th, a story on the protest in Washington, DC, against the US war with Iraq, we erroneously reported on *All Things Considered* that the size of the crowd was, and I quote, 'fewer than 10,000.' While Park Service employees gave no official estimate, it is clear that the crowd was substantially larger than that. On Sunday, October 27th, we reported on *Weekend Edition* that protest organizers estimated the crowd at 100,000. We apologize for the error." Despite this correction, the misinformational damage had been done.

Even with its substantial size, the protest received scant coverage in the *New York Times*, which devoted a single story to the demonstration. This article, which appeared on page eight, donned the misleading title: "Thousands March in Washington Against Going to War in Iraq."[44] The article also led off with the following lines: "Thousands of protesters marched through Washington's streets, chanting and waving banners against possible military action against Iraq. The rally was one of several held in American and foreign cities today. Fewer people attended than organizers had said they hoped for, even though after days of cold, wet weather, the sun came out this morning."[45] Even the DC Police Chief Charles Ramsey estimated the crowd to be much higher than 75,000, so saying "thousands" instead of "tens of thousands" or "a hundred thousand" was an egregious underestimation.

This tacit form of mass media underestimation was common. A *Washington Post* story about the massive anti-war protest in Florence, Italy was titled "Anti-War Activists Protest in Florence: Thousands Denounce U.S. Iraq Policy" despite the fact that over 400,000 people were in attendance.[46] Also, an example of relative disregard, this story was buried in the front section on page A26.

A few months later, in February 2003, the *Washington Post*, zeroing in on the protests in New York City, ran a story titled "In New York, Thousands Protest a War Against Iraq," which, once again, was misleading since between 100,000—the police estimate—and 400,000—the organizer estimate—were in attendance.[47] Major newspapers also failed to fully explain how a labyrinth of police barricades thwarted the efforts of tens of thousands of protesters to reach the site of the protest, thereby depleting the overall count. This protest, which occurred in concert with demonstrations in two hundred cities across the country and six hundred across the world, garnered a mere 370 words on NBC *Nightly News*. Anchor John Seigenthaler commented that protesters were in New York in "the thousands" and compared the massive protest in New York negatively with those in Europe, saying "the crowds [in the U.S. were] generally smaller than those in Europe."[48]

About a month later, in March 2003, the *New York Times* covered worldwide protests responding to the onset of U.S. hostilities in Iraq with a story entitled, "Thousands Denounce War and the United States in Cities Around the World."[49] Again, this was an understatement, since in reality more than a million people were in the streets around the world. A week earlier, the *Washington Post* severely underestimated a candlelight vigil that took place on the Mall, describing the crowd as 400 people when really there were several thousand.[50] The newspaper subsequently issued a correction in order to adjust its crowd estimate.

Protest coverage during to the build-up to Iraq War also suffered from false balance. For example, the NBC *Sunday Today Show* ran a short piece entitled "National Anti-war and Pro-war Protests Intensify," which reported in its entirety:

> War rallies are intensifying as the US inches closer to a possible inva-
> sion of Iraq. Thousands of anti-war protestors gathered in Los Angeles
> and Washington, DC, on Saturday. The crowds that gathered near the
> White House included about two dozen who were arrested allegedly
> for crossing a police line. While in Fort Bragg, North Carolina, about
> 1,000 people attended a rally to support the troops. Twenty thousand
> troops from Fort Bragg are currently deployed overseas. More protests
> nationwide are scheduled for later today.

By placing the two protests side by side like this, NBC viewers might be led
to believe that protests across the country were relatively even in terms of the
number of people attending.

False balance was especially evident after full hostilities began on 20
March 2003, and pro-war rallies sprouted up to counter the anti-war sentiments. In a *New York Times* article about the worldwide reaction to the
onset of the Iraq War—from the critical comments of Russian President
Vladimir Putin, French President Jacques Chirac, and Pope John Paul II to
U.S. flag burners in the streets of Athens—there were three accompanying
photographs from the United States. Of the three, one was a shot of supporters of the war who had gathered in Jackson, Mississippi, even though there
was no mention of such supporters in the actual article.[51] In an article that
appeared in the *San Francisco Chronicle*, discussion of numbers was dropped
entirely, as pro-war rallies and anti-war demonstrations were again placed
side-by-side. The lead of the story read, "While peace reigned in the streets
of San Francisco as anti-war protesters took a breather Sunday, flag-waving,
horn-honking citizens in other Bay Area cities filled the void with rallies to
support American troops and President Bush." The article never pointed out
that protests against the war were many times the size of the pro-war gatherings.[52] Although the article discussed both pro-war and anti-war events, the
title was "Troops, War Policy Supported at Local Rallies; Hundreds Show
Up in San Jose" and the accompanying photographs were both of war supporters. Following the war-related events that occurred in Washington, DC
on 12 April 2003, the *Washington Post* ran a number of articles. Taken together, counter-demonstrators who were in favor of war received roughly the
same number of column inches as anti-war protesters even though the latter
outnumbered the former by a 6 to 1 ratio.[53] In this time period, a number
of articles were published that examined the pro-war rallies, despite the relatively small numbers these events were drawing.[54]

Anti-war protesters also experienced mass media disregard. This could
be tied to the notion of the "institutionalization of protest," mentioned in
Chapter 1, whereby routinized protest activity is less in line with the journal-

istic norms and values that guide news production.[55] One prominent example
of such disregard involves the protests in Washington, DC in October 2002,
which was only covered by one story in the *New York Times*.[56] Although the
story that protesters were so numerous that they were able to form a thick
wall stretching two miles around the White House might have seemed "fit to
print," the *New York Times* essentially disregarded this concerted chorus of
anti-war sentiment. Considering 650 busloads of people came from around
the country and that organizers estimated over 200,000 attendees and police
100,000, one might have expected deeper coverage.

Among the prestige press, the *Wall Street Journal* was particularly notable for its disregard of anti-war protest, not publishing a single article that
focused on the massive worldwide protests that occurred in mid-February
2003. It also completely ignored the rally on 8 March in Washington, DC
that was sponsored by Code Pink.[57] It ran a single article on the large anti-
war protests that took place in DC in mid-March, and then virtually ignored
the protests that occurred there a month later, although in the run-up to the
April protest, the *Wall Street Journal* did run a story on police tactics for handling anti-war protests.[58] But the *Wall Street Journal* wasn't alone in its disregard. Neither ABC nor NBC news ran stories specifically on the January
2003 protests in DC or elsewhere, despite the sizable throngs in attendance.
NBC also failed to cover the Code Pink rally and march in Washington, as
did CBS, although CBS—in line with the personalization norm—did run
stories on the celebrities who were involved in Code Pink.

When it came to the Code Pink event, relative disregard was also present.
While the *Washington Post* covered the rally and march, which was attended
by a number of national celebrities and activists such as Alice Walker, Susan
Griffin, Michelle Shocked, Helen Caldicott, Maxine Hong Kingston, and
Terry Tempest Williams, it covered it in the Metro section.[59] This despite
the fact that the event culminated in the dramatic and noteworthy arrest of
Walker, Kingston, Code Pink organizer Medea Benjamin, and others.

By the time Code Pink and company had been relegated to the pages
of the Metro section, relative disregard had virtually become the *Washington
Post*'s standard operating procedure. In late October 2002, after the *Post*
consigned a 100,000-person protest to the Metro section, many readers
recognized a trend and contacted the newspaper in order to register their
complaints. This evoked a response from Ombudsman Michael Getler, who
summarized the coverage that the *Post* gave the protest in an early November
editorial:

> The *Post* didn't put the story on the front page Sunday. It put it halfway
> down the front page of the Metro section, with a couple of ho-hum

photographs that captured the protest's fringe elements. A photo of a larger crowd of demonstrators ran in the lower right-hand corner of the paper's front page. But that picture didn't have a headline. Rather, it was linked to a story and headline from Mexico about a meeting there between President Bush and the leaders of South Korea and Japan. The article was about problems dogging U.S. efforts to lead a multilateral coalition against Iraq and North Korea.

Getler went to the newspaper editors and asked why the story wasn't worthy of front-page coverage. They replied that space on the front page that day was highly competitive, and that, while it was a "close call," the protest story didn't make the cut. More specifically, Getler informed readers that the stories in competition with the DC protest story were "two stories about the horrendous attempt to rescue hostages from a Moscow theater, two follow-up stories to the sniper capture, and timely political stories about races in Maryland and Minnesota." In the end the protest article lost out to a "story from Mexico about the reported setbacks to two Bush initiatives."[60] The newspaper editors also reasoned that, since most people read the Metro section, such relegation was insignificant. However, the Ombudsman disagreed. "That sounds logical," he wrote, "but I'm with the complaining readers on this." He went on:

> Washington gets a lot of protest rallies, and most go into Metro. But this was one big demonstration—a lot bigger, these *Post* editors acknowledge, than they expected—and it was not about some narrow special interest. People had traveled here from all over the country. *Post* editors, in my view, fumbled this one, not because they are pro-war but because they were surprised at the turnout, and talked themselves into a compromise solution that pushed the story inside.[61]

This candid response, albeit laced with rationalizations, made explicit the newspaper's propensity for relative disregard of protests in the nation's capital.

But while this casual acknowledgement of systematic relative disregard of the anti-war movement was striking, it didn't seem to have much of an effect on subsequent coverage. In an ensuing round of national protests in December, in which demonstrators in 120 U.S. cities and 37 states held events in concert with International Human Rights Day, the *Post* featured a single Metro-section story on the events.

Why does mass media disregard matter to social movements and dissident citizens? Recent social-movement research has found that media attention plays a significant role in how protests are policed. "When protest becomes a blind spot in the public sphere, the likelihood of repression increases."[62] Importantly, Wisler and Giugni note:

> Social movements that are unable to make their voice heard in the public sphere are also more likely to experience repression than movements enjoying better access in the mass media. The police, in other words, modulate their action in response to the systematic outcome of the symbolic battle that affects protest movements and varies across them.[63]

So, being disregarded by the media leaves social movements and dissident citizens open to other forms of suppression. The political impacts can be even more devastating.

At the end of the day, the mass media are crucial in terms of how the general public comes to understand social movements and their adherents. Nevertheless, generally speaking, the role of the mass media has received very little attention in social-movement studies. By breaking down the mass media's role in the suppression of dissent into four main modes of suppression—(1) mass media manipulation, (2) bi-level demonization, (3) mass media deprecation, and (4) mass media underestimation, false balance, and disregard—I am attempting to address this gap in the understanding of social movements. In Chapters 2 through 13 of this book, I have offered a general framework for the suppression of dissent in the United States. Now, I'll shift my attention to the suppression of dissent in the post-9/11 era. In the following chapter, I explore how the twelve modes of suppression I have just laid out are relevant to understanding how the state and mass media have suppressed domestic activism after the attacks of 11 September 2001.

14
The Suppression of Dissent after 9/11

Karl Marx wrote in the *Eighteenth Brumaire*, "Men make their own history but they do not make it just as they please; they do not make it under circumstances chosen by themselves but under circumstances directly encountered, given, and transmitted from the past. The tradition of all the dead generations weighs like a nightmare on the brain of the living."[1] As this book has demonstrated, the suppression of dissent, as carried out by the state and mass-media, has a long, ignominious history in the United States. This chapter, which focuses on suppression after the terrorist attacks of 11 September 2001, explores how these well-established methods of suppression "weigh like a nightmare" on activists today.

Geoffrey Stone, author of *Perilous Times: Free Speech in Wartime*, writes that "like previous wartime leaders, members of the Bush administration have used fear to their political advantage and tarred their opponents as 'disloyal.'"[2] Heidi Boghosian, the Executive Director of the National Lawyers Guild, takes this critique a step further in *The Assault on Free Speech, Public Assembly, and Dissent* when she contends that in the wake of the 11 September attacks, "rather than protecting First Amendment rights of United States citizens and prosecuting police abuses as it ought to do, the Justice Department under Attorney General John Ashcroft has systematically encouraged these abuses and acted as a cheerleader for government officials using excessive force and abusing their authority against citizens engaged in free speech." She concludes that Justice Department misdeeds "have been so aggressive that rights of free assembly and free speech guaranteed by the First Amendment of the United States Constitution are simply no longer available to the citizens of this country."[3]

As we have seen, war affects the dialectic of restriction and resistance, with the state ratcheting the brackets of restriction when it feels threatened. Not surprisingly, after the attacks of 11 September, international terrorism became a powerful pretext for clamping down on domestic dissent. As social critic Kristian Williams put it, "Almost at once, when the planes hit the Twin Towers, the state's repressive apparatus moved into overdrive." Focusing on the historical continuity of the state's response, Williams notes that after September 11, "Official policy has become more aggressive...but none of this required a radical shift in the direction of government activity.

Instead, it brought the preexisting patterns into sharper focus and signaled to functionaries at every level of government that they need not be concerned, even in principle, with the rights or dignity of those they have been ordered to control."[4] Thus, a crucial corollary to preemptive belligerence on the international front is a knee-jerk lockstep at home that demands obedience, compliance, and conformity. Dissident citizens by definition refuse to mindlessly slide into alignment with these supposed social exigencies. Meanwhile, a burgeoning "security" apparatus at home—replete with a new bureaucratic wing, the Department of Homeland Security—seeks out and coerces diversions from the norm.

An important dimension to the suppression of dissent in the post-9/11 era is heightened secrecy in the everyday activities of the government. Geoffrey Stone finds the Bush administration's "obsession with secrecy" to be extremely problematic since "overboard assertions of secrecy cripple informed public discourse." According to Stone, a professor of law at the University of Chicago, "Excessive secrecy has been a consistent feature of the Bush administration, ranging from its refusal to disclose the names of those it detained after September 11 and its narrowing of the Freedom of Information Act, to its unprecedented closure of deportation proceedings and its redaction of 'sensitive' information from tens of thousands of government documents and Web sites."[5] Such state secrecy appears to be more about protecting the Bush administration from public scrutiny than combating terrorism or fighting crime. And, crucially, corruption thrives in hyper-secretive settings.

The suppression of dissent has almost always been difficult to detect, unless one is being suppressed directly by the state or mass media. But the Bush administration's borderline fixation on secrecy can also make the suppression of dissent all the more difficult to detect until long after the fact. Nevertheless, in this chapter I take the model I have presented in this book and apply it to the suppression of dissent in the post-9/11 era in order to see which modes of suppression are more common and which are less apparent.

Direct Violence

In November 2003, trade ministers from Chile to Canada assembled in Miami to discuss the possibility of forming a massive, hemisphere-wide free-trade zone called the Free Trade Area of the Americas (FTAA). While supporters of neoliberal capitalism found the idea of the FTAA to be a necessary step on the road to deepened, corporate-driven globalization, numerous protesters showed up in Miami to challenge this calculus by asserting that such trade deals would only bolster corporate coffers, exacerbate environmental degradation, and quicken the clip of job outsourcing.

Protesters were met in Miami by Police Chief John Timoney, who was no stranger to monitoring protests. Timoney was the same law enforcement official who headed zealous police efforts to quell dissent during the Republican National Convention in Philadelphia in 2000. Not coincidentally, the police in Miami used many of the same tactics police employed in Philadelphia, but in Miami they added a vicious, violent twist when police donning riot gear fired rubber bullets, tear gas, and pepper spray into the masses of protesters. Police also attacked protesters with batons, electric shields, and concussion grenades.[6] Legal observers from the National Lawyers Guild (NLG) witnessed "indiscriminate, excessive force against hundreds of nonviolent protesters." Police assaulted four legal observers from the NLG and arrested five, despite the clearly marked NLG uniforms.[7] Journalist Jeremy Scahill, who was shot with rubber bullets, dubbed the scene "a militarized zone."[8] Naomi Klein described the state's effort to intimidate this way: "Small, peaceful demonstrators were attacked with extreme force; organizations were infiltrated by undercover officers who used stun guns; buses of union members were prevented from joining permitted marches; people were beaten with batons; activists had guns pointed at their heads at checkpoints."[9] One disconcerted protester interviewed on *Democracy Now!* remarked, "I cannot understand why I don't have the right to protest in my own country. Why can't I do this? I have never gone to a rally before, political or any kind. And here I come, I see police presence, $8.5 million spent on this. We could have built an elementary school or something. I don't understand that. It makes me sick. Why are people shooting? No one's got guns, everyone's got cameras. People just want to get their voices heard."[10]

In the end, hundreds of people—including *Democracy Now!* producer Ana Nogueira—were arrested.[11] Soon community members created the Miami Civilian Investigative Panel (CIP), a board that investigated complaints against the Miami police and issued a public report. During pre-report testimony, Police Chief Timoney offered a consistent, standard-issue excuse for his police force's over-the-top behavior: he blamed protesters for starting the trouble. Timoney told the CIP members that "Police officers were assaulted with all sorts of objects from golf balls to bricks to a whole host of other weapons" including "Marbles and wrenches and nuts, lugs." He also said, "There may be some complaints of bruises and what have you" but "there were no head wounds as a result of police sticks across people's heads." Video shot by demonstrators and filmmakers—as well as numerous eyewitness accounts—contradicted the police chief's claims.[12]

In July 2006, the CIP issued its official report. It found that of the 219 arrests—"the overwhelming majority...misdemeanors"—only four resulted in conviction.[13] The report also found that protesters were profiled and unlawfully detained, searched, and arrested. After giving weak dispersal orders through ineffective bullhorns, police officers failed to provide adequate escape paths. The CIP also found that police deployed "non lethal weapons and munitions" in ways that were "inconsistent with the manufacturer's guidelines and user manuals, MPD [Miami Police Department] Departmental Orders, Standard Operating Procedures, and constitutional guarantees."[14]

Police Chief Timoney had told the CIP that pepper spray and Taser electric shock devices were preferable to batons. "I'll opt for the pepper spray or the Taser anytime," he said. Timoney's rosy testimony rang hollow against the brutal facts surrounding the case of Carl Kesser, a local filmmaker who was shot in the head with a non-lethal beanbag shot by police as they advanced on a group of activists. In a gory scene that was played on the evening news in Miami, Kesser's video camera jerked violently before blood splattered onto the camera's lens as he retreated with a pack of other journalists in an attempt to escape the wrath of the cops. Kesser underwent emergency surgery to remove the projectiles that split through his scalp and lodged themselves above his right eye.[15]

Kesser wasn't the only one victimized by the Miami Police Department's direct violence. Elizabeth Ritter, an attorney from Coral Gables, Florida, became frustrated with her inability to get to work since the police shut down the courthouse. She made a sign that read "Fear Totalitarianism" and joined ranks with the FTAA protesters. Soon after, police attacked her with a hail of rubber bullets as she tried to cover herself while lying in the street. This vicious attack against a non-violent demonstrator was caught on videotape. On a separate video, Broward County Sheriff's deputies were caught on tape praising each other for the draconian violence they unleashed on Ritter and others, whom they called "scurrying cockroaches." Referring to Ritter, whom they referred to as "the lady in the red dress," one sergeant said excitedly, "I don't know who got her, but it went right through the sign and hit her smack dab in the middle of the head!" His remark brought forth hearty hooting from his colleagues.[16] Broward County Major John Brooks was caught on video backslapping colleagues, saying, "I was so pumped up about how good you guys were." Brooks later apologized publicly for his callousness.[17]

FTAA protesters may well get the last laugh, though. Kesser sued the City of Miami, stemming from the nerve damage and partial paralysis of his face that he suffered from the police's beanbag weaponry. In the end, the city agreed to pay him $180,000. While Kesser said he probably only broke even after court and medical costs, he found hope in the fact that "there's probably 150, 170 cases behind me."[18] Regardless of the settlements earned by demonstrators, the police's vicious militarism gives protesters—and potential protesters—pause.

In Miami and elsewhere, police forces have been deploying "non-lethal" or "less-lethal" weapons as a supposed step in the humanitarian direction. But how humane are these weapons? A recent report by Amnesty International found that since June 2001, more than 150 people had been killed by tasers. The report stated, "the use of the tasers in many of the cases which resulted in death was excessive, amounting in some cases to cruel, inhuman or degrading treatment. In many of the cases reviewed by AI, those who came in contact with the police were not armed, or had already been restrained."[19] Police have used tasers to subdue activists. In September 2006 police shot a protester with a taser at an event called Human Rights Fest in Charlotte, North Carolina. Six additional demonstrators were arrested at the event, even though protesters had a permit.[20] The following month, two protesters were shot with a taser in Pittsburgh, where they were protesting the presence of Jeb Bush and Rick Santorum.[21]

Use of supposedly non-lethal weapons like tasers, beanbag rounds, and tear gas has become one facet of what many are now calling "The Miami Model" for crushing dissent.[22] This repressive model was thrumming full-throttle in Jacksonville, Oregon in October 2004 when protesters demonstrated President Bush's stopover during the presidential campaign season. Bush had just completed a campaign event in nearby Central Point and had driven to the Jacksonville Inn for dinner and to stay the night. Both pro-Bush and anti-Bush people showed up near the Inn to voice their opinions about the president. Approximately 200 anti-Bush protesters marched in front of the hotel and chanted slogans, which apparently Bush and his dining party could hear on the patio where they dined. Protest leaders had even made arrangements with local police that demonstrations would remain peaceful and confined to the sidewalk. Organizer Shelley Elkovich said, "This was billed as a very mellow family-friendly event, there was no civil disobedience planned, and we had this code of nonviolence."[23]

The state had different plans, however. Riot-gear clad police insisted that the protesters retreat a block. As one witness described it, "The riot police had formed a line from sidewalk to sidewalk and were moving towards us with their batons, yelling, 'Move back, move back.'" When demonstrators didn't move quickly enough, the police struck them with their batons and fired pepper balls at them. Michael Moss, a goat farmer who was participating in the event, described it this way: "When I turned my back on the police, they opened fire from point-blank range, probably three-to-four feet away. It sounded like something between a paint ball gun and a really loud lightbulb popping. It was pa-pa-pa-pa-pa, pa-pa-pa. I got hit six times." Moss first believed he was being pelted by rubber bullets until he felt the burning. "It felt like there was a red-hot branding iron being put on my back," he said, "and that's how it stayed for the remainder of the evening." Leisa Glass, who attended the rally with her young daughter, said that police "turned the event into something aggressive when it wasn't aggressive. They made me feel like I was not living in a free country. I felt I was living in some other place that was a non-democracy." Ralph Temple of the ACLU said at a post-event news conference, "You're supposed to use these weapons as a substitute for lethal weapons. You don't use them just to make people move." Paul Copeland, a board member of the Southern Oregon ACLU chapter, made the larger point: "More and more we're finding a militarization of police in the way that they relate to the citizens. We have to get the police to understand that dressing up as the army and assaulting citizens is not OK."[24] In July 2006, the ACLU filed a class action suit against the Secret Service and local police forces for violating citizens' constitutional rights.[25]

Public Prosecutions and Hearings

In the wake of the 9/11 attacks, the state has organized numerous terrorism-related prosecutions and hearings. Many of these rely on laws that make it a crime to provide material support to groups designated as terrorist organizations. Two prime examples of public prosecutions tied to terrorism investigations are the Lackawanna Six of Buffalo, New York and the Portland Seven from Oregon. Both cases were hyped by the U.S. State Department as breakthrough investigations and convictions involving high-value terrorist cells.

The Lackawanna Six—also known as the Buffalo Six—are six Yemeni-Americans who lived in the Buffalo area. Five of the six men had strong local roots, being born and raised in Lackawanna where they attended public schools, played in local soccer leagues, and started families. In the spring of 2001, the men attended an al-Qaeda-sponsored military training camp in Afghanistan where they viewed pro-al-Qaeda tapes and learned how to operate automatic firearms and explode bombs. The Justice Department also claimed they shared tea in Afghanistan with Osama bin Laden. Being from the United States, the men were used by the Bush administration as proof that Islamic terrorism could originate in the "homeland." Because of this, a journalist from the *Washington Post* wrote, "The 'Lackawanna Six' case embodied the nation's worst fears about the reach of Islamic terror networks."[26]

While the defendants were not accused of planning or engaging in any act of terrorism, they were charged with providing "material support" to a foreign terrorist organization, a crime with a maximum sentence of 10 years in prison and $250,000 fine. The Lackawanna Six surprised numerous observers by admitting so quickly to the crime. Defense attorneys for the Six later explained why their clients agreed to plead guilty in such speedy fashion. Attorney Patrick J. Brown said, "We had to worry about the defendants being whisked out of the courtroom and declared enemy combatants if the case started going well for us. So we just ran up the white flag and folded. Most of us wish we'd never been associated with this case."[27] Apparently, the prosecution had hinted heavily that if the Six didn't admit their guilt they could be locked up indefinitely as "enemy combatants" and prosecuted outside the civilian judicial system where they'd have fewer legal rights.[28] *Washington Post* reporter Michael Powell sums up the importance of this case: "The Lackawanna case illustrates how the post-Sept. 11, 2001, legal landscape tilts heavily toward the prosecution, government critics contend. Future defendants in terror cases could face the same choice: Plead guilty or face the possibility of indefinite imprisonment or even the death penalty."

Tapping into the heavily loaded vocabulary of terrorism, Attorney General Ashcroft, FBI Director Robert Mueller, and the prosecution repeatedly labeled the Six as members of a terrorist "sleeper cell." The arrests were heralded as a triumph for the retrofitted Bureau. Announcing the original arrests, Deputy Attorney General Larry Thompson said, "United States law enforcement has identified, investigated and disrupted al Qaeda-trained terrorist cell on American soil." In a news conference that afternoon in Buffalo, Governor George Pataki stated, "These arrests send a very important message: Terrorism is real, and not just in major cities." A couple months after that, President Bush's National Security Advisor Condoleezza Rice alluded to the Six when she said, "Victories are won every day. When a cell is broken up in Buffalo or when something is broken up in Singapore or broken up in Germany, those are victories in the war on terrorism." The president himself mentioned the Six in his State of the Union address, dubbing them an "Al Qaeda cell" that had been stopped in its tracks.[29]

Such anti-terrorist state hype was kicked into gear once again in another high-profile terrorism case, this one on the other side of the country in Portland, Oregon. In fall 2002, the FBI started to construct connections between al-Qaeda and Muslims living in Portland. In early October, FBI agents swooped in and arrested a handful of alleged terrorists with Oregon ties. The suspects were accused of conspiring to wage war against U.S. troops in Afghanistan and of providing support to al-Qaeda. Attorney General Ashcroft quickly organized a news conference to declare the indictments as a "defining day" in the "War on Terrorism."[30]

In many ways, those arrested in Portland led lives that were similar to members of the Lackawanna Six: They were practicing Muslims with young families, and all but one of them were born in the United States. Of the six in the initial indictment, five were men—Jeffrey Leon Battle, Ahmed Ibrahim

Bilal, Muhammad Ibrahim Bilal, Patrice Lumumba Ford, and Habis
Abdulla al Saoub—and one was a woman—October Martinique Lewis,
Battle's ex-wife. A federal grand jury in Portland charged them with con-
spiring to levy war against the United States, join the Taliban, and provide
services and support to al-Qaeda.[31] In Spring 2003, a final suspect—Maher
"Mike" Hawash—was added, rounding out the Portland Seven. Hawash, a
Palestinian-born U.S. citizen who was working as a contract engineer with
Intel, was snatched from his office on 20 March 2003.[32]

According to the indictment, in October 2001, the men traveled to
Hong Kong in hopes of making their way to Afghanistan through Pakistan.
Lewis, who did not make the trip, became involved when she wired money to Battle. According to the Justice Department, she wired him a total
of $2,130 in eight transactions "with the knowledge the money would be
used to support his attempt to reach Afghanistan." Their plans were foiled,
however, when Pakistani officials refused to grant them visas. Ultimately
the group decided to disband. Ford and Mohammed Bilal returned to the
United States in late 2001 and early 2002, Ashcroft said.[33] Only al Saoub
wended his way to the battlefield where he was killed in a gunfight with
Pakistani troops in October 2003.[34]

By the time al Saoub was killed, the other six members of the Portland
Seven had journeyed to the courtroom where they reached plea agreements.
By the end of 2003, all of them had been sentenced.[35] Hawash—who cooperated like "a prosecutor's dream witness"—received the lightest sentence: sev-
en years in federal prison.[36] Ahmed Bilal was given a ten-year sentence, while
his brother Muhammad received eight years for conspiracy and gun charges.
The Bilal brothers also cooperated with the government, although Hawash
was the state's superstar, even helping to secure guilty pleas for the relatively
compliant brothers. Two of the Portland Seven—Jeffrey Leon Battle and
Patrice Lumumba Ford—refused to cooperate with the authorities. They received the harshest sentences: 18 years in prison. October Martinique Lewis
was sentenced to three years in a work camp for her role in wiring money to
her ex-husband.[37]

At a news conference, Attorney General Ashcroft talked up the importance of the Portland Seven case, declaring the successful prosecution of the
Seven "cell" as a significant feather in the Bush administration's "War on
Terror" cap. He said, "The United States does not casually or capriciously
charge its own citizens with providing support to terrorists. But the terrorist
attacks on September 11th, 2001, serve as a constant, stark reminder that
America has enemies in the world…and sometimes the enemies are here at
home."[38] The FBI lists the Portland Seven case as one of a handful of "successes" on its "National Security Branch" web page.[39] In testimony to the

Senate Judiciary Committee in May 2004, FBI Director Mueller referred to "the successful dismantling of the 'Portland Seven' terror cell."[40]

Despite the government's best efforts to paint the Portland Seven as dangerous terrorists, not everyone was convinced. At his sentencing hearing Patrice Lumumba Ford explained why he wanted to go fight in Afghanistan: "I refused to stand passively in the face of policies, which inflicted such tremendous injustice death and destruction on Muslims." Directly addressing his young son, he said, "I hope you will understand that I could no longer watch these horrible things continue to happen to other children any more than I could watch them happen to you." According to Stanley Cohen, attorney for Lumumba Ford, his client was a principled man comparable to dissident leaders like Nelson Mandela, John Brown, and Malcolm X. He said, "The government has gone to great lengths to paint Mr. Ford in the worst light. These are complex, difficult times, and he is a complex man."[41] Lumumba Ford's family is no stranger to state suppression. His father, Kent Ford, was a Black Panther who was a leader in the Portland BPP in the 1960s and was held in perpetual suspicion by local police forces and the FBI.[42] Patrice Lumumba Ford may well have been a revolutionary in the mold of the Panthers. But in the hyper-charged atmosphere after September 11, such principled dissident claims are extremely difficult to make.

Employment Deprivation

As we have seen, dissident citizens can be fired—or at least threatened with termination—because of their radical politics. In the post-September-11 era, with many people on ideological edge, this mode of suppression was common across employment sectors.

After Hurricane Katrina struck the Gulf Coast of the United States in fall 2005, Laura Berg, a clinical nurse specialist in Albuquerque, New Mexico, wrote a letter to the *Alibi*, a weekly Albuquerque newspaper, criticizing how the Bush administration dealt with the hurricane and conducted the Iraq War. In her letter, she suggested that President Bush and members of his administration "should be tried for criminal negligence." Once the letter was published, the Veterans Administration (VA), where Berg worked, seized her computer and opened an investigation for "sedition." According to the ACLU, which took up the nurse's cause, VA human resources head Mel Hooker said in a letter dated in November 2005 that his agency was required to scrutinize "any act which potentially represents sedition." A VA spokesperson claimed the Administration would never disallow its employees "from exercising their freedom of speech" but Peter Simonson of the ACLU wasn't buying the VA's public-relations-ese. "From all appearances," he said in a press release, "the seizure of her work computer was an act of retaliation and a hardball attempt to scare Laura into silence."[43]

Jeff Bingaman, a Democratic Senator from New Mexico, jumped into the fracas, asserting that the VA's actions represented "a very real possibility of chilling legitimate political speech." In a letter to the Secretary of Veterans Affairs, R. James Nicholson, Bingaman wrote, "In a democracy, expressing disagreement with the government's actions does not amount to sedition or insurrection. It is, and must remain, protected speech. Although it may be permissible to implement restrictions regarding a government employee's political activities during work hours or on government premises, such employees do not surrender their right to freedom of speech when they enlist in government service."[44] Bingaman's point of view won out at the end of the day, as Berg kept her job and was cleared of any wrongdoing. Secretary Nicholson avowed, "Let me be clear: Her letter to the editor did not amount to sedition." Nicholson responded to Senator Bingaman, stating "The use of the word 'sedition' was not appropriate....No further action has been taken or will be taken related to the employee in this matter."[45] Berg responded to the whole matter by saying, "I did not sign away my First Amendment rights as a citizen...by choosing to serve in the federal government and choosing to serve veterans and care for people that have been wounded like this, you know. And this letter sounds like something from a totalitarian regime.... This was way out line."[46]

Numerous other workers have had their jobs threatened because of their political actions. One lighter example comes from Washington state, where a bus driver working for the Issaquah School District gave President George Bush the finger as his motorcade passed her and her bus-load of middle-school students. Congress member Dave Reichert, a Republican who was accompanying Bush at the time, reported the driver to the school superintendent, and the driver was let go. This is how Reichert himself described the incident at a Republican picnic in August 2006: "And as the motorcade went by, the president and I drove by on I-5, the president was having a great time. He was waving at everybody, he waved at the kids. He got the biggest kick out of the kids leaning out the window to say hello to the president of the United States. The sad part of it is though, we got to the last bus—and I won't tell you which school district this was—the bus driver flipped the president off." After the audience moaned in disapproval, Reichert said, "So the very next day, you know what I did? I called the superintendent of that school district and that bus driver no longer works for that school."[47] The bus driver, a 43-year-old single mother whose name has not been released, is teaming up with her union to fight her termination.[48]

As in the past, educators have experienced employment deprivation as part of the "War on Terror." In a high-profile case, Tariq Ramadan, a highly respected Swiss Muslim intellectual, was denied entry into the U.S. to take a position at Notre Dame University due to alleged ties to foreign terrorist organizations. Professor Ramadan originally had been granted a visa in 2004, but the State Department revoked it without explanation based on counsel from the Department of Homeland Security. The State Department eventually admitted it had rejected Ramadan's visa application, but claimed his political views were not a factor in its decision. Rather, State Department spokesperson Kurtis Cooper said, "A U.S. consular officer has denied Dr. Tariq Ramadan's visa application for providing material support to a terrorist organization." That "terrorist organization" was the Committee for Charity and Aid to Palestinians, a group based in France that Ramadan donated approximately $770 to in 2000. Ramadan figures the U.S. government has linked Committee for Charity and Aid to Palestinians to Hamas, which was designated a foreign terrorist organization by the U.S. government. Ramadan made his donation before Hamas was designated a foreign terrorist organization. In September 2006, the Bush administration rescinded the terrorism charges it had leveled against him, but the State Department continued to deny his entrance.[49]

Ramadan, who teaches Philosophy and Islamic Studies at Oxford University in England and who was named by *Time* magazine as one of the one hundred most likely innovators of the 21st century, said on *Democracy Now!* that he was denied entrance to the United States for political reasons, or more precisely, because of what he has been saying about the Bush administration. He said, "Of course, I'm critical about...the American policy in the Middle East. The unilateral support to Israel is, for me, problematic....You know, one thing which is really important to know is that during my interviews at the U.S. embassy in Switzerland, mainly the discussion was about my position on Iraq and my position on Palestine. And I was saying resistance is legitimate, even though I'm against the means they are using."[50]

Tariq Ramadan wasn't the only scholar barred from the United States based on politics. In a lesser known case, John Milios, an economics professor at the National Technical University of Athens, was denied admittance to the U.S. for a conference at the State University of New York at Stony Brook called "How Class Works." Federal authorities claimed there were visa irregularities with Milios's papers, even though he said he had used his visa numerous times in the past without any snags. He also said he "had just checked with the U.S. Embassy in Athens before coming to confirm that the visa was valid even though it was in the final six months of its 10-year duration." After arriving at John F. Kennedy International Airport in New York City, he was detained and grilled for hours. The character of his questioning was distinctly political, he said. Milios was sent home without attending the conference. Michael Zweig, a conference organizer, wrote in response to Milios's barring, "I am embarrassed to have to protest this unacceptable political intrusion into the flow of ideas and intellectual work across borders, a mission at the heart of any university's purpose." The exclusion of Milios, which was ignored by the mainstream press in the U.S., was front-page news in Greece.[51]

Scholars already inside the United States were also suffering from suppression, being denied tenure or promotion, getting flat-out fired, or undergoing microscopic scrutiny of their life's work. The Yale anthropology Department had hired one of the brightest young anthropologists in the field when it brought David Graeber to New Haven. Graeber was published widely, admired internationally for his work, and revered by his students. He was also an anarchist—and one who insisted on blending theory and practice. As he said in an interview,

> One thing that I've learned in academia is no one much cares what your politics are as long as you don't do anything about them. You can espouse the most radical positions imaginable, as long as you're willing to be a hypocrite about them. The moment you give any signs that you might not be a hypocrite, that you might be capable of standing on principle even when it's not politically convenient, then everything's different. And of course anarchism isn't about high theory: it's precisely the willingness to try to live by your principles.[52]

Yale officials said Graeber had issues showing up to class on time and turning in grades before their due date. They also professed Graeber's politics had nothing to do with the school's refusal to renew his contract in the fall of 2005. But Graeber begs to differ. He believes his anarchism—and his willingness to act on it—is what led to Yale's decision not to keep him on faculty. Everything seemed to be going fine for Graeber at Yale until 2001 when he left for sabbatical and became more involved in on-the-ground anarchist actions at global justice movement mobilizations. Upon his return to the university, some of his colleagues treated him differently, with a colder shoulder.[53] After he received word his contract would not be renewed, his students at Yale and his colleagues from around the world rallied in support of him through a letter-writing campaign and an online petition. His anthropology colleagues heaped praise upon him and his work, with colleagues like Maurice Bloch of the London School of Economics writing to the Yale administration that "It's extremely odd that one of the most brilliant anthropologists is being excluded from the department at Yale in such an extraordinary fashion."[54] None of this was enough, however, to alter the school's decision not to renew Graeber's contract, so he left Yale at the end of the 2005–2006 academic year.

At the end of the day, Graeber was better off than many scholars: he was offered a one-year sabbatical on the condition that he drop his complaint against their decision and then not return after his time off.[55] Stanley Aronowitz, professor at the Graduate Center of the City University of New York, said about the anarchist anthropologist, "I actually think places like Yale are not for people like David Graeber. He's a public intellectual. He speaks out. He participates. He's not someone who simply does good scholarship; he's an activist and a controversial person." While the *Wall Street Journal* attacked him for his "bourgeois ambitions" and his willingness to participate in "the very wage system he aims to abolish,"[56] Graeber could walk away from Yale with, as he put it, his "integrity intact."[57]

Another example of an academic losing his job in the post-9/11 era is Sami Al-Arian, a tenured computer-science professor at the University of South Florida (USF), who was fired based on his political commentary after the attacks of 11 September 2001. Shortly after the terrorist strikes, Al-Arian appeared on the Fox Television program "The O'Reilly Factor" where he was berated by the host, Bill O'Reilly, who suggested Al-Arian was a terrorist and called the fact that he was a college professor "a very disturbing situation." Said O'Reilly, "If I was the CIA, I'd follow you wherever you went." Following the show, a shower of hate mail and threatening phone calls were made to Al-Arian and USF. The university responded by holding an emergency board meeting to explore the suggestion made on "The O'Reilly Factor" that the school "may be a hotbed of support for Arab militants."[58] Shortly thereafter, Al-Arian was suspended from his position and ordered off campus for his safety and the protection of others. Meanwhile, the university hired lawyers to figure out how to fire Al-Arian. After the USF Board of Trustees voted 12 to 1 to terminate his employment, he was fired. His termination notice said that his "off campus conduct has caused disruption to the university." The next day, the Governor of Florida, Jeb Bush, issued an official statement asserting, "The taxpayers have no obligation to continue paying a teacher whose own actions have made it impossible for him to teach."[59] In an odd twist, Bill O'Reilly came to Al-Arian's defense, saying: "You don't sack a tenured professor for saying stuff you don't like." He also suggested that USF President, Judy Genshaft, should resign. "She's a coward," he said. Then, in February 2003, the Justice Department indicted Al-Arian and seven others with fifty charges, from racketeering to money laundering, as part of their involvement with a Palestinian Islamic Jihad terrorist organization.[60]

In an op-ed that appeared in the *Tampa Tribune*, USF President Judy Genshaft explained the decision for dismissal, saying that he was not fired because of the indictment. Rather, "We terminated him because his actions adversely affected the legitimate interests of the university. Regardless of whether he is guilty of criminal activity, he is clearly guilty of abusing his position as a faculty member. He has misused the university's name, reputation, resources and personnel."[61] So go the rationalizations of employment deprivation.

In early June 2003, a U.S. judge ruled that Al-Arian's case would not be heard until 2005, despite the defendant's desire to begin the trial as soon as possible. Al-Arian's co-defendants' lawyers want more time to more fully consider the evidence. Meanwhile, the American Association of University Professors voted to condemn USF for firing Al-Arian without first giving him a hearing before his faculty peers.[62]

Despite the pleas of his lawyer, Al-Arian was forced to remain in jail—and often in solitary confinement—until his trial, which finally got underway in the summer of 2005. Al-Arian's defense team tried to get the venue changed from the highly charged anti-al-Arian atmosphere in Florida, but was denied this motion by a federal judge. The judge acknowledged media coverage in the area had been "extensive" but not "so pervasive or insidious as to invoke or inflame the community."[63] Throughout the trial, Al-Arian—who had met with President Bill Clinton and who supported George W. Bush's bid for the presidency in 2000—was repeatedly accused by the prosecution of leading a double life as a college professor and a leader of Palestinian Islamic Jihad, "one of the most deadly terror organizations on earth."[64] During the trial, information surfaced that the FBI had tapped his telephones for nine years and had raided both his house and his office, making off with numerous boxes of his personal effects. After all this, Al-Arian was acquitted on eight of the seventeen counts of terrorism-related activities, and the jury deadlocked on another eight charges, causing a mistrial. The final outstanding charge against Al-Arian was for racketeering conspiracy. Thus, the Justice Department failed to achieve a single guilty verdict in a high-profile trial with more than 80 witnesses and 400 transcripts of FBI-intercepted phone conversations and facsimiles. According to the *St. Petersburg Times*, "The verdicts were a major defeat for the federal government, which characterized Al-Arian's indictment as a major case against terrorism, and a victory for Al-Arian's attorneys, who considered the government's case so weak they declined to put on a defense."[65] The supposed "Tampa terrorist cell" was actually a figment in the Bureau's terrorism-addled imagination.

In April 2006, Al-Arian signed an agreement with federal prosecutors, pleading guilty to a lesser version of one of the charges—conspiring to provide support to a Palestinian terrorist organization—and be deported from the United States.[66] But before he could even make travel plans, U.S. District Judge James Moody sentenced Al-Arian to four years and nine months in prison, the maximum allowable under the plea agreement and eleven months more than the prosecution was even asking for. Before Judge Moody handed down his sentence, Al-Arian read prepared remarks that said in part, "This process, your honor, affirmed my belief in the meaning [of] our democratic society. As I leave [the U.S.], I harbor no bitterness or resentment. I am grateful for the opportunities afforded the son of stateless Palestinian refugees."

The judge responded with vehemence that shocked many in the courthouse. He said, "As usual, you speak very eloquently. I find it interesting that here in public you praise this country, the same country that in private you refer to as the great Satan. But that's just evidence of how you operate in the face of your friends and neighbors. You are a master manipulator." The judge then went on a tirade: "Your only connection to widows and orphans is that you created them, even among Palestinians. You create them, not by sending your children to blow themselves out of existence. No. You exhort others to send their children. Your children attend the finest universities this country has to offer, while you raise money to blow up the children of others."[67]

As it turns out, the judge's language mimicked that of government informants who had participated in the trial. As one of Al-Arian's attorneys, Linda Moreno, noted on *Democracy Now!*, "one of the informants...was a paid F.B.I. snitch, who was thoroughly discredited. In cross-examination, we got him to agree that he lied in various documents, resumés, applications for work. And he would describe these lies in [the] colors of a rainbow. That was a white lie. That was a black lie. That was a red lie. So he was thoroughly discredited. But he made a very emotional statement when he was on the stand. He said that Dr. Al-Arian sent his son to Duke University, while he sent others to be blown up. We felt that the judge eerily paraphrased this discredited snitch on the stand, and it was of concern to us."[68]

Moreno's concerns undoubtedly were deepened when in mid-November 2006 Al-Arian was found guilty of contempt in federal court in Alexandria, Virginia. Al-Arian refused to respond to questions about a Virginia Islamic think tank—the International Institute of Islamic Thought, or IIIT—which the U.S. government claims is one of the big players in a terrorism-financing investigation. He said that answering questions could put his life in danger. By declining to answer questions, Al-Arian could have another eighteen months tacked onto his sentence.[69] Regardless of how many more months Al-Arian serves before he is deported, the Palestinian freedom movement has had the attention of one of its more eloquent spokespeople diverted. And, let's not forget, Sami Al-Arian lost his job.

A final case of post-9/11 employment deprivation involves Ward Churchill, a professor of Ethnic Studies at the University of Colorado–Boulder. Churchill, who has written extensively on the persecution of Native Americans and other groups striving for social justice, is an Indian himself and an AIM member of more than twenty years.[70] A longtime activist and scholar, Churchill has seen state and media suppression face-to-face on numerous occasions. In early 2005, he came under fire from journalists, state officials, his colleagues in academia, and the general public for an essay he wrote after September 11, 2001 called "Some People Push Back: On the Justice of Roosting Chickens." In this essay Churchill compared some of the victims of the terrorist attack to Nazi war criminal Adolf Eichmann, technocrats who, with their everyday actions, kept the apparatus of structural violence rolling forward. In January 2005, as he prepared to give a talk at Hamilton College in New York, the ideas in this essay were publicized and subsequently skewered in the press. As a result, a number of his speaking engagements were canceled.

The University of Colorado Board of Regents immediately called a special meeting to discuss Churchill's comments. Presuming guilt, Regent Cindy Carlisle slipped into attack mode, asserting, "I am appalled by Professor Churchill's comments. What can be done is a complicated legal issue involving First Amendment law. Once we receive advice from legal counsel, we will know what course of action may be taken." She vowed that "something should be done." Elected officials chimed in to castigate Churchill, with Republican U.S. Representative Bob Beauprez demanding his resignation and Democratic Representative Mark Udall condemning his ideas.[71] Colorado Governor Bill Owens demanded Churchill be fired and the Colorado legislature opened discussions on how to cut funding for the Ethnic Studies Department.[72] Churchill resigned as chair of the university's Ethnic Studies Department, although he vowed to continue to teach in the department.[73]

The University of Colorado then organized a special committee to investigate whether or not his statements were punishable. The committee concluded that the professor's controversial comments could not be grounds for his dismissal since his remarks and writings were protected by the First Amendment. However, the university's interim chancellor Phil DiStefano said the committee "concluded that the allegations of research misconduct related to plagiarism, misuse of others' work and fabrication have sufficient merit to warrant further inquiry."[74]

The university then referred the matter to the Standing Committee on Research Misconduct, which carried out an exhaustive, nit-picking assessment of Churchill's written work and public remarks. In mid-May 2006, the

12-member committee released a report detailing the findings of its investigation. The committee concluded that Churchill had engaged in "academic misconduct in the form of plagiarism." He was also condemned because he "relied at times on assertions made by 'researchers' with no formal qualifications, background, or training about the topics under consideration."[75] One of the cases of plagiarism involved Churchill's failure to properly cite a pamphlet that he originally co-authored with a Canadian environmentalist group called Dam the Dams Campaign. In subsequent iterations of the pamphlet, he did not cite the Dam the Dams group, although he credited individuals from the group at the end of his work for "assembling the original paper from which this essay was written."[76] The Committee also found him "disrespectful of Indian oral traditions when dealing with the Mandan/Fort Clark smallpox epidemic of 1837," because he "did not mention native oral sources in his published essays, but adduced them only retrospectively and disingenuously in an attempt to defend himself against charges of academic wrongdoing."[77] In the conversion of this information to the mainstream news, any nuance or detail found in the report was flattened into the simplistic charge that Churchill was an egregious plagiarist.

In late-June 2006, the University of Colorado announced it wanted to fire Churchill. In a secret vote, six members of the Standing Committee on Research Misconduct recommended Churchill's firing, while three supported suspension without pay. Two of the three suggested a five-year suspension for Churchill, while the third committee member recommended a two-year suspension. Interim chancellor DiStefano opted for firing.[78] Churchill appealed the decision, which triggered a confidential review process by the university's Privilege and Tenure Committee.[79] This process was still inching forward at the time this book went to print.

When Churchill was asked in an interview whether he was receiving support from his colleagues he replied,

> From some. It's a mixed reaction. Frankly, the bulk of my colleagues are trying to make up excuses to get out of the line of fire themselves. And I find that to be a somewhat understandable situation, but not really something that is in conformity with adherence to the principle of academic freedom, the protections of tenure. The whole structure that allows autonomous scholarship to occur is in jeopardy, when they can take a senior professor and run this kind of a charade in order to revoke tenure, to silence, when it's transparently the case that the entire investigation was convened to scrutinize speech. And they made no bones about it.[80]

The case of Ward Churchill demonstrates the lengths the state, its functionaries, and fellow travelers will go to crush the articulation of dissident
opinion.

Surveillance and Break-ins

After COINTELPRO was revealed to the public in the early-1970s, the FBI
allegedly tightened up its own investigative powers, placing checks on its
agents in order to prevent such egregious civil-liberties violations and targeted political suppression. Under mounting congressional pressure, Attorney
General Edward H. Levi placed limitations on Bureau investigative tactics
that violated First Amendment-protected activities. In order to open a criminal investigation, the Bureau had to show "specific and articulable" facts.
These relatively stringent regulations were quickly watered down by subsequent Attorney Generals William French Smith and Richard Thornburgh,
under the Reagan and Bush I administrations. Then came 9/11 and the
ever-opportunistic, arch-conservative John Ashcroft, who "effectively dis-
mantled" what was left of the Levi guidelines.[81]

Ashcroft's new FBI Guidelines of 2002 permitted a wide range of previously forbidden surveillance practices. Under the new guidelines, agents
could attend religious ceremonies open to the public and monitor online
activity in chat rooms and elsewhere. According to the Ashcroft guidelines,
to spot or thwart terrorism, "the F.B.I. is authorized to visit any place and
attend any event that is open to the public, on the same terms and conditions
as members of the public generally."[82] Such surveillance of constitutionally
protected political and religious activity could occur even if there was *no
objective evidence of wrongdoing.* And all this was happening under less and
less supervision from the FBI hierarchy as the Bureau moved to decentral-
ize its investigative apparatus. Numerous state and local police forces across
the country followed the Bureau's lead, weakening or flat-out eliminating
regulations on political surveillance.[83] Far-reaching changes like these raised
numerous eyebrows among civil libertarians, including Craig Eisendrath, a
senior fellow at the Center for International Policy think tank, who asserted,
"You can look at individual policies and say, 'This one may work, this one
may not.' But across the board, here's Ashcroft suspending civil rights again,
mainly of noncitizens. It's just a steady kind of move on the part of the administration."[84]

Such a "steady move" facilitated amped-up Bureau surveillance in numerous locales across the country. In particular, the anti-war movement has
been a prime focus of the state's massive, and ever-expanding, surveillance
apparatus. In November 2003, a confidential FBI memo surfaced, reveal-

ing a vast network of state surveillance. Although anti-war activists had long known they were under state scrutiny, journalist Eric Lichtblau noted, "The F.B.I. memorandum, however, appears to offer the first corroboration of a coordinated, nationwide effort to collect intelligence regarding demonstrations." In interviews with Lichtblau, Bureau officials said, "the intelligence-gathering effort was aimed at identifying anarchists and 'extremist elements,'" even though almost all anti-war protesters advocated non-violent tactics. The FBI memo, which circulated in October 2003, just before large anti-war protests, used the language of terrorism to describe dissidents, claiming, "Activists may also make use of training camps to rehearse tactics and counter-strategies for dealing with the police and to resolve any logistical issues." The memo also pressed local police "to be alert to these possible indicators of protest activity and report any potentially illegal acts" to the FBI's counterterrorism task forces, thereby tacitly linking anti-war activism to terrorism. In response, Anthony Romero of the ACLU said, "What the FBI regards as potential terrorism strikes me as civil disobedience."[85] Nevertheless, the state's linkage of activism to terrorism has become quite common in the post-9/11 political milieu.

By mid-2005, the FBI had collected thousands of pages on groups in the anti-war movement as well as their supporters. Reminiscent of the COINTELPRO era, the Bureau had created a nearly 1,200-page file on the ACLU and one twice that size on Greenpeace. In response to these revelations, John Passacantando, director of Greenpeace USA, stated, "If the FBI has taken the time to gather 2,400 pages of information on an organization that has a perfect record of peaceful activity for 34 years, it suggests they're just attempting to stifle the voices of their critics." Yet these documents, which were obtained under the Freedom of Information Act, were only a fraction of the documents produced by the Bureau on anti-war protest groups. The FBI also turned over portions of its files on United for Peace and Justice—a coalition of more than 1,000 anti-war groups—and the American Indian Movement.[86]

As the documents continued to trickle out of the Bureau, it became more and more obvious that the FBI was, in many instances, falsely equating anti-war activism with terrorism. This logic was clearly articulated in March 2006, when an FBI counterterrorism official gave a presentation at the University of Texas Law School that listed Foods Not Bombs and Indymedia as two groups terrorists might consort with.[87] In a further clarification of this conflation, the California Terrorism Information Center has continued to monitor anti-war protests, even after the previously discussed violent debacle at the Port of Oakland in 2003. As it turns out, CATIC was surveilling protests and then preparing reports, which it passed along to the Office of Homeland Security, the California Highway Patrol, and the California attorney general's office. Among other events monitored by CATIC were a demonstration by Women's International League for Peace and Freedom in Santa Barbara and a tame anti-war protest in Walnut Creek where even elected officials—like U.S. Representative George Miller—spoke out against the Iraq War.[88]

The surveillance of anti-war activists was also rampant in Denver, where local police, in conjunction with an FBI Joint Terrorism Task Force, targeted a Franciscan nun, a person promoting a documentary film that's critical of the FBI, and the American Friends Service Committee, a non-violent Quaker group the Denver police dubbed "criminal extremist."[89] The FBI also carried out "pretext interviews" of dissidents in Denver. Activist Sarah Bardwell, who underwent intensive Bureau questioning, said, "It's very clear to me that the purpose of those interviews was to intimidate activists in the Denver area from exercising their First Amendment rights."[90]

On the other side of the country, another FBI Joint Terrorism Task Force was surveilling a Pittsburgh peace group, the Thomas Merton Center. Documents obtained through the Freedom of Information Act detail the FBI spying, which the Bureau justified as terrorism-related.[91] In an FBI report from 29 November 2002 titled "IT [International Terrorism] Matters," the Bureau depicts the Merton Center as a "left-wing organization advocating, among many political causes, pacifism."[92] In response to the surveillance revelations, Tim Vining, the former head of the center, said, "We know, of course, that we're constantly having photographs taken of us. We've always suspected people at our meetings and at our large events. You know, this government has a history of spying on its citizens. We're not naive. But I think what's important is that we not allow this to get us to not trust one another or to live in fear and paranoia."[93] All this surveillance begs the question, asked by ACLU Executive Director Anthony Romero, "What is the chilling effect that will be felt by Americans all across the country if they think they will come under FBI scrutiny just by going to a protest?"[94]

But it's not just FBI surveillance that activists must contend with in the post-9/11 era. The Defense Department's electronic eye is also trained on domestic dissidents. In December 2005, NBC *Nightly News* broke the story that the Pentagon was spying on protesters in the United States as part of a massive intelligence-gathering program. Department of Defense spies even went as far as to record descriptions of vehicles outside "suspicious" meetings and events that the Pentagon considered "threats." Christopher Pyle, who during the Vietnam War-era was a whistleblower regarding the Pentagon's surveillance and infiltration of anti-war and civil rights groups, said about the database, "This is the J. Edgar Hoover Memorial Vacuum

Cleaner. They're collecting everything."[95] This database—which was called "TALON" (Threat and Local Observation Notice)—categorized protests like a March 2005 "Stop the War Now" rally in Akron, Ohio as "potential terrorist activity." The Talon database included at least 1,500 "suspicious incidents" that warranted deeper Pentagon surveillance, and the Pentagon kept these incidents on the books well after it was clear that these events did not pose a threat to the state.[96] An anti-war group's activities at a military recruiting fair on the University of California, Santa Cruz campus was logged in the database, as was a protest outside Halliburton's Houston offices in June 2004.[97] With the spirit of Posse Comitatus being whisked away like an old shirt, civil libertarians have a great deal to be concerned about.

The complex web of domestic surveillance does not end with the Department of Defense. In December 2005, it was revealed—after the *New York Times* sat on the story for a year for "national security reasons"—that President Bush secretly authorized the National Security Agency to listen in on telephone conversations and view email messages between people in the United States and supposed terrorists abroad. All this was done without the necessary warrants the Fourth Amendment demands. This revelation was especially alarming since the job of the NSA is to monitor communications abroad, not domestically in the United States. According to the *New York Times*, "Since 2002, the agency has been conducting some warrantless eavesdropping on people in the United States who are linked, even if indirectly, to suspected terrorists through the chain of phone numbers and e-mail addresses, according to several officials who know of the operation. Under the special program, the agency monitors their international communications."[98] Shortly thereafter, dissidents in the U.S. learned that the NSA—in a massive dataveillance operation that would slacken George Orwell's jaw—has also been secretly compiling tens of millions of domestic phone records into a national call database.[99]

As technology continues to advance, surveillance becomes more and more sophisticated. For instance, the *New York Times* reported in the fall of 2006 that the Department of Homeland Security has been funding a group of major U.S. universities to develop computer software that would allow the government to trace and track public opinion regarding U.S. leaders and policies through content analysis of newspapers, magazines, and other periodicals. According to a Homeland Security Department statement, the software—which government officials say is aimed at foreign, not domestic, media—is designed "to identify common patterns from numerous sources of information which might be indicative of potential threats to the nation." Yet despite this reassurance, articles in the database for this "sentiment analysis" include some from domestic sources like the *Miami Herald* and the *New*

York Times. Marc Rotenberg, executive director of the Electronic Privacy Information Center called the program "really chilling" and pointed out that "it seems far afield from the mission of homeland security."[100] "Chilling" indeed, and it doesn't take the imagination of an avant-garde poet to think up ways the program could be used to undermine dissent both in the United States and abroad.

Infiltration and the Use of Agent Provocateurs

State informants who worm their way inside social movements have continued to plague the practice of dissent after the attacks of 11 September 2001. To consider one example of an infiltrator damaging social-movement activity we must go back to the streets of Miami for the FTAA protests. Miami Mayor Manny Diaz pulled out all the stops as he teamed up with Police Chief Timoney to establish the "Miami Model," which included the use of undercover officers posing as protesters in order to gain intelligence and provoke problems within the global justice movement. Many of these infiltrators went out of their way to dress the part, donning clothes that protesters might wear. Some affixed signs to their backpacks that said things like "FTAA sucks." According to reporter Jeremy Scahill, union organizer Justin Molito "witnessed an incident between what appeared to be police provocateurs and protesters."[101] Scahill reported for *CounterPunch* that

> At one point during a standoff with police, it appeared as though a group of protesters had gotten into a brawl amongst themselves. But as others moved in to break up the melee, two of the guys pulled out electric tazers and shocked protesters, before being liberated back behind police lines. These guys, clearly undercover agents, were dressed like any other protester. One had a sticker on his backpack that read: "FTAA No Way." The IMC has since published pictures of people dressed like Black Bloc kids—ski masks and all—walking with uniformed police behind police lines.[102]

Activists can expect similar police maneuvering in the future, as the "Miami Model" gets exported to other locales. Apparently police departments from numerous cities in the U.S. sent their personnel to Miami to study the methods the Miami Police Department employed to crush dissent.[103]

Even before Miami, in late 2002, the Partnership for Civil Justice (PCJ), a DC-based public interest legal organization, unearthed evidence that DC police had an extensive and ongoing program of social-movement infiltration. After great persistence on the part of the PCJ, the DC police admitted that at least two undercover police officers had been instructed to infiltrate local protest groups. Activists also rooted out two additional agents provocateurs who recommended blowing up Potomac River bridges and calling in fake bomb threats.[104]

In Fresno, California, an undercover sheriff's detective named Aaron Kilner infiltrated a local activist group called Peace Fresno. Starting in the fall of 2003, Kilner began attending meetings, quietly taking notes without engaging in discussion or asking questions. Initially, Fresno County Sheriff Richard Pierce refused to address the question of whether Kilner was sent to the meeting as an infiltrator, yet he defended his right to assign undercover officers to monitor meetings if he so desired. Echoing Ashcroft's new guidelines for the FBI, and demonstrating the penchant to discuss dissidence and terrorism in consecutive breaths, Pierce stated, "For the purpose of detecting or preventing terrorist activities, the Fresno County Sheriff's Department may visit any place and attend any event that is open to the public, on the same terms and conditions as members of the public generally." Kilner's family said he would not have attended the meetings on his own time: He was a former College Republican with two young daughters and a dearth of free time. Peace Fresno only figured out Kilner was an infiltrator when they saw his photograph in the newspaper after he died in a motorcycle accident.[105]

Members of Peace Fresno, a group more known for book sales than pipe bombs, expressed dismay at the fact an infiltrator had wedged his way into their group. Kilner—who went by the name Aaron Stokes when working with the group—kept up with his membership dues. He participated in permitted protests and even took a bus trip with the group to Sacramento in the summer of 2003 to demonstrate against the corporatization of agriculture. He even served as group notetaker.[106] Camille Russell, an elementary school teacher and member of Peace Fresno, acknowledged, "We thought he was one of us, and when we read this, we felt betrayed. It's a very uncomfortable feeling. When we learned he was working for the anti-terrorism unit, we realized we were targeted because of our strong, vocal criticism of the Bush Administration."[107] Although California Attorney General Bill Lockyer vowed to investigate the case, the Fresno Sheriff plodded onward with increased infiltration, sending undercover officers to a speech given by an animal rights activist on the California State University–Fresno campus.[108]

In nearby Oakland, two police officers infiltrated anti-war groups, starting with the Port of Oakland event in April 2003, when police unleashed a wave of violence on demonstrators. Little did protesters know at the time, but while the beanbag bullets and wooden dowels were flying, two undercover members of the Oakland Police Department—Nobuko Biechler and Mark Turpin—were ducking and weaving in more ways than one. The two

informants were actually elected by anti-war activists to lead a subsequent
protest on 12 May 2003. After the rally, Deputy Police Chief Howard Jordan
indicated an interest in deepening infiltration practices. He told a city police
review board investigating the April 2003 protest event that "our ability to
gather intelligence on these groups and this type of operation needs to be
improved. I don't mean same-day intelligence. I'm talking about long-term
intelligence gathering." These comments came despite the fact that Attorney
General Lockyer created guidelines in the wake of the April 2003 protest asserting that law enforcement officials could not collect intelligence on activist groups unless they suspected that a crime had occurred. Mark Schlosberg
of the ACLU carried out a survey that found only eight of ninety-four law
enforcement agencies were aware of Lockyer's new rules and only six had
instituted written policies reflecting the guidelines.[109]

Environmentalists have also suffered from state agents and paid informants infiltrating their ranks. Since at least the mid-1990s environmentalists
have been victimized by what many call the "Green Scare," a powerful cocktail of state suppression reminiscent of the "Red Scares" of previous eras. A
prime ingredient in that cocktail is the embedding of informants in environmental groups or the flipping of former dissidents who abandon activist al-
legiances to cooperate with the state. Radical environmentalists have become
one of the FBI's top targets in the post-9/11 era, and the extraordinary laws
the state has promulgated to crush these dissidents will be discussed later.
For now I'll focus on how infiltrators destabilize radical environmentalism
from the inside, leaving it vulnerable to other forms of state suppression.

Despite the massive propaganda campaign proliferated by the state to
make environmentalists out to be "domestic terrorists," the "Green Scare"
hadn't turned out many high-profile legal victories for the state. The Earth
Liberation Front had been active in the late-1990s, but the "elves" had managed to elude the long arm of the state, by and large. Before December 2005
the state was floundering in its efforts to snatch up ELF activists engaging in
targeted economic sabotage. Then along came Jacob "Jake" Ferguson.

On 7 December 2005, operating under the codename "Operation
Backfire," the FBI scooped up seven environmental activists—Chelsea
Gerlach, Darren Thurston, William Rodgers, Kendall Tankersley (Sarah
Kendall Harvey), Kevin Tubbs, Daniel McGowan, and Stanislas Meyerhoff—
in four states. The Eugene, Oregon-based Civil Liberties Defense Center
(CLDC) called the arrests the beginning of "one of the largest roundups of
environmental and animal liberation activists in American history."[110] This
massive dragnet was largely based on the testimony of Ferguson who had become a paid informant of the state, and a talkative one at that. Lauren Regan,
a lawyer from the CLDC who represents numerous "Green Scare" non-coop-

erating defendants, said the case against those arrested in December would never have materialized were it not for informants. Regan said Ferguson—who was "an absolute full-throttle heroin addict" at the time—first told the FBI he played a central role in numerous eco-sabotage arsons and then wore a wire around the country recording incriminating conversations with other activists.[111] The FBI took full advantage of Ferguson's heroin addiction. Pressing him on his weaknesses and telling him they had proof he was involved in a 2001 arson at Romania Chevrolet in Eugene, they finally broke Ferguson, and he agreed to record conversations. According to the *Eugene Weekly*, Ferguson wore a wire to an Earth First! gathering, to the Public Interest Environmental Law Conference at the University of Oregon, and to private meetings with eco-activists.[112] Ferguson's cooperation with the state not only led to numerous arrests, but also set off a cascade of compliance with numerous eco-saboteurs now willing to talk in order to try to reduce their sentences. Such cooperation with the state led Jim Flynn, co-editor of the journal *Earth First!* to comment, "What's upsetting is how quickly people are folding and how namby-pamby and weak Earth First! looks when you compare it to the Black Panthers and the American Indian Movement, where people have held out for decades without talking. It just makes our movement look weak and soft and middle-class. For people like me, who have spent years in the movement, it's embarrassing. How will we recruit new people?"[113] Ferguson told the *Seattle Times* "I didn't roll; people rolled on me, and I was faced with a situation where I could go to jail for the rest of my life."[114] Ferguson has yet to be indicted on any charges, despite the fact he has admitted to more crimes than any of the defendants are being charged with. Sources say Ferguson is receiving between $50,000 and $100,000 for his role as a cooperative witness.[115]

According to attorney David Lane, "The federal government makes a living off tapes and snitches. It's absolutely standard operating procedure."[116] This "standard operating procedure" was also put to use in another "Green Scare" case in Northern California. The Sacramento Three—sometimes called the Auburn Three—are Zachary Jenson, Eric McDavid, and Lauren Weiner. They were arrested in January 2006 for allegedly plotting eco-sabotage in the Sacramento area. Weiner pleaded guilty to one count of conspiracy and told state authorities the actions they had planned would be carried out under the name of the Earth Liberation Front.[117] Both Lauren Regan and Portland Indy Media assert that a young government agent provocateur named "Anna" was instrumental in setting up the three defendants.[118] An FBI affidavit in support of the charges against the three, asserts that the Bureau has a "confidential source who is deeply embedded within the subjects 'cell.'" The affidavit also reveals that the FBI paid for this "confidential source" to rent a house in Auburn where the informant and the three defendants stayed for a short period of time. The house was chockfull of surveillance equipment. FBI Special Agent Nasson Walker, who testified at Weiner's bail hearing, said the agent provocateur was around twenty years old and has been paid by the Bureau approximately $75,000 plus expenses since 2004.[119] Were it not for infiltrators and agents provocateurs, the FBI's "Green Scare" arrest rate would be a shadow of its current self.

All this state infiltration is occurring in a context where the FBI has consistently and egregiously broken or ignored its guidelines for the use of informants. According to the Justice Department's Inspector General, Glenn Fine, almost nine out of ten cases he looked at involving informants made improper use of these sources. Many of Fine's issues included informants who were walking down the inflammatory path of the agent provocateur, engaging in illegal activity in order to ramp up the intensity or violence within a group's tactical repertoire. The Inspector General found that often FBI agents let informants engage in illegal activity without letting the prosecution know about it. Also, documentation of informant activity was erratic, incomplete, and clearly not up to snuff. With infiltrators freely breaking the law, the probability of agent-provocateur activities only increase.[120]

Black Propaganda

Given the extremes to which the state has gone in the wake of 9/11 to crush dissent—even above-board, wholly legal, nonviolent protest—at every opportunity, there should be little doubt that government forces have engaged in black propaganda in recent years. However, specific evidence that supports this state method of suppression is difficult to come by, even years after the fact. Given the customary lag time between government perpetration and public knowledge, it is not surprising that, at this point, I have not come across solid information supporting black propaganda actions on the part of the state. Time will tell with this mode of suppression.

Harassment and Harassment Arrests

Harassment and harassment arrests have emerged as staple suppressive tactics in the post-9/11 age. A great deal of this harassment has to do with the state's tight circumscription of space. Sze Tsung Leong's idea of "control space" is useful to understanding the Bush administration harassment of activists. Leong defines "control space" as "the desire to make space simultaneous with the irrationalities and vicissitudes of the market." While market mechanisms voraciously engulf public space, transmogrifying it into control space—what Leong dubs a mobile "cartography in continuous flux"—the state is also hard at work regulating space in the name of social order.[121]

Many of the common characteristics of harassment have been evident in the post-9/11 era, including preemptive attacks on activism, uncommonly high bails, extreme sentencing, and the fabrication of evidence. The state has also formed "snatch squads:" teams of undercover officers who swoop in on a specific activist, isolate the person, make a quick arrest, and cart the individual off immediately. "Snatch squads" were in operation at the World Economic Forum demonstrations in New York in 2002, at the FTAA protests in Miami in 2003, and at an anti-war protest in Washington, DC in April 2003.[122] The state also harassed dissidents through "pretextual searches and raids of organizing spaces," sometimes showing up with inspectors and bogus claims about housing violations and fire codes in order to close down mobilization centers.[123] While this harassment can force dissidents off the streets and into elaborate legal entanglements, harassment arrests often do not lead to indictments and, even when they do, activists many times are not convicted. Nevertheless, they are forced to expend significant resources defending themselves, resources they would much rather plunge into activism.

When President Bush travels the country, state functionaries sharply restrict who can come in contact with him, even when the president is supposedly making "public" appearances. As Bush campaigned for re-election in 2004, anti-Bush protesters were often scooped up by the police and Secret Service simply for exercising their First Amendment rights. In Cedar Rapids, Iowa two 55-year-old teachers—Christine Nelson and Alice McCabe—showed up at a Bush campaign event sporting a Kerry-Edwards button and a paper sign that read, "No More War." Three Secret Service agents, two county sheriff's deputies, and members of the Iowa State Patrol swooped in and arrested the two, handcuffing them and hauling them off to jail where they were strip-searched. The government defended its actions, saying the Republican Party had rented the public park in which the two were protesting, and thus the sidewalk on which they stood was considered private property.[124]

When Bush was in San Bernadino, California supporting the re-election bid of Governor Arnold Schwarzenegger, Thomas Frazier showed up donning two homemade signs that read "'Shock & Awe' = 'Maim & Murder'" and "Indict Bush—Crimes Against Humanity." He also carried bumperstickers that said, "Stop the Madness." As he left his car and walked toward the protest, Frazier was confronted by a San Bernadino Police Officer who, according to Frazier, "raced towards me screaming, 'No, no, no, no. Get there, get there!'" The policeman proceeded to confiscate the activist's signs and arrest him. Frazier wrote in a complaint lodged with the San Bernadino police that he was told, "You're being arrested for obstructing a police officer. Your sign could have been a weapon." The police report reads, "During a Presidential visit, the listed defendant entered a restricted area and did not comply with officer's request and demands. He was arrested for obstructing and delaying an officer."[125]

When President Bush made a campaign stop in Ashwaubenon, Wisconsin in July 2004, Jayson Nelson secured a ticket to watch the president speak. However, Nelson made the mistake of showing up at the Bush event with a t-shirt that read, "Kerry for President." Secret Service picked him out as he tried to enter and they gave him the boot. As he left, Secret Service officials halted him and, according to Nelson, "took my driver's license and wrote down my Social Security number and telephone number."[126] Nelson wasn't the only one plucked out of a pro-Bush crowd for his sartorial selection. In Medford, Oregon in October 2004, three teachers—Candice Julian, Tania Tong, and Janet Voorhies—showed up to a Bush speech with valid tickets issued by the Republican Party. They also sported t-shirts that read, "Protect our civil liberties." These weren't exactly rabble rousers bent on disrupting the president. Tong told the Associated Press, "We chose this phrase specifically because we didn't think it would be offensive or degrading or obscene." Nevertheless, they were escorted from the event and threatened with arrest.[127] These Bush administration rules are tantamount to the institution of tacit, new-wave loyalty oaths required for attending campaign events.

Not to be outdone, Vice President Dick Cheney's security team was also intolerant of even mild dissent. When Cheney went to Evansville, Indiana to campaign for a local politician, John Blair, an environmental activist, showed up with a sign that read, "CHENEY—19th Century Energy Man." Blair was approached by undercover police and asked to move over to an area that was being designated as a space for protesters. When Blair refused to do so, he was arrested for resisting law enforcement, a misdemeanor. The charges were eventually dropped. Blair later wrote, "this was a preemptive arrest to assure that no one going to the event would see any protesters let alone hear any protesters."[128] In 2006, another person was arrested for daring to penetrate Cheney's protective bubble. Steven Howards, an environmental consultant from Golden, Colorado stumbled upon Dick Cheney and his entourage at an outdoor mall. Unable to resist, Howards walked up to the Cheney and said, "I think your policies in Iraq are reprehensible." The Secret Service intervened and whisked Howards away, ultimately leveling misdemeanor harassment charges against him. A state judge later dismissed the case.[129] Howards remarked about the incident, "I was treated as though I was a convict, like criminal. It was horrifying for my kids." He also filed a civil suit against the Secret Service.[130]

In the post-9/11 world, even bumperstickers have ruffled the hackles of the state. In March 2006, Denise Grier, a nurse working in suburban Atlanta, was pulled over by Dekalb County law enforcement because of bumpersticker on her car that read, "I'm Tired Of All The BUSHIT." Grier was issued a ticket for breaking a state law that prohibits lewd or profane stickers and decals on vehicles. Grier said, "In my opinion, I was pulled over solely because the officer was pro-Bush, and this was an attempt to squash my right of free speech. The officer did not have any other reason to pull me over."[131] The lewd-sticker law had actually been ruled unconstitutional by a Georgia court in 1990, so Grier's ticket was eventually rescinded. Grier later sued Dekalb County for "emotional stress" resulting from the arrest.[132]

In the days before the 2004 Republican and Democratic National Conventions, the state trained its focus on dissidents who planned on doing more than affixing bumperstickers to their vehicles. The FBI went on an aggressive, preemptive rampage, sometimes even subpoenaing activists, as the Bureau tried to intimidate and gather intelligence on potential protesters before they even hit the streets. Using the pretext of potential violence, agents grilled activists as well as their friends and family members, asking them if they knew anyone who planned violence or disruption at the conventions. Tacitly admitting the FBI was keeping a modern-day rabble rouser index, an FBI spokesperson said, "We vetted down a list and went out and knocked on doors and had a laundry list of questions to ask about possible criminal behavior."[133] Chris Scheets, an anarchist from Missouri, was hounded for days by FBI agents. Ultimately Scheets and two fellow activists—Ben Garrett and Daniel Coate—were subpoenaed before a federal grand jury to answer questions about protests at the upcoming Republican National Convention in New York. They also received letters from federal prosecutors telling them they were targets of a "domestic terrorism" investigation. Scheets decided not to attend protests in New York and Coate, while vowing to remain active in dissent, he admitted, "this whole experience has made me more reluctant to go to protests, because I'm worried about what the FBI might do."[134] Three congressional Democrats labeled the Bureau's actions as "systematic political harassment and intimidation of legitimate antiwar protesters."[135]

The grand jury was also used as a coercive mechanism against Josh Wolf, a journalist who had shot video at an anti-capitalist demonstration in San Francisco in July 2005. Wolf was subpoenaed to face the grand jury and grilled about what he saw and captured on film, but he refused to testify or hand over his footage and was jailed for contempt.[136] He spent a month in jail before being released on bail and then ultimately sent back behind bars by the Ninth U.S. Circuit Court of Appeals, which rejected his appeal.[137] In early April 2007, after 225 days behind bars, Wolf was finally released from prison. This was an all-time record for journalists trying to protect their sources in the United States. Upon his release, Wolf told Amy Goodman of *Democracy Now!*, "A free press is not something that the government is very fond of, and they're going to do everything to try to stop that."[138]

Extraordinary Rules and Laws

In the wake of September 11, the state has promulgated numerous extraordinary laws and executed many exceptional rules. Across the United States, cities have passed ordinances that restrict protests and marches. Some localities charge exorbitant rates for protest permits and insist demonstrators take out liability insurance before permits are granted.[139] Sometimes permits are denied entirely based on "security" grounds, as happened in New York City at a massive anti-war rally in February 2003 where demonstrators were allowed to assemble but not march.[140]

In this section I will focus on four post-9/11 extraordinary laws and rules: (1) "designated protest zones"; (2) presidential signing statements; (3) the USA PATRIOT Act; and (4) the Military Commissions Act of 2006.

As we have seen, the Bush administration has a fixation with controlling space. One manifestation of this is the creation of "designated protest zones," or "free speech zones." The corralling of dissidents into "protest zones" that are often far from the event being protested has emerged as a common practice under the Bush regime.[141] This amounts to the quarantining of dissent, or in many cases, the literal penning of dissent. For example, at the 2004 Democratic National Convention in Boston, a "free speech zone" was created adjacent to the drop-off spot for busloads of convention delegates. Michael Avery of the National Lawyers Guild described the "free speech zone":

> The zone is large enough only for 1000 persons to safely congregate and is bounded by two chain link fences separated by concrete highway barriers. The outermost fence is covered with black mesh that is designed to repel liquids. Much of the area is under an abandoned elevated train line. The zone is covered by another black net which is topped by razor wire. There will be no sanitary facilities in the zone and tables and chairs will not be permitted. There is no way for the demonstrators to pass written materials to the convention delegates.[142]

Despite obvious constitutionality issues, a federal judge upheld the legality of the razor-wired zone, citing the safety of the convention delegates.[143]

Aside from rendering activists less effective, keeping them far away from the targets of their protest, these zones make activists look like caged animals that need to be penned off from the rest of society. When the media shows images of demonstrators rallying behind iron bars and barbed wire, it can't help the protesters' cause. And let's not forget, thanks to the First Amendment of the Constitution, the entire U.S. is supposed to be a "free speech zone."

Another remarkable piece in the Bush administration's suppression puzzle is the president's penchant for tacking questionable "signing statements" onto the bills he signs into law. In January 2006, Charlie Savage of the *Boston Globe* broke the story that President Bush had been issuing statements that not only undermine the power of Congress, but also quietly enhance the president's apparatus of state suppression. Savage described a presidential signing statement as "an official document in which a president lays out his interpretation of a new law—declaring that he will view the interrogation limits in the context of his broader powers to protect national security." Flashing the ever-trusty national-security trump card, Bush asserted that the statements were a way of "protecting the American people from further terrorist attacks." New York University law professor David Golove removed the layers of abstraction from the administration's rationale, asserting,

> The signing statement is saying "I will only comply with this law when I want to, and if something arises in the war on terrorism where I think it's important to torture or engage in cruel, inhuman, and degrading conduct, I have the authority to do so and nothing in this law is going to stop me." They don't want to come out and say it directly because it doesn't sound very nice, but it's unmistakable to anyone who has been following what's going on.[144]

While previous presidents have occasionally made use of signing statements, President Bush has made them part of his regular repertoire, issuing more than 800 of them by the end of 2006. All previous presidents combined had only attached 600 signing statements. Both the Congressional Research Service and the American Bar Association criticized the practice, denouncing it as an executive power grab, but Bush continued undeterred, signing the 2007 Military Budget Bill and tacking on a statement that challenged 16 provisions in it.[145] While many activists—and even members of Congress—have criticized Bush's use of signing statements in regards to foreign policy issues, fewer have recognized the immense potential such statements could have on the practice of dissent domestically. When Bush signed the re-authorization of the USA PATRIOT Act in March 2006, he fastened on a "signing statement" that asserts he need not pay heed to the Act's congressional oversight provisions. He wrote that he didn't need to obey provisions that might "impair foreign relations, national security, the deliberative process of the executive, or the performance of the executive's constitutional duties." The vague, slippery nature of this proclamation is glaringly apparent.[146]

The original USA PATRIOT Act—passed in a paroxysm of 9/11-induced haste—became the legislative centerpiece for not only combating terrorism, but also for squelching domestic political dissent. We shouldn't forget that USA PATRIOT is a propaganda-drenched acronym standing for Uniting and Strengthening America by Providing the Appropriate Tools Required to Intercept and Obstruct Terrorism. Geoffrey Stone calls it "opportunistic and excessive" in that it "smuggled into law several investigative practices that have nothing to do with fighting terrorism, but that law enforcement had for years tried unsuccessfully to persuade Congress to authorize."[147]

The PATRIOT Act is not a thing, but a process, and the contemporary assault on civil liberties did not begin in 2001. An important precursor to this law is the 1996 Anti-terrorism and Effective Death Penalty Act (AEDPA), which Cole and Dempsey dub "one of the worst assaults on the Constitution in decades."[148] The 1996 AEDPA, which President Bill Clinton helped ram through Congress, contained many shades and mechanisms that are either replicated or intensified in the PATRIOT Act, including: a shift of focus onto political activity, especially of people with non-mainstream beliefs and opinions; the resurrection of guilt by association as the paradigm for both criminal and immigration law; the loosening of FBI surveillance standards so that the Bureau might more easily surveil, investigate, and infiltrate political, religious, and ethnic groups; and the criminalization of peaceful—albeit dissident—activity by transforming support for the humanitarian and political activities of certain foreign-based groups into a federal crime.

Attorney General Ashcroft was heavily involved in the passage of the PATRIOT Act. When the bill was under consideration, he exerted substantial pressure on his former colleagues in Congress, essentially warning them that if they did not act quickly to adopt the Bush administration's anti-terrorism strategies (without amendment) they would have the blood of the victims of future attacks on their collective hands. Although the Act made significant amendments to over fifteen statutes, it was passed with very little debate. It was also passed without a House, Senate, or conference report. In the House, there was a full Committee mark-up, but no official testimony from opponents of the bill was allowed to be heard. In the Senate, the bill was never debated or marked up in Committee. After three weeks of secret, behind-the-scenes meetings between a shortlist of senators and the Bush administration, a bill was introduced in that chamber which housed almost all the President's wishes/demands. On 11 October, the bill passed the Senate after a fleeting debate that demonstrated that even those who voted for the bill had not actually read it since they were unaware of many of its provisions. Shortly thereafter, it was passed by the House, even though, according to Cole and Dempsey, "It is virtually certain that not a single member of the House read the bill for which he or she voted." Congress abandoned standard operating procedures and opted to not use a conference committee to hammer out the differences between the bills. As a result, it lacks background legislative history that often retrospectively provides the necessary statutory interpretation that comes in handy down the road.[149] President Bush signed the final bill, the USA PATRIOT Act, into law on 26 October 2001.

In *Silencing Political Dissent*, Nancy Chang argues that the PATRIOT Act sacrifices freedom on the altar of "national security" in three ways:

> First, the act places our First Amendment rights to freedom of speech and political association in jeopardy by creating a broad new crime of "domestic terrorism" and denying entry to noncitizens on the basis of ideology. Second, the act reduces our already low expectations of privacy by granting the government enhanced surveillance powers. Third, the act erodes the due process right of noncitizens by allowing the government to place them in mandatory detention and deport them from the United States based on political activities that have been recast under the act as terrorist activities.[150]

This big-picture critique points to serious civil-liberties issues for everyone in the United States.

Many provisions in the PATRIOT Act have little or nothing to do with terrorism. This is nowhere more evident than in Section 802 of the act, which creates the federal crime of "domestic terrorism." The PATRIOT Act defines "domestic terrorism" as "activities that involve acts dangerous to human life that are in violation of the criminal laws of the United States or of any State" that "appear to be intended" (1) "to intimidate or coerce a civilian population," (2) "to influence the policy of a government by intimidation or coercion," or (3) "to affect the conduct of a government by mass destruction, assassination, or kidnapping" occurring in the territorial United States.[151] The vagueness of this new legal category serves as a veritable vortex for dissident activity. Contentious protests, marches, rallies, and other actions are, by design, meant "to influence the policy of a government by intimidation or coercion" and sometimes the state's response to protests—even peaceful ones—creates situations that may be construed as "acts dangerous to human life."

Law professor Natsu Taylor Saito puts it this way in an *Oregon Law Review* article:

Many forms of social and political protest in the United States can now be classified as "domestic terrorism." Any serious social protest—such as demonstrations against the World Trade Organization, police brutality, or the war in Iraq—is, by definition intended to influence government policy and could easily be interpreted as involving "coercion." Such protests could qualify as acts of domestic terrorism if a law is broken (say, failure to obey a police officer's order) and life is endangered (perhaps by blocking an intersection).[152]

In fact, under the letter of the new law, acts of civil disobedience that take place in the United States could also be reconfigured as acts of "domestic terrorism," since they inherently meet many of the tenets of the term's definition. This means that actions that were formerly violations of local laws, like refusing to obey a police officer or disorderly conduct, are transformed into violations of federal anti-terrorism laws. As Chang notes, the definitional promiscuity inherent to Section 802 "allows the government to group nonviolent civil disobedience in the tradition of Thoreau, Gandhi, and King together with the Al Qaeda network's ruthless attacks on civilians, all under the single banner of terrorism."[153]

The PATRIOT Act also codifies the use of political ideology as legal criteria for entry into the United States. Section 411 of the act affects the ability of foreign nationals to practice dissent in the U.S., as it essentially establishes an ideological audition at the border in order to gain entry into the country. According to Section 411, delegates representing political or social groups, "whose public endorsement of acts of terrorist activity the Secretary of State has determined undermines United States efforts to reduce or eliminate terrorist activities" are barred from entering the country. Also, the law states that noncitizens who have utilized their "position of prominence within any country to endorse or espouse terrorist activity" or whose communication the Secretary of State has decided "undermines United States efforts to reduce or eliminate terrorist activities," may also be denied entry.[154] This section of the act imposes a guilt-by-association logic, and thus resembles the McCarran-Walter Act of 1952, which afforded the State Department the legal leverage to prohibit entrance to foreign speakers based on their political viewpoints. This Cold War relic was only repealed in 1990, and before that, it was used to prohibit entry to political-cultural workers like Pablo Neruda, Gabriel García Marquez, Ernst Mandel, Dario Fo, Carlos Fuentes, and many others.

Furthermore, the unchecked power of the Secretary of State to decide who is and who is not a foreign terrorist organization (FTO) is also deeply problematic, in that the determination process is drenched in politics that often have little to do with terrorism. Were FTO statutes in place during the 1980s, the Secretary of State may well have designated the African National Congress (ANC) an FTO, as politically motivated violence was part of the ANC's repertoire of resistance. Once marked as an FTO, Section 411 of the USA PATRIOT Act, if in place at the time, would have barred Nelson Mandela, as a leader of the ANC, from entering the U.S., even if he were coming to negotiate a peace treaty.

Section 411 also enlarges the category of noncitizens who can be deported because of their alleged participation in terrorism by loosening the definition of "terrorist activity." While terrorism is usually viewed as pre-planned, politically-driven violence carried out against civilians, Section 411 distends the definition to include all crimes that involve the use of "a weapon or dangerous device (other than for mere personal or monetary gain)."[155] As Chang points out, "Under this broad definition, a noncitizen who...grabs a knife or makeshift weapon in the midst of a heat-of-the-moment altercation or in committing a crime of passion may be subject to deportation as a 'terrorist.'"[156] The law's term "engaging in terrorist activity" has also been widened to include First Amendment activity that is directed toward furthering the wholly lawful political and humanitarian goals of a "terrorist organization." The definition of "terrorist organization" has also been expanded to mean any collection of two or more individuals who have engaged in violence or who threaten to engage in violence. As Cole and Dempsey point out, under such strategically slackened standards, "an alien who sent coloring books to a day-care center run by a designated [terrorist] organization would apparently be deportable as a terrorist, even if she could show that the coloring books were used only by 3-year olds."[157] This resurrection of "guilt by association" has myriad implications for foreign nationals in the United States, especially ones who have any interest in becoming activists.

The PATRIOT Act gives the government—and more specifically, the FBI—new and improved surveillance powers. These enhanced surveillance capabilities serve as a twenty-first century Orwellian how-to kit. Section 213 allows federal agents to carry out "sneak-and-peek searches"—surreptitious searches of an individual's home or office without showing a search warrant until after the search has already been carried out. This delayed notice may occur as long as the Bureau can show "reasonable cause to believe that providing immediate notification...may have an adverse result" (which they can, of course, do all the time). Notice that "reasonable cause" replaces the probable cause standard; this is a common feature of the PATRIOT Act. Section 213 applies to *all criminal investigations*, not simply terrorism investigations, despite the fact that the PATRIOT Act is supposedly designed to fight terrorism. In other words, Section 213 applies equally to Zacarias

Moussaoui and the community college student from your town who provides false information on her student loan application, whether she meant to or not.

In practice, under a "sneak-and-peek" warrant, an FBI agent can covertly enter your house when you are not there and can seize your possessions, copy, photograph, and/or alter them, and not tell you that s/he was there for a "reasonable period thereafter." Well, what exactly is the "reasonable period" before the FBI must notify you that it has stopped by? Actually, the term is undefined in the PATRIOT Act, although the Administration's *Field Guidance* booklet advises that this is a "flexible standard." In *Terrorism and the Constitution*, Cole and Dempsey report that the Justice Department interprets "reasonable period" to mean ninety days.[158]

Section 213 undercuts the well-established "knock and announce" principle that, in conformity to the Fourth Amendment, required law enforcement officials to inform the resident that a search was imminent before the search was actually carried out. It is worth noting that this new sneak-and-peek provision—an enormous expansion of FBI power—has virtually nothing to do with combating terrorism. Under the Foreign Intelligence Surveillance Act (FISA) the U.S. government already had the authority to carry out covert searches in international terrorism cases.[159] The PATRIOT Act's codification of sneak-and-peek searches, and its expansion to criminal investigations, is an extraordinary measure that could potentially routinize clandestine entries by law enforcement agents. Unlike other provisions in the PATRIOT Act, Section 213 is not scheduled to sunset.[160]

Other sections of the PATRIOT Act also complicate the practice of dissent: the government's access to records (Section 215); the tracking of Internet usage (Section 216); the rules for wiretapping and searches in foreign intelligence investigations (Section 218); and the stipulations on roving wiretaps (Section 206). Of these, Section 215 has received the most public attention. This section allows the FBI to obtain "any tangible things (including books, records, papers, documents, and other items)" as long as these items are "relevant" to a terrorism investigation. The law does not require the FBI to demonstrate that the records are those of a person linked to suspected terrorists. The original PATRIOT Act permanently gagged people who fulfill these orders, preventing them from telling anyone about the Bureau's inquiries.[161] For instance, it would be illegal for a librarian to let patrons know if the FBI had come by and requested their lending records. Under the re-authorized agreement that Congress passed in spring 2006, the length of the gag order was reduced from everlasting to a one-year period, after which information providers can challenge the restraint. This one-year gag order is being championed as a congressional compromise, a counterpunch to executive hegemony, but this is illusory since the government can trump such dissident challenges by simply asserting that disclosure could imperil national security or diplomatic relations. Moreover, to mount a successful challenge, the recipient would shoulder a high burden of proof, being forced to demonstrate the government had acted in bad faith.[162] The only-slightly-revised PATRIOT Act that Congress re-authorized is not a marked push of the pendulum back toward liberty and the ability to freely practice dissent.

A final, post-9/11 extraordinary law is the Military Commissions Act of 2006. This Act is yet another example of the Bush administration and a compliant Congress teaming up to use law to subvert the rule of law. Along with legalizing military tribunals, which the Supreme Court had outlawed in *Hamdan v. Rumsfeld,* this law rescinds habeas corpus rights for noncitizens, leaving them unable to challenge their detention in federal court. It also allows state agents to detain legal residents of the United States indefinitely without leveling charges or proof and without affording the person the possibility of challenging his or her detention. In other words, legal residents of the United States can be dubbed "enemy combatants" and shelved in detention centers at the executive's whim.[163] In an interview on National Public Radio, John Yoo, a former Bush administration lawyer and architect of the law, made it clear that the Act allowed the president to also designate U.S. citizens as enemy combatants and that "if you are an enemy combatant, there is no constitutional requirement that you get a criminal trial. You can be held until hostilities are over."[164] Again, much of the mainstream media's focus fell on how the Military Commissions Act affects non-citizens and detainees in Guantánamo, but the law has alarming potential to quash the dissent of activists working in the U.S., even legal residents and U.S. citizens.

Mass Media Manipulation

The George W. Bush administration has demonstrated a willingness to manipulate the media in direct, straightforward ways, even going as far as paying them for their pro-Bush services. Bush's Department of Education doled out $240,000 to media commentator Armstrong Williams to publicize the president's "No Child Left Behind" law. Williams produced a commercial in favor of Bush's educational policies, which he proceeded to air on his syndicated TV and radio programs. Armstrong also spoke positively of the law in his newspaper column and as a guest on cable television, yet he never revealed that he was receiving paychecks from the Bush administration. The contract obliged Williams "to regularly comment on NCLB during the course of his broadcasts" and to use his connections with black broadcast journalists "to encourage the producers to periodically address" the "No Child Left Behind" law. California Democrat George Miller, member of the House Education Committee, called Williams's work "propaganda…unethical, it's dangerous and it's illegal," adding it was "worthy of *Pravda*."[165]

Yet this was only the first among many revealed examples of the Bush administration paying off journalists to produce pro-Bush propaganda. Maggie Gallagher, a syndicated columnist, soon admitted to being on the take from the Department of Health and Human Services. She reportedly was paid $21,500 for her services.[166] Also, the Bush administration's Office of Cuba Broadcasting was caught paying journalists from *El Nuevo Herald*, a Spanish-language newspaper linked to the *Miami Herald*, to write material for Radio and TV Martí, stations the U.S. sponsors and transmits to Cuba that are fiercely critical of Fidel Castro and his government. One reporter from *El Nuevo Herald* received a whopping $175,000 since 2001.[167]

Then there's the case of Jeff Gannon. Gannon received White House media credentials from the Bush team. In return, he "asks softball questions to the president and his spokesman in the midst of contentious news conferences, and routinely reprints long passages verbatim from official press releases as original news articles on his website." Gannon, whose real name is James D. Guckert, wrote for the online source *Talon News*. He produced pro-Bush work and swerved the topics of press-conference discussions toward more Bush-friendly terrain. When Bush was being grilled about the improper payments of Armstrong Williams, Gannon injected the following question: "Senate Democratic leaders have painted a very bleak picture of the US economy. Harry Reid was talking about soup lines, and Hillary Clinton was talking about the economy being on the verge of collapse. Yet, in the same breath, they say that Social Security is rock solid and there's no crisis there. How are you going to work…with people who seem to have divorced themselves from reality?" According to Charlie Savage, Senator Reid "had never talked about soup lines. That was a phrase attributed to him in satire by Rush Limbaugh on his radio show."[168]

Journalists were in cahoots with the Bush administration in quieter, behind-the-scenes ways, too. In his book *State of Denial*, Bob Woodward revealed that in the immediate aftermath of the 11 September attacks, two key journalists secretly met with Bush and his advisors in order to concoct an effective response. Deputy Defense Secretary Paul Wolfowitz was the brain behind the plan. He wanted to assemble a super-star, super-secret mini-think tank to brainstorm strategies for dealing with massive crises like 9/11. He recruited Christopher Demuth, the president of the American Enterprise Institute, to pull together this small collection of intellectuals and strategists. Demuth later told Bob Woodward they agreed to participate only "if I promised it would all be kept secret." People in the group included Bernard

Lewis, a scholar of Islam; Mark Palmer, a former U.S. ambassador who specialized in dictatorships; Fareed Zakaria, *Newsweek International* editor and *Newsweek* columnist; Fouad Ajami, head of the Middle East Studies program at SAIS; Rumsfeld aide Steve Herbits; James Q. Wilson, a professor specializing in crime; and Reuel Marc Gerecht, a former CIA guy who worked in the Middle East. Reportedly, *Atlantic Monthly* writer Robert Kaplan was also in attendance. Kaplan defended his participation by stating, "everybody was in a patriotic fervor." Rumsfeld said the idea of the group was to "bring together some very fine minds on a highly confidential basis and provide intellectual content" for a post-9/11 world. [169] To many that sounds like a fancy way of saying "secret propaganda machine."

In terms of media coverage of the Iraq War, once again, the control of space was an issue. According to Rod Norland, who was *Newsweek*'s Baghdad bureau chief for two years, journalists were strictly managed in Iraq. He said in an interview with *Foreign Policy* magazine that "The restrictions on [journalists'] movements are very severe" and, if that weren't enough, "the military has started censoring many arrangements" with embedded reporters. The term "embedded reporters," which emerged with the U.S. invasion of Iraq in 2003, refers to journalists who travel and live with specific military units during armed conflict. Norland avowed that military officials, "want to know your slant on a story—they use the word slant—what you intend to write, and what you have written from embed trips before. If they don't like what you have done before, they refuse to take you. There are cases where individual reporters have been blacklisted because the military wasn't happy with the work they had done on embed."[170] Such intense control, especially in high-pressure situations where the journalists' lives were in danger, nudged them down the road of administration-friendly reporting. Certainly, it nudged them away from hot-button issues like anti-war sentiment within the military, which surely would have been given the Pentagon kibosh.

Some media workers were willing to admit the effects that Pentagon pressure was having on their writing and reporting. On CNBC, host Tina Brown said, "There was a lot of complaining during the war that the administration really intimidated the media into feeling really unpatriotic if they raised the voice of dissent." Then she asked CNN reporter Christiane Amanpour, "Do you think that we, in fact, in the media as much as in the administration drank the Kool-Aid when it came to the war, Christiane?" To the surprise of many, Amanpour spelled it out loud and clear: "I think yes. I think the press was muzzled and I think the press self-muzzled. I'm sorry to say but certainly television and, perhaps, to a certain extent, my station was intimidated by the administration and its foot soldiers at Fox News. And it did, in fact, put a climate of fear and self-censorship, in my view, in terms of—of the kind of broadcast work we did." When pressed by Brown whether there were stories that journalists were forbade from doing, Amanpour replied: "It's not a question of couldn't do it, it's a question of tone. It's a question of being rigorous. It's really a question of really asking the questions….I mean, it looks like this was disinformation at the highest levels."[171] In addition to Pentagon pressure, journalists must also contend with peer pressure. When told of Amanpour's remarks, Irena Briganti of Fox News remarked, "Given the choice, it's better to be viewed as a foot soldier for Bush than a spokeswoman for al-Qaeda."[172]

While many examples of government manipulation of the media have come to light, I have not come across hard evidence of journalists cooperating with the state to besmirch the reputations of activists in deliberate ways. As with black propaganda, sometimes such information takes time to slither its way to the surface.

Bi-level Demonization

Bi-level demonization is when the state publicly connects activists to a demonized group or individual from the international realm. This can be a specific international entity or it can be an abstraction like communism or terrorism. Whether the connections are real or imagined is beside the point. If the state is able to connect domestic activists with demonized enemies, the activists will experience a rougher road of resistance.

Bi-level demonization has been a central aspect to the Bush administration's squelching of dissent after September 11. Even in the immediate aftermath of the terrorist attacks, it became clear that bi-level demonization would be a central weapon in the war on dissent. The very day after the strikes, Don Young, a U.S. Congressman from Alaska, actually claimed that the global justice movement and radical environmentalists might have been responsible for the destruction of the Twin Towers. On the floor of Congress he stated, "If you watched what happened in Genoa, in Italy, and even in Seattle, there's some expertise in that field. I'm not sure they're that dedicated, but eco-terrorists—which are really based in Seattle—there's a strong possibility that could be one of the groups" responsible for the attacks.[173]

Bi-level demonization originated from the highest levels of government. In a general sense, President Bush and his minions have made an effort to paint their foes as indirect supporters of the ever-vague terrorist enemy. In late September 2006, while speaking to the Reserve Officers Association in Washington, DC, President Bush remarked that the logic of anti-war critics "buys into the enemy's propaganda."[174] Secretary of Defense Rumsfeld went as far as to compare opponents of Bush's Iraq policy to those who wanted to appease the Nazis before World War II.[175] Echoing this sentiment in the press—a key factor in bi-level demonization—the *New York Sun* editorialized, "There can be no question at this point that Saddam Hussein is an enemy of America....And there is no reason to doubt that the 'anti-war' protesters—we prefer to call them protesters against freeing Iraq—are giving, at the very least, comfort to Saddam Hussein." Thus, the *Sun* concluded, anti-war activists were guilty of treason.[176]

But terrorism, as an actual label, is more often affixed to specific groups. For instance, documents from a domestic terrorism symposium in Michigan that were secured through the Freedom of Information Act, made law enforcement in Michigan look like a modern-day Joe McCarthy, naming terrorist names like a banshee. Organizations that made the "terrorist" list included the affirmative action group By Any Means Necessary, the East Lansing Animal Rights Movement, and Direct Action. Tommy Simon of Direct Action was skeptical of the terrorist label. "What is a terrorist? The word is just a propaganda tool used to dissuade people from getting involved in activism—especially young people," he said.[177]

The word "terrorist" can indeed serve as a "propaganda tool," and the U.S. government has made much use of the term in recent years, especially in relation to animal rights groups like the Animal Liberation Front and Stop Huntingdon Animal Cruelty (SHAC), and environmental groups like the Earth Liberation Front. SHAC is an animal-rights group that formed in 1999. It focuses on Huntingdon Life Sciences, which they say is "synonymous with animal cruelty worldwide."[178] Although SHAC's web site asserts that it "does not encourage or incite illegal activity," the state and mass media have labeled it a "terrorist organization."[179] Deputy Assistant Director of the FBI's Counterterrorism Division couldn't have said it more clearly than when he testified in front of the Senate Committee on Environment and Public Works in 2005. He stated, "One of today's most serious domestic terrorism threats come from special interest extremist movements such as the Animal Liberation Front (ALF), the Earth Liberation Front (ELF), and Stop Huntingdon Animal Cruelty (SHAC) campaign." In his testimony, Lewis used phrases like "eco-terrorist," "eco-extremist," and "domestic terrorism threats."[180] This vocabulary of terror has been mimicked in the press without a second thought, with the *National Review* publishing an article titled, "In the Name of the Animals—America Faces a New Kind of Terrorism" and the *Sacramento Bee* offering headlines like "Eco-terror Sparks Anxiety: Builders on Guard against Environmental Radicals."[181]

Extraordinary laws like the Animal Enterprise Protection Act—which was amended by Congress in 2002 in order to make breaking the law on par with terrorism—have been used to prosecute members of SHAC, with the

first convictions coming in March 2006. SHAC's tactics fell under the pur-
view of the law, even though the activists who were convicted were never accused of perpetrating injury or engaging in violence or vandalism. Yet their
tactics—such as encouraging people to contact Huntingdon employees and
shareholders to try to get them to change their ways; publishing the names,
addresses and phone numbers of Huntingdon employees on the internet;
faxing black sheets to the company and its associates to clog up their fax
machines; and deluging the firms with emails to lock up their computer systems—were deemed punishable under the Act. Andrew Stepanian was the
first of SHAC convictions to go to prison. On *Democracy Now!* he said,

> At the end of the day, no one was hurt. SHAC USA, on their website,
> never advocated for anyone to be hurt. SHAC USA, at the bottom of
> every page, when you load up the html, always had a disclaimer that
> said that we do not advocate any form of violent activity, and in fact, we
> urge people that when they write letters or they send emails, that they're
> polite, they're to the point, they're not threatening in nature. And, obvi-
> ously, all that happened on the SHAC USA website was a legal form of
> reporting. It wasn't, "You go and go do this or go annoy these people or
> go harass these people," but rather, "These are the people that are sup-
> porting this laboratory. This is how they put bread on the table. And
> this is how this company exists." The website existed for a purpose, to
> say, "This company is an organism. And there are different things that
> feed this organism and keep it alive." Whether or not people took that
> information and did less than savory things or things that even made
> myself feel uncomfortable, well, that wasn't necessarily the business of
> SHAC USA to be responsible for. The only business that they had was
> reporting on the facts. And all that, no matter how uncomfortable you
> might say it is, is protected underneath the First Amendment.[182]

A New Jersey court begged to differ, though, and Stepanian was shipped
off to jail after receiving the maximum sentence—three years—under the
Animal Enterprise Protection Act. The convictions failed, however, to stamp
out animal activism. In September 2006, animal activists responded directly
to the convictions by releasing research animals from a lab in Massachusetts
called Capralogics. Camille Hankins, a spokesperson for the North American
Animal Liberation Press Office, said, "The government tried to send a message to activists and I think activists got a different message." She asserted
that the lesson animal activists took from the SHAC-7 case was that "if
you're going to be above ground and identifiable, you're going to go to jail,
so why not do activities in dead of night, protect your identity and not make

yourself a target of the government?" Hankins also predicted, "I think we're going to see a lot more of this."[183]

The Earth Liberation Front was also running into trouble with the law, after years of the government priming the "domestic terrorism" pump. After the first big set of indictments from "Operation Backfire" came down on 20 January 2006, the Justice Department held a press conference to hype the event. Attorney General Alberto Gonzales said the 65-count indictment "tells a story of four-and-a-half years of arson, vandalism, violence, and destruction claimed to have been executed on behalf of the Animal Liberation Front or Earth Liberation Front—extremist movements known to support acts of domestic terrorism." He added, "Today's indictment is a significant step in bringing these terrorists to justice."[184] FBI Director Mueller also used the "terrorist" label, claiming "Terrorism is terrorism—no matter the motive. The FBI is committed to protecting Americans from all crime and all terrorism, including acts of domestic terrorism on behalf of animal rights or the environment." He also said, "Today's indictment marks significant progress in our efforts to combat animal rights extremism and eco-terrorism."[185] Again, the media ran unquestioningly with the "terrorism" tag. The *Rocky Mountain News* of Colorado dredged up fear by opening a story with the following lead: "Friday's indictments won't completely crush the two shadowy eco-terrorist groups targeted by federal authorities."[186] The *Washington Post* conjured up international communism, describing the ELF's organizational system as "Maoist-style cells."[187] CNN casually referred to the "indictments of nearly a dozen people accused of eco-terrorism."[188]

Are the members of the ELF and ALF terrorists? They certainly don't fit the U.S. State Department's definition of terrorism—"premeditated, politically motivated violence perpetrated against noncombatant targets by subnational groups or clandestine agents, usually intended to influence an audience"—since their attacks do not target "noncombatants."[189] In fact, the ALF and ELF attacks do not target humans, and to date not a single person has been injured or killed.

The actions of these groups conform more snugly to the strikingly expansive definition of "domestic terrorism" found in Section 802 of the USA PATRIOT Act. But, as we know, this conspicuously vague part of the Act applies to virtually all domestic dissidents, whose actions are by definition designed "to influence the policy of a government by intimidation or coercion" and since sometimes the state's response to protests—even peaceful ones—can create situations that may be construed as "acts dangerous to human life." At the end of the day, as defiant as the ELF and ALF are, their activities would more accurately be characterized as "extreme vandalism" or "massive property destruction." Crimes, yes, but terrorism? No.[190]

Mass Media Deprecation

A basic tenet to successful activism is motivating people to puts their boots on the pavement for dissident actions both big and small. Yet, as the National Lawyer Guild's Heidi Boghosian notes, mass-media coverage can daunt activism "by depicting protesters as violent and by showing striking images of weapon-bearing police officers in riot gear well in advance of a given event. Such early media coverage of *anticipated* confrontations between police and protesters is now commonplace."[191] State officials feed this media framing by predicting protester-related problems. When the G-8 met in Georgia in May 2004, Governor Sonny Perdue went as far as to declare a state of emergency in the six counties near where the event was being held. Perdue justified his decree by alleging, "potential danger to the persons and property of this state from unlawful assemblages, threats of violence and otherwise."[192] Such characterizations—echoed through the media—only reinforce the equation that dissent means violence, disruption, and criminality.

Media priming was also prevalent in the lead-up to the 2003 FTAA protests in Miami. According to the City of Miami Civilian Investigative Panel's official report,

> For several months preceding the FTAA, the local media devoted considerable coverage to violent protests and wanton vandalism that had taken place in other locations where international economic conferences were held. Although not quantifiable, repeated television images of violent protesters at such events no doubt contributed to an apprehension that similar chaos and violence would befall the city of Miami during the FTAA.[193]

With media coverage portraying dissidents in a negative light even before protests actually occur, the press stacks the deck against effective activism.

Such deprecatory mass-media coverage doesn't stop once the protesters actually hit the streets, of course, as demonstrated by the case of anti-war crusader Cindy Sheehan. In April 2004, Sheehan's son Casey was killed in Sadr City, Iraq while serving in the U.S. military. After his death, Sheehan became increasingly active in the anti-war movement. In January 2005, she co-founded Gold Star Families for Peace, a group that offers support to the families of U.S. soldiers and that fights to end the Iraq War.[194] In August 2005, Sheehan hunkered down along the side of the road in Crawford, Texas near President Bush's ranch and held vigil, demanding to speak with the president. She was joined by others in what became known as Camp Casey, and their presence attracted significant media coverage, and, despite the fact she had lost a son to war, a great deal of the coverage was sharply critical of her. For instance, *Seattle Post-Intelligencer* columnist Robert L. Jamieson Jr. called Camp Casey "Sheehan's squatter stunt" and stated, "I deplore the disingenuous way Sheehan has politicized the death of a son who signed up to fight."[195] In a separate column, Jamieson infantilized Sheehan, calling her a "military mom turned antiwar poster child," and a dupe who "wants to make a public splash by allowing critics of the unjustified war in Iraq to use her as a human bazooka against Bush." He dismissed her dissent as "pathetic" and a "misguided spectacle."[196] And all this from someone who actually supported Sheehan's criticism of the Iraq debacle.

It should come as no surprise that supporters of the invasion of Iraq also attacked Sheehan. Fox's Bill O'Reilly regularly questioned Sheehan's integrity, asserting once that "It's obvious Cindy Sheehan has become a political player, whose primary concern is embarrassing the president. She is no longer just a protestor. I don't think she ever has been, by the way."[197] While not directly calling Sheehan's actions treasonous, O'Reilly used the grieving families of those killed in Iraq as a proxy to do just that, saying, "Some Americans who also lost loved ones in Iraq do indeed consider the woman's conduct treasonous." O'Reilly added implausibly that Sheehan was "associating with the most radical elements in this country" and that "we respect dissent, but we don't have time for extremism."[198] A common thread among conservatives was that the anti-war movement was using Sheehan, as James Bowman indicated in the *American Spectator*:

> There has been a left-wing anti-war movement since before the war even began, and it is now doing its utmost to batten on to Mrs. Sheehan in order to create the impression that it amounts to a grass-roots movement—an impression that the media are only too eager to promote. Moreover, they pretend to believe that Bush is making a big mistake by not meeting with her. I say "pretend" because they couldn't possibly believe this unless they also believe that a meeting with the President is what Cindy Sheehan really wants; and to believe that, they would have to be idiots.[199]

Conservative columnist Victor Davis Hanson accused Sheehan of anti-Semitism and then made the improbable connection between Sheehan and the racist right, asserting, "her antiwar venom could easily come right out of the mouth of a more calculating David Duke. Perhaps that's why he lauded her anti-Semitism." Continuing the comparison, he said the both Sheehan and the ultra-right "have embraced the paranoid style of personal invective" and "employ half-truths and spin conspiracy theories to argue that the war was unjust, impossible to win, and hatched through the result of a brainwashing of a devious few neocons."[200] It's interesting how a master of "the paranoid style of personal invective" used such paranoid invective as a way of casting aspersions.

The media also gave plenty of opportunity for others to vent venom toward Sheehan. The Associated Press quoted a counter-demonstrator who held a sign that read, "Help! I'm surrounded by America-hating idiots!"[201] A letter to the editor in the San Antonio Express-News said, "I think I speak for a large number of Americans when I say, 'Go home, Cindy Sheehan, and take your group of whiners with you.' Most of her anti-war protesters...come from generations of freedom abusers who think just because they were born here they deserve to have a warm and fuzzy feeling whenever they want it."[202] A letter to the editor in the Sacramento Bee stated, "The only thing Cindy Sheehan is accomplishing is to serve as another media-assisted prop for terrorists." Another letter writer expressed sympathy for Sheehan's loss before claiming, "Unfortunately, her honorable quest has been hijacked by her anti-President Bush 'handlers' and anti-war organizations who have turned a grieving mother's sincerity into a bash-Bush and embarrass-the-president media circus."[203]

Compared to most activists, Sheehan garnered loads of laudatory press. After all, as the mother of a fallen soldier, Sheehan had mainstream cred. Had she put forth a more radical perspective that cut straight toward the structural violence exerted by the state every day, from war to poverty to racism, one can only imagine what kind of malicious media coverage she would have stirred up.

Mass Media Underestimation, False Balance, and Disregard

In late-September 2005, more than 200,000 protesters took to the streets in cities across the United States to register their discontent with the war in Iraq. Such sentiment reflected public opinion polls at the time that found 67% of the population disapproving President Bush's handling of Iraq, 63% favoring complete or partial withdrawal of U.S. troops, and nearly seven in ten Americans believing that the military action against Iraq has either made people in the U.S. less safe from terrorism or has not made any difference in our safety level. Yet, if one were to consult many prominent U.S. newspapers, even the vigilant reader would struggle to detect such conspicuous anti-war attitudes. Although covering complex social issues is a challenging endeavor, mainstream press coverage of that weekend's protests was deficient in significant ways.

First, some newspapers succumbed to the seemingly logical practice of engaging in balance, offering the same number of articles on anti-war protesters and pro-war counter-demonstrators. Even though balanced coverage—telling "both" sides of the story—is widely considered a pillar of high-quality, professional journalism, it can actually be problematic when covering certain issues. In fact, as we know, balance can sometimes be a form of informational bias, elbowing us down the path of inaccuracy. Coverage of the anti-war protest in Washington, DC brought to light the shortcomings of mechanically employing balance. According to the most conservative estimates, anti-war protesters numbered 100,000, while pro-war counter-demonstrators totaled 200. In other words, there were 500 anti-war protesters for each counter-demonstrator. Yet, the *Los Angeles Times* featured two stories about the weekend protests, one focusing on each group. Such balance was common within individual articles, too. For instance, on 25 September the *New York Times* ran a 13-paragraph story about the DC protests in its National Edition, with counter-demonstrators featured or mentioned in six of the paragraphs. The *Oregonian* ran one story with one photo on the 100,000-person anti-war demonstration in Washington, DC. A small item about a related demonstration on bridges in Portland appeared on the same page and vastly undercounted attendance by estimating 100 people participated. Even the ombudsman later had to admit that there were at least 3,000, according to bridge operators with a bird's eye view. A counter-demonstration in Washington, D.C., drew only 400 people but was reported in a slightly longer story and larger photo in the *Oregonian*.[204]

A second weakness in protest coverage was injudicious story placement. Despite the fact that the DC protest was the largest since the war in Iraq began, both the *New York Times* and the *Los Angeles Times* relegated their accounts of the anti-war protest to page 26 and 22 respectively. In the *New York Times'* National Edition, the story appeared on page 14, following articles about worker protests in Dubai (page 4) and Vice President Cheney's surgery for an aneurysm behind his knee (page 11). The *Oregonian's* aforementioned story on the anti-war demonstration in Washington, DC appeared on page 10, while the counter-demonstration of only 400 people was reported on page 2. In an odd demonstration of priorities, the anti-war story was actually beaten out by a puff piece on page 3 about a rare pewter flagon that was recovered from theft in Maryland. This relative disregard of anti-war protest news affords the impression that such news is not a vital, burning issue of great importance. Burying anti-war articles in the back pages tacitly ghettoizes dissident citizenship.

Finally, the ideas and opinions of anti-war protesters were rarely included in the "hard news" about the war in Iraq. Rather, when such voices are granted admission in the pages of the national press, they appear in stories about protest and dissent or in feature pieces on the work of individual dissidents like Cindy Sheehan. Despite the fact that polls at the time revealed 50% of the U.S. public believing Iraq will never become a stable democracy and almost three in five Americans judging that the U.S. made a mistake sending troops to Iraq in the first place, such opinions rarely enter the "hard news" even if they would enrich and widen the national dialogue. Instead, major newspapers tend to rely on members of Congress, the president and military higher-ups as "hard-news" sources. Such sourcing can lead to an inside-the-Beltway mentality where viable alternatives, such as immediate extrication from Iraq, are never seriously considered.

State and mass-media suppression of dissent is thriving in the post-9/11 era. Examining the suppression of dissent after 11 September highlights continuity with previous methods of state and mass-media suppression and reminds us how interrelated the modes of suppression are when thrumming full-throttle in the real world. The intense, far-reaching suppression of dissent in the wake of 11 September also points to clear continuity with suppressive tactics of the past. The unmistakable resonances between Japanese internment during World War II and "preventative detention" of "enemy combatants" today, as well as between previous "Red Scares" and the current "Green Scare," are striking.

15
"Two Steps Ahead"

"Awareness is two steps ahead. Paranoia is two steps behind."
—Kim Marks, forest activist

"Now we don't want to go it alone. We want allies....We hope we shall never have to go it alone," declared a powerful U.S. politician. "At the same time," he continued, "we can't have allies who cringe and surrender in the face of an enemy threat or who lick the enemy's hand and furnish him with the weapons of war. A nation cannot be half loyal to the free world. Those allies and alleged allies must be for us or against us."

Sound familiar? Although hauntingly reminiscent of President George W. Bush's post-11 September speech in which he proclaimed, "Every nation, in every region, now has a decision to make. Either you are with us, or you are with the terrorists," the quote actually comes from a 1953 speech by Senator Joseph McCarthy, who at the time was assailing Communist China.[1] Just as McCarthy's persistent attacks on international Communism helped fashion an atmosphere conducive to the suppression of all leftist dissent in the United States, President Bush's with-us-or-against-us logic has set the table for the suppression of those who dissent during the so-called "War on Terrorism." Just as, under McCarthyism, all domestic dissent with a vaguely reddish hue was compressed into the convenient label "Communist," modern-day activism may be flattened into the new legal term "domestic terrorism," as delineated by the Bush regime and the USA PATRIOT Act. Side by side, the quotes from Bush and McCarthy highlight the rhetorical and ideological continuities that underpin the state's suppression of dissent. This book has tried to point out that there is also historical continuity in the methods the state and mass media have deployed to suppress dissent in this country. Especially in times of war—whether on countries, combatants, or concepts—these modes of suppression complicate the practice of dissent.

In the United States, the freedom of speech is held up as one of the most crucial pillars of free society. The tradition of free speech is considered by most people in the U.S. to be a non-negotiable aspect of democracy. Whether we actually live in a democracy—replete with representation for everyone and real-world equality for all—is highly debatable, especially since in moments of social peril—such as war—the much-cherished freedoms the U.S. was supposedly built on are often sacrificed on the altar of "national security." It is precisely when dissident citizens are adamantly challenging prevailing power relations and pushing forward with democratic principles and programs that the state utilizes suppressive tactics to crush—or at least muffle—this democratic impulse. We ought to be rigorously interrogating and vigorously deconstructing the assumptions buttressing the idea that the U.S. is in fact a democracy. Politics in the United States are writhing with contradiction, but often it is the honest exploration of contradiction that leads to innovative—and sometimes emancipatory—thought.

Lies, Damn Lies, and History

I.F. Stone famously said, "Governments lie. All governments lie." A possible corollary to this might be "Governments suppress dissent. All governments suppress dissent." Some governments use intensely coercive modes of repression while most nominal democracies are more often than not left with the alternative of more subtle forms of suppression.

Activism that challenges the power of the existing authorities, affects central institutions, or that exhibits innovative forms of protest is almost always met with efforts to suppress it. As U.S. Supreme Court Justice Lewis F. Powell aptly noted, "History abundantly documents the tendency of Government—however benevolent and benign its motives—to view with suspicion those who most fervently dispute its policies"[2] When confronted with dissident citizens engaging in oppositional practices both inside and outside the institutional pathways of political power, the state all too often engages in suppression in order to manage or eradicate them and, simultaneously, to lengthen or broaden its tenure. In *Paths to State Repression*, Christian Davenport notes that, "This finding has been supported with political-historical as well as statistical evidence considering most countries in the world over varied time periods from the late-eighteenth century to the present."[3] This is the case regardless of the political system in place, degree of wealth disparity, or level of economic development. *Beyond Bullets* shows how this propensity for the state to quell or channel dissent is most assuredly the case in twentieth and twenty-first century USAmerica.

It's a truism that the powerful exercise their power in order to maintain it. However, different contexts—whether historical or geographical—lead states to deploy different methods of suppression in order to decrease dissident threats on the homefront. In totalitarian societies, direct violence is an ever-available option, whereas in the context of the United States—where citizens in theory have a panoply of political and civil rights—direct violence is, by and large, politically unacceptable, at least in heavy, prolonged quantities. Therefore, the state relies on less obvious means.

Environmental historian Larry Lipin has said, "History gives us some distance to understand how human beings respond to evolving circumstances."[4] At the same time, as Sanjoy Banerjee writes, "History is interaction. What is called history is largely persons and groups commencing actions in response to previous actions by other persons and groups."[5] Taken together, these quotes help us understand the dialectic of resistance and restriction, whereby activists have responded and adapted to their suppression as they interact, whether they like it or not, with the state. In *Beyond Bullets*, I have traced this ongoing interaction, focusing on vibrant activism in the United States and how the state and media have attempted to dull it. In Chapters 2 through 13, I mapped out these processes of interaction one mode of suppression at a time. Along the way, I explored in detail the relations between dissidents and the mass media, since over time the mass media, as an institution, has become more and more important in the political realm in the United States. According to veteran journalist Salim Muwakkil, "News media are to a society what sensory perceptions are to an individual; they provide information necessary to accurately assess our situation and act accordingly."[6] The way dissent is framed by the media has massive implications not only for how the general public construes activism, but also how activist groups view themselves and each other. The upshot is that if social movements receive more positive coverage in mass-media outlets, they will vastly increase their chances of meeting their goals. If they receive denigrating, deprecatory coverage, on the other hand, bystander publics and potential recruits are less likely to support or join the movements, and group solidarity may be thrown into jeopardy.

With this in mind, I have identified the twelve modes of suppression that we have explored in the preceding pages. These techniques undermine the preconditions for effective collective action: maintaining solidarity and sustaining morale and commitment; attracting new recruits; creating, nurturing, and supporting activist leaders; generating preferably favorable media coverage; mobilizing support from potentially sympathetic "bystander publics;" and carving out the tactical freedom to pursue social-change goals, rather than having to put resources toward defensive maintenance needs. Clearly, many methods of suppression directly affect the ability of activists to meet these preconditions. Numerous forms of state suppression deplete the resources of activist groups. Others stigmatize activists in the public sphere and pit dissident groups against themselves and each other in highly divisive ways. Still others intimidate activists from taking future action.

Crisis

Walter Benjamin, in his "Theses on the Philosophy of History," wrote,

> The tradition of the oppressed teaches us that the "state of emergency"
> in which we live is not the exception but the rule. We must attain to a
> conception of history that is in keeping with this insight. Then we shall
> clearly realize that it is our task to bring about a real state of emergency,
> and this will improve our position in the struggle against Fascism. One
> reason why Fascism has a chance is that in the name of progress its op-
> ponents treat it as a historical norm.[7]

The state will always try to suppress dissent and try to pass such suppression off as normality or, at the very least, as necessary in the short term. And,
from the perspective of the committed activist, each moment feels vital and
crisis-like, where small decisions can have big consequences. The ability to
recognize—and even *foment*—the crisis amidst the generalized state of crisis
that extends backward through the decades is the key to pressing forward
with unpredictable, unprecedented dissent.

This can be extremely difficult, especially when the current state of affairs already feels like an unbearable crisis of oppressive proportions in which
the state holds ideological and cultural hegemony. Hegemony means ratcheting the brackets of "acceptable" discussion without anyone realizing that the
discursive brackets even exist. The idea of political and cultural hegemony is
unquestionably relevant in the United States where principled opposition to
capitalism—to name only one cutting critique of contemporary society—is
boxed out of mainstream discussions and information channels. To enter the
mainstream public sphere and speak out forcefully and fervently against capitalism is to risk forfeiting one's inclusion in that sphere. So go the machinations of hegemony and its relentless reproduction by and through each one of
us. When the state enjoys hegemony, the necessity of forcible forms of social
control becomes less pressing. Administrative and ideological control usually
does the trick.[8] Of course, sometimes the state falls back on blatant social
control, or what I've been calling direct violence, when absolutely necessary.

Related to hegemony, Michel Foucault wrote about the notion of a "disciplinary society" in which people police themselves and each other in place
of the state, yet in the state's interest. Discipline seeps into all the socio-cultural cracks in society, shaping the way we think and act. As he writes in
Discipline and Punish,

> discipline fixes; it arrests or regulates movements...it dissipates compact
> groupings of individuals wandering about the country in unpredictable

ways; it establishes calculated distributions. It must also master all the forces that are formed from the very constitution of an organized multiplicity; it must neutralize the effects of counterpower that spring from them and which form a resistance to the power that wishes to dominate it: agitations, revolts, spontaneous organizations, coalitions—anything that may establish horizontal conjunctions.[9]

In a sense, he's talking about the silence of violence, and how this violence surreptitiously slips into the deep structures of society, where it quietly casts anchor with little notice, becoming "normal" in institutions like prisons, schools, and the military. Through these institutions and other social relations, this silent violence infiltrates and becomes embedded in the everyday practices that everyone takes part in to various degrees.

In this context of hegemony and the "disciplinary society," Antonio Gramsci brings us back to Benjamin's concern with crisis when he writes in his *Prison Notebooks*, "The crisis consists precisely in the fact that the old is dying and the new cannot be born; in this interregnum a great variety of morbid symptoms appear."[10] It may feel like we're marinating in the "morbid symptoms" of silent, structural violence, but a principled, collective, ethical, politics is still possible, both within and among us. It is incumbent upon us that we respond to the silence of violence with radically new and ever-evolving forms of "counterpower."

Hope

On 10 September, the day before the attacks in Washington, DC and New York, Attorney General John Ashcroft rejected an FBI request for an additional $58 million to fund a strengthening of its counterterrorism effort.[11] Nevertheless, after September 11, Ashcroft may as well have legally changed his middle name to "Terrorism." He constantly yanked out the Justice Department soapbox to prattle about the perils of terrorism and the treacherous, yet-to-be-captured terrorists among us. In August 2003, Ashcroft even made like a rock star and embarked on a nationwide multicity tour designed to defend the PATRIOT Act. As one Justice Department official—who, incidentally, under the influence of hyper-secrecy, refused to be identified—put it, Ashcroft was going to "get out there and talk about the successes" of the Act in order "to set the record straight."[12] Alberto Gonzales, Ashcroft's successor, did the same song and dance when the PATRIOT Act was up for re-authorization in the spring of 2005. In his first policy speech as Attorney General, Gonzales claimed the PATRIOT Act "has helped prevent additional terrorist attacks." He also embraced the well-established tradition of issuing bland blandishments, saying he was in favor of "giving law enforcement the tools they need to keep America safe while honoring our values."[13] Meanwhile, in a paroxysm of decentralized dissent, more than 401 communities across the country—as well as the state legislatures in Alaska, California, Colorado, Hawaii, Idaho, Maine, Montana, and Vermont—have passed resolutions that condemn the PATRIOT Act and, in some cases, that refuse to enforce it, thereby creating PATRIOT-Act-free zones.[14] Such activism—replete with tangible results—is impressive, given our current context, and we would do well to take some hope from it.

This book aims to address the broader question of how—both historically and contemporarily—the state and mass media suppress the practice of dissent. I examine the actions that the state and mass media take—whether explicitly or tacitly, openly or surreptitiously, consciously or subconsciously—to diminish or discourage dissent. This book demonstrates that throughout the twentieth and twenty-first centuries, the state and mass media have relied on twelve modes of suppression in order to squelch dissent and maintain control. Yet, despite the seemingly gloomy nature of the topic, and the fact that I have been grappling with it intensely for years, I feel a deep sense of hope for the practice of dissent and acts of principled resistance in the United States.

Forest activist Kim Marks once told me, "Awareness is two steps ahead. Paranoia is two steps behind."[15] This book is meant to raise awareness and thus buoy dissent, not induce a paranoid, paralytic state of panicked inaction. *Beyond Bullets* is meant to be a pivot point in activist practice. It is my hope that activists will read this book and feel a sense of historical grounding as they come to understand that the state and media have a certain number of weapons in their cachet. Then, once dissident citizens know what these weapons are, they can more successfully strategize how to sidestep the sharper edges of suppression and become more effective activists. The state and its collaborators will never be able to fully suppress dissent.

This book is a concerted effort to not only identify, but ultimately to contest the boundaries that confine us; to challenge the discursive brackets that bind us; to collaboratively fashion a multi-pronged front of resistance that will bring us closer to social justice in its countless, gorgeous forms. As we do this, we might take heart from what Russell Banks wrote in *Cloudsplitter*, his work of historical fiction on the great abolitionist John Brown: "For even if we cannot know the ultimate consequences of our actions or inactions, we must nonetheless behave as if they do have ultimate consequences."[16] Fighting for change is hard work, especially when we're not even sure if our actions will lead to our desired, discernible outcomes. But there is one thing that most assuredly will *not* lead to our desired, discernible outcomes, and that is sitting on our hands and conjecturing as to whether our actions will lead to our desired, discernible outcomes.

In *Legacy of Suppression*, Leonard Levy notes, "The difficulty is that much of history lies in the interstices of the evidence and cannot always be mustered and measured."[17] In this book, I have tried to excavate these interstices, shining a spotlight on these half-hidden historical spaces. I have done this with a deep belief in the positive value of dissent, and with the hope that activists will be able to draw from the histories presented here to refine and recalibrate their own dissenting practices. If nothing else, I hope it prompts activists to reflect on their practice and to think of ways we might retool our strategies and tactics so we can maximize our effectiveness. Martin Luther King, Jr. once said, "Change does not roll in on the wheels of inevitability, but comes through continuous struggle." If it is meaningful social change we want, we must press forward with fire and passion, with resolution and grit, with knowledge and spirit, with fightback and counterpunch.

NOTES

1
The State, Mass Media, and Dissent

1   Katherine Bishop, "Environmentalists Hurt, Then Held, in Blast," *New York Times*, 26 May 1990, A1; Michael Taylor and Elliot Diringer, "2 Earth First! Members Hurt by Bomb in Car: Radicals Reportedly Suspected in Oakland Blast," *San Francisco Chronicle*, 25 May 1990, A1; Dean Congbalay, "Police Say Car Bomb Was in the Back Seat: How Earth First! Victims Became Suspects," *San Francisco Chronicle*, 28 May 1990, A2.

2   David Helvarg, *The War Against the Greens: The "Wise-Use" Movement, the New Right, and Anti-Environmental Violence* (San Francisco: Sierra Club Books, 1994), 331–334; David Cole and James Dempsey, *Terrorism and the Constitution*, 2d ed. (New York: New Press, 2002), 56–60. In June 2002, a federal jury awarded $4.4 million in damages to Bari and Cherney, ruling that their rights were violated by the local officers and FBI agents who arrested them. Bari did not live to see the results of this civil suit; she died of cancer in 1997. See Evelyn Nieves, "Environmentalists Win Bombing Lawsuit," *New York Times*, 12 June 2002, A18.

3   Helvarg, *The War Against the Greens*, 393, 397.

4   Dave Foreman, *Confessions of an Eco-Warrior* (New York: Crown Publishers, Inc., 1991), 128; Helvarg, *The War Against the Greens*, 395.

5   Helvarg, *The War Against the Greens*, 396, 395, 396; Deborah B. Balser, "The Impact of Environmental Factors on Factionalism and Schism in Social Movement Organizations," *Social Forces* 76 (1997): 206.

6   Foreman, *Confessions of an Eco-Warrior*. "Monkeywrenching" is a term that encompasses a wide range of activities, from the removal of surveyor stakes from logging roads to the destruction of logging and mining equipment to the insertion of spikes into soon-to-be-logged trees in order to destroy the saw blade (also known as the spiking of trees). The essential idea is to deliberately place a wrench in the plans of developers, loggers, miners, and others intent on laying claim to the environment.

7   David Snyder, "Theoretical and Methodological Problems in the Analysis of Governmental Coercion and Collective Violence," *Journal of Political and Military Sociology* 4 (1976): 277.

8   Also, while authoritarian states tend to depend more on suppression than con-
     cession, democratic regimes are more likely to use various combinations of sup-
     pression and concession, depending on the context. An important part of this
     context is the perceived level of threat that the social movement or dissident
     citizen poses to the social order.

9   Mayer Zald, "On the Social Control of Industries," *Social Forces* 57 (1978):
     83.

10   In offering this definition, Goldstein says that after reading hundreds of books
     and articles on suppression, he only came across one definition of political
     repression. This definition came from Alan Wolfe, who wrote that political
     repression is "a process by which those in power try to keep themselves in pow-
     er by consciously attempting to destroy or render harmless organizations and
     ideologies that threaten their power." See: Robert Justin Goldstein, *Political
     Repression in Modern America: From 1870 to 1976*, (Urbana and Chicago:
     University of Illinois Press, 2001), xxviii.

11   Jennifer Earl, "Tanks, Tear Gas, and Taxes: Toward a Theory of Movement
     Repression," *Sociological Theory* 21 (2003): 46.

12   For example, during the "War on Terrorism" a number of conservative groups
     have emerged in support of the war and against dissidents who have spoken
     out against the war. One example of such a group is Americans for Victory
     Over Terrorism (AVOT), which on 12 March 2002 released a list of professors,
     authors, legislators, and mass-media reporters that they consider to be "threats"
     because of statements they have made that question the War on Terrorism. This
     may signal an outsourcing of suppression from the government to non-govern-
     mental organizations (NGOs) and private groups (many former government
     officials are involved with AVOT, including former Secretary of Education.
     William Bennett). For AVOT's web site, see: http://www.avot.org/. Jennifer
     Earl has convincingly argued that more attention needs to focused on suppres-
     sion carried out by private groups. See: Jennifer Earl, "Controlling Protest:
     New Directions for Research on the Social Control of Protest," *Research in
     Social Movements, Conflicts, and Change* 25 (2004): 55–83.

13   Charles Tilly, *From Mobilization to Revolution*, (Reading, MA: Addison-
     Wesley, 1978), 100–102.

14   It also is in alignment with—and adds to the specification of—definitions
     from other studies that focus specifically on social movements. For instance,
     McAdam, Tarrow, and Tilly broadly define suppression—what they call "re-
     pression"—as "efforts to suppress either contentious acts or groups and or-
     ganizations responsible for them." See: Doug McAdam, Sidney Tarrow, and
     Charles Tilly, *Dynamics of Contention* (New York: Cambridge University Press,
     2001), 69. It also complements the definition offered by Michael Stohl and
     George A. Lopez in their study of governmental violence and repression: "the

use of coercion or the threat of coercion against opponents or potential opponents in order to prevent or weaken their capability to oppose the authorities and their policies." See: Michael Stohl and George A. Lopez, eds. *The State as Terrorist: The Dynamics of Governmental Violence and Repression* (Westport, Connecticut: Greenwood Press, 1984), 7.

15 This precondition is important, recent notions of leaderless resistance or action-oriented leadership aside. For more on leaderless resistance, see: Benjamin Shepard and Ronald Hayduk, eds. *From ACT UP to the WTO: Urban Protest and Community Building in the Era of Globalization* (New York: Verso, 2002), 52–53. For information about action-oriented leadership, see: Ronald Aminzade, Jack A. Goldstone, and Elizabeth J. Perry, "Leadership Dynamics and Dynamics of Contention," in *Silence and Voice in the Study of Contentious Politics*, ed. Ronald Aminzade et al (New York: Cambridge University Press, 2001), 152. As Aminzade, Goldstone, and Perry point out, "the role of leadership becomes [is] crucial at several points in actualizing the potential for protest and social change." Aminzade, Goldstone, and Perry, "Leadership Dynamics and Dynamics of Contention," 152. Therefore, "The public arrest of a few well-known members, perhaps the leaders, may produce the same symbolic effect as the arrest of all the members." John Wilson, "Social Protest and Social Control," *Social Problems* 24 (1977): 475.

16 I formed this list of preconditions for collective action by modifying Doug McAdam's set of "strategic hurdles" that social movements must overcome in order to be successful. Doug McAdam, "The Framing Function of Movement Tactics: Strategic Dramaturgy in the American Civil Rights Movement," in *Comparative Perspectives on Social Movements: Political Opportunities, Mobilizing Structures, and Cultural Framings*, ed. Doug McAdam, John D. McCarthy, and Mayer N. Zald (New York: Cambridge University Press, 1996), 339–340.

17 McAdam, Tarrow, and Tilly, *Dynamics of Contention*, 42, 43, 42, emphasis in original.

18 Kim Voss, "The Collapse of a Social Movement: The Interplay of Mobilizing Structures, Framing, and Political Opportunities in the Knights of Labor," in *Comparative Perspectives on Social Movements: Political Opportunities, Mobilizing Structures, and Cultural Framings*, ed. Doug McAdam, John D. McCarthy, and Mayer N. Zald (New York: Cambridge University Press, 1996), 227.

19 For example, see Donatella della Porta and Herbert Reiter, eds. *Policing Protest: The Control of Mass Demonstrations in Western Democracies* (Minneapolis: University of Minnesota Press, 1998) and John D. McCarthy, Clark McPhail, and Jackie Smith, "Images of Protest: Dimensions of Selection Bias in Media Coverage of Washington Demonstrations, 1982 and 1991," *American*

Sociological Review 61 (1996): 478–499.

20 For instance, although a study by Jennifer Earl, John D. McCarthy, and Sarah Soule notes, "The lion's share of academic attention has focused more on public protest policing," the authors go on to carry out a study on that very subject—protest policing—breaking down the policing of demonstrations into different types. Jennifer Earl, John D. McCarthy, and Sarah A. Soule. "Protest Under Fire? Explaining the Policing of Protest." *American Sociological Review* 68 (2003): 582.

21 Marwan Khawaja, "Repression and Popular Collective Action: Evidence from the West Bank," *Sociological Forum* 8 (1993): 50–51.

22 David Cunningham, *There's Something Happening Here: The New Left, The Klan, and FBI Counterintelligence* (Berkeley: University of California Press., 2004) and Earl, "Tanks, Tear Gas, and Taxes."

23 Ward Churchill and Jim Vander Wall also offer an early, important categorization of types of suppression, but they do so informally, and the mass media play only a minor role. Ward Churchill and Jim Vander Wall, *Agents of Repression: The FBI's Secret Wars Against the Black Panther Party and the American Indian Movement*, 2d ed. (Cambridge, MA: South End Press, 2002 [1988]).

24 Balser, "The Impact of Environmental Factors on Factionalism and Schism in Social Movement Organizations."

25 See: Michael Carley, "Defining Forms of Successful State Repression of Social Movement Organizations: A Case Study of the FBI's COINTELPRO and the American Indian Movement," *Research in Social Movements, Conflict and Change* 20 (1997): 151–176; David Cunningham, "State versus Social Movement: FBI Counterintelligence against the New Left," in *States, Parties, and Social Movements*, ed. Jack A. Goldstone (Cambridge: Cambridge University Press, 2003); and Cunningham, *There's Something Happening Here.*

26 Cunningham, "State versus Social Movement," 46.

27 A final example of a typology of suppression comes from Jennifer Earl who develops a multi-dimensional typology that, first of all, distinguishes between "coercion" and "channeling," with the latter defined as "more indirect repression, which is meant to affect the forms of protest available, the timing of protests, and/or flows of resources to movements." She also categorizes the repressors into three groups: (1) state agents with tight ties to national elites; (2) state agents with loose ties to national elites; and (3) non-state agents. The typology I offer in this book is more focused on suppression whereas some of the "unobserved" forms of "channeling" she discusses—such as U.S. tax laws that provide tax relief for non-profit organizations—swerve away from disruptive state repression and toward facilitative legal structures, or "channeling." Therefore, my typology is both more focused and more parsimonious. Additionally, I fully investigate the role of the mass media, whereas Earl sidesteps the repres-

sive role this crucial institution sometimes plays. See: Earl, "Tanks, Tear Gas, and Taxes," 48, 49.

28 Notable exceptions to this trend include: Todd Gitlin, *The Whole World Is Watching: Mass Media in the Making and Unmaking of the New Left* (Berkeley: University of California Press, 1980); Daniel Hallin, *The Uncensored War* (New York: Oxford University Press, 1986); and Melvin Small, *Covering Dissent: The Media and the Vietnam War Movement.* (New Brunswick, NJ: Rutgers University Press, 1994).

29 Mark Irving Lichbach, "Deterrence or Escalation? The Puzzle of Aggregate Studies of Repression and Dissent," *Journal of Conflict Resolution* 31 (1987): 268–269.

30 For an example of studies exploring the conditions affecting the use of political repression, see: Douglas Bwy, "Political Instability in Latin America: The Cross-Cultural Test of a Causal Model," *Latin American Research Review* 3 (1968): 17–66 and Conway W. Henderson, "Conditions Affecting the Use of Political Repression," *Journal of Conflict Resolution* 35 (1991): 120–142. For work that examines the timing of suppression, see: Will H. Moore, "Repression and Dissent: Substitution, Context, and Timing," *American Journal of Political Science* 42 (1998): 851–873 and Karen Rasler, "Concessions, Repression, and Political Protest in the Iranian Revolution," *American Sociological Review* 61 (1996): 132–152. On the scope and intensity of suppression see: Ted Robert Gurr, "Persisting Patterns of Repression and Rebellion: Foundations for a General Theory of Political Coercion," in *Persistent Patterns and Emergent Structures in a Waning Century.* ed. Margaret P. Karnes (New York: Praeger Special Studies for the International Studies Association, 1986) and Khawaja, "Repression and Popular Collective Action."

31 For the suppression of dissent in Germany and Northern Ireland, see: Ronald A. Francisco, "Coercion and Protest: An Empirical Test in Two Democratic States," *American Journal of Political Science* 40 (1996): 1179–1204. For suppression in Argentina, see: Laura Kalmanowieki, "Origins and Applications of Political Policing in Argentina," *Latin American Perspectives* 27 (2000): 36–56. For suppression in Iran, see: Rasler, "Concessions, Repression, and Political Protest in the Iranian Revolution." For suppression in Belarus, see: Larissa Titarenko, John D. McCarthy, Clark McPhail, and Boguslaw Augustyn, "The Interaction of State Repression, Protest Form and Protest Sponsor Strength During the Transition from Communism in Minsk, Belarus, 1990–1995," *Mobilization* 6 (2001): 129–150.

32 Charles Brockett, "A Protest Cycle Resolution of the Repression/Popular Protest Paradox," in *Repertoires and Cycles of Collective Action*, ed. Mark Traugott (Durham, NC and London: Duke University Press, 1995), 118.

33 Michael Hardt and Antonio Negri. *Empire* (Cambridge, MA: Harvard

University Press, 2000); Geoffrey R. Stone, *Perilous Times: Free Speech in Wartime from the Sedition Act of 1798 to the War on Terrorism* (New York: W.W. Norton & Company, 2004).

34 Giorgio Agamben, *Means Without End: Notes on Politics*, (Minneapolis and London: University of Minnesota Press, 2000), 133.

35 Ricardo Blaug, "New Theories of Discursive Democracy: A User's Guide," *Philosophy & Social Criticism* 22 (1996): 63.

36 Erik W. Doxtader, "Characters in the Middle of Public Life: Consensus, Dissent, and Ethos," *Philosophy and Rhetoric* 33 (2000): 337. Related to this, Doxtader characterizes the Jurgen Habermas's highly touted but heavily critiqued conception of the public sphere as an "idealistic account of public communication" that views "dissent as a transitory problem, best resolved when individuals abstract themselves from particular disputes and embrace a procedural ethic of consensus-building." In other words, a discourse ethic that is built on the foundation of consensus leaves little room for protracted dissent. In theory, this would not be problematic if barriers to participation—both material and knowledge-based—did not exist. See: Doxtader, "Characters in the Middle of Public Life," 344. For Jurgen Habermas's ideas on the public sphere, see: Jurgen Habermas, *The Structural Transformation of the Public Sphere: An Inquiry into a Category of Bourgeois Society* (Cambridge, MA: MIT Press, 1989).

37 McAdam, Tarrow, and Tilly, *Dynamics of Contention*, 7–8.

38 Nancy Fraser, "Rethinking the Public Sphere: A Contribution to the Critique of Actually Existing Democracy," in *Habermas and the Public Sphere*, ed. Craig Calhoun (Cambridge, MA: MIT Press, 1992), 117, 119, emphasis in original.

39 Habermas, *The Structural Transformation of the Public Sphere*.

40 Fraser, "Rethinking the Public Sphere," 122–123.

41 Fraser, "Rethinking the Public Sphere," 123.

42 Jane Mansbridge, "Using Power/ Fighting Power." *In Democracy and Difference: Contesting the Boundaries of the Political*, ed. Seyla Benhabib (Princeton, NJ: Princeton University Press, 1996).

43 Jules Boykoff, "Dissent," in *Encyclopedia of Activism and Social Justice*, ed. Gary L. Anderson and Kathryn Herr (Thousand Oaks, CA: Sage Publications, forthcoming).

44 Christian Davenport, ed. *Paths to State Repression: Human Rights Violations and Contentious Politics* (New York: Rowman & Littlefield Publishers, Inc, 2000) 1.

45 Frances Fox Piven and Richard A. Cloward, *Regulating the Poor: The Functions of Public Welfare* (New York: Vintage, 1971).

46 Cole and Dempsey, *Terrorism and the Constitution*, 16.

47 Stone, *Perilous Times*, 5.

48   James L. Gibson, "Pluralism, Federalism and the Protection of Civil Liberties,"
     Western Political Quarterly 43 (1990): 530.

49   Isaac D. Balbus, The Dialectics of Legal Repression (New York: Russell Sage
     Foundation, 1973); Ian F. Haney López, "Protest, Repression, and Race: Legal
     Violence and the Chicano Movement," University of Pennsylvania Law Review
     150 (2001): 205–244; Steven Barkan, "Legal Control of the Civil Rights
     Movement," American Sociological Review 49 (1984): 552–565; and Steven
     Barkan, Protesters on Trial: Criminal Justice in the Southern Civil Rights and
     Vietnam Antiwar Movements (New Brunswick, NJ: Rutgers University Press,
     1985).

50   See: Schenck v. United States. 249 U.S. 211. 1919. Also see Debs v. United States.
     249 U.S. 211. 1919.

51   Holmes actually brought this into the legal discussion earlier in a dissenting
     opinion he wrote for Abrams v. United States. Stone, Perilous Times, 207.

52   Schenck v. United States 249 US 47 at 52. 1919.

53   Robert K. Murray, Red Scare: A Study of National Hysteria, 1919–1920 (New
     York: McGraw-Hill Book Company, 1964) 272.

54   Goldstein, Political Repression in Modern America, 323.

55   Brandenburg v. Ohio, 395 US 444 at 447. 1969.

56   For example, see: NAACP v. Claiborne Hardware Co., 458 U.S. 886. 1982.

57   Healy v. James. 408 U.S. 169, 186. 1972.

58   Cole and Dempsey, Terrorism and the Constitution, 93.

59   Laird v. Tatum. 408 U.S. 1. 1972.

60   Howard Zinn, "Foreword," in Silencing Political Dissent, Nancy Chang (New
     York: Seven Stories Press, 2002), 11.

61   Cole and Dempsey, Terrorism and the Constitution, 212.

62   The transnational diffusion of ideas and information among dissident social
     movements has been facilitated by the increase in non-governmental organi-
     zations (NGOs) that are active in the international realm. All contemporary
     dissident movements are operating in a similar context, in that NGOs are an
     important part of the socio-political landscape. See: Pratap Chatterjee and
     Matthias Finger, The Earth Brokers: Power, Politics, and World Development
     (New York: Routledge, 1994). In fact, NGOs like Greenpeace and Global
     Exchange (groups involved in the modern-day global justice movement)
     are active dissident groups. The prevalence of NGOs has increased vastly
     since the 1970s, in large part because of the machinations of globalization,
     and this has improved the chances for NGO transnational mobilization.
     See: Kenneth Cmiel, "The Emergence of Human Rights in U.S. Politics,"
     Journal of American History 86 (December 1999): 1231–1250; Kathryn
     Sikkink, "Human Rights, Principled Issue-Networks, and Sovereignty in
     Latin America," International Organization 47 (1993): 411–441; Frances

Hagopian, "Democracy and Political Representation in Latin America in the 1990s: Pause, Reorganization, or Decline?" in *Fault Lines of Democracy in Post-Transition Latin America*, eds. Felipe Aguero and Jeffrey Stark (Miami: North/South Center Press, 1998); Donatella della Porta and Hanspeter Kreisi, "Social Movements in a Globalizing World: an Introduction," in *Social Movements in a Globalizing World*, ed. Donatella della Porta, Hanspeter Kriesi, and Dieter Rucht (London: MacMillan, 1999); Dieter Rucht, "The Transnationalization of Social Movements: Trends, Causes, and Problems," in *Social Movements in a Globalizing World*. According to Donatella della Porta and Hanspeter Kriesi, while "expanded capacity for cross-national communication will not automatically create transnational movements," the chances for such horizontal coordination between groups from different countries does increase. Della Porta and Kriesi, "Social Movements in a Globalizing World," 5.

63   Cole and Dempsey, *Terrorism and the Constitution*, 100.

64   Barbara Olshansky, *Secret Trials and Executions: Military Tribunals and the Threat to Democracy* (New York: Seven Stories Press, 2002); Cole and Dempsey, *Terrorism and the Constitution*.

65   Joy James, "Imprisoned Intellectuals: War, Dissent, and Social Justice," *Radical History Review* 85 (2003): 74–81; Jerry Markon, "Military to Watch Prisoner Interview: Hamdi's Lawyer Resents Monitoring," *Washington Post*, 31 January 2004, B3.

66   Melvyn P. Leffler, "National Security," *Journal of American History* 77 (1990): 143.

67   Murray Edelman, *Politics as Symbolic Action: Mass Arousal and Quiescence* (Chicago: Markham Publishing Company, 1971), 165–166.

68   Daniel Ellsberg, *Secrets: A Memoir of Vietnam and the Pentagon Papers* (New York: Penguin, 2002).

69   Goldstein, *Political Repression in Modern America*, 489.

70   See: *New York Times Co. v. Sullivan*. 376 U.S. 967. 1964. The Court's ruling that the newspapers could publish the Pentagon Papers did not settle the question of whether Ellsberg and Russo could be legally admonished under the Constitution for "liberating" the papers. Therefore, the FBI's massive manhunt for Ellsberg—who was in hiding underground—continued. A few days after the Supreme Court's decision in *New York Times Co. v. United States*, Ellsberg turned himself in. He was swiftly charged with multiple felonies and faced more than 100 years in prison if convicted. The judicial branch never was forced to rule on Ellsberg's case, however, after it was revealed that President Nixon's "plumbers" burglarized the office of Ellsberg's psychiatrist in order to turn up grist that could besmirch Ellsberg in the press. In 1973, the judge in the case dismissed all charges due to egregious government misconduct. See: Ellsberg, *Secrets*.

71 Richard B. Kielbowicz and Clifford Scherer, "The Role of the Press in the Dynamics of Social Movements," *Research in Social Movements, Conflicts and Change* 9 (1986): 71–96.

72 McAdam, "The Framing Function of Movement Tactics," 339.

73 Dominique Wisler and Marco Giugni, "Under the Spotlight: The Impact of Media Attention on Protest Policing," *Mobilization: An International Journal* 4 (1999): 172.

74 John D. McCarthy and Clark McPhail, "The Institutionalization of Protest in the United States," in *The Social Movement Society: Contentious Politics for a New Century*, ed. David S. Meyer and Sidney Tarrow (New York: Rowman & Littlefield Publishers, Inc., 1998) 84.

75 That is, if it is even taken up at all. Often protesters are ignored altogether. For example, McCarthy, McPhail, and Smith found that, in 1982, 13% of all protests in Washington, DC were covered by a major media outlet. In 1991, the coverage rate dropped to 7.1%. See: John D. McCarthy, Clark McPhail, and Jackie Smith, "Images of Protest: Dimensions of Selection Bias in Media Coverage of Washington Demonstrations, 1982 and 1991," *American Sociological Review* 61 (1996), 478–499. In a smaller mass-media market— Madison, Wisconsin—Oliver and Myers discovered that fewer than half of the protests (44%) that took place in this city in 1994 received next day coverage in the two Madison newspapers. Pamela E. Oliver and Daniel J. Myers, "How Events Enter the Public Sphere: Conflict, Location, and Sponsorship in Local Newspaper Coverage of Public Events," *American Journal of Sociology* 105 (1999), 38–87. In a separate study of the same city, Oliver and Maney widened their time scope to 1993–1996 and found 46% of message-based protest events received local newspaper coverage. See: Pamela E. Oliver and Gregory G. Maney, "Political Processes and Local Newspaper Coverage of Protest Events: From Selection Bias to Triadic Interactions," *American Journal of Sociology* 106 (2000): 463–505.

76 Robert W. McChesney, *Rich Media, Poor Democracy: U.S. Communication Politics in the 21st Century* (Urbana and Chicago: University of Illinois Press, 1999) and Robert W. McChesney, *The Problem of the Media: U.S. Communication Politics in Dubious Times* (New York: Monthly Review Press, 2004).

77 McChesney, *Rich Media, Poor Democracy*, 16.

78 Ibid., 281.

79 McChesney, *Rich Media, Poor Democracy* and W. Lance Bennett, *News: The Politics of Illusion*. 5th ed. (New York: Longman, 2002).

80 Martin Gilens and Craig Hertzman, "Corporate Ownership and News Bias: Newspaper Coverage of the 1996 Telecommunications Act," *Journal of Politics* 62 (2000): 383.

81   Anthony Corrado, "Elections in Cyberspace: Prospects and Problems" in *Elections in Cyberspace: Toward a New Era in American Politics*, ed. Anthony Corrado and Charles M. Firestone (Queenstown, MD: The Aspen Institute, 1996).

82   Robert W. Entman, *Democracy Without Citizens: Media and the Decay of American Politics* (New York and Oxford: Oxford University Press, 1989) 17.

83   Edward S. Herman and Noam Chomsky, *Manufacturing Consent: The Political Economy of the Mass Media* (New York: Pantheon, 1988) 1.

84   Michael Parenti affirms Herman and Chomsky's assessment, firmly rooting his own study of the corporate media in the larger structures of late capitalism. See: Michael Parenti, *Inventing Reality: The Politics of the Mass Media* (New York: St. Martin's Press, 1986).

85   Gitlin, *The Whole World Is Watching*, 10–12.

86   Jonathan Mermin, *Debating War and Peace: Media Coverage of U.S. Intervention in the Post-Vietnam Era* (Princeton, NJ: Princeton University Press, 1999); John Zaller and Dennis Chiu, "Government's Little Helper: U.S. Press Coverage of Foreign Policy Crises, 1945–1991," *Political Communication* 13 (1996): 385–405.

87   Patrick O'Heffernan, "A Mutual Exploitation Model of Media Influence in U.S. Foreign Policy," in *Taken By Storm: The Media, Public Opinion, and U.S. Foreign Policy in the Gulf War*, ed. W. Lance Bennett and David Paletz (Chicago: University of Chicago Press, 1994) 233.

88   Michael Schudson, *Discovering the News: A Social History of American Newspapers* (New York: Basic Books, 1978); Herbert Gans, *Deciding What's News* (New York: Pantheon, 1979).

89   See: Sharon Dunwoody and Hans Peter Peters, "Mass Media Coverage of Technological and Environmental Risks," *Public Understanding of Science* 1/2 (1992): 199–230 and Bennett, *News: The Politics of Illusion*.

90   A. Clay Schoenfeld, Robert F. Meier, and Robert J. Griffin, "Constructing a Social Problem: The Press and the Environment," *Social Problems* 27 (1979): 38–61.

91   Sharon Dunwoody, "The Science Writing Inner Club," in *Scientists and Journalists*, eds. Sharon Dunwoody, Sharon Friedman, and Carol Rogers (New York: Free Press, 1986).

92   Kielbowicz and Scherer, "The Role of the Press in the Dynamics of Social Movements," 76–77.

93   Stuart Hall, "The Determinations of News Photographs," in *The Manufacture of News: A Reader*, ed. Stanley Cohen and Jock Young (Beverly Hills, CA: SAGE Publications, 1973); Michael Parenti, "Methods of Media Manipulation," in *Twenty Years of Censored News*, ed. Carl Jensen (New York: Seven Stories Press, 1997).

94 William Gamson, *Talking Politics* (New York: Cambridge University Press, 1992); Shanto Iyengar, *Is Anyone Responsible?* (Chicago: University of Chicago Press, 1991).

95 David A. Snow and Robert D. Benford, "Collective Identity and Activism: Networks, Choices, and the Life of the Social Movement," in *Frontiers in Social Movement Theory*, ed. Aldon D. Morris and Carol McClurg Mueller (New Haven and London: Yale University Press, 1992): 137.

96 Robert W. Entman, "Framing: Toward Clarification of a Fractured Paradigm," *Journal of Communication* 43 (1993): 52.

97 Ibid., 55.

98 Daniel Kahneman and Amos Tversky, "The Psychology of Preferences," *Science* 246 (1982): 135–142; Donald Kinder and Lynn Sanders, "Mimicking Political Debate with Survey Questions: The Case of White Opinion on Affirmative Action for Blacks," *Social Cognition* 8 (1990): 73–103; Robert W. Entman and Andrew Rojecki, "Freezing Out the Public: Elite and Media Framing of the U.S. Anti-Nuclear Movement," *Political Communication* 10 (1993): 151–167; Murray Edelman, *The Politics of Misinformation* (New York: Cambridge University Press, 2001).

99 Murray Edelman, *The Symbolic Uses of Politics* (Urbana: University of Illinois Press, 1964) 15.

100 W. Lance Bennett, "An Introduction to Journalism Norms and Representations of Politics," *Political Communication* 13 (1996): 373–384; Bennett, *News: The Politics of Illusion*.

101 Pierre Bourdieu, *On Television* (New York: New Press, 1998); Gans, *Deciding What's News*; Bennett, *News: The Politics of Illusion*.

102 Holly Stocking and Jennifer Pease Leonard, "The Greening of the Media," *Columbia Journalism Review*, December (1990): 40.

103 Bennett, *News: The Politics of Illusion*, 45–50.

104 Ibid., 4.

105 Bennett explores how "indexing" occurred in mass-media coverage of U.S. funding for the contras in Nicaragua, while Zaller and Chiu explore a variety of "foreign policy crises" between 1945 and 1991, including the Cuban Missile Crisis, the Tet Offensive, the Soviet invasion of Afghanistan in 1979, and the first Persian Gulf War. Mermin considers a range of foreign policy moments after the Vietnam War. See: W. Lance Bennett, "Toward a Theory of Press-State Relations in the United States," *Journal of Communication* 40 (1990): 103–125; Zaller and Chiu, "Government's Little Helper"; and Mermin, *Debating War and Peace*.

106 This question may well be irresolvable, but such irresolvability has not dampened the enthusiasm with which scholars have tried to detect and isolate an ideological bias in the news. For works that assert a liberal bias in the mass media,

see S. Robert Lichter, Stanley Rothman, and Linda Lichter, *The Media Elite* (Bethesda, MD: Adler & Adler, 1986); L. Brent III Bozell and Brent H. Baker, *And That's the Way It Is[n't]: A Reference Guide to Media Bias* (Alexandria, VA: Media Research Center, 1990); Thomas R. Dye and Harmon Zeigler, *The Irony of Democracy, Millennial Edition* ed. (New York: Harcourt Brace College Publishers, 2000), and; Bernard Goldberg, *Bias: A CBS Insider Exposes How the Media Distort the News* (Washington D.C.: Regnery Publishing, Inc., 2002). For studies that observe a conservative bias, see Parenti, *Inventing Reality* and Herman and Chomsky, *Manufacturing Consent.*

107 Bennett, *News: The Politics of Illusion*, 45–50; Kielbowicz and Scherer, "The Role of the Press in the Dynamics of Social Movements," 75–76.

108 Iyengar, *Is Anyone Responsible?*

109 Jackie Smith, John D. McCarthy, Clark McPhail, and Boguslaw Augustyn, "From Protest to Agenda Building: Description Bias in Media Coverage of Events in Washington, D.C.," *Social Forces* 79 (2001): 1404, emphasis in original.

110 Jack A. Goldstone, "Bridging Institutionalized and Noninstitutionalized Politics," in *States, Parties, and Social Movements*, ed. Jack A. Goldstone (New York: Cambridge University Press, 2003), 21.

111 The state has also attempted to demobilize right-of-center groups such as the KKK (for example, see: U.S. Congress, Senate Select Committee to Study Government Operations with Respect to Intelligence Activities, *Final Report– Book II: Foreign and Military Intelligence*. 94th Congress, 2d sess. [Washington, DC: U.S. Government Printing Office, 1976] and Cunningham, *There's Something Happening Here*) and anti-abortion protesters (for example, see: Don Mitchell, *The Right to the City: Social Justice and the Fight for Public Space* [New York: Guilford, 2003], 42–51), even if with less vim, frequency, and vigor. Although I focus on left-of-center movements and their suppression, I believe, based on preliminary research, that the explanation presented in this book is equally applicable to right-of-center movements. That said, more empirical work needs to be done in order to test that claim.

112 The Church Committee—a Senate Select Committee established in January 1975 that issued a three-book report in April 1976 in response to alleged intelligence activity malfeasance—defined "black bag jobs" as "warrantless surreptitious entries for purposes other than microphone installation, e.g., physical search and photographing or seizing documents." See U.S. Congress.,Senate Select Committee to Study Government Operations with Respect to Intelligence Activities, *Final Report–Book III: Foreign and Military Intelligence*. 94th Congress, 2d sess. (Washington, DC: U.S. Government Printing Office, 1976) 355. Therefore surreptitious entries, or break-ins, constitute the wider category, and "black bag job" is a more specific term.

113 "Black propaganda" means creating false documents purporting to come from the target organization. See: Michael Linfield, *Freedom Under Fire: U.S. Civil Liberties in Times of War* (Boston: South End Press, 1990), 135; and Churchill and Vander Wall, *Agents of Repression*, 42. One should note the racialized language that is ingrained into the very vocabulary of suppression. "Black bag jobs," an FBI term, and "black propaganda" both evoke a racialized lexicon vibrating with history-drenched, race-based connotations.

2
Direct Violence

1   Joe Eszterhas and Michael D. Roberts, *Thirteen Seconds: Confrontation at Kent State* (New York: Dodd, Mead, & Company, 1970), 9.

2   Fred Halstead, *Out Now! A Participant's Account of the American Movement Against the Vietnam War* (New York: Monad Press, 1978), 537–538.

3   According to one SDS participant, Alan Canfora, SDS "started out with about six people in the fall of '68. By the time spring rolled around, two and three hundred were coming to their rallies." Bud Schultz and Ruth Schultz, *The Price of Dissent: Testimonies to Political Repression in America* (Berkeley: University of California Press, 2001), 353.

4   Eszterhas and Roberts, *Thirteen Seconds*, 14.

5   President's Commission on Campus Unrest, "The Report of the President's Commission on Campus Unrest" (Washington, DC: U.S. Government Printing Office, 1970), 233–238.

6   Goldstein, *Political Repression in Modern America*, 430. While most of these protests focused on the Vietnam War, a number of them took on a broader scope, addressing a wider array of social issues.

7   Eszterhas and Roberts, *Thirteen Seconds*, 13.

8   Abe Peck, *Uncovering the Sixties: The Life and Times of the Underground Press* (New York: Citadel Press, 1991), 236. Incidentally, this headquarters was never found.

9   Eszterhas and Roberts, *Thirteen Seconds*, 26.

10 James A. Michener, *Kent State: What Happened and Why?* (New York: Random House, 1971), 13.

11 President's Commission on Campus Unrest, "The Report of the President's Commission on Campus Unrest," 239–243.

12 Todd Gitlin, *The Sixties: Years of Hope, Days of Rage* (New York: Bantam Books, 1987), 409–410.

13 Kirkpatrick Sale, *SDS* (New York: Vintage Books, 1973), 635.

14 Halstead, *Out Now!*, 537.

15   President's Commission on Campus Unrest, "The Report of the President's Commission on Campus Unrest," 17, 244–245.

16   Ibid., 248–251.

17   Eszterhas and Roberts, *Thirteen Seconds*, 81–82.

18   Ibid., 84.

19   Ibid., 85.

20   President's Commission on Campus Unrest, "The Report of the President's Commission on Campus Unrest," 251–253.

21   Ibid., 253–54.

22   William A. Gordon, *The Fourth of May: Killings and Coverups at Kent State* (Buffalo: Prometheus Books, 1990), 24.

23   President's Commission on Campus Unrest, "The Report of the President's Commission on Campus Unrest," 254; Eszterhas and Roberts, *Thirteen Seconds*, 111.

24   Nancy Zaroulis and Gerald Sullivan, *Who Spoke Up? American Protest Against the War in Vietnam 1963–1975* (Garden City, NY: Doubleday & Company, Inc., 1984), 319.

25   Eszterhas and Roberts, *Thirteen Seconds*, 111–112.

26   Ibid., 116; Gordon, *The Fourth of May*, 25.

27   President's Commission on Campus Unrest, "The Report of the President's Commission on Campus Unrest," 253–259.

28   Gordon, *The Fourth of May*, 26–27.

29   Michener, *Kent State*, 331.

30   President's Commission on Campus Unrest, "The Report of the President's Commission on Campus Unrest"; Gordon, *The Fourth of May*.

31   Sale, *SDS*, 635–636.

32   Ward Churchill and Jim Vander Wall, *The COINTELPRO Papers: Documents from the FBI's Secret Wars Against Domestic Dissent* (Boston: South End Press, 1990), 221.

33   Gordon, *The Fourth of May*, 186.

34   Sale, *SDS*, 636.

35   President's Commission on Campus Unrest, "The Report of the President's Commission on Campus Unrest," 274. The students who were wounded were: Alan Canfora, John Cleary, Thomas Grace, Dean Kahler, Joseph Lewis, Donald MacKenzie, James Russell, Robert Stamps, and Douglas Wrentmore. See: Scott L. Bills, Bills (ed.), *Kent State / May 4: Echoes Through a Decade* (Kent, Ohio: Kent State University Press, 1982), 17.

36   Joseph Lewis, Personal Interview, 28 December 2006.

37   Eszterhas and Roberts, *Thirteen Seconds*, 176.

38   Sale, SDS, 636.

39   Dan Berger, *Outlaws of America: The Weather Underground and the Politics of*

Solidarity (Oakland: AK Press, 2006), 187.

40 Zaroulis and Sullivan, *Who Spoke Up?*, 319.

41 Linfield, *Freedom Under Fire*, 119.

42 Sale, *SDS*, 638; Halstead, *Out Now!*.

43 Linfield, *Freedom Under Fire*, 120; Ken Ellingwood, "Silence Breaks Over '68 Killing of Blacks at Southern College," *Oregonian*, 26 May 2003, A5.

44 Schultz and Schultz, *The Price of Dissent*, 349. For a thorough exploration and refutation of all the after-the-episode explanations offered by the National Guard after the event, see Gordon, *The Fourth of May*, 31–47.

45 Churchill and Vander Wall, *The COINTELPRO Papers*, 221.

46 Gitlin, *The Sixties*, 413.

47 Sale, *SDS*, 641; Joseph Lewis, Personal interview, 28 December 2006.

48 Ottavio M. Casale and Louis Paskoff, *The Kent Affair: Documents and Interpretations* (New York: Houghton Mifflin Company, 1971), 20.

49 "Kent State: The Day the War Came Home," A film produced by Ron Goetz and directed by Chris Triffo, Executive producer: Mark Mori (Landmark Media Inc., 2001).

50 Peck, *Uncovering the Sixties*, 239.

51 Gitlin, *The Whole World Is Watching*; Gitlin, *The Sixties*; Daniel Hallin "The Media, the War in Vietnam, and Political Support: A Critique of the Thesis of an Oppositional Media," *Journal of Politics* 46 (1984): 2–24; Small, *Covering Dissent*.

52 Peck, *Uncovering the Sixties*, 240.

53 Richard Hofstadter, "Reflections on Violence in the United States," in *American Violence: A Documentary History,* ed. Richard Hofstadter and Michael Wallace (New York: Alfred A Knopf, 1970), 3.

54 Robert L. Allen, *Black Awakening in Capitalist America: An Analytic History* (Garden City, NY: Doubleday & Company, Inc, 1969), 69.

55 *The Black Panther*, 3 January 1970, 5.

56 Schultz and Schultz, *The Price of Dissent*, 223.

57 Allen, *Black Awakening in Capitalist America*, 71.

58 Ibid., 70–71.

59 For the Panthers' 1966 "Party Platform and Program," see, among other places, *The Black Panther*, 10 January 1970, 19. The platform is also reprinted in Philip S. Foner, ed., *The Black Panthers Speak* (New York: Da Capo Press, 1995 [1970]), 2–4; and Allen, *Black Awakening in Capitalist America*, 71–73. The ten-point platform was seen by most Black Panthers, Fred Hampton included, to be a dynamic document that could and should be revised as the social conditions evolved. For instance, in a speech called "You Can Murder a Liberator but You Can't Murder Liberation," Hampton said, "Our ten point program is in the midst of being changed right now, because we used the word 'white'

when we should have used the word 'capitalist.' We're the first to admit our mistakes." Foner, *The Black Panthers Speak*, 143.

60　Manning Marable, *Race, Reform, and Rebellion: The Second Reconstruction of Black America* (Jackson, Mississippi: University Press of Mississippi, 1991), 110. Also see Charles Jones, ed., *The Black Panther Party Reconsidered* (Baltimore: Black Classic Press, 1998), 7.

61　U.S. Congress, Senate Select Committee to Study Government Operations with Respect to Intelligence Activities, *Final Report–Book II*, 10.

62　U.S. Congress, Senate Select Committee to Study Government Operations with Respect to Intelligence Activities, *Final Report–Book III*, 4. These COINTELPROs emerged out of the FBI's Communist Infiltration Program, or COMINFIL (see: U.S. Congress, Senate Select Committee to Study Government Operations with Respect to Intelligence Activities, *Final Report– Book II*, 48–49), which will be discussed in the context of the Bureau's surveillance of Martin Luther King, Jr.

63　Churchill and Vander Wall, *Agents of Repression*, 37.

64　"Mitchell Issues Plea on F.B.I. Files," *New York Times*, 24 March 1971, 24.

65　"Group to Publicize F.B.I.'s Informers," *New York Times*, 27 March 1971, 32 and Bill Kovach, "A Citizens Commission Writes to Seven Persons Who, It Says, Served as Informers for the F.B.I.," *New York Times*, 13 April 1971, 23.

66　Churchill and Vander Wall, *Agents of Repression*, 53.

67　Nikhil Pal Singh, "The Black Panthers and the 'Underdeveloped Country' of the Left," in *The Black Panther Party Reconsidered*, ed. Charles E. Jones (Baltimore: Black Classic Press, 1998), 79–80.

68　Noam Chomsky, "Introduction," in *COINTELPRO: The FBI's Secret War on Political Freedom*, ed. Nelson Blackstock (New York: Vintage Books, 1976), 12.

69　Schultz and Schultz, *The Price of Dissent*, 230.

70　Foner, *The Black Panthers Speak*, 259.

71　David Hilliard and Lewis Cole, *This Side of Glory: The Autobiography of David Hilliard and the Story of the Black Panther Party* (Boston: Little, Brown and Company, 1993), 259.

72　Jeff Gottlieb and Jeff Cohen, "Was Fred Hampton Executed?" *Nation*, 25 December 1976, 680.

73　Churchill and Vander Wall, *Agents of Repression*, 64, 68, 400.

74　In March 1968, the Rabble Rouser Index was renamed the "Agitator Index." The list was abandoned in 1971 because it was considered redundant after the creation of the multi-level Priority Apprehension Program, more commonly known as the "Security Index." See: U.S. Congress, Senate Select Committee to Study Government Operations with Respect to Intelligence Activities, *Final Report–Book II*, 89–93 and Frank Donner, *The Age of Surveillance: The*

Aims and Methods of America's Political Intelligence System (New York: Vintage Books, 1980), 167.

75   Roy Wilkens and Ramsey Clark, *Search and Destroy: A Report by the Commission of Inquiry into the Black Panthers and the Police* (New York: Metropolitan Applied Research Center, Inc., 1973), 20–21; U.S. District Court, Northern District of Illinois, Eastern Division, "Report of the January 1970 Grand Jury," 15 May 1970, 52.

76   Churchill and Vander Wall, *Agents of Repression*, xvi.

77   U.S. Congress, Senate Select Committee to Study Government Operations with Respect to Intelligence Activities, *Final Report–Book III*, 20.

78   Donner, *The Age of Surveillance*, 221; U.S. Congress, Senate Select Committee to Study Government Operations with Respect to Intelligence Activities, *Final Report–Book III*, 188.

79   U.S. District Court, Northern District of Illinois, Eastern Division, "Report of the January 1970 Grand Jury," 1, 68.

80   Schultz and Schultz, *The Price of Dissent*, 233.

81   U.S. Congress, Senate Select Committee to Study Government Operations with Respect to Intelligence Activities, *Final Report–Book III*, 222–223; Churchill and Vander Wall, *Agents of Repression*, 65, 71.

82   U.S. Congress, Senate Select Committee to Study Government Operations with Respect to Intelligence Activities, *Final Report–Book III*, 223.

83   Churchill and Vander Wall, *Agents of Repression*, 71–73; Schultz and Schultz, *The Price of Dissent*, 234; "Survivor Recalls Raid on Panthers," *New York Times*, 23 July 1972, 90.

84   U.S. District Court, Northern District of Illinois, Eastern Division, "Report of the January 1970 Grand Jury," 103.

85   Churchill and Vander Wall, *Agents of Repression*, 73.

86   Schultz and Schultz, *The Price of Dissent*, 226.

87   U.S. District Court, Northern District of Illinois, Eastern Division, "Report of the January 1970 Grand Jury," 135–137.

88   U.S. District Court, Northern District of Illinois, Eastern Division, "Report of the January 1970 Grand Jury," 5–47, 170–192; Todd Fraley and Elli Lester-Roushanzamir, "Revolutionary Leader or Deviant Thug?: A Comparative Analysis of the *Chicago Tribune* and *Chicago Daily Defender*'s Reporting on the Death of Fred Hampton," *The Howard Journal of Communications* 15 (2004): 147–167.

89   Fraley and Lester-Roushanzamir, "Revolutionary Leader or Deviant Thug?," 150.

90   John Kifner, "Police in Chicago Slay 2 Panthers," *New York Times*, 5 December 1969, 1.

91   They continued to assert this even though the last report filed (in late November) before the raid by their informant (William O'Neal) said that there were no illegal weapons in the flat. Nevertheless, the raid went forward, ostensibly to confiscate this illegal weaponry. So, in the end, in order to protect this valuable infiltrator, they lied and claimed they had another informant, too. See: Donner, *The Age of Surveillance*, 229.

92   Fraley and Lester-Roushanzamir, "Revolutionary Leader or Deviant Thug?," 150.

93   Peck, *Uncovering the Sixties*, 224.

94   Lillian S. Calhoun, "The Death of Fred Hampton," in *Government Lawlessness in America*, ed. Theodore L. Becker and Vernon G. Murray (New York: Oxford University Press, 1971), 38.

95   John Kifner, "Chicago Panther Mourned," *New York Times*, 10 December 1969, 37.

96   John Kifner, "5 Negroes Start Panther Inquiry," *New York Times*, 21 December 1969, 47.

97   John Kifner, "State's Attorney Makes Photographs of Black Panther Apartment Available to Newspaper," *New York Times*, 12 December 1969, 46.

98   Ibid., 46.

99   U.S. District Court, Northern District of Illinois, Eastern Division, "Report of the January 1970 Grand Jury," 206.

100 Ibid., 213.

101 Ibid., 233, 235.

102 Ibid., 219–220. As it turned out, there was even more legalistic legerdemain occurring than the Grand Jury was aware of at the time. According to Robert Justin Goldstein, "Chicago police who were questioned by the police investigators, it turned out, had been supplied both with the questions they would be asked and the answers they should give in advance." Goldstein, *Political Repression in Modern America*, 528.

103 Donner, *The Age of Surveillance*, 228.

104 Churchill and Vander Wall, *Agents of Repression*, 75.

105 Ibid.

106 FBI quoted in Donner, *The Age of Surveillance*, 229. Also see John Kifner, "F.B.I. Files Say Informer Got Data for Panther Raid," *New York Times*, 7 May 1976, 14.

107 Donner, *The Age of Surveillance*, 229–230.

108 U.S. District Court, Northern District of Illinois, Eastern Division, "Report of the January 1970 Grand Jury," 222.

109 Donner, *The Age of Surveillance*, 227.

110 Churchill and Vander Wall, *Agents of Repression*, 65, 397.

111 Donner, *The Age of Surveillance*, 229; Churchill and Vander Wall, *Agents of Repression*, 65, 68.

112 Churchill and Vander Wall, *Agents of Repression*, 66–68; Jeff Gottlieb and Jeff Cohen, "Was Fred Hampton Executed?" *Nation*, 25 December 1976, 681.

113 Schultz and Schultz, *The Price of Dissent*, 224–225.

114 Ibid.

115 Ibid., 225.

116 Churchill and Vander Wall, *Agents of Repression*, 49.

117 Calhoun, "The Death of Fred Hampton," 34.

118 Donner, *The Age of Surveillance*, 227; Churchill and Vander Wall, *The COINTELPRO Papers*, 139.

119 See: U.S. Congress, Senate Select Committee to Study Government Operations with Respect to Intelligence Activities, *Final Report–Book III*, 223 and John Kifner, "F.B.I. Files Say Informer Got Data for Panther Raid," *New York Times*, 7 May 1976, 14.

120 M. Wesley Swearingen, *FBI Secrets: An Agent's Exposé* (Boston, MA: South End Press, 1995), 88–89.

121 Churchill and Vander Wall, *The COINTELPRO Papers*, 140.

122 John Kifner, "F.B.I., Before Raid, Gave Police Plan of Chicago Panther's Flat," *New York Times*, 25 May 1974, 14.

123 Subsequent blood-work found no seconal in Hampton's bloodstream, but more reliable sources lend most credence to the first autopsy results. See: U.S. District Court, Northern District of Illinois, Eastern Division, "Report of the January 1970 Grand Jury," 104, 105.

124 Schultz and Schultz, *The Price of Dissent*.

125 Kenneth O'Reilly, *"Racial Matters" The FBI's Secret File on Black America, 1960–1972* (New York: The Free Press, 1989), 312.

126 Churchill and Vander Wall, *Agents of Repression*, 76.

127 Churchill and Vander Wall, *The COINTELPRO Papers*, 359.

128 U.S. Congress, Senate Select Committee to Study Government Operations with Respect to Intelligence Activities, *Final Report–Book III*, 195.

129 O'Reilly, *"Racial Matters" The FBI's Secret File on Black America, 1960–1972*, 303.

130 U.S. Congress, Senate Select Committee to Study Government Operations with Respect to Intelligence Activities, *Final Report–Book III*, 195–196.

131 "Retaliatory action" was quite possible, in light of Fort's history as "a seasoned felon who had been arrested twice for murder." See: O' Reilly, *"Racial Matters" The FBI's Secret File on Black America, 1960–1972*, 303.

132 U.S. Congress, Senate Select Committee to Study Government Operations with Respect to Intelligence Activities, *Final Report–Book III*, 197.

133 Donner, *The Age of Surveillance*, 228.

134 U.S. Congress, Senate Select Committee to Study Government Operations with Respect to Intelligence Activities, *Final Report–Book III*, 197.

135 Donner, *The Age of Surveillance*, 224.

136 Incidentally, Fred Hampton was not the only one who experienced an unenviable demise. Jeff Fort, who later changed his name to Malik, as the Blackstone Rangers became the Black P. Stone Nation and then the El Rukn tribe of the Moorish Science Temple of America before finally settling the simpler name El Rukn, was convicted in 1987 for conspiring to commit a terrorist act against the United States on behalf of Libya. Apparently, "El Rukn bought an antitank rocket from an undercover FBI agent, and the FBI implicated Fort as the mastermind of the entire terrorism-for-hire plot—even though he was incarcerated in Texas at the time, serving a thirteen-year sentence. He received eighty years on the conspiracy charges." See: O'Reilly, *"Racial Matters" The FBI's Secret File on Black America, 1960–1972*, 409–410 fn22.

137 Jones, *The Black Panther Party Reconsidered*, 7.

138 Michael E. Staub, "Black Panthers, New Journalism, and the Rewriting of the Sixties," *Representations* 57 (1997): 57, 58.

139 Ibid., 59.

140 John Fischer, "Black Panthers and Their White Hero-Worshippers," *Harper's*, August 1970.

141 Staub, "Black Panthers, New Journalism, and the Rewriting of the Sixties." For example, see Charlotte Curtis, "Black Panther Philosophy Is Debated at the Bernsteins," *New York Times*, 15 January 1970, 50 and an op-ed "False Note on Black Panthers," *New York Times*, 16 January 1970, 46.

142 Jane Rhodes, "Fanning the Flames of Racial Discord: The National Press and the Black Panther Party," *The Harvard Journal of Press and Politics* 4 (1999): 113–114.

143 "The Spirit of Lawlessness," *New York Times*, 7 May 1967, 228.

144 Fraley and Lester-Roushanzamir, "Revolutionary Leader or Deviant Thug?," 156.

145 Ronald Jacobs zeroes in on how the African-American press has historically been such a subaltern counterpublic. See: Ronald N. Jacobs, *Race, Media and the Crisis of Civil Society: From Watts to Rodney King* (Cambridge University Press, 2000).

146 Fred Hampton, "Excerpts from the Transcript of 'The Murder of Fred Hampton,' a Documentary Film," *New York Times*, 21 July 1971, 35.

147 Quoted in Berger, *Outlaws of America*, 120.

148 O'Reilly, *"Racial Matters" The FBI's Secret File on Black America, 1960–1972*, 315; Churchill and Vander Wall, *The COINTELPRO Papers*, 141.

3
Public Prosecutions and Hearings

1   William Kunstler, Politics on Trial: Five Famous Trials of the 20th Century (New York: Ocean Press, 2003), 15–49. The quote from Governor Dukakis appears on page 16.

2   Barkan, *Protesters on Trial*, 3–4.

3   Barkan, "Legal Control of the Civil Rights Movement"; Jennifer Earl, "You Can Beat the Rap, But You Can't Beat the Ride: Bringing Arrests Back into Research on Repression," *Research in Social Movements, Conflicts and Change* 26 (2005): 101–139.

4   Carey McWilliams, *Witch Hunt: The Revival of Heresy* (Boston, MA: Little, Brown and Company, 1950), 72.

5   David Caute, *The Great Fear: The Anti-Communist Purge Under Truman and Eisenhower* (New York: Simon and Schuster, 1978), 88.

6   Griffen Fariello, *Red Scare: Memories of the American Inquisition, An Oral History* (New York: Avon Books, 1995), 255–256.

7   Larry Ceplair and Steven Englund, *The Inquisition in Hollywood: Politics in the Film Community, 1930–1960* (Garden City, NY: Anchor Press/Doubleday, 1980), 244.

8   Fariello, *Red Scare*, 256.

9   Ceplair and Englund, *The Inquisition in Hollywood*, 255.

10 Walter Goodman, *The Committee: The Extraordinary Career of the House Committee on Un-American Activities* (New York: Farrar, Straus and Giroux, 1968), 203, 208–209.

11 Ibid., 203.

12 Eric Bentley, *Thirty Years of Treason: Excerpts from Hearings Before the House Committee on Un-American Activities, 1938–1968* (New York: Viking Press, 1971), 133.

13 Goodman, *The Committee*, 203.

14 Ceplair and Englund, *The Inquisition in Hollywood*, 257, 258, 259.

15 Goodman, *The Committee*, 205.

16 Bentley, *Thirty Years of Treason*, 78.

17 Goodman, *The Committee*, 191.

18 Ceplair and Englund, *The Inquisition in Hollywood*, 379–380.

19 Frank Donner, *The Un-Americans* (New York: Ballantine Books, 1961), 56.

20 Ceplair and Englund, *The Inquisition in Hollywood*, 259–260.

21 See: Fariello, *Red Scare*, 257; Ceplair and Englund, *The Inquisition in Hollywood*, 261. HUAC's October schedule of witnesses differed from the list of subpoenaed people that appeared the next day in the local newspaper, the *Hollywood Reporter*. The reasons for the discrepancies between the two

lists are unclear even to scholars who specialize in this topic. What follows
is HUAC's schedule of witnesses, divided by job. "Unfriendly" witnesses are
denoted by a †, while witnesses who were never called to testify are marked
with a *. Producers (7): Walt Disney, Eric Johnston, Louis B. Mayer, James
K. McGuinness, Dore Schary, Adrian Scott †, Jack Warner. Actors (7): Gary
Cooper, Adolphe Menjou, Robert Montgomery, George Murphy, Larry Parks
†*, Ronald Reagan, Robert Taylor. Writers (20): Alvah Bessie †, Bertolt
Brecht †, Richard Collins †*, Lester Cole †, Rupert Hughes, Gordon Kahn †*,
Howard Koch †*, Ring Lardner Jr. †, Emmet Lavery, John Howard Lawson
†, Richard Macaulay, Albert Maltz †, John Charles Moffitt, Fred Niblo Jr.,
Samuel Ornitz †, Ayn Rand, Howard Rushmore, Morrie Ryskind, Waldo Salt
†*, Dalton Trumbo †. Directors (7): Herbert Biberman †, Edward Dmytryk
†, Leo McCarey, Lewis Milestone †*, Irving Pichel †*, Robert Rossen †*, Sam
Wood. Others (3) Roy Brewer, Oliver Carlson, Lela Rogers. See: Ceplair and
Englund, *The Inquisition in Hollywood*, 439–440.

22 Bentley, *Thirty Years of Treason*, 110.
23 Ceplair and Englund, *The Inquisition in Hollywood*, 262.
24 Fariello, *Red Scare*, 261.
25 Ceplair and Englund, *The Inquisition in Hollywood*, 263.
26 Bentley, *Thirty Years of Treason*, 145, 147.
27 Ibid., 147.
28 Fariello, *Red Scare*, 257.
29 Athan Theoharis, *From the Secret Files of J. Edgar Hoover* (Chicago: Ivan R.
    Dee, 1991), 115.
30 Ted Morgan, *Reds: McCarthyism in Twentieth–Century America* (New York:
    Random House, 2003), 595.
31 Ceplair and Englund, *The Inquisition in Hollywood*, 266.
32 Victor S. Navasky, *Naming Names* (New York: Penguin, 1980).
33 Bentley, *Thirty Years of Treason*, 161–163.
34 Ibid., 155–156.
35 Ibid., 156–159.
36 Ceplair and Englund, *The Inquisition in Hollywood*, 283.
37 Ibid., 283–285.
38 Quoted in Dalton Trumbo, *The Time of the Toad: A Study of Inquisition in
    America and Two Related Pamphlets* (New York: Harper & Row, 1972), 19–
    20.
39 Bentley, *Thirty Years of Treason*, 209.
40 Ibid., 214.
41 Ibid.
42 Ibid., 220.
43 Ceplair and Englund, *The Inquisition in Hollywood*, 287.

44 Lardner's quote can be found in Fariello, *Red Scare*, 261. Ornitz's remarks are recorded in Ceplair and Englund, *The Inquisition in Hollywood*, 287.

45 Robert K. Carr, *The House Committee on Un-American Activities* (Ithaca, New York: Cornell University Press, 1952), 73.

46 Ceplair and Englund, *The Inquisition in Hollywood*, 287.

47 Carr, *The House Committee on Un-American Activities*, 74.

48 Ceplair and Englund, *The Inquisition in Hollywood*, 343.

49 Goodman, *The Committee*, 218.

50 Ellen Schrecker, *The Age of McCarthyism: A Brief History with Documents* (New York: St. Martin's Press, 1994), 217.

51 Navasky, *Naming Names*, 83–84.

52 Ceplair and Englund, *The Inquisition in Hollywood*, 297–298.

53 Schrecker, *The Age of McCarthyism*, 215–216.

54 Ellen Schrecker, *Many Are the Crimes: McCarthyism in America* (New York: Little, Brown, and Company, 1998), 327.

55 Lewis Wood, "Federal Jury Indicts 10 Film Men on Contempt of Congress Charges," *New York Times*, 6 December 1947, 1.

56 Caute, *The Great Fear*, 496–500; Ceplair and Englund, *The Inquisition in Hollywood*, 344–345; Schrecker, *Many Are the Crimes*, 324.

57 Ceplair and Englund, *The Inquisition in Hollywood*, 339.

58 Quoted in Ceplair and Englund, *The Inquisition in Hollywood*, 347–348.

59 Navasky, *Naming Names*, 84; Fariello, *Red Scare*, 263.

60 Lester Cole, *Hollywood Red: The Autobiography of Lester Cole* (Palo Alto, CA: Ramparts Press, 1981), 312.

61 Navasky, *Naming Names*, 371.

62 Ibid., 84.

63 Ceplair and Englund, *The Inquisition in Hollywood*, 355.

64 Bernard Dick, *Radical Innocence: A Critical Study of the Hollywood Ten* (Lexington, Kentucky: The University Press of Kentucky, 1989), 10. Dick analyzes each member of the Ten's art both before and after his experiences with HUAC.

65 Bud Schultz and Ruth Schultz, *It Did Happen Here: Recollections of Political Repression in America* (Berkeley: University of California Press, 1989), 110.

66 McWilliams, *Witch Hunt*, 71–72.

67 Ibid., 80.

68 Goldstein, *Political Repression in Modern America*, 361.

69 Ceplair and Englund, *The Inquisition in Hollywood*, 389.

70 Bentley, *Thirty Years of Treason*, 376–400.

71 Fariello, *Red Scare*, 298.

72 Carr, *The House Committee on Un-American Activities*, 365. For more specific examples of the cozy relationship between HUAC and the press during the

Hollywood hearings, see 366–384.

73   Ibid., 392.

74   Donner, *The Un-Americans*, 149.

75   Ceplair and Englund, *The Inquisition in Hollywood*, 281.

76   Bentley, *Thirty Years of Treason*, 122, 152.

4
Employment Deprivation

1   Goldstein, *Political Repression in Modern America*, 299–300.

2   Ellen Schrecker, *No Ivory Tower: McCarthyism and the Universities* (New York: Oxford University Press, 1986), 5. While this may well be true, it should be noted that Executive Order 9835 was part of a process whose "first modern statutory step" was taken in 1939 with the passage of the Hatch Act, which outlawed federal employees from belonging to a group that "advocates the overthrow of our constitutional form of government in the United States." See: Ralph S. Brown, *Loyalty and Security Employment Tests in the United States* (New Haven: Yale University Press, 1958), 21.

3   Truman's motives also had a lot to do with protecting himself politically against Republican attacks.

4   Goldstein, *Political Repression in Modern America*, xxxi, xxxiii.

5   Ibid., 300–301.

6   McWilliams, *Witch Hunt*, 27.

7   Linfield, *Freedom Under Fire*, 107; Herbert S. Parmet, *Eisenhower and the American Crusades* (New York: The MacMillan Company, 1972), 227; Nancy Chang, *Silencing Political Dissent* (New York: Seven Stories Press, 2002), 27.

8   Linfield, *Freedom Under Fire*, 83; Gary T. Marx, "External Efforts to Damage or Facilitate Social Movements: Some Patterns, Explanations, Outcomes, and Complications," in *The Dynamics of Social Movements: Resource Mobilization, Social Control, and Tactics*, ed. Mayer Zald and John D. McCarthy (Cambridge, MA: Winthrop Publishers, Inc, 1979), 100.

9   Donner, *The Age of Surveillance*, 27; Caute, *The Great Fear*, 270.

10   Schultz and Schultz, *The Price of Dissent*, 61.

11   U.S. Congress, Senate Select Committee to Study Government Operations with Respect to Intelligence Activities, *Final Report–Book II*, 42–44.

12   Howard Zinn, *A People's History of the United States* (New York: Harper & Row, 1980), 420.

13   Goldstein, *Political Repression in Modern America*, 302–303.

14   See the following court cases: *Baggett v. Bullitt*. 377 U.S. 360. 1964; *Elfbrandt v. Russell*. 384 U.S. 11. 1966; and *Keyishan v. Board of Regents*. 385 U.S. 589.

1967. *Keyishan v. Board of Regents* overturned *Adler v. Board of Education*. 342 U.S. 485. 1952.

15 Linfield, *Freedom Under Fire*, 108–110.

16 Alexander Cockburn, "The Tenth Crusade." *Nation,* 23 September 2002.

17 Caute, *The Great Fear*, 576.

18 Parmet, *Eisenhower and the American Crusades*, 234–235.

19 Caute, *The Great Fear*, 312–313.

20 Incidentally, the Los Angeles housing program Wilkinson was involved with disintegrated, and the Chavez Ravine area was converted into a baseball stadium for the Los Angeles Dodgers. See: Fariello, *Red Scare*, 531.

21 "Housing Aide Is Called" *New York Times*, 10 October 1952, 2; Cole and Dempsey, *Terrorism and the Constitution*, 5–6.

22 Caute, *The Great Fear*, 608; Fariello, *Red Scare*, 537–540.

23 Fariello, *Red Scare*, 468.

24 Ibid., 531.

25 Ibid.

26 "Contempt Sought for 2," *New York Times*, 9 August 1958, 33.

27 "A Year for Contempt," *New York Times*, 3 February 1959, 26.

28 Anthony Lewis, "High Court Backs House Committee in Contempt Issue," *New York Times*, 28 February 1961, 1.

29 Ibid. Justice Black went on to write, "Government by consent will disappear to be replaced by government by intimidation because some people are afraid that this country cannot survive unless Congress has the power to set aside the freedoms of the First Amendment at will. I can only reiterate my firm conviction that these people are tragically wrong. This country was not built by men who were afraid and it cannot be preserved by such men."

30 Wilkinson served nine months of the year-long sentence. His refusal to answer congressional questioning was rooted in the protection he claimed the First Amendment afforded him.

31 Fariello, *Red Scare*, 528–533.

32 Ibid. 537–538.

33 Schultz and Schultz, *It Did Happen Here*, 272.

34 Fariello, *Red Scare*, 536.

35 U.S. Congress, Senate Select Committee to Study Government Operations with Respect to Intelligence Activities, *Final Report–Book III*, 56.

36 Ibid., 56–57.

37 Stephen J. Schulhofer, *The Enemy Within: Intelligence Gathering, Law Enforcement, and Civil Liberties in the Wake of September 11* (Washington, DC: The Century Foundation, 2002), 55–56.

38 U.S. Congress, Senate Select Committee to Study Government Operations with Respect to Intelligence Activities, *Final Report–Book III*, 29, 56.

39   Schrecker, *No Ivory Tower*.

40   Fariello, *Red Scare*, 419. See also Linfield, *Freedom Under Fire*, 108; and Schrecker, *No Ivory Tower*, 84–218.

41   Schrecker, *No Ivory Tower*, 188.

42   Caute, *The Great Fear*, 414–484, 551–556; Schrecker, *No Ivory Tower*, passim; Fariello, *Red Scare*, 419–468.

43   W.S. DiPiero, "Politics in Poetry: The Case of Thomas McGrath," *New England Review* 17 (1995): 41.

44   Reginald Gibbons and Terrence Des Pres, eds., *Thomas McGrath: Life and the Poem* (Urbana and Chicago: University of Illinois Press, 1992), 44, 51.

45   Terrence Des Pres, *Praises & Dispraises: Poetry and Politics, the 20th Century* (New York: Viking, 1988), 152–153.

46   Frederick C. Stern, "An Interview with Thomas McGrath," in *The Revolutionary Poet in the United States: The Poetry of Thomas McGrath* (Columbia, MO: University of Missouri Press, 1988), 180.

47   Gibbons and Des Pres, *Thomas McGrath: Life and the Poem*, 50.

48   McGrath's statement in front of HUAC was reprinted in the *North Dakota Quarterly* 50 (Fall 1982): 8–9.

49   E.P. Thompson, "Homage to Thomas McGrath," in *The Revolutionary Poet in the United States: The Poetry of Thomas McGrath*, ed. Frederick C. Stern (Columbia, MO: University of Missouri Press, 1988), 110.

50   Donner, *The Un-Americans*, 61.

51   Schrecker, *No Ivory Tower*, 270.

52   Thompson, "Homage to Thomas McGrath," 110.

53   Schrecker, *No Ivory Tower*, 286.

54   Thompson, "Homage to Thomas McGrath," 111.

55   Schrecker, *No Ivory Tower*, 302.

56   Stern, "An Interview with Thomas McGrath," 181.

57   Caute, *The Great Fear*, 414–430, 444–445.

58   Michael Parenti, Personal Interview, 12 December 2006.

59   David Price, *Threatening Anthropology: McCarthyism and the FBI's Investigation of Anthropologists* (Durham: Duke University Press, 2004).

60   Michael Forrest Keen, *Stalking the Sociological Imagination: J. Edgar Hoover's FBI Surveillance of American Sociology* (Westport, Conn.: Greenwood Press, 1999), 6.

61   Churchill and Vander Wall, *The COINTELPRO Papers*, 198; Goldstein, *Political Repression in Modern America*, 522.

62   Bettina Aptheker, *The Morning Breaks: The Trial of Angela Davis*. 2d ed. (Ithaca and London: Cornell University Press, 1999), 2–3.

63   Angela Davis, *Angela Davis: An Autobiography* (New York: Random House, 1974), 217–218.

64 Scott P. Stimson, "Davis Returns," *Daily Bruin*, 18 October 1996.

65 Goldstein, *Political Repression in Modern America*, 522.

66 Stimson, "Davis Returns."

67 Aptheker, *The Morning Breaks*, 4.

68 "The Professor's Guns," *Time* magazine, 24 August 1970.

69 "Professor's Ouster Fought in Vermont," *New York Times*, 5 December 1971, 86.

70 Michael Parenti, *Against Empire* (San Francisco: City Lights Books, 1995), Chapter 10 and Goldstein, *Political Repression in Modern America*, 522–523.

71 Will Miller, "Introduction for Michael Parenti," University of Vermont, 9 April 1997. Available online at: http://www.uvm.edu/~radphil/uvmfirings.htm

72 "Others Under Fire," *Time* magazine, 17 January 1972.

73 Michael Parenti, Personal Interview, 12 December 2006.

74 For Morris Starsky, see Chomsky, "Introduction," 6–7; Churchill and Vander Wall, *The COINTELPRO Papers*, 55; Nelson Blackstock, *COINTELPRO: The FBI's Secret War on Political Freedom* (New York: Vintage Books, 1976), 175–176. For Peter Bohmer, see Goldstein, *Political Repression in Modern America*, 523; Churchill and Vander Wall, *The COINTELPRO Papers*, 200–203. For Bruce Franklin, see Churchill and Vander Wall, *Agents of Repression*, 96.

75 Laura Blumenfeld, "Dissertation Could Be Security Threat: Student's Maps Illustrate Concerns About Public Information," *Washington Post*, 8 July 2003, A1.

76 See: Fariello, *Red Scare*, 319–320; Schrecker, *No Ivory Tower*, 145; and R.C. Lewontin, "The Cold War and the Transformation of the Academy," in *The Cold War & the University: Toward an Intellectual History of the Postwar Years*, ed. David Montgomery (New York: The New Press, 1997), passim.

77 Ira Katznelson, "The Subtle Politics of Developing Emergency: Political Science as Liberal Guardianship," in *The Cold War & the University: Toward an Intellectual History of the Postwar Years*, ed. David Montgomery (New York: The New Press, 1997), 235.

78 Lewontin, "The Cold War and the Transformation of the Academy," 27.

79 Ami Chen Mills, *CIA Off Campus: Building the Movement against Agency Recruitment and Research* (Boston: South End Press, 1991), 32–41; Linfield, *Freedom Under Fire*, 134.

5
Surveillance and Break-ins

1 David Lyon, *The Electronic Eye: The Rise of Surveillance Society* (Minneapolis: University of Minnesota Press, 1994), ix.

2   David Lyon, *Surveillance Society: Monitoring Everyday Life* (Buckingham and Philadelphia: Open University Press, 2001), 2.

3   Brian Glick, *War at Home: Covert Action Against U.S. Activists and What We Can Do About It* (Cambridge, MA: South End Press, 1989), 53.

4   Document reprinted in Paul Cowan, Nick Egleson, and Nat Hentoff, *State Secrets: Police Surveillance in America* (New York: Holt, Rinehart and Winston, 1974), 138–141.

5   Churchill and Vander Wall, *Agents of Repression*, 39–40.

6   Marx, "External Efforts to Damage or Facilitate Social Movements," 98–99.

7   Donner, *The Age of Surveillance*, 3.

8   Electronic surveillance, in FBI slang is referred to as "Elsur." This procedure is more colloquially known as "bugging."

9   U.S. Congress, Senate Select Committee to Study Government Operations with Respect to Intelligence Activities, *Final Report—Book III*, 355.

10   Ibid., 361.

11   David J. Garrow, *The FBI and Martin Luther King, Jr.* (New York: Penguin, 1981), 154–155.

12   U.S. Congress, Senate Select Committee to Study Government Operations with Respect to Intelligence Activities, *Final Report—Book III*, 81.

13   Churchill and Vander Wall, *The COINTELPRO Papers*, 95.

14   Athan Theoharis, *Spying on Americans: Political Surveillance from Hoover to the Huston Plan* (Philadelphia: Temple University Press, 1978), 166–167.

15   J. Edgar Hoover, Federal Bureau of Investigation, "Memorandum from Director, FBI to SAC, Atlanta," 20 September 1957.

16   R.R. Nichols, Federal Bureau of Investigation, "Memorandum to Director Hoover—COMINFIL SCLC, IS-C," 1 October 1962.

17   G.H. Scatterday, Federal Bureau of Investigation, "Memorandum to Mr. A. Rosen," 22 May 1961.

18   Garrow, *The FBI and Martin Luther King, Jr.*, 41–43, 50.

19   Churchill and Vander Wall, *The COINTELPRO Papers*, 96.

20   Garrow, *The FBI and Martin Luther King, Jr.*, 46.

21   Jack Childs was a CP member-turned-informant who went by the name "Solo" at the FBI. The FBI went to great lengths to hide the identity of this valued infiltrator—even from the Church Committee. In 1975, the FBI told the Church Committee that "it cannot provide the Committee with the full factual basis for its charges on the grounds that to do so would compromise informants of continuing use to the Bureau." See: U.S. Congress, Senate Select Committee to Study Government Operations with Respect to Intelligence Activities, *Final Report—Book III*, 84–85.

22   Taylor Branch, *Pillar of Fire: America in the King Years, 1963–65* (New York: Simon & Schuster, 1998), 411.

23 U.S. Congress, Senate Select Committee to Study Government Operations with Respect to Intelligence Activities, *Final Report–Book III*, 85.

24 I certainly don't mean to give the Kennedys too much credit. In the context of the Cold War, they faced a great deal of international pressure to pass Civil Rights legislation. The U.S. with its egregious, codified racism looked appalling in the global south where the Cold War was being fought via proxies. I'm not arguing that the Kennedys were civil rights diehards who wanted desperately for African Americans to be on equal political footing as whites, rather they simply aimed to take the edge off the United States' blatant racism. A great deal of what they did to advance civil rights should be viewed through the prism of geopolitics.

25 Garrow, *The FBI and Martin Luther King, Jr.*, 44–45, 60–61; U.S. Congress, Senate Select Committee to Study Government Operations with Respect to Intelligence Activities, *Final Report–Book III*, 97.

26 Howell Raines, *My Soul Is Rested: Movement Days in the Deep South Remembered* (New York: G.P. Putnam's Sons, 1977), 430.

27 Donner, *The Age of Surveillance*, 12.

28 J. Bland, Federal Bureau of Investigation, "Memorandum to William Sullivan," 3 February 1962 and J. Edgar Hoover, Federal Bureau of Investigation, "Memorandum from Director, FBI to SAC, Atlanta," 11 May 1962.

29 U.S. Congress, Senate Select Committee to Study Government Operations with Respect to Intelligence Activities, *Final Report–Book III*, 87.

30 Section A of the Reserve Index is one step below the Security Index. For more details about these indexes, see U.S. Congress, Senate Select Committee to Study Government Operations with Respect to Intelligence Activities, *Final Report–Book III*, 436–447 and Theoharis, *Spying on Americans*, 43–64.

31 U.S. Congress, Senate Select Committee to Study Government Operations with Respect to Intelligence Activities, *Final Report–Book III*, 89–90.

32 Branch, *Pillar of Fire*, 526.

33 Ibid., 530.

34 See: U.S. Congress, Senate Select Committee to Study Government Operations with Respect to Intelligence Activities, *Final Report–Book III*. One must keep in mind, though, that at the time Sullivan said this, he was doing everything he could to exculpate himself from the emerging revelations about COINTELPRO. Also, Hoover was an easy target, as he had passed away in 1972.

35 It is worth noting that, when King made his critical comments about the FBI, the Bureau had already established a sizeable surveillance network to monitor his communication with Levison and O'Dell. According to Garrow: "The flood of memos on Stanley Levison and his influence on King had begun in January, 1962; the electronic surveillance of Levison by tap and bug had been

instituted in March, 1962; headquarters had started pressing the Atlanta and New York field offices to recommend a 'COMINFIL' investigation of SCLC in July, 1962; such a probe formally had been initiated in mid-October, 1962; and the first 'COINTEL' action against Jack O'Dell's tie to SCLC had occurred in late-October, 1962—all before King voiced his first criticism of the FBI's performance in Albany." See: Garrow, *The FBI and Martin Luther King, Jr.*, 84.

36 William C. Sullivan, Federal Bureau of Investigation, "Memorandum to AH Belmont," 30 August 1963.

37 U.S. Congress, Senate Select Committee to Study Government Operations with Respect to Intelligence Activities, *Final Report–Book III*, 100–102.

38 Ibid., 92.

39 Garrow, *The FBI and Martin Luther King, Jr.*, 91.

40 William F. Pepper, *Orders to Kill: The Truth Behind the Murder of Martin Luther King* (New York: Carroll & Graf Publishers, Inc., 1995), 113.

41 U.S. Congress, Senate Select Committee to Study Government Operations with Respect to Intelligence Activities, *Final Report–Book III*, 111–112, 318.

42 Ibid., 141–145.

43 Garrow, *The FBI and Martin Luther King, Jr.*, 104.

44 William C. Sullivan, Federal Bureau of Investigation, "Memorandum to AH Belmont," 8 January 1964.

45 J. Edgar Hoover, Federal Bureau of Investigation, "Memorandum from Director, FBI to SAC, Atlanta," 1 April 1964.

46 William C. Sullivan, Federal Bureau of Investigation, "Memorandum to AH Belmont," 24 December 1963.

47 Garrow, *The FBI and Martin Luther King, Jr.*, 106–107.

48 U.S. Congress, Senate Select Committee to Study Government Operations with Respect to Intelligence Activities, *Final Report–Book III*, 120, 318.

49 Ibid., 124–126.

50 Ibid., 140–144.

51 Roy Wilkins was a leader in the NAACP. He and King held divergent views on many civil rights issues, strategies, and tactics. The FBI had considered attempting to exacerbate the mutual antipathy between Wilkins and King into full-blown, public hatred. Wilkins met privately with the FBI's Cartha "Deke" DeLoach on 27 November 1964 to discuss the "derogatory" information that the FBI had on King. (See: U.S. Congress, Senate Select Committee to Study Government Operations with Respect to Intelligence Activities, *Final Report–Book III*, 162–163.) Such meetings are the grist of "black propaganda."

52 U.S. Congress, Senate Select Committee to Study Government Operations with Respect to Intelligence Activities, *Final Report–Book III*, 160; Garrow, *The FBI and Martin Luther King, Jr.*, 125–126.

53   Branch, *Pillar of Fire*, 556–557.
54   Donner, *The Age of Surveillance*, 245.
55   Ibid.; U.S. Congress, Senate Select Committee to Study Government Operations with Respect to Intelligence Activities, *Final Report–Book III*, 367–368.
56   U.S. Congress, Senate Select Committee to Study Government Operations with Respect to Intelligence Activities, *Final Report–Book III*, 126–130.
57   Garrow, *The FBI and Martin Luther King, Jr.*, 148–150.
58   Donner, *The Age of Surveillance*, 245.
59   Garrow, *The FBI and Martin Luther King, Jr.*, 207.
60   Ibid., 172.
61   Ibid., 173.
62   Churchill and Vander Wall, *Agents of Repression*, 55; Taylor Branch, *At Canaan's Edge: America in the King Years, 1965–1968* (New York: Simon & Schuster, 2006), 369.
63   Branch, *At Canaan's Edge*, 662, 668.
64   Garrow, *The FBI and Martin Luther King, Jr.*, 208.
65   E.J. Hughes, "A Curse of Confusion," *Newsweek*, 1 May 1967, 17.
66   "A Tragedy" *Washington Post*, 6 April 1967, 20.
67   "Dr. King's Disservice to His Cause," *Life*, 21 April 1967, 4.
68   J. Edgar Hoover, Federal Bureau of Investigation, "Memorandum from Director, FBI to Special Agents in Charge," 4 March 1968.
69   U.S. Congress, Senate Select Committee to Study Government Operations with Respect to Intelligence Activities, *Final Report–Book III*, 183.
70   J. Edgar Hoover, Federal Bureau of Investigation, "Memorandum from Director, FBI to Special Agent in Charge, Atlanta," 14 April 1969.
71   Garrow, *The FBI and Martin Luther King, Jr.*, 203.
72   William F. Pepper, *An Act of State: The Execution of Martin Luther King* (New York: Verso, 2003).
73   Pepper, *Orders to Kill*; Pepper, *An Act of State*; Garrow, *The FBI and Martin Luther King, Jr.*, 201.
74   Donner, *The Age of Surveillance*, 12.
75   U.S. Congress, Senate Select Committee to Study Government Operations with Respect to Intelligence Activities, *Final Report–Book III*, 360.
76   Ibid.
77   Ibid., 355.
78   Ibid, 360, emphasis added.
79   Ibid., 365–366.
80   Ronald Reagan, "Executive Order 12333—United States Intelligence Activities," in *Public Papers of the Presidents: Ronald Reagan, 1981* (Washington, DC: Government Printing Office, 1982).

81   Garrow, *The FBI and Martin Luther King, Jr.*, 218.

82   Raines, *My Soul Is Rested*, 427–428.

83   Schultz and Schultz, *It Did Happen Here*, 284.

84   Branch, *Pillar of Fire*, 557.

85   Donner, *The Age of Surveillance*, 6.

86   U.S. Congress, Senate Select Committee to Study Government Operations with Respect to Intelligence Activities, *Final Report–Book III*, 184.

87   Schultz and Schultz, *It Did Happen Here*, 288, 286.

88   Marx, "External Efforts to Damage or Facilitate Social Movements," 99.

89   U.S. Congress, Senate Select Committee to Study Government Operations with Respect to Intelligence Activities, *Final Report–Book III*, 183.

90   Ibid., 856.

91   Ibid., 35.

92   Theoharis, *Spying on Americans*, 164.

93   Churchill and Vander Wall, *Agents of Repression*, 54, 394.

94   Garrow, *The FBI and Martin Luther King, Jr.*, 127, 130; U.S. Congress, Senate Select Committee to Study Government Operations with Respect to Intelligence Activities, *Final Report–Book III*, 82.

95   Herbert Marcuse, *The One-Dimensional Man: Studies in the Ideology of Advanced Industrial Society* (Boston: Beacon Press, 1964), xv.

96   Noam Shoval and Michal Isaacson, "Application of Tracking Technologies to the Study of Pedestrian Spatial Behavior," *The Professional Geographer* 58 (2006): 172–183.

97   Gary T. Marx, *Undercover: Police Surveillance in America* (Berkeley, CA: University of California Press, 1988), 208.

98   Lyon, *The Electronic Eye*; Christian Parenti, *The Soft Cage: Surveillance in America from Slave Passes to the War on Terror* (New York: Basic Books, 2003).

99   Lyon, *Surveillance Society*, 3.

6
Infiltration, "Badjacketing," and the Use of Agent Provocateurs

1   U.S. Congress, Senate Select Committee to Study Government Operations with Respect to Intelligence Activities, *Final Report–Book III*, 228.

2   Ibid., 77.

3   Donner, *The Age of Surveillance*, 325, 327, 341–348; U.S. Congress, Senate Select Committee to Study Government Operations with Respect to Intelligence Activities, *Final Report–Book III*, 835–922.

4   Ibid., 228.

5   Donner, *The Age of Surveillance*, 137.

6   Ibid., 133–134. Active informers are rarely used in the courtroom since their identities would be revealed. Therefore, "the defector who has no future as a source is the preferred candidate for the witness stand." This also leads to witnesses being used more than once for different cases, or the "professional witness." Informants may serve in this role on a probationary level before becoming an informant from categories (1) and/or (2). Regardless of which category they fall into initially, it is mandatory for an informant to sign a document that s/he isn't an employee of the FBI and will therefore not publicly say that s/he is. This requirement allows the Bureau "to claim the fruits of his work while disclaiming responsibility for the manner in which he performs it—or even for his performing it at all."

7   Gary T. Marx, "Thoughts on a Neglected Category of Social Movement Participant: The Agent Provocateur and the Informant," *American Journal of Sociology* 80 (1974): 405.

8   Marx, "Thoughts on a Neglected Category of Social Movement Participant," 434.

9   Marx, *Undercover: Police Surveillance in America*, 155.

10   Marx, "Thoughts on a Neglected Category of Social Movement Participant," 416–418.

11   Marx, *Undercover: Police Surveillance in America*, 154.

12   U.S. Congress, Senate Select Committee to Study Government Operations with Respect to Intelligence Activities, *Final Report–Book III*, 235–239; 250.

13   Churchill and Vander Wall, *Agents of Repression*, 118.

14   John William Sayer, *Ghost Dancing the Law: The Wounded Knee Trials* (Cambridge, Mass.: Harvard University Press, 1997), 204.

15   Philip D. Roos, Dowell H. Smith, Stephen Langley, and James McDonald, "The Impact of the American Indian Movement on the Pine Ridge Indian Reservation," *Phylon* 41 (1980): 90–91.

16   Alvin M. Josephy, Jr., Joane Nagel, and Troy Johnson, *Red Power: The American Indians' Fight for Freedom*. 2d ed. (Lincoln, Nebraska: University of Nebraska Press, 1999), 16–21.

17   Robert Burnette and John Koster, *The Road to Wounded Knee* (New York: Bantam Books, Inc, 1974), 196.

18   Churchill and Vander Wall, *Agents of Repression*, 119.

19   Vine Deloria, Jr., *Behind the Trail of Broken Treaties: An Indian Declaration of Independence* (New York: Delacorte Press, 1974), 43.

20   The "Trail of Broken Treaties 20-Point Position Paper" can be accessed at the American Indian Movement's web site: http://www.aimovement.org/archives/index.html. A summary of the twenty points can be found in Josephy, Nagel,

and Johnson, *Red Power: The American Indians' Fight for Freedom*, 45–47.

21 Sayer, *Ghost Dancing the Law*, 30; Deloria, *Behind the Trail of Broken Treaties*, 56.

22 Deloria, *Behind the Trail of Broken Treaties*, 60.

23 Ibid., 59–60; Churchill and Vander Wall, *Agents of Repression*, 126.

24 Churchill and Vander Wall, *Agents of Repression*, 235.

25 Ward Churchill, *A Little Matter of Genocide: Holocaust and Denial in the Americas, 1492 to the Present* (San Francisco: City Lights Books, 1997), 11. Churchill, who has written extensively on the persecution of Native Americans and other groups striving for social justice, is an Indian himself and an AIM member of more than twenty years. A longtime activist and scholar, Churchill is no stranger to suppression. In early 2005, he came under fire for an essay he wrote after September 11, 2001 that compared some of the victims of the terrorist attack to Nazi war criminal Adolf Eichmann. Subsequently, a number of his speaking engagements were canceled and his employer, Colorado University, undertook an intensive, critical examination of his written work and public speeches. His situation will be considered in more detail in Chapter 14.

26 U.S. Congress, Senate Committee on the Judiciary, Subcommittee to Investigate the Administration of the Internal Security Act and Other Internal Security Law, *Revolutionary Activities Within the United States: The American Indian Movement*, 94th Congress, 2d sess. (Washington, DC: U.S. Government Printing Office, 1976), 16.

27 U.S. Congress, *Revolutionary Activities Within the United States*, 3.

28 John Kifner, "Security Chief for Militant Indian Group Says He Was a Paid Informer for F.B.I.," *New York Times*, 13 March 1975, 31; U.S. Congress, *Revolutionary Activities Within the United States*, 3, 10–11.

29 U.S. Congress, *Revolutionary Activities Within the United States*, 10–11; Churchill and Vander Wall, *Agents of Repression*, 220.

30 U.S. Congress, *Revolutionary Activities Within the United States*, 6–7.

31 Brand quoted in Churchill and Vander Wall, *Agents of Repression*, 223.

32 Kifner, "Security Chief for Militant Indian Group Says He Was a Paid Informer for F.B.I."

33 Sayer, *Ghost Dancing the Law*, 3–4.

34 Ibid., 10–11, 80.

35 Churchill and Vander Wall, *Agents of Repression*, 221, emphasis in original.

36 U.S. Congress, *Revolutionary Activities Within the United States*, 138.

37 Quoted in Sayer, *Ghost Dancing the Law*, 108–109.

38 Ibid., 109.

39 Churchill and Vander Wall, *Agents of Repression*, 255.

40 Sayer, *Ghost Dancing the Law*, 109.

41 John M. Crewdson, "Judge Says FBI Withheld Data on Indians," *New York Times*, 5 April 1975, 16; Kifner, "Security Chief for Militant Indian Group Says He Was a Paid Informer for F.B.I."; Sayer, *Ghost Dancing the Law*, 207.

42 Churchill and Vander Wall, *The COINTELPRO Papers*, 256.

43 Johanna Brand, *The Life and Death of Anna Mae Aquash* (Toronto: James Lorimer Publishers, 1978), 99.

44 Sayer, *Ghost Dancing the Law*, 211.

45 U.S. Congress, *Revolutionary Activities Within the United States*, 61.

46 Churchill and Vander Wall, *Agents of Repression*, 222.

47 U.S. Congress, *Revolutionary Activities Within the United States*, 61.

48 Peter Matthiessen, *In the Spirit of Crazy Horse* (New York: The Viking Press, 1984), 123; Kifner, "Security Chief for Militant Indian Group Says He Was a Paid Informer for F.B.I."

49 Kifner, "Security Chief for Militant Indian Group Says He Was a Paid Informer for F.B.I."

50 Matthiessen, *In the Spirit of Crazy Horse*, 123.

51 Sayer, *Ghost Dancing the Law*, 195; and "Prosecutors Cited for Indians' Trial," *New York Times*, 20 September 1974, 22.

52 Kifner, "Security Chief for Militant Indian Group Says He Was a Paid Informer for F.B.I."

53 Sayer, *Ghost Dancing the Law*, 293 n86; Churchill and Vander Wall, *The COINTELPRO Papers*, 391 n107.

54 Kifner, "Security Chief for Militant Indian Group Says He Was a Paid Informer for F.B.I."

55 Matthiessen, *In the Spirit of Crazy Horse*, 122.

56 Sayer, *Ghost Dancing the Law*, 207.

57 U.S. Congress, *Revolutionary Activities Within the United States*, 4.

58 Churchill and Vander Wall, *Agents of Repression*, 273.

59 Matthiessen, *In the Spirit of Crazy Horse*, 241.

60 Rex Weyler, *Blood of the Land: The Government and Corporate War Against First Nations* (Philadelphia: New Society Publishers, 1992), 170.

61 U.S. Congress, Senate Select Committee to Study Government Operations with Respect to Intelligence Activities, *Final Report—Book III*, 46.

62 Glick, *War at Home*, 43.

63 U.S. Congress, Senate Select Committee to Study Government Operations with Respect to Intelligence Activities, *Final Report—Book III*, 46.

64 Reprinted in Churchill and Vander Wall, *The COINTELPRO Papers*, 183–184.

65 Frank Donner, "Let Him Wear a Wolf's Head: What the FBI Did to William Albertson," *Civil Liberties Review*, April/May 1976; Donner, *The Age of Surveillance*, 191–194.

66 Document reprinted in Churchill and Vander Wall, *The COINTELPRO Papers*, 181–182.

67 Glick, *War at Home*, 43.

68 Churchill and Vander Wall, *Agents of Repression*, 212.

69 Ibid., 213.

70 Matthiessen, *In the Spirit of Crazy Horse*, 87.

71 Churchill and Vander Wall, *Agents of Repression*, 214.

72 Matthiessen, *In the Spirit of Crazy Horse*, 111.

73 Weyler, *Blood of the Land*, 91.

74 Matthiessen, *In the Spirit of Crazy Horse*, 111.

75 Ibid., 445.

76 Ibid., 146, emphasis in original.

77 Ibid.

78 Ibid., 252.

79 Churchill and Vander Wall, *Agents of Repression*, 215.

80 Weyler, *Blood of the Land*, 191–192; Alvin M. Josephy, Jr., *Now That the Buffalo's Gone: A Study of Today's American Indians* (New York: Alfred A. Knopf, 1982), 254.

81 Linfield, *Freedom Under Fire*, 135.

82 Marx, "Thoughts on a Neglected Category of Social Movement Participant," 404–405, emphasis added.

83 Churchill and Vander Wall, *Agents of Repression*, 47.

84 Goldstein, *Political Repression in Modern America*, 473.

85 Marx, "Thoughts on a Neglected Category of Social Movement Participant," 434.

86 "F.B.I. Agent Tells of S.D.S. Activity: Surprise Witness Heard at Tacoma Conspiracy Trial," *New York Times*, 6 December 1970, 79.

87 Goldstein, *Political Repression in Modern America*, 475.

88 "F.B.I. Agent Tells of S.D.S. Activity" 1970, 79.

89 "Informer Says FBI Paid for Spray Paint," *New York Times*, 8 December 1970, 52; Goldstein, *Political Repression in Modern America*, 475.

90 Weyler, *Blood of the Land*, 114.

91 U.S. Congress, *Revolutionary Activities Within the United States*, 11.

92 Matthiessen, *In the Spirit of Crazy Horse*, 123.

93 Churchill and Vander Wall, *Agents of Repression*, 223.

94 Ibid., 434 n27.

95 U.S. Congress, *Revolutionary Activities Within the United States*, 17.

96 Churchill and Vander Wall, *Agents of Repression*, 224.

97 U.S. Congress, *Revolutionary Activities Within the United States*, 154.

98 Ibid., 161–162.

99 Churchill and Vander Wall, *Agents of Repression*, 226.

100 Ibid., 227.

101 Reprinted in Churchill and Vander Wall, *The COINTELPRO Papers*, 300.

102 Matthiessen, *In the Spirit of Crazy Horse*, 126.

103 Sayer, *Ghost Dancing the Law*, 208.

104 Churchill and Vander Wall, *Agents of Repression*, 226.

105 Stephen Cornell, *The Return of the Native: American Indian Political Resurgence* (New York: Oxford University Press, 1988), 203.

106 Sayer, *Ghost Dancing the Law*, 5.

107 Cornell, *The Return of the Native*, 203.

108 U.S. Congress, *Revolutionary Activities Within the United States*, passim.

109 Ibid., 7, 63.

110 AIM was also repressed by Richard "Dickie" Wilson, the Pine Ridge Reservation tribal president, and his reactionary, thuggish Guardians of the Oglala Nation (GOONs). See: Churchill and Vander Wall, *Agents of Repression*, 127, 128, 182–197.

111 U.S. Congress, Senate Select Committee to Study Government Operations with Respect to Intelligence Activities, *Final Report–Book III*, 230.

7
"Black Propaganda" and the Creation of Schism

1 Churchill and Vander Wall, *Agents of Repression*, 42; Linfield, *Freedom Under Fire*, 135.

2 Churchill and Vander Wall, *Agents of Repression*, 42.

3 Document reprinted in Churchill and Vander Wall, *The COINTELPRO Papers*, 183–184, emphasis added.

4 U.S. Congress, Senate Select Committee to Study Government Operations with Respect to Intelligence Activities, *Final Report–Book III*, 187–188.

5 The precise percentage was 79%. See: Donner, *The Age of Surveillance*, 221; U.S. Congress, Senate Select Committee to Study Government Operations with Respect to Intelligence Activities, *Final Report–Book III*, 188.

6 U.S. Congress, Senate Select Committee to Study Government Operations with Respect to Intelligence Activities, *Final Report–Book III*, 40.

7 Ibid., 41–42.

8 O'Reilly, *"Racial Matters" The FBI's Secret File on Black America, 1960–1972*, 305; Amiri Baraka, *The Autobiography of Leroi Jones* (Chicago: Lawrence Hill Books, 1997), 355.

9   Scot Brown, *Fighting for US: Maulana Karenga, the US Organization, and Black Cultural Nationalism* (New York: New York University Press, 2003) 7, 8.

10 U.S. Congress, Senate Select Committee to Study Government Operations with Respect to Intelligence Activities, *Final Report–Book III*, 42.

11 Ibid., 43–44.

12 Ibid., 207.

13 Ibid., 45–46.

14 Peck, *Uncovering the Sixties*, 141.

15 Ibid., 142.

16 Linfield, *Freedom Under Fire*, 152.

17 Leroi Jones later changed his name to Amiri Baraka, as will be described below. See: Allen, *Black Awakening in Capitalist America*; and Baraka, *The Autobiography of Leroi Jones*.

18 Blackstock, *COINTELPRO*, 110–118; Marx, "External Efforts to Damage or Facilitate Social Movements," 104.

19 Blackstock, *COINTELPRO*, 134–135, 143–144.

20 Ibid., 126–127, 137–138, 145–146.

21 U.S. Congress, Senate Select Committee to Study Government Operations with Respect to Intelligence Activities, *Final Report–Book III*, 195; Donner, *The Age of Surveillance*, 228.

22 Allen, *Black Awakening in Capitalist America*, 46.

23 William L. Van Deburg, *New Day in Babylon: The Black Power Movement and American Culture, 1965–1975* (Chicago and London: University of Chicago Press, 1992), 171, 173.

24 Amiri Baraka, *Raise Race Rays Raze: Essays Since 1965* (New York: Random House, 1971), 136.

25 Brown, *Fighting for US*, 45–47.

26 Baraka, *The Autobiography of Leroi Jones*, 358.

27 Ibid., 387–388.

28 Baraka, *Raise Race Rays Raze*, 131.

29 Baraka, *The Autobiography of Leroi Jones*, 357, 359.

30 Brown, *Fighting for US*, 68–69. US created *Kwanzaa* in 1966.

31 Quoted in Allen, *Black Awakening in Capitalist America*, 140.

32 Van Deburg, *New Day in Babylon*, 173–174.

33 Earl Anthony, *Picking Up the Gun: A Report on the Black Panthers* (New York: The Dial Press, 1970), 75.

34 Baraka, *The Autobiography of Leroi Jones*, 357.

35 Allen, *Black Awakening in Capitalist America*, 141; Baraka, *The Autobiography of Leroi Jones*, 392.

36 Van Deburg, *New Day in Babylon*, 173.

37   Trayece Matthews, "'No One Ever Asks, What a Man's Place in the Revolution Is': Gender and the Politics of the Black Panther Party 1966–1971," in *The Black Panther Party Reconsidered*, ed. Charles E. Jones (Baltimore: Black Classic Press, 1998); Allen, *Black Awakening in Capitalist America*, 142–143.

38   Foner, *The Black Panthers Speak*, 50.

39   Brown, *Fighting for US*, 110.

40   Foner, *The Black Panthers Speak*, 50; Manning Marable, *How Capitalism Underdeveloped Black America* (Cambridge, MA: South End Press, 2000), 133–167. This even though US "rejected capitalism and advocated communalism and African socialism." See: Brown, *Fighting for US*, 110.

41   O'Reilly, *"Racial Matters" The FBI's Secret File on Black America, 1960–1972*, 308; Brown, *Fighting for US*, 93.

42   Hilliard and Cole, *This Side of Glory*, 171, emphasis in original.

43   Baraka, *Raise Race Rays Raze*, 129–130.

44   Gail Sheehy, *Panthermania: The Clash of Black Against Black in One American City* (New York: Harper & Row, Publishers, 1971), 17.

45   Floyd W. Hayes, III and Francis A. Kiene, III, "'All Power to the People': The Political Thought of Huey P. Newton and the Black Panther Party," in *The Black Panther Party Reconsidered*, ed. Charles E. Jones (Baltimore: Black Classic Press, 1998), 168.

46   U.S. Congress, Senate Select Committee to Study Government Operations with Respect to Intelligence Activities, *Final Report–Book III*, 40–41, 190; Document reprinted in Churchill and Vander Wall, *Agents of Repression*, 41; and Blackstock, COINTELPRO, 33.

47   Churchill and Vander Wall, *Agents of Repression*, 41; Blackstock, COINTELPRO, 33.

48   Hayes and Kiene, "'All Power to the People,'" 168–169.

49   Ibid.

50   Sheehy, *Panthermania*, 17.

51   Brown, *Fighting for US*, 97.

52   Churchill and Vander Wall, *Agents of Repression*, 42. Larry Watani-Stiner turned himself in to authorities in 1994 after hiding out in Surinam. He was shipped back to San Quentin prison. See Brown, *Fighting for US*, 97.

53   Donner, *The Age of Surveillance*, 222.

54   Swearingen, *FBI Secrets*, 83.

55   Brown, *Fighting for US*, 96–97.

56   Baraka, *The Autobiography of Leroi Jones*, 391–392.

57   U.S. Congress, Senate Select Committee to Study Government Operations with Respect to Intelligence Activities, *Final Report–Book III*, 190.

58   Ibid., 191. To see reprints of the FBI-drawn cartoons, see Blackstock, COINTELPRO, 34–35; Churchill and Vander Wall, *Agents of Repression*, 43;

Churchill and Vander Wall, *The COINTELPRO Papers*, 131.

59 U.S. Congress, Senate Select Committee to Study Government Operations with Respect to Intelligence Activities, *Final Report–Book III*, 191.

60 Kenneth O'Reilly and David Gallen, *Black Americans: The FBI Files* (New York: Carroll & Graf Publishers, Inc., 1994), 50.

61 U.S. Congress, Senate Select Committee to Study Government Operations with Respect to Intelligence Activities, *Final Report–Book III*, 191.

62 Ibid., 192.

63 O'Reilly, *"Racial Matters" The FBI's Secret File on Black America, 1960–1972*, 307.

64 U.S. Congress, Senate Select Committee to Study Government Operations with Respect to Intelligence Activities, *Final Report–Book III*, 192.

65 O'Reilly and Gallen, *Black Americans*, 50.

66 U.S. Congress, Senate Select Committee to Study Government Operations with Respect to Intelligence Activities, *Final Report–Book III*, 192–193, emphasis added; Chomsky, 10.

67 Brown, *Fighting for US*, 122.

68 Baraka, *The Autobiography of Leroi Jones*, 392.

69 U.S. Congress, Senate Select Committee to Study Government Operations with Respect to Intelligence Activities, *Final Report–Book III*, 193.

70 Ibid.

71 O'Reilly, *"Racial Matters" The FBI's Secret File on Black America, 1960–1972*, 307–308.

72 U.S. Congress, Senate Select Committee to Study Government Operations with Respect to Intelligence Activities, *Final Report–Book III*, 194, emphasis added.

73 Donner, *The Age of Surveillance*, 223.

74 Baraka, *The Autobiography of Leroi Jones*, 392.

75 Brown, *Fighting for US*, 123.

76 Sheehy, *Panthermania*, 21.

77 Brown, *Fighting for US*, 123, 120–121, 128.

78 Marx, "External Efforts to Damage or Facilitate Social Movements," 97.

79 Churchill and Vander Wall, *Agents of Repression*, 43–44.

80 U.S. Congress, Senate Select Committee to Study Government Operations with Respect to Intelligence Activities, *Final Report–Book III*, 35.

81 Donner, *The Age of Surveillance*, 224.

82 Van Deburg, *New Day in Babylon*, 302.

83 U.S. Congress, Senate Select Committee to Study Government Operations with Respect to Intelligence Activities, *Final Report–Book III*, 213–216.

84 Ibid., 192.

85 Churchill and Vander Wall, *Agents of Repression*, 42.

86   U.S. Congress, Senate Select Committee to Study Government Operations with Respect to Intelligence Activities, *Final Report—Book III*, 199.

8
Harassment and Harassment Arrests

1   Churchill and Vander Wall, *Agents of Repression*, 44.
2   Earl, "You Can Beat the Rap, But You Can't Beat the Ride."
3   Kim Marks, Personal Interview, 12 December 2006.
4   Glick,*War at Home*, 53–55; Craig Rosebraugh, *The Burning Rage of a Dying Planet: Speaking for the Earth Liberation Front* (New York: Lantern Books, 2004), 42–43.
5   Goldstein, *Political Repression in Modern America*, 493.
6   James Long, "Raid Seeks Information on Attacks Across West," *Oregonian*, 4 February 2000, C1; Rosebraugh, *The Burning Rage of a Dying Planet*; Leslie James Pickering, *The Earth Liberation Front: 1997–2002* (South Wales, NY: Arissa Publications, n.d.).
7   Mike Marqusee, *Redemption Song: Muhammad Ali and the Spirit of the Sixties* (New York: Verso, 1999).
8   Balbus, *The Dialectics of Legal Repression*, 13, 24.
9   Barkan, "Legal Control of the Civil Rights Movement," 558.
10   U.S. Congress, Senate Select Committee to Study Government Operations with Respect to Intelligence Activities, *Final Report—Book III*, 57.
11   Glick, *War at Home*, 55.
12   U.S. Congress, Senate Select Committee to Study Government Operations with Respect to Intelligence Activities, *Final Report—Book III*, 220–221.
13   Ibid., 221.
14   Jim Redden, "Police State Targets the Left," in *The Battle of Seattle: The New Challenge to Capitalist Globalization*, ed. Eddie Yuen, Daniel Burton Rose, and George Katsiaficas (Brooklyn: Soft Skull Press, 2001), 146.
15   Janet Wells, "$1 Million Bail Ordered for Protesters: Berkeley-Based Activist Allegedly Led Mayhem," *San Francisco Chronicle*, 5 August 2000, A3.
16   Francis X. Clines, "Convention Demonstrators Are Held on Very High Bail," *New York Times*, 5 August 2000, A8.
17   Redden, "Police State Targets the Left," 146; Francis X. Clines, "Bail Reduced for Man Accused of Leading Philadelphia Protests," *New York Times*, 8 August 2000, A18.
18   David Montgomery, "Protesters and Police Trade Accusations," *Washington Post*, 4 August 2000a, A23.
19   Churchill and Vander Wall, *Agents of Repression*, 400.

20　Eric Mann, *Comrade George: An Investigation into the Life, Political Thought, and Assassination of George Jackson* (Cambridge, MA: Hovey Street Press, 1972), 2; Aptheker, *The Morning Breaks*, 7.

21　*This Is What Democracy Looks Like*, Jill Freiburg and Rick Rowley, ed. (Cambridge, MA: Independent Media Center and Big Noise Films, 2000).

22　Cole and Dempsey, *Terrorism and the Constitution*, 38, 35–44.

23　Balbus, *The Dialectics of Legal Repression*, 233.

24　Manny Fernandez and David A. Fahrenthold, "Police Arrest Hundreds in Protests: Anti-Capitalism Events Cause Few Disruptions," *Washington Post*, 28 September 2002, A1; American Civil Liberties Union, "*Freedom Under Fire*: Dissent in Post-9/11 America," 2003. Available at: http://www.aclu.org/SafeandFree/SafeandFree.cfm?ID=12666&c=206.

25　Arthur Santana, "D.C. Council Probing Police Conduct in Protests," *Washington Post*, 29 April 2003, B3.

26　Carol D. Leonnig and Del Quentin Wilber, "D.C. Settles With Mass Arrest Victims: 7 Rounded Up in 2002 IMF Protest to Get $425,000 and an Apology," *Washington Post*, 25 January 2005, A1.

27　Halstead, *Out Now!*, 619, 618.

28　Ibid., 621.

29　Ibid., 623.

30　Churchill and Vander Wall, *Agents of Repression*, 51.

31　Alphonso Pinkney, *Red, Black, and Green: Black Nationalism in the United States* (New York: Cambridge University Press, 1976), 37.

32　Churchill and Vander Wall, *The COINTELPRO Papers*, 11.

33　Document reprinted in Churchill and Vander Wall, *The COINTELPRO Papers*, 12. Hoover was named the Director of the FBI in May 1924, when Attorney General Harlan Fiske Stone—in response to a public uproar over recent revelations of the extent of Bureau meddling with dissidents during World War I—instigated a major round of modifications in the Bureau hierarchy and on-the-ground Bureau practices. See Theoharis, *From the Secret Files of J. Edgar Hoover*, 2.

34　Pinkney, *Red, Black, and Green*, 49–50.

35　Ibid., 53.

36　Document reprinted in Churchill and Vander Wall, *The COINTELPRO Papers*, 12.

37　Hallin, "The Media, the War in Vietnam, and Political Support," 6.

38　Linfield, *Freedom Under Fire*, 146.

39　Peck, *Uncovering the Sixties*, xv.

40　Geoffrey Rips, *The Campaign Against the Underground Press* (San Francisco: City Lights Books, 1981), 51, 81–85.

41   Angus Mackenzie, *Secrets: The CIA's War at Home* (Berkeley: University of California Press, 1997), 3–4, 11, 19–25.

42   Ibid., 23.

43   U.S. Congress, Senate Select Committee to Study Government Operations with Respect to Intelligence Activities, *Final Report–Book II*, 93–96; U.S. Congress, Senate Select Committee to Study Government Operations with Respect to Intelligence Activities, *Final Report–Book III*, 835–922.

44   U.S. Congress, Senate Select Committee to Study Government Operations with Respect to Intelligence Activities, *Final Report–Book III*, 840.

45   Garrow, *The FBI and Martin Luther King, Jr.*, 105, 114. For other accounts of IRS abuse, as inspired by the FBI and CIA, see David Wise, *The American Police State: The Government Against the People* (New York: Random House, 1976), 322–351; Donner, *The Age of Surveillance*, 325–352; U.S. Congress, Senate Select Committee to Study Government Operations with Respect to Intelligence Activities, *Final Report–Book II*, 93–96; U.S. Congress, Senate Select Committee to Study Government Operations with Respect to Intelligence Activities, *Final Report–Book III*, 835–922.

46   Churchill and Vander Wall, *Agents of Repression*, 176.

47   Ibid.

48   Ibid.

49   Aptheker, *The Morning Breaks*, 16.

50   William Manchester, *The Glory and the Dream: A Narrative History of America, 1932–1972* (Boston and Toronto: Little Brown and Company, 1974), 1202–1203.

51   Churchill and Vander Wall, *Agents of Repression*, 95–96.

52   Howard Moore, Jr., "Angela—Symbol of Resistance," in *If They Come in the Morning*, Angela Y. Davis (New York: The New American Library Inc., 1971), 207.

53   Manchester, *The Glory and the Dream*, 1203.

54   Aptheker, *The Morning Breaks*, 21.

55   Churchill and Vander Wall, *The COINTELPRO Papers*, 364.

56   Moore, "Angela—Symbol of Resistance," 207.

57   "The Angela Davis Tragedy," *New York Times*, 16 October 1970, 34, emphasis added.

58   Aptheker, *The Morning Breaks*, 35.

59   Incidentally, the death penalty was reinstated in California in 1977.

60   Aptheker, *The Morning Breaks*, 136–153.

61   Ibid., 243.

62   Earl Caldwell, "Angela Davis Acquitted on All Charges," *New York Times*, 5 June 1972, 1.

63   Jack Olsen, *Last Man Standing: The Tragedy and Triumph of Geronimo Pratt*

(New York: Doubleday, 2000), 26.

64 Churchill and Vander Wall, *Agents of Repression*, 77.

65 Olsen, *Last Man Standing*, 34.

66 Ibid., 38.

67 Ibid., 35–42.

68 Churchill and Vander Wall, *Agents of Repression*, 79.

69 Ibid.

70 Glick, *War at Home*, 55–56.

71 Foner, *The Black Panthers Speak*, 257.

72 U.S. Congress, Senate Select Committee to Study Government Operations with Respect to Intelligence Activities, *Final Report–Book III*, 214.

73 Olsen, *Last Man Standing*, 43.

74 Foner, *The Black Panthers Speak*, 263.

75 Document reprinted in Churchill and Vander Wall, *The COINTELPRO Papers*, 156.

76 Churchill and Vander Wall, *Agents of Repression*, 79, 81.

77 Ibid., 407, emphasis added.

78 Olsen, *Last Man Standing*, 89.

79 Ibid., 97.

80 Churchill and Vander Wall, *Agents of Repression*, 85.

81 Olsen, *Last Man Standing*, 66.

82 Ibid., 71–75.

83 Churchill and Vander Wall, *Agents of Repression*, 87–88.

84 Don Terry, "Los Angeles Confronts a Bitter Racial Legacy in a Black Panther Case," *New York Times*, 20 July 1997, A14.

85 Churchill and Vander Wall, *Agents of Repression*, 91.

86 Olsen, *Last Man Standing*, 152.

87 Michael Taylor, "Ex-Panther Pratt Wins New Trial 25-Year Legal Battle in Politicized Case," *San Francisco Chronicle*, 30 May 1997, A1.

88 "Ex-Panther to Remain Free," *New York Times*, 17 February 1999, A11.

89 "Court Asked to Return Ex-Black Panther to Prison," *New York Times*, 16 December 1998, A28.

90 Todd Purdum, "Ex-Black Panther Wins Long Legal Battle," *New York Times*, 27 April 2000, A18.

91 Some of the FBI-drawn cartoons featuring Pratt are reprinted in Churchill and Vander Wall, *Agents of Repression*, 80.

92 For information on Maxwell Sanford, see Churchill and Vander Wall, *Agents of Repression*, 45–47. For information on the Republican National Convention, see Redden, "Police State Targets the Left," 139–146.

93 Aptheker, *The Morning Breaks*, 9–10.

9
Extraordinary Rules and Laws

1 Hardt and Negri, *Empire*, 16–17.

2 Agamben, *Means without End*, 138.

3 James L. Gibson, "Political Intolerance and Political Repression During the McCarthy Red Scare," *American Political Science Review* 82 (1988): 513.

4 Zinn, "Forward," 11.

5 Leonard W. Levy, *Legacy of Suppression: Freedom of Speech and Press in Early American History* (Cambridge, MA: Harvard University Press, 1964), vii, 258.

6 Michael Paul Rogin, *Ronald Reagan, the Movie* (Berkeley: University of California Press, 1987), 76.

7 Quoted in Chang, *Silencing Political Dissent*, 23.

8 Linfield, *Freedom Under Fire*, 43–44.

9 Quoted in Linfield, *Freedom Under Fire*, 76.

10 Ibid., 79–81.

11 Caute, *The Great Fear*, 245.

12 Fariello, *Red Scare*, 303; Caute, *The Great Fear*, 247–248.

13 Later, during the Reagan administration, the United States Information Agency (USIA) maintained a "blacklist" of U.S. citizens who should not, if at all possible, be allowed to travel to foreign countries to give speeches, due to their political stances. Included on the list were Coretta Scott King, Walter Cronkite, and Gary Hart. See Linfield, *Freedom Under Fire*, 161.

14 Caute, *The Great Fear*, 256.

15 Linfield, *Freedom Under Fire*, 106, 156; Rogin, *Ronald Reagan, The Movie*, 79.

16 Farley Mowat, *My Discovery of America* (Boston: The Atlantic Monthly Press, 1985).

17 Herbert Mitgang, *Dangerous Dossiers: Exposing the Secret War against America's Greatest Authors* (New York: D.I. Fine, 1988), 295–296.

18 Alan Gathright, "No-fly Blacklist Snares Political Activists," *San Francisco Chronicle*, 27 September 2002, A1.

19 Ira Berkow, "Rower With Muslim Name Is an All-American Suspect," *New York Times*, 21 February 2003, D2.

20 Wade Henderson, "No Justification for Racial Profiling," *San Diego Union-Tribune*, 21 March 2003, B11.

21 Gathright, "No-fly Blacklist Snares Political Activists," A1.

22 Rex W, Huppke, "Security Screeners 'Nab' David Nelsons," *Seattle Times*, 1 July 2003, A2.

23 The states with "red-flag" statutes (with their penalties in parentheses) were:

Alabama ($500 to $5000 fine); Arizona (6 months); Arkansas (6 months); California (6 months to 5 years); Colorado (1 to 10 years); Connecticut (6 months); Delaware (15 years); Idaho (1 to 10 years); Illinois (1 to 10 years); Indiana (5 years); Iowa (6 months); Kansas (18 months to 3 years); Kentucky (21 years); Massachusetts (6 months); Michigan (4 years); Minnesota (1 to 7 years); Montana (6 months to 5 years); Nebraska (3 years); New Jersey (15 years); New Mexico (6 months); New York (1 year); North Dakota (30 days); Ohio ($100); Oklahoma (10 years); Oregon (10 years); Pennsylvania (3 months); Rhode Island (3 months); South Dakota (30 days); Utah (1 to 10 years); Vermont (6 months); Washington (10 years); West Virginia (1 to 5 years); Wisconsin ($10 to $100). See: Linfield, *Freedom Under Fire*, 65–66, 219–220.

24 Goldstein, *Political Repression in Modern America*, x.

25 James L. Gibson, "Pluralism, Federalism and the Protection of Civil Liberties," *Western Political Quarterly* 43 (1990): 518.

26 American Civil Liberties Union, "*Freedom Under Fire*," 4.

27 Ibid., 11, 13.

28 Goldstein, *Political Repression in Modern America*, 105.

29 Ibid., 139.

30 Regin Schmidt, *Red Scare: FBI and the Origins of Anticommunism in the United States, 1919–1943* (Copenhagen, Denmark: Museum Tusculanum Press, University of Copenhagen, 2000), 177.

31 Quoted in Donner, *The Age of Surveillance*, 20).

32 Robert K. Murray, *Red Scare: A Study of National Hysteria, 1919–1920* (New York: McGraw-Hill Book Company, 1964), 68.

33 Murray B. Levin, *Political Hysteria in America: The Democratic Capacity for Repression* (New York: Basic Books, 1971), 38–50.

34 Linfield, *Freedom Under Fire*, 57.

35 William Preston, Jr., *Aliens and Dissenters: Federal Suppression of Radicals, 1903–1933* (Cambridge, MA: Harvard University Press, 1963), 211.

36 Murray, *Red Scare*, 196–197.

37 "249 Reds Sail, Exiled to Soviet Russia; Berkman Threatens to Come Back; Second Shipload May Leave This Week," *New York Times*, 22 December 1919, 1. It should be noted that Goldman and Berkman were not scooped up in the November raids. See Schmidt, *Red Scare*, 257–262.

38 "249 Reds Sail, Exiled to Soviet Russia; Berkman Threatens to Come Back; Second Shipload May Leave This Week," *New York Times*, 22 December 1919, 1.

39 Richard Drinnon, *Rebel in Paradise: A Biography of Emma Goldman* (Chicago: University of Chicago Press, 1961), 221; Murray, *Red Scare*, 206–208; Schmidt, *Red Scare*, 275. Drinnon notes that despite the fact that most commentators

considered the 249 anarchists, only 51 of them actually were. "Among the others there were 184 who allegedly advocated violent overthrow of government and 14 who were found guilty of moral turpitude or of being public charges." See Drinnon, *Rebel in Paradise*, 221.

40 Preston, *Aliens and Dissenters*, 217.

41 Ibid., 218.

42 "Raid from Coast to Coast," *New York Times*, 3 January 1920, 1.

43 For example, see Chang, *Silencing Political Dissent*, 39.

44 Murray, *Red Scare*, 213; Linfield, *Freedom Under Fire*, 57–58; Goldstein, *Political Repression in Modern America*, 157.

45 Linfield, *Freedom Under Fire*, 57–58; Goldstein, *Political Repression in Modern America*, 157.

46 Goldstein, *Political Repression in Modern America*, 162.

47 Article reprinted in David Brion Davis, *The Fear of Conspiracy: Images of Un-American Subversion from the Revolution to the Present* (Ithaca and London: Cornell University Press, 1971), 226–227.

48 Zinn, *A People's History of the United States*, 366.

49 Schmidt, *Red Scare*, 257.

50 Quoted in Preston, *Aliens and Dissenters*, 210.

51 Davis, *The Fear of Conspiracy*, 226.

52 At the same time, the Palmer Raids and the egregious violation of civil liberties that went along with them ended up radicalizing a group of wealthy, well-connected liberals on the East Coast who, led by Roger Baldwin, formed a watchdog organization that in 1920 transformed into the now-famous American Civil Liberties Union. See American Civil Liberties Union, *"Freedom Under Fire,"* 4.

53 Goldstein, *Political Repression in Modern America*, 284, emphasis in original.

54 Quoted in Goldstein, *Political Repression in Modern America*, 262–263.

55 Richard Drinnon, *Keeper of Concentration Camps: Dillon S. Myer and American Racism* (Berkeley: University of California Press, 1987), 6; Goldstein, *Political Repression in Modern America*, 267.

56 Drinnon, *Keeper of Concentration Camps*, 6.

57 Goldstein, *Political Repression in Modern America*, 267.

58 Greg Robinson, *By Order of the President: FDR and the Internment of the Japanese Americans* (Cambridge, MA: Harvard University Press, 2001), 128.

59 Ibid.

60 Drinnon, *Keeper of Concentration Camps*, 6–8; Chang, *Silencing Political Dissent*, 39.

61 John W. Dower, *War Without Mercy: Race & Power in the Pacific War* (New York: Pantheon Books, 1986), 49.

62 Drinnon, *Keeper of Concentration Camps*, 256, 8.

63 Robinson, *By Order of the President*, 119.

64 Drinnon, *Keeper of Concentration Camps*, 8.

65 Ibid., 9.

66 Ibid., 6, 10.

67 Goldstein, *Political Repression in Modern America*, 267.

68 Robinson, *By Order of the President*, 4–5, 134–146.

69 Linfield, *Freedom Under Fire*, 103.

70 Erica Harth, ed., *Last Witnesses: Reflections on the Wartime Internment of Japanese Americans* (New York: Palgrave, 2001), 153.

71 *Korematsu v. United States*. 323 U.S. 214, 223. 1944.

72 Robinson, *By Order of the President*, 180.

73 Ibid., 230.

74 Ibid., 251.

75 Linfield, *Freedom Under Fire*, 104.

76 Jeffrey F. Burton, Mary M. Farrell, Florence B. Lord, and Richard W. Lord, *Confinement and Ethnicity: An Overview of World War II Japanese Relocation Sites* (Seattle: University of Washington Press, 2002), 34.

77 Ibid., 46, 48.

78 Ibid., 46–47.

79 Ibid., 48.

80 Violet Kazue de Cristoforo and May Sky, *There Is Always Tomorrow: An Anthology of Japanese American Concentration Camp Kaiko Haiku* (Los Angeles: Sun & Moon Press, 1997), 275–279.

81 Barbara Takei, "Legalizing Detention: Segregated Japanese Americans and the Justice Department's Renunciation Program," *Journal of the Shaw Historical Library* 19 (2005): 76.

82 Draft resistance ran rampant through the internment camps. According to one study, "The best organized draft resistance was organized by the Fair Play Committee at the Heart Mountain Relocation Center, where 54 of 315 potential draftees did not show up for physicals." The leader of this organized resistance was shipped off to the Tule Lake Segregation Center. See: Burton, et al, *Confinement and Ethnicity*, 55.

83 Takei, "Legalizing Detention," 76.

84 Ibid., 76–78.

85 Ibid., 82–84, 81.

86 Gibson, "Political Intolerance and Political Repression During the McCarthy Red Scare," 520–521.

87 Drinnon, *Keeper of Concentration Camps*; Robinson, *By Order of the President*.

88 Mary Beth Sheridan and Brooke A. Masters. "More than 350 Held in Probe, Ashcroft Says," *Washington Post*, 25 September 2001, A1.

89 Schulhofer, *The Enemy Within*, 11.

90 Ibid., 12, emphasis in original.

91 Ibid., 13.

92 "Excerpt from Analysis of Detention of Foreigners After 9/11 Attacks," *New York Times*, 3 June 2003, A18.

93 President Bush's Military Order is available online at: http://www.whitehouse. gov/news/releases/2001/11/20011113-27.html

94 Olshansky, *Secret Trials and Executions*, 7, 63.

95 Elisabeth Bumiller, "Military Tribunals Needed In Difficult Time, Bush Says," *New York Times*, 20 November 2001, B5.

96 David Sanger, "President Defends Military Tribunals in Terrorist Cases," *New York Times*, 30 November 2001, A1.

97 Olshansky, *Secret Trials and Executions*, 18, 19.

98 Ibid., 12–14.

99 David Cole, "Why the Court Said No," *New York Review of Books*, 10 August 2006. Available online at: http://www.nybooks.com/articles/19212

100 Robin Toner, "Civil Liberty vs. Security: Finding a Wartime Balance," *New York Times*, 18 November 2001, A1.

101 William Glaberson, "The Tribunals: Closer Look at New Plan for Trying Terrorists," *New York Times*, 15 November 2001, B6.

102 Linfield, *Freedom Under Fire*, 91.

103 Schulhofer, *The Enemy Within*, 9.

104 Goldstein, *Political Repression in Modern America*, 265.

105 Linfield, *Freedom Under Fire*, 26–30; Chang, *Silencing Political Dissent*, 37–38.

106 Jerry Markon, "Moussaoui Prosecution Is Dealt Setback," *Washington Post*, 4 July 2003, A8.

107 William Haynes, "Enemy Combatants," Council on Foreign Relations, 12 December 2002. Available online at: http://www.cfr.org/publication. html?id=5312

108 Toner, "Civil Liberty vs. Security," A1.

109 "Americans May Be Held as 'Enemy Combatants,' Appeals Court Rules," *CNN*, 3 January 2003.

110 Common Article 3 of the Geneva Conventions asserts that detainees must be tried by a "regularly constituted court affording all the judicial guarantees which are recognized as indispensable by civilized peoples." See: http://www. genevaconventions.org

111 David Cole, "Why the Court Said No."

112 Charles Lane, "High Court Rejects Detainee Tribunals: 5 to 3 Ruling Curbs President's Claim Of Wartime Power," *Washington Post*, 30 June 2006, A1.

113 Kevin Johnson, "White House Renews Push for Tribunals," *USA Today*, 3 August 2006, 2A.

114 Michael A. Fletcher, "Bush Signs Terrorism Measure: New Law Governs Interrogation, Prosecution of Detainees," *Washington Post*, 18 October 2006, A4.

115 Dan Eggen, "Tough Anti-Terror Campaign Pledged: Ashcroft Tells Mayors He Will Use New Law to the Fullest Extent," *Washington Post*, 26 October 2001, A1.

10
Mass Media Manipulation

1   Rodger Streitmatter, *Mightier than the Sword: How the News Media Have Shaped American History* (Boulder, CO: Westview Press, 1997), 2, 234.

2   Edelman, *The Politics of Misinformation*, 113, emphasis added.

3   Kielbowicz and Scherer, "The Role of the Press in the Dynamics of Social Movements," 72.

4   Bert Klandermans, "The Social Construction of Protest and Multiorganizational Fields," in *Frontiers in Social Movement Theory*, ed. Aldon D. Morris and Carol McClurg Mueller (New Haven and London: Yale University Press, 1992), 79.

5   Gadi Wolfsfeld, *Media and Political Conflict: News from the Middle East* (Cambridge University Press, 1997), 13–55.

6   Sidney Tarrow, *Power in Movement: Social Movements and Contentious Politics* (New York: Cambridge University Press, 1998), 116.

7   McCarthy and McPhail, "The Institutionalization of Protest in the United States," 84.

8   Schudson, *Discovering the News*, 8.

9   Gans, *Deciding What's News*, 183; Bennett, *News: The Politics of Illusion*, 194.

10 The "emblem of American journalism" quote comes from Schudson, *Discovering the News*, 9.

11 Entman, *Democracy Without Citizens*, 31.

12 Brent Cunningham, "Re-thinking Objectivity," *Columbia Journalism Review* 42 (2003): 26.

13 Entman, "Framing: Toward Clarification of a Fractured Paradigm," 56.

14 M. Mark Miller and Bonnie Parnell Riechert, "Interest Group Strategies and Journalistic Norms: News Framing of Environmental Issues," in *Environmental Risks and the Media*, ed. Stuart Allan, Barbara Adam, and Cynthia Carter (New York: Routledge, 2000), 50.

15 Churchill and Vander Wall, *Agents of Repression*, 43.

16 Small, *Covering Dissent*, 13.

17 Tarrow, *Power in Movement*, 116.

18 For the suppression of the underground press, see Peck, *Uncovering the Sixties*

and Rips, *The Campaign Against the Underground Press*, 37–170. For the Schiller quote, see Herbert I. Schiller, *The Mind Managers* (Boston: Beacon Press, 1973), 49.

19 While implantation is rare, state spin-control is a daily reality in the world of news production. The state produces a plethora of information designed to frame the news in ways favorable to its interests. State officials stage events, make official announcements, and release waves of press releases, all in the hope of creating sympathetic spin. Such spin will be explored below in the chapters on bi-level demonization and mass media deprecation.

20 Gitlin, *The Whole World Is Watching*, 211–217, 4.

21 Daniel Chomsky, "The Mechanisms of Management Control at the *New York Times*," *Media, Culture & Society* 21 (1999): 579–199.

22 U.S. Congress, Senate Select Committee to Study Government Operations with Respect to Intelligence Activities, *Final Report—Book III*, 35.

23 Reprinted in Churchill and Vander Wall, *The COINTELPRO Papers*, 183–184.

24 Donner, *The Age of Surveillance*, 238.

25 U.S. Congress, Senate Select Committee to Study Government Operations with Respect to Intelligence Activities, *Final Report—Book III*, 36.

26 Ibid., 35–36.

27 For information on Fred Black, see Theoharis, *From the Secret Files of J. Edgar Hoover*, 168–169. For information on the Socialist Workers Party, see Blackstock, *COINTELPRO*, 95–99.

28 Richard Gid Powers, *G-Men: Hoover's FBI in American Popular Culture* (Carbondale: Southern Illinois University Press, 1983), 96–97, 131–132.

29 Ibid.

30 Special thanks goes to Bob Van Dyk for putting this book in my hands. See Edwin Johnson and J.R. White, *G-Man vs. The Fifth Column* (Chicago: Whitman Publishing Company, 1941), 208.

31 Donner, *The Age of Surveillance*, 240.

32 Wise, *The American Police State*, 200–201.

33 Garrow, *The FBI and Martin Luther King, Jr.*, 53–54, 61–62.

34 U.S. Congress, Senate Select Committee to Study Government Operations with Respect to Intelligence Activities, *Final Report—Book III*, 183.

35 Donner, *The Age of Surveillance*, 224.

36 U.S. Congress, Senate Select Committee to Study Government Operations with Respect to Intelligence Activities, *Final Report—Book III*, 218–219.

37 Ibid., 219.

38 Ibid., 220.

39 Ibid., 219–220.

40 Van Deburg, *New Day in Babylon*, 302.

41 Swearingen, *FBI Secrets*, 118.

42 Memo reprinted in Churchill and Vander Wall, *The COINTELPRO Papers*, 218.

43 U.S. Congress, Senate Select Committee to Study Government Operations with Respect to Intelligence Activities, *Final Report–Book III*, 219.

44 Memo reprinted in Churchill and Vander Wall, *The COINTELPRO Papers*, 218.

45 Swearingen, *FBI Secrets*, 120.

46 Document reprinted in Churchill and Vander Wall, *The COINTELPRO Papers*, 216.

47 David Richards, *Played Out: The Jean Seberg Story* (New York: Random House, 1981), 234.

48 Donner, *The Age of Surveillance*, 237; document reprinted in Churchill and Vander Wall, *The COINTELPRO Papers*, 216–217 and in Swearingen, *FBI Secrets*, 122–123.

49 Richards, *Played Out*, 241, 244.

50 Ibid., 248.

51 Ibid., 251.

52 Churchill and Vander Wall, *The COINTELPRO Papers*, 215; Richards, *Played Out*, 245.

53 Richards, *Played Out*, 253.

54 Ibid., 375.

55 Linfield, *Freedom Under Fire*, 71–75, 141–145.

56 John R. MacArthur, *Second Front: Censorship and Propaganda in the Gulf War* (New York: Hill and Wang, 1992).

57 This might seem like a minor indiscretion, but by this late point in his presidency, Eisenhower had formed a deeply distrustful relationship with the media. According to Craig Allen, the president believed "reporters had established a precedent for carrying press freedom to new and dangerous extremes" by publishing "sensitive information or material clearly designated as off-limits." See: Craig Allen, *Eisenhower and the Mass Media: Peace, Prosperity, & Prime-Time TV* (Chapel Hill and London: University of North Carolina Press, 1993), 187.

58 Sanford J. Ungar, *FBI* (Boston & Toronto: Little Brown and Company, 1976), 379.

59 Ibid., 379–380.

60 Aryeh Neier, "Surveillance as Censorship," in *The Campaign Against the Underground Press*, ed. Geoffrey Rips (San Francisco: City Lights Books, 1981), 14–15.

61 Small, *Covering Dissent*, 27.

62 Melvin Small, *Johnson, Nixon, and the Doves* (New Brunswick and London: Rutgers University Press, 1988), 64–65.

63 Kathleen J. Turner, *Lyndon Johnson's Dual War: Vietnam and the Press* (Chicago and London: University of Chicago Press, 1985), 174–175.

64 Sharon Downey and Karen Rasmussen, "Vietnam: Press, Protest, and the Presidency," in *Silencing the Opposition: Government Strategies of Suppression*, ed. Craig Smith (Albany, NY: State University Press of New York, 1996), 209.

65 Ibid.

66 Ibid.

67 Ross Gelbspan, *Break-ins, Death Threats and the FBI: The Covert War Against the Central America Movement* (Boston: South End Press, 1991), 123–124.

68 Bennett, *News: The Politics of Illusion*, 20–21.

69 Bill Carter and Felicity Barringer. "Networks Agree to U.S. Request to Edit Future bin Laden Tapes," *New York Times*, 11 October 2001, A1.

70 Bill Carter, "White House Seeks to Limit Transcripts," *New York Times*, 12 October 2001, B7.

71 Small, *Covering Dissent*, 13.

11
Bi-level Demonization

1 Murray Edelman, *Constructing the Political Spectacle* (Chicago and London: The University of Chicago Press, 1988), 75–76.

2 Ibid., 66.

3 Ibid., 78–79.

4 Zaller and Chiu, "Government's Little Helper"; Bennett, *News: The Politics of Illusion*.

5 Zaller and Chiu, "Government's Little Helper," 385.

6 For the "shook the nation" quote, see Zinn, *A People's History of the United States*, 240. For the "French Communism" quote, see Rogin, *Ronald Reagan, the Movie*, 64.

7 James R. Mock and Cedric Larson, *Words that Won the War: The Story of the Committee on Public Information, 1917–1919*, (New York: Russell & Russell, 1968 [1939]), 4.

8 Noam Chomsky, *Media Control: The Spectacular Achievements of Propaganda*, 2nd edition (New York: Seven Stories Press, 2002), 11–12.

9 Stephen Vaughn, *Holding Fast the Inner Lines: Democracy, Nationalism, and the Committee on Public Information* (Chapel Hill, NC: The University of North Carolina Press, 1980), 23.

10 Ibid, 5–6; Walter Lippmann, *Public Opinion* (New York: The Free Press, 1922), 158.

11   Vaughn, *Holding Fast the Inner Lines*, 12–14, 130–131.

12   Stuart Ewen, *PR! A Social History of Spin* (New York: Basic Books, 1996), 109.

13   For a short time, Creel was Denver's previous police commissioner. At one point he banned police officers from using guns and nightsticks, which sparked his critics to attack him as a "tramp anarchist" and a "crackpot." See: Stephen Vaughn, "First Amendment Liberties and the Committee on Public Information," *The American Journal of Legal History*, Vol. 23, No. 2 (April 1979): 105.

14   Vaughn, *Holding Fast the Inner Lines*, 24.

15   "Creel to Direct Nation's Publicity," *New York Times*, 15 April 1917, 1.

16   "Hysterical Saving A Peril to Nation," *New York Times*, 20 April 1917, 11.

17   George Creel, "Public Opinion in War Time," *Annals of the American Academy of Political and Social Science*, Vol. 78, Mobilizing America's Resources for the War (July 1918): 187.

18   "Government Daily Issues First Number," *New York Times*, 11 May 1917, 13.

19   Mock and Larson, *Words that Won the War*, 94, 93.

20   "Censor Creel Gives Out Rules for Newspapers," *New York Times*, 28 May 1917, 1.

21   Vaughn, "First Amendment Liberties and the Committee on Public Information," 107.

22   "Censor Creel Gives Out Rules for Newspapers," *New York Times*, 28 May 1917, 1.

23   Vaughn, "First Amendment Liberties and the Committee on Public Information," 107.

24   Creel, "Public Opinion in War Time," 187.

25   "Press Comment on the Censorship Plan," *New York Times*, 24 May 1917, 2.

26   Vaughn, *Holding Fast the Inner Lines*, 193–195.

27   "Government Asks Artists to Make War Posters," *New York Times*, 20 May 1917, SM8.

28   Creel, "Public Opinion in War Time," 188; Stephen Vaughn, *Holding Fast the Inner Lines*, 32.

29   Wilson quoted in "President Creates Advertising Agency," *New York Times*, 20 January 1918, 6.

30   Ibid.

31   Edward Bernays, (ed.), *The Engineering of Consent* (Norman, Oklahoma: University of Oklahoma Press, 1955).

32   Vaughn, *Holding Fast the Inner Lines*, 149.

33   George Creel, *Rebel at Large: Recollections of Fifty Crowded Years* (New York: G.P. Putnam's Sons, 1947), 163.

34   Vaughn, *Holding Fast the Inner Lines*, 31, 129, 128, 117.

35 Vaughn, *Holding Fast the Inner Lines*, 127, 116–123.

36 Mock and Larson, *Words that Won the War*, 125.

37 Creel, *Rebel at Large*, 164; Vaughn, *Holding Fast the Inner Lines*, 204–210.

38 "Will Issue War Booklets," *New York Times*, 20 June 1917, 2.

39 George Creel, *How We Advertised America* (New York: Arno Press, 1972 [1920]), 99.

40 Ibid., 5.

41 Harold D. Lasswell, *Propaganda Technique in the World War* (New York: Peter Smith, 1938), 221.

42 Edward Bernays, *Propaganda* (Brooklyn, NY: Ig Publishing, 2005 [1928]); Creel, *Rebel at Large*, 158.

43 Lasswell, *Propaganda Technique in the World War*, 195, 77.

44 Vaughn, *Holding Fast the Inner Lines*, 71–75.

45 Ibid., 3. Of these 8.5 million, 2.5 million were born in Germany and 6 million were second-generation German immigrants.

46 Ibid., 6.

47 Ibid., 78. Document reprinted on 80, italics in original.

48 Mock and Larson, *Words that Won the War*, 123.

49 Vaughn, *Holding Fast the Inner Lines*, 81.

50 Edward Bernays, *Public Relations* (Norman, Oklahoma: University of Oklahoma Press, 1952), 79.

51 Mock and Larson, *Words that Won the War*, 19.

52 Vaughn, *Holding Fast the Inner Lines*, 159, emphasis added.

53 Ibid., 234.

54 Ibid., 106.

55 Ibid., 228, 229.

56 "Creel Denounced in the House and Senate," *New York Times*, 10 April 1918, 8.

57 "Government May End Outrages by I.W.W.: Action Under Laws Dealing with Treason Expected—Evidence of German Plot," *New York Times*, 2 August 1917, 20.

58 "Blow at I.W.W.: 168 Are Indicted, Scores Arrested," *New York Times*, 29 September 1917, 1.

59 "100 Radical Papers May Be Suppressed," *New York Times*, 16 September 1917, 7.

60 Vaughn, *Holding Fast the Inner Lines*, 129, 130, 131.

61 Harold J. Tobin and Percy W. Bidwell, *Mobilizing Civilian America* (New York: Council on Foreign Relations, 1940), 16–17.

62 Creel, *How We Advertised America*, 14, 4.

63 Adolf Hitler, *Mein Kampf* (New York: Reynal & Hitchcock, 1941), 234, 235.

64 Ewen, *PR! A Social History of Spin*, 127.

65   Angela Davis, *Angela Davis: An Autobiography* (New York: Random House, 1974), 222.

66   Parmet, *Eisenhower and the American Crusades*, 227.

67   Glenn Frankel, "A Seer's Blind Spots: On George Orwell's 100th, a Look at a Flawed and Fascinating Writer." *Washington Post*, 25 June 2003, C1.

68   J. Edgar Hoover, *Masters of Deceit: The Story of Communism in America and How to Fight It* (New York: Holt, Rinehart and Winston, 1958), 8–9.

69   Hoover, *Masters of Deceit*, 9.

70   Paul Buhle, *Marxism in the United States: Remapping the History of the American Left* (London: Verso, 1987); Margaret Jayko, *FBI on Trial: The Victory of the Socialist Workers Party Suit Against Government Spying* (New York: Pathfinder, 1988).

71   Hoover, *Masters of Deceit*, 319.

72   Joseph A. Loftus, "McCarthy Sticks to Fight on Reds," *New York Times*, 10 July 1952, 21.

73   Of course, this isn't to say that the press in the late-1940s and early-1950s was exactly the same as the press today. There are many important differences between the two periods in terms of technology, economic pressures, and journalistic norms. See: Darrell M. West, *The Rise and Fall of the Media Establishment* (New York: Bedford/ St. Martin's, 2001); McChesney, *The Problem of the Media*.

74   "Hope of Peace Put in a Common Faith," *New York Times*, 24 September 1946, 12

75   "Chamber Opens Campaign To Oust Reds in U.S. Posts," *New York Times*, 10 October 1946, 1.

76   "Committee of Bar Would Expel Reds," *New York Times*, 25 February 1951, 44.

77   "Says Russia Plots to Rule the World," *New York Times*, 13 October 1946, 29.

78   Samuel A. Tower, "All Communists Here Are Spies, Budenz, Once Red, Tells Hearing," *New York Times*, 23 November 1946, 1.

79   "Calls Communists Here 'Soviet Spies,'" *New York Times*, 4 April 1946, 19.

80   Peter Kuznick, *Beyond the Laboratory: Scientists as Political Activists in 1930s America* (Chicago: University of Chicago Press, 1987), 211–218.

81   "Text of the President's Inaugural Address," *New York Times*, 21 January 1949, 4.

82   "Truman Calls Communism 'Crackpot' Political Theory," *New York Times*, 5 April 1951, 19.

83   "Soviet Peace Drive Seen as Deception," *New York Times*, 15 March 1950, 2.

84   James Reston, "General Asks End of All Prejudices," *New York Times*, 4 November 1952.

85   "Allies Scored at Service," *New York Times*, 31 May 1953, 16.

86   Loftus, "McCarthy Sticks to Fight on Reds," 21.

87   "Dies Submits Bill to Outlaw Reds," *New York Times*, 10 February 1953, 23; "Bush Stresses Red Menace," *New York Times*, 11 April 1955, 18.

88   Tower, "All Communists Here Are Spies, Budenz, Once Red, Tells Hearing," 1.

89   "Says Russia Plots to Rule the World," 29.

90   "Calls Communists Here 'Soviet Spies,'" 19.

91   "Budenz Says One Man Runs U.S. Communism," *New York Times*, 14 October 1946, 12.

92   C.P. Trussell, "Red 'Fifth Column' Mines Government, Budenz Testifies," *New York Times*, 3 August 1948, 1.

93   "'No Intention' of Resigning," *New York Times*, 2 August 1954, 7.

94   Joseph A. Loftus, "Eisenhower Signs Red Control Bill, Citing Protection." *New York Times*, 25 August 1954, 1.

95   Rogin, *Ronald Reagan, the Movie*, 72.

96   Gitlin, *The Whole World Is Watching*, 27–28, 116.

97   Jeane J. Kirkpatrick, "Communism in Central America: This Time We Know What's Happening," *Washington Post*, 17 April 1983, D8.

98   William M. LeoGrande, *Our Own Backyard: The United States in Central America, 1977–1992* (Chapel Hill and London: University of North Carolina Press, 1998), 639.

99   Mary McGrory, "Echoes of Red-Baiting," *Washington Post*, 12 June 1983, B1.

100 LeoGrande, *Our Own Backyard*, 215.

101 Philip P. Pan, "China Links bin Laden to Separatists; Report Details Attacks in Mostly Muslim Region," *Washington Post*, 22 January 2002, A8; Elizabeth Rosenthal, "Beijing Says Chinese Muslims Were Trained as Terrorists With Money from bin Laden," *New York Times*, 22 January 2002, A11.

102 In countries such as Russia, this process has deep historical roots. For instance, Stalin purged the old Bolsheviks based on the charge that they were German agents.

103 Carol Pogash and Chris O'Connell, "Antiwar Protest Turns Violent at Port of Oakland: Some Demonstrators Throw Rocks and Bolts at Police, Who Shoot Nonlethal Projectiles, Hitting Protesters as well as Some Longshoremen," *Los Angeles Times*, 8 April 2003, B1.

104 Chris O'Connell, "Panel to Probe Violence at Protest: Demonstrators Against the War in Iraq Complained the Police Fired Rubber Pellets and Other Items into a Crowd without Provocation," *Los Angeles Times*, 27 May 2003.

105 Ibid.

106 Ian Hoffman, "Lockyer: Don't Link Activists, Terrorists," *Oakland Tribune*, 21 May 2003.

107 Ibid., emphasis added.

108 See Section 802 of the USA PATRIOT Act. See: U.S. Congress. Uniting and Strengthening America by Providing the Appropriate Tools Required to Intercept and Obstruct Terrorism Act. Public Law 107-56. This section and other aspects of the PATRIOT Act will be taken up in greater detail later in the book.

109 Edelman, *Constructing the Political Spectacle*, 76.

12
Mass Media Deprecation

1   James Cox and Del Jones, "'This Weird Jamboree' Teamsters and Turtle Protectors on Same Side," *USA Today*, 2 December 1999, A1.

2   Hardt and Negri, *Empire*, 322.

3   The latter term is becoming more widely used. For example, see Benjamin Shepard, "Movement of Movements: Toward a More Democratic Globalization," *New Political Science* 26 (2004): 593–605 and Douglas Bevington and Chris Dixon, "Movement-Relevant Theory: Rethinking Social Movement Scholarship and Activism," *Social Movement Studies* 4 (2005): 185–208.

4   See: Arundhati Roy, "A Writer's Place in Politics," *Alternative Radio*, David Barsamian, ed., Amherst, MA., 15 February 2001.

5   For instance, see Jan Nederveen Pieterse, "Globalization and Collective Action," in *Globalization and Social Movements*, ed. Pierre Hamil, Henri Lustiger-Thaler, Jan Nederveen Pieterse, and Sasha Roseneil (New York: Palgrave, 2001). Social scientists Kevin Michael DeLuca and Jennifer Peeples try to sidestep the inappropriate label "anti-globalization" since, as they put it, "Such media labels are the first step to dismissing the protesters as Luddites, Nativists, simpletons, or unruly college kids who simply are against things and do not understand the realities of the world." Instead they employ the terms "fair trade" and "democratic globalization protesters." While I appreciate the spirit of such re-naming, I assert that fair trade is more of a movement within the larger movement and "democratic globalization protests" sounds like either protesters are disputing democratic globalization or that the protests are democratically organized, which is not always the case. See Kevin Michael DeLuca and Jennifer Peeples, "From Public Sphere to Public Screen: Democracy, Activism, and the 'Violence' of Seattle," *Critical Studies in Media Communication* 19 (2002): 125, 147.

6   Gaye Tuchman, *Making News: A Study in the Construction of Reality* (New York: The Free Press, 1978).

7   Entman, "Framing: Toward Clarification of a Fractured Paradigm," 52.

8   Sanford F. Schram and Joe Soss, "Success Stories: Welfare Reform, Policy Discourse, and the Politics of Research," *Annals of the American Academy of Political and Social Science* 577 (2001): 52.

9   Entman, "Framing: Toward Clarification of a Fractured Paradigm," 55.

10   Nayda Terkildsen and Frauke Schnell, "How Media Frames Move Public Opinion: An Analysis of the Women's Movement," *Political Research Quarterly* 50 (1997): 894.

11   Mike Moore, *A World Without Walls: Freedom, Development, Free Trade and Global Governance* (New York: Cambridge University Press, 2003), 15.

12   James H. Mittelman, *The Globalization Syndrome: Transformation and Resistance* (Princeton, NJ: Princeton University Press, 2000), 6.

13   Robin Broad, *Global Backlash: Citizen Initiatives for a Just World Economy* (Lanham, MD: Rowman & Littlefield Publishers, Inc., 2002). Many commentators have also asserted that globalization, as a general phenomenon, has a history that reaches back centuries. What were the international slave trade or colonialism, if not globalized phenomena of economic integration? See, for example, Broad, *Global Backlash*, 65–76.

14   Recent targets have expanded to include the G8, the Free Trade Area of the Americas (FTAA), and World Economic Forum (WEF).

15   The World Bank and IMF have largely abandoned the term "structural adjustment program" in favor of the phrase "Poverty Reduction Strategy Paper" (PRSP).

16   For a more detailed analysis of the major shortcomings of the WTO, IMF, and World Bank, see Michael Albert, "A Q & A on the WTO, IMF, World Bank, and Activism," *Z Magazine* (January 2000): 24–29.

17   Hardt and Negri, *Empire*, 397.

18   See Michael Albert and Robin Hahnel, *The Political Economy of Participatory Economics* (Princeton, N.J.: Princeton University Press, 1991); Robin Hahnel, *Economic Justice and Democracy: From Competition to Cooperation* (New York: Routledge, 2005); Michael Albert, *Parecon: Life after Capitalism* (New York: Verso, 2003).

19   John McMurtry, *Value Wars: The Global Market Versus the Life Economy* (London: Pluto Press, 2002), 165.

20   For additional alternatives to neoliberal capitalism, see Chapter 4 in Alex Callinicos, *Against the Third Way: An Anti-Capitalist Critique* (Cambridge, U.K.: Polity Press, 2001) and Jeremy Brecher, John Brown Childs, and Jill Cutler, eds., Global Visions: Beyond the New World Order (Boston: South End Press, 1993).

21   Dina Temple-Raston, "Protesters vs. Globalization, Part 2 Rallying Cries Echoing Seattle Arrive in D.C.," *USA Today*, 13 April 2000, 3B.

22   William Solomon, "More Form than Substance: Press Coverage of the WTO

Protests in Seattle," *Monthly Review* 52 (May 2000): 20. Solomon looks at only two newspapers—the *New York Times* and the *Los Angeles Times*—and draws from a total of 57 reports that appeared between 21 November and 21 December 1999. In general, his essay is more impressionistic than systematic.

23   Neil deMause, "Pepper Spray Gets in Their Eyes: Media Missed Militarization of Police Work in Seattle," *Extra!* (March/April 2000). Available online at: http://www.fair.org/index.php?page=1029. Like Solomon, deMause does not carry out a systematic or statistical analysis.

24   Rachel Coen, "For Press, Magenta Hair and Nose Rings Defined Protest," *Extra!* (July/August 2000). Available online at: http://www.fair.org/index. php?page=1037.

25   John Giuffo, "Smoke Gets in Our Eyes: The Globalization Protests and the Befuddled Press," *Columbia Journalism Review*, September/October 2001, 14.

26   DeLuca and Peeples, "From Public Sphere to Public Screen," 144, 141. The authors examine television (CNN, ABC, CBS, and NBC) and newspaper (*New York Times, Washington Post, Los Angeles Times*, and *USA Today*) sources between 28 November and 2 December 1999.

27   Andrew Rojecki, "Modernism, State Sovereignty and Dissent: Media and the New Post-Cold War Movements," *Critical Studies in Mass Communication* 19 (June 2002): 159.

28   These six newspapers constitute the "prestige press" in this study. The following three studies use similar prestige-press configurations to represent the influential elite press Lee Wilkens, "Between facts and values: print media coverage of the greenhouse effect, 1987–1990," *Public Understanding of Science* 2 (1993): 71–84; Craig Trumbo, "Constructing Climate Change: Claims and Frames in US News Coverage of an Environmental Issue," *Public Understanding of Science* 5 (1996): 269–283; and Maxwell T. Boykoff and Jules M. Boykoff, "Balance as Bias: Global Warming and the U.S. Prestige Press," *Global Environmental Change* 15: 2 (2004): 125–136.

29   I arrived at this total of 358 news packets through a two-step process that isolated relevant articles, op-eds, and TV reports. First, I carried out searches via *Lexis-Nexis* and *ABI/Inform* using the aforementioned search terms. This generated a preliminary collection of 732 news packets. Second, I read each article/report so I could detect and eliminate pieces that were extraneous or that considered the protests only peripherally. This second step also involved removing individual stories that, due to quirks in the search engines, were listed twice or more. Letters to the editor, cartoons, and articles that appeared in sections of the newspaper designed for children were also eliminated. This reduction method resulted in the purging of 374 cases, rendering a final universe of 358 relevant newspaper articles, op-eds, and television reports.

30   To measure coding reliability, two individuals independently coded a random

sample of forty media accounts ranging across media type and source. This reliability test led to a 92% coder agreement, a standard that meets accepted criteria for inter-coder reliability. See Allen Rubin and Earl Babbie, *Research Methods for Social Work*, 4th edition (Belmont, CA: Wadsworth, 2000), 192–194.

31 It is worth noting that, generally speaking, what the media really meant when it used the term "violence" was vandalism or property destruction.

32 Steven Greenhouse, "A Carnival of Derision to Greet the Princes of Global Trade," *New York Times*, 29 November 1999, A12.

33 George Lewis, "World Trade Organization To Meet Tomorrow In Seattle," *NBC Nightly News*, 29 November 1999.

34 Paul Waldman, "Why the Media Don't Call It as They See It," *Washington Post*, 28 September 2003, B4.

35 John Burgess and Steven Pearlstein, "Protests Delay WTO Opening; Seattle Police Use Tear Gas; Mayor Declares a Curfew," *Washington Post*, 1 December 1999, A1.

36 John Burgess and Steven Pearlstein, "WTO Ends Conference Well Short Of Goals; Ministers May Resume Talks Early Next Year," *Washington Post*, 4 December 1999, A1.

37 Burgess and Pearlstein, "Protests Delay WTO Opening," A1.

38 Sam Howe Verhovek, "Trade Talks Start in Seattle Despite a Few Disruptions," *New York Times*, 30 November 1999, A14.

39 Lynda Gorov, "Seattle Caught Unprepared for Anarchists," *Boston Globe*, 3 December 1999, A11.

40 Patrick McMahon and James Cox, "'Stop the WTO': Protesters say goal achieved," *USA Today*, 1 December 1999, 19A.

41 Jack Kelley, "In D.C., Police, Protesters Alike Say They're Prepared: Capital Braces for Weekend Demonstrations," *USA Today*, 13 April 2000, A4. CNN anchor Judy Woodruff's comments on the eve of the protests were typical of television coverage that adopted a comparative violence frame: "The anticipation has begun here in Washington as ministers for the World Bank and the International Monetary Fund arrive for their earlier spring meeting. The gathering, which begins Sunday, would normally pass almost unnoticed, but it has become a full-fledged media event as protesters vow to shut down the meetings and observers watch for a possible repeat of the violence in Seattle last fall." Judy Woodruff, "Anticipation Begins in Washington for Protests of IMF and World Bank Meeting," *CNN Worldview*, 14 April 2000.

42 Russ Mitchell, "Police In Washington, DC Ready for Protests against World Bank–IMF Meetings," *CBS Evening News*, 15 April 2000.

43 Frances X. Clines, "Washington Braces to Handle Flood of Globalization Protesters," *New York Times*, 11 April 2000, A5.

44   Dan Rather, "Protest Group Ruckus and What They Hope to Accomplish this Weekend in Washington, DC," *CBS Evening News*, 14 April 2000.

45   Bob Franken, "Police and Protesters Battle for Control of Washington," *CNN Worldview*, 16 April 2000.

46   Petula Dvorak and Michael E. Ruane, "Police, Protesters Claim Victory; Scattered Scuffles and Arrests Punctuate a Largely Peaceful Day," *Washington Post*, 17 April 2000, A1.

47   Alice Ann Love, "Police Raid Protest Headquarters, Say Bomb Material Found," Associated Press, 15 April 2000. Wyatt Andrews, "Police in Washington, DC, Ready for Protests against World Bank–IMF Meetings," *CBS Evening News*, 15 April 2000.

48   Kate Snow, "D.C. Officials Working to Ensure This Year's Meeting of Trade Ministers Not Marred by Violence," *CNN Worldview*, 15 April 2000.

49   Helene Cooper and Michael M. Phillips, "Antiglobalization Forces March in Washington; Police Respond Strongly," *Wall Street Journal*, 17 April 2000, A2.

50   Anne E. Kornblut, "Thousands in Protests against Finance Groups: IMF, World Bank Press on in DC," *Boston Globe*, 17 April 2000, A1.

51   Lee Cowan, "Protesters Battle Washington, DC Police in an Effort to Disrupt Meetings of World Finance Leaders," *CBS Evening News*, 16 April 2000.

52   Anne Swardson, "Trade Body Summit Targeted for Protests; Opponents Accuse WTO of Adding to the World's Ills, Not Helping Solve Them," *Washington Post*, 2 November 1999, A1.

53   John Cochran, "Seattle Police Crackdown On WTO Protesters," *ABC World News Tonight*, 1 December 1999. This sound byte was played repeatedly on television. On ABC television, reporter John Cochran linked this to a disruption of Christmas cheer, grimly noting, "Anyone walking through what should be streets thronged with Christmas shoppers found only destruction."

54   Judy Muller, "WTO Meeting Continues In Seattle Despite Protests," *ABC World News Tonight*, 2 December 1999.

55   "While the WTO Burns," *Wall Street Journal*, 2 December 1999, A22.

56   Andria Hall, "Washington D.C., Site of IMF and World Bank Protests, Heating Up," *CNN Worldview*, 15 April 2000. CNN consistently adopted this frame. In another segment, Bob Franken reported, "Police fully expect the demonstrators to try to block major roadways and disrupt rush hour traffic: a confrontation on still another front in their battle to really disrupt the financial practices of two organizations who claim their goal is to help the poor." See: Bob Franken, "Police and Protesters Battle for Control of Washington," *CNN Worldview*, 16 April 2000.

57   Helene Cooper, Jake Bleed, and Jerry Guidera, "Protesters Can't Stop World Bank Parley, But Do Disrupt Downtown Washington," *Wall Street Journal*, 18 April 2000, A20.

58 Steve Twomey, "Businesses Lock Up, Batten Down for Protests," *Washington Post*, 15 April 2000, A1. Not only did mass-media outlets report on the inconvenience that the protests presented to DC's citizenry and the projected pecuniary losses for local businesses, but they also discussed the costs that it would mean for the already financially beleaguered city. For instance, *CBS Morning News* noted that "Thirty-five hundred officers from six departments are on patrol" and that Washington, DC "spent $ 1 million on riot gear." Lisa Hughes, "Washington Prepares for Another Day of Protests Against the IMF and World Bank Meetings," *CBS Morning News*, 17 April 2000.

59 Brit Hume, "Political Headlines," *Special Report with Brit Hume*, Fox, 17 April 2000.

60 See: Steve Twomey, "Businesses Lock Up, Batten Down for Protests," *Washington Post*, 15 April 2000, A1; and "Protest Q & A," *Washington Post*, 17 April 2000, A6.

61 Robin Broad, "Of Magenta Hair, Nose Rings, and Naiveté," in *Global Backlash: Citizen Initiatives for a Just World Economy*, ed. Robin Broad (Lanham, MD: Rowman & Littlefield Publishers, Inc., 2002), 1.

62 These totals surely would have been higher had I not been working almost exclusively with television transcripts. Television images often feature this media frame, but with transcripts, such images rarely register.

63 Greenhouse, "A Carnival of Derision to Greet the Princes of Global Trade," A12.

64 Patrick McMahon, "WTO Under Fire on Many Fronts," *USA Today*, 29 November 1999, A6.

65 Katharine Barrett, "Protesters in Seattle Disrupting WTO Conference 'Looked Like a Group That Was Out of Control,' Says Jasinowski," *CNN Today*, 30 November 1999.

66 Brit Hume, "Political Headlines," *Special Report with Brit Hume*, Fox, 17 April 2000.

67 Jim Stewart, "Security in Washington Tightens in Effort to Deal with Numerous Groups of Protesters," *CBS The Early Show*, 14 April 2000.

68 Fred Francis, "Thousands of Protesters Converge in Washington Trying to Shut Down World Bank and IMF Meetings," *NBC Nightly News*, 16 April 2000.

69 David Montgomery, "Demonstrators Are United By Zeal for 'Global Justice,'" *Washington Post*, 16 April 2000, A1. This excerpt also serves as the quintessence of the amalgam of grievances frame, which will be discussed below. Similarly, Brit Hume of Fox News described the scenario in Washington, DC this way: "The scenes on the streets of Washington these past two days, richly reminiscent of the counter-culture of the '60s and '70s, have served as a reminder that some old ideas not only never die, they never quite even fade away.

The Vietnam era turned millions of young Americans off not only on the U.S. government but the U.S. system of government and on capitalism. More than a quarter of a century later, with the cold war over and capitalism and free markets spreading worldwide, young people are once more in the streets, wearing cotton bandanas and multi-colored hair." Guest David Horowitz said that what motivated these protesters was the search for a "narcissistic high." See: Hume, "Political Headlines," 2000.

70   Dvorak and Ruane, "Police, Protesters Claim Victory," A1.

71   Jack Kelley and Yasmin Anwar, "IMF Protests Fizzle in D.C. Drizzle," *USA Today*, 18 April 2000, 3A.

72   Jonathan Yardley, "They Doth Protest Too Much," *Washington Post*, 17 April 2000, C2.

73   Michael Kelly, "Imitation Activism," *Washington Post*, 19 April 2000, A27.

74   George Melloan, "Welcome to the Seattle World's Fair, Circa 1999," *Wall Street Journal*, 30 November 1999, A27.

75   David Frum, "Protesting, but Why?" *New York Times*, 19 April 2000, A23. Frum went on to say, "How could they be expected to trundle through the cold and wet to listen to some Andean Marxist dude rail against the privatization of the Bolivian waterworks in whatever language it is that they speak in Bolivia? So Round Two of the great mobilization against globalization ended in a squelch rather than in the photogenic violence of Seattle."

76   Joseph Kahn, "Seattle Protesters Are Back, With a New Target," *New York Times*, 9 April 2000, A6.

77   Kyra Phillips, "Anti-Globalization Protesters March Through Washington During IMF and World Bank Meetings," *CNN Sunday Morning*, 16 April 2000.

78   Darryl Fears, "Poetry Slams, Speeches, Posters, Rallies: All Efforts Fail to Get Black D.C. Activists Involved in IMF Fight," *Washington Post*, 15 April 2000, B1.

79   Helene Cooper, "Some Hazy, Some Erudite and All Angry—Diversity of WTO Protests Makes Them Hard to Dismiss," *Wall Street Journal*, 30 November 1999, A2.

80   Not only are protesters portrayed as uninformed when it comes to the causes they are contesting, but they have also been dubbed naïve for their willingness to be taken advantage of by interest groups with agendas. For example, an editorial in the *Wall Street Journal* asserted that "To begin with, we might stop referring to those who took to the streets on Tuesday as 'protesters'; it's far too generous a term. Plainly the Seattle activists are being used as shock troops by special interests trying to protect their own privileges at the expense of workers in the rest of the world." See: "While the WTO Burns," 1999.

81   James Cox and Del Jones, "'This Weird Jamboree' Teamsters and Turtle

Protectors on Same Side," *USA Today*, 2 December 1999, A1.

82 Juju Chang, "WTO Protests Lead to Seattle Curfew," *ABC World News Now*, 1 December 1999.

83 Francis X. Clines, "A New Age Protest Tackles Globalism With Polite Chants," *New York Times*, 14 April 2000, A13.

84 Brian Wilson, "Protesters Fail to Shut Down IMF/World Bank Meetings," *The Edge with Paula Zahn*, Fox, 17 April 2000.

85 Montgomery, "Demonstrators Are United By Zeal for 'Global Justice,'" A1.

86 George Melloan, "Welcome to the Seattle World's Fair, Circa 1999," *Wall Street Journal*, 30 November 1999, A27.

87 John Micklethwait and Adrian Wooldridge, "World Trade Organization; Skewered in Seattle; Fringe Protesters at Center of Global Mainstream," *Los Angeles Times*, 5 December 1999, 1.

88 Thomas L. Friedman, "Senseless in Seattle," *New York Times*, 1 December 1999, A23.

89 Hume, "Political Headlines," 2000.

90 See Alex Callinicos, *An Anti-Capitalist Manifesto* (Cambridge, UK: Polity Press, 2003).

91 Shepard, "Movement of Movements," 596.

92 Kate O'Neill, "Transnational Protest: States, Circuses, and Conflict at the Frontline of Global Politics," *International Studies Review* 6 (2004): 240.

93 Cox and Jones, "'This Weird Jamboree' Teamsters and Turtle Protectors on Same Side," A1.

94 "A Failure to Communicate; The World Trade Organization is Widely Misunderstood, and It Hasn't Helped Its Own Case. But It Isn't a Global Ogre," *Los Angeles Times*, 2 December 1999, 10.

95 Francis Fukuyama, "The Left Should Love Globalization," *Wall Street Journal*, 1 December 1999, A26.

96 Michael Medved, "Battle in Seattle: No, This Wasn't the '60s All Over Again," *USA Today*, 7 December 1999, 19A.

97 Jim Stewart, "Security in Washington Tightens in Effort to Deal with Numerous Groups of Protesters."

98 Twomey, "Businesses Lock Up, Batten Down for Protests,." A1.

99 Blake Morrison, "IMF Protesters' Goals as Varied as Their Styles," *USA Today*, 14 April 2000, A4.

100 James Taranto, "Global Village Idiots," *Wall Street Journal*, 18 April 2000, A18.

101 Joseph Kahn, "Global Trade Forum Reflects A Burst of Conflict and Hope," *New York Times*, 28 November 1999, A1.

102 Joseph Kahn, "Globalization Unifies Its Many-Striped Foes," *New York Times*, 15 April 2000, A7.

103 Fred Francis, "More Arrests and Disruptions Outside World Bank and International Monetary Fund Meetings," *NBC Nightly News*, 17 April 2000.

104 Hume, *Special Report with Brit Hume*, 1999.

105 Jim Sciutto, "Protesters Continue Attempts to Disrupt Talks of World Bank and International Monetary Fund," *ABC Good Morning America*, 17 April 2000.

106 "Protesters Target Institutions Most Able to Help the Poor," *USA Today*, 14 April 2000, A14.

107 Sebastian Mallaby, "D-Day in Washington," *Washington Post*, 24 March 2000, A23.

108 "Stopping the World," *New York Times*, 15 April 2000, A16. In another sweeping assertion, the *CBS Sunday Morning* show noted that "the same hodge-podge of protest groups" who were in Seattle would be in DC. These dissidents "all believe loans made by the World Bank support harmful trends in global trade and development." Wyatt Andrews, "Demonstrators in the Nation's Capital Hope to Disrupt World Bank and International Monetary Fund Meetings," *CBS Sunday Morning*, 16 April 2000.

109 Jim Stewart, "Thousands of People Gather in Washington to Protest Against Everything from World Trade to Defending Sea Turtles," *CBS Morning News*, 14 April 2000.

110 Gerald F. Seib, J.C. Conklin, and John Hechinger, "WTO—Clash in Seattle: Most Americans Don't Show Distrust of Free Trade," *Wall Street Journal*, 2 December 1999, A8.

111 DeLuca and Peeples, "From Public Sphere to Public Screen," 147, footnote 1.

112 Ibid., 139, 140.

113 Rojecki, "Modernism, State Sovereignty and Dissent," 161. In terms of mass-media sources, Rojecki looks at *USA Today*, CBS, and op-ed commentaries from the *New York Times*, *Los Angeles Times*, and *Washington Post*, whereas the present study considers a much wider range of news outlets.

114 DeLuca and Peeples, "From Public Sphere to Public Screen," 142.

115 The five-sentence test might have been too generous on my part. I even counted somewhat general statements like "demonstrators have descended on Washington to target the World Bank and IMF for joining forces with the WTO as part of a "global troika" exploiting workers and lesser-developed nations." See: Dina Temple-Raston, "Protesters vs. Globalization, Part 2 Rallying Cries Echoing Seattle arrive in D.C.," 3B. This *USA Today* article was one of two covering the World Bank / IMF protests that offered more than five sentences of explanation of movement goals and issues (the other appeared in the *Washington Post*). With Seattle coverage, a number of the articles that passed the five-sentence test only did so because President Bill Clinton, who spoke in Seattle during the WTO meetings, voiced many of the same critiques as the

protesters. See, for example, David E. Sanger, "President Chides World Trade Body in Seattle," *New York Times*, 2 December 1999, A1.

116 Of the eight in-depth newspaper accounts from Seattle, one appeared in the *Boston Globe*, two in the *Los Angeles Times*, four in the *New York Times*, and one in *USA Today*. While of the six television segments, one appeared on ABC, four on CNN, and one on Fox. As for the DC protests, the two in-depth newspaper articles were published in the *Washington Post* and *USA Today*, while both television segments were aired on CNN.

117 For an example, see George Lewis, "Seattle Still Under Curfew This Morning after Protesters of World Trade Organization Became Violent Last Night," *NBC Today*, 1 December 1999.

118 Furthermore, in the case of the World Bank / IMF protests in DC, three of the four in-depth stories appeared before any violence broke out in the streets.

119 Rojecki, "Modernism, State Sovereignty and Dissent," 167.

120 DeLuca and Peeples, "From Public Sphere to Public Screen," 140–143

121 John Kifner, "In This Washington, No 'Seattle' Is Found, by Police or Protesters," *New York Times*, 19 April 2000, A16.

122 Rojecki, "Modernism, State Sovereignty and Dissent," 166.

123 See: Jonathan Peterson, "A World of Difference in Trade Views; Economy: Question of Individual Rights versus Profits Raised as Nations Gather in Seattle," *Los Angeles Times*, 28 November 1999, 1; Temple-Raston, "Protesters vs. Globalization, Part 2 Rallying Cries Echoing Seattle Arrive in D.C.," 3B.

124 Malcolm Spector and John Kitsuse, *Constructing Social Problems* (Menlo Park, CA: Cummings, 1977).

125 Wisler and Giugni, "Under the Spotlight." 173.

126 Ibid., 181.

13
Mass Media Underestimation, False Balance, and Disregard

1 Small, *Covering Dissent*, 22, 172–173, 162.

2 Gitlin, *The Whole World Is Watching*, 82, 95, 28.

3 Oliver and Myers, "How Events Enter the Public Sphere," 72; Small, *Covering Dissent*, 20–21.

4 Scott Bowles, "Park Police Can Count On A Disputed Crowd Figure: Aerial Photos, Bus Tallies Crucial to Accuracy" *Washington Post*, 15 October 1995, B1.

5 Small, *Covering Dissent*, 22.

6 Bowles, "Park Police Can Count On A Disputed Crowd Figure," B1.

7 Sari Horwitz and Hamil R. Harris, "Farrakhan Threatens To Sue Park Police Over March Count," *Washington Post*, 18 October 1995, A8.

8   Sari Horwitz and Christopher B. Daly, "Scientist Fans March Dispute, Counts 870,000," *Washington Post*, 20 October 1995, A1.

9   Leef Smith and Wendy Melillo, "If It's Crowd Size You Want, Park Service Says Count It Out; Congress Told Agency to Stop, Official Says," *Washington Post*, 13 October 1996, A34.

10   Edelman, *The Symbolic Uses of Politics*; Bennett, *News: The Politics of Illusion*.

11   Ross Gelbspan, *The Heat Is On* (Cambridge, MA: Perseus Books, 1998), 57–58.

12   Entman, *Democracy Without Citizens*, 30.

13   Gans, *Deciding What's News*, 175.

14   Hallin, *The Uncensored War*, 68.

15   Small, *Covering Dissent*, 22.

16   Cunningham, "Re-thinking Objectivity," 26.

17   Pierre Bourdieu, *On Television*, 29.

18   Bennett, *News: The Politics of Illusion*, 46.

19   Gitlin, *The Whole World Is Watching*, 27.

20   Small, *Covering Dissent*, 55, 58, 69; Gitlin, *The Whole World Is Watching*, 114–115.

21   Roland Barthes, *Mythologies* (New York: Farrar, Strauss & Giroux, 1972), 110. For a compelling analysis that builds from the work of Barthes as it explores how photographs add "dimensions of meaning to a text," see Stuart Hall, "The Determinations of News Photographs," in *The Manufacture of News: A Reader*, ed. Stanley Cohen and Jock Young (Beverly Hills, CA: SAGE Publications, 1973).

22   Gitlin, *The Whole World Is Watching*, 47–48.

23   David L. Paletz and Robert M. Entman, *Media Power Politics* (New York: The Free Press, 1981), 128.

24   Oliver and Maney, "Political Processes and Local Newspaper Coverage of Protest Events," 465.

25   Shanto Iyengar and Donald R. Kinder, *News That Matters: Television and American Opinion* (Chicago and London: The University of Chicago Press, 1987); Lawrence Jacobs and Robert Shapiro, "Issues, Candidate Image, and Priming: The Use of Private Polls in Kennedy's 1960 Presidential Campaign." *American Political Science Review* 88 (1994): 527–540.

26   David Snyder and William R. Kelly, "Conflict Intensity, Media Sensitivity and the Validity of Newspaper Data," *American Sociological Review* 42 (1977): 105–123; Herman and Chomsky, *Manufacturing Consent*; Parenti, *Inventing Reality*; Entman, *Democracy Without Citizens*; Gans, *Deciding What's News*.

27   Oliver and Maney, "Political Processes and Local Newspaper Coverage of Protest Events"; Oliver and Myers, "How Events Enter the Public Sphere"; John D. McCarthy, Clark McPhail, and Jackie Smith, "Images of Protest: Dimensions

of Selection Bias in Media Coverage of Washington Demonstrations, 1982 and 1991," *American Sociological Review* 61 (1996): 488.

28 Jackie Smith, John D. McCarthy, Clark McPhail, and Boguslaw Augustyn, "From Protest to Agenda Building: Description Bias in Media Coverage of Events in Washington, D.C.," *Social Forces* 79 (2001): 1401.

29 McCarthy, McPhail, and Smith, "Images of Protest."

30 Oliver and Myers, "How Events Enter the Public Sphere," 51, 53.

31 Oliver and Maney, "Political Processes and Local Newspaper Coverage of Protest Events," 475, 481.

32 Oliver and Myers, "How Events Enter the Public Sphere," 72.

33 Downey and Rasmussen, "Vietnam: Press, Protest, and the Presidency," 193.

34 Small, *Covering Dissent*, 21. The mass media's disregard of social movements is not, of course, unique to the United States. For instance, Brian McNair demonstrates how in the 1980s the British press gave the peace movement "surprisingly little coverage." See: Brian McNair, *Images of the Enemy: Reporting the New Cold War* (New York: Routledge, 1988), Chapter 8, 159.

35 Edward S. Herman, "Diversity of News: Marginalizing the Opposition," *Journal of Communication* 35 (1985): 135–146; Herman and Chomsky, *Manufacturing Consent*.

36 Herman, "Diversity of News," 145.

37 Justin Lewis, *Constructing Public Opinion: How Political Elites Do What They Like and Why We Seem to Go Along with It* (New York: Columbia University Press, 2001), Chapter 2, 73, 66.

38 Daniel Hallin, "The Media, the War in Vietnam, and Political Support," 13, 14.

39 John Ward Anderson, "Poor Nations' Leaders Back Washington Protesters: Group Says IMF and World Bank Policies 'Stabilized Poverty,'" *Washington Post*, 16 April 2000, A31.

40 Another aspect of "relative disregard" dovetails with the previous mode of suppression: mass media deprecation. While protesters themselves—pink hair, piercings and all—may not be disregarded, often their ideas are.

41 Daniel Eisenberg, "We're Taking Him Out," *Time* magazine, 13 May 2002, 36.

42 Bob Woodward and Dan Balz, "'We Will Rally the World': Bush and His Advisers Set Objectives, but Struggled With How to Achieve Them," *Washington Post*, 28 January 2002, A1.

43 Nancy Marshall, "Protests Against a Possible War in Iraq Taking Place Around the Country," *NPR Weekend All Things Considered*, 26 October 2002.

44 Lynette Clemetson, "Thousands March in Washington Against Going to War in Iraq," *New York Times*, 27 October 2002, A8.

45 Ibid.

46   Daniel Williams, "Anti-War Activists Protest in Florence: Thousands Denounce U.S. Iraq Policy," *Washington Post*, 10 November 2002, A26.

47   Michael Powell, "In New York, Thousands Protest a War Against Iraq," *Washington Post*, 16 February 2003, A22.

48   John Seigenthaler, "American Protests against War with Iraq," *NBC Nightly News*, 15 February 2003. To NBC's credit, after making the negative comparison to European protests, Seigenthaler went on to say that the U.S. demonstrations "were among the largest anti-war protests seen in the U.S. since the Vietnam War."

49   Alan Cowell, "Thousands Denounce War and the United States in Cities Around the World," *New York Times*, 23 March 2003, B11.

50   Ian Shapira, "On the Mall, Songs of Old Carry Current Plea for Peace: Familiar Faces Protest Potential Action in Iraq," *Washington Post*, 17 March 2003, B1.

51   John Tagliabue, "Wave of Protests, from Europe to New York," *New York Times*, 21 March 2003, A1.

52   Michael Cabanatuan, Kevin Fagan, and Erin Hallissy, "Troops, War Policy Supported at Local Rallies," *San Francisco Chronicle*, 24 March 2003, W11.

53   Nancy Trejos and Timothy Dwyer, "Supporters Soldier On To Back Bush, Troops And Counter-Protests; Thousands Travel to Washington to Voice Views," *Washington Post*, 13 April 2003, A39; Manny Fernandez and Linda Perlstein, "Marchers Bring New Signs, Same Passion; War Protesters, Bush Supporters Rally in Washington," *Washington Post*, 13 April 2003, A25.

54   For example, see Douglas Jehl, "Across Country, Thousands Gather to Back U.S. Troops and Policy," *New York Times,* 24 March 2003.

55   McCarthy and McPhail, "The Institutionalization of Protest in the United States"; Bennett, *News: The Politics of Illusion.*

56   Clemetson, "Thousands March in Washington Against Going to War in Iraq," A8.

57   Code Pink describes itself as "a women initiated grassroots peace and social justice movement that seeks positive social change through proactive, creative protest and non-violent direct action." See: www.codepink4peace.org.

58   Robert Tomshow, Jim Carlton, and Dan Bilefsky, "The Assault on Iraq: Antiwar Protests Intensify in U.S., Abroad—Civil Disobedience Snarls Several American Cities; Big Rallies in Spain, Greece," *Wall Street Journal*, 21 March 2003, A6.

59   Sylvia Moreno and Lena H. Sun, "In Effort to Keep the Peace, Protesters Declare 'Code Pink,'" *Washington Post*, 9 March 2003, C1.

60   Michael Getler, "Listening to a Different Drummer," *Washington Post*, 3 November 2003, B6.

61   Ibid.

62   Wisler and Giugni, "Under the Spotlight," 184.

63   Ibid.

14
The Suppression of Dissent after 9 / 11

1   Karl Marx, *The Eighteenth Brumaire of Louis Bonaparte* (New York: International Publishers, 1991), 15.
2   Stone, *Perilous Times*, 551.
3   Heidi Boghosian, *The Assault on Free Speech, Public Assembly, and Dissent: A Lawyers Guild Report on Government Violations of First Amendment Rights in the United States* (Great Barrington, MA: The North River Press Publishing Corporation, 2004), 5.
4   Kristian Williams, *American Methods: Torture and the Logic of Domination* (Cambridge, MA: South End Press, 2006), 169, 170.
5   Stone, *Perilous Times*, 556, 557.
6   "Talks on free-trade zone draw protests in Miami," *Seattle Times*, 21 November 2003, A12.
7   Boghosian, *The Assault on Free Speech, Public Assembly, and Dissent*, 67.
8   Jeremy Scahill, "Mayhem in Miami," *Democracy Now!*, 21 November 2003.
9   Naomi Klein, "America's Enemy Within: Armed Checkpoints, Embedded Reporters in Flak Jackets, Brutal Suppression of Peaceful Demonstrators. Baghdad? No, Miami," *Guardian*, 26 November 2003.
10   Scahill, "Mayhem in Miami."
11   Ana Nogueira, "DN! Producer Ana Nogueira Among 250 Arrested in Miami FTAA Protests," *Democracy Now!*, 24 November 2003.
12   Kirk Nielsen, "Headbangers Ball: Claims that Police Didn't Aim at FTAA protesters' Upper Bodies Get a Black Eye," *Miami New Times*, 11 December 2003.
13   *City of Miami Civilian Investigative Panel Report on the Free Trade Area of the Americas Summit*, 20 July 2006. Available online at: http://ci.miami.fl.us/cip/Downloads/FTAAReport.pdf. See page 12 for conviction total (as of January 2006).
14   Ibid., 12.
15   Ibid.; Tristram Korten, "Pick Your Reality: Either FTAA Protesters Viciously Assaulted Police, or Police Viciously Assaulted Protesters." *Miami New Times*, 4 December 2003.
16   Ashley Fantz, "The FTAA Tapes: A Police Training Video Showed High-Ranking Broward Deputies Laughing about Shooting Rubber Bullets at a Coral Gables Attorney at the Free-Trade Summit," *Miami Herald*, 9 August 2006.

17 "Florida Police Chief Sorry For Laughing At FTAA Shooting Victim," *Democracy Now!*, 11 August 2006.

18 Michael Vasquez, "Miami to Pay $180,000 to Man Injured During Free Trade Protest," *Miami Herald*, 12 September 2006.

19 Amnesty International, "Amnesty International's Continuing Concerns about Taser Use," February 2006. Available online at: http://www.amnestyusa.org/countries/usa/document.do?id=ENGAMR510302006

20 "Police Shot Protester in NC With a Taser; Six Arrested," *Democracy Now!*, 26 September 2006.

21 Amy Goodman, "Police Shoot Protesters With Tasers at Pittsburgh Demo Against Jeb Bush & Sen. Rick Santorum," *Democracy Now!*, 9 October 2006.

22 Jeremy Scahill, "The Miami Model: Paramilitaries, Embedded Journalists and Illegal Protests," *CounterPunch*, 24 November 2003. Available online: http://www.counterpunch.org/scahill11242003.html

23 Matthew Rothschild, "Police Shoot Pepper Balls at Oregon Demonstrators," *McCarthy Watch*, 21 October 2004. Available online: http://www.progressive.org/mag_mc_pepper

24 Ibid.; Beth Quinn, "ACLU Decries Use of Force by Police at Bush Event," *Oregonian*, 7 January 2005, E5.

25 American Civil Liberties Union, "ACLU of Oregon Files Lawsuit Challenging Secret Service & Local Police Breakup of Demonstration During 2004 Bush Visit to Jacksonville," 6 July 2006. See: http://www.aclu-or.org/site/DocServer/moss_press_release_7_06.pdf?docID=1621

26 Michael Powell, "No Choice but Guilty: Lackawanna Case Highlights Legal Tilt," *Washington Post*, 29 July 2003, A1.

27 Ibid.

28 Amy Goodman, "As Sentencing in the Lackawanna 6 Case Begins, A U.S. Court Rejects Law That Criminalizes Unknowingly Supporting a Terrorist Organization," *Democracy Now!*, 4 December 2003.

29 Matthew Purdy and Lowell Bergman, "Where the Trail Led: Between Evidence and Suspicion; Unclear Danger: Inside the Lackawanna Terror Case," *New York Times*, 12 October 2003, 1.

30 Andrew Kramer, "U.S. Authorities Arrest Six Men on Terror Charges, Investigation Focused on Oregon," Associated Press, 4 October 2002.

31 Julie Sullivan, "Terror Case Stuns Those Who Know Suspects," *Oregonian*, 6 October 2002, A1. Habis Abdulla al Saoub—a Jordanian—was the one non-U.S.-born suspect.

32 Mark Larabee, "Hillsboro Man Faces Charges in Plot to Aid al-Qaida, Taliban," *Oregonian*, 28 April 2003, A1.

33 Andrew Kramer, "Federal Officials Accuse Six of Plotting to Fight U.S. Troops in Afghanistan," Associated Press, 5 October 2002.

34 Noelle Crombie, "Portland 7 Figure Gets 7 Years for Taliban Aid," *Oregonian*, 10 February 2004, A1.

35 Blaine Harden and Dan Eggen, "Duo Pleads Guilty to Conspiracy Against U.S.: Last of the 'Portland 7' Face 18 Years in Prison," *Washington Post*, 17 October 2003, A3.

36 Mark Larabee, "Hawash's Plea Gives Prosecutors Vital Voice," *Oregonian*, 9 August 2003, A1.

37 Noelle Crombie, "Portland 7 Figure Gets 7 Years for Taliban Aid," A1.

38 Harden and Eggen, "Duo Pleads Guilty to Conspiracy Against U.S.," A3.

39 See: http://www.fbi.gov/hq/nsb/nsb_brochure.htm. Visited 27 December 2006.

40 Robert Mueller, Testimony of Robert S. Mueller, III, Director, Federal Bureau of Investigation, Before the United States Senate Committee on the Judiciary, May 20, 2004. Available online: http://www.fbi.gov/congress/congress04/mueller052004.htm

41 Mark Larabee, "'Portland 7' Pair Explain Actions," *Oregonian*, 25 November 2003, A1.

42 Nick Budnick, "The Making of a 'Terrorist,'" *Willamette Week*, 16 October 2002.

43 "ACLU Wants Apology to VA Employee Investigated on 'Sedition,'" Associated Press, 1 February 2006; Miguel Navrot, "ACLU Protests VA 'Sedition' Memo to Nurse," *Albuquerque Journal*, 2 February 2006, A1.

44 "Bingaman Wants Probe into VA 'Sedition' Investigation of Nurse," Associated Press, 7 February 2006.

45 Matthew Rothschild, "'Seditious' VA Nurse Cleared," *McCarthy Watch*, 21 April 2006. Available online: http://progressive.org/mag_mc020806

46 Amy Goodman, "V.A. Nurse Accused of Sedition After Publishing Letter Critical of Bush on Katrina, Iraq," *Democracy Now!*, 2 March 2006.

47 Chris McGann, "Reichert Once Bragged He Ratted Out Bus Driver," *Seattle Post-Intelligencer*, 4 November 2006, A1.

48 Matthew Rothschild, "Union Appeals Firing of Bus Driver Who Flipped Off Bush," *McCarthy Watch*, 5 November 2006. Available online: http://www.progressive.org/mag_mc110506. Whether Congress member Reichert was telling the truth or engaging in some imaginary braggadocio is somewhat in question. Some say the bus driver was already on her way out the door.

49 "Muslim Scholar Barred by U.S. Denies Support For Terrorism," *New York Times*, 26 September 2006, A13.

50 Amy Goodman, "Bush Administration Says Prominent Muslim Scholar Can't Teach in the US Because He Donated to Palestinian Charity," *Democracy Now!*, 28 September 2006.

51 David Epstein, "Another Scholar Turned Back at JFK," *Inside Higher Ed*, 21

June 2006. Available online: http://insidehighered.com/news/2006/06/21/
milios. Zweig's statement is available in its entirety online at: https://naples.
cc.sunysb.edu/CAS/wcm.nsf/JohnMiliosStatement.pdf

52   Joshua Frank, "Without Cause: Yale Fires An Acclaimed Anarchist Scholar,
     An Interview with David Graeber," CounterPunch, 13 May 2005. Available
     online at: http://www.counterpunch.org/frank05132005.html

53   Matt Apuzzo, "Professor Points to Politics as Yale Fails to Renew Contract,"
     Associated Press, 23 October 2005.

54   Jamie Wilson, "Protests at Yale over Sacking of Rebel Professor," Guardian, 25
     October 2005, 22.

55   David Graeber, "Yale's Unusual Decision Left Me Little Recourse," Wall Street
     Journal, 13 January 2006, A13; Matt Apuzzo, "Anarchist Professor Drops
     Appeal, Will Leave Yale," Associated Press, 8 December 2005.

56   "Bourgeois Anarchy," Wall Street Journal, 3 January 2006, A24.

57   Karen W. Arenson, "When Scholarship and Politics Collided at Yale," New
     York Times, 28 December 2005, B1.

58   John Vaughan, "Fox News Program Links USF to Terrorists," Tampa Tribune,
     28 September 2001.

59   Richard Leiby, "Talking Out of School: Was an Islamic Professor Exercising
     His Freedom or Promoting Terror?" Washington Post, 28 July 2002, F1.

60   John Mintz, "Professor Indicted as Terrorist Leader," Washington Post, 21
     February 2003, A1.

61   Judy Genshaft, "USF Must Sever All Ties to Al-Arian," Tampa Tribune, 2
     March 2003, 1.

62   "Firing of Professor Draws Condemnation," Los Angeles Times, 15 June 2003,
     A18.

63   Elaine Silvestrini, "Judge Says Al-Arian Trial Stays In Tampa," Tampa Tribune,
     24 May 2005, Metro Section, 1.

64   Eric Lichtblau, "Ex-Professor Is Called Terrorist Leader," New York Times, 7
     June 2005, A3.

65   Meg Laughlin, Jennifer Liberto, and Justin George, "8 Times, Al-Arian Hears
     'Not Guilty,'" St. Petersburg Times, 7 December 2005, 1A.

66   Spencer S. Hsu, "Former Fla. Professor to Be Deported," Washington Post, 18
     April 2006, A3. This also meant federal prosecutors did not intend to retry
     Al-Arian on the eight counts that resulted in a mistrial.

67   Elaine Silvestrini, "Judge Rebukes, Sentences Al-Arian," Tampa Tribune, 2
     May 2006, 1.

68   Amy Goodman, "Daughter of Sami Al-Arian Says Family 'Devastated' by
     Father's Continued Imprisonment, Blasts Media Coverage," Democracy Now!,
     3 May 2006.

69   Meg Laughlin, "Al-Arian Gets More Prison Time," St. Petersburg Times, 17

November 2006, 4B; Jerry Markon, "Witness Is Silent in Terror Probe; Ex-Professor Says Grand Jury Testimony Would Endanger Him," *Washington Post*, 14 November 2006, B5.

70   Churchill, *A Little Matter of Genocide*, 11.

71   George Merritt and Howard Pankratz, "Prof's Essay Spurs Board Session," *Denver Post*, 31 January 2005, B1.

72   Michelle York, "Professor Is Assailed By Legislature And Vandals," *New York Times*, 3 February 2005, B6.

73   Howard Pankratz, "Ward Churchill Resigns as Head of CU's Ethnic-Studies Department," *Denver Post*, 1 February 2005, A1.

74   Arthur Kane, "Churchill Keeps His Job but a Second Probe Looms," *Denver Post*, 25 March 2005, A1.

75   University of Colorado, "Report of the Investigative Committee of the Standing Committee on Research Misconduct at the University of Colorado at Boulder concerning Allegations of Academic Misconduct against Professor Ward Churchill," 9 May 2006. Available online at: http://www.colorado.edu/news/reports/churchill/churchillreport051606.html. Quotations come from 87, 101.

76   Ibid., 86.

77   Ibid., 94.

78   Jennifer Brown, "CU Moves to Fire Churchill," *Denver Post*, 27 June 2006, A1.

79   Manny Gonzales, "Churchill Appeals Suggestion that CU Fire Him," *Denver Post*, 6 July 2006, B1.

80   Amy Goodman, "Ward Churchill Defends His Academic Record & Vows to Fight to Keep His Job at University of Colorado," *Democracy Now!*, 27 September 2006.

81   Stone, *Perilous Times*, 555.

82   Neil A. Lewis, "Ashcroft Permits F.B.I. to Monitor Internet and Public Activities," *New York Times*, 31 May 2002, A20.

83   Boghosian, *The Assault on Free Speech, Public Assembly, and Dissent*, 30.

84   Karen Branch-Brioso, "Looser Rules Spark Old Fears," *St. Louis Post-Dispatch* (Missouri), 2 June 2002, B1.

85   Eric Lichtblau, "FBI Scrutinizes Antiwar Rallies," *New York Times*, 23 November 2003, A1; Curt Anderson, "Groups Question FBI Protest Monitoring," Associated Press, 23 November 2003.

86   Eric Lichtblau, "Large Volume of FBI Files Alarms U.S. Activist Groups," *New York Times*, 18 July 2005, A12.

87   Nicholas Riccardi, "FBI Keeps Watch on Activists," *Los Angeles Times*, 27 March 2006.

88   Peter Nicholas, "State Tracked Protesters in the Name of Security," *Los Angeles Times*, 1 July 2006.

89 The ACLU had a thorough online resource that details the surveillance of activists in Colorado. See: http://www.aclu-co.org/spyfiles/chronology.htm. See also, Matthew Rothschild, "Red Squad Hits Denver," *McCarthy Watch*, 14 March 2002. Available online at: http://progressive.org/mag_mcdenver

90 Dan Eggen, "Protesters Subjected To 'Pretext Interviews': FBI Memo Shows No Specific Threats," *Washington Post*, 18 May 2005, A4.

91 "Pennsylvania Peace Group, ACLU Accuse FBI Of Improper Surveillance," *The Frontrunner*, 15 March 2006.

92 Paula Reed Ward, "Peace Group Claims FBI Spied on Activity," *Pittsburgh Post-Gazette*, 15 March 2006, B1.

93 Amy Goodman, "Newly Released Files Reveal FBI Spied on PA Peace Group Because of Antiwar Views," *Democracy Now!*, 15 March 2006.

94 Curt Anderson, "Groups Question FBI Protest Monitoring," Associated Press, 23 November 2003.

95 Brian Williams, "Pentagon Gathering Intelligence on US War Protestors," *NBC Nightly News*, 13 December 2005.

96 Eric Lichtblau, "Documents Reveal Scope of U.S. Database on Antiwar Protests," *New York Times*, 13 October 2006, A16.

97 Michael Isikoff, "The Other Big Brother," *Newsweek*, 30 January 2006. To see an actual TALON document, go to: http://progressive.org/images/articles/060703-dod_foia-2.pdf

98 James Risen and Eric Lichtblau, "Bush Lets U.S. Spy on Callers Without Courts," *New York Times*, 16 December 2005, A1.

99 Jules Boykoff, "Some Calm in the Eye of the Surveillance Storm?" *Common Dreams*, 19 May 2006.

100 Eric Lipton, "Software Being Developed to Monitor Opinions of U.S.," *New York Times*, 4 October 2006, A24.

101 Scahill, "Mayhem in Miami."

102 Scahill, "The Miami Model."

103 Ibid.

104 Boghosian, *The Assault on Free Speech, Public Assembly, and Dissent*, 30; David Montgomery, "Stirring a Cause: When Things Get Rough for Protesters, These Lawyers Go on the March," *Washington Post*, 12 May 2003, C1.

105 Diana Marcum, "Group Alleges Police Scrutiny: Peace Fresno Says Late Detective in Anti-terror Unit Was at Meetings," *Fresno Bee*, 3 October 2003, A1

106 Louis Galvan, "Peace Fresno Files Complaint Now-Deceased Deputy Is Accused of Infiltrating Group," *Fresno Bee*, 22 April 2004, B1.

107 Matthew Rothschild, "ACLU Seeks Info on Spying on Fresno Peace Group," *McCarthy Watch*, 4 February 2004. Available online: http://progressive.org/mag_mcfresno

108 Josh Richman, "Lockyer Vows Action on Police Spying," *Inside Bay Area*, 29 July 2006.

109 Demian Bulwa, "Oakland Police Spies Chosen to Lead War Protest," *San Francisco Chronicle*, 29 July 2006, B1.

110 Civil Liberties Defense Center, "The Green Scare." See: http://www.cldc.org/green.html Visited 20 December 2006.

111 Lauren Regan, Personal Interview, 19 December 2006.

112 Kera Abraham, "Flames of Dissent: The Local Spark that Ignited an Eco-sabotage Boom—and Bust, Part IV: The Bust," *Eugene Weekly*, 7 December 2006.

113 Ibid.

114 Hal Bernton, "An Activist-turned-informant: FBI's Break in Arson Attacks Shakes a Community to its Core," *Seattle Times*, 7 May 2006, A1.

115 Kera Abraham, "Flames of Dissent: The Local Spark that Ignited an Eco-sabotage Boom—and Bust, Part IV: The Bust"; "Green Scare: The Lauren Regan Interview," *SF Bay Area Independent Media Center*, 20 July 2006. Available at: http://www.indybay.org/newsitems/2006/07/20/18290048.php Visited 19 December 2006.

116 Alicia Caldwell, "'Snitch' Led to Suspects in Vail Fires," Associated Press, 25 December 2005.

117 Kim Minugh, "Second Guilty Plea in Eco-Terror Plot," *Sacramento Bee*, 20 July 2006, B2.

118 "Information on the Confidential Source in the Auburn Arrests," Portland Independent Media Center, 26 January 2006. Available at: http://portland.indymedia.org/en/2006/01/332740.shtml. Visited: 28 December 2006; Lauren Regan, Personal Interview, 19 December 2006.

119 Denny Walsh, "Bail Hearing Is Held in Eco-terror Case," *Sacramento Bee*, 21 January 2006, B1.

120 Eric Lichtblau, "FBI Found to Violate Its Informant Rules," *New York Times*, 13 September 2005, A14; Dan Eggen, "FBI Agents Often Break Informant Rules: Study Finds Confidentiality Breaches," *Washington Post*, 13 September 2005, A15.

121 Sze Tsung Leong, "Control Space," in Rem Koolhaas, Stefano Boeri, Sanford Kwinter, Nadia Tazi, and Hand Ulrich Obrist, *Mutations* (Barcelona: Actar, 2001).

122 Boghosian, *The Assault on Free Speech, Public Assembly, and Dissent*, 52–55.

123 Ibid., 24–28; Redden, "Police State Targets the Left."

124 Todd Dvorak, "Bush Dissenters Look to the Courts," *Milwaukee Journal Sentinel*, 23 July 2006.

125 Matthew Rothschild, "Bush Protester Arrested for Carrying Sign," *McCarthy Watch*, 29 January 2004. Available at: http://progressive.org/mag_mcsign2

126 Matthew Rothschild, "County Supervisor Booted from Bush Event for Wearing Hidden Kerry Shirt," *McCarthy Watch*, 22 July 2004. Available at: http://www.progressive.org/mag_mcshirt

127 Jeff Barnard, "Bush Rallies His Base in Southern Oregon," Associated Press, 14 October 2004; Matthew Rothschild, "Three Teachers Evicted from Bush Event for Wearing 'Protect Our Civil Liberties' T-Shirts," *McCarthy Watch*, 16 October 2004. Available at: http://www.progressive.org/node/2362

128 "Evansville Environmental Activist Arrested during Cheney Visit," Associated Press, 8 February 2002; John Blair, "Criticize Cheney, Go to Jail: Two Days in the Life of an Environmentalist," *CounterPunch*, 8 February 2002. Available at: http://www.counterpunch.org/blair1.html

129 Kirk Johnson, "Man Sues Secret Service Agent Over Arrest After Approaching Cheney and Denouncing War," *New York Times*, 4 October 2006, A22.

130 Amy Goodman, "Denver Man Sues Secret Service for Arrest After He Criticized Cheney on Iraq War," *Democracy Now!*, 5 October 2006.

131 "Questionable Bumper Sticker a Ticket to Free Speech Fight," Associated Press, 24 March 2006.

132 Daniel Yee, "Woman Sues DeKalb County over Ticket for Anti-Bush Bumper Sticker," Associated Press, 16 October 2006.

133 Eric Lichtblau, "FBI Goes Knocking for Political Troublemakers," *New York Times*, 16 August 2004, A1.

134 Eric Lichtblau, "Protesters at Heart of Debate on Security vs. Civil Rights," *New York Times*, 28 August 2004, A9.

135 The three congress members were John Conyers Jr. of Michigan, Jerrold Nadler of New York, and Robert C. Scott of Virginia. See: Eric Lichtblau, "Inquiry Into FBI Questioning Is Sought," *New York Times*, 18 August 2004, A16.

136 Jesse McKinley, "Blogger Jailed after Defying Court Orders," *New York Times*, 2 August 2006, A15.

137 Henry K. Lee, "Appeals Panel Sends Journalist Back to Prison," *San Francisco Chronicle*, 23 September 2006, B5.

138 Amy Goodman, "Imprisoned Journalist Josh Wolf Released After Record 225 Days in Jail," *Democracy Now!*, 4 April 2007.

139 Luis Fernandez, *Policing Protest Spaces: Social Control in the Anti-Globalization Movement*, (Unpublished PhD dissertation, Arizona State University, 2005), 59–60; Boghosian, *The Assault on Free Speech, Public Assembly, and Dissent*, 35–40.

140 Janny Scott, "Protesters Are Denied Potent Tactic of the Past," *New York Times*, 13 February 2003, B1.

141 Carol D. Leonnig, "Lawsuit Criticizes Secret Service," *Washington Post*, 24 September 2003, A27.

142 Michael Avery, "The 'Demonstration Zone' at the Democratic National Convention: An "Irretrievably Sad" Affront to the First Amendment," *Truthout*, 25 July 2004. Available at: http://www.truthout.org/docs_04/072504A.shtml

143 Jonathan Saltzman, "Judge Deplores But OKs Site for Protesters," *Boston Globe*, 23 July 2004, A1.

144 Charlie Savage, "Bush Could Bypass New Torture Ban: Waiver Right Is Reserved," *Boston Globe*, 5 October 2006, A2.

145 Charlie Savage, "Bush Signings Called Effort to Expand Power," *Boston Globe*, 4 January 2006, A1.

146 Amy Goodman, "Bush Signs Statements to Bypass Torture Ban, Oversight Rules in Patriot Act," *Democracy Now!*, 27 March 2006; Charlie Savage, "Bush Shuns Patriot Act Requirement: In Addendum to Law, He Says Oversight Rules Are Not Binding," *Boston Globe*, 24 March 2006, A1.

147 Stone, *Perilous Times*, 553.

148 Cole and Dempsey, *Terrorism and the Constitution*, 2.

149 Ibid., 51.

150 Chang, *Silencing Political Dissent*, 44.

151 U.S. Congress, *Uniting and Strengthening America by Providing the Appropriate Tools Required to Intercept and Obstruct Terrorism Act*, Public Law 107-56, Section 802.

152 Natsu Taylor Saito, "Whose Liberty? Whose Security? The USA PATRIOT Act in the Context of COINTELPRO and the Unlawful Repression of Political Dissent," *Oregon Law Review* 81 (2002): 1120.

153 Chang, *Silencing Political Dissent*, 112.

154 U.S. Congress, *USA PATRIOT Act*, Section 411.

155 Ibid.

156 Chang, *Silencing Political Dissent*, 62.

157 Cole and Dempsey, *Terrorism and the Constitution*, 153–154.

158 Ibid., 162.

159 In 1978, Congress passed the FISA, in order to establish a separate legal realm for "foreign intelligence" surveillance. FISA is only one of more than fifteen major statutes that the USA PATRIOT Act amends.

160 However, in July 2003, the House voted 309 to 118 to cut off funding for the part of Section 213 that allows the government to conduct sneak-and-peek searches of private property. The Senate has not followed the House's lead, though, and even if it does, it is questionable whether de-funding sneak-and-peeks will make a difference in the real world. Symbolically, though, the action may have some value.

161 U.S. Congress, *USA PATRIOT Act*, Section 215.

162 Jules Boykoff, "Patriot Acting: Congress, 'Compromise,' and the USA PATRIOT Act," *Common Dreams*, 16 February 2006.

163 Eric Mink, "Despite Act's Outrages, It's All Politics for Now," *Oregonian*, 8 October 2006, E10; Sheryl Gaye Stolberg, "President Signs New Rules To Prosecute Terror Suspects," *New York Times*, 18 October 2006, A20.

164 Steve Inskeep, "Yoo Defends Detainee Measure as 'Rules of War,'" National Public Radio, 4 October 2006.

165 Greg Toppo, "White House Paid Journalist to Promote Law," *USA Today*, 7 January 2005, 1A; Howard Kurtz, "Administration Paid Commentator: Education Dept. Used Williams to Promote 'No Child' Law," *Washington Post*, 8 January 2005, A1.

166 Anne E. Kornblut, "Third Journalist Was Paid To Promote Bush Policies," *New York Times*, 29 January 2005, A17.

167 Abby Goodnough, "U.S. Paid 10 Journalists for Anti-Castro Reports," *New York Times*, 9 September 2006, A9.

168 Charlie Savage and Alan Wirzbicki, "White House-Friendly Reporter Under Scrutiny," *Boston Globe*, 2 February 2005, A4.

169 Bob Woodward, *State of Denial* (New York: Simon & Schuster, 2006) 83–85; Amy Goodman, "Journalists Secretly Helped Bush Shape 9/11 Response," *Democracy Now!*, 9 October 2006.

170 "Seven Questions Covering Iraq," *Foreign Policy*, July 2006. Available online: http://www.foreignpolicy.com/story/cms.php?story_id=3525. Visited 13 October 2006.

171 Tina Brown, "Topic A with Tina Brown," CNBC, 10 September 2003.

172 Peter Johnson, "Amanpour: CNN Practiced Self-Censorship," *USA Today*, 15 September 2003.

173 "State's Delegation Favors Retaliation," Associated Press, 12 September 2001.

174 Marc Sandalow, "Bush Heads to California, Hitting Hard at War Critics, *San Francisco Chronicle*, 30 September 2006, A1.

175 Julian E. Barnes, "Rumsfeld Says Critics Appeasing Fascism," *Los Angeles Times*, 30 August 2006, A1.

176 Quoted in Eugene Volokh, "The Right to Oppose," *National Review*, 7 February 2003. Available at: http://www.nationalreview.com/comment/comment-evolokh020703.asp

177 To see the disclosed document, see: http://www.aclu.org/FilesPDFs/direct %20action%20foia%20document.pdf. See also Matthew Rothschild, "FBI, Michigan Police Tag Peace Group, Affirmative Action Group, and Others as 'Terrorist'" *McCarthy Watch*, 29 August 2005. Available at: http://www.progressive.org/mag_mc082905

178 Stop Huntingdon Animal Cruelty, "Frequently Asked Questions," http:// www.shac.net/SHAC/faq.html

179 Stop Huntingdon Animal Cruelty, "Who We Are," http://www.shac.net/ SHAC/who.html

180 John Lewis, "Statement of John E. Lewis, Deputy Assistant Director, Counterterrorism Division, Federal Bureau of Investigation, Before the Senate Committee on Environment and Public Works, 18 May 2005," Available online at: http://www.fbi.gov/congress/congress05/lewis051805.htm and http://epw.senate.gov/hearing_statements.cfm?id=237817

181 John J. Miller, "In the Name of the Animals—America Faces a New Kind of Terrorism," *National Review*, 3 July 2006; Andrew LePage, "Eco-terror Sparks Anxiety: Builders on Guard against Environmental Radicals," *Sacramento Bee*, 9 February 2005, D1.

182 Amy Goodman, "First Member of SHAC 7 Heads to Jail for Three Year Sentence," *Democracy Now!*, 3 October 2006.

183 Steve Mitchell, "Activists Threaten More Actions," *UPI*, 23 September 2006.

184 Alberto R. Gonzales, "Prepared Remarks for Attorney General Alberto R. Gonzales at the Operation Backfire Press Conference," 20 January 2006. Available at: http://www.usdoj.gov/ag/speeches/2006/ag_speech_0601201.html

185 Robert S. Mueller, "Prepared Remarks of Robert S. Mueller, III, Director, Federal Bureau of Investigation, Operation Backfire Press Conference," RFK Main Justice Building, Washington, D.C., 20 January 2006. Available online: http://www.fbi.gov/pressrel/speeches/mueller012006.htm

186 Charlie Brennan, "Shadowy Groups Difficult to Defeat," *Rocky Mountain News*, 21 January 2006, 4A.

187 Blaine Harden, "11 Indicted in 'Eco-Terrorism' Case," *Washington Post*, 21 January 2006, A3.

188 Daryn Kagan, "Eco-terrorism Indictments; Miners Trapped in West Virginia; Concerns Growing for American Journalist Jill Carroll," *CNN Live Today*, 20 January 2006.

189 The State Department's terrorism definition can be found online at: http://www.state.gov/s/ct/rls/crt/2000/2419.htm

190 Jules Boykoff, "'Terrorism' or Terrorism?: A Case of Selective Morality," *Common Dreams*, 29 January 2006.

191 Boghosian, *The Assault on Free Speech, Public Assembly, and Dissent*, 19–20, emphasis in original.

192 Don Plummer, "State of Emergency Set for G-8 Counties: Perdue Order Covers 6 Areas Near Summit," *Atlanta Journal-Constitution*, 22 May 2004, 3E.

193 *City of Miami Civilian Investigative Panel Report on the Free Trade Area of the Americas Summit*, 20 July 2006, 11.

194 For more information on Gold Star Families for Peace, see their web site: http://www.gsfp.org/

195 Robert L. Jamieson Jr., "Peace Mom Lights a Fire and a Furor," *Seattle Post-*

Intelligencer, 18 August 2005, B1. In this column, Jamieson also offers a thoughtful, nuanced argument as to why Sheehan should not be compared with civil-rights legend Rosa Parks, a comparison some commentators were drawing at the time.

196 Robert L. Jamieson Jr., "Mother's War Protest Veers onto Wrong Path," *Seattle Post-Intelligencer,* 13 August 2005, B1.

197 Bill O'Reilly, "The O'Reilly Factor: Talking Points Memo and Top Story," *Fox News,* 15 August 2005.

198 Bill O'Reilly, "The O'Reilly Factor: Talking Points Memo and Top Story," *Fox News,* 16 August 2005.

199 James Bowman, "Sheehan Is Believing," *American Spectator,* 22 August 2005.

200 Victor Davis Hanson, "The Paranoid Style," *National Review,* 26 August 2005.

201 Angela K. Brown, "More War Protesters, Bush Supporters Rally in Crawford," Associated Press, 13 August 2005.

202 "Your Turn: War, Focus: Cindy Sheehan," *San Antonio Express-News,* 4 September 2005, 4H.

203 "Letters: Protest and Patriotism," *Sacramento Bee,* 16 August 2005, B6.

204 Michael Arrieta-Walden, "Placement of Stories Sparks Charges of Bias," *Oregonian,* 2 October 2005, D1.

15
"Two Steps Ahead"

1   President George W. Bush, "Address to a Joint Session of Congress and the American People," United States Capitol, Washington, D.C., 20 September 2001. See: http://www.whitehouse.gov/news/releases/2001/09/20010920-8.html. More recently, and remarkably parallel with McCarthy's railings, Bush said, "No free nation can be neutral in the fight between civilization and chaos." See: Mike Allen. "Bush Urges Support for U.N.-Backed Multinational Force in Iraq," *Washington Post,* 13 September 2003, A16. For the McCarthy quote, see: "McCarthy Demands Boycott By Allies," *New York Times,* 24 September 1953 p. 10.

2   Quoted in Schulhofer *The Enemy Within,* 35.

3   Davenport, *Paths to State Repression,* 1.

4   Gabrielle Williams, "Q & A: Larry Lipin, Professor of History," *Pacific: The Magazine of Pacific University* 39 (Summer 2006): 11.

5   Sanjoy Banerjee, "Narratives and Interaction: A Constitutive Theory of Interaction and the Case of the All-India Muslim League," *European Journal of International Relations* 4 (1998): 178.

6   Salim Muwakkil, "Newspaper Editor's Resignation Reveals Growing Media Rifts," *Chicago Tribune*, 26 March 2001.

7   Walter Benjamin, "Theses on the Philosophy of History," in *Illuminations: Essays and Reflections* (New York: Schocken Books, 1968), 257.

8   Antonio Gramsci, *Selections from the Prison Notebooks* (New York: International Publishers, 1971).

9   Foucault, *Discipline and Punish*, 219.

10   Antonio Gramsci, *Selections from the Prison Notebooks*, 275.

11   See: Schulhofer *The Enemy Within*, 32.

12   Dan Eggen, "Ashcroft Planning Trip to Defend Patriot Act," *Washington Post*, 13 August 2003, A2.

13   R. Jeffrey Smith, "Attorney General Urges Renewal of Patriot Act: Gonzales Gives First Policy Speech," *Washington Post*, 1 March 2005, A2.

14   For updates on this total and to learn where local resolutions are in motion already, see the Bill of Rights Defense Committee's website at: http://www.bordc.org/.

15   Kim Marks, Personal Interview, 12 December 2006.

16   Russell Banks, *Cloudsplitter* (New York: Harper Collins Publishers Inc., 1998).

17   Levy, *Legacy of Suppression*, viii.

Bibliography

Abraham, Kera. "Flames of Dissent: The Local Spark that Ignited an Eco-sabotage Boom—and Bust, Part IV: The Bust." *Eugene Weekly*, 7 December 2006.

_____. "Flames of Dissent: The Local Spark that Ignited an Eco-sabotage Boom—and Bust, Part IV: The Ashes." *Eugene Weekly*, 21 December 2006.

"ACLU Wants Apology to VA Employee Investigated on 'Sedition'." Associated Press, 1 February 2006.

Adler v. Board of Education. 342 U.S. 485. 1952.

"A Failure to Communicate: The World Trade Organization is Widely Misunderstood, and It Hasn't Helped Its Own Case, But It Isn't a Global Ogre." *Los Angeles Times*, 2 December 1999, 10.

Agamben, Giorgio. *Means without End: Notes on Politics.* Trans. Vincénzo Binetti and Cesare Casarino. Minneapolis and London: University of Minnesota Press, 2000.

Albert, Michael. "A Q & A on the WTO, IMF, World Bank, and Activism." *Z Magazine* (January 2000): 24–29.

_____. *Parecon: Life after Capitalism.* New York: Verso, 2003.

Albert, Michael and Robin Hahnel. *The Political Economy of Participatory Economics.* Princeton, N.J.: Princeton University Press, 1991.

Allen, Craig. *Eisenhower and the Mass Media: Peace, Prosperity, & Prime-Time TV.* Chapel Hill and London: University of North Carolina Press, 1993.

Allen, Mike. "Bush Urges Support for U.N.-Backed Multinational Force in Iraq." *Washington Post*, 13 September 2003, A16.

Allen, Robert L. *Black Awakening in Capitalist America: An Analytic History.* Garden City, NY: Doubleday & Company, Inc, 1969.

"Allies Scored at Service." *New York Times*, 31 May 1953, 16.

American Civil Liberties Union. "*Freedom Under Fire*: Dissent in Post-9/11 America." 2003. Available at: http://www.aclu.org/SafeandFree/SafeandFree.cfm?ID=12666&c=206.

_____. "ACLU of Oregon Files Lawsuit Challenging Secret Service & Local Police Breakup of Demonstration During 2004 Bush Visit to Jacksonville." 6 July 2006. Available at: http://www.aclu-or.org/site/DocServer/moss_press_release_7_06.pdf?docID=1621

"Americans May Be Held as 'Enemy Combatants,' Appeals Court Rules." *CNN*, 3 January 2003.

Aminzade, Ronald, Jack A. Goldstone, and Elizabeth J. Perry. "Leadership Dynamics and Dynamics of Contention." In *Silence and Voice in the Study of Contentious Politics*, ed. Ronald Aminzade et al, 126–154. New York: Cambridge University Press, 2001.

Aminzade, Ronald et al, eds. *Silence and Voice in the Study of Contentious Politics.* New York: Cambridge University Press, 2001.

Amnesty International. "Amnesty International's Continuing Concerns about Taser Use." February 2006. Available at: http://www.amnestyusa.org/countries/usa/document.do?id=ENGAMR510302006

Anderson, Curt. "Groups Question FBI Protest Monitoring." Associated Press, 23 November 2003.

Anderson, John Ward. "Poor Nations' Leaders Back Washington Protesters: Group Says IMF and World Bank Policies 'Stabilized Poverty.'" *Washington Post*, 16 April 2000, A31.

Andrews, Wyatt. "Police in Washington, DC, Ready for Protests against World Bank-IMF Meetings." *CBS Evening News*, 15 April 2000a.

————. "Demonstrators in the Nation's Capital Hope to Disrupt World Bank and International Monetary Fund Meetings." *CBS Sunday Morning.* 16 April 2000b.

Anthony, Earl. *Picking Up the Gun: A Report on the Black Panthers.* New York: The Dial Press, 1970.

Aptheker, Bettina. *The Morning Breaks: The Trial of Angela Davis.* 2d ed. Ithaca and London: Cornell University Press, 1999.

Apuzzo, Matt. "Professor Points to Politics as Yale Fails to Renew Contract." Associated Press, 23 October 2005.

————. "Anarchist Professor Drops Appeal, Will Leave Yale." Associated Press, 8 December 2005.

Arenson, Karen W. "When Scholarship and Politics Collided at Yale." *New York Times*, 28 December 2005, B1.

Arrieta-Walden, Michael. "Placement of Stories Sparks Charges of Bias," *Oregonian*, 2 October 2005, D1.

"A Tragedy." *Washington Post*, 6 April 1967, 20.

Avery, Michael. "The 'Demonstration Zone' at the Democratic National Convention: An 'Irretrievably Sad' Affront to the First Amendment." *Truthout*, 25 July 2004. Available at: http://www.truthout.org/docs_04/072504A.shtml

"A Year for Contempt." *New York Times*, 3 February 1959, 26.

Baggett v. Bullitt. 377 U.S. 360. 1964.

Balbus, Isaac D. *The Dialectics of Legal Repression.* New York: Russell Sage Foundation, 1973.

Balser, Deborah B. "The Impact of Environmental Factors on Factionalism and Schism in Social Movement Organizations." *Social Forces* 76 (1997): 199–228.

Banerjee, Sanjoy. "Narratives and Interaction: A Constitutive Theory of Interaction and the Case of the All-India Muslim League." *European Journal of International Relations* 4 (1998): 178–203.

Banks, Russell. *Cloudsplitter*. New York: HarperCollins Publishers Inc., 1998.

Baraka, Amiri. *The Autobiography of Leroi Jones*. Chicago: Lawrence Hill Books, 1997.

_____. *Raise Race Rays Raze: Essays Since 1965*. New York: Random House, 1971.

Barkan, Steven. "Legal Control of the Civil Rights Movement." *American Sociological Review* 49 (1984): 552–565.

_____. *Protesters on Trial: Criminal Justice in the Southern Civil Rights and Vietnam Antiwar Movements*, New Brunswick, NJ: Rutgers University Press, 1985.

Barnard, Jeff. "Bush Rallies His Base in Southern Oregon." Associated Press, 14 October 2004.

Barnes, Julian E. "Rumsfeld Says Critics Appeasing Fascism." *Los Angeles Times*, 30 August 2006, A1.

Barrett, Katharine. "Protesters in Seattle Disrupting WTO Conference 'Looked Like a Group That Was Out of Control,' Says Jasinowski." *CNN Today*. 30 November 1999.

Barthes, Roland. *Mythologies*. Trans. by Annette Lavers. New York: Farrar, Strauss & Giroux, 1972.

Benjamin, Walter. *Illuminations: Essays and Reflections*. Trans. Harry Zohn. New York: Schocken Books, 1968.

Bennett, W. Lance. *News: The Politics of Illusion*. 5th ed. New York: Longman, 2002.

_____. "An Introduction to Journalism Norms and Representations of Politics." *Political Communication* 13 (1996): 373–384.

_____. "Toward a Theory of Press-State Relations in the United States." *Journal of Communication* 40 (1990): 103–125.

Bentley, Eric. *Thirty Years of Treason: Excerpts from Hearings Before the House Committee on Un-American Activities, 1938–1968*. New York: Viking Press, 1971.

Berger, Dan. *Outlaws of America: The Weather Underground and the Politics of Solidarity*. Oakland: AK Press, 2006.

Berkow, Ira. "Rower With Muslim Name Is an All-American Suspect." *New York Times*, 21 February 2003, D2.

Bernays, Edward (ed.). *The Engineering of Consent*. Norman, Oklahoma: University of Oklahoma Press, 1955.

_____. *Propaganda*. Brooklyn, NY: Ig Publishing, 2005 [1928].

_____. *Public Relations*. Norman, Oklahoma: University of Oklahoma Press, 1952.

Bernton, Hal. "An Activist-turned-informant: FBI's Break in Arson Attacks Shakes a Community to its Core." *Seattle Times*, 7 May 2006, A1.

Bevington, Douglas and Chris Dixon, "Movement-Relevant Theory: Rethinking Social Movement Scholarship and Activism." *Social Movement Studies* 4 (2005): 185–208.

Bill of Rights Defense Committee. http://www.bordc.org/

Bills, Scott L. (ed.). *Kent State / May 4: Echoes Through a Decade*. Kent, Ohio: Kent State University Press, 1982.

"Bingaman Wants Probe into VA 'Sedition' Investigation of Nurse." Associated Press, 7 February 2006.

Bishop, Katherine. "Environmentalists Hurt, Then Held, in Blast." *New York Times*, 26 May 1990, A1.

Blackstock, Nelson. *COINTELPRO: The FBI's Secret War on Political Freedom*. New York: Vintage Books, 1976.

Blair, John. "Criticize Cheney, Go to Jail: Two Days in the Life of an Environmentalist." *CounterPunch*, 8 February 2002. Available at: http://www.counterpunch.org/blair1.html

Bland, J. Federal Bureau of Investigation, "Memorandum to William Sullivan." 3 February 1962.

Blaug, Ricardo. "New Theories of Discursive Democracy: A User's Guide." *Philosophy & Social Criticism* 22 (1996): 49–80.

"Blow at I.W.W.: 168 Are Indicted, Scores Arrested." *New York Times*, 29 September 1917, 1.

Blumenfeld, Laura. "Dissertation Could Be Security Threat: Student's Maps Illustrate Concerns About Public Information." *Washington Post*, 8 July 2003, A1.

Boghosian, Heidi. *The Assault on Free Speech, Public Assembly, and Dissent: A Lawyers Guild Report on Government Violations of First Amendment Rights in the United States*. Great Barrington, MA: The North River Press Publishing Corporation, 2004.

Bourdieu, Pierre. *On Television*. Trans. Priscilla Parkhurst Ferguson. New York: New Press, 1998.

"Bourgeois Anarchy." *Wall Street Journal*, 3 January 2006, A24.

Bowman, James. "Sheehan Is Believing." *American Spectator*, 22 August 2005.

Bowles, Scott. "Park Police Can Count On A Disputed Crowd Figure; Aerial Photos, Bus Tallies Crucial to Accuracy." *Washington Post*, 15 October 1995, B1.

Boykoff, Jules. "Dissent." In *Encyclopedia of Activism and Social Justice*, ed. Gary L. Anderson and Kathryn Herr. Thousand Oaks, CA: Sage Publications, forthcoming.

———. "Some Calm in the Eye of the Surveillance Storm?" *Common Dreams*, 19 May 2006.

_____. "Patriot Acting: Congress, 'Compromise,' and the USA PATRIOT Act," *Common Dreams*, 16 February 2006.

_____. "'Terrorism' or Terrorism?: A Case of Selective Morality," *Common Dreams*, 29 January 2006.

Boykoff, Maxwell T. and Jules M. Boykoff. "Balance as Bias: Global Warming and the U.S. Prestige Press." *Global Environmental Change* 14 (2004): 125–136.

Bozell, L. Brent III and Brent H Baker. *And That's the Way It Is[n't]: A Reference Guide to Media Bias*. Alexandria, VA: Media Research Center, 1990.

Branch, Taylor. *Pillar of Fire: America in the King Years, 1963–65*. New York: Simon & Schuster, 1998.

_____. *At Canaan's Edge: America in the King Years, 1965–1968*. New York: Simon & Schuster, 2006.

Branch-Brioso, Karen. "Looser Rules Spark Old Fears." *St. Louis Post-Dispatch*, 2 June 2002, B1.

Brand, Johanna. *The Life and Death of Anna Mae Aquash*. Toronto: James Lorimer Publishers, 1978.

Brandenburg v. *Ohio*. 395 U.S. 444. 1969.

Brecher, Jeremy, John Brown Childs, and Jill Cutler, eds. *Global Visions: Beyond the New World Order*. Boston: South End Press, 1993.

Brennan, Charlie. "Shadowy Groups Difficult to Defeat." *Rocky Mountain News*, 21 January 2006, 4A.

Broad, Robin, ed. *Global Backlash: Citizen Initiatives for a Just World Economy*. Lanham, MD: Rowman & Littlefield Publishers, Inc., 2002.

_____. "Of Magenta Hair, Nose Rings, and Naiveté." In *Global Backlash: Citizen Initiatives for a Just World Economy*, ed. Robin Broad, 1–10. Lanham, MD: Rowman & Littlefield Publishers, Inc, 2002.

Brockett, Charles D. "A Protest Cycle Resolution of the Repression/Popular Protest Paradox." In *Repertoires and Cycles of Collective Action*, ed. Mark Traugott, 117–144. Durham, NC and London: Duke University Press, 1995.

Brown, Angela K. "More War Protesters, Bush Supporters Rally in Crawford." Associated Press, 13 August 2005.

Brown, Jennifer. "CU Moves to Fire Churchill." *Denver Post*, 27 June 2006, A1.

Brown, Ralph S. *Loyalty and Security Employment Tests in the United States*. New Haven: Yale University Press, 1958.

Brown, Scot. *Fighting for US: Maulana Karenga, the US Organization, and Black Cultural Nationalism*. New York: New York University Press, 2003.

Brown, Tina. "Topic A with Tina Brown." CNBC, 10 September 2003.

"Budenz Says One Man Runs U.S. Communism." *New York Times*, 14 October 1946, 12.

Budnick, Nick. "The Making of a 'Terrorist.'" *Willamette Week*, 16 October 2002.

Buhle, Paul. *Marxism in the United States: Remapping the History of the American*

Left. London: Verso, 1987.

Bulwa, Demian. "Oakland Police Spies Chosen to Lead War Protest." *San Francisco Chronicle*, 29 July 2006, B1.

Bumiller, Elisabeth. "Military Tribunals Needed In Difficult Time, Bush Says." *New York Times*, 20 November 2001, B5.

Burgess, John and Steven Pearlstein. "Protests Delay WTO Opening; Seattle Police Use Tear Gas; Mayor Declares a Curfew." *Washington Post*, 1 December 1999, A1.

_____. "WTO Ends Conference Well Short Of Goals; Ministers May Resume Talks Early Next Year." *Washington Post*, 4 December 1999, A1.

Burnette, Robert and John Koster. *The Road to Wounded Knee*. New York: Bantam Books, Inc., 1974.

Burton, Jeffrey F., Mary M. Farrell, Florence B. Lord, and Richard W. Lord. *Confinement and Ethnicity: An Overview of World War II Japanese Relocation Sites*. Seattle: University of Washington Press, 2002.

Bush, George W. "Address to a Joint Session of Congress and the American People." U.S. Capitol. Washington, D.C. 20 September 2001. Available at: http://www. whitehouse.gov/news/releases/2001/09/20010920-8.html

_____. "President Issues Military Order." 13 November 2001. Available at: http://www.whitehouse.gov/news/releases/2001/11/20011113-27.html

"Bush Stresses Red Menace." *New York Times*, 11 April 1955, 18.

Bwy, Douglas. "Political Instability in Latin America: The Cross-Cultural Test of a Causal Model." *Latin American Research Review* 3 (1968): 17–66.

Cabanatuan, Michael, Kevin Fagan, and Erin Hallissy. "Troops, War Policy Supported at Local Rallies." *San Francisco Chronicle*, 24 March 2003, W11.

Caldwell, Alicia. "'Snitch' Led to Suspects in Vail Fires." Associated Press, 25 December 2005.

Caldwell, Earl. "Angela Davis Acquitted on All Charges." *New York Times*, 5 June 1972, 1.

Calhoun, Lillian S. "The Death of Fred Hampton." In *Government Lawlessness in America*, ed. Theodore L. Becker and Vernon G. Murray, 34–47. New York: Oxford University Press, 1971.

Callinicos, Alex. *Against the Third Way: An Anti-Capitalist Critique*. Cambridge, U.K.: Polity Press, 2001.

_____. *An Anti-Capitalist Manifesto*. Cambridge, UK: Polity Press, 2003.

"Calls Communists Here 'Soviet Spies.'" *New York Times*, 4 April 1946, 19.

Carley, Michael. "Defining Forms of Successful State Repression of Social Movement Organizations: A Case Study of the FBI's COINTELPRO and the American Indian Movement." *Research in Social Movements, Conflict and Change* 20 (1997): 151–176.

Carr, Robert K. *The House Committee on Un-American Activities*. Ithaca, New York:

Cornell University Press, 1952.

Carter, Bill. "White House Seeks to Limit Transcripts." *New York Times*, 12 October 2001, B7.

Carter, Bill and Felicity Barringer. "Networks Agree to U.S. Request to Edit Future bin Laden Tapes." *New York Times*, 11 October 2001, A1.

Casale, Ottavio M. and Louis Paskoff. *The Kent Affair: Documents and Interpretations.* New York: Houghton Mifflin Company, 1971.

Caute, David. *The Great Fear: The Anti-Communist Purge Under Truman and Eisenhower.* New York: Simon and Schuster, 1978.

"Censor Creel Gives Out Rules for Newspapers." *New York Times*, 28 May 1917, 1.

Ceplair, Larry and Steven Englund. *The Inquisition in Hollywood: Politics in the Film Community, 1930–1960.* Garden City, NY: Anchor Press/Doubleday, 1980.

"Chamber Opens Campaign To Oust Reds in U.S. Posts." *New York Times*, 10 October 1946, 1.

Chang, Juju. "WTO Protests Lead to Seattle Curfew." *ABC World News Now.* 1 December 1999.

Chang, Nancy. *Silencing Political Dissent.* New York: Seven Stories Press, 2002.

Chatterjee, Pratap and Matthias Finger. *The Earth Brokers: Power, Politics, and World Development.* New York: Routledge, 1994.

Chomsky, Daniel. "The Mechanisms of Management Control at the *New York Times*." *Media, Culture & Society* 21 (1999): 579–599.

Chomsky, Noam. "Introduction." In *COINTELPRO: The FBI's Secret War on Political Freedom*, ed. Nelson Blackstock, 3–26. New York: Vintage Books, 1976.

———. *Media Control: The Spectacular Achievements of Propaganda*, 2d ed. New York: Seven Stories Press, 2002.

Churchill, Ward. *A Little Matter of Genocide: Holocaust and Denial in the Americas, 1492 to the Present.* San Francisco: City Lights Books, 1997.

Churchill, Ward and Jim Vander Wall. *Agents of Repression: The FBI's Secret Wars Against the Black Panther Party and the American Indian Movement*, 2d ed. Cambridge, MA: South End Press, 2002 [1988].

———. *The COINTELPRO Papers: Documents from the FBI's Secret Wars Against Domestic Dissent.* Boston: South End Press, 1990.

City of Miami Civilian Investigative Panel Report on the Free Trade Area of the Americas Summit. 20 July 2006. Available at: http://ci.miami.fl.us/cip/Downloads/FTAAReport.pdf

Civil Liberties Defense Center. "The Green Scare." Available at: http://www.cldc.org/green.html

Clemetson, Lynette. "Thousands March in Washington Against Going to War in Iraq." *New York Times*, 27 October 2002, A8.

Clines, Francis X. "Convention Demonstrators Are Held on Very High Bail." *New York Times*, 5 August 2000, A8.

_____. "Bail Reduced for Man Accused of Leading Philadelphia Protests." *New York Times*, 8 August 2000, A18.

_____. "Washington Braces to Handle Flood of Globalization Protesters." *New York Times*, 11 April 2000, A5.

_____. "A New Age Protest Tackles Globalism With Polite Chants." *New York Times*, 14 April 2000, A13.

Cmiel, Kenneth. "The Emergence of Human Rights in U.S. Politics." *Journal of American History* 86 (December 1999): 1231–1250.

Cochran, John. "Seattle Police Crackdown On WTO Protesters." *ABC World News Tonight*. 1 December 1999.

Cockburn, Alexander. "The Tenth Crusade." *Nation*. 23 September 2002.

Code Pink. http://www.codepinkforpeace.org

Coen, Rachel. "For Press, Magenta Hair and Nose Rings Defined Protest." *Extra!* (July/August 2000). Available at: http://www.fair.org/index.php?page=1037.

Cole, David and James Dempsey. *Terrorism and the Constitution*, 2d ed. New York: New Press, 2002.

Cole, David. "Why the Court Said No." *New York Review of Books* 53, no. 13, 10 August 2006. Available at: http://www.nybooks.com/articles/19212

Cole, Lester. *Hollywood Red: The Autobiography of Lester Cole*. Palo Alto, CA: Ramparts Press, 1981.

"Committee of Bar Would Expel Reds." *New York Times*, 25 February 1951, 44.

Congbalay, Dean. "Police Say Car Bomb Was in the Back Seat: How Earth First! Victims Became Suspects." *San Francisco Chronicle*, 28 May 1990, A2.

"Contempt Sought for 2." *New York Times*, 9 August 1958, 33.

Cooper, Helene. "Some Hazy, Some Erudite and All Angry—Diversity of WTO Protests Makes Them Hard to Dismiss." *Wall Street Journal*, 30 November 1999, A2.

Cooper, Helene, Jake Bleed, and Jerry Guidera. "Protesters Can't Stop World Bank Parley, But Do Disrupt Downtown Washington." *Wall Street Journal*, 18 April 2000, A20.

Cooper, Helene and Michael M. Phillips. "Antiglobalization Forces March in Washington; Police Respond Strongly." *Wall Street Journal*, 17 April 2000, A2.

_____. "IMF Protesters Prize Intensity Over Numbers." *Wall Street Journal*, 14 April 2000, A20.

Cornell, Stephen. *The Return of the Native: American Indian Political Resurgence*. New York: Oxford University Press, 1988.

Corrado, Anthony. "Elections in Cyberspace: Prospects and Problems." In *Elections in Cyberspace: Toward a New Era in American Politics*, ed. Anthony Corrado and Charles M. Firestone, 1–31. Queenstown, MD: The Aspen Institute, 1996.

"Court Asked to Return Ex-Black Panther to Prison." *New York Times*, 16 December 1998, A28.

Cowan, Lee. "Protesters Battle Washington, DC Police in an Effort to Disrupt Meetings of World Finance Leaders." *CBS Evening News*, 16 April 2000.

Cowan, Paul, Nick Egleson, and Nat Hentoff. *State Secrets: Police Surveillance in America*. New York: Holt, Rinehart and Winston, 1974.

Cowell, Alan. "Thousands Denounce War and the United States in Cities Around the World." *New York Times*, 23 March 2003, B11.

Cox, James and Del Jones. "'This Weird Jamboree' Teamsters and Turtle Protectors on Same Side." *USA Today*, 2 December 1999, A1.

Creel, George. "Public Opinion in War Time." *Annals of the American Academy of Political and Social Science* 78 (1918): 185–194.

_____. *How We Advertised America*. New York: Arno Press, 1972 [1920].

_____. *Rebel at Large: Recollections of Fifty Crowded Years*. New York: G.P. Putnam's Sons, 1947.

"Creel Denounced in the House and Senate." *New York Times*, 10 April 1918, 8.

"Creel to Direct Nation's Publicity." *New York Times*, 15 April 1917, 1.

Crewdson, John M. "Judge Says FBI Withheld Data on Indians." *New York Times*, 5 April 1975, 16.

Crombie, Noelle. "Portland 7 Figure Gets 7 Years for Taliban Aid." *Oregonian*, 10 February 2004, A1.

Cunningham, Brent. "Re-thinking Objectivity." *Columbia Journalism Review* 42 (2003): 24–32.

Cunningham, David. *There's Something Happening Here: The New Left, The Klan, and FBI Counterintelligence*. Berkeley: University of California Press, 2004.

_____. "State versus Social Movement: FBI Counterintelligence against the New Left." In *States, Parties, and Social Movements*, ed. Jack A. Goldstone, 45–77. Cambridge: Cambridge University Press, 2003.

Curtis, Charlotte. "Black Panther Philosophy Is Debated at the Bernsteins." *New York Times*, 15 January 1970, 48.

Davenport, Christian, ed. *Paths to State Repression: Human Rights Violations and Contentious Politics*. New York: Rowman & Littlefield Publishers, Inc., 2000.

Davis, Angela. *If They Come in the Morning*. New York: The New American Library Inc., 1971.

_____. *Angela Davis: An Autobiography*. New York: Random House, 1974.

Davis, David Brion. *The Fear of Conspiracy: Images of Un-American Subversion from the Revolution to the Present*. Ithaca and London: Cornell University Press, 1971.

Davis Hanson, Victor. "The Paranoid Style." *National Review*, 26 August 2005.

Debs v. *United States*. 249 U.S. 211. 1919.

della Porta, Donatella and Hanspeter Kreisi. "Social Movements in a Globalizing

World: An Introduction." In *Social Movements in a Globalizing World*, ed. Donatella della Porta, Hanspeter Kriesi, and Dieter Rucht, 3–22. London: MacMillan, 1999.

della Porta, Donatella and Herbert Reiter, eds. *Policing Protest: The Control of Mass Demonstrations in Western Democracies*. Minneapolis: University of Minnesota Press, 1998.

DeLoach, Cartha. Federal Bureau of Investigation. "Memorandum to John Mohr." 27 November 1964.

Deloria, Vine, Jr. *Behind the Trail of Broken Treaties: An Indian Declaration of Independence*. New York: Delacorte Press, 1974.

DeLuca, Kevin Michael and Jennifer Peeples. "From Public Sphere to Public Screen: Democracy, Activism, and the 'Violence' of Seattle." *Critical Studies in Media Communication* 19 (2002): 125–151.

deMause, Neil. "Pepper Spray Gets in Their Eyes: Media Missed Militarization of Police Work in Seattle." *Extra!* (March/April 2000). Available at: http://www.fair.org/index.php?page=1029

Des Pres, Terrence. *Praises & Dispraises: Poetry and Politics, the 20th Century*. New York: Viking, 1988.

Dick, Bernard. *Radical Innocence: A Critical Study of the Hollywood Ten*. Lexington, Kentucky: The University Press of Kentucky, 1989.

"Dies Submits Bill to Outlaw Reds." *New York Times*, 10 February 1953, 23.

DiPiero, W.S. "Politics in Poetry: The Case of Thomas McGrath." *New England Review* 17 (1995): 41–46.

Donner, Frank. *The Age of Surveillance: The Aims and Methods of America's Political Intelligence System*. New York: Vintage Books, 1980.

_____. "Let Him Wear a Wolf's Head: What the FBI Did to William Albertson." *Civil Liberties Review*, April/May 1976.

_____. *The Un-Americans*. New York: Ballantine Books, 1961.

Doxtader, Erik W. "Characters in the Middle of Public Life: Consensus, Dissent, and Ethos." *Philosophy and Rhetoric* 33 (2000): 336–369.

Dower, John W. *War Without Mercy: Race & Power in the Pacific War*. New York: Pantheon Books, 1986.

Downey, Sharon and Karen Rasmussen. "Vietnam: Press, Protest, and the Presidency." In *Silencing the Opposition: Government Strategies of Suppression*, ed. Craig Smith, 179–227. Albany, NY: State University Press of New York, 1996.

Drinnon, Richard. *Rebel in Paradise: A Biography of Emma Goldman*. Chicago: University of Chicago Press, 1961.

_____. *Keeper of Concentration Camps: Dillon S. Myer and American Racism*. Berkeley: University of California Press, 1987.

"Dr. King's Disservice to His Cause." *Life*, 21 April 1967, 4.

Duncan v. Kahanamoku. 327 U.S. 304. 1946.

Dunwoody, Sharon. "The Science Writing Inner Club." In *Scientists and Journalists*, ed. Sharon M. Friedman, Sharon Dunwoody, and Carol L. Rogers, 155–169. New York: Free Press, 1986.

Dunwoody, Sharon and Hans Peter Peters. "Mass Media Coverage of Technological and Environmental Risks: a Survey of Research in the United States and Germany." *Public Understanding of Science* 1 (1992): 199–230.

Dvorak, Petula and Michael E. Ruane. "Police, Protesters Claim Victory; Scattered Scuffles and Arrests Punctuate a Largely Peaceful Day." *Washington Post*, 17 April 2000, A1.

Dvorak, Todd. "Bush Dissenters Look to the Courts." *Milwaukee Journal Sentinel*, 23 July 2006.

Dye, Thomas R. and Harmon Zeigler. *The Irony of Democracy*, Millennial Edition, New York: Harcourt Brace College Publishers, 2000.

Earl, Jennifer. "Tanks, Tear Gas, and Taxes: Toward a Theory of Movement Repression." *Sociological Theory* 21 (2003): 44–67.

———. "Controlling Protest: New Directions for Research on the Social Control of Protest." *Research in Social Movements, Conflicts, and Change* 25 (2004): 55–83.

———. "You Can Beat the Rap, But You Can't Beat the Ride: Bringing Arrests Back into Research on Repression." *Research in Social Movements, Conflicts and Change* 26 (2005): 101–139.

Earl, Jennifer, John D. McCarthy, and Sarah A. Soule. "Protest Under Fire? Explaining the Policing of Protest." *American Sociological Review* 68 (2003): 581–606.

Edelman, Murray. *The Symbolic Uses of Politics*. Urbana: University of Illinois Press, 1964.

———. *Politics as Symbolic Action: Mass Arousal and Quiescence*. Chicago: Markham Publishing Company, 1971.

———. *Constructing the Political Spectacle*. Chicago and London: The University of Chicago Press, 1988.

———. *The Politics of Misinformation*. New York: Cambridge University Press, 2001.

Eggen, Dan. "Protesters Subjected To 'Pretext Interviews': FBI Memo Shows No Specific Threats." *Washington Post*, 18 May 2005, A4.

———. "FBI Agents Often Break Informant Rules: Study Finds Confidentiality Breaches." *Washington Post*, 13 September 2005, A15.

———. "Tough Anti-Terror Campaign Pledged: Ashcroft Tells Mayors He Will Use New Law to the Fullest Extent." *Washington Post*, 26 October 2001, A1.

———. "Ashcroft Planning Trip to Defend Patriot Act." *Washington Post*, 13 August 2003, A2.

"18-Month Hearing on Red Party Ends." *New York Times*, 15 August 1952, 22.

Eisenberg, Daniel. "We're Taking Him Out." *Time* magazine, 13 May 2002, 36.

Elfbrandt v. Russell. 384 U.S. 11. 1966.

Ellingwood, Ken. "Silence Breaks Over '68 Killing of Blacks at Southern College." *Oregonian*, 26 May 2003, A5.

Ellsberg, Daniel. *Secrets: A Memoir of Vietnam and the Pentagon Papers.* New York: Penguin, 2002.

Entman, Robert W. *Democracy Without Citizens: Media and the Decay of American Politics.* New York and Oxford: Oxford University Press, 1989.

_____. "Framing: Toward Clarification of a Fractured Paradigm." *Journal of Communication* 43 (1993): 51–58.

Entman, Robert and Andrew Rojecki. "Freezing Out the Public: Elite and Media Framing of the U.S. Anti-Nuclear Movement." *Political Communication* 10 (1993): 151–167.

Epstein, David. "Another Scholar Turned Back at JFK." *Inside Higher Ed*, 21 June 2006. Available at: http://insidehighered.com/news/2006/06/21/milios.

Eszterhas, Joe and Michael D. Roberts. *Thirteen Seconds: Confrontation at Kent State.* New York: Dodd, Mead, & Company, 1970.

"Evansville Environmental Activist Arrested during Cheney Visit." Associated Press, 8 February 2002.

Ewen, Stuart. *PR! A Social History of Spin.* New York: Basic Books, 1996.

"Excerpt from Analysis of Detention of Foreigners After 9/11 Attacks." *New York Times*, 3 June 2003, A18.

"Ex-Panther to Remain Free." *New York Times*, 17 February 1999, A11.

Ex Parte Milligan. 71 U.S. 2. 1866.

Ex Parte Quirn. 317 U.S. 1. 1942.

"False Note on Black Panthers." *New York Times*, 16 January 1970, 46.

Fantz, Ashley. "The FTAA Tapes: A Police Training Video Showed High-Ranking Broward Deputies Laughing about Shooting Rubber Bullets at a Coral Gables Attorney at the Free-Trade Summit." *Miami Herald*, 9 August 2006.

Fariello, Griffen. *Red Scare: Memories of the American Inquisition, An Oral History.* New York: Avon Books, 1995.

"F.B.I. Says Overthrow by Violence is Stalin Policy for Red Rule Here." *New York Times*, 30 July 1952, 1.

"F.B.I. Agent Tells of S.D.S. Activity: Surprise Witness Heard at Tacoma Conspiracy Trial." *New York Times*, 6 December 1970, 79.

Fears, Darryl. "Poetry Slams, Speeches, Posters, Rallies: All Efforts Fail to Get Black D.C. Activists Involved in IMF Fight." *Washington Post*, 15 April 2000, B1.

Fernandez, Luis. *Policing Protest Spaces: Social Control in the Anti-Globalization Movement.* Unpublished PhD dissertation, Arizona State University, 2005.

Fernandez, Manny and David A. Fahrenthold. "Police Arrest Hundreds in Protests:

Anti-Capitalism Events Cause Few Disruptions." *Washington Post*, 28 September 2002, A1.

Fernandez, Manny and Linda Perlstein. "Marchers Bring New Signs, Same Passion; War Protesters, Bush Supporters Rally in Washington." *Washington Post*, 13 April 2003, A25.

"Firing of Professor Draws Condemnation." *Los Angeles Times*, 15 June 2003, A18.

Fischer, John. "Black Panthers and Their White Hero-Worshippers." *Harper's*, August 1970.

Fletcher, Michael A. "Bush Signs Terrorism Measure: New Law Governs Interrogation, Prosecution of Detainees." *Washington Post*, 18 October 2006, A4.

"Florida Police Chief Sorry For Laughing At FTAA Shooting Victim." *Democracy Now!*, 11 August 2006.

Foner, Philip S., ed. *The Black Panthers Speak.* New York: Da Capo Press, 1995 [1970].

Foreman, Dave. *Confessions of an Eco-Warrior.* New York: Crown Publishers, Inc., 1991.

Foucault, Michel. *Discipline and Punish: The Birth of the Prison.* Trans. by Alan Sheridan. New York: Vintage, 1995.

Fraley, Todd and Elli Lester-Roushanzamir. "Revolutionary Leader or Deviant Thug? A Comparative Analysis of the *Chicago Tribune* and *Chicago Daily Defender*'s Reporting on the Death of Fred Hampton." *The Howard Journal of Communications* 15 (2004): 147–167.

Francis, Fred. "Thousands of Protesters Converge in Washington Trying to Shut Down World Bank and IMF Meetings." *NBC Nightly News.* 16 April 2000a.

———. "More Arrests and Disruptions Outside World Bank and International Monetary Fund Meetings." *NBC Nightly News.* 17 April 2000b.

Francisco, Ronald A. "Coercion and Protest: An Empirical Test in Two Democratic States." *American Journal of Political Science* 40 (1996): 1179–1204.

Frank, Joshua. "Without Cause: Yale Fires An Acclaimed Anarchist Scholar, An Interview with David Graeber." *CounterPunch*, 13 May 2005. Available at: http://www.counterpunch.org/frank05132005.html

Frankel, Glenn. "A Seer's Blind Spots: On George Orwell's 100th, a Look at a Flawed and Fascinating Writer." *Washington Post*, 25 June 2003, C1.

Franken, Bob. "Police and Protesters Battle for Control of Washington." *CNN Worldview.* 16 April 2000.

Fraser, Nancy. "Rethinking the Public Sphere: A Contribution to the Critique of Actually Existing Democracy." In *Habermas and the Public Sphere*, ed. Craig Calhoun, 109–142. Cambridge, MA: MIT Press, 1992.

Friedman, Thomas L. "Senseless in Seattle." *New York Times*, 1 December 1999, A23.

Frum, David. 2000. "Protesting, but Why?" *New York Times*, 19 April 2000, A23.

Fukuyama, Francis. "The Left Should Love Globalization." *Wall Street Journal*, 1 December 1999, A26.

Galvan, Louis. "Peace Fresno Files Complaint: Now-Deceased Deputy Is Accused of Infiltrating Group." *Fresno Bee*, 22 April 2004, B1.

Gamson, William. *Talking Politics*. New York: Cambridge University Press, 1992.

Gans, Herbert. *Deciding What's News*. New York: Pantheon, 1979.

Garrow, David J. *The FBI and Martin Luther King, Jr.* New York: Penguin, 1981.

Gathright, Alan. "No-fly Blacklist Snares Political Activists." *San Francisco Chronicle*, 27 September 2002, A1.

_____. "No-fly List Ensnares Innocent Travelers." *San Francisco Chronicle*, 8 June 2003, A1.

Gelbspan, Ross. *Break-ins, Death Threats and the FBI: The Covert War Against the Central America Movement*. Boston: South End Press, 1991.

_____. *The Heat Is On*. Cambridge, MA: Perseus Books, 1998.

Geneva Conventions. See: http://www.genevaconventions.org

Genshaft, Judy. "USF Must Sever All Ties to Al-Arian." *Tampa Tribune*, 2 March 2003, 1.

Getler, Michael. "Listening to a Different Drummer." *Washington Post*, 3 November 2003, B6.

Gibbons, Reginald and Terrence Des Pres, eds. *Thomas McGrath: Life and the Poem*. Urbana and Chicago: University of Illinois Press, 1992.

Gibson, James L. "Political Intolerance and Political Repression During the McCarthy Red Scare." *American Political Science Review* 82 (1988): 511–529.

_____. "Pluralism, Federalism and the Protection of Civil Liberties." *Western Political Quarterly* 43 (1990): 511–533.

Gid Powers, Richard. *G-Men: Hoover's FBI in American Popular Culture*. Carbondale: Southern Illinois University Press, 1983.

Gilens, Martin and Craig Hertzman. "Corporate Ownership and News Bias: Newspaper Coverage of the 1996 Telecommunications Act." *Journal of Politics* 62 (2000): 369–386.

Gitlin, Todd. *The Whole World Is Watching: Mass Media in the Making and Unmaking of the New Left*. Berkeley: University of California Press, 1980.

_____. *The Sixties: Years of Hope, Days of Rage*. New York: Bantam Books, 1987.

Giuffo, John. "Smoke Gets in Our Eyes: The Globalization Protests and the Befuddled Press." *Columbia Journalism Review*, September/October 2001, 14–17.

Glaberson, William. "The Tribunals: Closer Look at New Plan for Trying Terrorists." *New York Times*, 15 November 2001, B6.

Glick, Brian. *War at Home: Covert Action Against U.S. Activists and What We Can Do About It*. Cambridge, MA: South End Press, 1989.

Goldberg, Bernard. *Bias: A CBS Insider Exposes How the Media Distort the News.* Washington, DC: Regnery Publishing, Inc., 2002.

Gold Star Families for Peace. http://www.gsfp.org/

Goldstein, Robert Justin. *Political Repression in Modern America: From 1870 to 1976,* Urbana and Chicago: University of Illinois Press, 2001.

Goldstone, Jack A., ed. *States, Parties, and Social Movements.* New York: Cambridge University Press, 2003.

_____. "Bridging Institutionalized and Noninstitutionalized Politics." In *States, Parties, and Social Movements,* ed. Jack A. Goldstone, 1–24. New York: Cambridge University Press, 2003.

Gonzales, Alberto R. "Prepared Remarks for Attorney General Alberto R. Gonzales at the Operation Backfire Press Conference." 20 January 2006. Available at: http://www.usdoj.gov/ag/speeches/2006/ag_speech_0601201.html

Gonzales, Manny. "Churchill Appeals Suggestion that CU Fire Him." *Denver Post,* 6 July 2006, B1.

Goodman, Amy. "Daughter of Sami Al-Arian Says Family 'Devastated' by Father's Continued Imprisonment, Blasts Media Coverage." *Democracy Now!,* 3 May 2006.

_____. "Journalists Secretly Helped Bush Shape 9/11 Response." *Democracy Now!,* 9 October 2006.

_____. "Police Shoot Protesters With Tasers at Pittsburgh Demo Against Jeb Bush & Sen. Rick Santorum." *Democracy Now!,* 9 October 2006.

_____. "Bush Signs Statements to Bypass Torture Ban, Oversight Rules in Patriot Act." *Democracy Now!,* 27 March 2006.

_____. "First Member of SHAC 7 Heads to Jail for Three Year Sentence." *Democracy Now!,* 3 October 2006.

_____. "Bush Administration Says Prominent Muslim Scholar Can't Teach in the US Because He Donated to Palestinian Charity." *Democracy Now!,* 28 September 2006.

_____. "As Sentencing in the Lackawanna 6 Case Begins, A U.S. Court Rejects Law That Criminalizes Unknowingly Supporting a Terrorist Organization." *Democracy Now!,* 4 December 2003.

_____. "Ward Churchill Defends His Academic Record & Vows to Fight to Keep His Job at University of Colorado." *Democracy Now!,* 27 September 2006.

_____. "V.A. Nurse Accused of Sedition After Publishing Letter Critical of Bush on Katrina, Iraq." *Democracy Now!,* 2 March 2006.

_____. "Denver Man Sues Secret Service for Arrest After He Criticized Cheney on Iraq War." *Democracy Now!,* 5 October 2006.

_____. "Newly Released Files Reveal FBI Spied on PA Peace Group Because of Antiwar Views." *Democracy Now!,* 15 March 2006.

_____. "Police Shot Protester in NC With a Taser; Six Arrested." *Democracy*

Now!, 26 September 2006.

———. "Imprisoned Journalist Josh Wolf Released After Record 225 Days in Jail." *Democracy Now!*, 4 April 2007.

Goodman, Walter. *The Committee: The Extraordinary Career of the House Committee on Un-American Activities*, New York: Farrar, Straus and Giroux, 1968.

Goodnough, Abby. "U.S. Paid 10 Journalists for Anti-Castro Reports." *New York Times*, 9 September 2006, A9.

Gordon, William A. *The Fourth of May: Killings and Coverups at Kent State*. Buffalo: Prometheus Books, 1990.

Gorov, Lynda. "Seattle Caught Unprepared for Anarchists." *Boston Globe*, 3 December 1999, A11.

Gottlieb, Jeff and Jeff Cohen. "Was Fred Hampton Executed?" *Nation*, 25 December 1976, 680–684.

"Government Asks Artists to Make War Posters." *New York Times*, 20 May 1917, SM8.

"Government Daily Issues First Number." *New York Times*, 11 May 1917, 13.

"Government May End Outrages by I.W.W.: Action Under Laws Dealing with Treason Expected—Evidence of German Plot." *New York Times*, 2 August 1917, 20.

Graeber, David. "Yale's Unusual Decision Left Me Little Recourse." *Wall Street Journal*, 13 January 2006, A13.

Gramsci, Antonio. *Selections from the Prison Notebooks*. Trans. Quinton Hoare and Geoffrey Nowell Smith. New York: International Publishers, 1971.

Greenhouse, Steven. "A Carnival of Derision to Greet the Princes of Global Trade." *New York Times*, 29 November 1999, A12.

"Green Scare: The Lauren Regan Interview." *SF Bay Area Independent Media Center*. 20 July 2006. Available at: http://www.indybay.org/news-items/2006/07/20/18290048.php

"Group to Publicize F.B.I.'s Informers." *New York Times*, 27 March 1971, 32.

Gurr, Ted Robert. "Persisting Patterns of Repression and Rebellion: Foundations for a General Theory of Political Coercion." In *Persistent Patterns and Emergent Structures in a Waning Century*. ed. Margaret P. Karnes, 238–294. New York: Praeger Special Studies for the International Studies Association, 1986.

Habermas, Jurgen. *The Structural Transformation of the Public Sphere: An Inquiry into a Category of Bourgeois Society*. Translated by Thomas Burger and Frederick Lawrence. Cambridge, MA: MIT Press, 1989.

Hagopian, Frances. "Democracy and Political Representation in Latin America in the 1990s: Pause, Reorganization, or Decline?" In *Fault Lines of Democracy in Post-Transition Latin America*, eds. Felipe Aguero and Jeffrey Stark, 99–143. Miami: North/South Center Press, 1998.

Hahnel, Robin. *Economic Justice and Democracy: From Competition to Cooperation*.

New York: Routledge, 2005.

Hall, Andria. "Washington D.C., Site of IMF and World Bank Protests, Heating Up." *CNN Worldview*. 15 April 2000.

Hall, Stuart. "The Determinations of News Photographs." In *The Manufacture of News: A Reader*, ed. Stanley Cohen and Jock Young, 176–190. Beverly Hills, CA: SAGE Publications, 1973.

Hallin, Daniel. "The Media, the War in Vietnam, and Political Support: A Critique of the Thesis of an Oppositional Media." *Journal of Politics* 46 (1984): 2–24.

————. *The Uncensored War*. New York: Oxford University Press, 1986.

Halstead, Fred. *Out Now! A Participant's Account of the American Movement Against the Vietnam War*. New York: Monad Press, 1978.

Hampton, Fred. "Excerpts from the Transcript of 'The Murder of Fred Hampton,' a Documentary Film." *New York Times*, 21 July 1971, 35.

Haney López, Ian F. "Protest, Repression, and Race: Legal Violence and the Chicano Movement." *University of Pennsylvania Law Review* 150 (2001): 205–244.

Harden, Blaine and Dan Eggen. "Duo Pleads Guilty to Conspiracy Against U.S.: Last of the 'Portland 7' Face 18 Years in Prison." *Washington Post*, 17 October 2003, A3.

Harden, Blaine. "11 Indicted in 'Eco-Terrorism' Case." *Washington Post*, 21 January 2006, A3.

Hardt, Michael and Antonio Negri. *Empire*. Cambridge, MA: Harvard University Press, 2000.

Harth, Erica, ed. *Last Witnesses: Reflections on the Wartime Internment of Japanese Americans*. New York: Palgrave, 2001.

Hayes, Floyd W., III and Francis A. Kiene, III. "'All Power to the People': The Political Thought of Huey P. Newton and the Black Panther Party." In *The Black Panther Party Reconsidered*, ed. Charles E. Jones, 157–176. Baltimore: Black Classic Press, 1998.

Haynes, William. "Enemy Combatants." *Council on Foreign Relations*, 12 December 2002. Available at: http://www.cfr.org/publication.html?id=5312

Healy v. *James*. 408 U.S. 169, 186. 1972.

Helvarg, David. *The War Against the Greens: The "Wise-Use" Movement, the New Right, and Anti-Environmental Violence*. San Francisco: Sierra Club Books, 1994.

Henderson, Conway W. "Conditions Affecting the Use of Political Repression." *Journal of Conflict Resolution* 35 (1991): 120–142.

Henderson, Wade. "No Justification for Racial Profiling." *San Diego Union-Tribune*, 21 March 2003, B11.

Herman, Edward S. "Diversity of News: Marginalizing the Opposition." *Journal of Communication* 35 (1985): 135–146.

Herman, Edward S. and Noam Chomsky. *Manufacturing Consent: The Political Economy of the Mass Media*. New York: Pantheon, 1988.

Hilliard, David and Lewis Cole. *This Side of Glory: The Autobiography of David Hilliard and the Story of the Black Panther Party*. Boston: Little, Brown and Company, 1993.

Hitler, Adolf. *Mein Kampf*. New York: Reynal & Hitchcock, 1941.

Hoffman, Ian. "Lockyer: Don't Link Activists, Terrorists." *Oakland Tribune*, 21 May 2003.

Hofstadter, Richard. "Reflections on Violence in the United States." In *American Violence: A Documentary History*, ed. Richard Hofstadter and Michael Wallace, 3–43. New York: Alfred A Knopf, 1970.

Hoover, J. Edgar. *Masters of Deceit: The Story of Communism in America and How to Fight It*. New York: Holt, Rinehart and Winston, 1958.

_____. Federal Bureau of Investigation. "Memorandum from Director, FBI to Special Agent in Charge, Atlanta." 14 April 1969.

_____. Federal Bureau of Investigation. "Memorandum from Director, FBI to Special Agents in Charge." 4 March 1968.

_____. Federal Bureau of Investigation. "Memorandum from Director, FBI to SAC, Atlanta." 1 April 1964.

_____. Federal Bureau of Investigation. "Memorandum from Director, FBI to SAC, Atlanta." 11 May 1962.

_____. Federal Bureau of Investigation. "Memorandum from Director, FBI to SAC, Atlanta." 20 September 1957.

"Hope of Peace Put in a Common Faith." *New York Times*, 24 September 1946, 12.

Horwitz, Sari and Christopher B. Daly. "Scientist Fans March Dispute, Counts 870,000." *Washington Post*, 20 October 1995, A1.

Horwitz, Sari and Hamil R. Harris. "Farrakhan Threatens To Sue Park Police Over March Count." *Washington Post*, 18 October 1995, A8.

"House Group Maps War on U.S. Reds." *New York Times*, 30 March 1947, 7.

"Housing Aide Is Called." *New York Times*, 10 October 1952, 2.

Howe Verhovek, Sam. "Trade Talks Start in Seattle Despite a Few Disruptions." *New York Times*, 30 November 1999, A14.

Hsu, Spencer S. "Former Fla. Professor to Be Deported." *Washington Post*, 18 April 2006, A3.

Hughes E.J. "A Curse of Confusion." *Newsweek*, 1 May 1967, 17.

Hughes, Lisa. "Washington Prepares for Another Day of Protests Against the IMF and World Bank Meetings." *CBS Morning News*. 17 April 2000.

Hume, Brit. *Special Report with Brit Hume*. Fox, 29 November 1999.

_____. "Political Headlines." *Special Report with Brit Hume*. Fox, 17 April 2000.

Huppke, Rex W. "Security Screeners 'Nab' David Nelsons." *Seattle Times*, 1 July 2003, A2.

Huston, Luther A. "U.S. Reds Branded 'Puppets' of Soviet." *New York Times*, 21 October 1952, 1.

"Hysterical Saving A Peril to Nation." *New York Times*, 20 April 1917, 11.

"Information on the Confidential Source in the Auburn Arrests." *Portland Independent Media Center*. 26 January 2006. Available at: http://portland.indy-media.org/en/2006/01/332740.shtml

"Informer Says FBI Paid for Spray Paint." *New York Times*, 8 December 1970, 52.

Inskeep, Steve. "Yoo Defends Detainee Measure as 'Rules of War.'" National Public Radio, 4 October 2006.

Isikoff, Michael. "The Other Big Brother." *Newsweek*, 30 January 2006, 32–34.

Iyengar, Shanto and Donald R. Kinder. *News That Matters: Television and American Opinion*. Chicago and London: The University of Chicago Press, 1987.

Iyengar, Shanto. *Is Anyone Responsible?* Chicago: University of Chicago Press, 1991.

Jacobs, Ronald N. *Race, Media and the Crisis of Civil Society: From Watts to Rodney King*. New York: Cambridge University Press, 2000.

Jacobs, Lawrence and Robert Shapiro. "Issues, Candidate Image, and Priming: The Use of Private Polls in Kennedy's 1960 Presidential Campaign." *American Political Science Review* 88 (1994): 527–540.

James, Joy. "Imprisoned Intellectuals: War, Dissent, and Social Justice." *Radical History Review* 85 (2003): 74–81.

Jamieson Jr., Robert L. "Peace Mom Lights a Fire and a Furor." *Seattle Post-Intelligencer*, 18 August 2005, B1.

_____. "Mother's War Protest Veers onto Wrong Path." *Seattle Post-Intelligencer*, 13 August 2005, B1.

Jayko, Margaret. *FBI on Trial: The Victory of the Socialist Workers Party Suit Against Government Spying*. New York: Pathfinder, 1988.

Jehl, Douglas. "Across Country, Thousands Gather to Back U.S. Troops and Policy." *New York Times*, 24 March 2003, B15.

Johnson, Edwin and J.R. White, *G-Man vs. The Fifth Column*. Chicago: Whitman Publishing Company, 1941.

Johnson, Kevin. "White House Renews Push for Tribunals." *USA Today*, 3 August 2006, 2A.

Johnson, Kirk. "Man Sues Secret Service Agent Over Arrest After Approaching Cheney and Denouncing War." *New York Times*, 4 October 2006, A22.

Johnson, Peter. "Amanpour: CNN Practiced Self-Censorship." *USA Today*, 15 September 2003, 4D.

Jones, Charles, ed. *The Black Panther Party Reconsidered*. Baltimore: Black Classic Press, 1998.

Josephy, Alvin M., Jr. *Now That the Buffalo's Gone: A Study of Today's American Indians*. New York: Alfred A. Knopf, 1982.

Josephy, Alvin M. Jr., Joane Nagel, and Troy Johnson. *Red Power: The American Indians' Fight for Freedom.* 2d ed. Lincoln, Nebraska: University of Nebraska Press, 1999.

Kagan, Daryn. "Eco-terrorism Indictments; Miners Trapped in West Virginia; Concerns Growing for American Journalist Jill Carroll." *CNN Live Today,* 20 January 2006.

Kahn, Joseph. "Seattle Protesters Are Back, With a New Target." *New York Times,* 9 April 2000, A6.

_____. "Globalization Unifies Its Many-Striped Foes." *New York Times,* 15 April 2000, A7.

_____. "Global Trade Forum Reflects A Burst Of Conflict and Hope." *New York Times,* 28 November 1999, A1.

Kahneman, Daniel, and Amos Tversky. "The Psychology of Preferences." *Science* 246 (1982): 135–142

Kalmanowieki, Laura. "Origins and Applications of Political Policing in Argentina." *Latin American Perspectives* 27 (2000): 36–56.

Kane, Arthur. "Churchill Keeps His Job but a Second Probe Looms." *Denver Post,* 25 March 2005, A1.

Katznelson, Ira. "The Subtle Politics of Developing Emergency: Political Science as Liberal Guardianship." In *The Cold War & the University: Toward an Intellectual History of the Postwar Years,* ed. David Montgomery, 233–258. New York: The New Press, 1997.

Kazue de Cristoforo, Violet. *May Sky, There Is Always Tomorrow: An Anthology of Japanese American Concentration Camp Kaiko Haiku.* Los Angeles: Sun & Moon Press, 1997.

Keen, Michael Forrest. *Stalking the Sociological Imagination: J. Edgar Hoover's FBI Surveillance of American Sociology.* Westport, Conn.: Greenwood Press, 1999.

Kelley, Jack. "In D.C., Police, Protesters Alike Say They're Prepared: Capital Braces for Weekend Demonstrations." *USA Today,* 13 April 2000, A4.

Kelley, Jack and Yasmin Anwar. "IMF Protests Fizzle in D.C. Drizzle." *USA Today,* 18 April 2000, A3.

Kelly, Michael. "Imitation Activism." *Washington Post,* 19 April 2000, A27.

Kent State: The Day the War Came Home. A film produced by Ron Goetz and directed by Chris Triffo. Executive producer: Mark Mori. Landmark Media Inc., 2001.

Keyishan v. Board of Regents. 385 U.S. 589. 1967.

Khawaja, Marwan. "Repression and Popular Collective Action: Evidence from the West Bank." *Sociological Forum* 8 (1993): 47–71.

Kielbowicz, Richard B. and Clifford Scherer. "The Role of the Press in the Dynamics of Social Movements." *Research in Social Movements, Conflicts and Change.* 9 (1986): 71–96.

Kifner, John. "Police in Chicago Slay 2 Panthers." *New York Times*, 5 December 1969, 1.

_____. "Chicago Panther Mourned." *New York Times*, 10 December 1969, 37.

_____. "5 Negroes Start Panther Inquiry." *New York Times*, 21 December 1969, 47.

_____. "State's Attorney Makes Photographs of Black Panther Apartment Available to Newspaper." *New York Times*, 12 December 1969, 46.

_____. "F.B.I. Files Say Informer Got Data for Panther Raid." *New York Times*, 7 May 1976, 14.

_____. "F.B.I., Before Raid, Gave Police Plan of Chicago Panther's Flat." *New York Times*, 25 May 1974, 14.

_____. "Security Chief for Militant Indian Group Says He Was a Paid Informer for F.B.I." *New York Times*, 13 March 1975, 31.

_____. "In This Washington, No 'Seattle' Is Found, by Police or Protesters." *New York Times*, 19 April 2000, A16.

Kinder, Donald and Lynn Sanders. "Mimicking Political Debate with Survey Questions: The Case of White Opinion on Affirmative Action for Blacks." *Social Cognition* 8 (1990): 73–103.

King, Martin Luther, Jr. "Equality Now." *Nation*, 4 February 1962.

Kirkpatrick, Jeane J. "Communism in Central America: This Time We Know What's Happening." *Washington Post*, 17 April 1983, D8.

Klandermans, Bert. "The Social Construction of Protest and Multiorganizational Fields." In *Frontiers in Social Movement Theory*, ed. Aldon D. Morris and Carol McClurg Mueller, 77–103. New Haven and London: Yale University Press, 1992.

Klein, Naomi. "America's Enemy Within: Armed Checkpoints, Embedded Reporters in Flak Jackets, Brutal Suppression of Peaceful Demonstrators. Baghdad? No, Miami." *Guardian*. 26 November 2003.

Korematsu v. United States. 323 U.S. 214, 223. 1944.

Kornblut, Anne E. "Thousands in Protests against Finance Groups: IMF, World Bank Press on in DC." *Boston Globe*, 17 April 2000, A1.

_____. "Third Journalist Was Paid To Promote Bush Policies." *New York Times*, 29 January 2005, A17.

Korten, Tristram. "Pick Your Reality: Either FTAA Protesters Viciously Assaulted Police, or Police Viciously Assaulted Protesters." *Miami New Times*, 4 December 2003.

Kovach, Bill. "A Citizens Commission Writes to Seven Persons Who, It Says, Served as Informers for the F.B.I." *New York Times*, 13 April 1971, 23.

Kramer, Andrew. "U.S. Authorities Arrest Six Men on Terror Charges, Investigation Focused on Oregon." Associated Press, 4 October 2002.

_____. "Federal Officials Accuse Six of Plotting to Fight U.S. Troops in

Afghanistan." Associated Press, 5 October 2002.

Kunstler, William. *Politics on Trial: Five Famous Trials of the 20th Century*. New York: Ocean Press, 2003.

Kurtz, Howard. "Administration Paid Commentator: Education Dept. Used Williams to Promote 'No Child' Law." *Washington Post*, 8 January 2005, A1.

Kuznick, Peter. *Beyond the Laboratory: Scientists as Political Activists in 1930s America*. Chicago: University of Chicago Press, 1987.

Laird v. *Tatum*. 408 U.S. 1. 1972.

Lane, Charles. "High Court Rejects Detainee Tribunals: 5 to 3 Ruling Curbs President's Claim Of Wartime Power." *Washington Post*, 30 June 2006, A1.

Larabee, Mark. "Hillsboro Man Faces Charges in Plot to Aid al-Qaida, Taliban." *Oregonian*, 28 April 2003, A1.

_____. "Hawash's Plea Gives Prosecutors Vital Voice." *Oregonian*, 9 August 2003, A1.

_____. "'Portland 7' Pair Explain Actions." *Oregonian*, 25 November 2003, A1.

Lasswell, Harold D. *Propaganda Technique in the World War*. New York: Peter Smith, 1938.

Laughlin, Meg, Jennifer Liberto, and Justin George. "8 Times, Al-Arian Hears 'Not Guilty'." *St. Petersburg Times*, 7 December 2005, 1A.

_____. "Al-Arian Gets More Prison Time." *St. Petersburg Times*, 17 November 2006, 4B.

Lee, Henry K. "Appeals Panel Sends Journalist Back to Prison." *San Francisco Chronicle*, 23 September 2006, B5.

Leffler, Melvyn P. "National Security." *The Journal of American History* 77 (1990): 143–152.

Leiby, Richard. "Talking Out of School: Was an Islamic Professor Exercising His Freedom or Promoting Terror?" *Washington Post*, 28 July 2002, F1.

LeoGrande, William M. *Our Own Backyard: The United States in Central America, 1977–1992*. Chapel Hill and London: University of North Carolina Press, 1998.

Leong, Sze Tsung Control Space. In *Mutations*, eds. Rem Koolhaas, Stefano Boeri, Sanford Kwinter, Nadia Tazi, and Hand Ulrich Obrist, 185–195. Barcelona: Actar., 2001

Leonnig, Carol D. "Lawsuit Criticizes Secret Service." *Washington Post*, 24 September 2003, A27.

Leonnig, Carol D. and Del Quentin Wilber. "D.C. Settles With Mass Arrest Victims: 7 Rounded Up in 2002 IMF Protest to Get $425,000 and an Apology." *Washington Post*, 25 January 2005, A1.

LePage, Andrew. "Eco-terror Sparks Anxiety: Builders on Guard against Environmental Radicals," *Sacramento Bee*, 9 February 2005, D1.

"Letters: Protest and Patriotism." *Sacramento Bee*, 16 August 2005, B6.

Levin, Murray B. *Political Hysteria in America: The Democratic Capacity for Repression.* New York: Basic Books, 1971.

Levy, Leonard W. *Legacy of Suppression: Freedom of Speech and Press in Early American History.* Cambridge, MA: Harvard University Press, 1964.

Lewis, Anthony. "High Court Backs House Committee in Contempt Issue." *New York Times*, 28 February 1961, 1.

Lewis, George. "Seattle Still Under Curfew This Morning after Protesters of World Trade Organization Became Violent Last Night." *NBC Today.* 1 December 1999.

_____. "World Trade Organization To Meet Tomorrow In Seattle." *NBC Nightly News.* 29 November. 1999.

Lewis, Joseph. Personal Interview. 28 December 2006.

Lewis, John. "Statement of John E. Lewis Deputy Assistant Director, Counterterrorism Division Federal Bureau of Investigation Before the Senate Committee on Environment and Public Works." 18 May 2005. Available at: http://www.fbi.gov/congress/congress05/lewis051805.htm and http://epw.senate.gov/hearing_statements.cfm?id=237817

Lewis, Justin. *Constructing Public Opinion: How Political Elites Do What They Like and Why We Seem to Go Along with It.* New York: Columbia University Press, 2001.

Lewis, Neil A. "Ashcroft Permits F.B.I. to Monitor Internet and Public Activities." *New York Times*, 31 May 2002, A20.

Lewontin, R.C. "The Cold War and the Transformation of the Academy." In *The Cold War & the University: Toward an Intellectual History of the Postwar Years*, ed. David Montgomery, 1–34. New York: The New Press, 1997.

Lichbach, Mark Irving. "Deterrence or Escalation? The Puzzle of Aggregate Studies of Repression and Dissent." *Journal of Conflict Resolution* 31 (1987): 266–297.

Lichtblau, Eric. "F.B.I. Scrutinizes Antiwar Rallies." *New York Times,* 23 November 2003, A1.

_____. "Documents Reveal Scope of U.S. Database on Antiwar Protests." *New York Times*, 13 October 2006, A16.

_____. "F.B.I. Found to Violate Its Informant Rules." *New York Times*, 13 September 2005, A14.

_____. "Large Volume of F.B.I. Files Alarms U.S. Activist Groups." *New York Times*, 18 July 2005, A12.

_____. "Ex-Professor Is Called Terrorist Leader." *New York Times*, 7 June 2005, A3.

_____. "Inquiry Into F.B.I. Questioning Is Sought." *New York Times,* 18 August 2004, A16.

_____. "Protesters at Heart of Debate on Security vs. Civil Rights." *New York Times*, 28 August 2004, A9.

_____. "F.B.I. Goes Knocking for Political Troublemakers." *New York Times*, 16 August 2004, A1.

Lichter, S. Robert, Stanley Rothman, and Linda Lichter. *The Media Elite*. Bethesda, MD: Adler & Adler, 1986.

Linfield, Michael. *Freedom Under Fire: U.S. Civil Liberties in Times of War*. Boston: South End Press, 1990.

Lippmann, Walter. *Public Opinion*. New York: The Free Press, 1922.

Lipton, Eric. "Software Being Developed to Monitor Opinions of U.S." *New York Times*, 4 October 2006, A24.

Lissner, Will. "World Communists Warned To Ape Soviet Party Rules." *New York Times*, 11 July 1948, 1.

_____. "Expansion Is Key in New Red 'Line.'" *New York Times*, 29 May 1949, 10.

_____. "New U.S. Red Line Seeks Coalition." *New York Times*, 7 March 1954, 1.

Loftus, Joseph A. "12 U.S. Communists Indicted in Anti-Government Plot: Foster, Davis, Others Seized." *New York Times*, 21 July 1948, 1.

_____. "McCarthy Sticks to Fight on Reds." *New York Times*, 10 July 1952, 21.

_____. "Eisenhower Signs Red Control Bill, Citing Protection." *New York Times*, 25 August 1954, 1.

Long, James. "Raid Seeks Information on Attacks Across West." *Oregonian*, 4 February 2000, C1.

Love, Alice Ann. "Police Raid Protest Headquarters, Say Bomb Material Found," Associated Press, 15 April 2000.

Lyon, David. *The Electronic Eye: The Rise of Surveillance Society*. Minneapolis: University of Minnesota Press, 1994.

_____. *Surveillance Society: Monitoring Everyday Life*. Buckingham and Philadelphia: Open University Press, 2001.

MacArthur, John R. *Second Front: Censorship and Propaganda in the Gulf War*. New York: Hill and Wang, 1992.

Mackenzie, Angus. *Secrets: The CIA's War at Home*. Berkeley: University of California Press, 1997.

Mallaby, Sebastian. "D-Day in Washington." *Washington Post*, 24 March 2000, A23.

Manchester, William. *The Glory and the Dream: A Narrative History of America, 1932–1972*. Boston and Toronto: Little Brown and Company, 1974.

Mann, Eric. *Comrade George: An Investigation into the Life, Political Thought, and Assassination of George Jackson*. Cambridge, MA: Hovey Street Press, 1972.

Mansbridge, Jane. "Using Power/ Fighting Power." In *Democracy and Difference: Contesting the Boundaries of the Political*, ed. Seyla Benhabib, 46–66. Princeton, NJ: Princeton University Press, 1996.

Marable, Manning. *How Capitalism Underdeveloped Black America*. Cambridge, MA: South End Press, 2000.

————. *Race, Reform, and Rebellion: The Second Reconstruction of Black America*. Jackson, Mississippi: University Press of Mississippi, 1991.

Marcum, Diana. "Group Alleges Police Scrutiny Peace Fresno Says Late Detective in Anti-terror Unit Was at Meetings." *Fresno Bee*, 3 October 2003, A1.

Marcuse, Herbert. *The One-Dimensional Man: Studies in the Ideology of Advanced Industrial Society*. Boston: Beacon Press, 1964.

Markon, Jerry. "Moussaoui Prosecution Is Dealt Setback." *Washington Post*, 4 July 2003, A8.

————. "Jailing of Hamdi Upheld As Rehearing Is Denied." *Washington Post*, 10 July 2003, A10.

————. "Military to Watch Prisoner Interview: Hamdi's Lawyer Resents Monitoring." *Washington Post*, 31 January 2004, B3.

————. "Witness Is Silent in Terror Probe; Ex-Professor Says Grand Jury Testimony Would Endanger Him." *Washington Post*, 14 November 2006, B5.

Marks, Kim. Personal Interview. 12 December 2006.

Marqusee, Mike. *Redemption Song: Muhammad Ali and the Spirit of the Sixties*. New York: Verso, 1999.

Marshall, Nancy. "Protests Against a Possible War in Iraq Taking Place Around the Country." *NPR Weekend All Things Considered*. 26 October 2002.

Marx, Gary T. *Undercover: Police Surveillance in America*. Berkeley, CA: University of California Press, 1988.

————. "External Efforts to Damage or Facilitate Social Movements: Some Patterns, Explanations, Outcomes, and Complications." In *The Dynamics of Social Movements: Resource Mobilization, Social Control, and Tactics*, ed. Mayer Zald and John D. McCarthy, 94–125. Cambridge, MA: Winthrop Publishers, Inc, 1979.

————. "Thoughts on a Neglected Category of Social Movement Participant: The Agent Provocateur and the Informant." *American Journal of Sociology* 80 (1974): 402–442.

Marx, Karl. *The Eighteenth Brumaire of Louis Bonaparte*. New York: International Publishers, 1991.

Matthews, Traceye. "'No One Ever Asks, What a Man's Place in the Revolution Is': Gender and the Politics of the Black Panther Party 1966–1971." In *The Black Panther Party Reconsidered*, ed. Charles E. Jones, 267–304. Baltimore: Black Classic Press, 1998.

Matthiessen, Peter. *In the Spirit of Crazy Horse*. New York: The Viking Press, 1984.

McAdam, Doug. "The Framing Function of Movement Tactics: Strategic Dramaturgy in the American Civil Rights Movement." In *Comparative*

Perspectives on Social Movements: Political Opportunities, Mobilizing Structures, and Cultural Framings, ed. Doug McAdam, John D. McCarthy, and Mayer N. Zald, 338–355. New York: Cambridge University Press, 1996.

McAdam, Doug, John D. McCarthy, and Mayer N. Zald, eds. *Comparative Perspectives on Social Movements: Political Opportunities, Mobilizing Structures, and Cultural Framings*, New York: Cambridge University Press, 1996

McAdam, Doug, Sidney Tarrow, and Charles Tilly. *Dynamics of Contention*. New York: Cambridge University Press, 2001.

McCarthy, John D. and Clark McPhail. "The Institutionalization of Protest in the United States." In *The Social Movement Society: Contentious Politics for a New Century*, ed. David S. Meyer and Sidney Tarrow, 83–110. New York: Rowman & Littlefield Publishers, Inc., 1998.

McCarthy, John D., Clark McPhail, and Jackie Smith. "Images of Protest: Dimensions of Selection Bias in Media Coverage of Washington Demonstrations, 1982 and 1991." *American Sociological Review* 61 (1996): 478–499.

"McCarthy Demands Boycott By Allies." *New York Times*, 24 September 1953, 10.

McChesney, Robert W. *Rich Media, Poor Democracy: U.S. Communication Politics in the 21st Century*. Urbana and Chicago: University of Illinois Press, 1999.

———. *The Problem of the Media: U.S. Communication Politics in Dubious Times*. New York: Monthly Review Press, 2004.

McGann, Chris. "Reichert Once Bragged He Ratted Out Bus Driver." *Seattle Post-Intelligencer*, 4 November 2006, A1.

McGrory, Mary. "Echoes of Red-Baiting." *Washington Post*, 12 June 1983, B1.

McKinley, Jesse. "Blogger Jailed after Defying Court Orders." *New York Times*, 2 August 2006, A15.

McMahon, Patrick and James Cox. "'Stop the WTO:' Protesters Say Goal Achieved." *USA Today*, 1 December 1999, 19A.

McMahon, Patrick. "WTO Under Fire on Many Fronts." *USA Today*, 29 November 1999, A6.

McMurtry, John. *Value Wars: The Global Market Versus the Life Economy*. London: Pluto Press, 2002.

McNair, Brian. *Images of the Enemy: Reporting the New Cold War*. New York: Routledge, 1988.

McWilliams, Carey. *Witch Hunt: The Revival of Heresy*. Boston, MA: Little, Brown and Company, 1950.

Medved, Michael. "Battle in Seattle: No, This Wasn't the '60s All Over Again." *USA Today*, 7 December 1999, 19A.

Melloan, George. "Welcome to the Seattle World's Fair, Circa 1999." *Wall Street Journal*, 30 November 1999, A27.

Mermin, Jonathan. *Debating War and Peace: Media Coverage of U.S. Intervention in the Post-Vietnam Era.* Princeton, NJ: Princeton University Press, 1999.

Merritt, George and Howard Pankratz. "Prof's Essay Spurs Board Session." *Denver Post*, 31 January 2005, B1.

Michener, James A. *Kent State: What Happened and Why?* New York: Random House, 1971.

Micklethwait, John and Adrian Wooldridge. "World Trade Organization; Skewered in Seattle; Fringe Protesters at Center of Global Mainstream." *Los Angeles Times*, 5 December 1999, 1.

Miller, John J. "In the Name of the Animals—America Faces a New Kind of Terrorism." *National Review*, 3 July 2006.

Miller, M. Mark and Bonnie Parnell Riechert. "Interest Group Strategies and Journalistic Norms: News Framing of Environmental Issues." In *Environmental Risks and the Media*, ed. Stuart Allan, Barbara Adam, and Cynthia Carter, 45–54. New York: Routledge, 2000.

Miller, Will. "Introduction for Michael Parenti." University of Vermont. 9 April 1997. Available at: http://www.uvm.edu/~radphil/uvmfirings.htm

Mills, Ami Chen. *CIA Off Campus: Building the Movement against Agency Recruitment and Research.* Boston, South End Press, 1991.

Mink, Eric. "Despite Act's Outrages, It's All Politics for Now." *Oregonian*, 8 October 2006, E10.

Mintz, John. "Professor Indicted as Terrorist Leader." *Washington Post*, 21 February 2003, A1.

Minugh, Kim. "Second Guilty Plea in Eco-Terror Plot." *Sacramento Bee*, 20 July 2006, B2.

Mitchell, Don. *The Right to the City: Social Justice and the Fight for Public Space.* New York: Guilford, 2003.

Mitchell, Russ. "Police In Washington, DC Ready for Protests against World Bank-IMF Meetings" *CBS Evening News.* 15 April 2000.

Mitchell, Steve. "Activists Threaten More Actions." *UPI*, 23 September 2006.

"Mitchell Issues Plea on F.B.I. Files." *New York Times*, 24 March 1971, 24.

Mitgang, Herbert. *Dangerous Dossiers: Exposing the Secret War against America's Greatest Authors.* New York: D.I. Fine, 1988.

Mittelman, James H. *The Globalization Syndrome: Transformation and Resistance.* Princeton, NJ: Princeton University Press, 2000.

Mock, James R. and Cedric Larson. *Words that Won the War: The Story of the Committee on Public Information, 1917–1919.* New York: Russell & Russell, 1968 [1939].

Montgomery, David, ed. *The Cold War & the University: Toward an Intellectual History of the Postwar Years.* New York: The New Press, 1997.

Montgomery, David. "Protesters and Police Trade Accusations." *Washington Post*, 4 August 2000, A23.

_____. "Demonstrators Are United By Zeal for 'Global Justice.'" *Washington Post*, 16 April 2000, A1.

_____. "Stirring a Cause: When Things Get Rough for Protesters, These Lawyers Go on the March." *Washington Post*, 12 May 2003, C1.

Moore, Howard Jr.. "Angela—Symbol of Resistance." In *If They Come in the Morning*, Angela Y. Davis, 203–212. New York: The New American Library Inc., 1971.

Moore, Mike. *A World Without Walls: Freedom, Development, Free Trade and Global Governance*. New York: Cambridge University Press, 2003.

Moore, Will H. "Repression and Dissent: Substitution, Context, and Timing." *American Journal of Political Science* 42 (1998): 851–873.

Moreno, Sylvia and Lena H. Sun. "In Effort to Keep the Peace, Protesters Declare 'Code Pink.'" *Washington Post*, 9 March 2003, C1.

Morgan, Ted. *Reds: McCarthyism in Twentieth-Century America*. New York: Random House, 2003.

Morrison, Blake. "IMF Protesters' Goals as Varied as Their Styles." *USA Today*, 14 April 2000, A4.

Mowat, Farley. *My Discovery of America*. Boston: The Atlantic Monthly Press, 1985.

Mueller, Robert S. "Testimony of Robert S. Mueller, III, Director, Federal Bureau of Investigation, Before the United States Senate Committee on the Judiciary." 20 May 2004. Available at: http://www.fbi.gov/congress/congress04/mueller052004.htm

_____. "Prepared Remarks of Robert S. Mueller, III Director, Federal Bureau of Investigation Operation Backfire Press Conference." RFK Main Justice Building. Washington, D.C. 20 January 2006. Available at: http://www.fbi.gov/pressrel/speeches/mueller012006.htm

Muller, Judy. "WTO Meeting Continues In Seattle Despite Protests." *ABC World News Tonight*. 2 December 1999.

Murray, Robert K. *Red Scare: A Study of National Hysteria, 1919–1920*. New York: McGraw-Hill Book Company, 1964.

"Muslim Scholar Barred by U.S. Denies Support For Terrorism." *New York Times*, 26 September 2006, A13.

Muwakkil, Salim. "Newspaper Editor's Resignation Reveals Growing Media Rifts." *Chicago Tribune*, 26 March 2001.

NAACP v. *Claiborne Hardware Co.*, 458 U.S. 886. 1982.

Navasky, Victor S. *Naming Names*. New York: Penguin, 1980.

Navrot, Miguel. "ACLU Protests VA 'Sedition' Memo to Nurse." *Albuquerque Journal*, 2 February 2006, A1.

Nederveen Pieterse, Jan. "Globalization and Collective Action." In *Globalization and Social Movements*, ed. Pierre Hamil, Henri Lustiger-Thaler, Jan Nederveen

Pieterse, and Sasha Roseneil, 21–39. New York: Palgrave, 2001.

Neier, Aryeh. "Surveillance as Censorship." In *The Campaign against the Underground Press*, ed. Geoffrey Rips, 9–17. San Francisco: City Lights Books, 1981.

New York Times Co. v. *Sullivan*. 376 U.S. 967. 1964.

New York Times Co. v. *United States*. 403 U.S. 713. 1971.

Nicholas, Peter. "State Tracked Protesters in the Name of Security." *Los Angeles Times*, 1 July 2006, A1.

Nichols, R.R. Federal Bureau of Investigation. "Memorandum to Director Hoover—COMINFIL SCLC, IS—C." 1 October 1962.

Nielsen, Kirk. "Headbangers Ball: Claims that Police Didn't Aim at FTAA Protesters' Upper Bodies Get a Black Eye." *Miami New Times*, 11 December 2003.

Nieves, Evelyn. "Environmentalists Win Bombing Lawsuit." *New York Times*, 12 June 2002, A18.

Nogueira, Ana. "*DN!* Producer Ana Nogueira Among 250 Arrested in Miami FTAA Protests." *Democracy Now!*, 24 November 2003.

"'No Intention' of Resigning." *New York Times*, 2 August 1954, 7.

O'Connell, Chris. "Panel to Probe Violence at Protest: Demonstrators Against the War in Iraq Complained the Police Fired Rubber Pellets and Other Items into a Crowd Without Provocation." *Los Angeles Times*, 27 May 2003.

O'Heffernan, Patrick. "A Mutual Exploitation Model of Media Influence in U.S. Foreign Policy." In *Taken By Storm: The Media, Public Opinion, and U.S. Foreign Policy in the Gulf War*, ed. W. Lance Bennett and David Paletz, 231–249. Chicago: University of Chicago Press, 1994.

Oliver, Pamela E. and Gregory G. Maney. "Political Processes and Local Newspaper Coverage of Protest Events: From Selection Bias to Triadic Interactions." *American Journal of Sociology* 106 (2000): 463–505.

Oliver, Pamela E. and Daniel J. Myers. "How Events Enter the Public Sphere: Conflict, Location, and Sponsorship in Local Newspaper Coverage of Public Events." *American Journal of Sociology* 105 (1999): 38–87.

Olsen, Jack. *Last Man Standing: The Tragedy and Triumph of Geronimo Pratt*. New York: Doubleday, 2000.

Olshansky, Barbara. *Secret Trials and Executions: Military Tribunals and the Threat to Democracy*. New York: Seven Stories Press, 2002.

"100 Radical Papers May Be Suppressed." *New York Times*, 16 September 1917, 7.

O'Neill, Kate. "Transnational Protest: States, Circuses, and Conflict at the Frontline of Global Politics." *International Studies Review* 6 (2004): 233–251.

O'Reilly, Bill. "The O'Reilly Factor: Talking Points Memo and Top Story." *Fox News*, 15 August 2005.

———. "The O'Reilly Factor: Talking Points Memo and Top Story." *Fox News*, 16 August 2005.

O'Reilly, Kenneth. *"Racial Matters" The FBI's Secret File on Black America, 1960–1972*. New York: The Free Press, 1989.

O'Reilly, Kenneth and David Gallen. *Black Americans: The FBI Files*. New York: Carroll & Graf Publishers, Inc., 1994.

"Others Under Fire." *Time* magazine, 17 January 1972.

Paletz, David L. and Robert M. Entman. *Media Power Politics*. New York: The Free Press, 1981.

Pan, Philip P. "China Links bin Laden to Separatists; Report Details Attacks in Mostly Muslim Region." *Washington Post*, 22 January 2002, A8.

Pankratz, Howard. "Ward Churchill Resigns as Head of CU's Ethnic-Studies Department." *Denver Post*, 1 February 2005, A1.

Parenti, Christian. *The Soft Cage: Surveillance in America from Slave Passes to the War on Terror*. New York: Basic Books, 2003.

Parenti, Michael. "Methods of Media Manipulation." In *Twenty Years of Censored News*, ed. Carl Jensen, 27–32. New York: Seven Stories Press, 1997.

_____. *Inventing Reality: The Politics of the Mass Media*. New York: St. Martin's Press, 1986.

_____. *Against Empire*. San Francisco: City Lights Books, 1995.

_____. *Dirty Truths: Reflections on Politics, Media, Ideology, Conspiracy, Ethic Life and Class Power*. San Francisco: City Lights, 1996.

_____. Personal Interview. 12 December 2006.

Parmet, Herbert S. *Eisenhower and the American Crusades*. New York: The MacMillan Company, 1972.

Peck, Abe. *Uncovering the Sixties: The Life and Times of the Underground Press*. New York: Citadel Press, 1991.

"Pennsylvania Peace Group, ACLU Accuse FBI Of Improper Surveillance," *The Frontrunner*, 15 March 2006.

Pepper, William F. *An Act of State: The Execution of Martin Luther King*. New York, Verso, 2003.

_____. *Orders to Kill: The Truth Behind the Murder of Martin Luther King*. New York: Carroll & Graf Publishers, Inc., 1995.

Peterson, Jonathan. "A World of Difference in Trade Views; Economy: Question of Individual Rights versus Profits Raised as Nations Gather in Seattle." *Los Angeles Times*, 28 November 1999, 1.

Phillips, Kyra. "Anti-Globalization Protesters March Through Washington During IMF and World Bank Meetings." *CNN Sunday Morning*, 16 April 2000.

Pickering, Leslie James. *The Earth Liberation Front: 1997–2002*. South Wales, NY: Arissa Publications, n.d..

Pinkney, Alphonso. *Red, Black, and Green: Black Nationalism in the United States*. New York: Cambridge University Press, 1976.

Piven, Frances Fox and Richard A. Cloward. *Regulating the Poor: The Functions of*

Public Welfare. New York: Vintage, 1971.

Plummer, Don. "State of Emergency Set for G-8 Counties: Perdue Order Covers 6 Areas Near Summit." *Atlanta Journal-Constitution*, 22 May 2004, 3E.

Pogash, Carol and Chris O'Connell. "Antiwar Protest Turns Violent at Port of Oakland: Some Demonstrators Throw Rocks and Bolts at Police, Who Shoot Nonlethal Projectiles, Hitting Protesters as well as Some Longshoremen." *Los Angeles Times*, 8 April 2003, B1.

Powell, Michael. "No Choice but Guilty: Lackawanna Case Highlights Legal Tilt." *Washington Post*, 29 July 2003, A1.

⎯⎯⎯. "In New York, Thousands Protest a War Against Iraq." *Washington Post*, 16 February 2003, A22.

"President Creates Advertising Agency." *New York Times*, 20 January 1918, 6.

President's Commission on Campus Unrest. "The Report of the President's Commission on Campus Unrest." Washington, DC: U.S. Government Printing Office, 1970.

"Press Comment on the Censorship Plan." *New York Times*, 24 May 1917, 2.

Preston, William Jr. *Aliens and Dissenters: Federal Suppression of Radicals, 1903–1933*. Cambridge, MA: Harvard University Press, 1963.

Price, David. *Threatening Anthropology: McCarthyism and the FBI's Investigation of Anthropologists*. Durham: Duke University Press, 2004.

"Professor's Ouster Fought in Vermont." *New York Times*, 5 December 1971, 86.

"Prosecutors Cited for Indians' Trial." *New York Times*, 20 September 1974, 22.

"Protest Q & A." *Washington Post*, 17 April 2000, A6.

"Protesters Target Institutions Most Able to Help the Poor." *USA Today*, 14 April 2000, A14.

Purdum, Todd. "Ex-Black Panther Wins Long Legal Battle." *New York Times*, 27 April 2000, A18.

Purdy, Matthew and Lowell Bergman. "Where the Trail Led: Between Evidence and Suspicion: Unclear Danger: Inside the Lackawanna Terror Case." *New York Times*, 12 October 2003, 1.

"Questionable Bumper Sticker a Ticket to Free Speech Fight." Associated Press, 24 March 2006.

Quinn, Beth. "ACLU Decries Use of Force by Police at Bush Event." *Oregonian*, 7 January 2005, E5.

"Raid from Coast to Coast." *New York Times*, 3 January 1920, 1.

Raines, Howell. *My Soul Is Rested: Movement Days in the Deep South Remembered*. New York: G.P. Putnam's Sons, 1977.

Rasler, Karen. "Concessions, Repression, and Political Protest in the Iranian Revolution." *American Sociological Review* 61 (1996): 132–152.

Rather, Dan. "Protest Group Ruckus and What They Hope to Accomplish this Weekend in Washington, DC." *CBS Evening News*. 14 April 2000.

Reagan, Ronald. "Executive Order 12333—United States Intelligence Activities."
    In *Public Papers of the Presidents: Ronald Reagan, 1981*. Washington, DC:
    Government Printing Office, 1982.

Redden, Jim. "Police State Targets the Left." In *The Battle of Seattle: The New
    Challenge to Capitalist Globalization*, ed. Eddie Yuen, Daniel Burton Rose, and
    George Katsiaficas, 139–151. Brooklyn: Soft Skull Press, 2001.

Reed Ward, Paula. "Peace Group Claims FBI Spied on Activity." *Pittsburgh Post-
    Gazette*, 15 March 2006, B1.

Regan, Lauren. Personal Interview. 19 December 2006.

Reston, James. "General Asks End of All Prejudices." *New York Times*, 4 November
    1952.

Rhodes, Jane. "Fanning the Flames of Racial Discord: The National Press and
    the Black Panther Party." *The Harvard Journal of Press and Politics* 4 (1999):
    95–118.

Riccardi, Nicholas. "FBI Keeps Watch on Activists." *Los Angeles Times,* 27 March
    2006.

Richards, David. *Played Out: The Jean Seberg Story*. New York: Random House,
    1981.

Richman, Josh. "Lockyer Vows Action on Police Spying." *Inside Bay Area*, 29 July
    2006.

Rips, Geoffrey. *The Campaign Against the Underground Press*. San Francisco: City
    Lights Books, 1981.

Risen, James and Eric Lichtblau. "Bush Lets U.S. Spy on Callers Without Courts."
    New York Times, 16 December 2005, A1.

Robinson, Greg. *By Order of the President: FDR and the Internment of the Japanese
    Americans*. Cambridge, MA: Harvard University Press, 2001.

Rogin, Michael Paul. *Ronald Reagan, the Movie*. Berkeley: University of California
    Press, 1987.

Rojecki, Andrew. "Modernism, State Sovereignty and Dissent: Media and the New
    Post-Cold War Movements." *Critical Studies in Mass Communication* 19 (2002):
    152–171.

Roos, Philip D., Dowell H. Smith, Stephen Langley, and James McDonald.
    "The Impact of the American Indian Movement on the Pine Ridge Indian
    Reservation." *Phylon* 41 (1980): 89–99.

Rosebraugh, Craig. *Burning Rage of A Dying Planet: Speaking for the Earth Liberation
    Front*. New York: Lantern Books, 2004.

Rosenthal, Elizabeth. "Beijing Says Chinese Muslims Were Trained as Terrorists
    With Money from bin Laden." *New York Times*, 22 January 2002, A11.

Rothschild, Matthew. "Red Squad Hits Denver." *McCarthy Watch*, 14 March 2002.
    Available at: http://progressive.org/mag_mcdenver
    _____. "ACLU Seeks Info on Spying on Fresno Peace Group." *McCarthy Watch*,

4 February 2004. Available at: http://progressive.org/mag_mcfresno

_____. "Police Shoot Pepper Balls at Oregon Demonstrators." *McCarthy Watch*, 21 October 2004. Available at: http://www.progressive.org/mag_mc_pepper

_____. "'Seditious' VA Nurse Cleared." *McCarthy Watch*, 21 April 2006. Available at: http://progressive.org/mag_mc020806

_____. "Union Appeals Firing of Bus Driver Who Flipped Off Bush." *McCarthy Watch*, 5 November 2006. Available at: http://www.progressive.org/mag_mc110506

_____. "Bush Protester Arrested for Carrying Sign." *McCarthy Watch*, 29 January 2004. Available at: http://progressive.org/mag_mcsign2

_____. County Supervisor Booted from Bush Event for Wearing Hidden Kerry Shirt." *McCarthy Watch*, 22 July 2004. Available at: http://www.progressive.org/mag_mcshirt

_____. "Three Teachers Evicted from Bush Event for Wearing 'Protect Our Civil Liberties' T-Shirts." *McCarthy Watch*, 16 October 2004. Available at: http://www.progressive.org/node/2362

_____. "FBI, Michigan Police Tag Peace Group, Affirmative Action Group, and Others as 'Terrorist'." *McCarthy Watch*, 29 August 2005. Available at: http://www.progressive.org/mag_mc082905

Roy, Arundhati. "A Writer's Place in Politics." *Alternative Radio*. David Barsamian, ed. Amherst, MA. 15 February 2001.

Rubin, Allen and Earl Babbie. *Research Methods for Social Work*, 4th ed. Belmont, CA: Wadsworth, 2000.

Rucht, Dieter. "The Transnationalization of Social Movements: Trends, Causes, and Problems." In *Social Movements in a Globalizing World*, ed. Donatella della Porta, Hanspeter Kriesi, and Dieter Rucht, 206–222. London: MacMillan, 1999.

"Russia Cracks the Whip." *New York Times*, 12 July 1948, 18.

Saito, Natsu Taylor. "Whose Liberty? Whose Security? The USA PATRIOT Act in the Context of COINTELPRO and the Unlawful Repression of Political Dissent." *Oregon Law Review* 81 (2002): 1051–1131.

Sale, Kirkpatrick. *SDS*. New York: Vintage Books, 1973.

Saltzman, Jonathan. "Judge Deplores But Oks Site for Protesters." *Boston Globe*, 23 July 2004, A1.

Sandalow, Marc. "Bush Heads to California, Hitting Hard at War Critics." *San Francisco Chronicle*, 30 September 2006, A1.

Sanger, David E. "President Chides World Trade Body in Seattle." *New York Times*, 2 December 1999, A1.

_____. "President Defends Military Tribunals in Terrorist Cases." *New York Times*, 30 November 2001, A1.

Santana, Arthur. "D.C. Council Probing Police Conduct in Protests." *Washington*

Post, 29 April 2003, B3.

Savage, Charlie. "Bush Signings Called Effort to Expand Power." *Boston Globe*, 4 January 2006, A1.

———. "Bush Could Bypass New Torture Ban: Waiver Right Is Reserved." *Boston Globe*, 5 October 2006, A2.

———. "Bush Shuns Patriot Act Requirement: In Addendum to Law, He Says Oversight Rules Are Not Binding." *Boston Globe*, 24 March 2006, A1.

Savage, Charlie and Alan Wirzbicki. "White House-Friendly Reporter Under Scrutiny." *Boston Globe*, 2 February 2005, A4.

Sayer, John William. *Ghost Dancing the Law: The Wounded Knee Trials*. Cambridge, Mass.: Harvard University Press, 1997.

"Says Russia Plots to Rule the World." *New York Times*, 13 October 1946, 29.

Scahill, Jeremy. "Mayhem in Miami." *Democracy Now!*, 21 November 2003.

———. "The Miami Model: Paramilitaries, Embedded Journalists and Illegal Protests." *CounterPunch*, 24 November 2003. Available at: http://www.counter-punch.org/scahill11242003.html

Scatterday, G.H. Federal Bureau of Investigation. "Memorandum to Mr. A. Rosen." 22 May 1961.

Schenck v. *United States*. 249 U.S. 211. 1919.

Schiller, Herbert I. *The Mind Managers*. Boston: Beacon Press, 1973.

Schmidt, Regin. *Red Scare: FBI and the Origins of Anticommunism in the United States, 1919–1943*. Copenhagen, Denmark: Museum Tusculanum Press, University of Copenhagen, 2000.

Schoenfeld, A. Clay, Robert F. Meier, and Robert J. Griffin. "Constructing a Social Problem: The Press and the Environment." *Social Problems* 27 (1979): 38–61.

Schram, Sanford F. and Joe Soss. "Success Stories: Welfare Reform, Policy Discourse, and the Politics of Research." *Annals of the American Academy of Political and Social Science* 577 (2001): 49–65.

Schrecker, Ellen. *The Age of McCarthyism: A Brief History with Documents*. New York: St. Martin's Press, 1994.

———. *No Ivory Tower: McCarthyism and the Universities*. New York: Oxford University Press, 1986.

———. *Many Are the Crimes: McCarthyism in America* New York: Little, Brown, and Company, 1998.

Schudson, Michael. *Discovering the News: A Social History of American Newspapers*. New York: Basic Books, 1978.

Schulhofer, Stephen J. *The Enemy Within: Intelligence Gathering, Law Enforcement, and Civil Liberties in the Wake of September 11*. Washington, DC: The Century Foundation, 2002.

Schultz, Bud and Ruth Schultz. *The Price of Dissent: Testimonies to Political Repression in America*. Berkeley: University of California Press, 2001.

_____. *It Did Happen Here: Recollections of Political Repression in America.* Berkeley: University of California Press, 1989.

Sciutto, Jim. "Protesters Continue Attempts to Disrupt Talks of World Bank and International Monetary Fund." *ABC Good Morning America.* 17 April 2000.

Scott, James C. *Seeing Like a State: How Certain Schemes to Improve the Human Condition Have Failed.* New Haven: Yale University Press, 1998.

Scott, Janny. "Protesters Are Denied Potent Tactic of the Past." *New York Times,* 13 February 2003, B1.

Seib, Gerald F., J.C. Conklin, and John Hechinger. "WTO—Clash in Seattle: Most Americans Don't Show Distrust of Free Trade." *Wall Street Journal,* 2 December 1999, A8.

Seigenthaler, John. "American Protests against War with Iraq." *NBC Nightly News.* 15 February 2003.

"Seven Questions Covering Iraq." *Foreign Policy,* July 2006. Available at: http://www.foreignpolicy.com/story/cms.php?story_id=3525

Shapira, Ian. "On the Mall, Songs of Old Carry Current Plea for Peace: Familiar Faces Protest Potential Action in Iraq." *Washington Post,* 17 March 2003, B1.

Sheehy, Gail. *Panthermania: The Clash of Black Against Black in One American City.* New York: Harper & Row, Publishers, 1971.

Shepard, Benjamin and Ronald Hayduk, eds. *From ACT UP to the WTO: Urban Protest and Community Building in the Era of Globalization.* New York: Verso, 2002.

Shepard, Benjamin. "Movement of Movements: Toward a More Democratic Globalization." *New Political Science* 26 (2004): 593–605.

Sheridan, Mary Beth and Brooke A. Masters. "More than 350 Held in Probe, Ashcroft Says." *Washington Post,* 25 September 2001, A1.

Shoval, Noam and Michal Isaacson. "Application of Tracking Technologies to the Study of Pedestrian Spatial Behavior." *The Professional Geographer* 58 (2006): 172–183.

Sikkink, Kathryn. "Human Rights, Principled Issue Networks, and Sovereignty in Latin America." *International Organization* 47 (1993): 411–441.

Silvestrini, Elaine. "Judge Says Al-Arian Trial Stays In Tampa." *Tampa Tribune,* 24 May 2005, Metro Section, p. 1.

_____. "Judge Rebukes, Sentences Al-Arian." *Tampa Tribune,* 2 May 2006, 1.

Singh, Nikhil Pal. "The Black Panthers and the 'Underdeveloped Country' of the Left." In *The Black Panther Party Reconsidered,* ed. Charles E. Jones, 57–105. Baltimore: Black Classic Press, 1998.

Small, Melvin. *Johnson, Nixon, and the Doves.* New Brunswick and London: Rutgers University Press, 1988.

_____. *Covering Dissent: The Media and the Vietnam War Movement.* New Brunswick, NJ: Rutgers University Press, 1994.

Smith, Jackie, John D. McCarthy, Clark McPhail, and Boguslaw Augustyn. "From Protest to Agenda Building: Description Bias in Media Coverage of Events in Washington, D.C." *Social Forces* 79 (2001): 1397–1423.

Smith, Leef and Wendy Melillo. "If It's Crowd Size You Want, Park Service Says Count It Out; Congress Told Agency to Stop, Official Says." *Washington Post*, 13 October 1996, A34.

Smith, R. Jeffrey. "Attorney General Urges Renewal of Patriot Act: Gonzales Gives First Policy Speech." *Washington Post*, 1 March 2005, A2.

Snow, David A. and Robert D. Benford. "Master Frames and Cycles of Protest." In *Frontiers in Social Movement Theory*, eds. Aldon D. Morris and Carol McClurg Mueller, 133–155. New Haven and London: Yale University Press, 1992.

Snow, Kate. "D.C. Officials Working to Ensure This Year's Meeting of Trade Ministers Not Marred by Violence." *CNN Worldview*. 15 April 2000.

Snyder, David. "Theoretical and Methodological Problems in the Analysis of Governmental Coercion and Collective Violence." *Journal of Political and Military Sociology* 4 (1976): 277–293.

Snyder, David and William R. Kelly. "Conflict Intensity, Media Sensitivity and the Validity of Newspaper Data." *American Sociological Review* 42 (1977): 105–123.

Solomon, William. "More Form than Substance: Press Coverage of the WTO Protests in Seattle." *Monthly Review* 52 (2000): 12–20.

"Soviet Peace Drive Seen as Deception." *New York Times*, 15 March 1950, 2.

Sparks, Holloway. "Dissident Citizenship: Democratic Theory, Political Courage, and Activist Women." *Hypatia* 12 (1997): 74–110.

Spector, Malcolm and John Kitsuse. *Constructing Social Problems*. Menlo Park, CA: Cummings, 1977.

"State's Delegation Favors Retaliation." Associated Press, 12 September 2001.

Staub, Michael E. "Black Panthers, New Journalism, an the Rewriting of the Sixties." *Representations* 57 (1997): 53–72.

Stern, Frederick C., ed. *The Revolutionary Poet in the United States: The Poetry of Thomas McGrath*. Columbia, MO: University of Missouri Press, 1988.

_____. "An Interview with Thomas McGrath." In *The Revolutionary Poet in the United States: The Poetry of Thomas McGrath*, ed. Frederick Stern, 150–179. Columbia, MO: University of Missouri Press, 1988.

Stewart, Jim. "Security in Washington Tightens in Effort to Deal with Numerous Groups of Protesters." *CBS The Early Show*. 14 April 2000a.

_____. "Thousands of People Gather in Washington to Protest Against Everything from World Trade to Defending Sea Turtles." *CBS Morning News*. 14 April 2000b.

Stimson, Scott P. "Davis Returns." *Daily Bruin*, 18 October 1996.

Stocking, Holly and Leonard Jennifer Pease. "The Greening of the Media."

Columbia Journalism Review, 29 (1990): 37–44.

Stohl, Michael and George A. Lopez, eds. *The State as Terrorist: The Dynamics of Governmental Violence and Repression*. Westport, Connecticut: Greenwood Press, 1984.

Stolberg, Sheryl Gaye. "President Signs New Rules To Prosecute Terror Suspects." *New York Times*, 18 October 2006, A20.

Stone, Geoffrey R. *Perilous Times: Free Speech in Wartime from the Sedition Act of 1798 to the War on Terrorism*. New York: W.W. Norton & Company, 2004.

Stop Huntingdon Animal Cruelty. "Frequently Asked Questions." Available at: http://www.shac.net/SHAC/faq.html

Stop Huntingdon Animal Cruelty. "Who We Are." Available at: http://www.shac.net/SHAC/who.html

Streitmatter, Rodger. *Mightier than the Sword: How the News Media Have Shaped American History*. Boulder, CO: Westview Press, 1997.

"Stopping the World." *New York Times*, 15 April 2000, A16.

"Subversive Party." *New York Times*, 21 October 1952, 28.

Sullivan, Julie. "Terror Case Stuns Those Who Know Suspects." *Oregonian*, 6 October 2002, A1.

Sullivan, William C. Federal Bureau of Investigation. "Memorandum to AH Belmont." 30 August 1963.

_____. Federal Bureau of Investigation. "Memorandum to AH Belmont." 24 December 1963.

_____. Federal Bureau of Investigation. "Memorandum to AH Belmont." 8 January 1964.

"Survivor Recalls Raid on Panthers." *New York Times*, 23 July 1972, 90.

Swardson, Anne. "Trade Body Summit Targeted for Protests; Opponents Accuse WTO of Adding to the World's Ills, Not Helping Solve Them." *Washington Post*, 2 November 1999, A1.

Swearingen, M. Wesley. *FBI Secrets: An Agent's Exposé*. Boston, MA: South End Press, 1995.

Tagliabue, John. "Wave of Protests, from Europe to New York." *New York Times*, 21 March 2003, A1.

Takei, Barbara. "Legalizing Detention: Segregated Japanese Americans and the Justice Department's Renunciation Program." *Journal of the Shaw Historical Library* 19 (2005): 75–105.

"Talks on free-trade zone draw protests in Miami." *Seattle Times*, 21 November 2003, A12.

Taranto, James. "Global Village Idiots." *Wall Street Journal*, 18 April 2000, A18.

Tarrow, Sidney. *Power in Movement: Social Movements and Contentious Politics*. 2d ed. New York: Cambridge University Press, 1998.

Taylor, Michael. "Ex-Panther Pratt Wins New Trial 25-year legal battle in politicized case." *San Francisco Chronicle*, 30 May 1997, A1.

Taylor, Michael and Elliot Diringer. "2 Earth First! Members Hurt by Bomb in Car: Radicals Reportedly Suspected in Oakland Blast." *San Francisco Chronicle*, 25 May 1990, A1.

Temple-Raston, Dina. "Protesters vs. Globalization, Part 2 Rallying Cries Echoing Seattle Arrive in D.C." *USA Today*, 13 April 2000, 3B.

Terkildsen, Nayda and Frauke Schnell. "How Media Frames Move Public Opinion: An Analysis of the Women's Movement." *Political Research Quarterly* 50 (1997): 879–900.

Terry, Don. "Los Angeles Confronts a Bitter Racial Legacy in a Black Panther Case." *New York Times*, 20 July 1997, A14.

"Text of the President's Inaugural Address." *New York Times*, 21 January 1949, 4.

"Text of the Panel's Conclusions on Status of Communist Party in U.S." *New York Times*, 21 October 1952, 12.

"The Angela Davis Tragedy." *New York Times*, 16 October 1970, 34.

The Black Panther. 3 January 1970, 5.

Theoharis, Athan. *Spying on Americans: Political Surveillance from Hoover to the Huston Plan*. Philadelphia: Temple University Press, 1978.

_____. *From the Secret Files of J. Edgar Hoover*. Chicago: Ivan R. Dee, 1991.

"The Professor's Guns," *Time* magazine, 24 August 1970.

"The Spirit of Lawlessness." *New York Times*, 7 May 1967, 228.

This Is What Democracy Looks Like. Jill Freiburg and Rick Rowley, ed. Cambridge, MA: Independent Media Center and Big Noise Films, 2000.

Thompson, E.P. "Homage to Thomas McGrath." In *The Revolutionary Poet in the United States: The Poetry of Thomas McGrath*, ed. Frederick C. Stern, 104–149. Columbia, MO: University of Missouri Press, 1988.

Tilly, Charles. *From Mobilization to Revolution*. Reading, MA: Addison-Wesley, 1978.

Titarenko, Larissa, John D. McCarthy, Clark McPhail, and Boguslaw Augustyn. "The Interaction of State Repression, Protest Form and Protest Sponsor Strength During the Transition from Communism in Minsk, Belarus, 1990–1995." *Mobilization* 6 (2001): 129–150.

Tobin, Harold J. and Percy W. Bidwell. *Mobilizing Civilian America*. New York: Council on Foreign Relations, 1940.

Tomshow, Robert, Jim Carlton, and Dan Bilefsky. "The Assault on Iraq: Antiwar Protests Intensify in U.S., Abroad—Civil Disobedience Snarls Several American Cities; Big Rallies in Spain, Greece." *Wall Street Journal*, 21 March 2003, A6.

Toner, Robin. "Civil Liberty vs. Security: Finding a Wartime Balance." *New York Times*, 18 November 2001, A1.

Toppo, Greg. "White House Paid Journalist to Promote Law." *USA Today*, 7 January 2005, 1A.

Tower, Samuel A. "All Communists Here Are Spies, Budenz, Once Red, Tells Hearing." *New York Times*, 23 November 1946, 1.

_____. "Johnston Asserts Reds Are Seditious." *New York Times*, 28 March 1947, 15.

_____. "FBI Brands Communist Party a 'Fifth Column.'" *New York Times*, 27 March 1947, 1.

Trejos, Nancy and Timothy Dwyer. "Supporters Soldier On To Back Bush, Troops And Counter-Protests; Thousands Travel to Washington to Voice Views." *Washington Post*, 13 April 2003, A39.

"Truman Calls Communism 'Crackpot' Political Theory." *New York Times*, 5 April 1951, 19.

Trussell, C.P. "Red 'Fifth Column' Mines Government, Budenz Testifies." *New York Times*, 3 August 1948, 1.

Trumbo, Craig. "Constructing Climate Change: Claims and Frames in US News Coverage of an Environmental Issue." *Public Understanding of Science* 5 (1996): 269–283

Trumbo, Dalton. *The Time of the Toad: A Study of Inquisition in America and Two Related Pamphlets*. New York: Harper & Row, 1972.

Tuchman, Gaye. *Making News: A Study in the Construction of Reality*. New York: The Free Press, 1978.

Turner, Kathleen J. *Lyndon Johnson's Dual War: Vietnam and the Press*. Chicago and London: University of Chicago Press, 1985.

"249 Reds Sail, Exiled to Soviet Russia; Berkman Threatens to Come Back; Second Shipload May Leave This Week." *New York Times*, 22 December 1919, 1.

Twomey, Steve. "Businesses Lock Up, Batten Down for Protests." *Washington Post*, 15 April 2000, A1.

Ungar, Sanford J. *FBI*. Boston & Toronto: Little Brown and Company, 1976.

University of Colorado. "Report of the Investigative Committee of the Standing Committee on Research Misconduct at the University of Colorado at Boulder concerning Allegations of Academic Misconduct against Professor Ward Churchill." 9 May 2006. Available at: http://www.colorado.edu/news/reports/churchill/churchillreport051606.html

U.S. Congress. *Uniting and Strengthening America by Providing the Appropriate Tools Required to Intercept and Obstruct Terrorism Act*. Public Law 107-56.

U.S. Congress. Senate Select Committee to Study Government Operations with Respect to Intelligence Activities. *Final Report—Book I: Foreign and Military Intelligence*. 94th Congress, 2d sess. Washington, DC: U.S. Government Printing Office, 1976.

_____. Senate Select Committee to Study Government Operations with Respect to Intelligence Activities. *Final Report—Book II: Foreign and Military Intelligence*. 94th Congress, 2d sess. Washington, DC: U.S. Government Printing Office,

1976.

_____. Senate Select Committee to Study Government Operations with Respect to Intelligence Activities. *Final Report—Book III: Foreign and Military Intelligence*. 94th Congress, 2d sess. Washington, DC: U.S. Government Printing Office, 1976.

U.S. Congress. Senate Committee on the Judiciary, Subcommittee to Investigate the Administration of the Internal Security Act and Other Internal Security Law. *Revolutionary Activities Within the United States: The American Indian Movement*. 94th Congress, 2d sess. Washington, DC: U.S. Government Printing Office, 1976.

U.S. District Court. Northern District of Illinois, Eastern Division. "Report of the January 1970 Grand Jury." 15 May 1970.

Van Deburg, William L. *New Day in Babylon: The Black Power Movement and American Culture, 1965–1975*. Chicago and London: University of Chicago Press, 1992.

Vasquez, Michael. "Miami to Pay $180,000 to Man Injured During Free Trade Protest." *Miami Herald*, 12 September 2006.

Vaughan, John. "Fox News Program Links USF to Terrorists." *Tampa Tribune*, 28 September 2001.

Vaughn, Stephen. *Holding Fast the Inner Lines: Democracy, Nationalism, and the Committee on Public Information*. Chapel Hill, NC: The University of North Carolina Press, 1980.

_____. "First Amendment Liberties and the Committee on Public Information." *The American Journal of Legal History* 23 (1979): 95–119.

Volokh, Eugene. "The Right to Oppose." *National Review*, 7 February 2003. Available at: http://www.nationalreview.com/comment/comment-evolokh020703.asp

Voss, Kim. "The Collapse of a Social Movement: The Interplay of Mobilizing Structures, Framing, and Political Opportunities in the Knights of Labor." In *Comparative Perspectives on Social Movements: Political Opportunities, Mobilizing Structures, and Cultural Framings*, ed. Doug McAdam, John D. McCarthy, and Mayer N. Zald, 227–258. New York: Cambridge University Press, 1996.

Waldman, Paul. "Why the Media Don't Call It as They See It." *Washington Post*, 28 September 2003, B4.

Walsh, Denny. "Bail Hearing Is Held in Eco-terror Case." *Sacramento Bee*, 21 January 2006, B1.

Walz, Jay. "High Court Upholds Guilt of 11 Top U.S. Communists; Other Prosecutions Are Set." *New York Times*, 5 June 1951, 1.

_____. "Board Overrules Reds' Challenge." *New York Times*, 25 April 1951, 14.

Wells, Janet. "$1 Million Bail Ordered for Protesters: Berkeley-Based Activist Allegedly Led Mayhem." *San Francisco Chronicle*, 5 August 2000, A3.

West, Darrell M. *The Rise and Fall of the Media Establishment*. New York: Bedford/

St. Martin's, 2001.

Weyler, Rex. *Blood of the Land: The Government and Corporate War Against First Nations*. Philadelphia: New Society Publishers, 1992.

"While the WTO Burns." *Wall Street Journal*, 2 December 1999, A22.

Wilkens, Lee. "Between facts and values: print media coverage of the greenhouse effect, 1987–1990." *Public Understanding of Science* 2 (1993): 71–84.

Wilkins, Roy and Ramsey Clark. *Search and Destroy: A Report by the Commission of Inquiry into the Black Panthers and the Police*. New York: Metropolitan Applied Research Center, Inc., 1973.

Williams, Brian. "Pentagon Gathering Intelligence on US War Protestors." *NBC Nightly News* 13 December 2005.

Williams, Daniel. "Anti-War Activists Protest in Florence; Thousands Denounce U.S. Iraq Policy." *Washington* Post, 10 November 2002, A26.

Williams, Gabrielle. "Q & A: Larry Lipin, Professor of History." *Pacific: The Magazine of Pacific University* 39 (2006): 10–11.

Williams, Kristian. *American Methods: Torture and the Logic of Domination*. Cambridge, MA: South End Press, 2006.

"Will Issue War Booklets." *New York Times*, 20 June 1917, 2.

Wilson, Brian. "Protesters Fail to Shut Down IMF/World Bank Meetings." *The Edge with Paula Zahn. Fox*. 17 April 2000.

Wilson, Jamie. "Protests at Yale over Sacking of Rebel Professor." *Guardian*, 25 October 2005, 22.

Wilson, John. "Social Protest and Social Control." *Social Problems* 24 (1977): 469–481.

Wise, David. *The American Police State: The Government Against the People*. New York: Random House, 1976.

Wisler, Dominique and Marco Giugni. "Under the Spotlight: The Impact of Media Attention on Protest Policing." *Mobilization: An International Journal* 4 (1999): 171–187.

Wolfsfeld, Gadi. *Media and Political Conflict: News from the Middle East*. Cambridge University Press, 1997.

Wood, Lewis. "Federal Jury Indicts 10 Film Men on Contempt of Congress Charges." *New York Times*, 6 December 1947, 1.

Woodruff, Judy. "Anticipation Begins in Washington for Protests of IMF and World Bank Meeting." *CNN Worldview*. 14 April 2000.

Woodward, Bob and Dan Balz. "'We Will Rally the World'; Bush and His Advisers Set Objectives, but Struggled How to Achieve Them." *Washington Post*, 28 January 2002, A1.

Woodward, Bob. *State of Denial*. New York: Simon & Schuster, 2006.

Yardley, Jonathan. "They Doth Protest Too Much." *Washington Post*, 17 April 2000, C2.

Yee, Daniel. "Woman Sues DeKalb County over Ticket for Anti-Bush Bumper Sticker." Associated Press, 16 October 2006.

"Your Turn: War, Focus: Cindy Sheehan." *San Antonio Express-News*, 4 September 2005, 4H.

York, Michelle. "Professor Is Assailed By Legislature And Vandals." *New York Times*, 3 February 2005, B6.

Zald, Mayer. "On the Social Control of Industries." *Social Forces* 57 (1978): 79–102.

Zaller, John and Dennis Chiu. "Government's Little Helper: U.S. Press Coverage of Foreign Policy Crises, 1945–1991." *Political Communication* 13 (1996): 385–405.

Zaroulis, Nancy and Gerald Sullivan. *Who Spoke Up? American Protest Against the War in Vietnam 1963–1975*. Garden City, NY: Doubleday & Company, Inc., 1984.

Zinn, Howard. "Foreword." In *Silencing Political Dissent*. Nancy Chang, 11–12. New York: Seven Stories Press, 2002.

————. *A People's History of the United States*. New York: Harper & Row, 1980.

Index

OTHER TITLES AVAILABLE FROM AK PRESS

DANIEL COHN-BENDIT & GABRIEL COHN-BENDIT—Obsolete Communism: The Left-Wing Alternative

BENJAMIN DANGL—The Price of Fire: Resource Wars and Social Movements in Bolivia

DARK STAR COLLECTIVE —Beneath the Paving Stones: Situationists and the Beach, May '68

DARK STAR COLLECTIVE —Quiet Rumours: An Anarcha-Feminist Reader

VOLTAIRINE de CLEYRE—Voltarine de Cleyre Reader

CHRIS DUNCAN—My First Time: A Collection of First Punk Show Stories

BENJAMIN FRANKS—Rebel Alliances

EMMA GOLDMAN (EDITED BY DAVID PORTER)—Vision on Fire

DAVID GRAEBER & STEVPHEN SHUKAITIS—Constituent Imagination

DANIEL GUÉRIN—No Gods No Masters: An Anthology of Anarchism

GEORGY KATSIAFICAS—Subversion of Politics

KEN KNABB—Complete Cinematic Works of Guy Debord

KATYA KOMISARUK—Beat the Heat: How to Handle Encounters With Law Enforcement

PETER KROPOTKIN—The Conquest of Bread

RICARDO FLORES MAGÓN—Dreams of Freedom: A Ricardo Flores Magón Reader

SUBCOMANDANTE MARCOS—¡Ya Basta! Ten Years of the Zapatista Uprising

JOSH MACPHEE & ERIK REULAND—Realizing the Impossible: Art Against Authority

CRAIG O'HARA—The Philosophy Of Punk

ABEL PAZ (TRANSLATED BY CHUCK MORSE)—Durruti in the Spanish Revolution

RUDOLF ROCKER—Anarcho-Syndicalism

RUDOLF ROCKER—The London Years

RAMOR RYAN—Clandestines: The Pirate Journals of an Irish Exile

MARINA SITRIN—Horizontalism: Voices of Popular Power in Argentina

ALEXANDRE SKIRDA—Facing the Enemy: A History Of Anarchist Organisation From Proudhon To May 1968

ALEXANDRE SKIRDA—Nestor Makhno: Anarchy's Cossack

SUPPORT AK PRESS!

AK Press is a worker-run collective that publishes and distributes radical books, visual/audio media, and other material. We're small: a dozen people who work long hours for short money, because we believe in what we do. We're anarchists, which is reflected both in the books we publish and the way we organize our business: without bosses.

Currently, we publish about 20 new titles per year. We'd like to publish even more. Whenever our collective meets to discuss future publishing plans, we find ourselves wrestling with a list of hundreds of projects. Unfortunately, money is tight, while the need for books is greater than ever.

The **Friends of AK Press** is a direct way you can help. **Friends** pay a minimum of $20 per month (of course we have no objections to larger sums), for a minimum three-month period. The money goes directly into our publishing efforts. In return, **Friends** automatically receive (for the duration of their memberships) one free copy of every new AK Press title as they appear. **Friends** also get a 10% discount on everything featured in the AK Press Distribution catalog. We also have a program where groups or individuals can sponsor a whole book. Please contact us for details. To become a **Friend**, go to *www.akpress.org* and click on **Friends of AK** for more information.